Daring to Excel

THE FIRST 100 YEARS OF
SOUTHWEST MISSOURI STATE UNIVERSITY

BY DONALD D. LANDON

Southwest Missouri State University
901 South National Avenue
Springfield, Missouri 65804

International Standard Book Number: 0-9748190-1-8

Manufactured in the United States
Printing by Walsworth Publishing Company
Marceline, Missouri 64658

❀ Four Living Presidents ❀

Arthur G. Mallory   *Duane Meyer*   *Marshall Gordon*   *John H. Keiser*

Of the eight presidents who have served SMSU over the past 100 years, four are still living and have contributed valuable insight to the development of *Daring to Excel.*

The earliest to have served is also the youngest to have ever been selected as an SMSU president. In 1964, Dr. Arthur Mallory, at age 31, became the fifth president of what was then Southwest Missouri State College. He guided the institution through the turbulent 1960s, resigning in 1971 to become commissioner of education for the State of Missouri.

Dr. Duane Meyer, sixth president, succeeded Mallory in 1971 and brought to the office 16 years' experience at SMSU as a history professor, a dean of faculty and two stints as acting president. Dr. Meyer retired from the office in 1983 and is the only president to have resumed teaching after serving as president. At the end of his first year back in the classroom he was one of four university faculty to receive the SMSU Foundation Excellence in Teaching Award.

Dr. Marshall Gordon came to SMSU in 1983 from an 18-year career at Murray State University in Kentucky where he taught chemistry for 13 years. In 1975 he was appointed dean of the College of Environmental Sciences, vice president of university services in 1977, and acting president of Murray State in 1981. Dr. Gordon served as president at SMSU from 1983-92.

The first president to bring previous presidential experience to the task was Dr. John H. Keiser who spent 13 years as president at Boise State University in Idaho. Dr. Keiser, the eighth president of SMSU, came to the university in 1993.

Presidents in the earlier years included W.T. Carrington, appointed in 1906 but didn't begin service until 1907, Carrington left for Washington, D.C., in 1918 to serve in the Department of War Risk Management. President Carrington was succeeded by 33-year-old Clyde M. Hill of West Plains, a graduate of State Normal School #4 and a teacher of mathematics here. In 1926, President Hill left for Yale University where he later became dean of the College of Education. When Roy Ellis took the presidential reigns in 1926 at age 38, he began the longest tenure of any SMSU president retiring in 1961 after 35 years at the president's desk. The shortest tenure came with Ellis' successor, Dr. Leland Traywick, who was appointed president in 1961 and resigned in 1964.

❀ Essayists ❀

Dr. Robert H. Bradley came to SMSU in 1963 as an instructor of speech in the English and Speech Department. In 1971 he was named head of the Department of Speech and Theatre serving for 31 years until his retirement in 2002. A close associate of Dr. Leslie Irene Coger for nearly 30 years, Dr. Bradley has directed more than 100 theatre productions for SMSU Theatre, Tent Theatre and Springfield Little Theatre in his more than 40 years in Springfield. *(Essay on page 306)*

Dr. Robert Flanders arrived in Springfield in 1968 to serve as professor of history and head of the History Department. In 1979 he was appointed first director of the Center for Ozarks Studies, a novel research and public service division. He was co-director of *Sassafrass,* a theater-style multi-image presentation on the Ozarks, and executive producer of the documentary films *Shannon County: Home,* and *Shannon County: The Hearts of the Children.* Dr. Flanders has directed numerous cultural resource studies in the Ozarks region, and co-edited the quarterly magazine *OzarksWatch.* He retired from SMSU in 1995. *(Essay on page 181)*

Dr. Albert R. Gordon joined the Life Sciences Department at SMSU in 1969 after receiving his Ph.D. from Case Western Reserve University. He is currently a full professor in the Biomedical Sciences Department. Over the years at SMSU, Dr. Gordon has taught more than 30 different life science courses ranging from cell biology to human genetics. His current research interests are in the biology of aging. *(Essay on page 289)*

Dr. John H. Keiser was named the eighth president of SMSU in 1993 after serving as president of Boise State University for 13 years. His academic career started at Westminster College in Fulton, Missouri, where he taught history after completing a doctorate at Northwestern University. He served as vice president for academic affairs at University of Illinois in Springfield from 1971-78. *(Essay on page 353)*

Dr. Arthur Mallory was named fifth president of SMSU in 1964 succeeding President Leland Traywick. Dr. Mallory graduated from SMSU in 1954, joining presidents Hill and Ellis who also took undergraduate degrees here. After completing a doctorate in 1959 at the University of Missouri, Dr. Mallory served as assistant superintendent of schools in St. Louis County and served as a dean at the University of Missouri-St. Louis before coming to SMSU. In 1971 Dr. Mallory was named commissioner of education for the State of Missouri where he served until 1988. In 1991 he returned to SMSU to serve as dean of the College of Education, retiring in 1994. *(Essay on page 144)*

Andrea Mostyn serves as assistant director for university communications at SMSU. She holds a bachelor's degree in communication from Truman State University and a master's degree in public administration from SMSU. Andrea served as news editor for a small suburban newspaper in St. Louis before coming to Springfield where she has also held posts at the United Way of the Ozarks and Burrell Behavioral Health Center. *(Essay on page 365)*

Dr. Jon Moran served as head of the Philosophy Department at SMSU from 1991-2003. He came to SMSU after completing a doctorate at Tulane University in 1972. His areas of primary interest include American philosophy, ethics and philosophy of religion. *(Essay on page 249)*

Don Payton, a 1950 graduate of SMSU, returned to the university in 1956 to begin a 30-year career in public relations. He oversaw the development of the university's information services, publications, alumni relations and sports information services. His service virtually spanned the entire career of President Duane Meyer who arrived at SMSU in 1955. Payton was an inaugural inductee on the SMSU Wall of Fame in Plaster Student Union. *(Essay on page 272)*

Mark Stillwell is sports information director at SMSU, a post he has held since 1972. In 1998 he took on the added responsibilities of assistant director of Athletics for Public Relations. Mark oversees the information and publications effort for the 21-sport NCAA Division I intercollegiate athletics program, and has won more than 60 publications and writing awards during his career at SMSU. Prior to coming to the university, Mark served in the Navy and retired as a Captain in the U.S. Naval Reserve in 1991. *(Essay on page 92)*

Tina Stillwell has completed 30 years of service to SMSU. She graduated from SMSU in 1972 with a BA in writing. As a student, Tina was editor of the *Ozarko* in 1971. In 1974 she joined the SMSU staff as a publications assistant and in 1980 became assistant director of information services, serving under Don Payton. She was the first director of news services for the university serving from 1985-2003. She is currently manager of corporate support, outreach and volunteers for broadcast services. *(Essay on page 72)*

Tom Strong, a 1952 graduate of SMSU, has been practicing law in Springfield, Missouri, since 1957. Mr. Strong was a member of the first SMSU debate team to qualify for the National Debate Tournament at West Point in 1952. He and his partner, Yvonne Ray, reached the quarterfinals, bowing to the University of New Mexico team in a split decision. Strong and Ray were the final debate team coached by the venerable Virginia Craig who retired in 1952. Mr. Strong served on the SMSU Board of Governors from 1993-99. *(Essay on page 20)*

❧ Introduction ❧

I applaud the SMSU administrative decision to authorize the publication of a comprehensive history of the institution as a part of the upcoming Centennial Celebration. Such a document has, at the least, a dual benefit and may be seen as both pleasurable and practical.

For alumni, the history provides an opportunity to revisit favorite professors and to recall memorable events of their years on campus. Faculty and staff will remember good friends among their colleagues, some of whom have gone before them, and will relive amusing, inspiring and instructive episodes that occurred during their tenure.

A history such as this can inspire the individual reader to reconsider the years on campus and to ask helpful personal questions: Did I make optimum use of my time and talents while a student? Why did I major in psychology and not in agriculture or German? Was it a good decision to join a sorority or fraternity? Should I have married during my sophomore year? Should I have enlisted in the Army during the Korean War to avoid taking the Minimum Essentials Test in English?

In addition, this publication will be helpful to every department and program in the university as changes are made in our evolving programs. Institutional histories are often valuable for observing mistakes made and for charting improvements in the future of the institution.

It can also help an individual faculty and staff member, active or retired, to reconsider his or her career. Reading the manuscript caused me to ask many questions of myself and my life on campus: Was it worth the effort to change the college from a quarter system to a semester system? Should I have accepted the position of academic dean when it was offered in 1961? Should the Faculty Senate and the dean have used a different system to select the general education requirements for all baccalaureate degrees in view of the long and bitter battle that ensued?

Reading this insightful and detailed history will provide the reader an enjoyable experience in reliving and reconsidering his or her years on this campus known today as Southwest Missouri State University.

Duane Meyer
May 6, 2003

❧ Acknowledgements ❧

Scores of people have contributed the raw material out of which this book has been written. Their names are listed in the "Contributors" section at the end of the volume. Some of them wrote lengthy treatises on some aspect of the institution's development. Others wrote brief histories of their department. Others provided anecdotes, pictures, data collections and historical perspective through personal conversation and interviews. Their assistance has been invaluable.

During the research phase, I had the able help of Candida Arvizu who was working on a graduate degree in psychology. She digested hundreds of pages of recent *Southwest Standards* as well as organized the data from an extensive alumni survey.

Throughout the process an Advisory Committee read manuscripts, looked at layouts, debated perspectives, sat for interviews and generally provided moral support when the prospect of getting the story together looked grim. That group included Jim Anderson, Dr. Kenneth Brown, Jim Craig, Julie Ebersold, Dale Freeman, Dr. Gloria Galanes, Dr. Marshall Gordon, Dr. Russell Keeling, Dr. Arthur Mallory, Julie March, Dr. Duane Meyer, Dr. Jim Moore, Dr. Connie O'Neal, Don Payton, Dr. Denny Pilant and David Richards.

Rhonda Stanton, Dr. Connie O'Neal and Megan Patton contributed the expert's hand to edit the manuscript providing the writer an additional reason for humility.

The design of the book is the work of Amy Schuldt of the University Relations Publications staff. Her creative genius brought the pages to life. John Wall and Kevin White provided supportive assistance in gathering pictures spanning a century of time.

Paul Kincaid supervised the whole operation, giving advice, consolation, encouragement and support for four years while the birthing of the book was under way. His guiding hand was invaluable.

A sincere thanks to all who contributed to the creation of the centennial history.

Donald D. Landon
Author

❀ Preface ❀

While the history of Southwest Missouri State University is not unique inasmuch as scores of public universities across the country began as normal schools or teachers colleges, still the evolution of the *Shrine of the Ozarks,* as President Roy Ellis affectionately called the college, has distinguished itself in numerous ways, two of which stood out as its story unfolded: the institution has reflected a distinct commitment to place, and it has been driven by a powerful aspiration to excel.

At the beginning of the 20th century, the Ozarks was still a relatively isolated area of the state, decidedly rural, and struggling to bring the benefits of education to its scattered population. State Normal Schools were established in three other areas of Missouri more than 30 years before one was chartered for the Ozarks. Fortuitously, the site chosen for State Normal School #4 was the most urban of any of the other four normal school locations in the state. The choice of Springfield provided what came to be a metropolitan context in contrast to the locations of the other normal schools sited in Kirksville, Warrensburg, Cape Girardeau and Maryville. That metropolitan context has added a dynamic to the institution that is unique.

The institution's commitment to place is reflected in its leadership. Over its first 60 years, SMSU had but three presidents, all native sons, two of whom were graduates of the institution while it was still State Normal School #4. Its first president, W.T. Carrington, had already served as principal of Springfield High School before becoming state superintendent of schools. While in Jefferson City he developed a passion for improving rural education, commending him to lead the new normal school in Springfield in 1906. President Clyde Hill, who took the reins in 1918, grew up in

Howell County. A precocious lad, Hill became superintendent of schools in West Plains before he reached his 20th birthday. President Roy Ellis succeeded Hill in 1926 and went on to guide the institution for the next 35 years, one of the longest tenures of any college president in the country at the time. Ellis grew up on the border of Wright and Webster Counties, steeped in the traditions of the Ozarks, and acutely aware of this role education could play in the development of the Ozark Plateau and its people. These early leaders knew southwest Missouri as home and established links between SMSU and the Ozarks that have proved durable and constructive for a century.

The commitment to place is also seen in the professorate. By the 1930s, nearly half of the faculty carried SMSU credentials. They had come to school here, caught the vision of an educated citizenry, went on to do graduate work and returned to their alma mater. President Hill taught mathematics here before being named president. President Ellis taught economics and sociology. While the faculty has become much more cosmopolitan in recent years, many still carry undergraduate and graduate credentials from SMSU.

The curriculum shows a commitment to the needs of the Ozarks. Early on, the need was for trained teachers for rural schools, and the institution shaped the curriculum as well as its campus life around teacher preparation. It was soon apparent, however, that the developing Ozarks needed business and professional leaders, so the institution added a liberal arts component to the curriculum and developed a commerce department. Throughout the years the development of the Ozarks is mirrored in the evolution of the curriculum including the addition of a dozen graduate programs in health related areas over the past decade to serve the growing regional health care industry.

As the world becomes a global community, the Ozarks are becoming transformed. Politics are still local, but the vision is becoming global. A physicist in Temple Hall is working on sensors that will detect biological and chemical weapons. A health and physical education professor in McDonald Arena is developing the structure of the Ozarks Public Health Institute, which will have the capacity to become a first responder to an attack from weapons of mass destruction. The commitment to place follows the place into the global community.

A second characteristic present from the beginning in 1905 has been the drive to excel. In the early years, this drive was fueled in part by the institution's rivalry with neighboring Drury College. The humble normal school coveted the status of college and suggested in its early *Bulletin* that it would be better named a "teachers college" because of the quality of its curriculum and the credentials of its faculty. Once it achieved that status in 1919, and even before it became a state college in 1946, it was hearing the word "university" fall from the lips of visiting dignitaries and visionary faculty. The status quo was always seen as temporary.

The commitment to excel quickly became part of the institution's culture. It was established early in the classrooms of Dr. Virginia Craig, Professor Jim Shannon and Professor Norman Freudenberger. It was established by pioneering coaches Arthur Briggs and Andrew McDonald. Dr. Leslie Irene Coger inspired students to excel on stage. Dr. Craig expected excellence from her debaters. The culture of excellence drew outstanding faculty who in turn drew students with high aspirations. The striving for excellence pushed athletics into Division I competition; created an SMSU Foundation to support greatness; sent debaters to West Point, drama students overseas on USO tours, and the Bruin Pride Band to Macy's parade; and generated a proposal to the Legislature that gave SMSU a statewide mission in public affairs.

Rivalry has evolved under the commitment to excel as well. In the beginning it was with the local campus across Jordan Creek, which already held the coveted title of college. A century later the rivalry seems to be with the state's flagship institution, the University of Missouri, which has systematically resisted SMSU becoming Missouri State University. In 2002 the change was blocked by a Senate filibuster. In 2003, the resistance included an alternative bill sponsored by the Columbia Senator to bring SMSU into the University of Missouri system. In 2004, the University of Missouri claimed to own the historical rights to the name "Missouri State University" during the filibuster. The striving to excel has pushed the envelope at the highest levels.

Trying to grasp the genius of an institution is a challenging task, in part because what you see is so much a function of where you stand as you look. I have not tried to hide the fact that I have labored within these walls for nearly 30 years. That shapes, in part, where I have stood as I have written. Fortunately, I have had access to an Advisory Committee of 16 knowledgeable folks from the community and the university, four of whom were former presidents or acting presidents of SMSU. Some on the Committee have been associated with the university for more than half its lifetime, which yielded helpful historical perspective. While I acknowledge my debt to them for their advice and assistance, I must take responsibility for the content of the book.

From the outset it was clear that this could not be a scholarly history. That is clearly beyond my capacity. Someone else sometime needs to do that. What I have attempted to do is write the story of the institution, particularly as students experienced it. I have relied heavily on student publications to provide that perspective. My purpose is similar to that of President Roy Ellis who, 40 years ago, sat down to write the history of the first 60 years, titled *Shrine of the Ozarks*. His wish then was "to water the green meadows of memory for former students of the college." I join him in that wish.

Donald D. Landon
Author

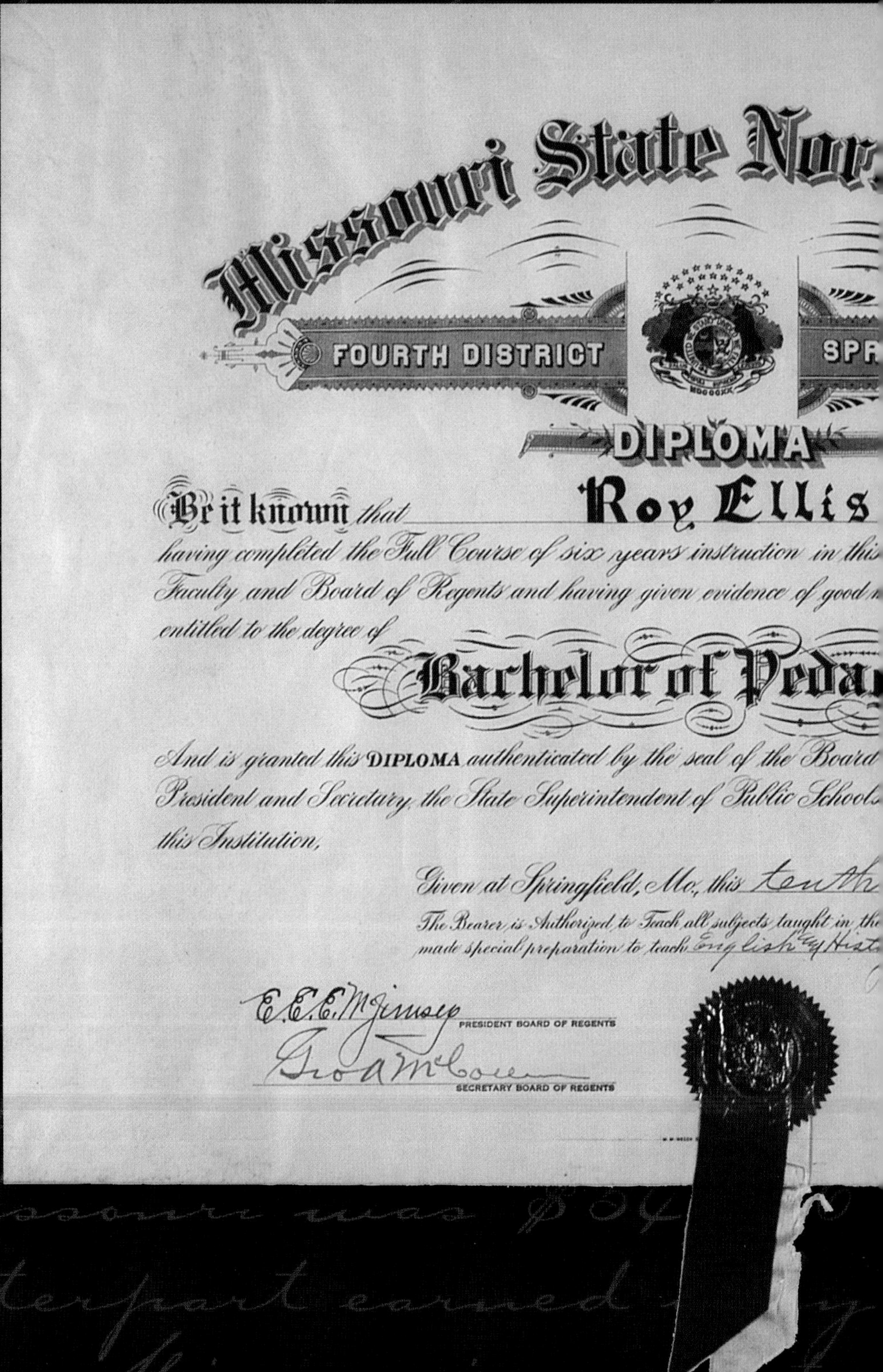

Missouri State Nor...

FOURTH DISTRICT   SPR...

DIPLOMA

Roy Ellis

Be it known that

having completed the Full Course of six years instruction in this...
Faculty and Board of Regents and having given evidence of good...
entitled to the degree of

Bachelor of Peda...

And is granted this **DIPLOMA** authenticated by the seal of the Board...
President and Secretary, the State Superintendent of Public Schools...
this Institution,

Given at Springfield, Mo., this tenth...

The Bearer is Authorized to Teach all subjects taught in the...
made special preparation to teach English & Hist...

E. E. E. M.Jimsey
PRESIDENT BOARD OF REGENTS

Geo. A. McCow...
SECRETARY BOARD OF REGENTS

1905-1919

Missouri State Normal School, Fourth District

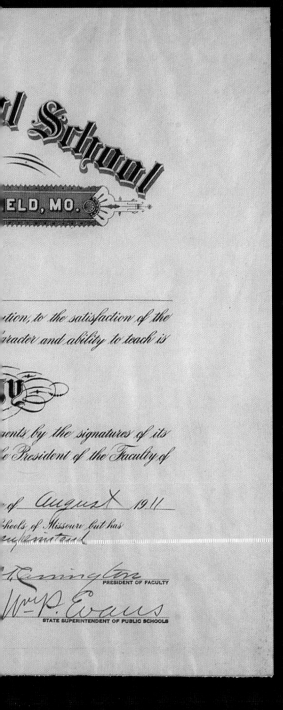

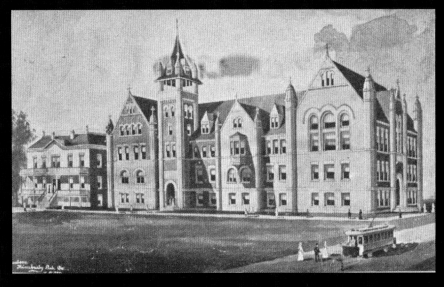

Contents

1905-1919

Missouri State Normal School, Fourth District

W.T. Carrington, the first president of State Normal School #4, was serving as state superintendent of schools in Jefferson City when called to launch the Normal School in Springfield in 1906. He had previously served as principal of Springfield High School. His tenure at the Normal School continued until 1918 when he left to work in the office of War Risk Insurance in Washington, D.C. President Carrington earned an A.B. degree from Westminster College, an A.M. from McGee College and a Master of Scientific Didactics from Kirksville Normal School. He died in 1937.

"The Springfield State Normal School is not an experiment." That declaration, published in the October 1906 *Bulletin*, captured the sentiment of a fledgling institution that had the heady experience of enrolling 543 students in its first term in the summer of 1906. It was the second largest enrollment of any of the five state Normal Schools, three of which had been in existence for more than 30 years. Brimming with enthusiasm, possessing confidence about its mission, and boasting a location, which its October 1909 *Bulletin* described as "a veritable health resort," State Normal School #4 in Springfield was positioning itself early to be a leader in higher education in Missouri.

ABOUT THE TIMELINE

Three timelines are provided to put the development of the university in context. While the events chosen for the timelines were arbitrary, hopefully they provide insight into the period described.

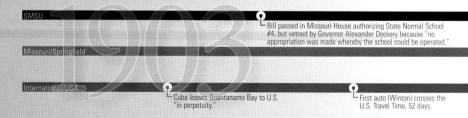

SMSU

Missouri/Springfield

International/USA

Bill passed in Missouri House authorizing State Normal School #4, but vetoed by Governor Alexander Dockery because "no appropriation was made whereby the school could be operated."

Cuba leases Guantanamo Bay to U.S. "in perpetuity."

First auto (Winton) crosses the U.S. Travel Time, 52 days.

Completed in 1909, Academic Hall (now Carrington Hall) was the first building on the Normal School Campus. This 1918 picture shows the circle drive from National Avenue.

Its third president, Dr. Roy Ellis, himself a student in the early years, recalls the heady atmosphere. "State Normal #4 indulged few doubts and harbored no inferiority complexes. It pulsated with vigor and glowed with ambition. It faced the future with courage."

Even before the first term in the summer of 1906 was over, the July *Bulletin* boasted that "no institution ever opened under more favorable auspices." It continued by explaining that the three sister institutions, which opened more than 30 years earlier in Kirksville, Warrensburg and Cape Girardeau "began with few students" and struggled with "a sentiment in favor of training teachers for public school work (that) was not strong." So, it argued, "a new Normal School established in Missouri today does not

go through the stages of development necessary thirty years ago." In fact, the 1906 *Bulletin* declared, "The Fourth District Normal School sprang into existence full grown, in its first term, the second largest in the state."

So indeed, from the school's perspective, it was not an experiment. In some respects it was building on the hard work done earlier in other places. Being a late-comer in the Normal School era may have been a disservice to the citizens of the 22 counties in southwest Missouri who had to wait to have the opportunity for higher education, but the delayed beginning clearly took many of the uncertainties out of the enterprise. And it led its enthusiastic founders to claim that State Normal School #4 "was equal to the best from its very beginning." Clearly, the insti-

tution "indulged few doubts and harbored no inferiority complexes."

The Place of Normal Schools in Higher Education

Normal Schools occupy an interesting, if not brief, period in American educational history. By 1800 the public had begun to realize that qualifications for teaching should exceed the vague requirement of being a "fit person." Many understood that the knowledge of subject matter didn't necessarily carry with it the ability to teach. What was needed, the experts said, was an institution situated between the common school and the university, solely dedicated to the preparation of teachers.

By the end of the Civil War, education had become a critical issue in the United States. The industrial revolution

1904

First football game west of the Mississippi played under the lights occurs in Springfield, Missouri, where Springfield Normal School defeats the Indians of Talequah, Indian Territory, 11-0.

Library system opens in Springfield.

Orville Wright flies aircraft with a petrol engine in first documented, successful, controlled powered flight.

World's Fair opens in St. Louis, commemorating the Centennial of the Louisiana Purchase.

N.Y. Subway opens.

The first faculty at State Normal School #4 included (1) Dr. Virginia Craig, English; (2) W.E. Vaughn, English; (3) Clayton Kinsey, vocal music; (4) C.E. Marston, geography; (5) Cora Louise Boehringer, education; (6) D.T. Kizer, biology and agriculture; and (7) Elizabeth Park, mathematics. John Taylor (not pictured), founder of Springfield Normal School and Business College, also taught briefly.

had created the need for a far better educated workforce, and the strivings for a democratic society clearly called for an educated citizenry. Educational needs were particularly acute in rural areas where often half of the population was illiterate.

In Missouri, throughout most of the 19th century, education was conceived as a private, family, church or neighborhood responsibility. Public schools were thought of as places "where the poor shall be taught gratis." Many people did not want the state designing the curriculum, training teachers or setting standards. However, maintaining the tradition of private education was becoming difficult in the face of the overwhelming need to educate the masses to participate in the emerging industrial age.

The Plight of Education in Rural Areas

Not only were the public schools poorly distributed, particularly in rural areas, but those that did exist were poorly staffed. W.T. Carrington, state superintendent of education at the turn of the century, confessed, "It's a stubborn fact (that) persons with only a fair knowledge of the common school branches (of learning), and no professional training, are in charge of about 40 percent of the rural schools in the state." Even as late as 1914, a Carnegie Commission report on Missouri Normal Schools noted that "the burden of rural teaching falls on women, many of whom have no more than one year of high school."

Not only were teachers poorly prepared, they were in desperately short supply, particularly in rural areas. For years after the Civil War, Missouri was importing most of its teachers from neighboring states. The desire of Missouri citizens to have "home teachers for home schools" resulted in hiring thousands of local people with minimal teaching preparation. In 1905

1905

SMSU

Missouri/Springfield — St. Louis police tried new investigation method, fingerprints.

First training facility for nurses opened as Springfield Hospital, which later became Springfield Baptist Hospital.

International/USA

there were 17,036 teachers licensed in Missouri, but only one in four had any Normal School or college work.

The rural problem was exacerbated by city schools regularly raiding rural districts for their best qualified and most experienced teachers. Pay differentials made the quest simple. In 1905 the average annual salary of a city teacher in Missouri was $549.06 while the rural counterpart earned only $221.58. Southwest Missouri rural teachers fared much worse than the average. Barry County paid an average of only $210; Douglas, $153; Phelps, $190; Stone, $167; Taney, $130; and Wright, $137. So rural teachers gladly abandoned their one-room schools and subsistence salaries for the better conditions and pay in the cities.

Superintendent Carrington put the supply problem in perspective by reporting that if all students graduating from all Missouri colleges in 1905 were to go into teaching, they would satisfy only about 10 percent of the demand. Moreover, if all high school graduates joined the college graduates going into teaching, the demand would still not be met.

The shortage of teachers and the minimal levels of preparation combined to produce a profile of academic achievement in rural areas that profoundly distressed Superintendent Carrington. While eight years of schooling was the norm over the state in 1905, only 50 percent of rural students remained in school through the fourth grade. Only 10 percent persevered through the eighth grade, and a mere 5 percent ever entered a high school classroom.

So in 1905 when State Legislators authorized the establishment of Normal Schools in the southwest and northwest

---

Rural Education, 1900

"It is a stubborn fact that persons with only a fair knowledge of the common school branches and no professional training are in charge of about forty percent of the rural schools of the state."

∞

W.T. Carrington, 1900
State Superintendent of Schools

Missouri districts, they were responding to a critical need to both increase the supply and broaden the qualifications of those going into public school teaching, particularly in rural areas.

Origin of the Normal School

Experiments with the Normal School idea had already occurred in Prussia with its seminaries and in France with its Ecole Normal in the early years of the 19th century. By 1839 the first Normal School in the United States had been established in Massachusetts. Appropriate candidates for the teaching profession at the time were high school students who were given focused instruction in pedagogy. Prior to the Civil War, some American high schools actually had Normal departments dedicated to teacher training.

A Surprising Spelling Bee

Spelling bees were regular events at the beginning of school after Christmas vacation. The event in 1913 was noteworthy because a scientist out-spelled the head of the English Department.

"Euphorbiaceous" cried out the announcer to Dr. Virginia Craig, head of the English Department and only Ph.D. on the faculty. "It was so quiet one could almost hear the twinkling of the stars as Miss Craig hesitated, spelled, and missed the word," recalled Roy Ellis.

The next contestant was D.T. Kizer, a botanist and doctor of medicine, who quickly spelled the word correctly. The surprised audience speculated that the contest had been deliberately rigged against Miss Craig!

~

Normal School Dress

In the early years, school dress was quite formal as many of the pictures suggest. Men were expected to wear coats to class regardless of the weather. Those who appeared without them were often sent home to dress properly. Tailored wool suits cost $15 at Glasgow's. Good shoes from Royal Shoe Store were $2.50. Students often worked all summer to buy clothes for school in the fall.

Legislature passes bills authorizing establishment of Normal School #4 in Southwest District on March 17, and Normal School #5 in Northwest District on March 25.

Diemer Theater opens on North Jefferson.

Bayer aspirin first marketed.

Las Vegas, Nevada is founded.

"Education has taken the place of war as the means by which one nation dominates another."

Genevieve Campbell
Student, 1914 *Standard*

The 1906 *Bulletin* of State Normal School #4 in Springfield endorsed the view that "a high school course and thorough pedagogical training… prepare(s) one for efficient teaching in any grade or any kind of school." The norm by that time, however, was the two-year college course leading to the Bachelor of Pedagogy degree granting a lifetime teaching certificate. Therefore, when State Normal School #4 started in Springfield in the summer of 1906,

it was much like a high school and a junior college combined. It included 15-year-olds who were seeking their first high school classes and were studying alongside experienced teachers in their 20s and 30s who were seeking lifetime certification or a college degree. A challenging mix, to say the least!

Choosing Springfield as the Site for Normal School #4

The authorizing and locating of State Normal School #4 is itself an intriguing story. Thirty years after Normal Schools had been established in Kirksville, Warrensburg and Cape Girardeau, pressure was mounting on the state Legislature to establish a similar institution in the southwest district of the state. Two authorizing resolutions had been passed by the Legislature during Governor Alexander Dockery's administration, but both were vetoed because "no appropriation was made whereby the law could be operated."

Normal Schools established in Missouri just after the Civil War had to struggle to survive. Meager funding by the state and weak public

support combined to make the Normal Schools' work difficult. But by 1904 attitudes were changing. Prior to that, Normal Schools were technically rated as high schools, even though their true character was quite different. But by 1904, they were authorized to offer 18 units of work, the last eight being equivalent to the first two years of college.

So by 1905 with a new governor in Jefferson City and a growing consensus that Normal Schools had much to contribute to the solution of educational problems in the state, the prospects appeared much brighter. The highly respected superintendent of schools in Kansas City, J.M. Greenwood, was joined with John Kirk, former state superintendent of education and then president of Kirksville State Normal School, and with W.T. Carrington, state superintendent of education, to lobby the Legislature on behalf of establishing two new State Normal schools. On March 17, 1905, the Missouri General Assembly authorized the establishment of State Normal School #4 in the southwest district, and a week later authorized the establishment of State

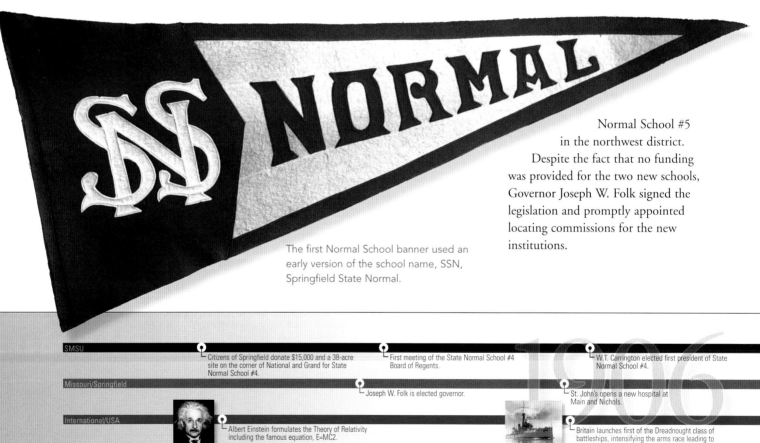

The first Normal School banner used an early version of the school name, SSN, Springfield State Normal.

Normal School #5 in the northwest district. Despite the fact that no funding was provided for the two new schools, Governor Joseph W. Folk signed the legislation and promptly appointed locating commissions for the new institutions.

SMSU
Citizens of Springfield donate $15,000 and a 38-acre site on the corner of National and Grand for State Normal School #4.

First meeting of the State Normal School #4 Board of Regents.

W.T. Carrington elected first president of State Normal School #4.

Missouri/Springfield
Joseph W. Folk is elected governor.

St. John's opens a new hospital at Main and Nichols.

1906

International/USA
Albert Einstein formulates the Theory of Relativity including the famous equation, $E=MC^2$.

Britain launches first of the Dreadnought class of battleships, intensifying the arms race leading to World War I.

A Bizarre Bidding Process Locates the School

Locating State Normal Schools was left to a bizarre bidding process authorized by the state in 1870. Communities wishing to locate the school within their boundaries would make a bid composed of a campus site and a cash subsidy. Kirksville outbid Chillicothe in 1870 to locate State Normal School #1 there. The price was $76,400. Warrensburg won over Sedalia for Normal School #2 with a bond-issue-based bid of $173,000. Cape Girardeau won out over Ironton for Normal School #3 with a bid of $54,865. The competition was heated, and the losers complained loudly.

Locating State Normal School #4 in the southwest district in 1905 engaged the same mechanism with similar strife. Seven communities in the district entered the competition: Webb City, Pierce City, Monett, Aurora, Lebanon, Marshfield and Springfield. The locating Commission appointed by Governor Folk was headed by Chancellor W.E. Chaplin of Washington University in St. Louis. Joining the chancellor were four other commission members, all from outside the southwest district. They included J.P. Greene, president of William Jewell College in Liberty; J.F. Cook, former president of LaGrange College; T.M. Johnson, a member of the Osceola School Board, and O.D. Gray, editor of *The Leader* in Sturgeon.

Toward the end of July 1905, the Commission had visited most of the sites and received their bids. Webb City boasted an existing private normal school with a rather pretentious building available. J.T. Woodruff, a leading businessman in Springfield, recalled that while Springfield was still in the

running, it had not yet made a bid. A group of citizens was organized through the Springfield Club (precursor of the Chamber of Commerce) to identify eligible sites and escort Commission members on a tour.

Traveling in horse-drawn cabs, the Commission visited the Williams tract northeast of the city and the Dobbs farm on the southwest border of Springfield. Upon leaving the Dobbs farm and traveling north on National Boulevard to visit the site of a private Normal School operated by John Taylor, the cab containing Chancellor Chaplin passed the Headly tract on the west side of National just north of Grand. The beautifully wooded tract caught the chancellor's attention and he asked why that tract was not offered. "It might be if the Commissioner would care to consider it," replied Woodruff, who was riding with the chancellor in his cab. Reining the horses to a halt, the commissioners got out, climbed over a wire fence and walked up to the center of the tract. "We stopped at a point where the Administration Building now stands," John Woodruff recalled. "The Chancellor turned to me and said, 'Now, this property appeals to me! We may want to look it over again.'"

A Deal Is Struck

That night the Commission went to Lebanon by train, returned to Marshfield the next day, and the following day came back to Springfield, where they met privately with the Springfield Club group. They stated that the Headly tract on National Boulevard "was the best they had seen." Furthermore, "They preferred Springfield over any of the other contending

First summer term enrolls 543 students.
Fall term enrolls 173.

Library opens with 600 volumes.

A mob lynches three Negroes on the public square in Springfield initiating an exodus of many Blacks from the city.

Elfindale Academy opens in Springfield, called St. de Chantal Academy.

Filmmaker John Huston born in Nevada, Missouri.

Great San Francisco earthquake.

Construction begins on the Panama Canal.

Springfield Normal School, established by John Taylor in 1893, built an impressive building east of Springfield on Pickwick near Cherry. When State Normal School #4 was established in Springfield in 1906, Taylor cheerfully turned over his Normal School students to the new institution. He rented the attractive building to the state for three years while Academic Hall was being built on National Avenue. He built a new building on the corner of Jefferson and Walnut to house his Business College.

earlier visits to Chancellor Chaplin in St. Louis. So, that evening the Commission made a proposal to Springfield rather than receiving one from the city of 23,000 residents. "If you would give the Headly property to the state and $25,000 in money," Woodruff recalls Chaplin saying, "they would locate the school in Springfield." The negotiating group agreed to terms "without much hesitation."

The property was readily available since one of the owners, John T. Woodruff, was present in the meeting. Raising the $25,000, however, was a different matter. But with the deal so nearly done, city representatives called a public meeting for the following evening "at which there were present not less than 200 handpicked men and women, all tremendously interested in the project," reported Woodruff. An agreement had been drafted to be signed by the citizens of Springfield, guaranteeing the gift of the land and the money — $25,000 in cash.

As the meeting opened, Chancellor Chaplin made a presentation outlining the advantages to the city of having such a school in its midst. Others on the Commission also spoke briefly. Then Senator McDavid read the agreement to be signed by the citizens guaranteeing the gift of the land and the money. At that juncture, Woodruff recalled, "We closed the doors of the auditorium and announced emphatically that no person would be permitted

towns," according to Woodruff.

As it turned out, the Headly tract had been purchased some months earlier by Woodruff, M.C. Baker and William H. Johnson, who had platted it for a residential subdivision. They had paid $15,000 for the 38-acre property, according to Woodruff.

Apparently the Commission was determined to locate State Normal School #4 in Springfield, perhaps even from the beginning of the bidding process. Senator F.M. McDavid had worked assiduously to that end with

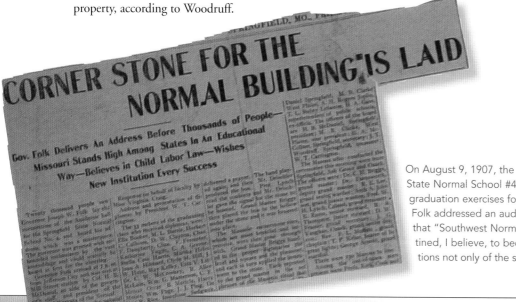

On August 9, 1907, the cornerstone for the first building on the State Normal School #4 campus was laid. The ceremony followed graduation exercises for the class of 1907. Governor Joseph W. Folk addressed an audience estimated to be 20,000, declaring that "Southwest Normal has a bright future before it and is destined, I believe, to become one of the great educational institutions not only of the southwest, but of the state."

SMSU

Carrington Literary Society organized with Dr. Virginia Craig, sponsor. W.E. Vaughn appointed sponsor of Bentonian Literary Society.

First athletics team (baseball) organized on campus.

Clyde Hill elected president of first graduating class.

Missouri/Springfield

Missouri Historical Review first volume published.

Burge Deaconess hospital opens on North Jefferson.

International/USA

More than 1 million immigrants pass through Ellis Island.

1907

This was the *Ozarko* cartoonist's characterization of the Normal School faculty in 1909.

to leave until each and every one had signed the agreement."

Every member of the appointed Commission to locate State Normal School #4 filed by and signed the document. "After this," stated Woodruff, "there was a rush on the part of nearly everyone to sign." There were, however, a few cautious citizens who positively refused to sign the instrument. But, according to Woodruff, "Their objections were to no purpose; before leaving that meeting all had signed, no one escaped."

With the papers signed, the Commission went into executive session and entered of record an order establishing State Normal School #4 in Springfield. Some 10 years later, a team from the Carnegie Foundation for the Advancement of Teaching studied the Normal Schools of Missouri, and while

the Foundation found the schools' operation exemplary, they found the process for their siting deplorable. Rolla succeeded in getting the School of Mines by pledging $75,000 to the state through a bond issue but then defaulted on the bonds. The city went to court and argued, successfully, that the whole system of bidding for state institutions was unconstitutional.

In spite of the complaints and bitterness on the part of its competitors who felt that Springfield had really never made a bid, by July 26, 1905, Springfield was designated as the location for State Normal School #4. Governor Folk immediately appointed a Board of Regents consisting of H.B. McDaniel, Springfield; M.B. Clarke, West Plains; A.H. Rogers, Joplin; T.L. Rubey, Lebanon; J.M. Earp, Lamar, and Chancellor Chaplin, St. Louis. The Board convened on September 7, 1905, and elected McDaniel, president; Clarke, vice president; G.A. McCullom, secretary, and J.T. Woodruff, treasurer.

The First President Is Selected

The decision to hire Carrington as the first president of the fledgling institution was a stroke of genius on the part of the Board. Carrington was thoroughly familiar with Springfield, having served as principal of its high school from 1887-92 and again from 1895-99. He left to become state superintendent of education, where he was serving when the Board elected him president of State Normal School #4 in January 1906.

Carrington himself was a product of State Normal School #1 in Kirksville, where he took a Master of Scientific Didactics degree. His A.B. degree was from McGee College, and he did addi-

On Naming the School

While the Legislation that created a state Normal School in southwest Missouri identified the institution as Missouri State Normal School, Fourth District, early references to the school identified it by several names. Because it acquired the normal school students and many of the faculty from John Taylor's Springfield Normal School and Business College, some early accounts refer to the school as Springfield State Normal School. There were even variations on the early school Bulletins. The cover page carried Missouri State Normal School, Fourth District as well as Fourth District State Normal School. Other literature referred to the school as State Normal School, Southwest District and State Normal School #4. We have chosen to use the latter because of its brevity and readability, not to settle the question of what the official name was. The diplomas settled that by identifying the institution as Missouri State Normal School, Fourth District.

First intercollegiate basketball game played. Normal girls defeat Drury girls.

YMCA conducts campus revival.

Doling Park was purchased from James Doling for $50,000 by The Springfield Amusement Company.

First Ziegfeld Follies show.

tional work at Westminster College and the University of Missouri. He was a passionate advocate for Normal Schools in Missouri and pleaded their case repeatedly before the State Legislature. While he was a man of great vision, he also was quite willing "to start from where he was rather than from where he might wish he were," according to Roy Ellis, a student at the time of Carrington's service and subsequently the third president of the new institution.

Carrington had broad experience in both teaching and educational administration. Reading his reports to the Legislature while serving as state superintendent, one catches his passion for improvement of the public school system, his concern for the plight of rural schools, and his determination to enhance the dignity and respect for the teaching profession.

The First Session, Summer 1906

When and how do we start? Since President Carrington would not be available until his services as state superintendent ended January 1, 1907, the Board faced the vexing question of when and how the school should open. The only money available was the $25,000 pledged by the people of Springfield. The dedicated site provided 25 acres of beautiful trees and 13 acres of tillable ground, but no buildings. The State Legislature would not convene again until 1907; consequently, it would be at least a year before any state funds would be available.

Nevertheless, the Board, in a bold move, announced that the first term would begin June 11, 1906, just six months away. Since it would be a summer term, the school expected a reasonable enrollment of practicing teachers eager to extend their certification and acquire additional skills. The expectation for a "reasonable enrollment" turned out, in fact, to be a gross underestimate. Records show 543 students attended that first session.

To answer the question of where the classes might be held, the Board turned to John H. Taylor, who operated the private Springfield Normal School and Business College. Established in 1893 to provide both teacher training and business training, the school had built an impressive four-story brick building east of Pickwick and north of Cherry streets in 1894 close to where "the poor farm" had been.

A fiercely independent institution, Springfield Normal and Business College described itself in its 1900-01 *Bulletin* as "self supporting. It is not compelled to beg at church doors nor legislative halls…no denominational bias can secure a place on its faculty."

Taylor was an astute businessman. He understood immediately that he could hardly compete with a publicly supported school, so he embraced the fledgling State Normal School #4, delivered his Normal students to its classes and five of his faculty to its staff, leased his facilities to the state for the summer, and subsequently, relocated his Business College downtown to the southeast corner of Jefferson and Walnut streets.

The good will of John Taylor extended even to helping the summer

SMSU

Normal Debating Club organized.

Legislature appropriates $302,000 of which $225,000 is earmarked for construction of Academic Hall.

Cornerstone for Academic Hall laid before an audience of 20,000.

Missouri/Springfield

Colonial Hotel opens. First building in Springfield built with a steel framework.

International/USA

Bakelite, the first wholly synthetic plastic, patented.

Daily newspaper comic strip introduced in *San Francisco Chronicle* — "Mutt and Jeff."

The first session of the State Normal School #4 occurred in the summer of 1906 with an enrollment of 543 students, of whom 84 percent were experienced public school teachers. This panoramic view includes both faculty and students.

session get under way. The "sub-normal" or high school students took their classes that first summer on Taylor's campus. He served as director of the "sub-normal" program. However, the "Normal Department" classes met in the Springfield High School, which had been leased for the summer for $290. E.E. Dodd, principal of the high school, served as director.

Considerable excitement attended the opening of the summer session for the new school. The Frisco Railroad offered a special round-trip rate of one and one-third of its regular one-way fare from any of its stations to Springfield for the summer term. Drury College offered dormitory space at 50 cents to $1 per week. Because no state money was yet available, students were asked to pay $6 in tuition for the summer session from which faculty salaries would be paid, as well as a $6 incidental fee to pay for building rental and asso-

ciated administrative expenses. Meals on campus would be $2.25 per week.

By the time June 11, 1906, arrived, the enrollment had exceeded the highest expectations and even the fondest hopes of those who planned for the opening session. Of the 543 students enrolled, 84 percent were experienced teachers. In its first session, State Normal School #4 had the second largest enrollment of the five state Normal Schools. All 22 counties in the southwest district were represented, as were 31 other counties in the state. Students from five surrounding states and Indian Territory registered for classes as well. The enrollment response seemed to underline the founders' assertion that this "is not an experiment!"

While the session was clearly not an experiment from the students' perspective, it may have looked a little different to the faculty. Recruited from Taylor's Normal School, Springfield

Scientific Lab Equipment in 1912

With the completion of Academic Hall in 1909, Normal School #4 began acquiring the most modern and up-to-date equipment for its laboratories. According to the 1912 *Bulletin*, the equipment included:

Geography Lab: Relief maps, physical maps, Johnson Commercial map, full set of weather observational material including a Government Fortin type of mercurial barometer rain gauge, "sling" psychometer, hygrodeik, Alluard hygrometer, 1,000 lantern slides, MacIntosh College Bench Lantern, 20-inch Jones relief globe, and individual stereoscopes for students.

Biology Lab: 24 student desks supplied with gas and water connections, full set of anatomical models, a rare collection of artistically mounted birds, 12 compound microscopes, a projecting microscope, Spencer sliding microtome, full set of stands and balances.

Physics Lab: Atwood's machine for falling bodies, oil seal vacuum pump, ammeters, volt meters, watt-meter transformers, three working engine models, one-half horse power gas engine dynamo set, full set of "X-Ray" tubes, a standard four-inch induction coil for vacuum tube work, wireless telegraphy, wireless telephone, large size Wimshurst static machine and a Toepler-Holz static machine.

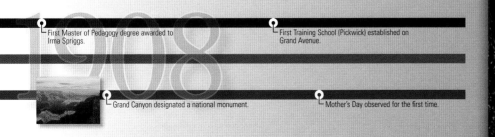

First Master of Pedagogy degree awarded to Irma Spriggs.

First Training School (Pickwick) established on Grand Avenue.

1908

Grand Canyon designated a national monument.

Mother's Day observed for the first time.

The Perils of Mechanization

When W.T. Carrington began his duties as President of State Normal School #4 in January 1907, he traveled to campus in a surrey drawn by a sorrel horse. He transported both students and visiting dignitaries from the Frisco Railroad station to campus in the surrey. However, he soon joined the motoring public with a Model T Ford. The transition from reining a horse to operating a motor-driven vehicle proved hazardous. During those first years, Carrington broke his arm twice cranking the vehicle to start it. There were no electric starters on the early Model Ts.

He often took staff and faculty members on Sunday afternoon excursions in the vehicle. One faculty member, upon returning from such a ride, admitted he "had never believed in a special dispensation of Providence until he had ridden with Mr. Carrington!"

High School, Drury College and neighboring schools, the faculty were told their salaries would range from a guaranteed minimum to a maximum, depending upon the funds available from tuition. As it turned out, they all received the minimum figure. Highest paid faculty were those borrowed for the summer from other colleges or Normal Schools. They earned between $100 and $150 a month. A young high school teacher from St. Charles, who was just finishing her doctorate in English from the University of Pennsylvania, was paid $60 a month for the summer session. The modest salary notwithstanding, Virginia Craig stayed with the school for the next 46 years and helped shape the culture and traditions of the institution throughout its first century.

The Normal School #4 ended in the black. Fees collected totaled $4,040 and bills paid totaled $3,950, leaving a balance of $90 on hand to begin the fall term.

Location Proves Fortuitous

"The locating Commission made no mistake" in establishing State Normal School #4 in Springfield, according to the July 1906 *Bulletin*. In fact, the *Bulletin* declared, "No institution ever opened under more favorable circumstances."

Indeed, establishing the school in Springfield was a fortuitous decision and contributed greatly to the "favorable circumstances" attending the opening session. Springfield was a growing community serving as a market center to southwest Missouri. It had all the characteristics that pointed toward an urban metropolitan future. The Frisco Railroad had helped to put the city on the map and served to connect it with its rural surroundings, as well as to

urban centers across the state. At the time, Springfield was the fifth largest city in the state after St. Louis, Kansas City, St. Joseph and Joplin. None of the other Normal Schools were located where metropolitan possibilities of such magnitude existed.

Yet, one is struck with the enthusiastic endorsement of Springfield when

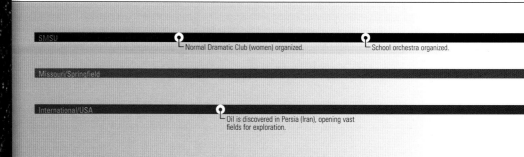

SMSU
Normal Dramatic Club (women) organized.
School orchestra organized.

Missouri/Springfield

International/USA
Oil is discovered in Persia (Iran), opening vast fields for exploration.

This 1911 photograph shows President W.T. Carrington at his desk in Academic Hall.

only three months earlier, on Easter weekend, the city was the scene of a brutal lynching that took the lives of three innocent black citizens. A raging white mob had hanged the young men from a tower on the town square beneath a replica of the Statue of Liberty and then burned their bodies, terrifying the large black community of the city. Many of them fled in fear for their lives in only a matter of hours; most never to return. That no mention was ever made of this traumatic event in *Bulletins* or other publications of State Normal School #4 gives some insight into the prevailing attitude

toward African Americans in southwest Missouri, as well as much of the rest of the nation, during the first half of the 20th century. It was an attitude which became reflected in school debate topics, humor columns, team mascots and entertainment venues in the young school for many years.

In 1905, Springfield was experiencing the first privately owned automobiles sharing the streets with horses and wagons. The city had just replaced mule-drawn trolley cars with electric models, which traveled more than 14 miles of track across the city, including a route to Taylor's Normal School on Pickwick.

Electric streetlights illuminated 160 street corners, and 2,400 telephones rang in homes and businesses in the 11-square-mile city. Five thousand five hundred people worked in 125 factories, which produced $8 million worth of products annually. The Frisco Railroad was becoming a major force in the community, with a $1.34 million annual payroll.

City government was headed by James Blair, a Democrat, who was paid $1,000 a year for his services. A.L. Loveless received $60 a month to keep the peace. In 1905, the City Council was busy passing an ordinance "requir-

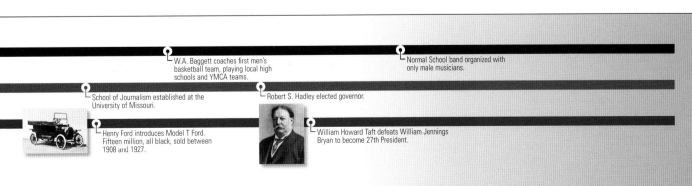

W.A. Baggett coaches first men's basketball team, playing local high schools and YMCA teams.

Normal School band organized with only male musicians.

School of Journalism established at the University of Missouri.

Robert S. Hadley elected governor.

Henry Ford introduces Model T Ford. Fifteen million, all black, sold between 1908 and 1927.

William Howard Taft defeats William Jennings Bryan to become 27th President.

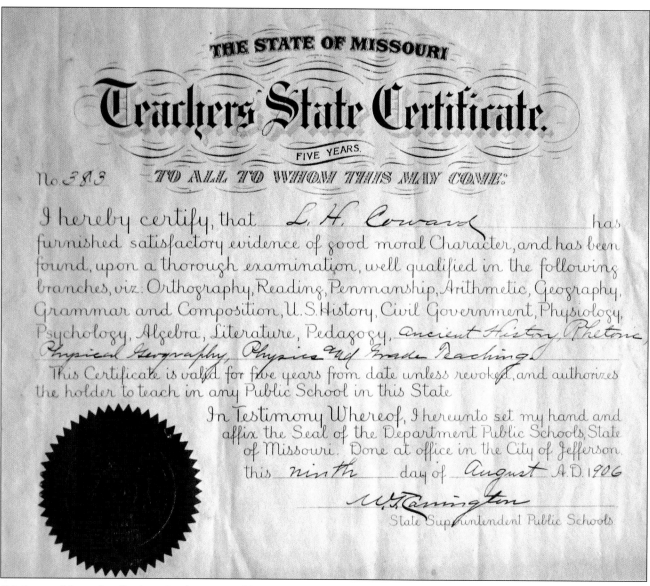

THE STATE OF MISSOURI

Teachers State Certificate.

FIVE YEARS.

No. 383   TO ALL TO WHOM THIS MAY COME:

I hereby certify, that *L. H. Coward* has furnished satisfactory evidence of good moral Character, and has been found, upon a thorough examination, well qualified in the following branches, viz: Orthography, Reading, Penmanship, Arithmetic, Geography, Grammar and Composition, U.S. History, Civil Government, Physiology, Psychology, Algebra, Literature, Pedagogy, *Ancient History, Rhetoric, Physical Geography, Physics and Grade Teaching.*

This Certificate is valid for five years from date unless revoked, and authorizes the holder to teach in any Public School in this State.

In Testimony Whereof, I hereunto set my hand and affix the Seal of the Department Public Schools, State of Missouri. Done at office in the City of Jefferson, this *ninth* day of *August* A.D. 1906

W.T. Carrington
State Superintendent Public Schools

This is one of the earliest Teachers Certificates issued by State Normal School #4, awarded on August 9, 1906, at the end of the first summer session.

ing all able bodied men to support their wives and children," and declared it against the law to "throw water from passing trains on persons gathered to watch them."

Springfield had a growing educational establishment at the time. Drury College had been founded in 1873; a first class high school had been in place for many years, and a private Normal School and Business College was operating in the city. A Carnegie Library was being built between the high school and Drury College, and 10 doctors were opening a new hospital downtown.

State Normal School #4 itself became an enthusiastic booster of the community, claiming "the school has an ideal location. We have no sickness among the student body. The air is purer and the sun shines brighter than in any other school center in the state."

1909

SMSU

Academic Hall completed. Normal School #4 moves to National and Grand campus.

First *Ozarko* yearbook published.

Missouri/Springfield

Springfield's first auto race.

International/USA

Geronimo, Apache Indian leader, dies.

National Association for the Advancement of Colored People (NAACP) founded.

First Fall Term Registers 173

On Tuesday, September 4, 1906, surreys were dispatched to the Frisco station to pick up students arriving by train for the opening of the first regular fall term. Trolley cars arrived at regular intervals at the old Normal School near Pickwick and Cherry, discharging their passengers with books, baggage and baffled looks. Groups of students crowded around the venerable Normal School building and began registering for classes and getting acquainted.

Actually, there were two schools in operation at the site. Taylor's Business College students were there, as were State Normal School #4 students. The mingling of two institutions seemed to pose little problem. By the end of the first day, 173 students had enrolled for classes in State Normal School #4, ending the anxiety about who would be enrolling for classes after the students at the summer session returned to their schools across the Ozarks.

By the winter term, the enrollment had grown almost 40 percent to 240, and the spring term enrollment had grown another 65 percent to 397. The summer term of 1907 had 726 students,

a growth of 33 percent over the first session in 1906. Fortunately, by March of 1907, Taylor was able to move his Business College into its new quarters downtown, leaving State Normal School #4 in full possession of the rented Pickwick facility. At the same time, the school was lobbying the Legislature aggressively for funds to build Academic Hall on the National Boulevard site selected earlier as "ideal for a college of 2,000 students."

Throughout the fall term of 1906, Professor C.E. Marston of the Science Department served as director of the Normal School, while President Carrington was finishing his duties in Jefferson City. Carrington arrived in Springfield in January 1907, and he immediately began planning for the development of the new campus at National and Grand and assessing student transfer credits to position them for certification as soon as possible.

No one knew better the desperate need for trained teachers, particularly in the rural schools of southwest Missouri. Carrington shared the belief of John Taylor that the function of a Normal School was

"to educate, not graduate," a peculiar notion to 21st century students. But the focus then was clearly on gaining certification. Professional certification loomed larger than an academic degree in the early days. That focus would change quickly, but in the winter and spring terms of 1906-07, Carrington was busy applying presidential scrutiny to students transferring credits from other schools. In those days, President Carrington also was the registrar and typically followed the rule of practicality in getting students qualified to teach. Evaluating transfer credits from a second- or third-class high school was more of an art than a science. Another difficult problem he encountered was the need to schedule classes and provide credits for teachers who enrolled in the

Clyde Milton Hill from West Plains, Missouri, became the second president of State Normal School #4, serving from 1918-26. He graduated with the first Normal School class in 1907 with a Bachelor of Pedagogy degree and went on to earn his A.B. degree from Drury and A.M. and Ph.D. from Teachers College, Columbia University. He joined the Yale University faculty as professor of secondary education in 1926 and later headed the university's Education Department, from which he retired in 1954.

First electric streetcar reaches campus.

Roy Ellis enrolls as a freshman at Normal School #4.

Men's basketball team plays first intercollegiate games with Drury, Warrensburg and Marionville College.

Springfield's Landers Theatre opens.

Sigmund Freud visits U.S. for the first and last time.

By the fall of 1908, a fully uniformed, 15-piece Normal School band, under the direction of Walter C. Schricker, was entertaining at chapel, athletics contests, assemblies and the autumn picnic.

middle of the spring semester because their local schools closed in March or early April to accommodate the planting season. Flexibility and creativity were the requisite skills for a successful Normal School president in those days, and W.T. Carrington qualified.

Carrington's "peculiar but practical way" of counting credits succeeded in presenting a graduating class at the end of the 1907 summer session, just over a year after the institution opened. Thirty-three students received their Bachelor of Pedagogy degree at that first commencement. One of them, Clyde M. Hill, was destined to succeed Carrington as president when the institution was on the threshold of becoming a State Teachers College in 1918.

The First Faculty

Eight pioneering faculty members guided the academic effort during that first regular term in the fall of 1906. They taught daily from 8:20 a.m. until 3:50 p.m., conducting seven 50-minute classes with an hour and 20 minutes for lunch. Their load was not only heavy, but it was also diverse. Virginia Craig, the only faculty member with a Ph.D., taught seven preparations daily, beginning with American classics and followed by beginning Latin, Shakespeare, Caesar, history of literature, and prose and poetry. She ended her day teaching Cicero. D.T. Kizer, who had a medical degree from Starling Medical College, began his day teaching zoology. He then turned to American history and American government, U.S. history, physiology, and ended his day with physics.

It was the opinion of many at the beginning of the 20th century that a well-educated person could encompass all the fields of knowledge. Whether that assumption explained the disciplinary diversity in teaching loads in the early years or necessity mothered that invention is difficult to say. In any event, it appears that Carrington held the view that a faculty member should be able to teach just about any subject in the curriculum, and teaching assignments seemed to reflect that view. Nearly everyone who joined the staff in those days took his turn teaching algebra.

Selecting faculty, according to the July 1908 *Bulletin,* was based on three considerations: (1) evidence of "thorough scholarship," (2) "special preparation and adaptation to the work," and (3) youth with experience. Earned degrees, as the July 1907 *Bulletin*

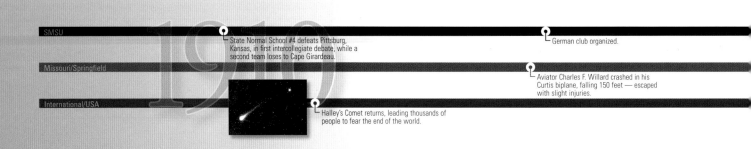

SMSU

State Normal School #4 defeats Pittsburg, Kansas, in first intercollegiate debate, while a second team loses to Cape Girardeau.

German club organized.

Missouri/Springfield

Aviator Charles F. Willard crashed in his Curtis biplane, falling 150 feet — escaped with slight injuries.

International/USA

Halley's Comet returns, leading thousands of people to fear the end of the world.

stated, were also important. "Every member of the faculty is a graduate of a high grade institution and has his well-earned degree. There is not a complimentary degree in the list." However, in examining faculty appointments over the first several years, the emphasis clearly lay in the direction of experience, not credentials.

That's not to suggest that faculty were indifferent to the need for improvement. By the end of the second year, State Normal School #4 *Bulletins* were reporting on faculty efforts to improve their preparation. C.E. Marston spent several months in the British Isles, Germany and Switzerland studying first-hand the geography — "physical, industrial and commercial." Upon his return, Marston spent a semester at the University

of Wisconsin. Ira Richardson, from the education faculty, completed a year at Teachers College at Columbia University in New York. Stella Harris also completed a year at Teachers College where she studied manual arts. Mr. Clayton P. and Mrs. Lula Kinsey of the music faculty spent a year in Germany "among the masters of music."

Carrington saw the opportunity for the school to "grow our own" credentialed faculty. In 1913 he recommended to the Board that after three years of service, faculty be given study and travel leaves with school support. For the next 60 years, the institution assisted scores of promising faculty in completing their terminal degrees under the "grow our own" philosophy.

Faculty compensation during that first fall term in 1906 reflected the plight of a state institution without state support, but a faculty committed to making State Normal School #4 the best in the state. Monthly salaries were at the minimum guaranteed level — $90 for administrators/teachers J.A. Taylor and C.E. Marston. Cora Boehringer drew $75 a month, as did Virginia Craig. D.T. Kizer received $70, and Elizabeth Park and W.E. Vaughn survived on only $50 a month for the first term. As the winter term began, the expectation for state funding in 1907 increased salaries to $150 a month for Taylor and Marston, $118.75 for Boehringer and Craig, $100 for Kizer, and $85.33 for Park and Vaughn.

As enrollments increased each year, faculty grew well beyond the "original eight."

As early as 1907, six new faculty were added. These included W.A. Daggett, librarian; Norman

Dr. Anna Lou Blair joined the Normal School Foreign Languages Department in 1908 and taught German and French for 49 years, retiring in 1957. She headed the department from 1943-57.

Freudenberger, Latin; A.P Temple, science; and B.M. Anderson, history and political economy. By 1910, there were 32 faculty members including several who would prove to be definitive shapers of the institution: Anna Lou Blair teaching German, J.W. Shannon teaching history and Clyde M. Hill in mathematics.

Faculty reputations were established quickly among students. As a student, Roy Ellis remembers George Melcher teaching trigonometry in 1909 in Academic Hall. "In his boundless enthusiasm for the grandeur of mathematics, he drew a graph of a cosine clear around the room, skipping windows and doors. Professor Melcher stood back in awe of this concept and explained how he could prolong that graph endlessly into space if he had a blackboard long enough." Not many students shared Melcher's rapture, however. "Most of us," recalled Dr. Ellis,

---

First Regents Scholarships offered to top high school graduates in 22-county area.

Corliss Buchanan appointed first athletics director.

Irvington Dormitory opens under a lease agreement with the school.

First electric lights in a Springfield home.

St. Agnes church dedicated.

First official wireless telegraph message transmitted between land and airplane.

Mexican Revolution and Civil War begins.

Baseball made an early start at Normal School #4. The 1909 team, pictured above, had a .666 season with intercollegiate competition wins over Warrensburg Normal School and Drury. The feature game of the year, which the Bears lost 13-11, was with the University of Arkansas. "That one would probably not have been lost had it not been for the poor generalship and stage fright in the first part of the game," explained the *Ozarko* editor. The team finished the season with a .234 batting average.

"were too sleepy from three hours spent on the assignment to partake of the pleasures of even so grand a concept."

Professor Norman Freudenberger's Latin recitations also qualified for student comment. A 1912 *Southwest Standard* writer made a poetic observation:

All the people dead who wrote it,
All the people dead who spoke it,
All the people die who learn it,
Blessed death, they surely earned it!

Student Characteristics

Who were these early students who recited Latin, graphed cosines, debated the enfranchisement of women, and wondered if football would ever be included in the sports venue of State Normal School #4? For the most part, they were residents of the 22-county southwest Missouri district with a scattering from other counties, from neighboring states and from Indian Territory. While a large percentage were from Greene County, most were from rural areas where the privileges of high school were virtually unknown.

Admission requirements for the fall term in 1906 said simply, "Any person 15 years of age who holds a teacher's certificate or diploma or certificate of graduation from any public or state school or other accredited institution will be admitted and classified without examination." Subsequent *Bulletins* set the minimum age at 16, but it is instructive to note that people of that tender age were already teaching in one-room schools throughout the Ozarks in the first two decades of the 20th century. Early photos of student organizations document the considerable range in the ages of students. Admission requirements by 1915 had been modified by the additional requirement that students "must furnish satisfactory evidence of good moral character," although it is not clear exactly how that was to be done.

The Common Man's School

Family incomes for Normal School students were modest. A survey by the Carnegie Foundation for the Advancement of Teaching in 1914-15 shows 82 percent of the students' families had incomes of less than $1,000 a year. A mere 2 percent reported incomes above $3,000. Almost three-fourths of the students' fathers were farmers. Eleven percent were in trades, 5 percent in manufacturing and 8 percent in professional service. Seventy-two percent of Normal School student families had five or more children.

Normal School students were not oblivious to their modest economic profile. They made a virtue of it. They emphasized the democratic character of the institution, its organizations, and its mode of operation. They extolled the fact that its clubs were open to anyone who met the standards. They celebrated the fact that many of their teachers came from modest Ozark communities, and that even the presidency of their school could be won by the hard work and perseverance of common folk.

In many respects the Normal School was itself a democratizing institution. It gave access to higher and professional education to people who could neither afford private or public colleges or universities, nor qualify for admission to such schools because of the limited opportunities for schooling beyond common school in their home areas. The Normal School literally lifted peo-

SMSU

— Hugh McIndoe of Joplin and W.M. Wade of Ozark added to Board of Regents.

— 150 students enrolled in Normal Conservatory of Music, Voice and Piano Departments.

Missouri/Springfield

— State capitol burns after being hit by lightning.

— Woodruff office building opens.

— Champ Clark elected Speaker of U.S. House of Representatives.

— Missouri becomes first state to provide aid to mothers with dependant children.

International/USA

ple into an opportunity for achievement, an opportunity most seized vigorously.

As early as 1914 the democratic atmosphere of the school caught the imagination of students. Genevieve Campbell wrote in *The Southwest Standard* about the virtues of a democratic environment in contrast to aristocratic settings with their fraternities and secret societies. Such settings, she argued, create "false standards of social selection…and a disposition to pick the wealthy rather than the worthy."

Another student in 1917 boasted, "It is not the man who can show the fattest purse nor the girl who wears the richest gowns that is the leader in our affairs…. It is brains and personality that distinguish one here…. In almost every classroom this democratic spirit prevails."

To emphasize the commitment to egalitarian values, the class of 1913 voted to wear caps and gowns for graduation. "They eliminate invidious distinctions," was the rationale given. The 1914 class reversed the decision. The 1915 class reaffirmed the cap and gown decision, and it has remained the tradition now for nearly 90 years. The struggle to maintain the democratic atmosphere is a thread which runs through the entire history of the first century of the school.

Moving to the New Campus

While the opening of State Normal School #4 was not to be understood as an experiment, it had to be understood as a venture of faith. Starting with no state money and a 38-acre campus without a building, the Board and the president found themselves exhibiting a great deal of trust in both divine providence and the welcoming community. For the first $2^{1}/_{2}$ years, the hospitality of John Taylor and his Springfield Normal School and Business College provided solutions. Students were taught in adequate classrooms in the four-story Normal School building near Pickwick and Cherry.

Two dormitories also were available on the old campus. Room and board cost $2.75 a week. Many students took advantage of the dormitory space. Others boarded with private families near the school for $3 a week. There was housing for at least 300 students in the immediate vicinity of the old Normal School.

While the temporary quarters were much appreciated, school officials understood it as a stop-gap measure at best. They were anxious to have the first building erected on the new

Football team finishes season 1-4, with a win over Drury.

Training school renamed Greenwood school in honor of Kansas City Superintendent of Schools, Dr. J.M Greenwood, considered by President Carrington to be "Missouri's greatest educator."

Irving Berlin composes "Alexander's Ragtime Band."

Standard Oil Company broken up by anti-trust suit (Sherman Antiturst Act)

First Indianapolis 500 Race won by Ray Harroun with an average speed of 75 m.p.h.

At a time when most young women in America did not finish high school, Virginia Craig had completed her doctoral studies at the University of Pennsylvania. At a time when most southwest Missourians spoke "hillbilly," Dr. Craig was teaching Latin at a newly formed Normal School in Springfield. At a time when women were not allowed to vote, Dr. Craig was an outspoken socialist.

When I enrolled at Southwest Missouri State College in the summer of 1949, I found that everything I had heard about Dr. Craig was an understatement; even the wittiest debater appeared half-witted in comparison. Yet Dr. Craig did not act superior; she could establish a rapport with the most immature student or the most sophisticated statesman. Dr. Craig was undoubtedly the funniest person I have ever known. Her debaters loved to mock her high-pitched voice, her habit of smacking her lips as she talked and the hilarious things she said.

Virginia Judith Craig was born in Maryville, Missouri, on January 14, 1878, to Silas and Annie Maria Craig. A photograph of her birth home shows a neat, one-story frame house, probably consisting of three or four rooms. A picture of Virginia at 11 years, 7 months depicts a petite, auburn-haired girl with fine features and keen, intelligent eyes. She had two sisters, both of whom also became teachers.

At age 16, Virginia moved to Springfield with her parents and sisters, graduated from Drury College in 1901 with a major in mathematics, then switched her graduate study to English because she felt that would give her more contact with people. She obtained a master's degree from Washington University in 1904 and a Doctor of Philosophy Degree from the University of Pennsylvania in 1906. Her doctoral thesis, "Martial's Wit and Humor," shows where her interest lay.

When the State Normal School #4 opened in Springfield in 1906, it had only one teacher with a Ph.D. degree — Virginia Craig, who was paid $60 a month for teaching literature and Latin in the summer term. She was head of the Speech and English Department from the inception of the school until her retirement on July 1, 1952. She wrote the first school song, edited the college *Catalog*, sponsored the Carrington Literary Society, and wrote its marching song.

Dr. Craig was a member of the Springfield branch of the American Association of University Women and twice served as its president. In 1930, she published a nationally recognized book, *The Teaching of High School English.* She was the first woman named as president of the school's chapter of the American Association of University Professors. In 1948, she was named "Missouri's Woman of Achievement," and in 1951, "Springfield's Woman of the Year." She was listed in "Who's Who in America" at a time when very few women received that recognition. In 1952, Dr. Craig was one of 13 Springfieldians elected to serve on a commission to draw up the new city charter.

Perhaps Dr. Craig is most famous for her work in forensics. She supervised the Normal Debating Club, the Webster Forensic Society, interclass debates, intercollegiate debates and oratorical contests. During her tenure as debate coach, there was no college with a consistent record of tournament victories to compare with that of SMS. Dr. Craig's teams participated in interstate oratorical contests as early as 1914. Intercollegiate debate began in earnest in 1932 at the Winfield, Kansas, tournament, where her team reached the semifinals. Two months later, at Conway, Arkansas, her students brought home the school's first interstate debate championship. As one of Dr. Craig's debaters, I can attest to the fact that she demanded complete intellectual honesty, no tricks, no plagiarism, thorough research, learning both sides of the issue and memorizing countless arguments on every conceivable point and sub-point.

A few months shy of her 98th birthday, Dr. Craig, a Presbyterian, said, "I have no ambition to live to be a hundred. My goal is to be a good Christian, and that's not easy." She treated her body as a temple; she did not smoke or use alcohol and was a physical fitness addict — her principle exercises were walking and bicycling long distances.

For many decades Dr. Craig lived at 815 E. Belmont upon land which is now, appropriately, part of the university campus. When she died on March 26, 1976, at 98 years of age, she was one of the richest people in America; not in money, but in the respect and admiration of the thousands of people whose lives she touched. ❀

38-acre campus, which would accommodate up to 2,000 students. The Legislature responded, generously providing $302,000 for the 1907-08 biennium of which $225,000 was earmarked for the construction of the first building.

When it was clear that Governor Folk would sign the appropriation, the July 1907 *Bulletin* published "cuts and floor plans of what is proposed for the best Normal School plant in the country." Actually, the cuts and floor plans were for three buildings: Academic Hall, Science Hall and Pedagogy Hall. The full dream of three completed buildings wasn't realized until 1930, but work on Academic Hall began on May 1, 1907.

On August 10, 1907, the cornerstone was laid, witnessed by some 20,000 proud and inspired students, citizens and dignitaries. Folk addressed the sun-drenched crowd for more than an hour on the progress of the state in the matters of education. During its construction "countless excursions were made by both staff and students to see the new building site." Roy Ellis recalls that "it was viewed with something of the same longing as Moses is said to have viewed the Promised Land."

On Monday morning, January 4, 1909, following Christmas vacation, students, faculty and staff "trudged across unpaved streets, along muddy paths to the new building." According to the *Springfield Leader,* "It was the intention of the faculty to have students assemble at the old building as usual that morning and march over to the new Academy (Academic) Hall where classes will do their work from now on." President Carrington and members of the faculty made speeches in the

library where students had assembled "urging them to show appreciation for what the state had done for them by immediately beginning to delve into their books."

Students, however, had a different plan. They had decided the day would be a holiday, in celebration of the move. So they "marched around the hall, went through every room in the building, roamed over the campus and wound up taking an excursion to the powerhouse. They returned to the Academy (Academic) Building through the tunnel connecting with the powerhouse. A council of war was held, and it was decided by the (student) leaders that the student body should march to the city, leaving the faculty to discuss the situation."

The students did march to the Square, where they gave "lusty Normal yells" and sang college songs. Some added noise to the demonstration "by beating pieces of tin."

The move to Academic Hall marked "the beginning of a new period in the history of the school," declared the *Bulletin* of 1909. "The period of foundation is over, and the school is prepared to do its work, and to stand in comparison…with the best Normal Schools in the State." The structure was, indeed, elegant. Built along pure Greek lines of a smooth, white limestone that is almost marble, the front of the structure featured a row of massive Ionic columns. The interior finish spared no pains. Quarter-sawed oak trim, tile and marble corridor floors, and hard maple floors in the classrooms combined to give an elegance that immediately impressed the visitor. The *Bulletin* was not bashful in declaring "The building is, in appearance

and arrangement, and in material and construction, perhaps the best school building of the state."

Solving the Housing Problem

When Academic Hall opened in January 1909, campus enrollment was nearing the 500 mark. The temporary arrangement at the old Normal School ended, but the problem of housing students became more acute with no dormitories available on the new campus. However, creative solutions abounded. "Boarding Clubs," cooperative arrangements with local householders, developed as early as 1907. Springfield builders, anticipating the need for student housing, had moved into the area earlier, building some 100 dwellings within a few hundred yards of the new campus. East of National was the "Pickwick Addition," an 80-acre subdivision with about 60 families, half of whom had new homes, and, according to *The Standard,* "nearly all accommodate Normal students." To the north was "Irvington," a 40-acre subdivision with 40 new homes all erected between 1907-09. "Driving Park," a 40-acre subdivision on the west side of the campus, was formerly a fairgrounds, but by 1909 it had "30 neat cottage homes."

Townsfolk and Normal School officials worked together to establish policies to govern housing accommodations. Men and women were not to be accommodated in the same house. All houses had to be "approved dwellings" by the school for the use of students.

The first actual dormitories constructed for the use of State Normal School #4 were built by the Irvington Hall Dormitory Company, a group organized among the faculty. Two frame

SMSU

Missouri/Springfield

Springfield's heaviest recorded snowfall — 20 inches in 18 hours.

International/USA

Madam Marie Curie awarded the Nobel Prize for chemistry for the second time.

Lenin founds the Russian Socialist Democratic Workers' (Bolshevik) party.

1912

Looking Back

Describing the Scientific Method 1912 *Bulletin*

"The student of science relies not on authority but on experiment in gaining the information sought. This carries with it the inestimable value of accurate observation, logical inference, and "cause to result" reasoning. Such work trains in originality.... The rapid progress of science in this age of scientific achievements renders authority, though valuable, of less worth than in the days of Aristotle."

~

Getting an Auditorium and Gymnasium

The 1911 General Assembly appropriated $65,000 to add an auditorium wing to the west side of Academic Hall. It provided a much-need gymnasium and auditorium space. The 1912 *Bulletin* describes the addition as "the best school auditorium in the State having 1,150 opera chairs, the best on the market, with room for 300 extra chairs in emergencies. The stage is large, having a pipe organ costing $5,000 and room for choruses of 200 voices and a large orchestra. The gymnasium will be 54 feet by 78 feet. It will be equipped for use by both men and women."

buildings were constructed at a cost of $15,000. The buildings were rented to the school for $150 a month. Irvington Hall accommodated 64 women in the fall of 1910 when it opened. It was described as "admirably managed and environed, heated by steam, lighted by electricity, well ventilated and has six toilet rooms with a bathtub in each supplied by both hot and cold water." Not wanting to antagonize citizens who also boarded Normal students, the *Bulletin* assured patrons that Irvington Hall "does not take the place of the many excellent private boarding places which can be had at about the same price ($2.50 per week)."

Other entrepreneurs entered the market providing dormitory space as well. In January 1914, it was announced that work would begin immediately on the Lombard Apartments: a three-story, private dormitory structure with a café, "and all the conveniences of a first class college dormitory." The Town/Gown partnership in providing housing continued for 45 years. It was 1950 before the school built its first residence hall.

Establishing Early Traditions

While schools are, in part, known by the "bricks and mortar" spread across their campuses, a far better insight into their character is seen in the traditions built by their students and faculty. Long before Academic Hall rose from the ground on the new campus, Normal students were selecting the building blocks of tradition. Early in the school year of 1906-07 a joint committee of faculty and students was formed to consider school colors and "select an animal which would be the emblem of athletic teams." Maroon and white were chosen as school colors,

establishing a continuing tradition.

Equally as durable was the choice of a Bear to lead athletics teams to victory. The idea for the Bear came primarily from the state seal which includes two erect bears facing the center of the design. The Normal Bear and the Drury Panther became symbols of an intense athletics rivalry in the early years. The Bear was not always triumphant, but according to one student, it did possess a distinct advantage. "You can tie a knot in a panther's tail, but not in a bear's tail." That perceived advantage fueled the imagination of cartoon makers and sports reporters throughout the early years.

Joining the enthusiasm over the school colors and mascot, Dr. Virginia Craig and Professor Clayton Kinsey collaborated to produce the first school song. It reflected the confidence and ambition of the fledgling institution as it proclaimed that Normal, of our grand old state, was "The pride of Ozark Hills.

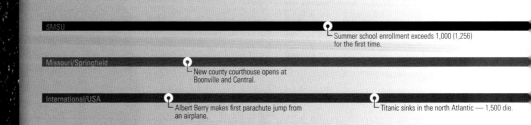

SMSU
Summer school enrollment exceeds 1,000 (1,256) for the first time.

Missouri/Springfield
New county courthouse opens at Boonville and Central.

International/USA
Albert Berry makes first parachute jump from an airplane.
Titanic sinks in the north Atlantic — 1,500 die.

No school in all the world so great."

To record the proud history of the school, a number of early student publications surfaced, two of which survived. In 1909 the first *Ozarko* yearbook appeared with Florence Silsby as editor and Ralph Anderson as business manager. Anderson was a debater, class orator, star student-athlete and aspiring poet. His poem in the first *Ozarko* no doubt provided the name for the publication. In it he extolled the virtues of the Ozarks, and in the closing line he was searching for a work to rhyme with "know." So a solution suggested itself quickly, and he penned the words, "That grandest land in all the world is that of "Ozarko." So he coined a word and established a tradition.

In January 1912 the first issue of *The Southwest Standard*, a monthly magazine containing the news and literary work of students, appeared. The publication was a project of the senior class. It represented "the characteristics of the senior — part as serious and part as humorous, but the whole filled with school spirit."

Martha Mellor was appointed the first editor by President Carrington; she was assisted by J.A. Oliver as business manager. Associate Editor Luther Adamson of Lawrence County is credited with naming the publication. Like other aspects of the new institution, the paper suffered no inferiority complex. In explaining the choice of the name *Standard,* the editor referred to the definition of the word in the Century Dictionary, which emphasized its referring to a measure of quality or value. The writer went on to say, "The above definition means that *The Standard* is a magazine established by the law of necessity…. To it all other

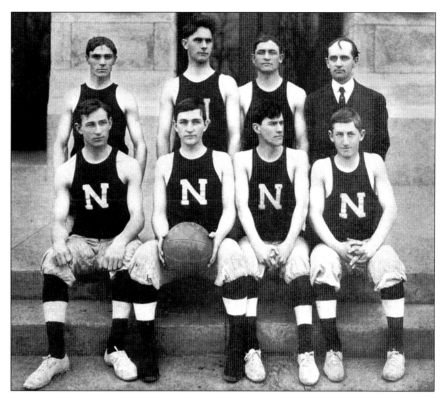

Coach W.A. Daggett, who also served as Normal School librarian, led his cagers to a 9-2 season in 1909. Scoring 370 points to their opponent's 205, the "grizzlies" as they were often called then, won the City Championship, defeating the Acorn Club, Springfield High School, and on March 5, "before the largest crowd to ever witness a basketball game in Springfield,…defeated Drury 37-17."

schools would do well to refer in case they desire to properly construct, test or regulate their own official organs as regards the extent of their influence, the quantity and quality of their contents and their permanent value to the subscriber." *The Standard* has had almost a century to live up to that challenge!

The 8-by-5 inch publication was more like a magazine than a newspaper when it was first published. Its original format consisted of 32 pages, six of which were advertisements located not on news pages but on the back pages. Subscriptions in 1912 were listed in the newspaper as 75 cents per year, with single copies costing a dime. The

Board of Regents offered funding for the publication, but the paper declined saying, "*The Standard* is proud of the position which it has attained among school papers. But it is no less proud of the fact that it has been able to attain this position without the financial aid which the Board of Regents so kindly placed at our disposal." Subscriptions to the paper grew quickly. In the second edition, the editor reported, "We now have a subscription list of nearly four hundred and it is still growing." While subscriptions assisted in funding the paper, advertising was the main source of support.

Arthur Briggs joins faculty in physical education. Coaches football and basketball and serves as athletics director.

The Southwest Standard begins publication under supervision of English faculty.

"Old" Missouri Intercollegiate Athletic Association established.

Auditorium wing completed on Academic Hall.

Teddy Roosevelt visits Springfield.

Woodrow Wilson defeats William H. Taft for the U.S. Presidency.

Coached by Elizabeth Park, Normal School mathematics instructor, the 1908-09 girls basketball team, according to the *Ozarko*, had "the most successful season in the history of Normal." The girls lost to Marshfield High School, won twice against the Springfield YWCA, and dropped their final game against Morrisville College.

The Beginnings of the Forensic Tradition

The confluence of a strong student interest in public speaking and the powerful teaching of Dr. Virginia Craig produced a forensic tradition that brought national attention to the Ozarks. "It seemed that just about every student in those days aspired to emulate Cicero or Daniel Webster," recalled Roy Ellis. The beginning of the oratorical tradition lay in the literary societies, which, in the opening years, were the primary source of extra-curricular activities and entertainments for Normal School students. Dr. Craig served as sponsor of the Carrington Literary Society. She possessed an uncanny skill in coaching aspiring orators. Craig matched that skill with an infectious enthusiasm which led students in oratory and debate to become virtual disciples.

Early on, oratorical contests and debates occurred between the campus literary societies. But early in the spring of 1910, intercollegiate debate got under way with two Normal School teams competing against a Pittsburg, Kansas, team at Springfield, and a Springfield State Normal School team in Cape Girardeau. Springfield debaters prevailed over the Kansas team, but lost in Cape Girardeau.

The growing interest in forensic activities disclosed a set of Normal School student aspirations that came to characterize the school as a leader in the state. A writer in a 1916 *Standard* expressed it well: "Today in the world at large there is no great or prominent leader who has not considerable ability as a public speaker, and who does not owe his leadership, in a large degree, to this ability." Many of the graduates of the school who have become leaders and prominent public figures spent some years in the forensics program on campus.

Debate and oratory as extra-curricular activities also went a long way in integrating the lessons of the classroom. Analytic skills were cultivated as contestants listened to the arguments of their competitors to find flaws in reasoning or irrelevance in evidence. Thought necessarily precedes speech in reasoned argument, so debaters typically gave thoughtful preparation to presenting their own case.

Then debate also focused student attention on problems of their contemporary world. Debate topics over the years are a veritable lexicon of public policy issues facing the country. In the early years of the 20th century, labor unrest occurred in city after city across the nation, disrupting the economy, pitting workers against their employers and leaving a trail of injury and death as combat became mortal. With this as the backdrop, students in State Normal School #4 were debating the proposition "that Boards of Arbitration with compulsory power should be established to settle disputes between employees and employers."

Not all debate, however, was wrestling with vexing policy problems. Normal School students also debated whether bachelors over the age of 35 should be taxed to support old maids, and whether cornbread was more important than biscuits in contributing to the advance of civilization. We have no record of the judges' decision in either of those contests.

SMSU

Missouri/Springfield — Elliot W. Major is elected governor. | State flag adopted.

International/USA — 16th Amendment ratified enabling U.S. Congress to impose federal income taxes. | Prizes are included in Cracker Jack candy boxes for the first time. | Canberra becomes capital of Australia.

Establishing the Athletics Tradition

The athletics tradition has contributed powerfully to the stature and character of the school over its century-long history. It inherited a sports tradition from John Taylor's old Normal School, which had the distinction in 1904 of playing the first football game under the lights west of the Mississisppi. Bolstering the sports tradition inherited from the old Normal School was a clear commitment on the part of the new State Normal School #4 "to send our pupils out in better physical condition than when they enter our school." To accomplish this, the school pledged to "encourage many sports and much living out of doors."

The pledge was fulfilled. The first athletics team to be organized on campus was a baseball team in 1906. There

The athletics rivalry between the Bears and their cross-town rivals, the Drury Panthers, was intense. *Standard* cartoonists exploited the possibilities of the Panther's long tail. In the 1915-16 season, the Bears defeated the Panthers in football, basketball and track — a record three knots!

was no athletics budget, but there were a host of supportive people who signed a subscription list to purchase uniforms and equipment for the players. Heading the list of donors was Dr. Virginia Craig, who gave a magnificent $5, the equivalent of nearly two full days' pay at the summer rate of compensation that first year.

Several intramural basketball teams, both boys and girls, played that first year, as well. The first actual intercollegiate athletics contest for the new school was a women's basketball game with Drury. Charles E. Marston, who directed the school most of that first year while President Carrington was finishing his work in Jefferson City, told the girls he would treat them to an oyster supper "at one of the fancier restaurants" if they were to prevail over their cross-town rival. They did, impressively, and he did as promised.

While the commitment to sports and physical well-being was unequivocal on the part of State Normal #4, there was hesitation about football. The 1907 *Bulletin* explained, "So far the Normal School has not organized a football team. It is not sure it is a desirable game for a Normal School to foster. For the present it prefers to give attention to those games that reach a larger number and appeal to students who need more moderate and less strenuous exercise."

But students had a dissenting opinion on the matter. The first *Ozarko* in the spring of 1909 needled the administration with a facetious fall athletics schedule for 1908, which showed Normal beating Phelps School in mumble-peg, 6-4; Normal losing to Pickwick 9-2 in tiddledywinks; and Normal being dispatched in Ping-Pong[TM] by the YMCA Intermediates.

Why Not Football?

The *St. Louis Star,* in 1909, reported the visit of a delegate of the Federated Women's Clubs to the Normal School Campus in Springfield. She reported that a student told her, "Our Normal School in Springfield is one of the finest in the country, and we are unique in that we do not believe in football. We have never organized a football team because we do not consider it a desirable game for a Normal School to foster, but we have basketball and tennis to our heart's content."

The delegate went on to comment, "He was a husky lad to whom kicking a goal would be as easy as a problem in simple addition. Just then a group of male students appeared, athletic looking fellows with strength of muscles characteristic of the rural districts from which many of them come. There were no narrow-chested youths who had had the street for a playground, but broad shouldered men who had developed the brawn of the fields. Therefore the absence of a football team is not for lack of muscular material."

First May Day Festival celebrated.

First Bachelor in Education degree given to Onita Woody.

Graduating class first to wear caps and gowns.

First Springfield Park Board was appointed.

Springfield's Convention Hall opens.

Igor Sikorsky becomes first person to pilot a four engine aircraft.

Working One's Way Through School

At least one-third of all Normal School students worked to help pay for their schooling. Among them were such illustrious alumni as Finis Engleman, Earl Greer, Milford Greer, Kathryn Harrison, Chester and Lester Barnhard, John Lounsbury, Leonard Oliver and Henry Detherage. Those who worked for the school were paid 15 cents an hour. The rate stayed the same until 1930 when it was raised to 25 cents an hour.

~

History Teacher Becomes Economist for Chase National Bank

The first full-time history teacher at State Normal School #4 was B.M. Anderson, who came to the school in 1907 from the University of Missouri, where he graduated Phi Beta Kappa. Anderson stayed on until 1911. He finished a doctorate in economics, taught at Harvard and served as economist for Chase National Bank in New York City for many years.

The fall season was climaxed on Thanksgiving Day with the annual marble game with Stephens Female College, Normal prevailing 62-12.

Student interest in the football question grew to the point where the Bentonian Literary Society sponsored a debate in the spring of 1909 on the question of whether or not State Normal #4 should have a football team. Harry Knight affirmed the proposition, and David Lewis opposed it. Knight won the debate and went on to captain the first football team, which took the field in the fall of 1909, coached by Walter Langston. The team played on a field on the northwest corner of the young campus, known then as "the orchard." It would later be occupied by Fruedenberger Residence Hall. Only two of the 14 players had any experience with the game. They played three high school teams that first year — Monett, Springfield and Aurora — and won. However the two games with Drury didn't turn out so well. The first intercollegiate football victory came at the expense of Pittsburg, Kansas, on Thanksgiving, 6-0.

Corliss Buchanan coached football in 1910 and 1911. Arthur W. Briggs came to the Normal School in 1912 having graduated from YMCA College in Springfield, Massachusetts. A vigorous man from a long line of whalers out of New England, Briggs was to become legendary both as a coach and as a physical education instructor. But his first

season as football coach was tough. His line averaged only 160 lbs., and the schedule called for a contest with the University of Arkansas, which pummeled the Bears 100-0. The only football victory that year was over the Verona town team. Coach Briggs decided to take his team out of competition for a year to emphasize the building of the fundamentals of the sport for his student-athletes.

By 1914, Arthur Briggs had put together a virtual football "machine." The team went undefeated and outscored their combined opposition 154-0 in six contests. The competition, admittedly, was modest — two high schools, Marshfield and Monett, and three small colleges, Marionville, Pittsburg, Kansas, and Kansas School of Mines at Weir City.

By 1915 the Bears were ready to meet their cross-town rivals over whom they had yet to be victorious. The season opener at Marionville College was a breeze, a 97-0 victory for the Bears. A week later Rolla overwhelmed the Normal team 51-20. At halftime Coach Briggs assembled his bruised and buffeted team asking, "Are you all here?" "I'm not," Finis Engleman replied. "I left an ear and part of a finger on the 25-yard line." But by Thanksgiving the team was ready to meet the Panthers of Drury. All week long a series of pep meetings had been held to practice yells and songs to boost the Bears to victory. The day arrived, but Coach Briggs was ill, forcing the team to go forward without him.

This is what the Bears' football equipment looked like, circa 1915.

SMSU
Fall enrollment reaches 537.

Missouri/Springfield

International/USA
There is a near-riot at the premiere of Stravinsky's ballet *The Rite of Spring* in Paris.

Only two members of the Bears' 1909 football team had any experience playing the game before suiting up for coach Walter Langston and manager W.E. Vaughn of the English faculty. Padding afforded little protection for the inexperienced team, but they produced a winning season, defeating high schools in Springfield, Monett and Aurora, as well Pittsburg, Kansas, Manual Training School. Drury College handed the Bears two losses in the cross-town rivalry.

The field at Drury that day was a literal mud hole due to heavy rain, but the grandstand and sidelines were filled with enthusiastic spectators including Virginia Craig who had arrived a half-hour before game time. A.P. Temple and Norman Fruedenberger excitedly beat a path up and down the sidelines. James Shannon's hat sailed into the air at frequent intervals. The game was a fiercely fought punting duel. Normal kicked 47 times, Drury 51. Tackling was as difficult as running in the rain-soaked field, but at the end the score was Normal 15, Drury 7.

The celebration began that evening with a banquet for the Bears. It spilled over into the next day as students refused to settle down from parading the halls and singing "March, march on down the field!" Roy Ellis recalled that "Dean Marston, realizing it was futile to retain custody of their bodies when their minds were obviously elsewhere, declared a holiday until the following Monday."

The sports rivalry with Drury had become legendary by 1915-16, and in that year State Normal School #4 accomplished a spectacular triumph — winning over Drury in football, basketball and track! Three knots had been tied in the Panther's tail!

Basketball in the early years had been handicapped by lack of facilities. Practices could be scheduled only two periods a week at the YMCA. W.A.

Daggett, school librarian, coached the men's team. Elizabeth Park assisted with the women's teams. Despite the fact that the school's first intercollegiate sports contest had been between the women's basketball team and Drury's girls, women's intercollegiate sports faded rather quickly. In 1910 there was no mention of a women's basketball team. The 1911 *Ozarko* shows a picture of the women's team, but no story. In 1913 there appeared to be only interclass games with both the men's and women's teams competing. In 1914, women's basketball was back, boasting an undefeated season playing Springfield High School, Walnut Grove High School, Marionville College,

└ Pipe organ installed in Academic Hall.

└ Greenwood school adds high school division.

└ Greenwood School relocated to Kingshighway

└ Henry Ford introduces the moving assembly line.

A forensic or athletics victory over cross-town rival Drury College was frequently an occasion for a "holiday" from classes.

Drury College and Crescent College.

But beginning in 1915, there is no mention of women's intercollegiate competition in either the *Ozarko* or *The Standard*. With the organization of the "old" Missouri Intercollegiate Athletic Association (MIAA) in 1912 and its exclusive scheduling of men's contests, women's intercollegiate athletics competition ceased. It would be 50 years before women's intercollegiate athletics would start again. The "old MIAA" was a loose collection of about a dozen public and private four-year schools in Missouri. Membership in the league changed often, and there was no consistent schedule of games or opponents for member schools. The league operated primarily for football, men's basketball, and later track.

In the meantime, men's basketball, also under the leadership of Arthur Briggs, was picking up speed. In 1915, State Normal #4 played its first full season of intercollegiate play, winning five and losing six. The Drury rivalry heated up as the Panthers drubbed the Bears twice. The 1916 season saw the Bears defeat Drury twice and place second in the

MIAA conference. By the 1917 season, Normal had a scoring machine in place. Despite losing to Drury 28-27, the Bears won their first conference basketball championship.

Baseball suffered much the same fate as women's basketball. It had a vigorous start in 1906-07 and winning seasons in 1908 and 1909 and again in 1913. In 1912 the baseball team played its first full season of intercollegiate competition with a 5-5 record. Without the inclusion of baseball in the newly organized MIAA Conference, the Bears struggled to find competitors in 1913. They beat the Springfield Painter's Union but lost to Drury three times. Their last games were played in 1914. Baseball, like women's athletics, would wait 50 years to return to campus.

Intercollegiate track competition started slower but lasted longer than baseball. High school interest in

track and field events was widespread throughout the Ozarks, so in 1910 the Normal School sponsored a track meet for area high schools. Intramural track appeared in 1912 with a Field Day for contests between literary societies, boarding clubs and other student groups. W.A. Daggett won the 100-yard faculty foot race in 15 seconds flat. The fastest student ran it in 11 seconds. By 1914 the Field Day had become an interclass event with sophomores winning, closely followed by juniors and freshmen. Seniors also ran.

Intercollegiate track competition started in 1915 with a triangular meet with Drury and Rolla, the Bears doing no better than third. However, in the last meet of the season where the Bears were matched against seven other collegiate teams, they finished fourth. In 1916 the Bears improved by defeating Drury and claiming second in the conference.

Coach Briggs' 1915 track squad found intercollegiate competition tough. In a triangular meet with Drury and Rolla on May 8, the Bears finished last. A week later they defeated the Pittsburg, Kansas, thinclads. The climactic intercollegiate meet on May 21 included eight colleges, the Bears finishing fourth. However, Paul Boyd distinguished himself by winning the two-mile race in 10 minutes and 44 seconds. "I could have done better," Boyd remarked, "but I had to sit down in the third lap and take a rock out of my shoe."

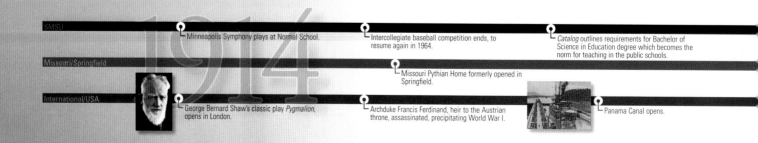

SMSU
Minneapolis Symphony plays at Normal School. / Intercollegiate baseball competition ends, to resume again in 1964. / *Catalog* outlines requirements for Bachelor of Science in Education degree which becomes the norm for teaching in the public schools.

Missouri/Springfield
Missouri Pythian Home formerly opened in Springfield.

International/USA
George Bernard Shaw's classic play *Pygmalion,* opens in London. / Archduke Francis Ferdinand, heir to the Austrian throne, assassinated, precipitating World War I. / Panama Canal opens.

Finis Engleman made a 1917 fashion statement with his Bear basketball uniform. The 1917 *Ozarko* described Engleman as "the best basketball center in the state. He has seldom, if ever, been out-jumped, and he uses good head-work which helps in winning a game. Finis is a good floor worker; he guards closely and can shoot baskets with perfect ease."

Athletics competition contributed richly to institutional identity and school spirit. The chief architect of the athletics program was Arthur Briggs. In addition to directing the entire program, Mr. Briggs, at one time or another, coached every sport the institution had, and did so successfully. His 20-season tenure with the football Bears saw the teams post a record of 76-58-11. At the close of the university's first centen-

nial, that victory total had never been exceeded by any other football coach. His basketball tenure lasted only nine seasons, but the 105-32 record his teams produced in the sport achieved a .766 winning percentage, a feat exceeded by only one coach whose tenure was longer than a single season.

Throughout the early years, faculty and students alike crowded the bleachers, lined the sidelines and hung from the balconies to cheer for their Bears. The Bears' struggles were their struggles. Their triumphs were the school's triumphs. They had the sense they were building a tradition.

Building a Music Tradition

Joining debate and athletics in the establishment of early traditions was the music department headed by Clayton Kinsey and his wife, Lula. Clayton Kinsey was among the faculty who moved to State Normal #4 from the old Springfield Normal School in the fall of 1906. As early as 1907 a Normal Choir and a Glee Club had made their appearance. In the fall of 1908, a 15-piece school band was organized under the direction of Martin C. Schricker. Pictures of the group indicate they were without uniforms, but not without enthusiasm. They were part of the pep squad playing at athletics events and the annual picnic as well as more formal performances at chapel periods. The first band contained only male musicians. By 1909 they had added a 16th member and acquired smart uniforms.

A Normal School orchestra also made its appearance in 1908 with eight members. It was directed by Sidney Meyers. Vocal music developed quickly. The Choral Club gave several classic

All Normal Schools in Missouri expand curricula to offer four full years of college work.

First business courses are taught by J.D. Delp.

Red traffic lights introduced in Cleveland, Ohio.

"St. Louis Blues" music published by W.C. Handy and Harry Pace.

Looking Back

Faculty Credentials

In 1907, among the 15 full-time faculty members at the Normal School, only five had master's degrees or higher. There were only seven Ph.D.s teaching in all of Missouri's State Normal Schools at the time. Virginia Craig held the only Ph.D. in Springfield throughout the normal school era (1905-19). By 1919 the proportion of master's degrees among Normal School faculty had increased from 26.6 percent to 29.8 percent, and the number of bachelor's degrees decreased from 53.3 percent to 29.8 percent. A second Ph.D. joined the faculty 1924. Francis Todd H'Doubler carried a Ph.D. in bacteriology from the University of Wisconsin and an M.D. degree from Harvard.

Marketing Springfield Normal

When Roy Ellis was an elementary school student in Wright County, he recalled using school tablets from Springfield Tablet Company which were emblazoned with big letters, "With Springfield Normal, Learn it Right!" The slogan advertised the private Normal School under John Taylor, which would soon give up its teacher training program to the new State Normal School #4. Ellis came to Springfield in 1909 and graduated from the Normal School in 1911.

The State Normal School Choral Club in 1915 boasted 100 members. Directed by Professor C.P. Kinsey, the singers produced *Ruth*, a cantata by Gaul, and *Melusina*, by Hoffman, during the 1914-15 season. In the background is the pipe organ, which was featured in Academic Hall auditorium.

contatas in 1912 and then courageously undertook Handel's *Messiah* for its capstone event at the Landers Theater downtown. It was joined by the 60-piece Minneapolis Symphony and four noted soloists. The chorus, directed by Clayton Kinsey, numbered 200 voices and in the tradition of modest understatement, the 1912 *Bulletin* described the event as "the best musical entertainment ever given in Springfield." The campus visit of the Minneapolis Orchestra began a tradition that continued for several years.

Rules for Student Conduct

The traditions being established were rooted in a campus ethic that was clearly no-nonsense. Teachers were held to high standards of moral conduct in the communities they served, and the Normal School assumed those seeking entrance to the profession were well grounded in moral principle. Consequently, the first *Bulletin* to include a section on General Regulations contained four rules, each about attendance, and only one dealing with student conduct. It said simply, "Students are prohibited from attending billiard rooms, pool rooms and similar places of resort." The prohibitions appear to have been designed as much to protect the institution's reputation as student welfare.

There was no need for a statement about smoking or drinking. It was assumed that students understood that such behavior was entirely inconsistent with a teacher training academy. By July 1907 those assumptions were made explicit. The *Bulletin* happily reported that, "So far it has not become necessary to formulate any rules of conduct, nor indulge in any espionage. Students conduct themselves as members of a law abiding community and each takes pride in the good name of the community." The *Bulletin* went on to warn any potential student that "they must be able to practice self-restraint when necessary." That *Bulletin* also relaxed the strictures on billiard rooms and pool rooms by generalizing the prohibition saying, "Attendance at questionable resorts and participation in questionable amusements and practices are strictly prohibited." There seemed to

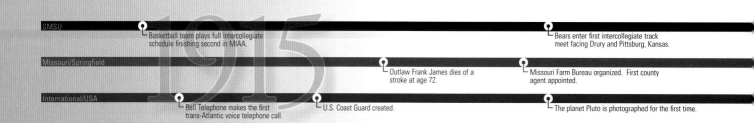

1915

SMSU
Basketball team plays full intercollegiate schedule finishing second in MIAA.
Bears enter first intercollegiate track meet facing Drury and Pittsburg, Kansas.

Missouri/Springfield
Outlaw Frank James dies of a stroke at age 72.
Missouri Farm Bureau organized. First county agent appointed.

International/USA
Bell Telephone makes the first trans-Atlantic voice telephone call.
U.S. Coast Guard created.
The planet Pluto is photographed for the first time.

be no need to be explicit in either of these prohibitions. Everyone knew what was "questionable."

Religion Plays a Central Role

The moral consensus of the period was built out of the devout religious conservatism found throughout the Ozarks. It was no accident that the first two organizations established on campus were the Young Men's Christian Association and the Young Women's Christian Association. These organizations reinforced what had been learned at home and in churches throughout the region. Nor was it a coincidence that the three assembly periods scheduled each week were called "chapel." The Wednesday assembly period was reserved for local ministers and other religious leaders to deliver advice and encouragement in living the circumspect life. Nor was it unusual to hear President Carrington deliver a devout prayer from the lectern of a state educational institution. It wasn't that there was an indifference to

church/state issues that have come to trouble our times, it was simply that there was an assumption that Protestant piety and national patriotism were inextricably tied together.

Religious revivals were routinely held on campus as was regular *Bible* study. The 1907 *Bulletin* declared "we are especially proud of the three Christian Associations. The Normal has the banner Christian Endeavor organization in Springfield. More than one-half of the students are regular participants." The *Bulletin* goes on to report on the revivals sponsored by the YMCA and YWCA (Y), indicating that "two-thirds of the young men who were not church members made the confession and joined one of the 30 (local) churches."

"Some have called the state schools irreligious, un-Christian. Not here!" boasts the Normal School *Bulletin*. "No church school has ever had a stronger Christian spirit among its student body — a spirit devoid of denominationalism." The claims may seem exaggerated, but the evidence suggests that the strong Christian orientation was pervasive. The President delivered lectures on the practice of prayer; the faculty sponsored Y groups and spoke at Christian Endeavor meetings, and students attended "Chapel" regularly and took strong initiative in planning *Bible* study and Christian witness activities. The January 1908 *Bulletin* reports the results of such pervasive religiosity. "A high moral, a high religious tone runs through the school. It is practically a self-governing body of students.... Students vie with each other in contributing to the good order and happy demeanor of the entire student body."

The *Bulletin* concludes that there

The debate program at Normal School #4 started in 1906 with competition between literary societies and debating clubs. By 1917, competition had become intercollegiate with all five state normal schools vying for honors.

was little need for rules for expulsion. "Now and then a student of low ideals or unworthy spirit enrolls. The surroundings bring such into harmony with this school spirit or he voluntarily withdraws," claims the *Bulletin*. "Only twice during the past year has it become necessary for the school authorities to suggest to students that they would better to withdraw."

Such idyllic conditions ultimately give way to harsher realities, but it is clear that State Normal School #4 saw the Christian vocation and the teaching profession co-terminus in the early years. Its diplomas bore the guarantee of "good moral character" for those

First varsity letters awarded to student-athletes.

Legislature appropriates $250,000 for education building, which is later redirected to Warrensburg to replace a building destroyed by fire.

Fall term enrollment reaches 555. Summer term, 1,622.

Missouri Day established by the 48th General Assembly

Cornerstone laid for new capitol building in Jefferson City.

German submarines sink Allied and neutral shipping in the Atlantic, including the Lusitania, with a loss of 1,198 lives.

Margaret Sanger founds the first American birth-control clinic in Brooklyn, New York.

1905-19 Missouri State Normal School, Fourth District   31

Looking Back

Snapshot of the U.S. circa 1905

Life expectancy: 47 years

Homes with bathtubs: 14 percent

Cost of a three-minute telephone call from Denver to New York: $11

Paved roads: 144 miles

Average wage: 22 cents an hour

Babies born at home: 95 percent

Physicians practicing without a college education: 90 percent
(They attended medical schools described by the press and the government as "substandard.")

Population of Las Vegas: 30

Adults classified as illiterate: 10 percent

Marijuana, heroin and morphine: available over the counter at drug stores

Total murders recorded in the entire United States: just over 200

Recruitment Tool, 1907

"The campus will be planned by a skilled landscape gardener and made the most beautiful spot in this, the brightest and sunniest land on earth. The Ozark country has the best climate and everything here contributes to health, comfort, and good cheer."

Normal School *Bulletin*
April 1907

who carried it, and at the end of its sixth year declared "no school was ever more earnest, industrious, conscientious and circumspect than the Fourth District Normal; during the past six years nothing unseemly has marred the peace, happiness or good name of the school."

The Student Experience

Student response to the Normal School experience was clearly enthusiastic. Those who arrived by train in the early years were met at the Frisco depot by older students dressed in maroon and

white. Surreys carried their baggage to campus, where they were helped to settle into dormitories or approved local homes.

Most of the early students had their educational credentials examined personally by President Carrington. He learned their names, outlined their class schedules and calculated their credits toward the coveted certificate or degree. Faculty were described as scholarly and likely to demand thorough work of the students. But the 1907 summer *Bulletin* also reassured the students that the faculty "know what constitutes proper effort and will not demand unreasonable things."

The daily schedule was tightly structured with 50-minute classes beginning at 8:00 a.m. The lunch intermission went from noon until 1:20 p.m. There were daily "chapel" exercises at 10:00 a.m. On Monday the assembly was devoted to lectures and discussion by the faculty. Typical of the activities was a lecture by Professor Shannon on "Lincoln, The Man," a discussion by Professor Irion on the "Philosophy of Democracy," and a lecture by Professor Temple on "The Life

The first cup awarded in debate competition on the Normal School campus shows that the Carrington Literary Society prevailed in 1909, 1910, 1911, 1914 and 1915, while the Bentonians were victorious in 1912 and 1913.

SMSU

Bertha Wells begins teaching Latin in the Foreign Language Department.

Missouri/Springfield

International/USA

Albert Einstein completes his general theory of relativity.

Franz Kafka publishes *The Metamophosis*.

and Work of Thomas Edison." These co-curricular chapel assemblies were all-school meetings, which built a sense of community among students and enriched their formal class work with interesting and useful information.

The Wednesday chapel was devoted to religious programs, often sponsored by the Y groups and supported by the local ministerial alliance. The programs were typically devotional in nature, and sometimes featured out-of-town speakers including national figures such as Rabbi Samuel Mayerberg. Attendance at chapel was monitored by faculty, and students who became notable by their absence were counseledto

be present next time.

The Friday assembly was planned as an entertainment program provided by on-campus musical groups, literary societies, and guest visits by the likes of pianist Percy Grainger, the Charles Coburn Players and the St. Louis Symphony. Occasionally faculty gave demonstrations of the practical applications of their fields of knowledge.

On Tuesday and Thursday, the assembly periods were devoted to "section work." "Section work" was remedial academic work, and students were assigned to a particular section based on the faculty's assessment of their needs. The July 1907 *Bulletin* promised

students, "There will be sections for word-study, for current events, for callisthenic drills, for study of sanitation and decoration, for penmanship, for correct speech, for memory games, etc."

Weekday evenings were understood to be study times. Friday night was the appointed time for Literary Societies to meet while Saturday was reserved for school social events.

Planning the student experience was deliberate and detailed. The *Bulletin* in the fall of 1906 promised that "every precaution will be taken and every encouragement given to the end that right social, religious, and literary influences surround the student." To

Literary Societies were among the first organizations established at State Normal School #4. In the fall of 1906, the Carrington Literary Society was organized with Dr. Virginia Craig as the sponsor. It joined the Bentonian Literary Society, which had been organized earlier at John Taylor's Normal School. Dr. Craig can be seen in the middle of the third row.

Football Bears complete an undefeated season.

Bears celebrate first athletics sweep over Drury winning in football, basketball and track.

Professional Golfers Association (PGA) is formed.

Louis Brandeis becomes the first Jewish justice appointed to the Supreme Court.

The Bentonian Literary Society enjoyed the distinction of being five years older than any Literary Society at State Normal #4. It was organized in the fall of 1901 at John Taylor's private Normal School. The 1907 Society pictured above consisted of 25 men and 25 women "whose names were rigidly investigated by a committee and voted on by secret ballot...insuring a high grade of scholastic qualification for admission."

accomplish these ends, school officials called upon the YWCA, YMCA and the established Literary Societies.

The YWCA was the first group to form with 22 charter members, adopting the motto, "Every Girl for Christ." Quickly thereafter the YMCA took shape and defined its objectives as, (1) fostering *Bible* study, (2) training men for Christian service, (3) promoting fellowship and aggressive Christian work, and (4) leading men to devote their lives to Christian ideals.

The Place of Literary Societies

Literary Societies were the shapers and carriers of Normal School culture in the early years. They were the center of campus social life and defined its content with thoughtful precision. Programs were planned to develop self-expression. The arts and literature were tools to that end. And, of course, debate and oratory became important components of the Literary Society experience. The Bentonian Society was inherited from the old Normal School and was named in honor of Missouri's distinguished Senator, Thomas Hart

Benton. The Bentonians hosted the famous debate on the football question in 1909. On the same program Scott Smith gave an oration and Luther Adamson offered a whistling solo.

A second Literary Society was quickly organized in the fall of 1906 with Dr. Virginia Craig as the advisor. The Carrington Society, like the Bentonians, had colors, a motto, and a rousing marching song written by Dr. Craig. It was customary for the societies to gather elsewhere on campus when a debate or oratorical contest was scheduled, and then march into the audi-

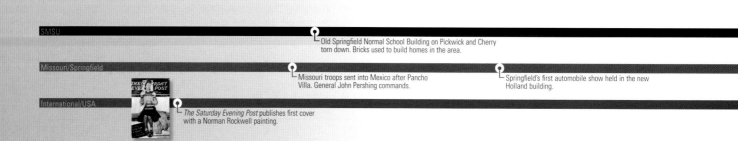

SMSU

Old Springfield Normal School Building on Pickwick and Cherry torn down. Bricks used to build homes in the area.

Missouri/Springfield

Missouri troops sent into Mexico after Pancho Villa. General John Pershing commands.

Springfield's first automobile show held in the new Holland building.

International/USA

The Saturday Evening Post publishes first cover with a Norman Rockwell painting.

torium amid the sound of cadenced yells and rousing cheers, much like an athletics contest.

The Literary Societies were very competitive. They "rushed" promising new students and engaged each other in every kind of competitive endeavor. They were joined in this activity by the Boys' Normal Debating Society and the Girls' Normal Dramatic Club. So valuable were the experiences in the Literary Societies that the school required every student seeking the Regents Certificate to be an active society member for at least one term or, failing that, the student must add one-third additional credit to his class schedule. For the Bachelor of Pedagogy degree, the student must show three terms of Literary Society activity or take one full extra unit of credit. The *Bulletin* for July 1907 reflected the esteem with which these societies were held by claiming that they "offer the best opportunity for cultivating self control and the spirit of initiative."

The Literary Societies played an enormously important role in the formative years of the institution. By World War I and the end of the Normal School period, they had begun to wane in the face of rival organizations, particularly the four class organizations that picked up the debating tradition. But the culture of State Normal School #4 was clearly shaped in the activities of the Literary Societies.

Clubs and Organizations

Student organizations quickly proliferated on the Normal campus. Within 10 years, the initial three had become 19. Additional literary societies were organized, disciplinary clubs were added, and even county clubs were

established to provide a sense of home to students from outlying areas. The Alumni Association was established in 1907 immediately upon the granting of degrees to the first graduates. A German Club was organized in 1910, as was the Pickle Club, which led in comic action and fun for its members

promoting vinegar as its favorite drink and sour grapes as the club fruit. A Mathematics Club formed in 1912. The Scribbler's Club organized the next year to write the senior class play.

The expansion of clubs and organizations did nothing to destroy the democratic ideal of the young school.

This Buster Brown notebook was the Bentonian Literary Society's cash book for 1910. It records that initiation into the society cost 50 cents and yearly dues were 25 cents.

D.T. Kizer, M.D., and professor of biology, identifies tobacco as a health risk.

Southwest Standard becomes an independent student newspaper.

First fountain built in front of Academic Hall, a gift of the class of 1916.

Streetcar strike called in Springfield.

First female, Jeannette Ranken of Montana, elected to Congress.

One millionth Model T is produced by Ford.

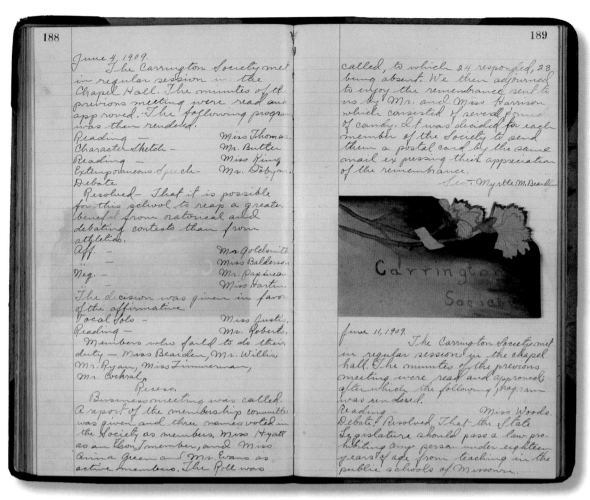

This book of minutes from the Carrington Literary Society reports that on June 4, 1909, the society engaged in a debate, "Resolved: That it is possible for this school to reap greater benefit from oratorical and debating contests than from athletics." The affirmative, argued by Inez Balderson and Mr. Goldsmith, prevailed.

Access to organizations was open to all, and a sense of dignity was felt by these people whose origins were ordinary but whose school-inspired dreams and aspirations were indeed bold.

Social Traditions Established

Lest it be thought that the Normal School students spent their entire week poring over books, memorizing speeches, researching debate topics, preparing Literary Society programs and developing strategies to fully Christianize the campus, they also participated in "campusology," an unlisted course in the *Bulletin* but engaged in by most students; it was a favorite. Articles about it appeared in *The Standard*. As Roy Ellis recalled as a student, "cupid lurked in every billowing bower and rode on every whispering breeze."

The fun occasions were both spontaneous and planned. School picnics became a tradition. The entire student body was transported five miles in horse-drawn wagonettes to Steury's Cave east of Springfield, where they spent the day exploring, playing games, competing in all kinds of contests and consuming huge baskets of picnic fixings. Halloween was celebrated with an all-girls planned party for the boys. Valentine's Day was reversed with the boys planning a school-wide party for the girls. Games and singing were the primary entertainment.

Dancing had a quite spontaneous beginning on campus. In the early years, while it was not prohibited by regulation, dancing was frowned upon by President Carrington and thus was never a part of school parties — that is, until 1911. After the Halloween party that year, a group of students and faculty were visiting in what is now the registrar's office in Carrington Hall. Someone in the group started playing the piano, and quite spontaneously, Professor Shannon and his wife got to their feet and began moving rhythmically across the floor. Others watched in amazement. As the ice was broken, others moved cautiously to the floor to join the Shannons, and dancing started at State Normal School #4. Professor Shannon explained to the startled company that he was from Wisconsin, "where everything turns into a dance!" Jim Shannon and his wife became guest chaperones at campus dances for years after that event. "I guess we went to hundreds of them," he recalled.

Practical jokes added to the fun of the early years. Dr. Craig was known to take a dim view of the early silent movies. She rarely passed up an opportunity to declare their degenerative effect on culture. Some students managed to get a snapshot of Dr. Craig and Miss Mary Woods visiting on a campus sidewalk. They then went to the old Jefferson Theater and took a photograph of the billboard advertising a double feature "thriller-chiller" show for the day. They managed to superimpose one negative over the other so that the resulting picture showed these two venerable and highly-respected teachers standing in front of the Jefferson Theater excitedly reading the sensational movie menu!

Student pranks were sometimes fueled by class rivalries. In fall of 1910, members of the sophomore class climbed inside the 100-foot-tall smokestack beside the powerhouse and mounted their class pennant at the top. The next morning the juniors shot it down with shotgun blasts and mounted

their own pennant atop the stack. The following night a coalition of rival groups climbed the stack and captured the pennant. Roy Ellis remembered "there was a lot of traffic up and down the inside that smokestack" despite the fact that "the cleats were loose and the soot was blinding."

Pageantry played a prominent role in campus life in the early years. Arthur Briggs spearheaded much of this effort including the May Day celebration initiated in 1913. The first May festival was held west of Academic Hall. The May Pole Dance was done by 16 young women from the Literary Societies. A gymnastic exhibition was done by a group of young men. Even Greenwood School youngsters marched in the colorful event. Wave Brown was the first May Queen.

By 1915, the May Poles had multiplied to nine, and an Indian Club torch drill was added to the festivities. In 1917, 50 May Poles were wound in a dramatic display of pageantry. Crowning of the May Queen and winding of the May Poles continued for 30 years.

In trying to revive the May Day and Joyland pageants in 1947, Louise Miller wrote a stirring tribute in *The Standard* to their place in school life. "These two events were outstanding in Springfield and outstanding in the lives of those who took part…. More than 1,000 college and Greenwood students marched, danced and wound the May Poles in honor of the newly crowned Queen of May. The gorgeous array of color, movement and grace was climaxed by the sight of 50 multi-colored May Poles being wound simultaneously before breathless spectators."

The student experience evolved quickly in the early years. In its open-

Grade Distribution, 1913-14

Grade	Collegiate Division	High School Division	All
A	32%	25%	29%
B	47%	44%	46%
C	9%	13%	11%
Conditioned	1%	3%	2%
Half Credit	2%	3%	2%
Failed	3%	6%	4%
Dropped	6%	6%	6%

~

Missouri Population Data, 1910

Missouri was the seventh-largest state in the union in 1910 with 3.25 million citizens. Five percent were African American. Sixty percent of the population lived in rural areas. Occupations for people 10 years of age and older were listed as: Agriculture and Forestry, 35.5 percent; Manufacturing, 23.6 percent; Trade, 11.1 percent; Domestic and Personal Services, 9.8 percent; Transportation, 7.1 percent; Clerical, 5 percent; Professional Services, 4.7 percent; Mining, 2.1 percent; and Public Service, 1.1 percent.

Roy Ellis joins faculty to teach economics and sociology.

Booster Club organized, forerunner of Student Government.

Missouri and Kansas National Guards consolidate to form 35th Division.

Three children claim to see the Virgin Mary near Fatima, Portugal.

Congress passes the 18th Amendment, banning the manufacture and sale of alcoholic beverages.

By 1916 Greenwood Training School was operating on campus out of a bungalow just southwest of Academic Hall, where Pummill Hall now stands. While training of the hand and mind were important to Greenwood teachers, the *Ozarko* reported that "they realize that the chief aim of education is character development."

ing terms, many of the Normal students considered themselves as "temporary," staying just long enough to get a teaching credential and not doing much advanced work. But the summer 1909 *Bulletin* noted that not only more students were doing advanced work, but also "more noteworthy than this is the fact that the general spirit of the student body has changed." Whereas in the very beginning, students were interested primarily in one thing — how much they could get out of school in the least possible time, now 2¹/₂ years later "the student is interested in the school itself, has a pride in the institution, is willing to work for it, is pleased with the progress of other students, takes active part in the clubs, societies, athletics teams and other school activities." In a word, the school had become a community.

Academic Standards Established

The success in molding a community was being matched in the academic life of State Normal School #4. In the summer of 1906, 84 percent of those enrolled were experienced teachers. But when the fall term opened, things were vastly different. Eighty-five percent of those enrolled were in the "sub-normal" curriculum, the equivalent of high school work. The admission policy in 1906-07 stated it clearly, "You can begin where you are." Thus an eighth grade credential or even a third grade certifi-cate admitted a student if he was deemed capable of eventually doing advanced work.

The "elementary" department gave work at the junior and senior level of high school plus some professional courses that led to the county certificate qualifying the student to teach the elementary grades in rural school districts. The "advanced normal" department was equivalent to the first two years of college with extensive professional training in pedagogy. Upon completion of the two-year program, the student received the Bachelor of Pedagogy degree and a lifetime teaching certificate. So in the earliest years, the Normal School simultaneously consisted of refresher work in the common

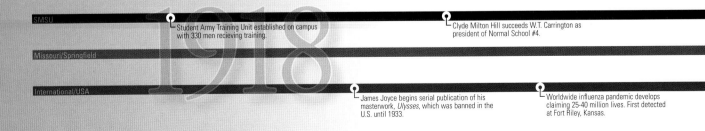

SMSU

Student Army Training Unit established on campus with 330 men recieving training.

Clyde Milton Hill succeeds W.T. Carrington as president of Normal School #4.

Missouri/Springfield

International/USA

James Joyce begins serial publication of his masterwork, *Ulysses*, which was banned in the U.S. until 1933.

Worldwide influenza pandemic develops claiming 25-40 million lives. First detected at Fort Riley, Kansas.

school curriculum, high school work and two years of college work. The norm for teachers at that time was the two-year Bachelor of Pedagogy degree.

But change occurred quickly. Standards increased and by 1914 teachers had moved from the two-year Bachelor of Pedagogy degree to the four-year Bachelor of Education degree. As early as 1908, State Normal School #4 had awarded a Master of Pedagogy degree to Irma Spriggs, symbolizing its academic aspirations. But despite the rising standards and the institutional aspirations, Normal Schools across the state continued some teaching on the high school level and certifying people to teach in rural schools who had not yet completed the Bachelor of Pedagogy degree.

As early as 1908, the A.B. degree (Bachelor of Arts) was listed in the *Bulletin* reflecting the ambitions of State Normal School #4. In 1910 it listed the Bachelor in Education degree anticipating the four-year degree becoming the norm. And in 1913 it actually awarded that degree to Onita Woody.

Despite the striving for higher standards, the school started with people where they were. In 1913, after seven graduation exercises, 798 students had completed high school, 411 had received the Bachelor of Pedagogy diploma and two had received the four-year Bachelor of Education degree.

Those receiving the full four-year Bachelor of Education degree steadily increased so that by 1915 nine were receiving the diploma, and in 1919, the final year of the Normal School period, 25 candidates took the degree.

The Curriculum Evolves

With standards for teaching rising, the Normal School curriculum expanded, as well. In the fall term of 1906, a total of 48 courses were offered including "subnormal" or high school studies. Eleven of those courses were in pedagogy, nine in science, eight in mathematics, seven in history and civics, five in English, two in foreign languages and six in special subjects including music and manual arts. By the end of the Normal School period in 1919, the total number of courses had increased four-fold to 240. The vast majority (179) were college level. High school offerings stood at 61.

The commitment to teacher education remained powerful, including an ambitious extension program that sent faculty into towns and villages of southwest Missouri to teach night courses for the benefit of working teachers. In the fall of 1906, Professor Boehringer taught special methods in towns adjacent to Springfield. Dr. Craig taught literature in addition to her seven-course load on campus. By the fall of 1907, 156 teachers had enrolled in extension work in eight different locations. That number swelled to 350 by 1919. Correspondence courses were offered to those beyond the reach of extension work.

There were other curricular challenges coming from the southwest district, as well. The region was primarily rural, so farm problems were indigenous to family life here. Seeking to serve area needs, the Normal School organized the first "Short Term in Agriculture" to run from February 8 to 13 in 1909. Teachers were expected to attend the sessions since it was seen as important "to understand the conditions of (the) district…(and) to work effectively for the betterment of the rural home and rural society." The invitation was extended to all farm families throughout the district to hear the lectures and see the demonstrations. They were advised that, "The school has an excellent stereoptican and some of the lectures will be illustrated, thus simplifying the work."

Another excursion into the practical skills occurred in 1914 with the addition of commercial courses to help those interested in business. J.D. Delp led the charge and helped to organize a Department of Commerce in 1918.

Normal School Aspirations

The Normal School mission evolved rapidly at the beginning of the 20th century. State Normal School #4 in Springfield was established some 65 years after the first American Normal School was organized in Massachusetts and about 35 years after the first was set up in Missouri. Originally, Normal Schools were seen as the intermediate

State Normal School #4 has largest enrollment of any Normal School in Missouri.

First rural demonstration school established.

Department of Commerce established.

U.S. Post Office permits shipping of baby chicks by parcel post.

Influenza epidemic closes schools, churches, amusement centers and all public gathering places in Springfield.

Irving Berlin writes "God Bless America," and then shelves it until 1939 when it becomes the unofficial anthem of World War II.

Normal Dictionary

Advice:

That which everyone has and everyone gives, but no one will take.

Conscience:

A small voice which on beginning to speak up finds that the line is already busy.

Defeat:

What Normal gave Drury.

Elated:

The feelings of one who did not flunk.

Freshman:

A novice biped.

Hat:

A brain shade.

Heck:

A polite word for girls.

Latin:

An antique but everlasting rock upon which are wrecked the students' brightest hopes for all future intelligence.

Music:

The offering given by the ukelele.

Mercy:

Something unknown in the History and English Departments.

Obtuse:

Mr. Temple.

Rational:

A characteristic of Miss Craig.

step between the common or elementary school where education ended for most people, and the college or university where a select few studied. In 1910 only 3 percent of the population were college graduates as compared to 1998, when nearly one in four had college degrees. Only 13 percent of the population in 1910 had completed high school, compared to 83 percent in 1998.

So, for many, the Normal School was a high school with a teacher training focus. It prepared students to teach the elementary grades. Colleges prepared students to be teachers for high schools. But those distinctions between normal schools, high schools and colleges were beginning to fade by the time State Normal School #4 opened in Springfield. It wasn't officially called a college, yet from the outset it offered a two-year college degree.

While it was clear that the assigned mission of State Normal School #4 was to "qualify students for efficient teaching in the public schools of the state," in the earliest (1906) *Bulletin* it suggested that "the institution would better be called a teachers college," than a Normal School. True, it still offered high school courses and "as an academy it must offer the best instruction in secondary grades such as mathematics, the languages, literature, history and the sciences." But, the *Bulletin* continued, "as a college it must offer work leading to the liberal arts and of such character as to develop scholarship and culture."

So State Normal School #4 originated in a time of transition when the distinctions between normal schools and colleges were disappearing and the standards for teacher certification were rising. The fact that teachers were increasingly understood as the bearers of culture to rural settings, their train-

ing necessarily included "both scientific and practical knowledge of agriculture, horticulture (and) how to make homes more sanitary and attractive." Thus the first *Bulletin* in 1906 announcing the opening of State Normal School #4 declared its ambition "to improve conditions in every district in southwest Missouri," a mission much broader than teacher education.

The drumbeat for recognition as a legitimate member of the higher education community grew louder as the years went by. In 1907, the October *Bulletin* declared, "This institution is in reality a 'teachers college.'" It was joined by Kirksville Normal School

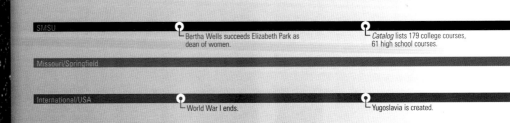

SMSU — Bertha Wells succeeds Elizabeth Park as dean of women. — *Catalog* lists 179 college courses, 61 high school courses.

Missouri/Springfield

International/USA — World War I ends. — Yugoslavia is created.

describing itself in 1909 as "the people's college," and Cape Girardeau expanding its mission beyond teacher training.

The struggle to become a collegiate institution involved curriculum as well as name. There had been a long discussion about the kind of training teachers needed. Some felt pedagogy courses should be the focus of their training. Others felt academic work should be emphasized so teachers could draw from a broad knowledge base to produce good teaching. In their view, teaching methods do not a teacher make.

The January 1908 *Bulletin* weighed in on this debate saying, "The purpose of the State Normal School is to educate and train teachers for the public schools of Missouri. We purposely put *educate* before *train* to put more emphasis on that phase of the work for the present." It is noteworthy that the first building on the State Normal School campus in Springfield was named Academic Hall, a clear signal of the direction in which the new institution was heading.

About the time Academic Hall was opened in 1909, the school *Bulletin* announced, "about one-fifth of its energy" was devoted to pedagogy, and "one-fourth of its effort (going) to subjects that are directly or indirectly related with industrial training…all pointing toward the preparation of young men and young women for better living, better homemaking." Presumably the remaining 55 percent of institutional effort went into academic subjects.

Students also were discerning the need for broader and deeper education. Genevieve Campbell, writing in the 1914 *Standard* observed that, "Education has taken upon itself all the great problems of society…. We have found it cheaper to educate the Indian

This was the education process as seen by Atlantic Brown, art editor, 1914 *Ozarko*.

than to fight him; wiser to teach the Negro than to keep him ignorant." She concludes her argument with a flourish. "The spirit of democracy has revolutionized the idea of the learned professions. Democracy is saying that education is for use, not for adornment, and that not knowledge, but applied knowledge is power."

So the envelope was being pushed from many directions. Not all Normal School students aspired to be teachers. Increasingly students sought academic credit toward a degree rather than hours toward certification. Moreover, local communities began to see the district Normal School as a place where their youth could prepare for college or even pursue collegiate studies and earn a degree rather than prepare for a teaching career. Then, too, the Jeffersonian ideal of an educated electorate was gaining ground. Democracy was a vocation and it required knowledge, judgment

and understanding on the part of its citizens. And finally, the debate over academic versus professional studies was generating heat among some Normal School faculty, which added to the pressure to redefine the mission.

World War I and the Normal School Experience

While State Normal School #4, under the visionary leadership of W.T. Carrington, was defining itself as an educational leader in the state, world events were roiling the waters in the nation's capitol. War had broken out in Europe in 1914. There was an ongoing debate about the role of the United States in European conflicts. An oratorical contest on campus in 1913 heard a moving speech by a student on "The Futility of War." By 1914, debate topics were honing in on war issues. Questions of neutrality, retrenchment of Naval construction, the probability of world peace, mandatory conscription for military service, the importance of aircraft to war, adoption of universal military training for all young men 18-25 years of age, and the timeliness of disarmament all came up for debate on campus.

But the impact of the war went beyond the arguments of the debaters. By 1916-17 school enrollment began dropping as young men were called

1919

Lunchroom opened in northwest corner of Academic Hall ground floor.

League of Women Voters organize in St. Louis.

Paris Peace Conference founds the League of Nations and negotiates the Treaty of Versailles, laying the groundwork for World War II.

Prohibition Amendment ratified by vote of the states.

1905-19 Missouri State Normal School, Fourth District   41

into military training. On April 2, 1917, Normal School students gathered in the Auditorium of Academic Hall to express their support for President Woodrow Wilson and Congress as they consulted about entering the war. The school orchestra played patriotic songs. Ms. Theodosia Callaway addressed the student body about what women could do for the nation if war were declared. Then Professor Shannon took the floor and spoke of history, heritage and democratic values. When he had finished "no person present could help feeling a great love for the country," according to *The Standard* reporter.

At 1:00 o'clock that day, with classes canceled, the entire student body and faculty gathered in front of Academic Hall bearing flags and banners preparing to march to the Square downtown. Arthur Briggs organized the 600 marchers into squads, drilled them in a coordinated salute to the flag, and then set them to marching downtown.

"The march was a pretty impressive sight," according to *The Standard.* "With 600 men and women marching in military order, to military music, and at the same time displaying scores of our nation's flag, it made a scene long to be remembered." The procession was led by a lavishly decorated automobile bearing "The Goddess of Liberty" impersonated by Florence Dunlap and "Uncle Sam" by M.A. Gray.

Arriving at the Square, the 600 marchers came together at the center and sang "America," to the delight of local citizens. When the song ended, at the command of Briggs, the flag on the Landers Building was saluted smartly by dedicated marchers.

The war became a preoccupying reality for the next 21 months. War projects sprang up all over campus with classes in food conservation, surgical dressings and knitting. The Red Cross, organized in Springfield in April 1917, led many campus initiatives in preparing comfort kits and medical supplies for soldiers overseas. It also taught sewing classes where garments for hospital workers and war refugees were assembled.

The Board of Regents weighed in on the war issue by voting unanimously to immediately eliminate German from the curriculum. That decision led to the collapse of the students' German Club.

A New President Selected

The war was costly in other ways as well. It drew students and some faculty from the campus. And it also cost the school its first president. Carrington went to Washington, D.C., to serve in the Department of War Risk Insurance in 1918. He had launched a new school with ringing success.

It was on course to become the largest of the State's Normal Schools when his successor, Clyde Milton Hill, took the reins.

President Hill, like President Carrington, was a native Ozarker. Raised in West Plains and a Normal School graduate in that first class of 1907, Clyde Hill had returned to State Normal School #4 to teach mathematics in 1909. He headed the Mathematics Department from 1912 to 1918. When he accepted the presidency of the school, he was only 32-years-old, the youngest president in the history of the school, and the youngest college president in the country at the time.

As President Hill began his first year as chief administrator, it would turn out to be the last year for State Normal School #4. In 12 months, the institution would shed its Normal School identity and become what it described itself as 13 years before, a state teachers college.

In its first 13 years it had enrolled more than 10,000 students. Most were from the Ozarks and other counties in Missouri. Some were from adjoining states and Indian Territory, and a few came from abroad. The addition of State Normal School #4 had not only substantially enhanced the opportunity for education for Ozarks families, it had also enhanced the reputation of its host city, Springfield. Jonathon Fairbanks, one-time superintendent of schools in Springfield, wrote in 1914 that "Springfield was called the Athens of the Ozarks owing to her numerous and splendid educational institutions, especially since State Normal School of District #4 was located here."

Springfield itself had changed in

This was the Normal School graduation ring, 1914.

SMSU
└ Normal School #4 becomes Southwest Missouri State Teachers College.
└ Bachlor of Pedagogy degree dropped. BS in Education becomes the norm for all the teachers.

Missouri/Springfield
└ Governor Frederick D. Gardner signs law granting presidential suffrage to women.
└ Last saloon closes in Springfield because of prohibition.

International/USA

└ First non-stop flight across the Atlantic completed by John Alcock and Authur Whitten Brown.

With the arrival of Arthur Briggs to head the physical education program in 1912, the Physical Training Department began producing a variety of pageants and festival events including the May Day Carnival. In addition to crowning a Queen of May, the festival featured a May Pole dance. Over the years as many as 30 poles were wound by Greenwood pupils and Normal School students. The event drew hundreds of spectators from the community.

those 13 years. Automobiles were rapidly replacing the horse and buggy on city streets. By 1915 there were 821 registered in town. By 1918 Springfield had the largest railroad shops in the state, employing more than 2,000 workers. One of the largest wagon factories in the country was located here, along with other firms making furniture, iron castings, stoves, harnesses, clothing, flour, bread, macaroni, butter, ice cream and books.

With the end of World War I in late 1918, the formative era for State Normal School #4 had also ended. A new campus had been established. A fine building had been built. Traditions

had been established that would guide the institution for decades, and the school had commended itself to both the citizens of the Ozarks and educational leaders across the state. Under the leadership of a young new president, it was poised to become a fully collegiate institution, nationally accredited, and recognized for its program excellence and student achievements.

The founders were vindicated. "The Springfield State Normal School is not an experiment." ∎

BS in Commerce degree first listed in the *Catalog.*

AB degree added to degree programs.

Theodore W.H. Irion named registrar.

Missouri becomes 11th state to ratify 19th Amendment giving suffrage to women.

Details of Black Sox scandal in baseball breaks publicly, for alleged fixed World Series of 1919.

Lincoln's Inn in London admits the first women bar student.

FOR VICTORY

BUY
UNITED
STATES
WAR
BONDS
AND
STAMPS

THE·SOUTHWEST·MISSOURI·STATE
IN·THE·CITY·OF·SPRIN

TO · ALL · PERSONS · TO · WHOM · THESE · PRESENT
BE · IT · KNOWN · THAT

STELLA YOWE

HAVING COMPLETED THE · STUDIES · AND · SATIS
FOR · THE · DEGREE · O

BACHELOR·OF·SCIENCE·I

HAS · ACCORDINGLY · BEEN · ADMITTED · TO · THAT
RIGHTS · PRIVILEGES · AND · IMMUNITIES · THE
IN · WITNESS · WHEREOF · WE · HAVE · CA
LIFE · CERTIFICATE · TO · TEACH · IN · THE · PUBLIC ·
MISSOURI · TO · BE · SIGNED · BY · THE · PRESIDENT · O
SUPERINTENDENT · OF · SCHOOLS · AND · THE · PRES
THE · BOARD · OF · REGENTS · AND · THE · COLLEGE · SEA
IN · THE · CITY · OF · SPRINGFIELD · ON · THE · FIFTH · DA
OF · OUR · LORD · ONE · THOUSAND · NINE · HUNDRED · A

J. Glaser
PRESIDENT · BOARD · OF · REGENTS

J.C.Mann
SECRETARY · BOARD · OF · REGENTS

Southwest Missouri
State Teachers College

ACHERS·COLLEGE
IELD

Y · COME · GREETING

THE · REQUIREMENTS

DUCATION

GREE · WITH · ALL · THE
NTO · APPERTAINING
· THIS · DIPLOMA · AND
OLS · OF · THE STATE · OF
E · FACULTY · THE · STATE
T · AND · SECRETARY · OF
BE · HEREUNTO · AFFIXED
· AUGUST · IN · THE · YEAR
TWENTY · FOUR

UPERINTENDENT · OF · SCHOOLS

DENT · OF · THE · FACULTY

Contents

1919-1946

Southwest Missouri State Teachers College

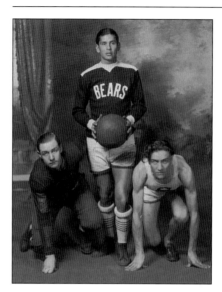

By the State Teachers College period, Bear athletics teams had begun to win state and regional championships. In 1923-24 Captain Efton "Heavy" Henderson (left) led the football Bears to a 7-2 season, which included scaring the University of Missouri Tigers in a 0-10 loss. Clyde L. "Chief" James' basketball Bears suffered only one loss in the season, 22-21 at the University of Arkansas. The track squad also took MIAA honors that spring under the leadership of Raymond D. Lipe (right).

Despite the fact that Normal School #4 had been operating only a dozen years, it was already chafing under the burden of an uncomplimentary image associated with normal schools. *The Standard* editor stated the irritation in his January 15, 1918, edition. "Many people have long had the impression that the student body of the Normal School was not equal in ability or scholarship to that of a college or university," the editor complained. "These people think that the student body is composed of immature students who are taking lower grade work, and women teachers who teach in the rural schools."

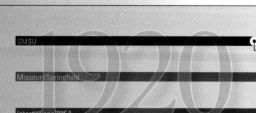

SMSU

Demonstration schools opened in Webster, Douglas, Lawrence, Jasper, Wright, Howell and Greene Counties.

Department of Sociology and Economics established with Roy Ellis as head.

Missouri/Springfield

International/USA

U.S. population reaches 105,710,620, with the majority living in cities for the first time.

The chafing under the normal school image was made more acute because just across Jordan Creek to the north was another institution carrying the coveted title of "college." Drury had been on the scene since 1873, and it had educated the children of many of Springfield's leading families. It stood at the top of the local higher education pecking order, a point of irritation to Normal students.

By the time State Normal School #4 was established, the normal school era across the country was drawing to a close. Historically, Normal Schools provided the training for teachers of the elementary grades. High school teachers were typically trained in colleges and universities. But by the early years of the 20th century, the number of high schools was increasing more rapidly than the supply of teachers from colleges and universities. So Normal Schools began building more liberal arts into their curricula in hopes of contributing to the supply of high school instructors. As the normal school mission changed to include this new task, so did its name. Normal Schools across the nation became teachers colleges.

State Normal School #4 anticipated this as early as 1907 when it called attention to the need to include "college training in a normal school." As early as 1906, it was building a liberal arts core into its curriculum leading it to declare, quite frankly, "This institution would better be called a Teachers College."

Internal steps were being quickly taken to help escort the young institution into the coveted ranks of "colleges." By 1908 it was offering enough advanced work to award Irma Spriggs and Mrs. W.W. Bagley the Master of Pedagogy degree. The same year, its *Bulletin* sketched the requirements for an

A.B. (Bachelor of Arts) degree. In 1913, a Bachelor of Education degree had been awarded to Onita Woody. By 1914, the Normal School #4 *Bulletin* was carrying a vocabulary typical of a collegiate institution, including the requirements for a Bachelor of Science in Education degree. The very next year, nine students were listed as earning that four-year degree.

So by 1919 when the Missouri General Assembly granted all state Normal School Boards the option of changing their institutional names to State Teachers Colleges, Normal School #4 was fully prepared and savoring the moment. The fall 1919 *Bulletin* matter-of-factly declared, "From the beginning, the school has maintained profes-

Mrs. Ellenora Linney was the first woman appointed to the Board of Regents of the college. She served from 1925-31, assisting in writing the Board's By-Laws, which were approved in 1927. Her husband, W.B. Linney, was a prominent attorney in Springfield.

sional and academic courses of the rank and character offered by the best teachers colleges. The recognition of this fact has brought about the change to the truer name, the Southwest Missouri State Teachers College."

The process of changing normal schools into teachers colleges was also hastened by the formation of accrediting associations. The North Central Association of Colleges and Secondary Schools had formed as early as 1896, and by 1902 it had proposed standards that would allow accreditation to high schools only if their teachers were college graduates. This standard, combined with the increasing demand for high school teachers, resulted in the rapid upgrading of many normal schools to become teachers colleges. That transition in Missouri was completed in 1919.

Shortly after State Normal School #4 became Southwest Missouri State Teachers College in July 1919, Governor Frederick D. Gardner came to Springfield and complimented the college declaring, "in the efficiency of its faculty and the excellence of its curriculum, the college today ranks as

Student government established by college administration.

French Club and Story Telling Club organized.

Marie Byrum becomes first woman to vote in Missouri history.

Sinclair Lewis publishes satirical novel, *Main Street*, pillorying Midwestern small town life and attitudes.

S. W. Missouri State Teachers College Looking From S.E. Part of Campus.

one of the best in the country." *The Standard* editor joined the parade of praise and spoke of the future saying, "Our ambitions for the college are only partly attained…. There is prevalent everywhere…an earnest desire for bigger things."

The move from normal schools to teachers colleges was picking up momentum all around the country. By 1933, rising expectations for teachers and the more rigorous standards for their training had changed nearly all normal schools into teachers colleges.

For Southwest Missouri State Teachers College in Springfield, however, the new name and new status was not understood as a destination. Rather it was seen as an interim step in a much larger evolutionary scheme. In 1924, *The Standard* editor, while praising President Clyde Hill on his excellent leadership, declared, "Fortunate indeed will be Southwest Teachers College and

Springfield if we can keep (President Hill) with us until our institution is a full-fledged university." Board of Regents President Ignace Glasser picked up the theme in his recitation of the accomplishments of the school saying, "It will be but a question of a few years until 'The University of the Southwest' will be an accomplished thing." The 1924 *Ozarko* chimed in with its own assessment noting, "in the past 25 years we have seen the phenomenal growth of the future 'University of the Ozarks.'"

This sense of destiny informed the thinking of faculty, students and administrators from the very beginning. While their vision was clearly prophetic, it would take nearly 50 years to fulfill.

Academic Changes
New Degrees Added
The name change to State Teachers College caught on quickly. College publications adopted STC as the

abbreviated form. Local newspapers alternated between calling athletics teams "Bears" and/or "Teachers." But while the official designation suggested the continuation of a teacher training mission, the institution had already broadened its definition by attracting students with interests other than teaching. The 1919 *Bulletin* advertised an A.B. degree for "young men and women who wish a full collegiate course undetermined by specific professional aim." The *Bulletin* also advertised pre-medical and pre-legal courses saying, "the resources provided by the State of Missouri are at the service of those who may desire to do the first two years' work of a legal or medical course at the Teachers College. All the courses needed for this purpose are provided." This was more than idle talk, for the first A.B. degree was awarded in 1920. By 1926, the liberal arts degree was awarded to 20 students, and for the

SMSU
College library swells to 20,000 volumes.

Missouri/Springfield
The $60 million "good roads" amendment passes Legislature.
Springfield Boy Scout Band formed in city.

International/USA
Warren G. Harding elected U.S. President.
First regular radio broadcasts begin in East Pittsburgh, Pennsylvania.

1921

A view of the front of Academic Hall from National Avenue showing the circle drive as it appeared in the 1920s.

next 20 years nearly 10 percent of all degrees awarded was the A.B. degree, reflecting the establishment of a sound liberal arts tradition in the midst of a regional teachers college.

The broadening of the educational vision was propitious. While the need for trained teachers in the southwest district remained acute, the need for an affordable liberal arts education for citizens of the area was also acute. The growth of the liberal arts within a teachers college, however, also raised questions. One of the local newspapers editorialized about the problem of teachers colleges, one-third of whose students "do not intend to teach." Concern was also raised about teachers colleges competing for students with the state university. But *The Standard* editor replied that for most STC stu-

dents, the University of Missouri was simply not affordable. Moreover, while well-trained teachers were still a premium, by the 1930s the overall shortage of teachers had lessened making the liberal arts offerings a valuable relief valve for a declining market in the teaching profession. The Great Depression further contributed to that decline as many who lost jobs in business and industry resorted to teaching to keep bread on the table. *The Standard* editor in 1932 saw what was shaping up when he said, "We hesitate to predict the future of teacher's training institutions. The outlook is dark for those which issue only B.S. in Education degrees." The editor went on to point out that the State Teachers College in Maryville had just added an A.B. degree to its offerings, realizing that another tran-

sition was already beginning, even though it would take another world war and the G.I. Bill to force the issue.

From Certificates to Diplomas

One of the most dramatic changes taking place in the years following the name change was the shift from awarding teaching certificates to awarding college diplomas. It had only been a dozen years since President Carrington lamented that the "overvaluation of degrees and diplomas continues to menace sound education." He was echoing John Taylor's dictum that the function of a normal school was "to educate, not to graduate."

What was making these statements so ironic now was the achievement of the ends both men so diligently sought. Better educated and better qualified teachers through state certification were their goals and as those goals were approached, the norm shifted from cer-

Legislature appropriates $250,000 to build second building (Education) on campus.

Madame Luiza Tetrazzini, world-class soprano, comes to STC for concert.

WEW, Missouri's first radio station, broadcasts from St. Louis, second oldest in country.

Don Sebring's portrayal of "college heroes" in the 1926 *Ozarko* gives us a glimpse of campus culture during the "Roarin' Twenties."

tificates and 60- and 90-hour diplomas to four-year college degrees.

To be sure, STC continued to award certificates and diplomas to those who sought them. But the trend for teachers was clearly in the direction of a four-year college degree, the Bachelor of Science in Education.

While the first four-year collegiate degree was awarded in 1913, by 1915 nine candidates had earned the degree. Roy Ellis recalls that those early degree winning graduates were honored by being individually called to the president's office to receive their diplomas. By the summer of 1919, when the school name was changed, 25 students were summoned to the president's

office to receive their Bachelor of Science in Education diploma. That same year the Bachelor of Pedagogy degree was dropped, and STC was fully engaged in *both* educating and graduating students.

Throughout the STC period there was also a growing interest in preparation for careers in business. A Bachelor of Science in commerce degree was first outlined in the 1919 *Catalog*, then dropped until 1940. However, a commerce major and minor were available by the time the school name was changed. In 1925, 13 students had graduated with a major in commerce, and by 1933 the Commerce Department was the largest elective department in the college.

While the college continued to provide teacher certification programs based on earned hours, degree fever caught on quickly. In the period between 1919-45, 4,538 bachelor's degrees were awarded. In 1926, 252 students were awarded the coveted B.S. in Education degree, a 10-fold increase in just seven years. That record was not surpassed until 1939 when 253 degrees were awarded.

High School Department Closed

Despite the achievement of full college status in 1919, admission to STC still remained open to students wanting to complete their high school training. The High School Department remained in place until 1927 when it was dropped, ending a historic era. Local high schools were developing throughout the district, and by that time the number of high school enrollments at STC had dropped significantly. F.B. O'Rear's statistical summary for the years 1919-26 showed high school enrollments dropping from 896 in 1920-22 to 304 in 1924-26, a decline of over 66 percent. Apparently many of those who enrolled as high school students did not graduate since only 117 high school diplomas were issued between 1906-26. Many of the high school students probably took only enough work to obtain a rural teaching certificate. More than 700 of those were issued between 1906 and 1926.

A high school survey conducted in the southwest district about the time of the name change not only reflected the growing interest in college education, but also foreshadowed the direction the college would take in the years ahead. Of the 1,009 respondents to the survey, 92 percent indicated they wanted to attend college. When asked about careers they wished to prepare for, 27 percent indicated business, 24 percent indicated teaching, and 12 percent said the liberal arts. Other preferred areas included engineering, 10 percent; domestic science, 9 percent; music, 9 percent; medicine, 4 percent; and law, 3 percent. So while teaching as a career still ranked high, other disciplines and the liberal arts were rapidly gaining ground.

SMSU
└ "S" club organized for campus student-athletes, Finis Engleman, first president.
└ Homecoming celebration established.

Missouri/Springfield
└ Centennial Road Law passed creating Missouri highway system.

International/USA

└ Adolph Hitler becomes leader of Nazi party.

The first building exclusively for classrooms was the Education Building, located southeast of the Administration Building. Designed to house Greenwood Laboratory School as well as the education faculty, the building was started in 1922. This picture, looking west, was taken on July 10, 1922, just 17 days before the cornerstone was laid.

"It was with Mr. Hill's thoughts, ideas, and plans, the result of five years of conscientious toil, that were incorporated into this structure, which will stand forth, for all time, attesting to the fact that we have for a President, a practical idealist, under whose guidance, some say our institution will become 'The University of the Ozarks.'"

∾

Ozarko editor, 1924, on the occasion of the completion of the Education Building

The survey did not indicate whether respondents were male or female, but O'Rear's statistical data showed fall enrollments between 1920-26 to be approximately 40 percent men and 60 percent women. When lower male enrollments in the spring and summer terms were factored in, the percentage shifted to 30 percent men and 70 percent women for the entire year. So the student body continued to be predominantely female, and while other degrees were beginning to be offered, the vast majority of graduates took teaching degrees.

Enrollment Growth

Enrollments at STC grew rapidly during the 1920s. The period between 1920-30 saw a 52 percent growth, the second largest in the entire history of the institution. Even before the beginning of the teachers college period,

the school had established itself as the largest of the state's five normal schools and was second only to the University of Missouri in total enrollment for any college or university in the state.

Summer schools had surpassed the 1,000 student mark as early as 1912. By 1923, summer enrollment passed the 2,000 mark. Summer school remained the highest enrolled term in the school year well into the 1950s reflecting the large number of teachers enrolling to advance their careers and renew their certification.

But fall term enrollments showed dramatic increases as well. Between 1918-22, fall term enrollments virtually doubled, and that occurred on a campus with less classroom space per student than any of the state colleges or universities.

Enrollment during the STC years fluctuated broadly as families responded

to the end of World War I, coped with the Great Depression and then saw World War II on the horizon. With the end of World War I in 1918, the fall enrollment stood at 500 students. By 1923, the enrollment had virtually doubled to 997. Relative prosperity across the country and the opportunity to earn full collegiate degrees fueled the growth. By 1931, a record enrollment of 1,406

College acquires radio broadcasting and receiving set from Westinghouse.

Arthur M. Hyde elected governor.

Leaded gasoline developed to solve engine "knocking."

A 14-year-old boy receives first basic insulin injection treatment for diabetes.

1922

"As we look backward over the footprints in the sand of time, we see the annals of Southwest Missouri State Teachers College richly emblazoned upon the history of education of Southwest Missouri, and as we look out across the untrampled sands of the future, we see on the not distant horizon a leader among leaders in the educational institutions of the time — our own beloved Southwest Missouri State Teachers College — a true mecca of learning, of guidance and of inspiration!"

∾

1925 Ozarko

By 1920 the Agriculture Department was the proud owner of a New Franklin tractor, which assisted in tilling the garden plot on the west side of the campus.

students made STC the sixth largest teachers college in the nation. But shortly thereafter, the Great Depression began to be felt in the Ozarks and enrollment declines began dropping student numbers so that by 1934-35, fewer than 1,000 students were on campus. In 1935, enrollment started an upward trend again reaching a record 1,615 in the fall of 1939.

By 1940, the unsettled conditions of World War II again turned the enrollment trend line down. At first, the decline was gradual, but by 1942 the loss was 700 students from the 1939 record. By 1945 the decline had become severe with only 517 regularly enrolled students, a loss of almost 70 percent.

It is ironic that the enrollment at the end of the STC era in 1944-45 was only 17 more than the enrollment at the beginning of the era in 1919, despite the dramatic growth between the two dates. The institution was commending itself broadly to its service

area, but the twin adversaries of the Depression and war delayed or changed the college plans of thousands of students.

Enrollment demographics at the beginning of the STC period show that nearly 85 percent of the students came from the 22-county southwest district. About 15 percent came from elsewhere in the state and other surrounding states. Dunklin County in southeast Missouri regularly sent quite a number of students to Springfield because the STC quarter system was more compatible with cotton raising than the semester plan at Cape Girardeau. Other states were represented as well. In 1938, when Howard "Red" Blair came to STC as football coach, he brought students from his home in Mt. Vernon, Ohio. One of those native Ohioans, James Mentis, became an SMS football coach in 1965. But by far, the bulk of the students came from Springfield and Greene County — almost 40 percent of the total. That pattern persisted throughout the STC years.

SMSU
— Cornerstone laid for second (Education) building on campus.

— Edwin Markham lectures on campus.

Missouri/Springfield
— Springfield Park Board agrees to buy Dickerson Estate for $23,000 to create Dickerson Park Zoo.

International/USA
— *Reader's Digest* first published.

— Annie Oakley breaks women's trap shooting record hitting 98 out of 100.

— British imprison Mahatma K. Gandhi in India.

By July 1, 1923, the Education Building was moving toward completion. A formal "open house" for this second building constructed on the SMS campus was held on April 15, 1924. An estimated 8,500 visitors toured this "state-of-the-art" facility, which boasted a large gymnasium, swimming pool and innovative classrooms for the teacher training program.

Campus Growth

Education Building Added to the Campus

While the beginning of the fall semester in 1919 featured a new institution name, it retained the old Normal School look. One classroom building completed in 1909, designed to serve 300 students, was crammed with 500 eager learners, taxing Academic Hall to the limit. There had been no expansion of campus facilities since 1912 when a west wing was added to Academic Hall at a cost of $66,000. The wing provided a much needed gymnasium, as well as an auditorium, which featured a $4,000 pipe organ.

Even before Academic Hall was completed in 1909, the Legislature had been besieged by requests from Springfield for additional facilities to house the education program and Greenwood school. The Legislature responded in 1915, setting aside funds for the second building. However, those plans literally went up in smoke. In February 1915, a fire in Warrensburg destroyed the main Normal School building there requiring Springfield to yield to the desperate needs of its older sister campus. But by 1920, the situation in Springfield was also desperate. Roy Ellis recalled that the "ends of corridors, the coal bin and the green house" were all pressed into service as classrooms.

Relief finally came in 1921 when the Legislature appropriated $250,000 for the Education Building, which had been functionally designed by President Hill and was destined to become a model for similar buildings across the country. However, the legislative appropriation fell almost $50,000 short of the cost of constructing and equipping the building. While the college was grateful for the appropriation, it found itself scrambling to find the additional $50,000 to make the building a reality.

By July 27, 1922, enough work was done to allow the cornerstone to be laid, and a crowd of 4,000 gathered to celebrate the event. They witnessed the placement of the metal cornerstone box filled with a college *Catalog*, an *Ozarko*, a *Southwest Standard*, copies of the local newspapers, a roster of the "S"

Football competition with Drury ends with a 28-0 STC win.

Football team finishes season undefeated, MIAA Conference champions.

Nationwide railroad strike idles 3,000 in Springfield.

Central Bible College opens in Springfield.

Benito Mussolini takes power in Italy.

1919-46 Southwest Missouri State Teachers College   53

Construction of the Science Hall started on October 21, 1924. By May 1, 1925, when this picture was taken, foundations were in place and the cornerstone was laid. Science Hall housed the departments of science, agriculture, mathematics, foreign languages and home economics. All sections of the building were not completed until 1930.

Men's Club, a *Bible*, current coins from a penny to a dollar, and letters from the Board of Regents and the construction company. Some 21 months later, the building was completed and a formal opening on April 15, 1924, was held welcoming more than 8,500 people to tour the state-of-the-art facility.

The building was designed to house 390 pupils, 30 per grade from kindergarten through high school. The innovative classroom/conference room/office concept outlined by President Hill

was widely copied across the country.

Excavating for the basement was a herculean task for the equipment of the day. The basement provided a gymnasium with a 46-foot by 81-foot playing floor seating some 1,800 persons, including 600 in balconies on each end. It served not only Greenwood training school, but also physical education classes for college men and women and college basketball games. At the time, it was the most modern and the largest gymnasium in the state. The

gymnasium incorporated many innovative ideas, including glass backboards for the basketball goals so spectators could see from any angle. A 20-foot by 50-foot swimming pool, which ranged from three to eight feet in depth, was also placed in the basement.

It appeared, however, that nature was intent on having its own swimming pool in the building. Shortly after the building was completed a heavy rain produced several feet of water in the basement. A wet-weather spring that

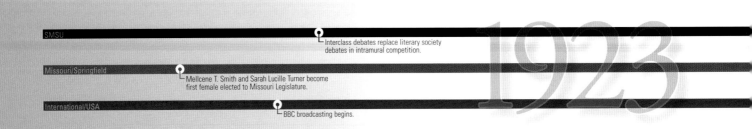

SMSU
Interclass debates replace literary society debates in intramural competition.

Missouri/Springfield
Mellcene T. Smith and Sarah Lucille Turner become first female elected to Missouri Legislature.

International/USA
BBC broadcasting begins.

1923

flowed diagonally across the campus and under the building turned out to be the problem. So the walls and floor were waterproofed. But the problem persisted. The pressure of the water under and around the building was so great that when a steel pipe was driven into the ground north of the building, an artesian well-like stream spurted several feet into the air. The solution finally came when a deep drain was built to Grand Avenue carrying the water away.

In reality, the Education Building wasn't completed until 1955 when the last name was carved on the frieze around the top of the building. Each college graduating class, beginning in 1923, decided on a name to be added to the frieze. The names represent a virtual "Who's Who" of education — people who expanded the boundaries of knowledge or made a noteworthy contribution to pedagogy. Not surprisingly, the first class to contribute a name chose as it patron educator Horace Mann, founder of normal schools in America, and the man who encouraged Missouri to establish normal schools as early as 1856 when he addressed the first session of the Missouri State Teachers Association. A tour around the building today will reveal names going back to the golden age of Greek philosophy (Socrates and Aristotle) as well as contemporary local heroes such as W.T. Carrington and Dr. J.M. Greenwood, superintendent of schools in Kansas City at the time of the founding of State Normal School #4. Other names appearing on the freize include Rousseau, Pestalozzi, Comenius, Harris, Spencer, Herbart, Baldwin, McMurry, Copernicus, Cyrus Pierce, McGuffey, James, Erasmus,

Cornerstone laying for the Science Hall, the third facility built on campus, was held May 1, 1925. Under the direction of Masonic Order, Deputy State Grand Marshall W.W. Martin officiated at the ceremonies. Among items included in the cornerstone were silver coins of 1924 and photographs of faculty members' infants born during the period of the construction.

$250,000 appropriated by Legislature for Science Building.

Board of Regents terminates all intercollegiate athletics contests with Drury.

The Hawthorn named Missouri State Flower.

Lee DeForest demonstrates process by which the sound track is imprinted on movie film opening the opportunity for sound movies.

Looking Back

First "Air Mail" Delivery in Southwest Missouri

On June 21, 1921, the largest crowd ever assembled in Springfield up to that time gathered on the State Teachers College football field to witness the Centennial Pageant celebrating 100 years of statehood.

While the Pageant itself was a spectacle, the manner in which it was publicized was perhaps yet more spectacular. Ralph Snavely, an STC student and veteran of World War I, owned a biplane which he kept on a corner of the football field northwest of the campus. Snavely volunteered to distribute 25,000 handbills advertising the Centennial Pageant over southwest Missouri. And he would do it by air!

On Friday, June 17, Snavely climbed into his flying machine with 25,000 handbills and several free tickets to the Pageant. With only 100 yards of runway space, Snavely revved the engine, released the brake and headed down the center of the football field. He cleared the tree tops and the power lines and swerved to miss the 125-foot smokestack beside the powerhouse.

Throughout the day he flew at tree-top level over 17 communities dropping handbills and free tickets to startled observers below. Twenty-five years later, Snavely was a Brigadier General in the Air Force.

The new concrete stadium for football was completed in 1941. Designed for 5,000 spectators, the stadium was a Federal Works Progress Administration (WPA) project valued at $75,000. The college contributed one-third of its cost.

Dewey, Jefferson, Hall, Locke, Thorndike, Descartes, LaSalle, Ritter, Susan Blow, Webster, Parker, Eliot, Barnard, Bacon and Froebel.

Science Building Added

The original campus plan described in the 1907 *Bulletin* called for three major buildings to comprise the central campus of State Normal School #4. Only Academic Hall was completed within the normal school period. At the same time the Legislature was appropriating funds for the Education Building, the STC Board of Regents reported to the General Assembly that the conditions

for teaching the sciences and allied subjects were totally inadequate.

"Agriculture," they reported, "is taught in poorly-lighted and poorly-ventilated quarters in the powerhouse." They went on to declare that domestic science and arts "occupy two small basement rooms wholly inadequate to this work." Their report described a single room, 22-foot by 30-foot room that housed all the biological sciences, and a similar sized improvised room that housed the chemistry lab. Sewing classes were crammed into the attic of Academic Hall.

The same report was shared with

the Legislature again in 1923, and that year a $250,000 appropriation was passed to construct and equip a Science Building. That would complete the plan envisioned in 1907 with Academic Hall flanked on the southeast by the Education Building and on the northeast by the Science Building.

The cornerstone for the Science Building was laid on May 1, 1925. The box contained some uncommon items, including a student directory and pictures of faculty babies born during the building's construction. The day itself turned out to be quite uncommon, for while the cornerstone ceremony was in

SMSU
Bears win conference titles in football and track.
STC plays University of Missouri in football, losing 10-0.

Missouri/Springfield

International/USA
President Harding dies suddenly — Calvin Coolidge succeeds him.
U.S. Steel offers 8-hour workday.

By 1942, the campus consisted of four major buildings, an athletics stadium and an Olympic size outdoor swimming pool, all contained within the original 38 acres. The view above is looking west from National Avenue.

progress a telegram from the governor was delivered to the platform stating that funds for the completion of the building were being withheld because of a revenue shortfall. A month later the Board had to borrow $29,325 to pay for work already completed.

The work stoppage was a devastat-ing blow to everyone, and the builder, Stewart-McGehee Construction Company of Little Rock, sued the college for damages due to the delay. The suit was unsuccessful. Later, however, the college joined the con-struction company in petitioning the Legislature for relief. The funds were finally released and the upper two floors were completed in 1927 at a cost of $278,392. The lower floor was not completed until 1930 at a cost of $38,479. But by 1930, the Department of Agriculture was out of the powerhouse; biology and chemis-try classes were taught in specifically

Dr. James Naismith, "father of basketball," addresses students and faculty.

First Health Office established in Education Building. Dr. F.T. H'Doubler, Sr. provides physician services.

Shrine Mosque dedicated.

Massive earthquake in Tokyo and Yokohama kills more than 500,000.

Equal Rights Amendment first proposed by Alice Paul, head of the National Women's Party.

1919-46 Southwest Missouri State Teachers College 57

designed classrooms; home economics was out of the attic and the Foreign Language Department occupied new space on two floors.

The vision of 1907 was now complete. Three Carthage limestone buildings formed a quadrangle area looking out on to National Boulevard. But an important lesson was learned. Providing campus space was going to be a struggle. Need was not the decisive factor in Jefferson City. State economics and regional politics would forever be factors in shaping capital appropriations for state colleges and universities.

Physical Education Facilities Added

While the first decade of STC saw the completion of two academic buildings, the decade between 1930 and 1940 saw the completion of the first physical education facility. Coach Arthur Briggs had been dreaming and

planning for this since 1912 when he arrived on campus from Springfield, Massachusetts.

In 1930, the athletics field was moved from its traditional spot on the northwest corner of the campus to the southwest corner, bordering Grand and Kings streets, where the college orchard and garden had been for more than 20 years. The enterprise involved extensive grading to provide appropriate drainage. It also introduced lights to the field resulting in a period of exclusively night football games for the Bears.

The stadium on the west side of the field was completed in 1941 as part of a Depression era Works Progress Administration (WPA) project. Estimated to cost $75,000 when built, the project cost the college just $25,000. The remainder was covered by government grants, which provided employment to local citizens who were

without work in the 1930s. When the new stadium, accommodating 5,000 spectators, was completed on the west side of the field, the old and rickety wooden bleachers were moved to the east side of the new athletics field where students, cheerleaders and the band were assigned to boost the Bears to victory.

That idea didn't set well with students. A *Standard* editorial, titled "Whose New Stadium?" complained about the comfortable new stadium seating for spectators, while students, band members, drum corps and cheerleaders were relegated to the rickety bleachers behind the team on the east side. "Yes, the old bleachers felt exactly the same," complained the editor. "Freshman girls, unused to the perils and thrills of bleacher-climbing, mounted the rickety structures with trepidation in their hearts, and their hearts in their mouths, expecting to slip at any moment on one of the warped boards that shimmied and bounced each time a foot was placed upon it." While the students were not *forced* to sit on the east side bleachers, the editor continued, "they were made to feel unpatriotic to their team if they did not. With the college band, the drum corps and the cheerleaders situated on the east side of the field, no college student but a social outcast would have felt at home sitting in the new stadium." The editor concluded his protest by saying, "We believe that all STC students should be entitled to sit on the west side of the playing field, and that the band should accompany them there. Money from our incidental fees is used to support football games, so we should like to see places reserved for STC students in the new stadium." Sixty years

On a bitterly cold February 6, 1939, the cornerstone for the new Health and Recreation Building was laid. The arena, shown above, was the scene of the Bears' basketball victory over the University of Missouri Tigers, 35-32, in 1941, the first season for the new facility.

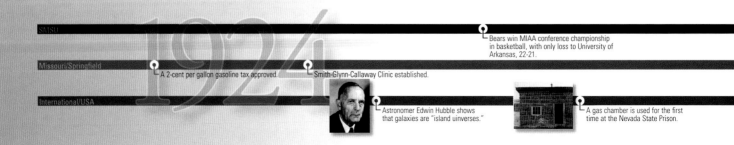

1924

SMSU

Bears win MIAA conference championship in basketball, with only loss to University of Arkansas, 22-21.

Missouri/Springfield

A 2-cent per gallon gasoline tax approved. Smith-Glynn-Callaway Clinic established.

International/USA

Astronomer Edwin Hubble shows that galaxies are "island uinverses." A gas chamber is used for the first time at the Nevada State Prison.

MUSIC HALL, STATE-TEACHER'S COLLEGE, SPRINGFIELD, MISSOURI

OA3525

After Greenwood Laboratory School moved out of the bungalow into the Education Building in 1924, the bungalow became the Music Hall, home of the Conservatory and the music faculty.

later, students, band and cheerleaders remain in the east bleachers.

Health and Recreation Building

While the Depression years created many hardships for the college and its students, it did facilitate building projects financed in part by the Public Works Administration (PWA) and WPA federal grants providing employment for area workers. The college had long needed a physical education building. Arthur Briggs had gathered data and visited physical education plants over the country for 25 years. He envisioned a plant built of Carthage stone, matching Academic Hall and the Education and Science buildings. It would have two gymnasiums — one on the west for men and another on the east for women. The women's gym was planned with a large fireplace to accommodate social gatherings as well as a large patio at the east entrance. The layout for the building was inspired by Soldier's Field and the Art Museum in Chicago. A sketch of the Soldier's Field

building hung in Arthur Briggs' office for years.

The State Legislature appropriated $178,000 for the building in 1937, but Governor Stark withheld the funds until state revenues justified their release. The break-through came in 1938 when the Federal Government provided $199,391 to supplement the state appropriation of $188,000, and $55,700 in local funds. In October 1938, a huge power shovel broke ground. On February 6, 1939, the cornerstone for the 54,499-square-foot Health and Recreation Building was laid. President Roy Ellis remembered it as a bitterly cold day, accounting for "the brevity of the address by Colonel S.E. Trimble, President of the Board, and me as President of the College." The dedication was broadcast over radio station KWTO. As with previous buildings, the cornerstone box contained items perceived to be of interest to future users of the building. It included a 1938-40 college *Catalog*,

a 25th anniversary issue of *The Standard* in addition to a current issue, a Springfield daily newspaper, 1939 stamps, silver half dollars, quarters and dimes, as well as a sampling of Missouri mills. The box also included a listing of all faculty, staff and students who were members of the Masonic order.

When the $443,091 building was completed in 1940, it was and remained for years an outstanding example of facility planning for college physical education. Arthur Briggs had dreamt of the day when such a facility would grace the STC campus. Long before the building was even designed, he predicted to associates that the day would come when he would sit in an opera chair at STC and watch a basketball game. In the spring of 1941 Coach Briggs settled comfortably into an opera chair and watched Coach Andy McDonald's basketball Bears defeat the University of Missouri Tigers, 35-32, in the brand new arena. Three thousand one hundred and ninety-nine other opera chairs were filled that night with delirious fans watching the splendid victory unfold.

The Health and Recreation

Ground broken for new Science Building.

Fall enrollment exceeds 1,000 for the first time (1,053).

St. Louis Cardinal Jesse Haines no-hits Boston Braves, 5-0.

King Tut's tomb is opened.

Paul Robeson and Mary Blair appear in Eugene O'Neil's controversial play *All God's Chillun Got Wings*, a direct attack on American racism.

Native Americans granted citizenship in the U.S.

Building was not only the largest and most expensive building on the campus in 1940, but it was also the premier arena in the City of Springfield, surpassing even the Shrine Mosque, which had 2,500 seats. When portable seats were added to the fixed seats in the Health and Recreation Building, it could accommodate an audience of 5,000.

Over the years, the arena has hosted outstanding basketball by championship Bear teams, concerts by world-renown artists such as Van Cliburn, and speeches by such national leaders as Vice President Al Gore. The dreams of Arthur Briggs continue to unfold in the building he designed and that was named for his colleague Andy McDonald.

The Swimming Pool Saga

Long before the Health and Recreation Building was under construction in 1938, excavation for an Olympic-sized swimming pool was started immediately north of where the arena would stand. It was to be 70 feet by 165 feet, vary in depth from 42 inches to 16 feet, and hold 965,000 gallons of water. It would be one of only two pools in the United States adequate for Olympic contest events; the other was located in Los Angeles, California.

Again the dark side of the Depression produced a bright side for the college. The pool was a WPA project providing employment for dozens of area workers. Construction began in 1935 with WPA workers using picks and shovels to excavate the site. Debris was carted away in wheelbarrows. The construction process was anticipated to be slow given the fact that WPA workers could work only 13 days a month. But the project dragged on much longer than anticipated.

After many starts and delays, the pool remained unfinished a full six years after excavation began. In July 1941, *The Standard* lamented its unfinished condition noting that "several non-corrosive materials are necessary for the completion of the pool. It's now impossible to get them because of government priority. They are needed for defense purposes." Finally though, in the summer of 1942, STC students were able to take their first dip in the pool. Its enameled brick finish and lavish underwater lighting system made it an exhibit piece. Initially, it was planned to be an enclosed pool, part of the Health and Recreation Building, but by the time it was finished, those plans were abandoned.

The finishing of the swimming pool completed the major building projects of the STC years. The period started with Academic Hall standing proudly at the center of the east side of the campus. By 1924, a sister building stood to the southeast housing Greenwood and the education program, and in 1927 a second sister building stood to the northeast housing the sciences. The physical education facilities began the development of the west side of the campus between 1930-42. So by the beginning of World War II, physical facilities were in place, but their utilization took an unanticipated turn as the campus mobilized for the war effort.

Teacher Education and Greenwood School

A noteworthy development of the STC period was the maturing of the teacher education program. Throughout STC history, more than 90 percent of all the graduates took degrees in education

In 1928 the college cafeteria, located on the first floor of the Administration Building, was remodeled and enlarged to accommodate the growing campus. President Ellis declared it should be operated exclusively for the benefit of students. Welcoming the new facility, the 1929 *Ozarko* said, "Here, 'over the teacups' the social and intellectual life of the student body is enriched."

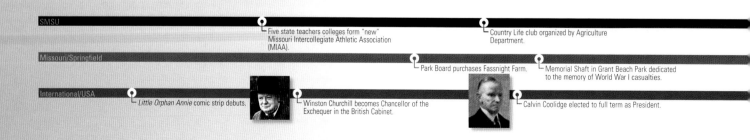

SMSU

Five state teachers colleges form "new" Missouri Intercollegiate Athletic Association (MIAA).

Country Life club organized by Agriculture Department.

Missouri/Springfield

Park Board purchases Fassnight Farm.

Memorial Shaft in Grant Beach Park dedicated to the memory of World War I casualties.

International/USA

Little Orphan Annie comic strip debuts.

Winston Churchill becomes Chancellor of the Exchequer in the British Cabinet.

Calvin Coolidge elected to full term as President.

and the majority went on to teach in the schools of southwest Missouri.

It was an exciting time in the field of learning. John Dewey, among many others, had fostered a revolution called "Progressive Education." In fact, Dewey, in 1896, organized an experimental school at the University of Chicago where he could test his theories about teaching and learning. That experimental school idea spawned a host of lab schools and training schools all over the country. When Normal #4 started, it established a "training school" at Pickwick School, located near the present site of Rountree School, on Grand just east of National.

In 1910, when the Normal School had moved to Academic Hall, a bungalow was built on Kings Street, just across the street from where the swimming pool is now located. It would house the "training school," and it would be named in honor of Dr. J.M. Greenwood, a close friend of W.T. Carrington and Superintendent of Schools in Kansas City. The bungalow housed grades one through 12 in those early years. In 1914 grades one, two, nine and 10 were moved into Academic Hall to provide room for the growing enterprise. In 1916, the bungalow was moved to the present site of Pummill Hall, just south of Academic Hall. In keeping with the experimental tradition of the progressive movement, a kindergarten was added to Greenwood in 1918.

In the meantime, the college had expanded its list of demonstration schools throughout the district giving many rural schools the opportunity to participate in the educational ferment going on in Springfield. Sunshine School was "adopted" in 1917 and STC

student teachers were sent there for six weeks of practice teaching.

By 1918, there were demonstration schools near Marshfield, Joplin, Ava, Willow Springs, Mountain Grove and Strafford, as well as Oak Grove school east of Springfield. Willard was added to the list in 1924.

By the time Greenwood school moved into the new Education Building and the bungalow had become home to the Conservatory, the teacher training process was becoming refined. Students were required to take two terms of practice teaching in Greenwood or one of the demonstra-

tion schools. The facilities in the new Education Building provided profound encouragement to the faculty. The kindergarten classroom, for example, was a spacious room on the ground floor with a fireplace and tasteful interior decoration, a far cry from the cramped conditions of the bungalow. The 1924-26 *Catalog* described the innovations including a room that "has been especially designed for observation of classes. The amphi-theatrical arrangement of the seats makes possible complete observation of class procedure. The curved walls provide an acoustic device which insures that the voices of children will carry perfectly."

Nearly every faculty member on campus was involved in some way with the preparation of teachers. The push was toward qualifying students for the B.S. in Education degree. The once popular Regents Certificate was dropped after 1933. The 60-hour and 90-hour diplomas ultimately were phased out as well. Curricula were organized and focused according to grade level with a special curriculum for rural teachers.

Some evidence of the progressive attitude present in the teacher-training program was the administration of IQ tests to Greenwood students. In one report, three students were ranked well below 100 (average), while "several measured 155 to 175, genius level." The scores were reported to parents, but not to students.

Technology had begun its appearance in the Greenwood classrooms as well. Two radios with victorola attachments enabled classes in 1930 to hear "the philharmonic from New York, Walter Damrasch conducting," as well as "addresses from government officials

1925

First female, Ellenora V. Linney, appointed to Board of Regents.

Plans are announced for the Kentwood Arms Hotel.

Nellie Taylor Ross of Wyoming becomes first female governor in the U.S.

Crossword puzzles become popular.

1919-46 Southwest Missouri State Teachers College 61

1921 Football

When the 1921 Bears took the field against Missouri Wesleyan College of Cameron, Missouri, to open the season, 25 players suited up. The average weight of the team was only 168 pounds. Only one player weighed as much as 200 pounds. He also was the tallest at 6'1". Three players weighed in at only 150.

Eighty years later when the Bears traveled to Lawrence, Kansas, to kick off the 2001 season against the University of Kansas, 89 players were on the roster. Their average weight was 224 — 56 pounds heavier than the 1921 team. Sixty-four of the 89 players topped the scales at 200 pounds or more. The heaviest, Elliot Smith, carried 340 pounds into the opposing line. Sixty-nine percent of the players (61) were six feet tall or taller. Jeff Bristol towered at 6'7".

Virgil Cheek was team captain in 1921. According to the *Ozarko*, he handled the team well. Cheek was credited with playing an "efficient offensive game, especially in running interference." But his genius was defense. "It was almost impossible for an opposing team to gain consistently around his end," according to the yearbook. Four years later, W. Virgil Cheek returned to the college to teach business courses and eventually head up the Business Department from 1940-55.

in Washington, D.C."

Honor Day was established at Greenwood in 1926 and remains a cherished tradition. In that year the student body elected a Fair Greenwood and a First Citizen from members of the senior class. Outstanding students in scholastics, forensics, athletics, music and journalism were inducted into the "Order of the Rose." In 1946, the First Citizen was replaced by Sir Greenwood. The "Order of the Rose" continues to be a mark of distinction among Greenwood graduates. Over the years, Greenwood has nurtured national leadership in science (Dr. Robert Moon and the Manhattan Project), in women's issues (Dr. Paula Caplan), and in sports (Payne Stewart, professional golf), as well as in other fields.

Accreditation Achieved

It's not surprising that in the midst of this ferment and growth, examiners from the North Central Accrediting Association were invited to visit the STC campus in 1927. Despite its pretentious new name, STC was regarded as no more than a junior college until North Central could assess the quality of its work and accredit it as a full collegiate, degree-granting institution.

The accrediting association allowed teachers colleges to choose between three accrediting options: (1) accept a junior college ranking; (2) refuse any ranking; or (3) apply for full recognition. STC chose the latter option, and when the report was given, the college was given full accreditation as a teachers college and full accreditation as a baccalaureate liberal arts institution.

When the North Central report arrived, *The Standard* exploded with the headline "STC is given highest

rank in North Central Association." The story that followed began with the lines, "This college has been accredited with a full scholastic rating which places it on the same level as any other college in the U.S." Was the editor looking north across Jordan Creek when he wrote that lead sentence? Who knows,

Teaching Is Basic

"Teaching is basic to all other professions. When we are regaled with the achievements of statesmen who have swayed the destinies of nations, of disciples of science who have stayed the ravages of disease, of engineers who have drained the dismal swamps and spanned our rivers with arches of steel, let us answer in the heroic words of Superintendent McHenry, 'Yes, we make those fellows.'"

President Roy Ellis'
greeting to students
September 10, 1930

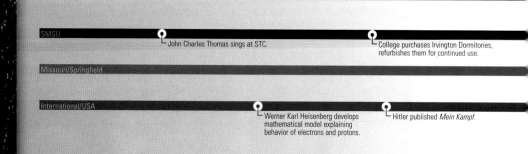

SMSU — John Charles Thomas sings at STC. — College purchases Irvington Dormitories, refurbishes them for continued use.

Missouri/Springfield

International/USA — Werner Karl Heisenberg develops mathematical model explaining behavior of electrons and protons. — Hitler published *Mein Kampf*.

but respectability had been won at the hands of the most rigorous of examiners, the North Central Association.

STC was among the first group of 12 teachers colleges to be accredited by North Central. In a return visit in 1932 North Central identified STC as one of the six best teachers colleges in the U.S., and Greenwood School was described as "one of the country's best planned and conducted training schools."

Native Sons Become President
Clyde Milton Hill
Guiding the rapid ascent of the young institution was a series of leaders whose roots were decidedly local, but whose vision embraced the best practices in the growing field of higher education. John T. Woodruff, the first treasurer of the Board of Regents, called attention to "the native sons" who had grasped the reins and "conducted the affairs of the school." For him it was fortuitous that W.T. Carrington, "a native Missourian, a home product," was selected as the school's first President.

Carrington's successors, Clyde Hill and Roy Ellis, had their roots thrust deeply into the culture of the Ozarks. Clyde Milton Hill succeeded President Carrington in 1918. He was only 32 years of age but had already made a name for himself in education. A precocious lad, Hill graduated from high school in West Plains when he was only 15, began teaching in Howell County when he was 16, and was appointed as superintendent of schools in West Plains before he was out of his teens. He was president of the first graduating class at Normal School #4 in 1907, and three years later he was on the mathematics faculty. In 1912, he became head of the Mathematics Department.

Clyde M. Hill became the second president of STC succeeding W.T. Carrington who left for Washington, D.C., at the end of World War I. A precocious youth, Hill became superintendent of West Plains schools before he reached his 20th birthday. He was only 32 when he was tapped to succeed President Carrington. President Hill's personal greeting to STC students in the 1922 *Ozarko* reflects his high expectations for the young school.

Observing the difficult transition required of students moving from the elementary grades to high school, Hill began to advocate the establishment of a transitional period which would be called "Junior high school." In 1916 the

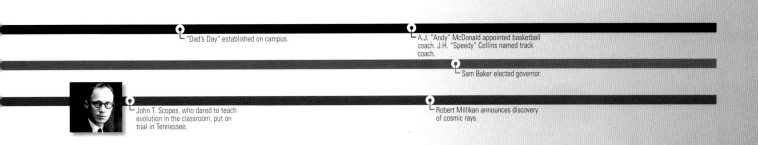

"Dad's Day" established on campus.

A.J. "Andy" McDonald appointed basketball coach. J.H. "Speedy" Collins named track coach.

Sam Baker elected governor.

John T. Scopes, who dared to teach evolution in the classroom, put on trial in Tennessee.

Robert Millikan announces discovery of cosmic rays.

Clear Evidence

"Well, I'll stick to basketball. I can tell when the ball goes through the hoop."

∽

Ralph Snavely, student-athlete, debater and airplane pilot on the occasion of losing a debate he was sure he had won in 1921. Snavely went on to become a General in the Army Air Force during World War II.

State of Vermont called him to introduce the junior high school concept into their educational system, a unique innovation for the time.

Hill returned to State Normal School #4 in 1918 to become its second president and to escort the institution into its state teachers college period. In 1925, when President Hill took a year's leave to complete his doctoral studies at Columbia University, *The Standard* observed that, "His purpose in life has been to serve his fellowmen and the growth of STC from a small college to a young university."

In many respects, Hill was a charismatic leader. His exceptional social skills, combined with his intellectual gifts, put him at the forefront of a host of local organizations. He was a 32nd degree Scottish Rite Mason, a Shriner, president of the Springfield Rotary Club, president of the Greene County Health Association, and president of

the Missouri State Teachers Association. He served as an elder in the First Presbyterian Church and on the Board of Governors of the Springfield Chamber of Commerce.

The 1923 *Ozarko* was dedicated to President Clyde Milton Hill, who by this time had become very popular among students. They saw him as a "wise administrator, able leader, progressive educator, whose kindly friendliness and humor, whose devotion to the students, and whose vision for a broadening field of service for the Teachers College, have endeared him to us all."

Hill was a practitioner of Christian piety, reflecting again his Ozark roots. He prayed publicly at STC events, lectured on the virtues of prayer, and occupied the pulpit in local churches on occasion. In his welcome to the students in the fall of 1925, he admonished them, "do not neglect your religious life just because you are away from home. You will need the influence of the church of your choices more here, perhaps, than at home."

Hill's watch at STC was dynamic. Between 1918-26 total annual enrollment increased more than 200 percent. Instructional staff increased 88 percent. Increasing numbers of faculty were earning terminal degrees. Academic standards were increasing leading to a laudatory accreditation report by the North Central Association in 1927. Graduates from STC were being readily accepted into graduate programs at the best universities across the country. In collaboration with local leaders in the field of music, President Hill brought some of the finest artists of the era to Springfield.

Despite the warm embrace of students and local citizens, President

Hill had his critics. Some faculty complained of favoritism and a flagrant misuse of funds. A former student alleged that a football player was paid for work he never did. By 1925, a cloud hung over the Hill administration. The state auditor made a visit to campus and while President Hill was cleared of any wrongdoing, the auditor's report found a great deal of room for improvement in the administration of the college.

President Hill completed his doctorate in the spring of 1926, but did not return to the college. He accepted a position at Yale University as professor of secondary education and college administration. He resigned his post at STC on July 23, 1926.

During President Hill's absence, his critics had been busy making a case against his leadership. When he resigned, they turned their attention to the Board of Regents who had begun the search for a replacement. The critics were primarily public school superintendents and principals from some rural areas in the Ozarks. Superintendent N.E. Viles of Neosho appeared to lead the dissidents who claimed to represent 200 schools throughout the district.

Roy Ellis

The critics felt that the Board was leaning toward appointing Roy Ellis to be the new president. In their view, Ellis was unsatisfactory because he had been "groomed by President Hill to succeed him." They circulated a petition demanding that the Board find a president "who bears a national reputation in the field of education, who has a doctor's degree in that field of endeavor, and who comes from the outside and who is neutral." While Roy Ellis was

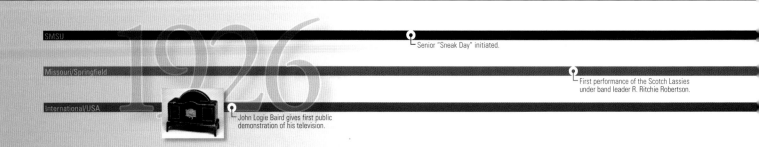

SMSU

Senior "Sneak Day" initiated.

Missouri/Springfield

First performance of the Scotch Lassies under band leader R. Ritchie Robertson.

International/USA

John Logie Baird gives first public demonstration of his television.

The Country Life Club was organized in 1924 by the agriculture, home economics and rural life departments, to promote interest in country life in the Ozarks. On April 24, 1924, the club sponsored the first "Dairy Day," the occasion for this picture.

not named in the petition, it was clear that it was intended to discredit him.

The dissident schoolmen increased the pressure on the Board by threatening to boycott the institution if their demands were not met. They would neither hire its graduates to teach in their schools, nor send their graduates to enroll at STC, unless someone was chosen "from the outside and who is neutral." The Board was in a difficult position, but it refused to be blackmailed by the threats of the dissidents. It had assessed the situation and decided that Roy Ellis would lead the growing college. He was appointed acting president on July 23, 1926, and on April 1, 1927, was given the full responsibilities of presidency.

Roy Ellis had no sooner taken the reins when Governor Baker slashed $67,000 from the 1926-27 budget of the college because of a state revenue shortfall, President Ellis' first task was to respond to a budget crisis. There

were not many options. That size of a shortfall required cuts in faculty. Eighteen were released at the end of the spring semester. Ellis tried to limit the hardship by releasing several whose spouses were also on the faculty thereby enabling the retention of others who were the single source of income for their families.

But some of those released were outraged at what they called the "cold-blooded animosity of the president." T.J. Walker, who had taught rural education since 1913, was convinced he was released because, "I had enough honor to say, when asked, that Roy Ellis was not a suitable man to head the institution." On May 15, 1927, the dissident schoolmen struck again in support of Walker's allegations. Thirty-one superintendents and principals from the southwest district demanded that President Ellis resign because of his actions in dismissing 18 faculty. But Ellis stood firm. The Board stood firm.

Local businessmen in Springfield rallied to support the beleaguered president against what they called the "guerilla attacks" of the dissidents. Governor Sam Baker gave his backing to the new administration as well.

The institution's third president had a difficult beginning, but he quickly commended himself to the district by not only solving the budget woes that threatened to destroy the young college, but also by leading it through a successful accreditation process by both the North Central Association and the American Association of Teachers Colleges, which identified it as one of the nation's leading teacher training institutions.

The Board felt vindicated as it saw the enrollment grow, the financial condition stabilize and the academic quality of the institution complemented under the leadership of "a native son," a man who was born in Seymour and grew up in the valley of the Wood Fork of the Gasconade River, where he learned from his Baptist preacher father "to do the things that were right even if it took the hide off your back."

Roy Ellis, like Clyde Hill, started teaching at a young age in Wright County. He was immersed in Ozark life and, in 1909 came to Normal School #4 in Springfield where he graduated in 1911. George Wattle, one of his classmates in 1910, remembers Ellis as a serious student. "He always seemed to have some books under his arm; wore rather short trousers, low shoes and white sox."

Ellis went on to earn an A.B. and B.S. in Education at the University of Missouri and a master's degree at Harvard in 1917. He returned to State Normal School #4, as did Hill, as a

First spring commencement held with 60 graduates. First faculty academic procession at commencement ceremonies.

National Geographic takes first natural-color undersea photos.

Houdini stays in coffin under water for one hour.

Gertrude Ederle, first woman to swim the English Channel, sets a new record time: 14 hours and 39 minutes.

1919-46 Southwest Missouri State Teachers College 65

THE FACULTY

HEADS OF DEPARTMENTS

Lives of great men sometimes bore us;
They can make our lives so punk,
When departing they leave behind them,
Facts that we must learn—or flunk.

Over the Hills of Germania
And through the valleys of Gaul
He leads the plodding Latin student
And makes him learn it all.

Will argue any question, either side,
And if you agree with him,
Your chances are slim,
For he'll switch to the other side.

Her hobby is five minute speeches on
the freedom of speech and of the press.
She believes that the time will come when
men will beat their swords into billard
cues and their spears into golf clubs.

He has an inspiring way
That makes men train three hours a day.

The 1925 *Ozarko* portrayed leading faculty and their idiosyncracies. Top to bottom: James Shannon, history; Norman Freudenberger, Latin; Roy Ellis, economics and sociology; Dr. Virginia Craig, English; Coach Arthur Briggs, physical education.

faculty member. Ellis taught economics and sociology from 1917 until he was appointed acting president in 1926-27.

President Ellis' classmates not only remember his thirst for knowledge and his short trousers, but they also had him figured out to become a judge on the Supreme Court. By the 1930s, Roy Ellis had become a leader in higher education throughout Missouri, chairing the President's Conference for more than 30 years and attracting the attention of the *Kansas City Star,* which described him as "a hillbilly school master who has risen in the world of education." He took the cause of the state teachers colleges to the Legislature and persuaded them to give the institutions better treatment. As a student in the late 1930s, Katherine Alexander Gilroy remembers that she "was in awe of him."

Like his predecessor Clyde Hill, Roy Ellis came to the presidency still working on his doctoral degree. He finished it in 1930 at Columbia University. His dissertation was published and titled "A Civic History of Kansas City, Missouri." The *Kansas City Star* reviewed the book and described it as addressing questions such as, "How was the city born, named, spanked and coddled? What civic and business habits did it develop and why?" The reviewer assured prospective readers that "Mr. Ellis…will not mislead you with fiction, nor bore you with unimportant facts."

President Ellis remained at his post for 35 years, one of the longest tenures of any college president in the nation at the time. He developed a profound respect for the contribution the college was making to the Ozarks. In 1936, he wrote in the *Ozarko*: "The surrounding scene was indeed a fertile field for the founders of an educational enterprise of this character. Round about stretched the vast and beauteous expanse of the Ozarks, stocked with a strong and sturdy race in whose hearts there burns a ceaseless yearning for learning and for culture…. Teachers College has made this educational interest of the Ozarks pulsate with new power and new life. The teachers who have been trained

SMSU

President Hill resigns to accept a position at Yale University. Roy Ellis appointed acting president.

Missouri/Springfield

Gillioz Theater opens.

International/USA

Henry Ford announces the 40-hour, five-day work week.

Ernest Hemingway publishes *The Sun Also Rises.*

Hirohito becomes Emperor of Japan.

Professor A.P. Temple began his career at SMS in 1907 teaching physics and chemistry. A graduate of Ohio Wesleyan, he also did graduate work at the University of Chicago. Temple introduced visual education at the college, using slides and films in his classroom. He also pioneered the development of radio on campus. An avid sportsman, Temple often supplied his table and others with game.

here have not only found in their own hearts a new vision of life, but they have also carried this vision into every nook and corner of the Ozarks. Teachers College is indeed the Shrine of the Ozarks."

That vocabulary of the sacred summed up the feelings of another homegrown leader for the institution. As we will subsequently see, that language was not peculiar to Roy Ellis.

Board of Regents

The genius of Ozark leadership for STC was not confined to the President's office. The Regents were also of Ozark stock and took a deep interest in the growing institution. During the lean Depression years, the Legislature proposed that the boards of all state educational institutions be consolidated into one central board in order to save money. The idea did not set well in Cape Girardeau, Kirksville, Marysville, Warrensburg or Springfield. The colleges were taking shape around the needs and interests of their constituencies, and that principle would not be sacrificed to the dubious proposition that a single governing board would be more economical. The consolidation idea ultimately died in committee.

The local boards were also breaking new ground. In 1925, the first woman was appointed to Southwest Missouri State Teachers College Board of Regents. Elenora Linney, wife of W.B. Linney, a Springfield attorney, joined five men from Houston, Mountain Grove, Carthage, Bolivar and Springfield, to help chart the course for STC.

A Homegrown Faculty

If the administration had a peculiarly homegrown look to it, by the STC years the faculty had certainly acquired that look as well. An ever increasing number of students returned to their alma mater as teachers. As early as 1914, eight of the 37 total faculty had taken undergraduate work at State Normal School #4. By 1919, when the school became STC, more than one-third of the instructors had taken degrees from State Normal School #4. The trend continued so that by 1922 a full 45 percent of the instructional staff were graduates of the school. By 1932 the proportion had increased to 46 percent.

A Cheerleader from the Stands

Fans who witnessed the 1941 Homecoming football game with Kirksville won't soon forget Paul Shelton, man-of-the-hour for STC students and Springfield sports enthusiasts.

Paul graduated from State Teachers College in 1932, but maintained a keen interest in campus events, including athletics. By 1941 he had grown weary of passive spectators at Bear athletics events.

During the Homecoming game with Kirksville, Paul could take it no longer. The Bears had lost their 13 point lead and nobody was working the crowd.

So he charged out of the stands and appointed himself cheerleader. Racing up and down in front of the 6,500 fans, thrusting his fists into the air and calling for action from the crowd, Shelton managed to bring the stands alive. Cheers rang out. Fans stomped and shouted.

"It made me so darn mad! All those students and other people sitting up there wanting to yell or do something for the team and there was nobody who wasn't afraid to lead them in a yell. I had to do something!" he explained at the time.

He must have made a difference. The Bears came back in the last three minutes to beat the Bulldogs 19-13, and go on to an undefeated season!

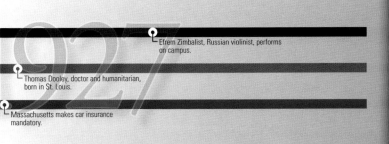

1927

Efrem Zimbalist, Russian violinist, performs on campus.

Thomas Dooley, doctor and humanitarian, born in St. Louis.

Massachusetts makes car insurance mandatory.

"THE QUADRANGLE", STATE TEACHER'S COLLEGE, SPRINGFIELD, MISSOURI

OA3527

Such a development spoke well for the contagious enthusiasm the school generated among students, and it provided a faculty with deep commitments to the institution. Nonetheless, by the end of Roy Ellis' career as president in 1961, many were beginning to think that the school was suffering from the considerable inbreeding. So the faculty encouraged the Board to look outside the institution for its new president.

The "homegrown" tradition at STC was augmented by a faculty development plan initiated by President W.T. Carrington. He allowed faculty educational leaves after three years of service to assist teachers in completing their graduate work. Immediately upon becoming a full collegiate institution in 1919, more and more STC faculty were engaged in summer studies or educational leaves to achieve terminal degrees, as had both President Hill and President Ellis.

In 1937, provision was made for educational leaves with pay, which assisted many faculty in advancing their training. The policy provided three months of study after 12 terms of work. While the policy was not a vested right, it was a privilege granted generously by the Board to promising faculty.

For the first 18 years, Virginia Craig was the only faculty member with an earned doctorate in her discipline. In 1924, Francis Todd H'Doubler joined the science faculty bringing a doctorate in bacteriology from the University of Wisconsin. A doctorate in economics was added in 1926 with the arrival of R.D. Thomas, also from Wisconsin.

But the road to doctorates was long and arduous. By 1931 only one-fourth of the faculty had earned the coveted degree. Ten years later just more than 30 percent had completed their work. But by 1936, the investment the institution had been making

was paying off. Eighty percent of the faculty had earned a terminal degree appropriate to their field, with 55 percent holding doctorates. By the end of the STC period in 1944-45, the college stood in the upper quartile of similar North Central colleges in the number of faculty holding doctorates.

While highest professional credentials were being pursued by the faculty, it was also organizing itself to assist in administering the college and encouraging professional standards among its members. When W.T. Carrington took over the duties of president in 1907, he was simultaneously the chief administrator, dean of faculty, registrar, business manager, auditor and superintendent of the physical plant. The evolution of administrative staff was slow. Until 1918 the faculty acted as a committee-of-the-whole, sharing administrative tasks under the president's direction. But in that year, the Faculty Council was put in place to assist in administering the affairs of the school. Its 16 members included academic department heads, the dean of women, and the registrar, all overseen by the president. They acted as an executive committee of the faculty. A Faculty Senate, as such, was still more than four decades away.

However, with the organization of the Faculty Council there was also

SMSU

Roy Ellis appointed third president.

F-Square club organized.

Missouri/Springfield

Bluebird named state bird.

International/USA

Flooding Mississippi River leaves 600,000 homeless.

AT&T gives first demonstration of television, broadcasting the image and voice of Herbert Hoover.

Charles Lindbergh completes first solo transatlantic flight in "The Spirit of St. Louis," flying from New York to Paris in 33 hours and 29 minutes.

the creation of a Faculty Club where instructors could discuss issues and problems of common concern. At an early meeting of the club, Dr. Virginia Craig spoke on constructing exams for both the secondary and college students. Anna Lou Blair spoke on "War and Languages." Arthur Briggs spoke on "Play and the Play Movement," while L.L. Alexander lectured on the "Implications of the Smith-Hughes Act."

Faculty wives discovered their common interests and concerns and founded the College Dames in 1919. Over the years the Dames have provided service to the institution and scholarship assistance to students.

In 1944, the faculty chartered the first American Association of University Professors (AAUP) chapter on campus. Headed by Drs. Donald Nicholson, Virginia Craig and James Snapp, the chapter brought faculty into the wider circle of academics across the nation with a focus on professional standards, faculty rights and responsibilities and other issues affecting faculty welfare.

During the first 50 years of faculty work, there was no such thing as tenure. Faculty were hired on a year-to-year basis. In fact, it wasn't even until 1934 that a classification system was developed. A faculty committee assisted in the process of defining faculty ranks, based primarily on the amount of training and length of service. The plan provided that the professor rank went to department heads, those with an earned doctorate who had served five years or more or possessed "the equivalent of a doctor's degree and had 10 years or more of service credit." Three years of graduate technical training was considered the equivalent of the doctorate.

Associate Professors included those with the doctorate, but less than five years of service, those with the equivalent of the doctorate but less than 10 years service, and those with at least two years of advanced study and 15 years of service. Assistant Professors included those with at least two years of advanced work and less than 15 years of service.

The introduction of a classification system into faculty work is not without its problems. When a pecking order is defined, there is always some tension between one's estimation of his or her own qualities and the grant of status by his or her peers. But as President Roy Ellis pointed out, the faculty in 1934 "knew what their 'portion' under the plan was, whether or not it might be just what they wished their portion to be." It seemed to work well for the time and wasn't modified until 1962.

Faculty Scholarship

While it wasn't mentioned in the 1934 plan, research was a component of faculty work for a growing number of instructors in the STC years. Early in her career Dr. Virginia Craig was writing textbooks on teaching methods for English instructors. In 1924, J.D. Delp, head of the Commerce Department, was converting his master's thesis into a textbook on accounting.

Dr. Clarence Koeppe of the Geography Department was among

Professor Temple's persistent advocacy of the use of visual technology resulted in the college undertaking the production of a technicolor film of STC life in 1942. Three STC faculty check over the college's motion picture equipment. From left to right: Dr. R.W. Martin, chemistry; Dr. Allen G. Douglas, chemistry and biology; and Dr. Chauncey Goodchild, biology.

Bears defeat Southwest Baptist College of Bolivar 94-0 in football, the highest score ever achieved by an SMS football team.

College granted first accreditation by North Central Association. Accredited both as a liberal arts college and a teachers college.

High school credit courses dropped from STC curriculum, except as offered at Greenwood.

Babe Ruth sets a major league record with 60 homeruns in a single season.

First-class stenographic equipment was available to students at STC during the late 1930s and early 1940s for improving typing skills in preparation for secretarial careers.

the more prolific scholars. In 1932, he was writing a geography text for first year college students in collaboration with a colleague at the University of Illinois. He was also conducting a study of wheat yields and climate changes in Kansas. Koeppe was also interested in mathematical geography and wrote a book on the subject. In 1935, he published the first wall map of climate regions throughout the world with notations in English. It climaxed six years of work and was published by A.J. Nystrom and Company of Chicago.

Walter Cralle was among the many who came to STC with a master's degree and full ambition to clear the doctorate hurdle. Cralle chose the University of Minnesota for his doctoral studies and was encouraged to do his dissertation research on the Ozarks. He completed the study in 1934 and titled his paper "Social Change and Isolation in the Ozark Mountain Region of Missouri." He commented on the speed of change in the Ozarks saying, "There are survivals of the primitive culture in the Ozarks, but they linger only, like the last remnant of the snow of spring." Dr. Cralle derived a paper from his dissertation which was published in the January 1936 issue of the *American Journal of Sociology*, a leading journal of the discipline. He sought to set the record straight in the article by arguing that "the Ozarks is neither urbanized to the degree depicted in Chamber of Commerce literature, nor is it the illiterate, lawless or even super-rural civilization so frequently depicted in the fiction allegedly pertaining to the area."

Other disciplines were engaging in scholarly production in the 1930s as well. Dr. Virgil Cheek's doctoral dissertation on "Objectives of Bookkeeping in Secondary Schools" was published in condensed form. Dr. Nettles, of the history department, wrote 18 biographical

SMSU

Missouri/Springfield

International/USA

1928

Women's Athletic Association replaces Spartan Club for women student-athletes.

70   *Daring to Excel: The First 100 Years of Southwest Missouri State University*

For nearly a half-century, students carried their academic records with them on cards naming the course they completed, the grade they received, their attendance record and the signature of their instructor. Students kept their own transcript of college work by adding class cards to their ring binders. The card below, issued to Irene Pearl Williams in the summer of 1926, shows she did above average work in Principles of Economics taught by soon-to-become president, Roy Ellis.

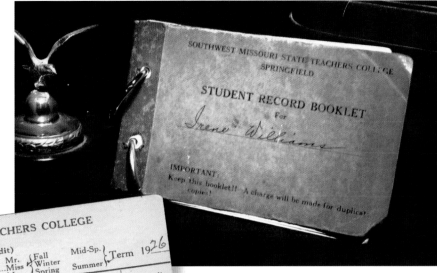

install receiving sets so they may take advantage of the opportunity to hear music and speeches from STC." On October 26, 1922, Professor Temple arranged for the broadcast of the STC football game with Tarkio College. It was a play-by-play broadcast, the first in the college's history, and to the delight of the broadcaster and the fans, the Bears triumphed, 50-0.

Temple, himself, was amazed at the technology. He wrote in *The Standard*, "Did you ever get a thrill? If you never have you are due such excitement when you listen on the radio telephones. All of a sudden one hears the piercing tones of enchanting music coming from some great city far away…. Peculiar buzzing sounds in the forms of dots and dashes are sometimes heard. This may be a message from some local station or it may be official news coming from Washington, D.C. Some people rather suspect the veracity of the whole affair; but it is no longer a thing to be doubted or questioned, for in our own laboratory, where many of you have sat in class and pondered and wondered over such complexities the wonderful

sketches of important figures in the history of Missouri for publication in *A Dictionary of American Biography*. Dr. B.B. Bassett, professor of economics, published extensively on education for citizenship and was appointed Research Fellow at University of Iowa. Just before World War II, Dr. Lester V. Whitney, who taught physics and math, was studying the angular distribution of diffused light in natural water. His findings were published as *Bulletins* for college classwork.

Few were as enthusiastic about emerging communications technology

as Professor A.P. Temple of the science department. He pioneered the introduction of the first radio receiver and transmitter at STC in 1921. Wireless telephony and telegraphy promised to bring the best speeches, the finest concerts, the most provocative lectures delivered anywhere in the U.S. to the STC campus. Moreover, it would allow STC to broadcast its programs to listeners across the country. He tirelessly promoted wireless radio throughout the college service area. "It is the wish of the science department," he said, "that high schools of the surrounding area

Lunch room in Administration Building becomes a cafeteria serving three meals a day.

First annual Farm Week held by Agriculture Department.

The Chillicothe Baking Co. announces the marketing of sliced bread.

Amelia Earhart becomes first female to fly the Atlantic.

1919-46 Southwest Missouri State Teachers College 71

BERTHA WELLS

by Tina Stillwell '72

I t's been said she couldn't have carried a stick as big as her reputation. Her era at SMSU spanned World War I, the Great Depression, World War II, the Korean War, and three university presidents. If you were a student, you didn't complain to her, and you didn't want to be called to her office. She had a keen nose for alcohol at school events, and she didn't much like purple punch or dancing cheek-to-cheek. Although she was classified as the dean of women, she also served as dean of men, dean of students, housing director and social director during much of her 40-year tenure (1915-55).

She was Miss Bertha Wells. Dean Bertha.

Bertha Wells' association with SMSU goes back to the summer of 1906, when she enrolled at what was then State Normal School #4. After receiving a B.Pe (Bachelor of Pedagogy) degree in 1909, she taught Latin and German at Lamar High School for four years. She earned an A.B. degree from Drury College in 1915 and became a Latin instructor at Normal School #4 that same year. Wells became the acting dean of women in 1918 and dean of women in 1924.

One of her responsibilities was inspecting and approving private rooming houses for STC women. "She served as the intermediary with the landladies," said Dr. Richard Wilkinson, professor emeritus of psychology (1939-70). "Of course those were the days when no boys were allowed in the living room, the girls had to be in by 9:00 p.m., and three or four girls lived in a house."

Wilkinson recalled Dean Bertha's encounters with students with disciplinary problems who had been called into her office on the second floor of the Administration Building. "She sat in a wicker rocker and had a rocker for the student," he noted. "The more serious the case, the harder she would rock."

Dean Bertha was responsible for the fraternities and sororities on campus. She also issued the keys and kept a pass key for the walls of lockers in the Administration Building, Siceluff Hall and Hill Hall. The locker numbers and renters were contained in the famous "blue book" in her office.

With dark, short, finger-waved hair, Dean Bertha came across as prim and proper. Conservative in dress, she often wore a necklace or family broach. The dean had a "mature" build, and, at times, seemed taller than her approximate 5-foot 6-inch stature. "Bertha left no doubt in anyone's mind

she had the final say on the social scene," said Don Payton, '50.

"She was absolutely lovely, polite and charming at the social events," Jeanne Craig Stinson, '50. "You would go and greet the chaperones, introduce your date, and get a cup of punch. People were well dressed and well behaved. In those days, what a school administrator said was the word. We did precisely what we were told to do." "The boys practiced gallantry on her, and she loved it," added E.E. "Jimmy" Johnson, '49.

Dean Bertha guarded her privacy. One of the few people on campus who became closely acquainted with her was Ruth Button Greenlee, '39, who served as her assistant for almost a year after Greenlee graduated from STC. "She was a character," Greenlee said of her former boss. "Although she was stiff and stern on the outside, she was a 'softy' underneath. If you were straight with her, she was straight with you."

Dean Bertha never married. She lived with her sister, Carolyn Wells Lawing, on Roberson Street in a big, old-fashioned, two-story house with a parlor. They tended a vegetable garden out back. Dean Bertha is described in the 1930 edition of the *Ozarko* as "a person of rare ability and understanding and a blessing to S.T.C." The yearbook entry continued, "...she also has a strong and undying belief in the possibilities and the judgment of youth. She is greatly responsible for the democratic atmosphere which prevails in the school."

The Dean Bertha epoch ended when she retired from her position at SMS in the summer of 1955. SMS' first dorm, Women's Residence Hall, was renamed Wells House in July 1967. In 1969 the SMS Alumni Association honored the dean emeritus with an award of appreciation during Homecoming. At the time she had been a resident of the nursing home section of Cox Medical Center for two years and was confined to a wheelchair. Her award was accepted by Neil Wortley, '50, the administrator at Cox Medical Center, who later presented it to her.

The remarkable woman who had given generously of her time to four decades of SMS students as a teacher, friend, counselor and loyal supporter of all wholesome college activities died in April 1972 at age 92, but she clearly lives on among the legends of SMSU history. ✿

results are being manifest daily."

Temple was also an innovator with film. In the summer of 1923, he produced a film documenting the experience of a student in summer school. He titled the film (what else?) "College Life in the Ozarks." It included buildings, residence life, agriculture classes complete with livestock, Greenwood first graders at play, the May Day Celebration and an off-campus visit to Phelps Grove Park. The entire campus gathered at the end of summer school to see the documentary.

The experiments with technology and the research into diffused light would hardly have been possible in the early years. In 1906, faculty members taught seven classes a day, each a 50-minute period. Typically, each period represented a different preparation. By 1910, the load had been lightened, but only slightly. Six 45 minute class sessions per day was the mean. But finally, in 1916, the Missouri Educational Conference set a statewide standard of teaching 18 clock hours per week. That standard remained until 1963.

The First Retirements

By the time the Great Depression struck the country, there were faculty who had been teaching for 30 years with no clear view of what they would do when age and infirmity made teaching difficult. The first to retire was Dr. D.T. Kizer, a trained physician who taught in the science department until 1936. His retirement was atypical however. He showed up outside President Ellis' office at regular intervals asking for things to do on campus. Ellis admits that Dr. Kizer's restless quest for things to do soon exceeded his ingenuity in devising tasks. He finally had to

tell Professor Kizer, "When I have more for you to do I'll contact you."

But Kizer's retirement did bring into focus the need for a college policy. So in 1939 the Board adopted what they called "The Limited Service Plan." It provided that at age 66, the teaching load would be reduced 25 percent with a corresponding reduction in salary. At age 70, there was a 50 percent teaching load allowed, and at age 72, one could teach only a quarter load. At age 74, one was mandated to stop teaching. A stipend of $50.00 per month was given in 1939, and it was raised from time to time. The plan was unique to the college with no support given by the state. But it soon became clear that the stipend was not adequate, nor was it feasible for faculty to save sufficiently to provide for their own retirement. So by the end of the STC era, the retirement issue had become acute. Fortunately, in 1945, the State Public School Retirement plan came into being and faculty quickly embraced the opportunity to join that plan.

While retirement plans were being made by some other faculty, most started as energetic young folks and were in their prime during the STC years. Dr. Virginia Craig, for one, was becoming a legend in her own time. The 1925 *Ozarko* humorously described her hobby as "five minute speeches on the freedom of speech and the press." The *Ozarko* went on to say that "she believes the time will come when men will beat their swords into billiard cues and their spears into golf clubs."

Dr. Craig and Mrs. H.B. Wherriet of Joplin collaborated to write a play in 1922. It was titled *A Camel's Nose*, a farce dealing with "a modern day sex problem." It was described by those

who saw it as "a clever comic satire on a social condition that has existed down through the ages." No one was surprised that the play was part of a crusade to set social issues right. That was Dr. Craig's stock-in-trade.

First Dean of Women

By the time the Normal School had become a teachers college, it needed a person to manage its busy social calendar and in Victorian style, watch out for the welfare of the young women on campus. Bertha Wells was appointed to that job in 1918. She taught Latin and German and was known for her no-nonsense approach to student affairs. Like Dr. Craig, her manner of operating became legendary. In chaperoning social club dances, she stood at the door of the gym and inspected each entering couple for their proper credentials and for banned substances on the person. The inspection often included an early version of the breathalyzer — she asked the couples to breathe into her face. Alcohol, consequently, was rarely a problem at STC parties.

Her jobs as Dean were legion. She oversaw "rushing for the social clubs, helped find employment for 200 or more girls each year, allocated, inspected, and kept track of 1,380 lockers, scheduled social events, served as final arbiter in disputes between students and landlords, operated the lost and found service, chaperoned at least three parties a week, approved guest lists for formal dances, inspected rooms offered by local families for housing students, and administered a disciplinary code, which was unwritten but clearly understood by every student who met her."

Toward the close of the STC period, another person arrived on

Power plant burns eight tons of coal a day to heat campus in cold weather.

Bears capture both conference football and basketball crowns.

Alexander Fleming discovers penicillin.

Dubble Bubble bubble gum is invented by Walter E. Deimer.

Herbert Hoover elected U.S. President.

Aviation became part of the STC curriculum in the fall of 1939 as a result of the Civilian Pilot Training Act passed by Congress earlier that year. One venturesome woman, Sue Woodruff, joined 19 men in the training and is shown here in the cockpit of the single engine trainer.

faculty was not thoroughly integrated in the early years. The women had organized for themselves a Faculty Women's club. As Roy Ellis remembers, "The administration, as well as other men on the staff, have suffered from severe attacks of curiosity as to what went on in that organization." Among the publicized events were annual "frolics" which were described as "refreshingly audacious." One such "frolic" in 1937 found the faculty women transforming themselves from teachers into Hollywood movie stars and celebrities. Floy Burgess of home economics fame transformed herself into Mae West at the frolic. She was outfitted "in a form-fitting dress trimmed with red jewelry." As she paraded before the audience she walked coyly from Nelson Eddy (Alice Harrison) to Fred Astaire (Olive Galloway) "muttering in a deep, low tone, 'c'm up and see me some time.'"

Men of the faculty hardly matched the audacity of the women, but they did have their events where they did "male things." In 1935, 25 faculty men went for a weekend outing to Presbyterian Hill, near Hollister. Friday night they spent playing cards and telling stories. Saturday the men fished and hunted and prepared the evening meal from the success of their separate quests. Fish and quail were served, and Professor Pummill was recognized for bagging the largest number of quail. President Ellis was unable to join the men for their fun, but he sent a box of El Producto cigars for their enjoyment.

Grading and the Curriculum

With the name change in 1919, there also came a change in the grading system. Up to that time, student grades were expressed in percentages: 90 per-

campus who was also to become legendary. Leslie Irene Coger joined the faculty in the fall of 1943 and was described in *The Southwest Standard* as "a charming, vivacious young woman." She came from Huntsville, Arkansas where she served as drama coach. Her training began at Central College in Conway, Arkansas, and subsequently included work at the School of the Ozarks in Point Lookout, Missouri, Crescent College in Eureka Springs,

Curry School of Expression in Boston, College of the Ozarks in Clarksville, Arkansas, the University of Arkansas, and Northwestern University. At the end of her first year of service at STC, *The Standard* marveled at her "energetic leadership" and observed that "the visibility of the drama program increased dramatically" upon her arrival on campus. That energy and creativity marked Dr. Coger's work for the next 40 years.

It is of interest to observe that the

cent was considered excellent work, 80 percent was good, 70 percent was passing, and a grade of 60 to 69 percent could, at the option of the teacher, be made up. A grade below 60 percent signified course failure.

In 1919, a system of letter grades was adopted in which a grade of "E" suggested excellent work, "S" was superior, "M" was medium or average, "I" was inferior but passing, "U" was unsatisfactory or failing, "D" was delayed, and "EX" was excused or dropped. The system was based on the Max Meyer Curve, which suggested that 5 percent of the assigned grades should be excellent, 20 percent superior, 50 percent medium or average, 20 percent inferior but passing, and 5 percent U or failing.

At the end of the 1919-20 academic year, the actual grade distribution approximated the Meyer Curve, but over time adjusted in the direction of greater liberality. Current observers describe the trend as "grade inflation" and characterize it as one of the serious problems of contemporary academic life. Grade distributions for the STC years are summarized below.

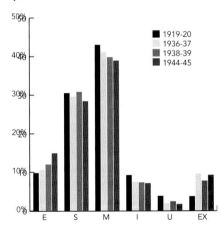

In 1930, STC followed the lead of the University of Missouri in creating a novel system of excess and diminished credit in grading. The idea was to strengthen academic effort by adding to the grade earned the incentive of extra credits accumulated. So a person earning an "E" in a 2.5 semester hour course would actually be given 3 semester hours credit. Earning an "S" would result in 2.75 credit hours earned. An "M" would earn the assigned 2.5 hours, but if the student received an "I" grade, they would receive diminished credit of 2.25 semester hours for the course. Under this system, if a student could maintain "E"s and "S"s during each term, they would be able to graduate in less than four years. This system of grading was used throughout the later part of the STC era and was only dropped in 1961 when all Missouri state colleges and universities adopted a common grading system without the excess and diminished credit innovation.

As the school developed policies dealing with scholastic probation, graduation requirements and graduation honors, it also established a credit point system which enabled the computation of grade point averages and credit accumulation toward graduation. This system went into effect in 1928. An "E" grade carried three credit points per semester, the "S" carried two, while the "M" carried one credit point per semester. In 1933, a new wrinkle was added which reflected the previous idea of diminished credit. For courses failed, a full credit would be deducted from the student's accumulated credits, thus creating the need to replace that credit lost with credit points earned by higher grades. It is still a central feature of the grading and credit earning system in the 21st century.

34 Years to Find a 4.0 Student

The first student to graduate from SMS with a 4.0 grade point average was Dorothy Martin, daughter of STC Chemistry Professor and Mrs. Robert W. Martin. The year was 1940. Dorothy went on to earn a Ph.D. in physical chemistry at the University of Illinois in 1945 and quickly gained an international reputation in the field of combustion. She joined Avco Corporation in 1956 becoming Vice President for Research where she guided development activities in eight technology-based divisions.

The second person to graduate with a 4.0 came 24 years later when Lyna Lee Montgomery received an A.B. degree from SMS in 1964. She went on to earn a Ph.D. in 1967 and joined the faculty of the University of Arkansas.

Only two students reached that lofty goal in the first 60 years of the institution's history.

STC wins first intercollegiate debate tournament.

University of Kansas City incorporated.

Vatican City becomes a sovereign state.

Curriculum Innovations

The evolution of grading systems reflects, in part, the evolution of the curriculum and the academic experience of the student in the STC period. In 1923, Lee Morris described changes that had occurred since 1913. "In 1913, few people, comparatively, were regular college students. Irregular classification was common. The majority were doing high school work." According to Morris, "Had they been asked to what class they belonged, they would have been unable to tell you just as the pupils in the rural school of 15 years ago were unable to tell you to what grade they belonged." Morris also observed that in the Normal School days "the courses were loosely organized and lacking in uniformity." But by 1923, it was his opinion that, "the

courses represent the last word in curriculum planning. (They) are closely affiliated with the content and requirements of all the colleges and universities of the land." Morris continued his assessment by lauding the superior quality of students coming to STC. "Along with the phenomenal growth in numbers has come a student body that is the height of intelligence. The students are well organized…. Everybody knows where he is in the course and what he is doing."

Faculty in the 21st century marvel at such a description, hyperbole notwithstanding, but STC was indeed different than State Normal School #4. The normal school started its work with six departments and a dozen faculty. By 1919 there were 58 faculty staffing a dozen departments, five divisions, and a conservatory of music. There was also a system of majors and minors and a form of general education, which distributed students' studies over a variety of disciplines in addition to their major.

Moreover, teaching innovations were occurring across the disciplines. Professor Temple was pioneering the use of films in science courses. He showed movies on zinc, copper, pottery production, old Mexico and Fox News pictures. A *Standard* headline in 1922 declared, "Greatest Educational Film Here This Week." Temple had secured a film showing the building, operating and functioning of every part of the automobile. By the summer of 1923, Temple was showing feature films in the college auditorium for the entertainment of students, including *Over The Hill, A Connecticut Yankee in King Arthur's Court* and *Crystal Jewels*. As head of the science department, Temple declared, "It is (my) most earnest desire

to extend this most modern method of instruction throughout the Southwest District."

Geography students were leaving the classroom for field trips to study mining in Joplin, eastern Kansas and northeast Oklahoma. They continued their travels to West Plains, Mammouth Springs, Poplar Bluff, Portageville, Cape Girardeau, St. Louis and Columbia to study geology, timber, soils, minerals and other resources of the region.

In the late 1930s, Congress passed the Civilian Pilot Training Act extending to colleges and universities the opportunity to include aviation as part of their curriculum. STC joined the ground-training component and produced graduates who scored well above the norm on national tests. Twenty students were taking the training in 1940, including one pioneering woman, Sue Woodruff.

In a lecture to faculty in 1925, Professor M.A. O'Rear summarized what he took to be the important trends in education. He emphasized the role of science in improving educational techniques with particular focus on standardized testing and measurement of learning. The measurement of intelligence and an emphasis upon practical learning were noted as significant advances. O'Rear also cited what he called "a concern for the spiritual side of education." "Children," he said, "must be taught to appreciate art, music, literature and value the ideals and habits of good conduct."

Professor E.E. Dodd appeared to take O'Rear seriously. In the late 1920s, he designed what turned out to be an extremely popular course titled "Personality Training." Highly practical, it launched many an STC student into

SMSU

Missouri/Springfield

International/USA

└ Historian/Philosopher Will Durant lectures at STC.

└ Springfield celebrates its Centennial.

└ Robert Goddard launches first instrumented, liquid-fueled rocket.

└ Stock market crash initiates worldwide economic depression.

Professor Norman Fruedenberger came to State Normal School #4 in 1907 to head the foreign language department. He received an A.B. degree from the University of Missouri in 1900 and a master's from Harvard in 1902. His interests were broad including archaeology and science. His Latin classes were legendary. The 1938 *Ozarko* described him saying, "His zeal in his work is unsurpassed, yet he has not become a mere robot, carrying out inflexible decisions. Instead, he is another human, more understanding and sympathetic than most, yet one of flesh and blood, as are we."

more confident social relationships and increased the proportion of men and women who sought and successfully achieved campus dates.

Responding to the religious orientation of the area, the college introduced a *Bible* course in 1937. Taught by the eminently qualified local minister, Rev. F.W.A. Bosch, the course met with immediate success, enrolling 186 the first semester. The course later became the focus of an Attorney General's ruling concerning the separation of church and state.

The evidence of curriculum development and academic experimentation was seen throughout the campus as STC explored the implications of its newly won collegiate status.

Town/Gown Courtship

Just three months before State Normal School #4 acquired its new status as a full collegiate institution, women in Missouri gained a new right as voters in all elections. Women's suffrage had been an issue for decades across the country and in July 1919 the 21st amendment to the constitution was ratified empowering women throughout the nation.

While women were acquiring the right to vote, the city of Springfield was becoming a thriving urban center. The 1920 census counted 39,631 citizens, a 70 percent growth from the turn of the century and the establishment of the Normal School. Industrial development and the railroad had drawn workers to the city from rural areas and across the country. The industrial expansion across America carried with it labor troubles in many cities. The year 1919 was marked by labor conflicts unparalleled in the nation's history. Massive strikes crippled steel and coal industries. Normally tranquil sectors of labor such as police and theatre were convulsed as well. Whole cities and regions

were virtually shut down by strikes. In 1922, railroad shop workers went on strike across the country resulting in 3,000 men in Springfield's Frisco shops being out of work. The strike crippled the local economy.

In the early 1920s, baseball, the national pastime, came to Springfield as the St. Louis Browns established a Western Association farm team that played in White City Park. For 20 years, the local citizens saw St. Louis Browns and Cardinals players move up through the minor leagues into major league prominence.

In 1929, commercial air travel made its debut in Springfield. American Airlines and TWA scheduled flights into the downtown airport. It had only been 13 years since the first recorded airplane flight came to Springfield. Katherine Stenson, a woman stunt flyer, entertained local citizens from the fairgrounds field near Phelps Grove Park in 1916. By 1942 citizens approved a bond issue to build a new airport west of the city to accommodate the growing number of flights into the city.

The 1920s also saw the building of the Kentwood Arms Hotel to accommodate the growing commercial activity of the city. John Woodruff built the facility while he was building Hickory Hills golf course on the far east side of the city.

The pace of development in the

First cigarette ad appears in *The Southwest Standard*.

Henry Caulfield elected governor.

Admiral Richard Byrd flies over South Pole becoming the first person to fly over both poles.

Game of BINGO is invented by Edwin S. Lowe.

Science building completed.

American Airlines is established.

Queen City of the Ozarks was clearly accelerating. In 1933, the Springfield Civic Symphony was organized by James P. Robertson. A year later, the Springfield Little Theater was founded by a group of new graduates from Senior High School. The Springfield Traction Company retired street cars in 1936 and introduced a fleet of buses. In 1939, the Kraft Cheese Company opened a milk processing plant on Mill Street. Kraft was to become one of the largest employers in the city. That same year, John Ramey opened a supermarket on the corner of Glenstone and Sunshine, one of the first in the country. The world premiere of "Jesse James" with Tyrone Power, Henry Fonda, Randolph Scott and Nancy Kelly opened at the Gillioz Theatre in 1939. Local citizens jammed the theater to see the movie since dozens of Springfieldians had served as "extras" when the movie was being shot near Pineville and Noel.

The Standard editor in 1926 sensed the massive changes taking place in Springfield and declared, "The pioneer American institutions are passing! The little one-room log school house has given way to the consolidated district. The crossroads Blacksmith shop is now a filling station and the city livery stable is a garage. The country store has moved to town along with the church in the wildwood...." But despite the massive changes occurring in the environment, the 1932 *Standard* editor still saw "a city which dreams in drowsy somnolence of tradition even while it meets the requirements of modern commerce.... It was on the square that Wild Bill Hickock, the most picturesque ruffian of the old untamable west, fought a death battle with Dave

Tutt. (It) boasts one of the largest farm produce plants in the world and at the same time has along its streets high pressure salesmen walking alongside bearded, patriarchal hillsmen, the direct descendants of men who crossed the sea to fight their way across a continent."

While observing this scene in 1933, one could also have dropped by the Frisco Station and for a 10 cent ticket seen the largest sea mammal ever captured. A 68-ton finback whale was on display. Measuring 55-feet long, the creature required 38 barrels of embalming fluid to preserve it. The heart alone weighed 1,268 lbs.

In the midst of all that excitement, there was a graceful dance going on between the Springfield Chamber of Commerce and STC. The Chamber had discovered that 1,600 students spending $40 a month added up to nearly a $1 million enhancement of the local economy. So as early as 1923, students were invited to become student members of the Chamber at $4.00 a year. *The Standard* encouraged the idea saying, "the Chamber of Commerce and STC can cooperate for a better community."

The dance continued into 1924 with M.V. Carroll, secretary of the Springfield Chamber of Commerce, writing a letter to the editor declaring STC to be "a valuable asset to the community." He joined others in observing that STC "is virtually the University of the Ozarks, such is its commanding influence and usefulness." He suggested that with faculty salaries, institutional overhead and maintenance, and student expenditures, "STC will compare favorably with the largest industrial institution." He stated that "a large majority of citizens do not realize the magnitude

of the business which the institution delivers to them, hence do not properly appreciate it."

But for all the economic benefits STC was bringing to the community in the early 1920s, its primary benefit, according to Mr. Carroll, was establishing "a point of contact" between Springfield and "thousands of bright, ambitious, earnest young women and young men from homes scattered throughout an area larger than some states of the union." Such connections and acquaintances formed here "reach back home; ideals and the knowledge of new and better methods acquired here are widely disseminated, and I verily believe," said Mr. Carroll, "that the ultimate beneficial results will overshadow in worth and influence the day-by-day dollars and cents fruition now discernable."

College Services to the Region

The benefits to Springfield of STC's presence were indeed more than economic. Students saw community service as part of their vocation as learners. The annual Joyland Christmas celebration at the college with its pageantry, music and drama benefited low-income families in and around the city. By 1926, the Joyland celebration was drawing more than 3,000 people and was held in the Shrine Mosque. The Springfield Kiwanis club assisted with the production, which featured Greenwood students. Two-hundred-fifty families were helped from the proceeds of the event.

In March 1927, two dozen STC students climbed into Joe Worrel's new Studebaker bus and rode to Green Forest, Arkansas, to assist the tornado ravaged town.

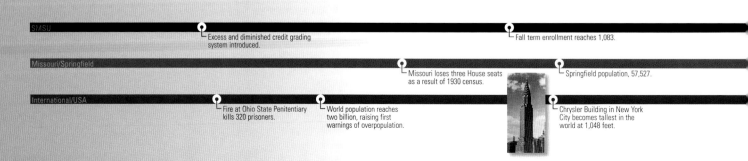

SMSU

Excess and diminished credit grading system introduced.

Fall term enrollment reaches 1,083.

Missouri/Springfield

Missouri loses three House seats as a result of 1930 census.

Springfield population, 57,527.

International/USA

Fire at Ohio State Penitentiary kills 320 prisoners.

World population reaches two billion, raising first warnings of overpopulation.

Chrysler Building in New York City becomes tallest in the world at 1,048 feet.

Farmers throughout southwest Missouri were a special focus of the college. Even in the Normal School period, special agricultural demonstrations and conferences were held to assist farmers throughout the area coax their land into higher productivity. In the 1930s, an Agricultural Improvement Program was held over a three-day period promoting scientific agriculture in the Ozarks. The program drew 500 Ozark farmers in 1938. The next year it drew more than 1,000 to hear several agriculture faculty from MU speak, as well as Paul Shepherd from the Fruit Experiment Station in Mountain Grove. By 1942, the popular event drew 2,000 visitors.

In 1933, more than 9,000 visitors had come to campus where meetings were hosted for teachers, farmers, school boards and musicians, to name a few. By 1940, the visitors to such events had grown to more than 18,000.

In addition to people coming to campus, faculty were continuing to reach out to the area. President Ellis reported the extra-curricular effort of faculty in 1930-31 included 76 forensic contests judged consuming 460 hours and 6,650 miles of travel. In addition, faculty officiated at 18 athletics contests, delivered 30 commencement addresses, and made 113 Extension Division trips, together totaling 40,477 miles of travel from campus.

Extending coursework into the outlying reaches of the southwest district was a service provided by the college from its earliest days. Extension and correspondence courses were a popular option for teachers and others who were unable to attend regular classes at the college. Between 1918 and 1922, more than 3,500 students had received instruction through the Extension Division. Extension classes typically met on Saturdays in such places as West Plains, Ava, Cassville, Crane, Greenfield, Lebanon, Pineville, Stockton and Nevada.

In addition to extension and correspondence courses, the college provided library books to patrons throughout the district. Faculty frequently gave speeches in outlying communities as well as attended meetings associated with their disciplines. *The Standard* reported that during the 1919-20 academic year, 55,859 persons were direct beneficiaries of the college's outreach to the region.

As you would expect, a State Teachers College would cultivate a very close relationship with area schools. The Southwest Teachers Association meetings were often held on campus with more than 2,000 in attendance. High School basketball tournaments, music festivals and contests, track meets, annual sport and athletics carnivals, oratorical contests and debate tournaments were all hosted regularly by the college. Area schools were drawn into a close community by these scheduled events. By 1927, 17 of the 22 county superintendents in the STC service area had graduated from or taken work at STC, creating a solidarity between college and communities in the area.

Besides driving to remote sections of the service area to provide assistance to citizens, the college quickly adopted radio as a tool for outreach. Members of the agriculture faculty had a regular 7:00-7:15 morning program on KWTO to discuss matters of interest to farmers. Professor Alexander is credited with helping to get the poultry industry going in the Ozarks through his radio broadcasts. Cultural programs were also offered over radio. Sunday evenings featured music, and Wednesday evenings featured informative and entertaining presentations by faculty. In 1939, Anna Lou Blair and Woodrow Denny talked about the history of the college. Mary Keeth lectured on South America, and Donald Nicholson and J.D. Bounous discussed opportunism and fascism in Italy.

Radio station KGBX also was a host for STC program outreach. In 1938, a series of lectures from the science department faculty included such features as, "The Secret of the Sun's Energy," "Madame Curie," "Sir Isaac Newton" and "Will the World Run Down?"

Deborah Weisel, head of the Art Department, founded the Art Study Club in Springfield in 1926. It was incorporated into the Springfield Art Museum in 1928. The club made art purchases for the museum, the first of which was a landscape by Mary Butter. By 1980, the collection encompassed 400 paintings, 53 drawings, 800 prints, and a large number of

First football game "under the lights" on campus at new football field.

Pi Beta Chi, honorary science fraternity founded.

First and Calvary Church held first service at new building on Cherry and Dollison.

The Effects of the Repeal of Prohibition

In April 1933, 46 students on campus were questioned about the probable effects of repealing the Prohibition Amendment to the Constitution. When asked if the return of beer to the country would increase drunkenness, 38 of the 46 surveyed said "no." When asked if beer would create a problem at college social functions, either on or off campus, 37 of the 46 asked said "no," with one student adding, "Not with Miss Wells on the job!"

~

STC Humor

"If all the red ink used by the English department in correcting papers were changed into wine, the 18th Amendment would have to be repealed."

"If kissing is as unsanitary as Dr. Kizer says it is, the average span of life would be 19 days."

"If all the energy used by Marvin Ward doing the Charleston were changed into heat, it would warm the social hall for three months."

1926 Ozarko

sculptures and photos. Weisel brought the Art Department into national prominence in the early 1930s when it was recognized in *Parnassus* — an art magazine published by the College Art Association of America. STC was listed for recognition along with art departments at Yale, Princeton, Brown, Harvard, NYU, Vassar, Wellesley, Mt. Holyoke, Bowdon and Dartmouth.

Professor Weisel is also credited with helping to design the Benton Avenue viaduct in Springfield. Initial plans were for the viaduct to be a straight structure. Weisel suggested that a curved structure would add interest and beauty to the city's architecture.

Visiting Artists and Lecturers

The cultural enrichment of the community was a special concern of President Hill who collaborated with the Civic Music Association to bring to STC and the community the leading musicians of the era. Many of these musicians came as featured artists during the annual Music Festival sponsored by STC for aspiring musicians from area high schools.

Featured artists from the 1919 Music Festival were Rudolph Ganz, pianist, and Carolina Lazzari, contralto. By 1920, more than 2,500 were attending the Festival. They sat spellbound as operatic soprano Amelita Galli-Curci from the Metropolitan Opera Company in New York sang selections from *La Traviata, Rigoletto* and *Romeo and Juliet*. The following year, Luisa Tetrazzini, Italian coloratura soprano, was the guest artist.

President Hill helped create a golden age of music for the college in the 1920s. In 1922, the famed Irish tenor John McCormack came to the campus.

Poet Vachel Lindsay visited campus during the 1930-31 academic year and made a profound impression on students with his eloquence. Cartoonist Mitchell Sanford described him as "the poet who took us to the sky."

During his concert the audience was invited to join him in singing familiar tunes. The popularity of the musical events exceeded the seating capacity of any facility on campus, so the McCormack concert, as well as others, was held in Convention Hall in downtown Springfield. While it had seating capacity, the convention hall had little else to commend it for music concerts, so it was with great relief that the Shrine Mosque was finished in 1923 at a cost of $600,000. The mosque would seat 2,500 people. It also had a huge stage, second only to the Metropolitan Opera House stage in New York City. The hall was outfitted with what was at the time the largest pipe organ west of the Mississippi River.

In addition to John McCormack, musical events for 1922 included the St. Louis Symphony; Cydena Van Gorin of the Chicago Opera Company; a presentation of Mozart's opera "The School for Lovers"; Emma

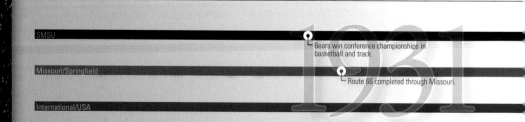

SMSU

Bears win conference championships in basketball and track.

Missouri/Springfield

Route 66 completed through Missouri.

International/USA

1931

Calve of the Metropolitan; Thurlow Lieurance, a collector and composer of Indian music; Louis Gravene, baritone; Maier and Pattison, pianists; and Glovanie Martinelli, America's leading tenor. The budget for concerts in 1922 totaled $12,000, a substantial investment in cultural enrichment.

The following year's budget for music programs was $13,200 and it featured Mary Garden, soprano ($3,500), and Jascha Heifetz, violinist ($2,500). The San Carlos Opera Company staged *Madame Butterfly* for the enjoyment of the community. Season tickets for six scheduled concerts sold for $6.50.

When Percy Hemus appeared in concert at the college in 1922, Professor Temple had arranged to broadcast the event as a "tribute to Marconi." Band enthusiasts were thrilled when John Philip Sousa's band played two concerts at the Shrine Mosque. In 1924-25 the program schedule featured John Charles Thomas, baritone, and Fritz Keisler, violinist. In 1927, Reinold Werrenrath, baritone, Efrem Zimbalist, distinguished Russian violinist, and the Minneapolis Symphony all visited Springfield as part of the STC concert series.

Even during the Great Depression, the concert series continued with pianist Percy Grainger, ensembles from the St. Louis Orchestra, and a variety of vocal and instrumental concerts. In 1940, violinist Isaac Stern played in the STC auditorium with "exceptional tone quality and intensity of feeling."

Visiting Lecturers

While musical sophistication was occurring on the STC campus, intellectual stimulation was also occurring through the scheduling of visiting lec-

A common joke among STC students in the 1920s was the quantity of red ink used by the English department.

turers. In 1925, the English Club sponsored the appearance of Alfred Noyes, described at the time as "the greatest living English poet." Noyes had just published the second part of his epic trilogy "The Torch Bearers."

Just a week after the crash of the stock market in 1929, the famed historian and philosopher Will Durant visited STC. He had just published his *Story of Philosophy* and was working on his monumental *The Story of Civilization*, which was published in 1935. Known for his love of democracy and his candor about its abuses, Durant told his STC audience, "America has let democracy mean the election of any fool to office."

In 1930, Vachel Lindsay came to campus described as "one of America's greatest poets and a fighter for social justice." Twenty-five years earlier, at about the time Normal School #4 was established, Lindsay was tramping like a troubadour through the South and West exchanging his poem "The Tree

of Laughing Bills" for bed and board. The tradition continued at STC. Lindsay chanted a number of his well-known poems, including "General Booth's March Into Heaven," to the generous applause of his appreciative STC audience.

Carl Sandburg visited the campus in the spring of 1931 and remarked afterward that STC students "give off an atmosphere of youth and gaiety in greater degree than many other institutions of learning." *The Standard* reported that "strumming his guitar, he gave us a new version of history, a singing history of America." Sandburg spoke candidly to his student audience, suggesting that the major problems they had to solve were about themselves: "What's worth living for and what's worth dying for?" When he lectured at STC, Sandburg was writing *Mary Lincoln, Wife and Widow*, a sequel to his popular biography *Abraham Lincoln: The Prairie Years*.

Although he did not lecture at STC, poet Edward Markham visited Springfield in 1935. Dr. Virginia Craig was invited to a dinner party with Markham at the home of Drury College President Thomas W. Nadal. Dr. Craig reported the visit to her students as "one of the most enjoyable evenings of my life." She described Markham as being "a delightful conversationalist with a greatly cultivated sense of humor."

The great Olympic runner Dr. Glenn Cunningham lectured at STC in 1939 on "Running Around the World." After the assembly he joined students for a run around the track as well as talking to Arthur Briggs' and Florence Bugg's physical education classes.

In reviewing the convocations and concerts during the STC period, one is

Poet Carl Sandburg lectures on campus.

Tennis added to intercollegiate sports.

State Highway Patrol established.

Nevada legalizes gambling.

The Star-Spangled Banner adopted as national anthem.

Empire State Building opens.

1919-46 Southwest Missouri State Teachers College 81

struck with the rapid development of a cosmopolitan outlook on campus. For most STC students, the axis of the universe went through the Ozarks. Their opportunity to discover the breadth of the world's culture and the depth of the world's understanding came through their dedicated faculty who had broken the bonds of provincialism and arranged the parade of musicians, playwrights, authors and lecturers who mounted the convocation platform from year to year. This parade of cultural events left a legacy of appreciation and understanding to the community as well as the students.

Racism

*The Standard*s and the *Ozarko*s published in the Normal School and State Teachers College periods demonstrate the degree to which the institution and its students mirrored the attitudes and practices of the day. This is particularly evident to a 21st century reader who finds racial jokes and caricatures crude and offensive.

The period between 1890-1930 is seen by many as the low point in race relations in America. The passage of Jim Crow laws, the vigilante justice expressed in frequent lynchings, and the general disregard for the black citizen as a person, expressed a profound prejudice typical of many white Americans. Between 1889-1903, every week, on the average, two Negroes were lynched by mobs — hanged, burned and mutilated. Three black citizens were lynched in Springfield on Easter weekend in 1906, just 60 days before the opening of State Normal School #4. No mention of the event is found in school publications in the early years. Indicative of the strong feelings in

Springfield at the time, brass medallions were struck commemorating the event as an "Easter Offering." The medallions were said to have been worn as part of a white woman's necklace. The medallions are pictured on page 84 in Harris and Phyllis Dark's *Springfield of the Ozarks: An Illustrated History*.

After World War I, black Americans expected to share in the fruits of the victory since more than 400,000 of them served in the military, 1,353 as commissioned officers. More than 9,000 black Missourians served in the armed forces. But instead of sharing in the fruits of victory, they reaped a harvest of hate as they streamed north to fill the labor gap created by the halt in immigration in 1914. Immediately following the war, labor strikes occurred throughout the industrial cities of the north, and Blacks were often recruited by corporations as strike-breakers further intensifying the white disdain for black workers.

Missouri had mandated a segregated school system in its 1875 constitution. A Missouri Supreme Court decision written by Justice Francis M. Black in 1890 expressed the prevailing sentiment: "Color carries with it natural race peculiarities." Black citizens in Missouri were customarily prohibited from joining whites in hotels, restaurants, theaters and hospitals. A 1914 report issued by the Missouri Association for Social Welfare summed up the situation by saying, "So much of the problem lies in the unthinking, inconsiderate attitude of white people that no specific remedies for present conditions can be proposed which in themselves offer any solution."

The perceived freedom to abuse black citizens was rooted in part in the neglect of black Americans by white politicians. That neglect was interpreted by many lawless whites as a license to harrass Blacks. Missouri's tradition of lynching is an infamous example. Between 1900-31, mobs in Missouri lynched 22 men, 17 of whom were black.

The anti-black sentiment was pervasive across the state. The University of Missouri was forced to cancel plans for a triangular track meet with the University of Wisconsin and Notre Dame in April 1939. Missouri had banned Wisconsin's black hurdler, Ed Smith, from competing in the meet which led Wisconsin to withdraw. Notre Dame pulled out of the meet, in protest of Missouri's action.

The Ku Klux Klan fanned the prejudicial fires in the 1920s. The Klan claimed to control 400,000 votes across Missouri. It was very active in Springfield in the 1920s, claiming 3,000 members in the city. At the time it owned and held its meetings in Percy

SMSU

Fifty percent of faculty hold terminal degrees in their field.

Missouri/Springfield

Amelia Earhart visits Springfield.

International/USA

NBC and CBS start television broadcasting.

Yangtze River in China floods; 3.7 million die.

Japanese Army invades Manchuria.

Cave north of Springfield. The cave has since gotten new owners and a new name — Fantastic Caverns.

It is this antipathy toward Blacks generally throughout the state that provides the context for the sentiments expressed and the actions taken at State Normal School #4 and, subsequently, STC. Not infrequently, humor published in *The Standard* was at the expense of Blacks. (Of course there were no Blacks on campus until after 1954). On January 24, 1924, *The Standard* published "A Darky Soldiers Love Letter," which mocks the stereotypical inability of the black soldier to spell, punctuate or otherwise communicate in writing. The letter is prefaced by a statement from H.E. Nettles who claims to have come into possession of the letter as a censor in the Army. He states, "This particular Negro soldier in question, I was in a position to know, had never been within 40 miles of the front, nor had he been elsewhere in France. The letter was so unique in the exaggerations and absurdities that I could not refrain from making an exact copy of it." The opportunity to humiliate a black soldier was too great a temptation to resist, and apparently *The Standard* editor saw it as entertainment for his readers.

During the STC Literary Society years, it was commonplace to entertain with readings capturing what was believed to be typical black speech patterns. In January 1917, "Miss Freeman entertained the (Normal Debating) society with a darky dialect Christmas selection." That same year, *The Standard* reported that "Theda Pyland so cleverly represented an old colored mammy that few recognized her." Minstrel shows were common place

on the STC campus in the 1930s. *The Southwest Standard* reported in January 1936 that the "whole Tri-C bunch was in blackface."

In 1924, Parsifal Cobb reported to his Social Problems class on "The Status of the Negro in the South." "The Negro is not treated as badly by the Southerners as is commonly believed in other sections," reported Cobb. The Negro, Cobb claimed, is not molested "as long as he stays where he belongs and does not try to cause trouble." Mr. Cobb added that, "when a Negro got out of his place, he was seldom able to get back into it." Professor E.E. Walker was reported as complimenting Mr. Cobb, "because his report was not influenced by that well-known Southern race prejudice, but was given from an unbiased, frank, open, broad-minded point of view."

Debate topics on campus frequently dealt with matters of race. In the spring of 1917, students debated the proposition "that the free Negro

is a greater menace to the South than the Negro slave was." In 1920 the Bentonian society debated the notion "that the Negro should be given primarily an industrial education." In 1925, the proposition "that the American Negro should be colonized" was debated on campus. In 1941, art students at STC made a series of recommendations to city leaders for improvement of the city. One of the recommendations was to "gather all Negroes to live near Silver Springs." Antipathy toward black Americans even crept into observations by college officials. President Ellis in greeting the summer class of 1938 said, "The Ozark highland is unique in its charm and beauty. Its people present a degree of racial homogeneity which could be hardly matched anywhere else in America."

Despite the denigrating attitudes toward black Americans found on campus in the early years, there were other voices calling for understanding, justice and tolerance. In 1924, the second place prize in interclass oratory went to Blanche Gorman who spoke passionately on "Justice for the Negro." A lively conversation about "the Negro problem" was found in letters to the editor in 1925. The first formal on-campus discussion of race relations was sponsored by the Polity Club in 1927 with Professor Walter Cralle's encouragement. The Reverand G.I. Nick Miller, a black pastor of the Gibson Chapel Presbyterian Church, addressed the club on the evening of January 26, 1927. *The Standard* reported Miller as "emphasizing that (he) had no intention of arousing any bitter feelings between the races, but he wished to make a plea for more toleration for the

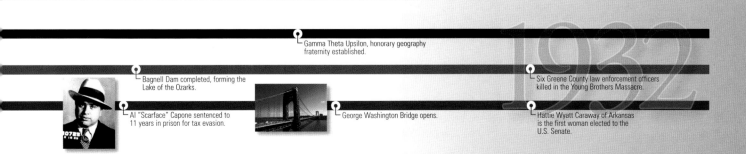

Gamma Theta Upsilon, honorary geography fraternity established.

Bagnell Dam completed, forming the Lake of the Ozarks.

Al "Scarface" Capone sentenced to 11 years in prison for tax evasion.

George Washington Bridge opens.

Six Greene County law enforcement officers killed in the Young Brothers Massacre.

Hattie Wyatt Caraway of Arkansas is the first woman elected to the U.S. Senate.

1932

Negro people." The reporter continued, saying, "Various interesting facts regarding the progress of the Negro race were given by the speaker." Students from Springfield's (black) Lincoln High School were invited to the Polity Club event. A month later, Professor Cralle spoke to the STC YMCA on the same topic, and a boys quartet from Lincoln High School sang.

In 1931, Wave Hix entered the interclass oratorical competition with a speech titled "A Plea for the Negro." A year later, the joint YM and YWCAs

of Drury and STC held an inter-racial banquet where 25 nations were represented. Townspeople and students were invited and the Lincoln High School Quartet again sang. In 1933, the YMCA invited George Skidmore, a local attorney, to speak on the topic "Is Lynching Justifiable?" Among his comments was the observation that "most of the vices the Negro has, he has picked up from whites."

Throughout the 1930s, even while antipathy toward Blacks was clearly present on campus, there was a discernable movement toward greater understanding of African Americans. In 1934, the English/Dramatic Club discussed Negro literature with the assistance of Miss Rollins from Lincoln High School. A boys sextet from Lincoln sang for the group. That same year, A.L. Jackson, an STC graduate, accepted the Superintendency of Stillman Institute in Tuscaloosa, Alabama, a black school with six white and six black instructors. Another STC graduate, Lyle Owen ('27), wrote an article in *Common Ground* in 1944 urging that race not be used as a basis for discrimination because "we all are related." Owen was recognized as an authority on economic issues and held faculty positions at the University of Wisconsin and Carnegie Institute of Technology in Pittsburgh.

While the process was slow and arduous, STC, along with the region and the country, was feeling its way toward a better understanding of the issues of race.

Debate Comes of Age

The STC period from 1919 to 1946 was framed by two world wars, punctuated by prosperity in the 1920s and

then a Great Depression in the 1930s. Radicalism and labor unrest, race riots, vigilantism, prohibition, the Scopes trial in Tennessee, and corruption in government all made front-page news during the period. That mix of circumstances gave debaters a great deal of grist for the argumentation mill and STC debaters embraced the opportunity enthusiastically.

In 1920, debaters were sharpening their arguments over whether all foreign immigration to the U.S. should be prohibited by federal law, and whether or not the government should own, control and operate all coal mines. Debaters also tackled the question of whether labor unions were to the benefit or detriment of the nation. Even movies entered the debate scene. Were they ultimately beneficial or detrimental to the welfare of the country?

The convulsive effects of strikes and labor unrest after World War I led debaters to argue whether government ownership and operation of the railroads was in the national interest, and whether or not all labor disputes should be settled by binding arbitration. There was also debate over a minimum wage law for women in Missouri, as well as the abolition of the death penalty in the state.

The trauma of World War I had produced an isolationist movement in the country that fueled a debate on the question of a constitutional amendment forbidding any declaration of war or placing of troops on foreign soil except as authorized by a popular referendum.

In the middle 1920s there were debates over higher education policies as well. In 1925, the question of whether or not publicly supported colleges and universities should refuse to

SMSU
Percy Grainger entertains at STC.
Pan-Hellenic Council organized to coordinate campus social activities.

Missouri/Springfield

International/USA
Lindbergh baby kidnapped and killed.   Ford introduces the V-8 engine.

Cheerleaders were a fixture at all Bear athletics events during the STC years. In 1931-32, Paul Fultz, Tasker Brooks and Claude Meador led the varsity yells with help from Isom Richardson and Margaret Guinn (not pictured). The *Ozarko* reported, "At each game...the cheerleaders were out in their bright sweaters and gleaming trousers. They sweated until their trousers no longer glistened; they yelled until they were hoarse; they leaped and cavorted until their muscles were sore, and all of this to arouse the student body to do likewise and help the team on to victory."

recognize secret societies (fraternities and sororities) was argued. Debaters also asked whether, on the whole, intercollegiate athletics were detrimental to higher education in the U.S. In 1927, debaters crossed swords over the proposition that discrimination against married women as teachers was contrary to the best interests of the public schools. As early as 1929, debaters questioned whether the volume and method of the present system of installment buying was socially and economically sound.

By the time the Great Depression was being felt across the country and Franklin Delano Roosevelt was elected to implement his New Deal, debate turned to domestic, political and economics issues. Should the amount of property owned by any one person be limited by federal statutes to a definite sum? Should congress enact laws for the centralized control of industry? Should the powers of the president be substantially increased as settled policy? Should Congress be empowered by a two-thirds vote to override any 5-4 decision of the Supreme Court? Should the U.S. cease using public funds for the purpose of stimulating business?

As the threat of a second world war developed in Europe in the middle 1930s, debate shifted focus again to the role of the U.S. Vigorously debated in the late 1930s was the proposition: Should the U.S. follow a policy of strict economic and military isolation toward all nations outside the western hemisphere engaged in armed, international or civil conflict?

The debate topics offered a stimulating array of issues to a growing cadre of STC debaters. Despite the fact that literary societies were in decline by the early 1920s, debate did not decline with them. Interclass competition became the new context for honing argumentation skills, and the interest in debate soared. With the institution achieving full collegiate status and the focus shifting from certification to graduation, students began understanding themselves as members of a particular academic class progressing toward the coveted degree. Therefore, interclass contests became the preparatory route to intercollegiate competition.

By the early 1930s, debate tournaments began evolving as the successor to statewide and interstate contests. As early as 1932, STC sent contestants to tournaments in Winfield, Kansas and Conway, Arkansas. The Winfield Tournament held December 8 and 9 gave an enormous boost to STC debaters as they reached the semi-final round. Two months later, the debate team went to Conway, Arkansas, where it won its first interstate tournament. Marion Bennett and Malcom Magers brought home the coveted silver cup. One year later, Dr. Craig's debaters returned to Winfield, Kansas, to enter one of the largest debate tournaments in the nation. *The Standard* announced the result with a screaming headline; "S.T.C. Wins Debate Tournament!" The story outlined the impressive victory. "Winning over 72 of the finest debate teams in the middle west was the record made by Marion Bennett and Rex Ballinger in winning the largest debate tournament in the United States." Four hundred debaters from 60 colleges had come to Winfield to vie for the prize won by Bennett and Ballinger. Included in the group were two men from Greeley, Colorado, who hitch-hiked 750 miles to represent their

Fees raised to $20 a term.

STC ranks 6th in size among nation's teachers colleges.

Amelia Earhart completes first solo non-stop transatlantic flight by a female.

1919-46 Southwest Missouri State Teachers College   85

Jack Russell (49) goes up against a Warrensburg opponent as the Bears conclude a 15-4 season in 1938-39. Coach McDonald's cagers were still in the defensive play mode typical of the basketball at the time. The Bear's highest game score was 42 against Kirksville. The lowest was 15 in a losing match to the Oklahoma Aggies. The Bears' season average was 31 points a game.

school in the tournament.

Bennett had just won first honors in the State Peace Oratorical contest in Jefferson City earlier that year. His oration, "Civilization or Catastrophe," was chosen as one of the 12 best among 155 colleges and universities and was published by Ohio and Illinois Councils of Churches.

By the middle and late 1930s, STC teams were participating in debate tournaments throughout the Midwest and establishing remarkable records. In 1936-37, STC debaters entered tournaments in Missouri, Oklahoma and Kansas. Twenty-seven different debaters had won 20 out of 27 debates. Career wins up to that point were 47 for William Henry, 32 for Roy Daniel, eight for Charles Killingsworth and seven for Darwin Lewis.

The victories kept piling up. In 1938-39, Horace Haseltine and Woodrow Denny won 44 debates in eight tournaments, while Jack Powell and R.A. Ellis won eight debates in three tournaments. In the women's division, Rose Shirley Hinrickson and Ellen Bernice Stewart won 16 debates.

The decade ended with a banner year for STC debaters. In 1939-40, Horace Haseltine and Woodrow Denny went through eight rounds undefeated at Ada, Oklahoma. They then defeated the University of Oklahoma in the finals. Later that year, they defeated Texas Christian University at the Waco Tournament and went on to win the Midwest tournament at Norman, Oklahoma and the Grand Eastern Tournament at Rock Hill, S.C. where they defeated teams from New York University, Duke, the University of Florida, Washington and Lee, Clemson and American University. Over that

SMSU
Indoor track added to intercollegiate athletics.

Missouri/Springfield
Outlaws Bonnie and Clyde kidnap Springfield policeman Tom A. Persell at north end of Benton Ave. viaduct.

International/USA
Franklin Delano Roosevelt elected U.S. President.
Construction on Golden Gate Bridge begins.
Adolph Hitler, leader of Nazi party, becomes Chancellor of a German coalition cabinet.

1933

entire year, the debate squad won 131 of 175 debates. Haseltine and Denny won 67 of their 76 debates. A record number of students were involved in the program in 1939-40.

By the decade of the 1940s, STC was known around the country as a formidable power in forensic competition, paving the way for its hosting the first tournament in Springfield. Drury and STC co-hosted the Missouri State Forensic meet in 1942 with 12 Missouri colleges and universities competing.

Athletics Achievements

Forensic teams were not alone in their ability to win. STC athletics teams were capturing conference titles and playing full university opponents with some success. Arthur Briggs was the athletics director, football coach, basketball coach and head of the physical education program when Normal School #4 became Southwest Missouri State Teachers College in 1919. He had graduated in 1891 from YMCA College at Springfield, Massachusetts, where Dr. James Naismith had invented the game of basketball. Naismith was invited to attend the 1923 high school basketball tournament held at STC, and in the course of his visit he made an address at a special assembly. Roy Ellis remembered his description of the now-famous game he invented. "Originally, a team consisted of eight players, two centers, two 'wings' (forwards), two guards, one 'goal' and one 'home.' Baskets were of wire netting. They

In 1930, the athletics field was moved from the northwest corner of the campus to its current location. Floodlights were installed and night games began at STC. As the 1931 Ozarko cartoon infers, games under the lights were not entirely satisfactory.

were carried by the team and hung on the wall for the game. The baskets were closed at the bottom so that when a goal was made, the ball had to be retrieved with a ladder. The first baskets were nailed to the corners of an indoor track, which just happened to be 10 feet from the floor."

The game of basketball was much refined by 1923. But throughout the early years, it was

primarily a defensive contest. In 1922-23, the STC average game score was 29.3 points to their opponents 21.8 points. In those days, of course, there was no shot-clock, no three point shot, and no one-and-one free throws, so scoring between 20 and 30 points in a game was the norm. In 1934, STC defeated Pittsburg State Teachers College by a score of 7–6, a low-scoring school record. Fifteen and one-half minutes had elapsed before there was a point scored by either team. All six points scored by the Gorillas were by field goals. The Bears scored only two field goals in the entire game — both long, outside shots. With only two minutes to play, the score was tied 6-6.

Prior to 1923, all Missouri colleges played in the Missouri Intercollegiate Athletic Association Conference — the "old MIAA" as it was called. In 1923, the conference split and formed a conference exclusively for Missouri state colleges and another for Missouri private colleges. The STC basketball team in 1923-24 was undefeated in the new conference and lost only one game during the entire season, that to their first full university opponent, the University of Arkansas. Earlier in the year in their first meeting, the Bears triumphed over the Razorbacks, 38-31. But in the return match, the Bears lost, 22-21.

Coach Briggs stepped aside as basketball coach at the end of the 1923-24 season and after only one year each under Chester Barnhard and Donald Holwerda, the cage program was turned over to another man who was to become

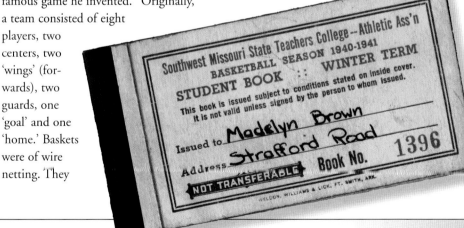

1940-41 student basketball ticket book with remaining coupons.

"Hazing" of freshman class discontinued.

State "Peace Oratorical Contest" won by Marion Bennett.

Charles Lindbergh visits Springfield.

President Roosevelt temporarily closes all banks and airs his first "Fireside Chat."

President Roosevelt declares, "the only thing we have to fear is fear itself."

Federal Deposit Insurance Corporation (FDIC) created.

The 1942 track squad posted a winning season prevailing in three of four dual meets and placing second in the MIAA Conference Outdoor Meet hosted by STC. One of the star performers was Orville Pottenger who excelled in throwing the discuss and running the low hurdles. Pottenger returned to SMS in 1961 as head football coach.

an SMS legend. Andrew J. "Andy" McDonald played both football and basketball at the University of Kansas for Forrest C. "Phog" Allen, including the 1922 national championship basketball team. He came to STC fully intending to create a winning tradition. He succeeded in producing conference championship teams in 1927-28, 1930-31, 1933-34 and 1934-35. In the years McDonald's teams did not win the conference title, they were usually found in the runner-up spot.

There was a particularly savory moment for Coach McDonald's cagers on December 13, 1940, when the Missouri Tigers traveled to Springfield to confront the Bears in the first game scheduled in their new arena. The Tigers broke out to an early lead, scoring six points in the first three minutes. By halftime, the score was 19-11 in favor of the Tigers. But the Bears came back after the halftime break determined to close the gap. Within eight minutes, the Tigers led by only two

points, 27-25, but then pulled ahead 31-25. In the final three minutes, however, the Bears fought back to win 35-32, sending the Tigers home with a new respect for basketball at STC.

In 1937, the Bears made their first national affiliation when they joined the NAIB (National Association for Intercollegiate Basketball). STC made its first foray into national tournament competition at the end of the 1938-39 basketball season when Coach McDonald's hoopsters were selected for the first time to play in the NAIB tournament in Kansas City's Municipal Auditorium. The Bears took a 15-5 record to Kansas City where they lost to East Texas State, 68-45.

STC got back into national tournaments in 1942-43 when the Bears suffered a 72-44 loss to Murray State in the first round of the NAIA (National Association of Intercollegiate Athletics), which had succeeded the NAIB. The NAIA became home for the Bears for nearly 20 years. The Bears scored their first-ever win in a national tournament at the end of the 1948-49 season when they defeated the University of Portland, 66-59, in the first round before losing to Beloit College, 66-47, in the second round.

Football, like basketball, came into its own during the STC years. The bitterest rivalry remained with Drury, the cross-town foe. Prior to 1919, the record was in Drury's favor, but by 1921, the Bears were winning regularly. In 1922, the Bears won the "old MIAA" conference championship, defeating Drury in the process, 28-0. That was the last football game played against the cross-town rival. That remarkable 1922 Bear team, led by captain Paul Matthews, amassed a season total of 288 points to their opponent's 18.

With most of the same players back in 1923, the Bears again won the conference championship. But that year they ventured for the first time into full university competition. They scheduled a game in Columbia on October 6, 1923, against the University of Missouri Tigers. A train chartered from Springfield carried 150 fans as well as the Bruin Band to Rollins field.

Throughout the first half, the teams struggled against each other without success. The Tigers' yardage came on line plunges, the Bears' on end runs. Finally, in the third quarter the Tigers scored a touchdown and a field goal to win the game, 10–0. *The Standard* headline carried the sentiment of the STC fans — "Bears Win Morally but Lost Score-ally." The venture into university football territory did seem to be a moral victory, and it encouraged *The Standard* to declare that STC "proved herself to be in the same class with the largest universities in the country." The 1920s also saw the Bears amass the largest football score in the history of the school. The Bears defeated Southwest Baptist College in Bolivar, 94–0 in 1927.

Conference affiliation for STC athletics teams changed in 1924. The "old MIAA" was reformulated as the Missouri Intercollegiate Athletic

Coach Howard "Red" Blair achieved the longest winning streak in SMS football history. In 1941 his team went undefeated and unscored upon. Above, Coach Blair talks over some game strategy with (from left) Dean George, "Hank" Williams, and Bill Long prior to the 1942 game with Winfield, Kansas.

Looking Back

The Education Advantage, 1933

In July 1933, President Walter Williams from the University of Missouri spoke at STC reminding students of the value of their investment in higher education. He pointed out that persons with an elementary school education reach their peak earning capacity at age 45 when they can expect to earn $1,700 a year. High school graduates do better reaching their top earning capacity at age 55 when they can expect an annual income of $2,800. College graduates reach their peak earning at age 65 when on average, their annual income will be $6,200. By age 65, the average income of persons with an elementary education will have dropped to $1,375, and a high school graduate's earnings will have declined to $1,975. The MU president reminded students of the select company they were joining — only 4.5 percent of the population had college degrees in 1933.

Forty-six percent of faculty are graduates of Normal School or STC.

Guy B. Park becomes governor.

KWTO goes on the air.

William Rockhill Nelson Art Gallery opens in Kansas City.

Native American Player Receives National Recognition

In 1923-24, he worked his way up from substitute to top scorer for the Bear's basketball team. According to the *Ozarko*, "We were never in doubt about winning as long as 'Chief' remained in the game." His regular position was forward, "but he plays everywhere." In his last year of competition "Chief" was rated as one of the best players in the state, "and his opponents generally used two men in guarding him."

Who was this player that "terrorized the MIAA as no athlete had up to that time?" He was Clyde L. James, from Seneca, Missouri. A half-blood Native American, incorrectly described in advance press clippings as "a full-blooded Modock brave," "Chief" was a remarkable student-athlete competing in several sports in addition to basketball between 1921 and 1925. He was one of the first Bear cagers to score consistently in double figures. He scored 34 points in a 75-18 rout of Ozark Wesleyan College of Carthage in the fall of 1924. On one six-game road trip he made 40 consecutive free throws.

James went on to play AAU basketball for 22 years after leaving STC. He played for the Tulsa Oilers, then later the Phillips 66 Oilers, helping them win two national titles.

By 1926, the track squad coached by J.H. "Speedy" Collins was becoming a formidable competitor in the MIAA conference. Joe Cherry handled the pole vaulting chores with considerable success; although, the picture suggests that the higher the vault, the greater the risk as one fell into what appears to be a modestly padded pit. The Bears defeated the University of Arkansas in a dual meet that year 72^1/$_2$ to 56^1/$_2$.

Conference and the charter members were the state teachers colleges in Kirksville, Maryville, Warrensburg, Cape Girardeau and Springfield. The private colleges in the state went their own way and formed the MCAU (Missouri College Athletic Union). Early league competition in the new MIAA included football, basketball and track. Travel was by train or car, and there were years in which schools would go on the road and play their entire league basketball schedule on a single trip. The trip could last as long as a week.

With the organization of the new MIAA conference, the football rivalry shifted from Drury to the Missouri Miners at Rolla who joined the conference in 1934. Over the years the Miners were often the featured opponent on Thanksgiving Day. In the early days, conference rules were not as complete as they needed to be, so the 1927 game with Rolla was canceled because

the teams could not agree on contract terms. There was disagreement whether a player could play more than four years or play as a post-graduate student. There was also a transfer issue. Could a transferring student play if he had not been in residence at least 18 weeks? Conference rules soon settled such issues.

Beginning in 1930, football became a night game at STC. The new football field, located just southwest of the three main campus buildings, was dedicated September 19, 1930. Four thousand fans gathered under the floodlights to watch the Bears play Shurtliff College of Alton, Illinois. Despite the fact that both fans and players were unanimous that daylight was better than floodlights, evening football games persisted.

By 1941, the entire sports scene at STC gained a new momentum with the addition of a permanent stadium

SMSU

Missouri/Springfield

International/USA

Pittsburg State defeats Bears 7-6 in lowest scoring basketball game in college history.

Horton Smith, Springfield golf pro, wins Masters Tournament.

Alcatraz officially becomes a federal prison.

It Happened One Night, a Frank Capra film, released.

"Education is as necessary in the 'New Deal' as in any social scheme, for our schools are the powerhouses of history."

∞

President Roy Ellis, 1934

seating 5,000 football fans and a new basketball arena accommodating more than 3,000 spectators in opera chairs. Both structures were WPA projects providing employment for local craftsmen and first-rate accommodations for Bear student-athletes. The basketball facility included a large gymnasium in the center portion, offices for coaching and teaching staff, locker rooms and small gyms on the east and west sides of the main playing floor. The original scoreboards in the arena were manually operated. They proved not to be fast enough for Coach McDonald's fast-scoring combination. In 1929, Coach Briggs designed an electric scoreboard, which was operated from the scorer's table. A clock was on the face of the scoreboard with players' names posted on the side of the board. An electric light flashed alongside the name of the player

who scored a basket. The new arena set the standard for the entire state at the time it was built.

The football stadium located directly south of the arena was constructed at an original cost of $60,000. It included permanent seating on the west side along with a small press box. A locker room and other facilities were located in a concourse beneath the seating area. The new stadium was opened on September 19, 1941, with the Bears scoring a lopsided 46-0 victory over Southeastern Oklahoma State.

In 1934, after 22 years of coaching football at STC, Arthur Briggs handed the reins to Andy McDonald. By this time Briggs had become recognized as the dean of Missouri athletics coaches. Beginning with a football team in 1912 that had only three experienced players, and which lost to Drury 96–0, Coach Briggs went on to amass the best winning record of any college coach in the state.

McDonald filled in as football coach for four years until Howard H. "Red" Blair came in 1938. Blair was a native Ohioan, a graduate of Mt. Vernon, an Ohio high school, where he garnered all-state football honors three times. He played football at Ohio

In the late 1930s, swimming was the only intercollegiate sport open to women. Here, Georgiana Davis is executing a fine jack knife as she practices for the next meet. Davis was coached by Margaret Putnam, who along with Florence Bugg, supervised an extensive intramural program for women including soccer, volleyball, tennis, archery, field hockey and esthetic dancing.

State, earning honors as an all-Big Ten halfback. He graduated and went on to coach at Akron Central High and then at Akron University for nine years. He returned to Ohio State as an assistant coach in 1936 and was recruited by STC in 1938.

Coach Blair had a disappointingly short, but memorable, career as coach at STC. Just two years after he arrived, his team captured the conference championship. By 1941, the team had built an 18-game winning streak when an incident

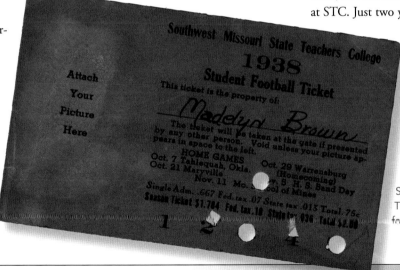

Student Football Season Ticket for 1938. Cost, $2 for five games.

Bears win 5th MIAA basketball championship.

Arthur Briggs retires from coaching duties.

Orchesis, dancing club, organized.

Springfield Little Theater founded by graduates of Senior High School. First production, Oscar Wilde's, *The Importance of Being Earnest.*

Midwest becomes "dust bowl" as a result of catastrophic drought.

Bonnie and Clyde killed in Louisiana.

Indian Reorganization Act encourages native American self-government.

1919-46 Southwest Missouri State Teachers College   91

Arthur W. Briggs was a coaching and administrative pioneer in the very early days of SMS athletics, and his service to the college extended for nearly 40 years. Coming to SMS less than a decade into the school's existence, he wore dual hats as the first full-time SMS director of athletics and also as head of the physical education department. At one time he coached every sport SMS had, and he remains the winningest football coach in SMS history as the school reaches its centennial.

SMS got its sports beginnings with the establishment of basketball in 1908, followed by football and baseball a year later. In 1912, the school entered into a loose association of some 15 of the state's four-year small colleges, an arrangement known as the "old MIAA." The need quickly arose for an athletics administrator to oversee both the sports programs and the new league affiliation. Mr. Briggs came to SMS to take over as coach of all three sports, and he served as athletics director from 1912 until 1938. He also taught and served as physical education department head from 1912 until his death in 1949.

A graduate of YMCA College in Springfield, Massachusetts, Briggs arrived at SMS with *The Standard* heralding his coming by noting, "statistics show that only three percent of the time of (SMS) students is spent in physical education (as) we grow wiser and weaker. The new teacher should be qualified to give a certain amount of physical instruction as well as mental." A native of the North Shore of Massachusetts, Briggs was a descendant of a long line of whalers, and he had no use for anyone who wasn't physically fit. He was a stern and demanding taskmaster but remained popular with his players. After a winless (0-4) football season in 1912, Briggs took his team out of competition for a year to concentrate on fundamentals. When the Bears returned to action in 1914, they went undefeated (6-0) and captured the first SMS state gridiron championship.

Briggs guided SMS to its second state championship in football with his unbeaten (7-0) team in 1922. The Bears that year steamrolled their opponents by a combined score of 308-18

with four shutouts in seven games against a schedule that included Northwest Missouri State, Southeast Missouri State, Tarkio, Missouri Wesleyan, Central Wesleyan, Culver-Stockton and Drury. SMS streamlined its athletics affiliation in 1924 when the MIAA realigned itself with only the state schools as charter members. SMS won its first MIAA gridiron crown under Briggs in 1928. He stepped aside from football after the 1933 season with a record of 76-58-11 for his 20 SMS seasons.

Arthur Briggs gained much of his other notable coaching success in basketball. From 1913 to 1923, his SMS teams amassed a nine-year record of 105-32, and the Bears recorded winning seasons every year of his SMS tenure. He posted a .766 winning percentage that remains the second highest of any SMS basketball coach whose tenure lasted more than one season.

One of Mr. Briggs's successors as director of athletics is Bill Rowe, who took over the position in 1982 when SMS elevated its athletics program to a Division I status. Of Briggs, Rowe observes, "I wasn't privileged to know Mr. Briggs, but his overall tenure of nearly 40 years to athletics and to physical education and the contributions he made in that time were remarkable. He did so many things, from coaching several sports, to directing the athletics department, to leading the physical education department. In those days, the program was operating literally on a shoestring. People who competed for SMS on teams Mr. Briggs coached had tremendous regard for him as a coach and as a person."

Mr. Briggs's leadership included overseeing the detailed planning and subsequent construction of the new SMS football stadium and new basketball arena in the 1939-41 time period. The SMS football stadium was named Briggs Stadium in his honor from 1970 until 1991. The street now approaching the stadium from the west is known as Briggs Street, and the top scholar-athlete on the football team, based on leadership, scholarship and athletics achievement, has been selected to receive the Arthur Briggs Award each year since 1991. Mr. Briggs was inducted into the SMS Athletics Hall of Fame in 1978. ❀

with Coach Blair attracted national attention. The Bears were playing the Tallequah, Oklahoma, Redmen. The Bears came from behind to tie the score 14–14 with 3:30 left to play. They called for an onside kick in hopes of recovering the ball and having a final opportunity to score. The Bears caught the Redmen flat-footed with the onside kick, and the Bears' Russell Kaminsky downed the ball on the Tallequah 49 yard line. During a mild protest by the Tallequah coach, "Red" Blair walked out onto the field and told the referee that indeed Kaminsky had touched the ball just before it crossed the 50-yard-line, invalidating the play. On the strength of that report, the officials reversed their decision, requiring the Bears to kick-off again. Tallequah, with explosive power, returned the ball to their own 48-yard line. Then, in straight power plays, they put the ball into the STC end zone with only 45 seconds remaining.

In those 45 seconds, the Bears fought back furiously from their 35-yard-line. Two passes later the Bears were on the Redmen's 11-yard-line. A quick huddle and a pass to Gene Rimmer put the Bears in the Redmen's end zone and the arms of one official went up declaring a touchdown. But the official timer said, "No, boys, the game ended a half-second before that play started."

The Standard writer reported, "Springfield fans will not, can never, forget the drama-laden atmosphere that engulfed some 6,500 witnesses as they watched Coach Howard "Red" Blair virtually sacrifice his team's 18-game winning streak, excellent chances for a Bowl game, innumerable honors that accompany victories — for the sake of

sportsmanship, as he graciously reversed the unanimous decision of three officials." That 18-game winning streak remains the longest in school history.

At the time, the Bears were one of only three teams in the nation to go unbeaten through the 1940 and 1941 seasons. The other two, Minnesota and Wittenburg of Springfield, Ohio, finished the 1941 season undefeated. Coach Blair guided the Bears through three magnificent seasons. They went 7-1-1 in 1939, a perfect 10-0 in 1940, and 8-3 in 1941.

By 1942, World War II was making in-roads into the football program. Very few lettermen returned, and by 1943 it was apparent that football would have to be put on hold for the duration of the war. From 1944 until the end of the war, Coach Blair was loaned to Springfield High School.

When Blair returned after the war, he was in declining health, suffering from a heart ailment. Roy Ellis remembered him coaching in his last season "from a chair on the field." He died November 30, 1947.

Basketball, like football, was interrupted by the war. After the 1942-43 NAIA trip, the Bears did not play basketball again for two seasons.

The success of the Bear's football and basketball teams during the STC years was matched by Bear track squads. From 1921-25 the thinclads won successive conference championships. During the 1925 season, track coaching duties were taken over by J.H. "Speedy" Collins who guided the squad for the next 22 years. His runners shared the conference title with Kirksville in 1931. The Bears captured the indoor conference meet in 1932 and the outdoor meet in 1933. In

1928, two STC runners entered the Olympic tryouts. Natalie Briggs placed fourth in the 100-meter race in St. Louis and first in the 400-meter relay. Victor Fite captured first in the 5,000-meter run. While neither made the Olympic team, they demonstrated the growing stature of STC athletics.

Tennis was added to the MIAA sports competition in 1931. Walter Cralle guided the tennis hopefuls in the early years. In both 1931 and 1935, the Bears won the conference singles tournament. From 1936 to 1940 they won both the singles and doubles tournaments.

Golf was added to MIAA competition in 1934. Andy McDonald provided it enthusiastic leadership. The Bears won the conference championships the first year and continued to win again in 1940 and 1941.

Women's Athletics

Women's athletics continued to operate under the handicap of being excluded from MIAA conference competition. Basketball teams were organized in the early 1920s and played area high school teams, Drury and Marionville College. A unique form of intercollegiate competition was started in 1929 with the creation of Play Day. Women's athletics teams were invited to the Warrensburg campus where they competed in a variety of sports. However, the teams assembled at the event were mixed, with representatives from different schools. "The play is not to be competition between schools," explained *The Standard*. "Competition will only be between color teams selected regardless of school."

Despite being denied intercollegiate play, women student-athletes took their efforts as seriously as the men.

Homecoming parade resumes after a 10-year hiatus.

Faculty ranks introduced including instructor, assistant professor, associate professor and professor.

The "Long March" of the Red Army in China claims 45,000 lives.

Interclass play became the focus for women. In 1925, STC women student-athletes organized the Spartan Club to promote athletics competition in field hockey, volleyball, basketball, track, softball and swimming. There was a College State Letter in Athletics which could be earned by accumulating 1,000 points through participating in a variety of sports, hiking 100 miles, passing badge tests, and displaying sportsmanship and scholarship. The first two STC women to earn the recognition were Dorothy Thomas in 1925 and Fern Pennington in 1926. In 1927, Lillian Caudle, Lucille Peters and Ella Hanshaw were awarded the letter.

The Spartan Club developed procedures by which women could also earn the coveted STC letter for athletics, identical to the letter earned by the men. The women would earn a letter by making three different teams in interclass competition in softball, soccer, basketball or hockey. In 1927, "for the first time in the history of STC, the girls are to be given College Letters for Athletics," reported *The Standard*. Twenty-five were awarded.

Two people regarded as pioneers in women's athletics at SMS arrived on the scene in 1930. Florence Baker Bugg taught physical education and organized the Girls' Athletic Association at Greenwood School as well as the Physical Education Majors (PEM) Club at the college. She also took a leading role in College Play Days. Much of that early competition was organized by Margaret Putnam who coached all the STC women's teams in Play Day events. Putnam also served as sponsor of the PEM Club, the Women's Athletic Association and the intramural program.

Interclass competition among women student-athletes were spirited affairs. In 1926, the first women's interclass track meet was held. The sophomores won the event. The 60-yard dash was run in 8.4 seconds, the 110 in 13.5 seconds, and the quarter-mile relay finished in 1:05. The winning mark in high jump was 4 feet, broad jump, 14 feet 1 inch. The throwers put the shot 26 feet 4 inches, the javelin traveled 77 feet, and the winning discus throw sailed 80 feet and 10 inches.

In 1928, the Spartans affiliated with the Women's Athletic Association, a national organization promoting women's athletics. In 1937, the women's swim team competed in the AAU Indoor Swimming Championships in Kansas City, and by 1941 STC women were competing in golf and tennis in addition to other WAA sports.

Athletics competition in the 1920s also included faculty-student contests. Coach Briggs and his faculty basketball team were quickly dispatched by the student team in 1922. But in 1928, the faculty upset the students in the annual track meet. Big Walter Cralle captured 18 points in the meet competing in several events. Dr. Kizer set a faculty record putting the shot.

Rivalry between STC and Drury

As any sports fan knows, team rivalries can be intense. Such was the case between STC and Drury. It began with the 96–0 shellacking given the Bears by the Panther's football team in 1912. The Bears had little success against Drury until 1915 when the Bears won, 15–7. The following year the game ended in a 7–7 tie, and in 1917 Drury again prevailed, 19–0.

Basketball competition was similarly intense. In 1908-09, the Bears won two of the three games with the Panthers, but the initial success didn't last. In 1914-15, Drury won all three contests. The next year the Bears won twice.

By the time the Normal School became STC in 1919, Drury–STC athletics contests were drawing capacity crowds. Students were creating yells to urge their teams to victory. Many of those yells were team specific. *The 1923 Standard* listed several including:

*Oh me! Oh my! Won't we black that
Panther's eye!
Won't he holler, won't he wail,
When we twist that Panther's tail!!
Eat that Drury Panther Up,
Eat that Drury Panther Up,
Eat that Drury Panther Up,
Grrr-ah! Grrr-ah! Bears!*

In 1922, the Bears swept the competition with Drury, winning football, basketball and track. The symbol of the victorious year was a Panther with three knots tied in his tail.

The sentiments in the yells themselves were enough to stir emotions among the spectators, but when the game was hotly contested, as most were, fans frequently exchanged insults and ended up in brawls. *The Standard* captured some of the feeling when the basketball Bears, in January 1923, were defeated in a Drury home game. "On January 19, we journeyed across the pseudo-river Jordan and unwillingly conceded a game to Drury 19 to 23. It was not, strictly speaking, a game, but a battle royal between two organized groups of friends urged on to deeds of daring by a howling mass composed of two bloodthirsty student bodies as set upon victory as any Roman mob that ever watched its gladiators fight for life in the arena." Just 60 days earlier, 6,000 howling fans had watched the

SMSU
Construction begins on AAU regulation Olympic size swimming pool.

Missouri/Springfield
Harry S. Truman becomes U.S. senator from Missouri.

International/USA
First Sugar Bowl and Orange Bowl games.

1935

Bears gain a 28–0 Thanksgiving Day football victory over the Panthers.

But by this time the rivalry had become overheated and in 1923, the STC Board of Regents halted all inter-collegiate athletics contests between the two schools. The ban was not lifted until 1975 when the SMS Board of Regents authorized the university to schedule men's basketball games with Drury "if it wished to do so." Competition commenced in 1977 with the Bears winning, 76-74. The following year, Drury triumphed. Close contests were the rule throughout the late 1970s and early 1980s. By 1984, when the Bears were competing in Division I, they overwhelmed the Panthers 61-41, ending again the Drury-SMS basketball rivalry.

The truth of the matter was that the sports rivalry was only the top of the iceberg. Despite the fact that Drury officials had been active in securing State Normal School #4 for Springfield, when the new institution arrived it clearly carried competitive implications for Drury. Initially, the Normal School was seen as academically inferior to the established college. And, indeed, it was, given the fact that it had not yet achieved collegiate status. But it rankled Normal School students to be described as an inferior class. Taunts were frequently exchanged. When students were asked in 1928 whether athletics relations should be resumed with Drury, Marguerite Teeter replied, "I think two colleges in the same town should have friendly relations. However, this cannot be done until Drury respects our school and organizations and stops calling us the 'Yap House.'"

The issue of respect was indeed part of the picture. Even after athlet-

ics relations between the schools were terminated, conflicts between student groups continued. Roy Ellis remembered "hedge apples…used as confetti" and STC students "purloining the ancient canon from its pedestal on the

Drury campus." While Ellis remembered them as "innocent pranks," *The Standard* pictured the encounters as dangerous, demeaning and inappropriate. Clashes between student groups broke out in 1935 when groups of students from each institution marched through the rival's campus much like Catholic marches through Protestant neighborhoods in Belfast. "There's no excuse for the annual tour of the campus of the rival," declared *The Standard*. "It's time to bury the hatchet and get on with life!" In November of that year, student leaders from each campus met to see what they could do to stop the clashes.

But again in 1937, *The Standard* was reporting that "minority factions carried on a minor war" with hedge apples, tear gas, sidewalk painting, and "dares." Apparently some Drury students stole an STC football sign and dared STC students to "come and get it." About 50 youths, some from high school, led by a non-student, attacked Drury's "Barn." Fighting broke out in the street and police were called to disperse the crowd by using tear gas. Additional tear gas was used near the College Inn where the fracas continued. Marion Preston Emerson remembers several students being injured in that encounter. Again student leaders were called together to find common ground.

In 1939, Drury challenged STC to a basketball game, but STC students were forced to refuse because of the Board's edict in 1923. *The Standard* reported that "Drury taunts us as cowards," and went on to advocate acceptance of the challenge. But it didn't happen. The ban held firm.

The Standard editorialized again in 1940 that "friendly rivalry and

Bears win conference basketball championship.

Toyohiko Kagawa, Christian leader and social reformer from Japan, visits campus.

Boulder Dam completed.

Alcoholics Anonymous (AA) founded by two former alcoholics.

1919-46 Southwest Missouri State Teachers College　95

horseplay makes sense, but not the cry for blood." It expressed the hope that "civilization is creeping insidiously into Springfield's college life." Student leaders at STC continued to discourage what they called the "Jordan Follies" and "the nocturnal visits across the viaduct." A turning point in the rivalry came in 1940. On December 21 that year, STC hosted an intercollegiate basketball tournament to which Drury was invited. Baker University and Upper Iowa were also invited. The tournament was structured so that Drury and STC exchanged opponents, but did not play each other. Earlier in the season, Drury's basketball team came to the new field house and cheered for the Bears as they defeated the Tallequah Indians, 24–10.

While athletics competition was off the table, forensic competition with Drury was featured in 1940. Radio Station KGBX aired a debate between Horace Haseltine and Woodrow Denny of STC and Henry Duncan and Bill Reese of Drury. In a non-decision contest, the teams tackled the timely proposition, "Resolved: That a policy of isolation should be adopted." The debate was intense, but civil.

So the brittle edge to the relationship between the schools during the late STC years softened, but the issue of respect has been slow to resolve. Students coming to STC defined themselves as "democrats," people valuing their commonplace backgrounds and inclusive habits. They defined their cross-town rivals as exclusive in habit and selective in relationships, all of which tended to perpetuate the chasm between the institutions.

Student Organizations
The Growth of Social Clubs
The issue of exclusivity was not just a Drury–STC issue. By the 1920s, the STC campus itself was struggling with issues of inclusion and exclusion. For some, the long standing democratic tradition was being challenged by the emergence of social clubs on campus, which began looking very much like sororities and fraternities.

The *Catalog* was very clear about college policy stating that "the organizations to which the college gives recognition are distinctly democratic. Standards of membership are definitely announced, and any student who can meet the announced standards is eligible. In no case is membership based on personal or social selection."

That policy stayed in the *Catalog* until 1949, but the growth of "unrecognized organizations" during the STC years was dramatic. In fact, as early as 1917, a men's club called Knights of the Road was organized. In 1921, it changed its name to the Key and Dagger Club and stated its purpose as "supporting athletic activities." By 1925, 16 Key and Dagger Club men were living together in a house at 871 Kingshighway, near the northwest corner of the campus. A year later it was called a "local social fraternity" by the *Ozarko*. Other clubs began popping up quickly. In 1929, the Tri-C's organized and purchased a home at 802 Kickapoo. Two women's clubs also appeared that year — the Dianas and F-Squares.

The emergence of social clubs that recruited pledges and selected members on a purely individual basis was certainly not within college policy, but such clubs began to play an increasingly

important role in the social life of the institution. The contradiction between the official policy and the emerging practice was a concern for *The Standard* editor in 1930 who quoted the policy and then asked, "But then what does it mean if such a (unrecognized) club gives a dance that the guest list must be approved by the Dean of Women, faculty must act as chaperones, and formals must be given in the school gym? One club even has a faculty sponsor." *The Standard* argued for policy clarification declaring that, "The only attribute of the existing order seems to be that the clubs are kept in the adolescent stage. Official recognition would mean development and maturity. It seems time for something definite to be done — for some positive step in one direction or the other to be taken. At least tell us what constitutes recognition."

By the fall of 1930, men were being initiated into the KD and Tri-C clubs, gaining their membership on "personal and social selection" principles. The clubs were entertaining their prospective pledges at "smokers" and scheduling a variety of entertainment for potential new members.

Four women's clubs were engaging in "rush" activities as well and it did, indeed, appear that the "democratic" commitment of the institution was being compromised by a growing club-based exclusivity.

Back in 1912, *The Standard* published an acerbic piece against fraternities saying,

> *"Organized primarily for social purposes, the fraternity has gradually acquired power until today it practically dominates the majority of our schools, colleges and universities…. The secret society, no matter what its*

Association for Childhood Education founded.

National Labor Relations Act passed, affirming the right of labor to organize and bargain collectively.

Social Security Act passed by Congress.

Adolph Hitler announces "Nuremberg Laws" against Jews.

Among the rapidly growing organizations on the STC campus was The Story Telling Club shown here with students from Greenwood in 1922. Their story telling skills were a fitting complement to their classroom teaching skills.

name and purpose, has no place in our system of education, whether it is high school, Normal or university. It is contrary to all principles of democracy, fair play and common sense." Such a diatribe had to be addressed, at least in part, to Drury the crosstown rival, since in 1912, virtually all Normal School students were members of literary societies with clear democratic values. There was no apparent interest in social clubs, and the "democracy" of the new campus was extolled as a primary virtue.

But things had changed by 1924. Student Neil Clarke makes an impassioned plea on behalf of fraternities that year in *The Standard*, declaring that, "there are freakish relics in this wonderful institution of ours who are against everything from stacomb and rouge down to safety razors, rubber heels and radios.... Because one is an accomplished student or a weak-mind-

ed bookworm, it does not necessarily follow that he could make or hold friends." Two weeks later, Eula Roberts responded, "Fraternities hinder democracy for they favor cliques. They divide a school, for no one can belong to more than one such association. In a state school especially, there should be no conditions favoring cliques. If we could have just one fraternal organization, one including all our students, it would be well! But that is impossible. Give other colleges their fraternities and sororities, but let ours be the Bears of STC."

By the 1930s, however, the momentum in the direction of independent social clubs was growing. Ten such clubs existed in 1933. By 1940, 300 students belonged to 11 clubs, five for men and six for women. By 1941, the men's Key and Dagger Club had affiliated with the Sigma Tau Gamma national fraternity, the first STC social club to affiliate with a national orga-

nization. President Ellis signed the petition despite the policy statement in the *Catalog*. About the same time, ABZ, a women's club, announced its affiliation with a national sorority, Delta Sigma Epsilon. The trend continued throughout the 1940s.

In many respects, the emergence of social clubs divided the campus. An opponent of social clubs in 1930 advised freshmen through *The Standard*, "If you are one of the rushed freshmen, it hasn't taken you long to find out what 'fellowship and brotherhood, loyalty,' and such terms mean. If you are one of the 'great unrushed' it may take you longer to learn about them. You may even be on campus two weeks before you learn that two or three club houses that face the campus on the south and east are not universal hangouts or rally rendezvous. Only the privileged few may enter those front doors. You may deliver their groceries and stoke their furnaces for a long time and never catch a glimpse of the waxed floors and radios that furnish entertainment for the members.... Being only fair, however, it is necessary to state

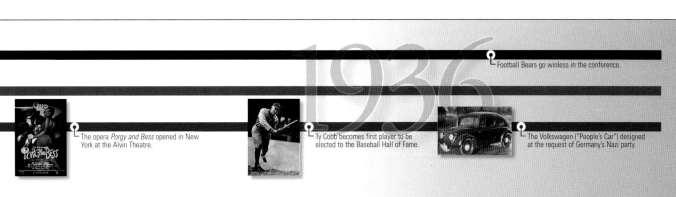

1936

Football Bears go winless in the conference.

The opera *Porgy and Bess* opened in New York at the Alvin Theatre.

Ty Cobb becomes first player to be elected to the Baseball Hall of Fame.

The Volkswagen ("People's Car") designed at the request of Germany's Nazi party.

Bruin Booster Mary Spellman, left, was a proud member of the 1938-39 Bruin Boosters whose history went back to 1927 when campus women organized a marching club to support the Bears' athletics teams. Key players in promoting school spirit, the Boosters, with their well-executed drills, brought cheers from the stands at athletics events and pep rallies, Joyland and May Day performances. Physical Education instructor Margaret Putnam coached the 40-member squad.

over into campus politics and campus elections. Roy Wert, *Standard* editor in 1931-32, deplored the degree to which campus elections were dominated by club interests. He started his editorial year by encouraging students to "vote for people whose interests are beyond the club to which they belong." In 1932, 14 of 16 elected to the *Ozarko* "who's who" section were from campus social clubs reflecting the growing power of "unrecognized" but nonetheless "institutionally regulated" student organizations. By 1933, "independents" had captured several positions in student body elections reversing a trend where social club candidates had dominated campus politics. *The Standard* editor observed, "The clubs had tasted power so long it was beginning to be nauseating."

The college took an early interest in the activities of these social clubs, particularly their "hazing" or "hellweek" activities. In 1932, the Panola girls were requiring their pledges to wear seven stockings on one leg, carry an uncooked egg for all their teachers to sign, wear makeup on only one side of their face, roller skate between classes, carry an onion and eat half of it during the day, wear four earrings on one ear, and put their arms in slings and put patches over their eyes.

The Felix Fidelis boys were required to wear different costumes daily, wear their clothes backwards and wear their overcoats all day. In 1940, they could be seen wearing unmatching shoes, wool sweaters against bare skin, lipstick, and signs declaring their pledge status. They also carried a shoe-shine kit, chewing gum and cigarettes for the benefit of their active brothers. The KD's could neither talk to nor date girls,

that if you have come to college wanting to spend money and have a glorious time, and go many places, you can do just that by accepting your pledge to this or that social club." Signed: "One who knows." Social club defenders were quick to reply. John Gillespie, identifying himself as "one who ought to know" answered, "Once more the criticism of one of our 'sour grapes' at the college has challenged the realm of fraternities and sororities at STC. We have no quarrel with students who do not wish to belong to social fraternities

and sororities, but it seems that these same members must howl so much about lack of democracy and then go meowing their way through four years of college life with their own little clique which lacks only the name to make them equal to those whom they criticize so severely and whose method of discriminating is by far more socially desirable than the kind the little meowers use."

Campus Politics
The rift between the independents espousing the democratic way and the social club members defending their right of selective association spilled

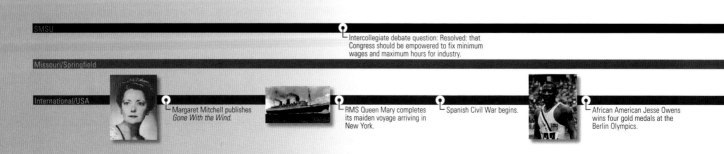

Intercollegiate debate question: Resolved: that Congress should be empowered to fix minimum wages and maximum hours for industry.

Missouri/Springfield

International/USA

Margaret Mitchell publishes *Gone With the Wind.*

RMS Queen Mary completes its maiden voyage arriving in New York.

Spanish Civil War begins.

African American Jesse Owens wins four gold medals at the Berlin Olympics.

shave nor wash their hair for a week.

Despite being "unrecognized," the clubs were clearly college regulated. Rushing rules in 1942 included a ban on drinking, forbade dates on weeknights, and required an "M" (C) average in classes. Rushing rules also carried an expectation to show respect and courtesy in all activities, including relations with "independents." Girls were admonished to "conduct yourself as a lady at all times." Everyone must study a minimum of two hours daily. Clubs were also required to schedule their initiations at the same time — the second week in December — "in order not to disrupt the dignity of the school over a longer period than is necessary."

The struggle to maintain democratic traditions in the midst of a fragmenting student body was not easy. In 1934, *The Standard* pointed out the unfairness of having all formal dances at the school sponsored by the social clubs, which meant many students would be excluded from the festivities. It was proposed that formal dances be sponsored by college classes which meant all class members were invited. At first the suggestion was deemed impractical, but by March 1934 an all-school prom sponsored by the junior class was held.

Changing Campus Organizations

The whole structure of student organizations went through dramatic change in the STC period. The solidarity around campus literary societies so typical of the Normal School years had declined by the end of World War I. *The* 1919 *Standard* editor commented on the decline of interest saying, "It's a deplorable fact that the students and faculty of (the school) are not 'square' in their boosting. Either that is the case, or their idea of relative values is askew. What we refer to is the difference in enthusiasm over athletic and literary contests. More than 90 percent of the faculty and students of the school attended both the recent basketball games and yet hardly 75 percent were present at the oratorical contest a few evenings later! What is wrong?"

By 1920, only three literary societies were active and by 1922, their sponsorship of the forensic program was taken over by the academic classes. *The* 1922 *Standard* attributed the decline of the literary societies to the movies. "The bold movie posters and bright lights of the city must be equaled or

Drum Major Helen Davison models the new STC Band uniforms that arrived late in the fall of 1939 along with Drum Majorette Patsy Lynes, daughter of band conductor Winston E. Lynes. Boasting 67 players and 14 instrument groups, the band played regularly at athletics contests, pep rallies and senior class play night, as well as giving concerts in several southwest Missouri communities.

counterbalanced by an equally strong impelling attraction, or the movie will get the crowd." The explanation was obviously too simple, but it did show an awareness of both a changing world and a changing student body. Nothing more is heard of the literary societies after 1925.

A plethora of other organizations emerged, more attuned apparently to the diversity of students' interests and to the growth of the curriculum. Discipline-based clubs were already emerging in the Normal years. In 1910, both the Normal Dramatic Club and the German Club (Der Deutsch Verein)

Biology offerings expand to 20 courses.

Anti-war sentiment builds on campus.

State Conservation Commission established.

British Broadcasting system launches first regular television service.

First *Life* magazine published by Henry Luce.

Meekee Wright was the first woman elected student body president at SMS. She served during the 1928-29 academic year, and, along with Harry Hedley, was chosen as a Commencement Speaker. A history major, Spartan, and member of the YWCA cabinet, Meekee hailed from Rover, Missouri.

were formed. A Mathematics Club formed in 1912 as did the Philomena Glee Club. A Home Economics Club was organized in 1913. By the STC period, students studying both French and Spanish had organized clubs to advance their foreign language skills. Honorary clubs in the various disciplines were organized as well. In 1923 the Omicron Club was formed for STC students in forensics. Gamma Theta Upsilon was organized in 1930 for geography students.

By 1927, there were 26 different organizations vying for students' interest and participation. Four were religious organizations, 10 were discipline related, three were built around athletics interests, two were related to forensic interests while music, service and fellowship were the foci of other groups. By 1930, student organizations numbered 34, and by 1940 there were more than 40.

The proliferation and differentiation of organizations on campus was noteworthy during the STC years. While the campus was still a community, it was beginning to learn what it meant to be "a community of communities." Athletics came closest to mobilizing the whole student body, but even that struggled at times to compete with the diversity of activities and interests developing among students.

The Birth of Student Government

Student government, until 1920, operated as a pure democracy. There were no student officers, cabinet, senate, or other evidence of representative government. It appears that relations between students and school administration were good and that communication between the faculty, administration and students was very open. The bureaucracy was very thin and the interaction was clearly intimate.

When student government did finally appear in 1920, it came at the request of the college administration, not the students. In fact, excitement over student government remained virtually nonexistent leading *The Standard* editor in 1931 to say "It has been carried on dutifully as a responsibility rather than enthusiastically as a privilege."

The first Student Council elected in 1920 included R.W. Martin, president of the student body (and later professor of chemistry at STC), Gladys Matthews, representative-at-large, and class officers Horace K. Robins (seniors), Freda Marshall (juniors), W.V. Cheek (sophomores), and Paul Matthews (freshmen). R.W. Martin wrote the first constitution for student government in 1921, which wasn't rewritten until 1941.

The 1923 *Ozarko* documents the decline of the Literary Societies during the STC years. With the emphasis upon college degrees rather than teaching certificates, the four college classes became the basis for many competitive activities including debate and athletics as well as social events.

Student Council functions in the early years included appointing the editors of *The Standard* and the *Ozarko*, planning student assemblies, student activities, school advertising, monitoring student conduct, entertaining visitors and advising faculty on school policy. By 1940, the responsibilities had expanded to include planning freshman orientation, planning "play nights," organizing all school social events and pep assemblies, assisting with registration and helping plan Homecoming.

Not all Student Councils took their work seriously. In 1928, *The Standard* called student government "a failure. Their neglect in assuming this duty and privilege has become a very serious matter," according to the edi-

tor. The student body president then resigned, and his newly elected replacement also resigned. Finally on January 24, 1929, the student body elected Meekee Wright to head the Student Council, the first female in the history of the school to be elected to the position. Wright was a history major, member of the YWCA, the Spartans and the English Club, and was "a senior noted for her unusual ability." She also was selected, along with Henry Hidley, to speak at the 1929 commencement.

It's not clear how frequently women sought elective office in the Student Council, but it was nine years later before another woman, Marguerite Noble, was elected student body president. Then Mary Burns was elected to the post in 1943-44.

Rules of Conduct

How much monitoring of student conduct the Student Council did is also not clear. But the tradition of the Normal School years continued through the STC years — no written disciplinary code. In the middle 1920s there was a Freshman Red Book published by the Student Council that served as an orientation guide for new students. It contained the school calendar, gave library and locker instructions, approved boarding places, listed all campus organizations, school songs and yells and schedules of athletics contests. Then there was a section on campus rules. By 1932, the Red Book was rewritten and contained what it called "friendly instructions, not rules." *The Standard* reported that the new edition was "radically different from the previous system which consisted briefly of hard and fast rules of Thou Shalt and Thou Shalt Not." No Red Books have been located enabling us to see what was encouraged and what was forbidden during the Roaring Twenties and the more sober Thirties.

In 1935, the Key and Dagger Club ran into trouble as it initiated Charles Killingsworth, an honor gradu-

As this 1931 *Ozarko* cartoon infers, social clubs became a dominant force in the political and social life of the campus during the STC years. Despite the fact that the clubs were not granted official recognition until much later, they set the agenda for campus activities in the 1930s.

Powerhouse Appetite

In the winter of 1937, 10 to 12 tons of coal were burned daily to help keep the four campus buildings warm. One truck operated 24 hours a day to keep the bins full. The slack coal was fed into the burners by two automatic stokers. A 125-foot smokestack alongside the powerhouse created enough draft to sweep a child off his or her feet.

~

The Uncompleted Gift

Class gifts were commonplace during STC years. The class of 1923 left as its gift, plans to build a 135- to 150-foot high monument, located equidistant from the three main buildings and surmounted by a clock. Apparently, the primary contribution of the Class of 1923 was the plan. *The Standard* reported that "succeeding classes will complete the monument." They haven't.

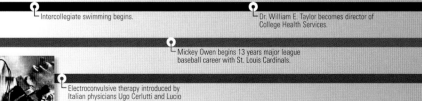

Intercollegiate swimming begins.

Dr. William E. Taylor becomes director of College Health Services.

Mickey Owen begins 13 years major league baseball career with St. Louis Cardinals.

Electroconvulsive therapy introduced by Italian physicians Ugo Cerlutti and Lucio Bini for treatment of mental illness.

Cartoon from *Springfield Newspapers*, December 11, 1938, depicting Dr. Virginia Craig on one of her frequent "hikes" to Hollister from Springfield. According to Lyle Owen, Dr. Craig was a great believer in physical fitness. "She was particularly famous for phenomenal walking.... Sometimes the walks were as far as all of those rough, winding, hilly miles from Springfield to Hollister, more than 50 miles in those old road-meandering days." In 1920 she made the walk alone in three days, staying the two nights with farm families in Ozark and Walnut Shade. In the summer of 1921 Mary Alice Wood joined Dr. Craig on a hike to Hollister that took only two days. In succeeding years Craig and Wood make the walk five additional times. They always returned to Springfield on the train.

ate of Springfield High School. The club administered a goodly portion of plaster-of-paris on Killingsworth and left him quite a distance from the city to walk home. He was not injured, but President Ellis was not entertained. He said, "the school will try to persuade the club to modify its practices in order to avoid further embarrassment to themselves and to the school."

On another occasion, local citizens apparently came to Dean Wells to ask her to prevent dancing at the college. They saw it as dangerous to the morals of the young. By this time (1930),

dancing had become a virtual institution at the college and was a centerpiece of the entertainment venue. Dean Wells apparently did pass the issue on to the Student Council who subsequently "advised students to conduct themselves properly at dances so dancing can continue."

In 1933, a set of dance regulations were formed by representatives of the social clubs. The rules included requiring that the guest list be approved by Dean Wells before any invitations were sent out, that no verbal invitations could be issued, and that drinking

was forbidden. The rules also created a disciplinary council composed of one member from each social club, a member of the Student Council, an independent student and the dean of women, which would hear cases and administer penalties for misconduct at dances.

One can observe the loosening of standards in the STC era by remembering that the 1906 *Bulletin* warned students against frequenting billiard halls, but by the 1930s, ads in *The Standard* were inviting students to the Woodruff Billiard Parlor.

Occasionally, students took it upon themselves to advise the college about rules. In 1925, one student wrote *The Standard* declaring, "I have written a petition which I am going to present to President Hill, but before I present it to him, I want the signature of every loyal STC student on it.... My plan... is...that all college girls and boys be prohibited from having dates together at night or during school hours. STC is an institution of higher learning, and it is up to us as loyal students to uphold the high standards and fame of our school and prevent its degrading into a matrimonial agency."

Responses to his proposal came quickly. One writer declared such a proposal would "divide the school into two separate units, one, a penitentiary for men, and the other a penitentiary for women." Another declared that if he could not "date any and all possible girls at any and all times, he could not possibly remain in school, even for the rest of the term!" *The Standard* editor joined the conversation by calling attention to the fact that Park College north of Kansas City had expelled a student for kissing a woman, "all of which," he said, "would lead us to con-

SMSU
STC joins National Association of Intercollegiate Basketball.

Missouri/Springfield
Streetcars end service in Springfield.
Missouri death penalty changed from hanging to gas chamber.
First Ozark Empire Fair opens near Dickerson Park Zoo.

International/USA
Joe Louis defeats James A. Braddock in Chicago to become world heavyweight boxing champion.
Sino-Japanese War begins.

clude that STC is not such a bad place after all!"

The most contentious issue during the STC years was smoking. As Roy Ellis recalled, "It was hardly an issue at first. It just wasn't done. I think it could fairly be said that President Carrington would have hesitated to hire a teacher who was a habitual smoker." But as time passed and cigarettes became more popular, the non-smoking tradition began to crumble. Cigarette butts began appearing in campus restrooms and along the sidewalks. The first cigarette ad on campus appeared in *The* April 4, 1929 *Standard*. Camels were portrayed as the smoker's choice. The ad appeared again in the May 2 issue, the same issue that complained about the prevalence of smoking on campus.

Efforts were certainly made to curtail smoking on campus. But as the habit grew more popular and campus social clubs entertained with "smokers," it became clear that maintaining the no smoking tradition was a lost cause. Letters to the editor encouraged abandoning the tradition. President Ellis observed that he had "never seen an institution where smoking was permitted that wasn't littered up. If students started smoking on campus within a week they would be smoking in the buildings," he said.

By 1937, it was proposed that smoking be kept out of classrooms, but not forbidden on campus. Nevertheless, President Ellis pointed out that while "no one will be expelled for smoking on campus…anyone who makes a habit of it will probably be spoken to."

Despite the fact that at least one-half of the student body used tobacco in the 1930s, by 1939 a balloting among students indicated the desire for a no-smoking policy on campus. The Student Council passed such a resolution, but it appears that it went up in smoke. In 1941, *The Standard* editor plaintively asked, "Why class as a school tradition what amounts to an empty phrase as far as large numbers of students are concerned? Unless students themselves will enforce the (non-smoking) custom, there seems little use in pretending to maintain it."

Other traditions were changing as well. The Normal School years saw students dress rather formally, with men wearing coats even on the hottest days. Roy Ellis recalled that students who appeared in class without coats "were likely to be sent out to get one." But in the STC period, clothing became more casual. In 1941, there was a debate over the propriety of women wearing slacks. *The Standard* conducted a poll eliciting a variety of comments including York Wolf's; he said, "It's none of my business. I don't care. They can wear slacks if they want to." But Paul Brackley saw it differently. "No, I definitely don't like them," he said. "I suppose they might be worn to a picnic, but certainly to no other place." Women weighed in on the matter as well. "Males shouldn't be selfish with their pants," declared

The Joyland Christmas festival featuring 400 Greenwood students dancing, singing and performing drills had grown so popular that in 1925 it was moved to the newly-constructed Shrine Mosque. The colorful event was witnessed by 3,000 people. A giant choir composed of singers from several local churches and the De Molay band assisted in the Arthur Briggs production. Proceeds from the festival assisted 250 local families with Christmas provisions.

Pi Omega Pi, national honorary commerce fraternity, established.

Lloyd C. Stark elected governor.

Snow White and the Seven Dwarfs, first full-length animated movie, becomes worldwide hit.

Arthur Briggs retires as athletics director and becomes head of the Physical Education Department.

Springfield City Flag made official.

1919-46 Southwest Missouri State Teachers College   103

May Day festivals at the college were started by Arthur Briggs upon his arrival in 1912. The 1925 festival was titled "Wonderland." Staged outdoors, several thousand spectators were escorted through Wonderland's magic as more than 1,000 performers conducted "A Trip to the Moon." May Queen Violet Harvey presided over the festivities. Thirty-six May Poles were wound. The climax of the festival came as Greenwood students did mass calisthenics and a star drill. "The rhythm and accuracy of the entire ensemble was little short of phenomenal," according to the *Ozarko*.

Anna Marcy. "They are quite comfortable." No doubt the "Roaring Twenties" introduced a more liberated attitude on campus about dress, norms of conduct and the extent of personal freedom.

Developing Traditions

While changes were occurring in the college, 28 years after its founding writers could still speak of the traditions that were developing in the young institution. According to *The Standard* editor, in the summer of 1933, democracy headed the list of those durable traditions. He emphasized that "every recognized organization has standards of membership and is open to any student." What he didn't mention, of

course, was the proliferation of social clubs whose membership selection policies were clearly undemocratic. Despite their "unofficial" status, they, too, were becoming a campus tradition.

The democratic tradition, nevertheless, was clearly evident in student initiative. The election of their own officials, the editing of their own publications, and the planning and conducting of their own social affairs were all seen as democracy at work. The freedom to attend or not attend regular weekly assemblies was also viewed as an important democratic principle, even though frequent complaints were raised about the declining interest in assembly programs. The absence of a complex

disciplinary code reflected a democratic reliance on student initiative in responsible decision making.

There were traditional events, as well, that helped profile the institution. Mother's and Dad's Day in October, the All-School Picnic at Doling Park in October, the Christmas Joyland celebration with Greenwood children participating, and the annual May Day Festival with more than 1,000 participating had all established their places in the life of the college. The Class Day for Seniors with the lighted candle ceremony at dusk, the unveiling of the name of the famous educator to be added to the Education Building freize and the announcing of the class

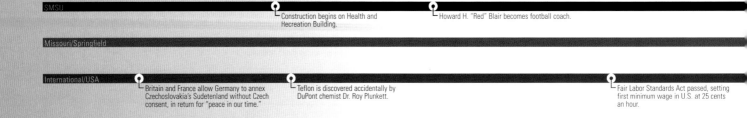

gift were always memorable events. Homecoming, first established in 1921, was becoming a featured event each year with alumni reunions, football, a play by the College Theatre and, beginning in 1940, the selection of a Homecoming Queen.

The campus became known for its pageantry during the STC years. Arthur Briggs developed the tradition, starting with the May Day festival in 1913, the year after he arrived. In 1921, the centennial year of Missouri statehood, Briggs produced the State Historical Pageant, referred to by many as "the biggest event of the year in Springfield."

For 30 years, the May Day festival mobilized the campus and drew thousands of town folks to witness the winding of the May Poles, the marching and dancing of Greenwood students and the crowning of the May Queen. In 1920, 30 May Poles were wound. Marion Preston Emerson ('38) recalls the winding process and the complex color designs produced by the dancers. "Participants alternated girl and boy with eight winding at each pole. The boys wore white pants and shirts. The ribbons were of two colors. When everyone at the pole danced in the same direction, the pole took on the appearance of a peppermint stick. When four danced clockwise and the other four danced counter clockwise, squares in color appeared on the poles. The last dance was more varied leaving a complex pattern on the pole which was left wound."

Pageantry had a central place on campus until the war years. The last May Day celebration occurred in 1943 as did the last Joyland Christmas celebration. Neither was renewed after the end of the war.

The Great Depression

"By the late 1920s aircraft symbolized speed, modernity and youthful heroism, images epitomized by the 1922 solo flight of Charles A. Lindbergh from New York to Paris," according to historian Philip Jenkins. "Together with the emerging skyscraper landscape of the great cities, aircraft represented the futuristic dream of a new society based on constant technological innovation and unlimited consumer prosperity."

But the dream began unraveling with the October 29, 1929, crash of the stock market and the subsequent wave of bank and business failures. Some numbers help to tell the story. In the middle 1920s, the unemployment rate in the U.S. fell to under 2 percent. Prospering business and a buying public put almost everyone to work. But by 1935, one in four Americans was without work. Industrial production fell to 40 percent of capacity. The stock market was at one-tenth of its pre-crash level. In 1933, 13 million people were unemployed.

In rural Missouri, farmers had only half the purchasing power they had in the 1920s, and they received only 56 percent of what they were paid for commodities in 1922. Many could not pay property taxes so their farms were sold for the tax debt. Eighteen thousand farms were seized for foreclosure between 1930-34. Farm conditions reached utter desperation between 1933-36 when drought and high winds turned the central plains into a dust bowl.

The prosperity and hope engendered in the 1920s gave way to the Great Depression, which dwarfed in scope all previous economic downturns in the country. Springfield suffered

He Knew Business: Lee H. Morris

When Lee H. Morris graduated from STC in 1924, he didn't have to look far for a job. President Hill hired him to manage the college bookstore. His business savvy became quickly apparent. In 1927 President Ellis named him business manager for the college and in 1930 he took on the additional responsibility of treasurer for the Board of Regents. He retired from both positions in 1961 after 37 years of distinguished service.

During the depression years when financial management was a key to college survival, Lee Morris played a key role. He not only managed the institution's resources astutely, he helped hundreds of students remain in school by providing them jobs on campus.

Recognized nationally by being elected President of the National Association of Educational Buyers in 1934, Morris is credited with modeling purchasing practices for educational institutions nationwide throughout the 1930s.

Known for his hearty laugh, his love of cribbage and his secret desire to own a parrot and a jaybird, Morris served throughout the entire Ellis era.

Last all-school picnic held.

New Federal building opens at Boonville and Central.

Orson Welles broadcasts H.G. Wells' *The War of the Worlds*, convincing many in the radio audience that martians had landed and were warring with humans.

Working Their Way through School

In the spring of 1926, a survey was conducted on campus revealing that more than one-third of the students were working to earn part or all of their college expenses. On the average, students worked 24 hours a week, although some reported working a full 40 hour week in addition to attending their classes. Nearly half exchanged labor for board and room with local families. Women typically helped with household chores including cleaning, cooking and child-care. Men did odd jobs around the home. Many students worked in local businesses as clerks or office assistants. The going rate was 30 cents an hour.

~

Occupational Research

The Rural Sociology class in 1923 conducted a research project in which 4,800 rural high school graduates in the southwest district were asked about their occupation. The largest number (1,048) reported themselves as housewives. Following closely were 906 who said they were teachers. About 16 percent identified themselves as college students while 258 (5 percent) said they were farmers. When asked who were community leaders, they named bankers, merchants and farmers. The survey also reported the cost of a stay in any of Springfield's four hospitals was $3.50 a day.

Delmar Pachl, 1932 *Ozarko* cartoonist, portrays resilient STC as it fights to survive during the Great Depression.

along with the rest of the country, but not as dramatically. *The Standard* called it "one of the most prosperous cities in the U.S." during the Depression years. Yet, despite its relatively favorable situation, the 57,527 people living in Springfield in 1930 clearly felt its impact. Both Drury and STC found their enrollments shrinking and their budgets tightening. President Roy Ellis once remarked to a colleague about the Depression that, "To qualify as a college administrator in those days, it reminded me of the rule of the barber's guild in the middle ages. Before a barber could set up shop for himself, he had to be able to take a small cake of soap and whip it up into a barrel of lather."

The biennial state budget for STC for 1930-32 was $529,500. But the financial situation of the state required a 25 percent cut reducing the state allocation to $394,000, and the budget for 1933-34 was projected to be

yet lower — no more than $286,000. Complicating the college's financial situation was the failure of more than 40 banks in southwest Missouri, making student fee payments difficult.

By 1932, North Hall and Irvington Hall were closed "since they were no longer financially self-supporting." Numerous private homes were opened to students in the area, and families were happy to have the supplemental income from boarding students. The college subsidized the *Ozarko* so students could purchase it for $1.00 from the bookstore rather than allow it to fold.

In 1933, in what was described as an economy move, the Missouri House passed a bill vesting control of all teachers colleges, Lincoln University, the School for the Blind and the School for the Deaf under one central governing board. Governor Park supported the elimination of local boards, but after heavy lobbying by all five teachers col-

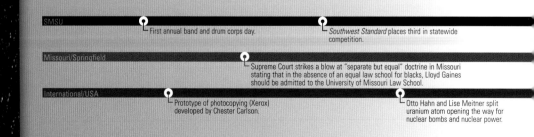

SMSU
First annual band and drum corps day.
Southwest Standard places third in statewide competition.

Missouri/Springfield
Supreme Court strikes a blow at "separate but equal" doctrine in Missouri stating that in the absence of an equal law school for blacks, Lloyd Gaines should be admitted to the University of Missouri Law School.

International/USA
Prototype of photocopying (Xerox) developed by Chester Carlson.
Otto Hahn and Lise Meitner split uranium atom opening the way for nuclear bombs and nuclear power.

leges, the Senate defeated the bill and local boards remained intact.

While teachers in the public schools retained their employment, many took severe cuts in pay. Greene County property valuation dropped drastically, forcing a 40 percent cut in pay for teachers throughout the county. Summer enrollments at STC dropped significantly because many teachers had not been paid for several months by their bankrupt school boards.

The hardships were felt by the STC faculty as well. On Friday, February 17, 1935, the Board ordered an immediate 10 percent cut in all faculty salaries, which were already the lowest of all the five teachers colleges in the state. Retrenchments had already been made in library hours and custodial staff, and all building improvements were curtailed. In April, another 10 percent cut in faculty salaries was ordered by the Board, but this time faculty holding the Ph.D. were exempted and they took less than a 10 percent cut. President Ellis requested a full 20 percent cumulative cut in his own salary to match the sacrifice of most of the faculty.

Salary recovery for the faculty was slow. By April 1934, salaries were increased to 83.33 percent of the base rate prior to the first reduction in February 1933. By April 1936, faculty had recovered to 90 percent of the base and by September of that year, they were at 100 percent of the base rate. The median salary for STC faculty in 1929 was $2,513 for 11 months service. A decade later it stood at $2,837.

Students experienced pay cuts as well. The hourly pay for work on campus in 1933 was 30 cents an hour. In July 1933 it was dropped to 25 cents. Four years later students were returned to the 30 cents an hour rate.

Not only were faculty and students struggling to cope, even college graduates had a particularly grim outlook. By the early 1930s the teaching profession had become overcrowded largely as a result of people losing their jobs elsewhere in the economy and taking up teaching as a stop-gap measure. School boards suffered significant declines in tax revenues, which led not only to lowered teacher salaries, but also to a reduction in teaching positions. A national survey reported that less than 20 percent of the class of 1931 were able to secure teaching positions. At STC, only 12 of 105 graduating seniors obtained jobs.

In July 1933, State Superintendent of Schools Charles Lee visited STC and outlined the dismal picture for schools in Missouri. More than 1,800 months of teaching service were donated by rural teachers during 1932-33. Had that not have been the case 1,600 rural schools would have shut down early for lack of funds. Two thousand school districts closed the term with deficits. One-half of all high school teachers donated at least a month of service to the state. For 1933-34, salary cuts ranged from 15 percent to 40 percent. Looking ahead, Superintendent Lee anticipated one-third of all rural school districts would be unable to have an eight month term and still pay teachers $50 a month. Most high school teachers would earn less than $500 a year for 1933-34. Despite these grim projections, most teachers stayed on to teach. Even a poorly paid job was better than none, they reasoned.

The Standard editor gave some advice to graduating seniors in 1936. "Now that I have finished college, what does society have to offer me? That question is asked by more than a few young people as the day of graduating from college draws near. No high-flown phrases can minimize the seriousness of the situation wherein thousands of American youths are thrown upon a cruel and heartless world which has no jobs to offer." But, the writer went on to suggest, "A great many more opportunities are awaiting capable young people than they really think. If youth is determined, it can make a place for itself. Preparation, determination and concentration upon a goal should insure a college graduate an opportunity to show his wares. If he fails…well, it cannot be laid at the door of the system." While the editor's encouragement to graduates is to be admired, we have no evidence how many bought into his "blame the victim" perspective.

The New York Times surveyed 24 colleges to assess the impact of the Depression on campuses across the country. Their chief finding was a change in students' attitudes. The carefree joy typical of campus life in the 1920s had modulated. Students were more focused on books and blackboards. They were buying used books, asking for scholarships, living in low-priced dormitory rooms and looking for jobs to support themselves while in school. Similar results were found at STC where *The Standard* reported in 1933, "This year has been different in mode of student life — it's fashionable to be thrifty. A sense of obligation to self and parents (has) settled down on coeds and collegians.

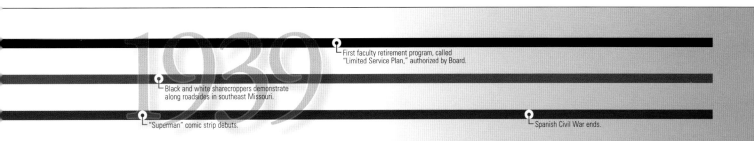

First faculty retirement program, called "Limited Service Plan," authorized by Board.

Black and white sharecroppers demonstrate along roadsides in southeast Missouri.

"Superman" comic strip debuts.

Spanish Civil War ends.

Student Opinion on the New Deal

In the spring of 1940, *The Standard* conducted a survey of students' attitudes toward many of President Roosevelt's New Deal programs. By a 53% to 47% margin, those surveyed were against New Deal policies. When asked about specific policies, students were even more explicit. Despite the many direct benefits of the Public Works program to both the campus and workers in southwest Missouri, 65 percent were opposed to it. They were even more opposed to the agriculture program, power projects such as the Tennessee Valley Authority, and direct relief programs. However, a majority of students were in favor of the Social Security Act, Roosevelt's foreign policy and reciprocal trade pacts.

By the 1940s the need for space on campus for socializing and recreation had become acute. In the fall of 1942, President Ellis opened a space in the Administration Building for students to gather and socialize. Betty Short, Gene Wilkerson, "Snookie" Orr, Marjorie Moore and Harry Dark initiated the new recreation room on the day it opened in 1942.

The carefree attitude of flaming youth has received a severe jolt. Industry has again become a cardinal virtue."

Fall semester enrollment peaked at STC in 1931 with 1,406. By 1934-35 it had dropped by 34 percent to 923. Summer enrollment drops were even more dramatic. From a high of 2,055 in 1931, enrollment dropped 42 percent to 1,181 in 1934. By 1936, the trend was reversed with gains being made every year thereafter leading *The Standard* to declare, "The large enrollment is definite proof that 'Ole Man Depression' has left."

By 1937, even job opportunities were improving. For teachers, it was back to the 1929 levels. What wasn't present, however, was significant improvement in teacher salaries.

"New Deal" Help At STC

Ironically, it took the desperation of the Great Depression to produce some significant gains for the STC campus. In an effort to provide employment for the more than 14 million who were out of work, the Roosevelt administration poured billions of dollars into public works projects that resulted in significant capital improvements across the country. From 1933-37, federal grants of $862,880,012 were made to Missouri alone. At STC, the

SMSU
Glenn Cunningham lectures on "Running Around the World."
Cornelius Vanderbilt lectures on the possibility of war.

Missouri/Springfield
Kansas City boss, Tom Pendergast convicted of income tax evasion.
McDonnell Aircraft Corporation established by J.S. McDonnell.

International/USA
Food stamps are first issued.
Pan American Airways offers world's first transatlantic passenger service.

football stadium was built as a Works Progress Administration project with only $25,000 coming from local funds. The Health and Recreation Building, completed in 1940, benefited also from $200,000 in federal grants through the WPA and the Public Works Administration. The swimming pool, so long under construction, was also a WPA project for which the college contribution was only $26,000. Extensive remodeling and repairs were done in Academic Hall as a result of a grant by the Civil Works Administration. Defective plaster was replaced, walls were repainted, and woodwork was refinished. The President's Office was remodeled and a partition was put in the Dean's Office to allow for private conferences. A two-story concrete fireproof vault was built, new lighting fixtures were installed and restrooms were relocated. One hundred and fifty-six

men were employed in the process, the majority of whom were STC students needing work to stay in school.

Students kept close tabs on their expenditures during the Depression years. Elsie Mantels Leamers remembers Dr. Cheek requiring students to keep a record of their expenditures, allowing the college to publish estimates of college costs for prospective students. In 1932, the average student spent $340 in three terms, which included board and room. Local students living at home spent an average $110 for the year.

Incidental fees at the college were increasing from $6.00 per term in 1906 to $11.00 per term by the beginning of the STC period. In 1924, fees were raised to $12.50 per term for boys and $13.00 for girls. The additional 50 cents for girls was for "privileges in case of illness," the first instance of a health service assessment. By 1931, fees had

jumped to $20 per term.

The challenge of the 1930s was to finding ways to assist students in meeting the cost of a college education. A number of federal programs were initiated during the Depression, which supported students in college as well as helped graduates find employment. Graduates from the home economics program in 1934 were hired by the Civil Works Administration (CWA) to teach cooking, clothing selection and parenting skills to southwest district rural families, some of whom had incomes of no more that $35.00 a year. Those graduates worked in Anderson, Bakersfield, Rolla, Thayer, Stockton, Lebanon, Bolivar, Buffalo and Neosho.

A variety of other New Deal programs gave employment to STC students. Twenty students were given CWS jobs involving a variety of research projects in 1924. Some stud-

Incidental Fee Receipt issued to Madelyn Brown on September 11, 1940. Fees at the time were $20 a quarter.

Students vote "no smoking" policy on campus.

New field house opens for use.

Civilian pilot training begins on STC campus.

World War II begins with German invasion of Poland.

To escape bombing raids, 650,000 children evacuate from London to rural England.

Nylon stockings go on sale for first time in U.S.

ied college and public school curricula including pupil progress reports while others surveyed the social and educational interests of students. Sociological and economic aspects of community life in the Ozarks, as well as price trends and standards of school equipment and supplies, were assigned to others. Some students did research on Ozarks insect life, particularly stophylindae, while others researched Missouri history. The entire enterprise was supervised by Dr. Harry Wise, assisted by Stanley Oliver.

Need-based grants were given to 106 students in 1934 through the MERA program. Forty-three boys and 63 girls received $15.00 a month in exchange for working at various tasks around the college. Some compiled data on social problems, adult education and weather conditions in the Ozarks. Others conducted industrial surveys and compiled course materials for non-readers. Several worked on entertainment projects including band and glee club concerts, as well as plays and pageants on Missouri history. Selected students assisted French instructor J.D. Bounous to record the Waldensian dialect.

National Youth Administration (NYA) allotments were also given each year during the Depression to assist students working their way through school. The grants provided $15.00 a month for 50 hours of work or $7.50 for 25 hours. Drought conditions in 1935 increased the 1936 allotment by 50 percent. Three hundred and twenty-seven students applied for NYA assistance, which represented 34 percent of the entire student body. Grants were given to 158, 14 percent of the student body. NYA grants continued until 1943. In 1940, the 135 recipients had to take the "oath of allegiance" as a condition for receiving the grant. The oath was an intensification of the anti-fifth-column movement developing across the country.

The Civilian Conservation Corps (CCC) also had a presence on the STC campus during the latter years of the Depression. The CCC provided training for young men in useful jobs and is estimated to have directly benefited one in seven young men. In 1940, some 47,186 enrollees found jobs through the skills learned in CCC Camps. While learning vocations and skills, they also took academic subjects.

Thousands earned grammar school or high school diplomas. Some earned college degrees. In 1941, 46 CCC boys from the camp in Springfield took classes at STC in American history, psychology, Spanish, algebra,

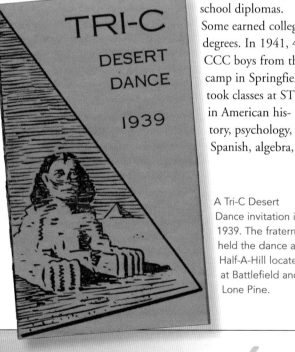

A Tri-C Desert Dance invitation in 1939. The fraternity held the dance at Half-A-Hill located at Battlefield and Lone Pine.

English and trigonometry.

Without federal programs providing grants to students, enrollment declines during the Depression years would have been much more dramatic than they were. Hundreds were assisted each year with campus jobs and monthly stipends. However, despite the assistance received and the benefits provided, by 1940, student opinion on the value of many New Deal initiatives to cope with the Depression was divided. Conservative attitudes were skeptical of governmental solutions to economic and social problems.

The Student Experience

The student experience during the STC years ran the gamut of emotions. It started with the elation over the end of World War I and the designation of the school as a full collegiate institution. The Roaring Twenties introduced a more liberal spirit and powerful challenges to traditional campus ways. Then the Great Depression cast its pall over the college, moving students to sober reflection on their ability to stay in school and their job prospects if they persevered to graduation. As that cloud began to lift, another appeared on the horizon. Echoes of war reverberated from Europe and soon the college was witnessing its men going off to serve in the military, and campus life was wrenched into a war-readiness mood that penetrated every aspect of the student experience.

So the STC years spanning just over a quarter century were times of triumph and tribulation. Student life was somewhat like a roller coaster from the confidence and enthusiasm of the 1920s to the sobriety of the 1930s and then to the anxieties of the 1940s. But

1940

SMSU — Alpha Phi Omega service fraternity organized on campus.

Health and Recreation Building (McDonald Arena) completed.

Missouri/Springfield

International/USA — In *Gaines v. Canada*, U.S. Supreme Court rules that "separate but equal" must mean facilities are of equal standard for both black and white students.

students managed. They studied; they played; they courted; they celebrated — all the things that define the unique experience of college life.

With the emergence of a clearer academic class structure during the STC years, the orienting of freshmen to college life became the (unofficial) task of the sophomores. As early as 1915, freshman naivete had become a topic of lively discussion and prescription, as outlined in this 1915 *Ozarko* limerick:

> *A woodpecker lit on a freshman's head,*
> *And straightway began to drill;*
> *He bored away for half-a-day,*
> *And then he broke his bill.*

It's unclear exactly when sophomores began "mentoring" freshmen, but early in the 1920s accounts of sophomore "guardianship" of hapless freshmen began appearing in *The Standard*. Wearing red hats became a distinguishing mark for freshmen, which made them easy prey for any sophomore who wished to make life miserable for them. The Student Council in 1922-23 voted to make the red hats mandatory for all freshmen until Thanksgiving, when their initiation would be considered complete. The red caps were officially discarded during halftime at the Thanksgiving football game, as were the red hair ribbons worn by freshmen girls.

The "orientation" (initiation) of freshmen by sophomores bordered on "hazing." As early as 1924, the "evils of the caste system" were written up in *The Standard*, including the abuse of freshmen women who were sometimes paddled in mixed company. Paddles were used to enforce freshmen "regulations," which were typically written by sophomores. They included dress regulations calling for "sobriety and

A record number (700) freshmen enrolled in the fall of 1931 creating a problem for the modest sized sophomore class who traditionally initiated (hazed) the freshmen identified by their red caps.

simplicity." Loud socks, suspenders and neckties were outlawed by the sophomores who removed them whenever they were detected on a freshman. "The green plebe must content himself with plain open collar, colorless sox [sic] or rolled trouser legs, and the inevitable red cap," reported *The Standard*.

Sophomores were free to order freshmen to sing a college song, quote rules from the handbook, do "the ridiculous calisthenics of buttoning," or run the gauntlet in pencil races where freshmen pushed pencils with their noses. Sophomores were forever on the search for hapless freshmen to discipline. In 1927, some went downtown to the Square and tried to enforce the rules on

what turned out to be non-STC students. A brawl erupted.

The hazing abuses were such that in 1933, the college began publishing its own "Manual of Friendly Information" for new students. The red cap tradition had been dropped the previous year, and hazing began to wane. President Roy Ellis reported his suspicion that the decline of hazing was connected to the growing size of the freshmen class. He recalls that "One autumn, a group of sophomores who appeared paddle-in-hand to discipline an assemblage of freshmen on the site of the present stadium, found themselves completely engulfed in a horde of freshmen armed with rubber hoses, sticks, and all forms of improvised weapons." The sophomores, he recalled, were soundly walloped. "Maybe they did not really 'retreat,'" he observed, "but they did 'retire to prepared positions.'"

While the sophomore mission to "orient" freshmen did not disappear altogether, by 1938 more elaborate plans for orienting new students were under way. According to *The Standard*, "The incoming freshman class this year should be pardoned for feeling a sense of pride in the fact that more elaborate preparations have been made for its induction into the life of the college than have been made for the reception of any other class in the history of the college." Three full days were spent escorting 625 freshmen through the intricacies of academic life. They took placement tests, were advised about majors by departmental staff, met with the Student Council, learned school yells at a pep assembly, and met Coach

Howard "Red" Blair. Each incoming freshman was also assigned a faculty advisor to help "solve not only instructional problems but personal problems as well." On the final day they began registering for classes.

Life in Irvington Hall

Getting into the housing business was not high on the list of priorities for either the Normal School or its successor, Southwest Missouri State Teachers College. Building dormitories involved funds the institution did not have as well as requiring oversight the administration was reluctant to get involved in. Nevertheless, a faculty group built two residences called Irvington Hall in 1910 and leased them to the College for $150 a month. More than 50 women were accommodated there.

Despite the fact that the college had not yet developed a written disciplinary code, and its behavioral expectations for students were usu-

ally expressed in a short paragraph in the *Bulletin,* life in Irvington Hall was tightly regimented. The first item listed on the sheet of *Regulations for Irvington Hall* had to do with "hours." Meal-time hours were to be honored precisely as posted. In case students were late for a meal for reasons acceptable to the matron, they could report after the meal hour, "provided they serve themselves and wash their own dishes." After the dinner meal, from 6:30-7:30, girls were to report for recreation. "It is expected that students participate in some kind of wholesome recreation at this time. This regulation is made in the interest of health and school work," according to the Irvington Hall matron.

At 7:30 p.m., the Hall atmosphere changes. "After 7:30, study conditions must prevail throughout both halls." According to the *Regulations,* "A violation of this regulation shall be treated as a gross indifference to the wishes of ambitious, earnest students and therefore will be treated as a most serious offence [sic]." The anticipated penalties

The parlors of Irvington Hall, college residence for girls in 1922, were hospitality centers for women and their friends during the early STC years.

SMSU
└ Football Bears complete an undefeated season.

Missouri/Springfield
└ Missouri non-partisan court plan established.

International/USA
└ Dr. Charles Richard Drew, an African American physician, appointed director of "Blood for Britain" project.
└ Franklin Delano Roosevelt elected to unprecedented third term as U.S. President.

The STC campus was served by electric trolleys, which stopped on the west side of the Administration Building in 1922.

are not listed.

Young men could appear at Irvington Hall only on Saturday and then only by invitation. The co-ed recreation hour ended at 10:30 p.m. "Too frequent requests for exceptions to regulations on the part of any individual student shall be considered as sufficient evidence to merit a special investigation of the general standing of the student in the college," the *Regulations* warned.

Not only were residents expected to be "regular in church attendance," but they were also expected to show "proper reverence...for the Sabbath day." This included maintaining "a spirit of quiet during the day, both in and out of the dormitories." More specifically, "It is not expected that students will practice upon the piano or other musical instruments or play inappropriate selections which may not only disturb the residents of the dormitory, but may prove quite offensive to

the neighborhood." "Absolute quiet" was prescribed for the hours between 2:00 and 4:00 p.m. on Sunday.

Dormitory residents were also reminded of the Chaperon rules. "It is expected that the young women of the dormitory will not partake of meals in public restaurants as guests of young men, without a chaperon, except in the case of relatives and then the kinship should not be closer than that of a cousin." The *Regulations* went on to declare that, "Under no conditions will a resident of the dormitory be permitted to go to the (railroad) station unless she is accompanied by someone who is approved by the matron." And then, finally, "It is understood that no resident of the dormitory will go automobile riding after night with young men, *under any conditions whatsoever.*" Period!

The Victorian atmosphere dissolved over time. The Irvington women of 1915 would have startling

Looking Back

Spectator Conduct

Richard Wilkinson, professor emeritus of Psychology, remembers the rules of conduct governing the behavior of players and spectators at STC basketball games in the late 1930s. From a player's point of view, there could be no such thing as a "physical" game. Any type of body contact with an opposing player resulted in a foul. Contests were low scoring affairs with an emphasis on defensive strategies. "During play fans remained so quiet you could hear the players' breathing," recalls Wilkinson. Only when the team scored would the crowd come alive, and then with applause. Immediately thereafter the crowd fell silent again as if watching a chess game. Free-throws were tried in absolute silence. Waving anything behind the goal or attempting to distract the shooter was out of the question.

Basketball Bears beat University of Missouri 35-32 in new arena.

"Lend-lease" program initiated to help Britain by lending supplies to be paid for later.

Popular student hangouts during the STC years included The Bear's Den, Varsity Inn, and the Tea Cup Inn.

conversations with Blair-Shannon women of 2004.

"Campusology" Popular

A popular course, taught exclusively by students, and offered at odd hours and in a variety of settings was dubbed "Campusology." Dean Wells asked the groundskeeper in 1921 to "trim the trees to spruce up the campus." Students understood her request as a way of improving her line of sight in monitoring "campusology." Another site for observing the popular course was in the library, despite the fact that that site

Cartoonist Sidney Hicks portrays the naïve freshman who hasn't yet discovered the tedium of the weekly all-school assemblies.

was never designed for such activity. A *Standard* writer in 1933 observed: "College dates having their derivation in the library are very amusing to observe. Every night we may observe a surplus of the fair sex spending much time to catch the attention of one of the less numerous date possibilities that occasionally wander through the library…. In numerous cases, eyes would stay on the book the individual was pretending to study for only a short interval, then glance around the room, back to the book, and then would follow a conference with some nearby sympathizer, resulting in an 'Ah! There he is in the book line,' or 'Do you think he has seen me yet?' which continues until the majority find that they have failed again, and rise slowly as they proceed to carry their own books home."

The local newspaper took note of the frequent show of affection between students and published an article about necking in one of its Sunday editions in November 1933. It posed the question, "Was necking necessary to be popular on campus?" Students were quick to respond. "Girls, as a rule, like to neck," replied an experienced man. "My grandmother says she never kissed until she was engaged," responded a woman,

"but moderns say 'How do I know if I want to be engaged if he has never kissed me?'"

Among the more popular times for this "campusology" course was 10:00 a.m. on Wednesdays, the scheduled hour for the campuswide assembly. While the assembly gathered in a faithful few, others would be scattered across campus socializing or gathering at one of the favorite off-campus hangouts to visit and arrange dates. Valiantly in defense of the assemblies, *The Standard* editor argued that "the benefits derived from attending chapel may even more than repay one for missing a séance on campus."

Declining interest in the weekly assemblies plagued the college for most of the STC period. It must be acknowledged, however, that the task of planning a weekly event that would attract the majority of students was, indeed, challenging. And the faculty committee who worked at this task did so with ingenuity. In 1933, a variety of lecturers including Joseph Wood Krutch, literary critic, and Dr. Elmer Eckblaw, polar explorer, appeared on campus. In 1936, Dr. Harry C. White of the University of Kansas gave STC students their first experience with television. He brought a huge cathode tube to campus and "set a stream of electrons in movement

SMSU

Football stadium seating 5,000 completed.

Board authorizes assessment of parking fines for first time.

Missouri/Springfield

International/USA

114   *Daring to Excel: The First 100 Years of Southwest Missouri State University*

within the tube under a force of 5,000 volts. The demonstrator wrote figures and letters on a transmitter and they were reproduced by the light inside the tube," according to *The Standard* reporter. "This," said Dr. White, "is the forerunner of television. Television, when perfected, will put an end to war forever," he predicted.

Despite the fascinating demonstrations and thoughtful speakers, weekly assembly attendance waned until finally in 1945 *The Standard* editor asked, "How soon will weekly assemblies be discontinued?" The student paper complained as well about student apathy.

Of course, student apathy did not originate at STC. It has been a perennial complaint of campus newspaper editors across the country. As one reads *The Standard* throughout the 1920s

Hal Rhea was among the student grounds-keepers in the spring of 1938 who earned 30 cents an hour mowing, weeding, spading and trimming. The reel mower, staple for the time, led Rhea to feel he was "all wound up in his job."

and 1930s, there are repeated calls for more school spirit, better support of athletics contests, greater participation in student government elections and broader participation in assembly programs. The problem never disappeared.

The Movie Craze

Student apathy was, of course, but a euphemism for other developing interests. When there are two dozen student organizations, a dozen social clubs plus an array of attractions developing downtown, it became more difficult to mobilize the entire campus for an athletics event or a literary society debate as happened during the Normal School years. Back then, the campus was smaller, the organizations fewer and the sense of community more immediate.

By the time of the name change in 1919, movies had become an attraction for students. The college bought its first projector in 1919 and contracted for 10 top films including *Vanity Fair, Vicar of Wakefield, David Copperfield, The Last Days of Pompeii, Little Mother Hubbard Travel Pictures,* and *Cannibals of the South Sea Islands.* The debate over the artistic value of movies was heating up on campus, and *The Standard* suggested "the appreciation for art on the screen is a development. The inferior will be discarded only after the superior has been demonstrated."

Quite indifferent to the debate, students took to the movies at the local theaters with enthusiasm. Silent movies had been shown for years. The first talking movie to be shown in Springfield was "The Home Towners," screened at the Landers in 1928.

So popular were movies with students that they initiated a "theater-storming" tradition in the late 1920s

and early 1930s. Large groups of students would come to a theater en-mass, forcing their way in without buying the 10-cent ticket. In 1932, students stormed the Paramount Theater, provoking criticism by the local paper, which considered the practice dangerous. In 1934, students tried to crash the Electric Theater but were resisted by employees. Irritated at the theater's lack of cooperation with their "occasional fun," students boycotted the Electric. After the freshman bonfire that year, the Electric was ready to allow itself to be stormed, but no one appeared. The students stormed the Mozark instead.

Throughout the 1940s, movies continued to be a popular pastime. Movie reviews were a regular feature in *The Standard*, thanks to the pen of Jean Heyle who must have seen hundreds between 1943-45. Moreover, dancing continued to grow in popularity among students after its accidental introduction by the rhythmic Shannons in the normal school period. Social clubs

Key and Dagger social club affiliates with Sigma Tau Gamma, becoming first fraternity on campus.

United Nations conceived in a conversation between President Roosevelt and Prime Minister Winston Churchill.

Germany invades Russia and begins 900-day siege of Leningrad. More than one million die of malnutrition or starvation.

One of the biggest events of the STC year was the annual school picnic. In 1926 the event was held September 30, at Doling Park. A series of special streetcars loaded students at 8:30 a.m. at the Tea Cup Inn for the trip to the park. Activities throughout the day included class contests featuring a tug-of-war, in which the sophomores prevailed, and the famous "tilting match," which was won by the seniors.

sponsored frequent dances, and when there were no dances on campus, folks went to local night spots such as The Wagon Wheel, The Anchor, Lurvic's, and Half-a-Hill. With the building of the Shrine Mosque in 1923, another popular entertainment venue opened. Students could hear Carl "Deacon" Moore and his sensational NBC orchestra for $1.00 a couple in 1939.

As yet there was no student union or similar gathering place for students during the STC years, so students popularized local hangouts on the edge of campus. During the 1920s, Ye Old Colony Shoppe sold toilet articles, candy and school supplies, as well as served a popular lunch. By the 1930s, Varsity Inn, The Teacup Inn and the Bears Den were all popular gathering places. In 1934, the Teacup Inn became the College Inn under the management of Mrs. Angie Ordway. The remodeling process destroyed the old haunts and loafing places familiar to students, but in their place came a waxed and polished floor just right for dancing. Music was furnished by a large radio, and the College Inn became a favorite hangout. It wasn't until 1943 that a student

lounge was opened on campus. That year the gymnasium in Academic Hall was remodeled to include a dance floor. The décor was a loyal maroon and ivory, and furnishings included a nickelodeon and a record player. It was opened from 8:00 a.m. to 5:00 p.m. daily.

Annual School Picnic

One of the venerable traditions at the college was the annual school picnic, which started during the early normal school years. In those early years it was held east of Springfield at Turner's Station or Sequiota Park. Chartered trains transported students to the day-long event. Sequiota Cave was a popular feature with its long rows of commercial mushroom beds.

During the STC years, the picnic was moved to Doling Park where streetcar transportation at seven cents a person was provided by the Springfield Traction Company. Doling Park provided a host of recreational activities — boating, swimming, roller skating, dancing, hiking, horseshoes, caving, swings, teeter-totters plus student-invented games and contests of all kinds. The traditional contests drawing the most attention were between freshmen and their "mentoring" sophomores. The tug-of-war was the feature event. In 1932, to the groans of the

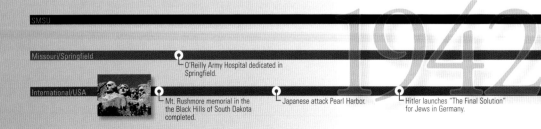

SMSU

1942

Dr. E. Stanley Jones, missionary to India, visits campus.

Missouri/Springfield

O'Reilly Army Hospital dedicated in Springfield.

International/USA

Mt. Rushmore memorial in the the Black Hills of South Dakota completed.

Japanese attack Pearl Harbor.

Hitler launches "The Final Solution" for Jews in Germany.

The annual school picnic was a day-long affair. Boating on the lake, exploring the cave, dancing and roller skating prepared appetites for the box lunches. According to the 1926 *Ozarko*, "The mess call was sounded and all sorts of amusements were speedily abandoned. Two wiggling crooked lines waited for their hand-outs." Those who finished their boxes first were free to get another until all the lunch boxes were gone.

crowd, the tug-of-war had to be called off because no one remembered to bring a rope!

Many remember the annual picnic as the highlight event of the year. A *Standard* reporter described the scene. "If you could have strolled through Doling Park between the hours of nine in the morning and five in the afternoon on the first day of October (1930), you would have beheld a scene of unrestrained fun and frivolity which is enacted but once a year. The revelers, nearly six hundred in number, were…students and faculty members of State Teachers College released for the day from the serious business of getting and giving an education."

Toward the end of the day after a sumptuous lunch had been served and competitive energies were declining, students took to the boats and gathered at the middle of the lake where they sang favorite songs to the accompaniment of ukuleles. On occasion, live orchestras provided music to dance by.

As the college enrollment grew, it became more difficult to make the annual picnic an "all school" event. With classes canceled for the day, students began to think of optional activities. Less than half of the students chose the picnic. Cost may also have been a factor. In 1932, when the

Depression pinch was being felt by many, the 40-cent ticket for the picnic was undoubtedly an issue. As ticket sales declined, the faculty voted not to hold the annual picnic after 1937. Thus the "arcadian outing," as it was called, became a memory.

New Traditions Develop

As old traditions became memories, new traditions developed capturing the spirit of the maturing institution. The physical education department had sponsored an Athletics Carnival for area high schools for a number of years. Competitive events of all kinds brought more than 1,000 high

First war blackout exercise on campus.

President Roosevelt signs Executive Order, sending Japanese Americans to internment camps for the duration of the war.

Construction of the Alaska Highway begins.

Food and gasoline first rationed in U.S.

Helicopter makes first cross-country flight.

HOW TO WORK YOUR WAY THROUGH SCHOOL

With no college-owned dormitories to house students, townsfolk rented rooms, some of which were sparingly heated according to the 1922 *Ozarko*.

school athletes to the STC campus for three days. The 1924 Carnival was special, however. For the first time, women student-athletes were invited to compete. The language of the April 3, 1924, *Standard* is instructive:

"Women's rights will be observed for the first time and they will have a place in the three day event." More than 50 schools entered the competition.

While Homecoming celebrations were held in earlier years, the

Homecoming tradition as we know it today with a play in the college theater, an alumni meeting, banquet or luncheon, football game and dance, all started in 1921. The crowning of the Homecoming Queen became a highlight in 1940. "To be Homecoming Queen," President Roy Ellis remembered, "to ride in triumph around the track and be crowned at the game, and to reign over the homecoming dance, was one of the greatest honors that could come to an SMS girl." The first Homecoming queen was Polyanna Coble, who was elected to the honor in 1940. She was followed by Lillian Darby in 1941 and Betty Scarbrough in 1942.

Students in the early 1920s experienced the traditional all-school Halloween and Valentine's Day parties, as well as class parties and the Faculty Reception. Social club dances were just beginning then with the "S" club leading the way. By 1931, social club dances had become a center-stage piece of the social calendar, particularly their spring formals. The TNTs, Panolas, KDs, Merry-go-Rounds, Dianas, and TriCs all planned elaborate formal dances with invitation lists cleared by Dean Bertha Wells who also scrutinized couples at the door.

The selection of the *Ozarko* Queen became another exciting tradition during the STC years and "one of the most sought after honors in student circles," according to President Ellis. The first *Ozarko* Queen was selected in 1922. Wilma "Snooks" Meyer, a sophomore from Springfield, received the honor. In 1926, students, in a primary election, nominated four women to be candidates for *Ozarko* Queen. The *Ozarko* editor, Charles Wyman,

When the Normal School moved to National Avenue campus in 1909, there were no college dormitories to house students. However, residential subdivisions were developing around the campus providing room and board for out-of-town students. In 1910, a faculty group built two units of dormitory housing and subsequently leased them to the college. The venture did not succeed for the investors. In the early 1920s the college purchased the buildings and refurbished them. This 1925 picture shows these earliest dormitory buildings including North Hall and Irvington Hall, which housed a total of 64 women. Social Hall provided space for student social gatherings. These facilities were closed in 1932.

confessed his inability to choose a winner from among the four beauties. "Owing to the diversified opinion as to who should be selected beauty queen" writes Mr. Wyman, "and realizing that many would be disappointed if any one person was to select the queen, the editor…took the liberty of naming all four candidates beauty queens."

Over the years the *Ozarko* Queen selection process varied. In 1933, Robert Montgomery, stage and screen star, selected four finalists from a bevy of candidate pictures sent by the *Ozarko* staff. In 1931, queen candidate photos were sent to "one of the largest fraternities at the University of Chicago." The Phi Kappi Psi men posted the pictures on the wall of the frat house and after several days announced their choice as Lila Hillyer. In 1939, 12 Queen candidates' pictures were sent to George B. Petty, an illustrator

for *Esquire Magazine*, who selected Mary Belle Mercer as the winner. James Montgomery Flagg, artist and author, who subsequently designed posters for the war effort, selected the 1938 *Ozarko* Queen. The last *Ozarko* Queen selected before the end of World War II was Peggy Pummill. In 1943, three service men — Ray Weber, a soldier from Cleveland, A.S. Michaels, a sailor from Minneapolis, and Roy Gilmore, a marine from San Diego — made the choice.

While some women were being recognized in Queen contests, others were banding together to support men in STC athletics contests. In 1928, the Bruin Booster Club (all women) was organized "to promote school spirit and loyalty and support varsity athletics." This organization quickly drew members. Booster uniforms were designed and the Bruin Boosters soon made their appearance performing marching drills

between halves of athletics contests. By 1938, the Bruin Boosters were traveling away from home to support the Bears. That year, 44 girls chartered a car on the Frisco and headed for Maryville where the Bears were playing basketball. Included in the trip was a ride on the famed Burlington Zephyr from St. Joseph to Kansas City. The Zephyr had recently been a featured exhibit at the Chicago World's Fair.

Working To Pay Expenses
Part of the student experience during the STC years was working to help pay college expenses. The college itself employed more than 100 students during the late 1920s and early 1930s. The cafeteria, bookstore, library and switchboard all had student workers. Others worked as groundskeepers, custodians or maintenance assistants. Some assisted faculty in clerical and grading tasks.

1943

Debate program curtailed for duration of war.

Last May Day Festival celebrated.

Women in the workforce increase 50 percent. *Rosie the Riveter* becomes popular tribute song.

The Pentagon completed in Arlington, Virginia.

Women's Marine Corp created.

Despite the large number who worked for the college, a far greater number worked in town. Some delivered papers, others worked in stores including Kresge's, Woolworths, The Town and Country Variety Store, Rubenstein's Men's Wear, Barth's, Ryer's Jewelry, the Gillioz Theater, J.C. Penney's, Heers and Grant's Picture Frames.

Others worked for their room and board in the homes of local families. Elizabeth Bryant Craw remembers rooming "with a prominent, wealthy Springfield family. My main job was caring for their 6-year-old son. I did some cooking and a bit of housework. I got room and board and $1.00 a week (for cafeteria meals). Twenty cents paid for a generous meal. I was included in most of the family activities and entertaining. I enjoyed it."

Most students exchanged four hours of work a day for board and room in local homes. The college pay scale was 15 cents an hour during the Normal School years, but by 1930 it was 25 cents, and by 1931 it was raised to 30 cents.

Student Housing

The abundance of local housing and the reluctance of the Legislature to invest state money in student housing kept college dormitory construction in the distant future. Two frame house dormitories built during the Normal School period by a faculty group, The Irvington Hall Dormitory Company, fell on hard times in the 1920s and were ultimately bought by the college, refurbished and re-opened in 1925. The two buildings, at 810 and 812 South Hampton, were designed to house girls — 36 in South Hall and 24 in North Hall. In 1922, a brick apart-

Dr. William E. Taylor was the college's first full-time school physician. By 1939 he was on the way to establishing a model clinic program that provided services to the entire campus. He gave physical exams to all entering freshmen and provided medical services to all athletics teams. He was the son of John Taylor, founder of Springfield Normal School and Business College in 1894.

ment house at 873 E. Madison, just west of Hampton, was leased by the college to serve as a social center and dormitory. It accommodated 15 women. A hospital unit was established on the second floor, supervised by a trained nurse. The first director of social life for the campus, Katherine Aagensen, was housed in the building as well.

Dormitory life for the women was emphatically inclusive, according to the November 13, 1924, *Standard*. Perhaps reacting to the growth of selective social clubs on campus, *The Standard* declared, "There are various classes of girls at the dormitory: new girls, old girls, cocoa drinkers, coffee drinkers; temporary spinsters, permanent spinsters; those who dance at a party, those who play games at a party; those who hike, those who do not

hike; those who have dates, those who do not have dates; freshmen, sophomores, juniors, seniors; those who have bobbed hair, those who do not have bobbed hair yet; those who are taking English I, those who are not taking English I; those who would vote for LaFollete, those who would not vote for David; those who would vote for Coolidge. Any girl can make friends at the dormitory who belongs to any of the classes named above."

Despite the inclusiveness, the dormitory enterprise went no better for the college than it did for the Irvington Hall Dormitory Company. Overhead expenses were high. After several years of precarious operation, the two frame buildings were closed down. In January of 1933, a *Standard* reporter visited the abandoned buildings and wrote:

SMSU

Leslie Irene Coger begins teaching at STC.

Air Corps Cadet Training School established on campus.

Missouri/Springfield

International/USA

Postal Zone System invented.

Battle of Kursk, greatest tank battle in history, continues for a full week.

120   *Daring to Excel: The First 100 Years of Southwest Missouri State University*

"Edgar Allen Poe could have found material for at least one spooky story in the now-deserted dormitory which stands locked and empty, but fully furnished and absolutely quiet except for many small sounds common to empty places. The house has for a number of years been the scene of youthful feminine activity, but the rooms seem now almost aghast at being disturbed by anyone entering even for inspection purposes. Down in the basement recreation room stands a grand piano with only the keyboard closed. A victrola still has on it Wrigley's Radio Drama. Appropriately enough it grinds out somewhat reluctantly, 'How do you do?' In the stack of records are such fairly recent favorites as 'Song of the Nile,' 'There ought to be a Moonlight Saving Time,' and 'Someone Stole My Gal.' An occasional venture into highbrow included a red-seal recording of 'Humoresque.' At the end of the room the red chairs and davenports are stacked. And mingled dismally with them are tables and even a mahogany tea table. On the first floor a reception room and parlor are furnished for immediate occupancy and so far the curtains have only a small accumulation of dust…. A thermometer in the hall volunteers the unnecessary information that the temperature is now 47 degrees. A few cobwebs in the corner add a dramatic touch of desolation."

Before the dormitories closed, rules were liberalized, allowing girls to be out until 10:00 p.m. instead of 7:30 p.m. Hours were 11:15 on Friday, Saturday and Sunday. Men could be entertained in the reception room with dancing, cards and other games until 10:00 p.m.

any night.

A variety of meal plans were available for students during the STC era. Some cooperative arrangements off campus served three meals a day for $4.50 a week in 1921. In 1924, the College Café on Dollison served 14 meals for $3.50. The college also operated a cafeteria in the basement of Academic Hall. In the early 1920s it served primarily lunch, but in 1928 the cafeteria was refurbished and began serving three meals a day. All food service was consolidated in the new cafeteria, and dormitory meals were discontinued. Mrs. L.B. Minard managed the cafeteria and oversaw the baking of pies and cakes and other features. During 1936, when budgets were tight, a student could purchase a lunch of spaghetti and meatballs, green beans and fresh baked apple pie for 20 cents. The cafeteria regularly served two kinds of meat, five vegetables, three salads, pudding, iced tea, coffee, ice cream and cantaloupe. It was planned as a not-for-profit enterprise and operated as such until food service was moved to the Student Union in 1951.

Health Services
What has come to be a model student health care system began modestly, if not accidentally, when one of the original eight faculty members during the normal school days was a medical doctor. Dr. David T. Kizer received his medical training at the Ohio State University, but was teaching physiology, history and agriculture at State Normal School #4 in 1906. He gave students free and informal medical advice in the early years and administered eye exams.

Only in 1916 did the *Catalog* identify Dr. Kizer as the school physician. The first actual "health office" was established in the Education Building in 1923. The room was equipped with a chair, a desk and a file cabinet. Dr. F.T. H'Doubler Sr., a local physician, worked part-time out of this office. In 1925, Dr. Ralph V. Ellis was appointed school physician and biology instructor. The health office was moved to Academic Hall and upgraded to include an examination table, sterilizer, and "all the contemporary tools of the trade." The health services were offered at no charge to students. During the five years Dr. Ellis served as college physician, William E. Taylor was enrolled as a pre-med student at STC. Taylor was a son of John Taylor, founder of Springfield Normal School and Business College in 1894. Besides taking biology classes under Dr. Ellis, Bill Taylor helped out in the health office and developed an early interest in student health work.

Taylor took his medical training at Rush Medical College, graduating in 1934. He returned to Springfield where he established a private practice as well as practicing part-time on campus in the varsity athletics office. In 1936, Taylor was appointed city physician. During that year a typhoid epidemic, 75 home birth deliveries, and a 35-pound weight loss caused him to rethink his priorities, and he accepted the STC offer to become full-time director of college health in 1937. Health service was still free to students. Under Dr. Taylor's guidance, each freshman was given a physical exam including a chest x-ray, hemoglobin and blood sugar screening, and a urinalysis test. By 1938, a nurse, Pearl

A graduation ring from the class of 1941, Southwest Missouri State Teachers College.

Pitts, was added to the health office where daily visits were increasing rapidly. By 1941, 2,264 visits were made to the health office during the fall term in addition to the 547 physicals given to freshmen and transfer students. More than 40 visits a day became the standard. Dr. Taylor initiated a college-wide tuberculosis testing program in 1941 and found that 50 percent of those taking the exam tested positive indicating TB bacilli were present in the body. Compared to the then-current national rate of 35 percent testing positive, the higher incidence in this region led to the establishment of a permanent TB screening program at the college.

In 1940, the health office was again moved, this time to the ground floor of Academic Hall where two classrooms were remodeled into office, examining rooms and an x-ray unit. State-of-the-art equipment was added to the new spaces making the health service a model for college campuses of the time.

Campus Religious Life

Religion continued to play a prominent role on campus during the STC years. Local ministers made regular appearances at student assemblies. Dr. Leake, from the South Street Christian Church, addressed students in the first assembly of the fall term in 1922. The *Standard* reported him "pleading from the depths of his soul for bigger, better, cleaner lives." Local ministers were invited to campus on Tuesdays and Thursdays for private conferences with students. Student prayer meetings were held from 1:00-1:20 p.m. on Tuesday in room 30 of Academic Hall.

The YMCA and the YWCA continued a vital Christian presence on campus. A 1928 religious census by the YWCA indicated Methodists and Baptists were the largest denominations on campus, each claiming more than 200 members. The Christian Church showed 150 members. President Hill frequently gave encouragement to the Y groups, and on at least one occasion addressed them on the subject of prayer. In 1921, President Hill led a procession of 600 students along with Mr. Meyers' STC band to the tabernacle downtown to hear the famous Christian orator, Bob Jones. President Hill and the students entered the tabernacle singing "Onward Christian Soldiers."

Other national religious leaders visited campus, including Bishop Arthur J. Moore, who spoke at the Shrine Mosque. In the early 1940s, a Religious Emphasis Week was instituted on campus with guests such as Daniel Poling, editor of the *Christian*

Ads featuring professional athletes who were in the Armed Forces during World War II appeared in *The Standard* from 1943 through 1945.

SMSU
First G.I. Bill veterans enroll.

Missouri/Springfield
Battleship Missouri christened.

International/USA
NFL legalizes coaching from the bench.

1944

122   *Daring to Excel: The First 100 Years of Southwest Missouri State University*

Herald, Dr. Willard Trueblood, Quaker leader, and Dr. E. Stanley Jones, missionary to India for 27 years.

In 1937, religion courses were introduced on campus. Dr. F.W.A. Bosch, pastor of Westminister Presbyterian Church, was hired to teach courses on the Old and New Testaments. His courses were popular and enjoyed heavy enrollments. Even though the campus understood "religion is a subject which can be touched only lightly in the regular classes" because of "establishment of religion" issues in the U.S. Constitution, it wasn't until 1950 that serious constitutional questions were raised about the *Bible* courses taught by Bosch.

Graduate Clyde Miller delivered one of the commencement addresses in 1926 on the topic "The College Student's Religion." He declared that while the college student is not altogether orthodox, he "is not irreligious…. In fact, the college student is much like the unorthodox Jesus, going beyond doctrinal quarrels, creeds, and ceremonies and focusing on the great commandment, 'Thou Shalt love thy neighbor as thyself.' His thinking was more about humanity and less of choirs, candles and programs. We claim the ideals of open-mindedness, tolerance and sympathy. We can, by following the Great Commandment, bring to realization the era of peace on earth and goodwill toward men."

The Spectre of War

While fondly hoped for, peace on earth was not to be. By the end of the 1930s, campus concern over the Depression, drought and financial woes was being replaced by anxiety over events abroad and at home. While the German jug-

gernaut was rolling across Europe, Americans were witnessing daring rallies by the far right, a dangerous fifth column threatening to subvert the United States and possibly resorting to sabotage in the event of war. Domestic fascists held daring torchlight rallies complete with swastika flags.

By mid-1940, virtually all the Allied powers had been crushed by the German war machine with the exception of the impoverished and embattled Britain. Despite the tragedy unfolding in Europe and the prospect of the European continent being wholly ruled by Germany, Americans wanted no part in the war. Throughout 1940 and 1941, the American people engaged in a passionate debate that involved issues more fundamental than at any time since the Civil War and slavery. As Philip Jenkins, Penn State historian points out, "Intervention was opposed by the America First Committee, an umbrella organization composed of conservatives in alliance with some liberals, religious leaders and pacifists…. The movement…raised critical questions…about the nature of executive power in matters of foreign policy, and the official use of propaganda and deceit to achieve what is believed to be a desirable political end."

The debate was feverish. It touched on such basic issues "as the nature of the United States, the ethnic basis of political power, and the degree to which the nation had liberated itself from a European and specifically British political orientation." In the midst of the debate, President Roosevelt was seeking ways to assist beleaguered Britain which led many to see his international policies "as reckless buccaneering cynically designed to provoke a war,

The sale of war bonds and stamps was an ongoing enterprise at STC in the 1940s. A booth was set up in the Administration Building in 1942 to sell war bonds and stamps three days a week. In 1942, STC sponsored a bond drive in the community resulting in $685,425 in pledges.

contrary to the overwhelming weight of public opinion."

As early as 1936, *The Standard* weighed in on the debate, advocating Congress pass a mandatory neutrality law saying "no financial interest, nothing save actual invasion, warrants our going to war." The editor called attention to the tragedy of World War I, "where combating nations spent $113 million a day, at a cost of $25,000 for each of the 9 million lives lost." The editor reminded his readers that 65 percent of the national budget is spent paying for old wars, 20 percent preparing for new wars, leaving only 15 percent to be spent on civil departments — law enforcement, education, public health, etc.

The momentum for non-involvement was assisted by campus visits of such notables as Admiral Richard Byrd, who told an October 1936

American Association of University Professors (AAUP) chapter organizes on campus.

Dr. Virginia Craig resigns as head of English Department.

General Omar Bradley of Moberly commands troops in Europe.

Meat rationing ends in U.S.

Allies invasion of Normandy commences. Hitler retaliates with a rain of terror on England with V-1 rockets.

Roosevelt signs *G.I. Bill of Rights*.

Nelson Potter first pitcher suspended for throwing spitballs.

Tribute to the Armed Forces

During the Christmas season in 1942, President Roy Ellis wrote a poetic tribute to the "Valiant Sons of STC" who were serving in the armed forces around the world. The tribute was printed in the 1942 *Ozarko*.

Shattered altars, crumpled spires,
Blackened chimneys,
smoldering fires,
Darkened harbors, phantom ships,
Muffled footsteps, silent lips,
Flash of gun-fire, shriek of shell,
Planes, tanks, roaring hell,
Muttered oaths, ringing cheers,
"Blood and sweat" and
burning "tears,"
Southern sun and northern light,
Coral Sea and Baffin Bight,
Jungles green and desert sand,
Guadalcanal and Samarkand,
Valleys wide and mountains high,
Belem, Bagdad, Sinai,
Dakar, Derna, Mozambique,
Frederickshap and Reykjvik,
Trimming sails on every sea,
Bering, Barents, Caribee:
Today our hearts go out to thee,
Valiant Sons of STC.

student audience, "I believe in peace — I expect to spend the rest of my life working for it." A year later, General Smedley D. Butler, former Commandant of the Marine Corps, gave a spirited address to students calling war "a racket." The only ones who profit, declared Butler "are the sellers of war materials."

About the same time, the American Legion proposed establishing an ROTC unit in Springfield Senior High School as a means of creating national readiness for war. *The Standard* editor went ballistic, declaring, "The strong taint of fascism and militarism which envelopes the ROTC behooves thinking people to be extremely skeptical as to the wisdom of establishing a local unit…as a matter of self-protection, we must therefore unequivocally vocally oppose the ROTC."

In 1939, STC campus attitudes toward war were surveyed. Sixty percent believed "war cannot be justified on any grounds." Sixt Britain. Dr. Virginia Craig spoke for the negative saying that such an initiative "would give Roosevelt virtual dictatorial power."

While campus sentiment was clearly anti-war, the growing threat of both the German and Japanese aggressions confronted everyone with sobering realities. Cornelius Vanderbilt Jr., who had interviewed a variety of European leaders prior to the outbreak of hostilities in 1939, told STC students that year, "This thing is certain. War will go on until a new ideology conquers or civilization is annihilated."

In the fall of 1940, President Ellis' greeting to students acknowledged the threat of war but encouraged them to continue their studies. He called

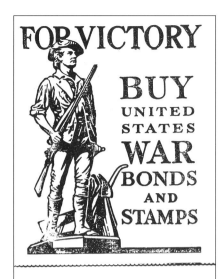

This famous Minuteman advertisement summoning citizens to buy war bonds and stamps was seen in virtually every issue of *The Standard* between 1942 and 1945.

upon them to be alert to the threats to democracy and the need to defend the nation against enemies both within and without.

While the debates and the struggle to be neutral continued, the realities were increasingly compelling. Suddenly came the electrifying news on December 7, 1941, that Pearl Harbor had been attacked. The attack crippled the Pacific fleet, but it also galvanized the American people. The debates stopped. A patriotism unseen for generations mobilized citizens, families, neighborhoods, communities, institutions and organizations into a vast war effort. Together they became, in Tom Brokaw's words, "The Greatest Generation" — men who fought on the front lines and men and women who staffed factories and offices in support of those who fought. Folks at home who planted victory gardens, collected rubber, scrap metal, and copper wire,

SMSU

45 percent of entering freshmen declare they do not plan to become teachers.

Missouri/Springfield

International/USA

Anne Frank arrested.

Army Air Force cadets in training at STC used the football field for their calisthenics in the spring of 1943. By the end of the war the field was so packed down by the activities of the cadets, Coach Blair doubted if it were suitable for football.

were part of that generation, as were families who found ways to live with meager rations of meat, canned goods and sugar, and people who went without tires, white shirts, gasoline and heating oil. The mobilization touched everyone.

On the day after war was declared, President Ellis declared "neither the college, not its faculty, nor its student body will shirk or evade any duty or opportunity in the face of the present situation. We are 100 percent in on the united effort. We will fit into the general plans and accept willingly and cheerfully our assignment, whatever it may be."

The College Mobilizes for War

Those assignments became clear pretty quickly. In February, STC was named as a Center for Civilian Morale Service, one of four in the state and one of 140 nationwide. Dr. Walter Cralle, who had just returned from a leave, was appointed as full-time director of Defense Activities. The college became a center for gathering and disseminating vital war information. Speakers from both the faculty and student body were sent throughout the district to advise citizens about the progress of the war and how they might assist in seeing it through to victory.

While studies would continue at

the college, the context of those studies had radically changed. The awareness of war, the sacrifices needed to win it, and the role of an educated citizenry in times of crisis, all punctuated classroom discussions. President Roosevelt expressed the situation well when he said, "We cannot always build the future for our youth; we can build youth for the future. That itself is a component part of national defense."

The prospects of military service for graduating seniors at STC posed a troubling question for *The Standard* editor. "Is a college education worthwhile in a world as befuddled as the one of today?" he asked. "When the

Annual Christmas "Joyland" program dropped after 33 consecutive celebrations.

Franklin Delano Roosevelt elected to a fourth term as U.S. President. Harry Truman elected Vice President.

Yalta Conference held and Spain agrees to fight the Japanese once Germany is defeated.

stormy troubles of the world subside…there will be a greater need than ever before for college trained men and women…. The wrongs of the world cannot be made right until we learn to think clearly and act wisely." So students were encouraged to hang on, complete their degrees, serve nobly and return to help shape an improved version of international life.

War Changes Curriculum

Early in 1942, course changes were occurring in response to the war situation. Dr. Donald Nicholson prepared a one hour course titled "Introduction to War Problems." The science department prepared a new course on preventive medicine and hygiene. The University of Missouri offered defense training courses on the STC campus at no charge. They were designed particularly for men and women who were not eligible for military service, but who could contribute by working in defense industries. The course included surveying, industrial accounting, cost accounting and topographical drafting. The Navy introduced the V-1 program at STC, which enabled graduates to be admitted to officer candidate school.

The college revised its scheduling system so that a high school graduate entering STC in the fall of 1942 could finish the degree in three years. Two-hundred students called "45ers" were admitted under this program. An August intersession was added to help men finish their degrees as well as help with the teacher shortage. A Civilian Pilot Training program was set up involving 240 hours of ground school training in 10 different disciplines as well as 35-45 hours of actual flying. Five faculty provided the training to over 200 students.

Concert pianist Percy Grainger, who at the time was living in

Early in 1943, STC was selected as a preliminary training school for U.S. Army Air Force cadets. In February, 500 pilot candidates arrived on campus to begin their training. Their instructors are shown with President Ellis and Dr. Walter Cralle. Left to right; Lieutenant Harold C. Anderson, Lieutenant John E. Connelly, President Ellis, Dr. Cralle, Major H.O. Fichte, Lieutenant John E. McCadden Jr., and Lieutenant James Spangler.

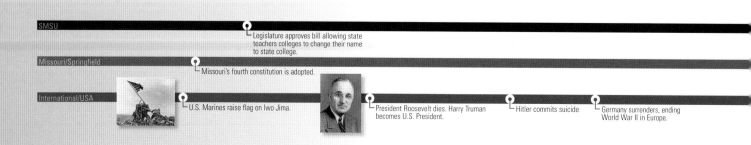

SMSU

Legislature approves bill allowing state teachers colleges to change their name to state college.

Missouri/Springfield

Missouri's fourth constitution is adopted.

International/USA

U.S. Marines raise flag on Iwo Jima.

President Roosevelt dies. Harry Truman becomes U.S. President.

Hitler commits suicide

Germany surrenders, ending World War II in Europe.

Springfield, advocated that the college "ban all enemy music as part of its war effort." This would involve German, Italian and Japanese music. *The Standard*, however, did not embrace the idea. "We hope no one will misunderstand us and accuse us of unpatriotism. It's merely that we regard any attempt to boycott those nations we are fighting as futile and childish. Such an idea is reminiscent of World War I, when schools ceased teaching the German language. It's all to the credit of STC that the teaching of German and French has been continued despite the enmity of those nations…. Why destroy the work of Bach and Goethe because of the terror of Adolph Hitler?"

A year later *The Standard* editor took occasion to respond to a speech delivered by Senator Tom Stewart on May 22, 1943, proposing to revoke the citizenship of Americans of Japanese ancestry. "I do not believe," declared the Senator, "that there stands today upon the free soil of the United States of America, one single, solitary Jap, one single solitary person with Japanese blood in his veins, but what there stands a man who will stab you in the back."

The Standard editor again took the high ground by noting that post-war reconstruction would not be helped by engendering hate between warring nations. "Our national agencies in this war have, in a sense, prevented mob-spirited hatred, as evidenced in the last war by the anti-German violence. By many means they have attempted to draw forth the nation's fighting spirit without directing it toward the common citizen in our enemy nations; they have emphasized that we are fighting a particularly powerful and despised influence rather than a hated nation-

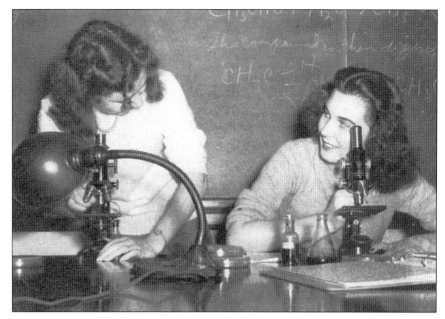

Ozarko editors in 1943 announce, "there is a future for women in biological and chemical research." Jean Treadway (left) and Irene Powell are discovering some of the revelations of the microscope in the biology lab.

ality, or nationalities. By leading us along a careful course of thought they have intended to facilitate postwar reconstruction." The STC Student's Christian Association also sent a letter to Senator Stewart protesting the prejudicial content of his speech.

Enrollments Decline

The war profoundly impacted student enrollment. Not only did it drop from a high of 1,615 in the fall of 1939 to only 517 in the fall of 1944, leaving a student body only one-third its previous size, but the ratio of women to men continued to drop until in the fall of 1944 it stood at eight to one. The impact on campus social life was palpable. *The Standard* editor, in February 1945, complained that "class spirit has reached a new low here at the college. Of all the classes, only the seniors so far have had a meeting or

planned a party. In former years, the lounge and the gym were in use several times a week by various groups. Now it is seldom that it is used at all in the evening."

The loss of men to the military was the largest source of enrollment decline, but some students dropped out of school to take jobs in defense plants around the country as well. Faculty were not spared service in the military. At least seven were called to active duty, including Richard Wilkinson, Robert Howe, John E. Webb, C.E. Koeppe, Harry Siceluff, William E. Taylor and James Cozad. Dr. Koeppe entered the army as a Lieutenant Colonel and commanded the Signal Corps school at Camp Crowder, training 30,000 corpsmen.

The STC Band normally boasted more than 70 members, but by 1943 its numbers were down to 43, and the

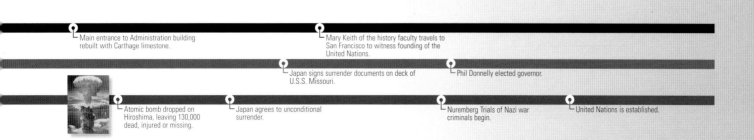

Main entrance to Administration building rebuilt with Carthage limestone.

Mary Keith of the history faculty travels to San Francisco to witness founding of the United Nations.

Japan signs surrender documents on deck of U.S.S. Missouri.

Phil Donnelly elected governor.

Atomic bomb dropped on Hiroshima, leaving 130,000 dead, injured or missing.

Japan agrees to unconditional surrender.

Nuremberg Trials of Nazi war criminals begin.

United Nations is established.

Dr. Walter O. Cralle, STC sociologist, was appointed Coordinator of War Activities for the college in 1942. He served as the conduit through which vital defense information was communicated to the college and the surrounding area. Cralle also planned campus programs that supported the war effort.

usual trips scheduled to area towns were restricted to save fuel and help the war effort. As early as 1942, football scheduling became difficult as one school after another dropped the sport to conserve resources. STC played Memphis State, Murray State and Rockhurst in 1942 to fill in for canceled games. Homecoming was dropped in 1943, but a huge bonfire was enjoyed on the 29th of October with several former students present who were home on furlough.

Campus adjustments to war occurred in both expected and unexpected places. As early as 1940, the German Club voluntarily discontinued their activities in respect for the anti-German feeling on campus and in the community. A year after the attack on Pearl Harbor, the campus rehearsed its first blackout in preparation for air raids. At 10:00 p.m. on Monday,

December 14, 1942, all the lights on campus were extinguished and stayed off until 10:20 p.m. A set of administrative rules for campus blackouts was distributed from President Ellis' office. Instructions for extinguishing incendiary bombs were issued. Students were organized for clerical and courier service in the event of attack. Faculty and students were all blood-typed in 1942 as part of preparedness measurers, and in January of that year the campus went on Daylight Saving Time to conserve power.

Service in Support of the War

Gearing up to help the war effort brought a new sense of mission to the shrinking campus. The 1943 *Ozarko* captured its essence. "Through the strife and chaos of a world at war, service has become the watchword of

college students everywhere. Students at STC pledge an alert allegiance to their school and their country and stand firm in the belief that those who serve shall be served."

The pledge was translated into action day after day, week after week. One thousand books were collected on campus in early 1942 as part of the Victory Book Campaign to provide servicemen overseas with good reading material. Students were also signing up for civilian defense duties ranging all the way from spotting enemy aircraft to preparing first aid kits. Fifty-four students took first aid courses in preparation for emergencies. The Red Cross organized a knitting initiative on campus coordinated by Mary E. Davis. Seventy-five garments were completed to keep servicemen warm during the winter months. Instruction in home nursing and nutrition were given to dozens of students who pledged to assist in Civilian Defense. Arthur Briggs volunteered to co-chair the Greene County unit of the State Council of Defense.

Even before Pearl Harbor, STC students were entertaining troops at Fort Leonard Wood. Isolated from any urban centers, the Fort welcomed STC students who volunteered to bring instrumental music, singing and humor to recruits in training.

In addition to the service activities in support of the war effort, there were campus War Bond drives and the sale of defense stamps. Giving financial support to the war effort included buying 10 cent defense stamps, pasting them in a book until $18.75 in value had accumulated and then exchanging the book for a War Bond worth $25.00 at maturity. Coach "Red" Blair, as a tribute to servicemen who lettered in

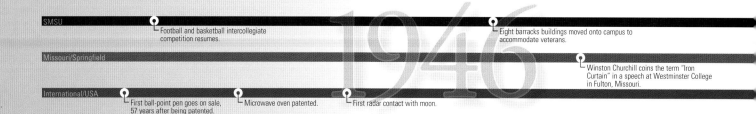

SMSU
Football and basketball intercollegiate competition resumes.

Eight barracks buildings moved onto campus to accommodate veterans.

Missouri/Springfield

Winston Churchill coins the term "Iron Curtain" in a speech at Westminster College in Fulton, Missouri.

International/USA
First ball-point pen goes on sale, 57 years after being patented.

Microwave oven patented.

First radar contact with moon.

athletics competition since he came to STC in 1938, dedicated a War Bond to each of them. The dedications were broadcast over the KGBX sportscast every other day.

Defense bonds and stamps were sold three days a week on campus in booths staffed from 9:00 a.m. to 4:00 p.m. by student volunteers. The first week's sales in February 1942 amounted to $38.35, but by 1943, the momentum had picked up, and STC sponsored a two-week effort in the community climaxed with a Bond Queen and a dance. A total of $685,425 in bond pledges was raised. The Alpha Phi Omega service fraternity secured $254,925 in pledges while Alpha Beta Zeta obtained $221,750. It was the largest amount raised in Springfield during the 4th War Loan Campaign.

Throughout the war years, *The Standard* ran ads and cartoons encouraging citizens to buy bonds through a payroll savings plan. One cartoon pictured heavyweight boxing champion Joe Lewis administering knock-out blows to every ring opponent, with the tag line "Help KO the Axis! Invest 10 percent of your income in War Bonds."

The spirit of sacrifice and service was not only seen in students' foregoing a soda at the College Inn to buy defense stamps at the booth in Academic Hall, it was also seen in the Delta Sigma Club announcing the cancellation of their Spring Formal in order to purchase war bonds. The club notified the campus that they would forgo all entertaining during the year in order to give more assistance to the war effort. The Dianas held a script dance with all the proceeds going to defense bonds. The Alpha Phi Omegas bought defense stamps, and when they had

accumulated enough to exchange the book for a bond, they gave the bonds to the Veterans of Foreign Wars post to benefit war widows. The Panolas and several other social clubs canceled their traditional Christmas parties in order to give more money to the war effort.

In 1942, the Delta Sigma Epsilon girls sponsored a script dance, held a rummage sale, and engaged in other fund-raising activities as they gathered $1,600 to purchase an ambulance as a Christmas gift to the Red Cross. They also made "utility kits" for servicemen without families. The kits included cigarettes, playing cards, gum, pencils, razors and blades. Other clubs rolled bandages, took Advanced First Aid courses from the Red Cross, knitted sweaters and taught nutrition to area families.

Early in 1942, the Secretary of the Navy sought volunteers in Missouri to build 15,000 model airplanes for military training purposes. The planes were models of current aircraft, both Allied and Axis. The smallest had a wingspan of 5.5 inches, the largest 25 inches. They were constructed to rigid standards that included details of form and marking. In addition to training spotters for civilian defense, the planes were used in training air and ground personnel in recognition, range estimation, and determination of "cones of fire." A workshop in the STC Science Building was set up where 150 of the models were constructed by STC volunteers under the direction of E.V. Thomas. After passing rigid inspection by the Navy, the planes were entered into the training program and their builders were given certificates of appreciation.

While volunteers were building model airplanes on campus, the college was also training aviators for

the war. The Army, Navy, and War Manpower Commission selected 2,812 colleges and universities across the country to become specialized training centers for the military. STC was included on the list.

Air Corps Cadets on Campus

Early in the war, STC was selected as an Air Corps Cadet Training School. In February 1943, 250 Army Air Corp cadets arrived on campus, taking over the new Health and Recreation Building, spreading their cots out on the arena floor, and turning the ladies' powder room into a barbershop. *The Standard* declared, "Teachers' College Has Gone To War!" as it announced the arrival of the cadets who would spend a month or so on campus and then be replaced by a new contingent.

In reality the Army training unit constituted "a college within a college." The contingent was commanded by five officers and taught by a dozen new faculty members. Their day began at 6:00 a.m. and ended at 10:00 p.m. Course loads were 60 percent heavier than those carried by STC students. Over a period of five months, the men had 180 class hours of physics, 80 hours of math, 60 hours of geography, English and current history, 24 hours of military courtesy, 20 hours of medical aid and 10 hours of flying instruction. It also included 140 hours of military drill, which, by the time the program was over, had packed the surface of the STC football field so hard, Coach Blair wasn't sure it could ever recover. In addition to daily classes, three hours of supervised study was scheduled. The cafeteria in Academic Hall was turned over to the military, sending students scrambling for meals for most of 1943

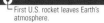
Board officially changes name to Southwest Missouri State College.

Physics major introduced.

First U.S. rocket leaves Earth's atmosphere.

Weight Watchers forms.

First bikini bathing suit displayed in Paris.

into early 1944.

With the STC women to men ratio reaching eight to one by 1943, the presence of 250 uniformed Air Force cadets on campus was an unanticipated benefit of the war. While there were strict socialization rules circumscribing the activities of service men on campus, the men did add significantly to campus morale.

The cadets were an enterprising group. In April 1943, they staged a musical variety show on campus displaying clearly professional talent. One of the cadets was an actor who had played in *Gone with the Wind* and other pictures. One was the son of a Hollywood producer. Another was a professional dancer. With limited seating available, the show was open only to cadets and their dates. The lucky STC students who got asked as dates to the show were considered a very elite group by the somewhat jealous unasked observers. In November 1943, the Air Corps unit sponsored a Thanksgiving formal dance in the field house. It was preceeded by a buffet dinner of chicken and ham. During the evening the dance floor was awash in dress uniforms and formal gowns moving to the sounds of Jerry Pettit's Orchestra. It was a memorable night for many lonely STC women.

By June 30, 1944, the sound of cadenced marching and the bright khaki uniforms disappeared from campus. After some 15 months of adding an unforgettable touch to STC life, the cadet program ended. *The Standard* editor summed up campus feeling: "Since the first khakis appeared more than a year ago, this group has become almost a necessary part of college life. These young men have filled the places

of our own, not far-away boys, as nearly as this could be done."

Shortly after the departure of the Air Corps Cadets, however, the Health and Recreation Building was pressed into military service as a rehabilitation unit for ambulatory patients from O'Reilly General Hospital. Seventy-six convalescing service men took up residence here in August 1944. Similar sized groups were rotated in and out of the building until December 1945. While the purpose was recuperation and not training, there was some instruction in physical education. Many of the men returned to limited duty in their units while others were given discharges.

The Health and Recreation Building showed considerable wear and tear as a consequence of its use by the military. Repeated scrubbing of the playing floor with soap and water had rotted it out. But the building was repaired and available for classes by March 1946. The playing floor, however, wasn't replaced until August of that year.

Academic life at the college reflected the effects of the war as well. A shortage of scientifically trained technicians to help run the war plants producing planes, tanks, guns and munitions produced a federal college loan program to help keep science majors in school. Students in engineering, physics and chemistry could obtain grants to supply full college expenses in exchange for accepting a technical position in industry upon graduation.

By the end of 1943, women were shouldering more than 20 percent of the industrial work burden supporting the war effort. Companies like Curtis-Wright were recruiting women to become engineer cadets at leading universities.

By 1943, many former students were visiting campus while on furlough from the armed forces. Student body president Bill Perkins and Emma Lou Burns welcome officer Eddie Michael who was STC student body president in 1942.

The company paid up all the school expenses and provided $10.00 a week in spending money. Beginning salaries for graduates at Curtis-Wright ranged between $135-$150 a month in 1943.

Even before the outcome of the war was certain, STC students were discussing how to manage their lives and the world in the postwar period. In June 1942, the YMCA and the defense office at the college sponsored a student forum on "Postwar Reconstruction." Students from STC, Drury, Central Bible Institute and Springfield Senior High School gathered to share ideas on political, social and economic issues facing the nation. More than 100 attended the event. Such forums were also aired over radio station KTTS. The weekly, 30-minute programs were planned by Dr. Cralle's war activities office.

As early as the fall of 1944, the college began to see harbingers of a new era. Five discharged veterans enrolled

SMSU

Enrollment increases from 728 to 1,614.

Willard Graff appointed administrative dean.

Missouri/Springfield

International/USA

Dr. Benjamin Spock's *Common Sense Book of Baby and Child Care* is published.

130   *Daring to Excel: The First 100 Years of Southwest Missouri State University*

at STC under the new G.I. Bill. The initial G.I. Bill provided one year of college plus whatever additional time the service man spent in the military. The government paid tuition, incidental and lab fees, student activity fees, medical fees, books and all supplies up to $500 a year. A $50 monthly stipend was given for personal expenses, room and board. Seventy-five dollars was allotted to married students. The educational benefits extended for seven years beyond the date of discharge.

A Rehabilitation Bill gave similar benefits to those with at least a 10 percent war-related disability. Qualified candidates were provided $85.00 for personal expenses and a full four years of college work regardless of the length of their military service. Donald Nicholson of the History Department was given oversight responsibilities for programs for veterans. In the spring of 1945, J.D. Inmon was appointed as advisement officer for veterans.

Those first five veterans returning under the G.I. Bill in the fall of 1944 witnessed a remarkable year. They saw the intensification of the war effort in Springfield, even as victory seemed in sight. Renewed efforts to save paper spread over the city. The streets were darkened at night to save precious fuel. Then on April 12, 1945, while hundreds of thousands of servicemen were still on their way overseas, the nation was numbed with the announcement of the unexpected death of President Franklin D. Roosevelt, Commander-in-Chief of the most powerful military force in the world. Missourians took pride in the stalwart Harry S. Truman, a native son, as he assumed the responsibilities of presidency. The momentum toward victory was unrelenting.

Just over three weeks after Truman assumed the Presidency, V-E (Victory-in-Europe) Day was proclaimed. On May 8, the campus and the city of Springfield spilled into the streets for an unrestrained celebration. The Nazi threat was crushed. Two months later, the first atomic bomb was successfully tested in New Mexico heralding the nuclear age, a new era in human history. Just three weeks later, on August 6, the bomb was dropped on Hiroshima, displaying a military destructive force never before witnessed on earth. On August 14, 1945, Japan surrendered unconditionally and World War II was over. But ironically, the weapon that ended the second World War would fuel a cold war that would last for decades.

Those first five veterans who enrolled in the fall of 1945 witnessed the dizzying events of that academic year. They were the first of a virtual army of veterans who would march onto the STC campus in the years following the war. Their presence would change the school — its name, its direction, its self-understanding, its rules and its policies. The challenges of change were not new to the school despite the fact that it was only 40 years old, but the scale of change looming before it was unprecedented. ■

Looking Back

A Dandelion Pageant

Long before the first building graced the SMS campus in 1909, the 38-acre tract was known for its profuse crop of dandelions. As the campus began developing, a variety of strategies to stop the annual parade of dandelions were tried but none succeeded. Finally, in 1924, someone proposed a novel solution. Dismiss classes for a day at the peak of the dandelion season and engage students in a contest of dandelion digging.

When the appointed day in May arrived, four candidates had been nominated for Dandelion Queen honors. The *Ozarko* reported that students armed themselves with "rusty Case knives, clothes pins, safety razor blades, and other modern garden instruments" as they waited for the bugle to sound starting the contest. Each dug dandelion with roots attached delivered to the scorers table represented a vote for one of the queen candidates. It's not reported how many of 1,053 students took to the field with their digging tools, nor is it reported how many dandelions were dug. But when the bugle sounded ending the contest, Ruba Willet, representing the Country Life Club, was crowned dandelion queen. The YMCA served lunch to the hungry diggers, after which a Dandelion Pageant climaxed the festive day.

The Board of Rege

The Southwest Missour

Upon the nomination of the faculty

Floyd Dow Deidik

the degree of

Bachelor of Scien

Given under the seal of the College a
State of Missouri, on this nineteenth
the year of Nineteen Hundred an

J. L. Johnston
President, Board of Regents

1946-1972

Southwest Missouri
State College

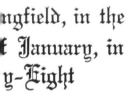

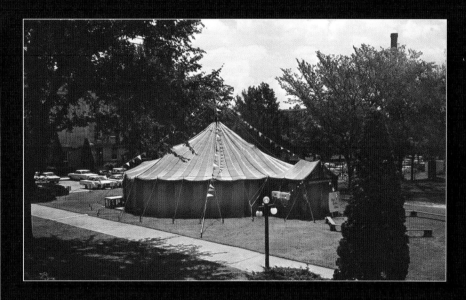

Contents

1946-1972

Southwest Missouri State College

The first on-campus housing consisted of four Army barracks moved from Alva, Oklahoma, at the end of World War II. The units were reserved for veterans and their families. Marvin Looney, pictured above, occupied a room in one of the single-veteran's units in 1947. The rent ($15 per month) included daily maid service.

The end of World War II left the United States forever changed. It emerged from the conflict as the greatest economic and military power on the planet — indeed in human history. "Superpower" entered our vocabulary to describe the American supremacy. With a nuclear monopoly and an unprecedented financial structure, the nation was poised to lead the world throughout the second half of the 20th century.

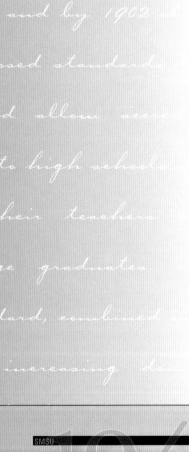

SMSU

Missouri/Springfield

International/USA

Legislature appropriates $467,500 for housing, food service and social facilities.

Edwin Herbert Land produces the Polaroid Land Camera.

The flood of veterans enrolling in the college at the end of World War II required the formation of a Veterans Committee consisting of (left to right) Dr. Harry Wise, professor of education and head of the education department and Greenwood Training School, Jim Inmon, director of veterans affairs, and Dr. Donald Nicholson, professor of history.

More than 16 million men and women had served in the military between 1941 and 1945. Nearly 300,000 had died in battle. More than 100,000 others had perished from other causes. Three million women had been involved in war production increasing the proportion of women in the workforce from 27 percent to 35 percent.

The gigantic war effort mobilized by Presidents Franklin Delano Roosevelt and Harry S. Truman had a profound effect on the entire structure of American society. A geographic shift of power from the eastern to the western U.S. was effected through war production. But the most far-reaching effect was the revolution of higher education achieved through the G.I. Bill.

Colleges and universities underwent a transformation unlike any other in their history. Millions of veterans who flooded onto their campuses to prepare for peacetime productivity created a revolution in facilities, faculties, curricula, and campus dynamics. The storm hit Southwest Missouri State Teachers College as it did every other college and university in the country.

A New Name

While many colleges and universities picked up after the war with their name and identity intact, Southwest Missouri State Teachers College (STC) began the new era with a new name that carried a distinctly new identity. As early as 1943, the Southeast Missouri State Teachers College Board of Regents in Cape Girardeau approved the idea of changing its name to Southeast Missouri State College since increasing numbers of its graduates were entering professions other than teaching. Three

other State Teachers Colleges, including Southwest, joined Southeast in petitioning the Legislature for the name change. Only Kirksville refused to endorse the idea, but the bill died in committee.

The momentum for a name change, however, did not die. In October 1944, the Southwest Missouri State Teachers Association went on record favoring a name change to Southwest Missouri State College. President Ellis had already written about the logic of a name change in the *Peabody Journal of Education.* He said the trend for teachers colleges across the nation to change their name to state colleges "merely recognizes what has already happened. The evolution from a specialized function to that of general college training has been a natural outgrowth of the demands made upon such colleges by their service areas." He went on to point out that 45 percent of the entering freshman class at STC in the fall of 1943 indicated they did not plan to teach.

Students weighed in on the issue as well. Gene Brooks, a 1944 senior said, "I find it hard to explain why I am attending a Teachers College when I am not planning to be a teacher." Bill Revis, a music major declared, "Over half of us here don't plan to teach."

But when STC led the charge in the 1945-46 General Assembly for a name change for all state teachers colleges, it was careful not to offend the State University in Columbia. The Committee of the Faculty pointed out "that this does not in any way mean this college has the ambition to become a state university. It is the wish of those connected with the college to see it grow into one of the best four-year colleges in the U.S. and to leave

Enrollment reaches 1,910.

Springfield Newspapers plant destroyed by fire.

Jackie Robinson breaks baseball's color barrier joining the Brooklyn Dodgers.

The Marshall Plan for European recovery begins.

1946-72 Southwest Missouri State College   135

graduate and final professional work to Missouri's capable university."

While the statement intending to neutralize MU's fears that a name change would create ambitious competitors apparently succeeded, it was hardly prophetic, as subsequent developments will show. But the Legislature was satisfied and passed Senate Bill No. 7 granting permission for all the State Teachers Colleges to drop "Teachers" from their names. In January 1946 President Ellis stated that "the name change should take effect around July or August depending upon the time of legislative adjournment."

The quest for a name change appeared very early on campus. In 1944, students noticed that benches facing National Avenue had "State College" inscribed on them. When President Ellis was asked why, he coyly answered, "I really don't know." But he went on to say that students should have a role in deciding on the new name. They experimented with Missouri State College, Southwest State College, and Southwest Missouri State College. A campus poll showed Southwest Missouri State College was the student choice. On May 22, 1946, the Board of Regents passed a resolution changing the name to Southwest Missouri State College "whenever the Senate bill becomes law." The Senate Bill became law in July, so on July 19, 1946, the Board officially renamed the institution Southwest Missouri State College, and SMS quickly replaced STC as the abbreviated title.

Elements of a New Era

World War II had enormous implications for the college. At the beginning of the war in Europe in 1939, the col-

lege boasted an enrollment of 1,615. In 1943 the enrollment had plummeted to 465, just one more student than was enrolled in 1911, a precipitous 71 percent loss in just four years. But the turn around was just as dramatic. By 1946 when the name change became effective, enrollment had recovered to the 1939 level with 1,614 students on campus.

Veterans enrolled by the hundreds, taking advantage of the G.I. Bill. The college accommodated the veterans by admitting them whether or not they had high school diplomas. Eighteen terminal vocational courses were added to the curriculum to serve veterans who preferred vocational training to the traditional four-year degree.

The faculty and administration recognized that the college was in a new era. Not only were veterans' needs driving institutional priorities, but constituents throughout the Southwest District showed a quickened interest in higher education. In the 1948 *Catalog*, a report by the faculty and administration outlined the philosophy, objectives and functions of the "new" institution. It affirmed the intention to address *all* the educational needs of southwest Missouri in cooperation with other institutions. While preparation of teachers would continue to be a major function, the college would emphasize liberal education and prepare students to enter professional schools. It would also offer a two-year vocational program, and increase evening courses and Saturday conferences.

The report also affirmed the importance of balanced development of the whole person through higher education, a clear move toward a liberal arts orientation. It also affirmed the intent to make the college experience contrib-

ute to character development, enabling graduates to participate constructively in a democratic society and fulfill their civic and social responsibilities.

While the college was gearing up to respond to its new mission in radically new times, it could hardly have anticipated the parade of events that would continue to reshape its character. The Cold War and the Korean Conflict would soon come, as would the Civil Rights Movement, the Vietnam War, race riots, counter-culture, free-speech and campus upheavals, all confirming that education would be sorely tested during the state college era.

Desegregation of Schools and Colleges

Missouri's 1945 Constitution declared "separate schools shall be provided for white and colored children." Consequently, most public schools and all public colleges and universities were segregated until the Supreme Court ruling in 1954 overturned the "separate but equal" principle. While the heritage of segregated schools in Missouri was deeply rooted in its southern orientation, by the 1950s the state was sufficiently diverse in outlook that school integration proceeded without the difficulties experienced in neighboring states to the south.

Since the end of the Civil War, Missouri had provided higher education for black citizens at Lincoln University in Jefferson City. As early as 1949 a bill introduced in the Missouri General Assembly would permit black citizens to enroll in Missouri state colleges and universities. In response to the bill, two petitions were circulated on the SMS campus: one in support of the bill and the other opposing it. The

SMSU

Agriculture club organizes.

Missouri/Springfield

International/USA

India wins its independence from Great Britain.

Captain Chuck Yeager breaks the sound barrier flying over 700 m.p.h.

136 *Daring to Excel: The First 100 Years of Southwest Missouri State University*

Negro Girl Admitted As Regents Declare End Of Segregation

"HOW GREEN ARE OUR PASTURES—AT SMS?"

With one Negro student accepted for admission, and at least three others planning to enroll for fall-term classes, the first effects of Friday's Board of Regents decision to abolish racial segregation are being felt, while various campus organizations are now "setting their sights" to comply with the ruling.

According to Registrar Guy Thompson, the transcript of Freda Marie Thompson, 1954 salutatorian at Lincoln High School, was received early in July before the Board of Regents made the desegregation decision. However, as soon as the ruling was passed, Thompson reported that a letter of acceptance was written to the 18-year-old girl.

Goler Collins, Jr., principal of Lincoln High reports that at least three other girls plan to apply for fall-term admission—one of them Freda Thompson's older sister, Betty. Betty, a 1953 graduate, attended Kansas City Junior College this year.

The other girls—also sisters— are both Lincoln valedictorians. Elizabeth Ann Payton, the 1954 honor students, and her sister, Rose, 1953 valedictorian, will have their high school transcripts

(Continued on PAGE FOUR)

The four Negro girls who plan to enroll in SMS next fall are pictured above, superimposed on a background of the "A" building. In the front row are Rose Payton, 1953 Lincoln High School valedictorian, and Betty Thompson, another 1953 graduate. Standing back of her sister is Lincoln's 1954 valedictorian, Elizabeth Ann Payton, and this year's salutatorian, Freda Marie Thompson, whose transcript has already been accepted by Registrar Guy Thompson.

Senior Events Highlighted By Gift Of Picture

The Southwest Standard announces the end of segregation on campus in the summer of 1954.

opposing petition was sponsored by a group calling themselves "Defenders of American Ideals." Marv Summers, responded to the group in a letter to the editor saying, "Since when has it become an American ideal to discriminate against the Negro?"

In Missouri there were several suits brought by black citizens seeking admission to state colleges and universities on the grounds that Lincoln University did not provide comparable opportunities for college work. In the fall of 1950, Mary Jean Price, a graduate of Lincoln High School in Springfield, sought admission to

SMS to get a teaching degree with an emphasis in library science. Lincoln University did not offer the requisite courses, so she based her request for admission to SMS on the basis of previous rulings that Lincoln must either offer equivalent courses and programs or the black student must be admitted to a white school. SMS sought a declaratory judgment from the Greene County Circuit court on the merits of Miss Price's petition. The Court denied her petition.

In 1953 *The Standard* couldn't resist taking a poke at its cross-town rival *Drury Mirror*, which had pub-

lished an editorial titled "Let's Keep Drury Strong." The editorial criticized those who sought admission to Drury for Negroes saying, "Considering that Missouri is still thought of as a southern state, it stands to reason that the public sentiment would be against such a move. Would south Missouri residents want to send their children to a school with this policy?" What really irked *The Standard* editor was the *Mirror* statement, "Take also into consideration that within a few years SMS will be required to admit Negroes and when this happens, there will be a great number of students who will come to

Future Teachers of America Chapter formed.

U.N. approves creation of new state of Israel in Middle East for settlement by Jews.

Howdy Doody makes his first appearance on television.

Mohandas K. Ghandi killed by a Hindu fanatic opposed to reconciliation with Muslims.

1948

1946-72 Southwest Missouri State College 137

$2 Will Cover A Date in 1949

According to a college survey in 1949, if you have two bucks in your pocket you can ask a girl on a date. Seventy-seven percent of the girls surveyed thought $2 was all you should be expected to spend. If you were lucky, you might pick a date from the 23 percent who don't expect you to spend over $1. Where to go with the date? To a dance, 60 percent of the girls said. Second choice was to a show. Some liked skating. A few were happy with a simple stroll. What to do when the date ended? More than half of the boys expected a good-night kiss. Only 31 percent of the girls thought that was a good idea.

~

Kinsey Report Available

In October 1948, the library announced that one of its newest acquisitions was the Kinsey Report, a book titled "Sexual Activity of the Human Male," by Kinsey, Pomeroy, and Martin. It was available for the asking, but put on permanent reserve to accommodate the anticipated demand.

Drury to avoid this situation."

The Standard editor seized upon the contradiction between the headline and the content of the editorial. "That's the gist of it. That's how the writer proposes to keep Drury strong — by playing on the prejudices of people, and by capitalizing on recent moves of the State Legislature to open the doors of state colleges to Negroes." In a final caustic comment, *The Standard* writer suggested that "when Negroes are finally admitted to state colleges, SMS will be willing to accept them. And those who feel they are too good to associate with Negroes can go to the campus with the forty acres of Christian atmosphere." In fairness to Drury, *The Standard* editor also pointed out that both candidates for its student body presidency supported an end to racial segregation.

When the Supreme Court issued its desegregation order on May 17, 1954, there was already considerable pressure on the SMS administration to act. A group of faculty sent a letter to President Ellis prior to the June 25, 1954, Board meeting urging him to "effect the early ending of segregation, and to award the regular Board of Regents scholarships to high-ranking Negro high-school graduates." Dr. Richard Haswell, head of the English Department, said that "it is high time for the racial barriers to be lowered." He said he "regretted not having Negroes in his class before now."

Students were also weighing in on the matter. When asked, "Are you in favor of admitting Negroes to SMS?" Jackie Cooper, a freshman, replied, "Yes, I am. I believe that there shouldn't be any race barriers in the U.S. because if we treat the Negroes like they are

underprivileged it'll make them easier prey for the communists." John Prater, a sophomore, replied, "Yes. I believe that any of them going to college will have standards as high as our own." Lolla May Patter, a junior, had a different opinion. "No, because I don't believe in mixing races in Missouri. It wouldn't work in Missouri." But Cathy Cochran, writing in the July 2, 1954, *Standard,* tells of her own prejudice developed as a southerner, and then declares, "With the elimination of segregation in our schools, we have the opportunity to make democracy work on an individual basis. We must not let this opportunity escape us."

Despite the Supreme Court ruling, SMS took no action, awaiting the Missouri Attorney General's opinion about how the ruling would affect the state's segregated schools. Thus, a July 9, 1954, *Standard* editorial complained that "A lot is being said about the segregation problem on the SMS campus nowadays, but little is really being done." It went on to point out that two state colleges had already opened their classes to Negro students. "SMS can gain nothing now by declining into an agonizing period of indecision."

The wait was not long. At the Board meeting of July 16, 1954, a resolution was passed expressing the consensus of the Board "that segregation based on racial differences shall be, and is hereby, immediately abolished upon the College Campus, and Negro students, otherwise eligible, shall be admitted to the college henceforth upon proper application made." There was no more indecision. In fact, the Board added a paragraph to the resolution indicating it was effective immediately and "the Administration of the

SMSU

Basketball Bears rated top defensive team in the nation among small colleges.

Missouri/Springfield

International/USA

College is hereby directed to take any and all necessary action to implement this decision."

By July 23, one Negro student was already accepted for admission. Freda Marie Thompson, Salutatorian of the 1954 class at Springfield's Lincoln High School, had her transcript in Registrar Guy Thompson's office before the Board's decision. On the day the decision was made, a letter of acceptance was sent to the 18-year-old girl. Goler Collins Jr., Principal of Lincoln High School, reported that three other graduates planned to apply for admission to fall classes. One was Freda Thompson's older sister, Betty, who was attending Kansas City Junior College. The other two, also sisters, were Lincoln Valedictorians. Elizabeth Ann Payton and her older sister, Rose, were reported to be preparing their transcripts for the SMS registrar.

Earlier in July, when asked if he expected many Negro students to enroll at SMS, President Ellis said, "(they) would probably prefer to attend Lincoln University in Jefferson City."

The admission of Negro students, as difficult as it was to finally achieve, was to be the least difficult of the desegregation tasks facing the college. The more difficult part was the social adjustment of the campus. Mary Lou Bilsborough, social director, stated that the "success depends upon the adjustment of the students. The facilities of the Student Center will be open to all students attending SMS." For students who were used to segregated eating establishments, hotels, movie theaters and the like, desegregation would be a clear challenge.

Bill "Dell" Dellastatious, SMS athletics director, declared that as far as athletics participation was concerned, "we'll treat 'em just like any other student. There's a place for all in a state supported school." He offered the opinion, however, that he didn't expect any Negroes on varsity teams for a while. "But anyone who proves his worth will be considered." Dellastatious expected that it was more likely to have Negro basketball players than football players, at least for a while. "Negro high schools in this area are too small to maintain football teams," he said.

So the summer of 1954 introduced a set of challenges to the college it had never faced before. The homogeneity celebrated in 1938 would be lost in the ensuing years. Instead, the campus would learn to celebrate the virtues of diversity.

The Challenges of Growth

While growth had been an institutional theme since 1907 when the college nearly doubled its 1906 enrollment, it could hardly have anticipated what would happen in its State College years. To begin with, college enrollment jumped 122 percent in a single year, from 1945 to 1946, a record that still stands. Fueling that powerful growth, of course, was the return of veterans. Many of them had been college students before entering the Armed Forces. Others went directly from high school into the service. Now, with the G.I. Bill to assist them, veterans invaded college campuses across the nation.

As early as 1944 there were already five veterans enrolled. The next year there were 25. By 1946 there were 316, including several women. Mary Davidson was the first Women's Army Corps veteran to enroll. A tall, vivacious brunette, Mary had spent 19 month overseas in England and France.

Registration for classes was an exercise in anxiety during the SMS years. After standing in line for 30 minutes, as you neared the table to pick up a class card providing you a perfect schedule for the next semester, inevitably the "keeper of the cards" would go to the board closing the section you had chosen. Of course, changing one class seems to have a domino effect and forces most if not all of your classes to change. Dr. Holt Spicer, pictured above, was occasionally the bearer of bad news.

By the fall of 1946 the veteran count had increased to 720, nearly half of the campus, and by 1948 it peaked at 734. Despite peaking in 1948, the veteran influx continued on through the 1950s so that by 1957, there were still more than 400 studying under the G.I. Bill.

The veteran constituency was transforming the campus atmosphere. Many of them felt they had helped change the 20th century from a time

Industrial Education building erected on campus from military surplus.

Apartheid formalized by white majority in South Africa.

In response to Soviet blockade of Berlin, U.S. and Great Britain begin airlift of food and fuel to West Berlin.

President Truman desegregates the Armed Forces.

of darkness to one of light. Stephen Ambrose wrote, "that was the great achievement of the generation who fought World War II on the Allied side. As of 1945 — the year in which more people were killed violently, more buildings destroyed, more homes burned than any other year in history — it was impossible to believe in human progress…. But slowly, surely, the spirit of those GIs handing out candy and helping bring democracy to their former enemies spread, and today it is the democracies — not the

totalitarians — who are on the march. Today, one again can believe in progress, as things really are getting better. This is thanks to the GIs…. That generation has done more to spread freedom — and prosperity — around the globe than any previous generation."

The college honored these men and women as heroes, and it reshaped itself to help these veterans become citizen-teachers, citizen-chemists, citizen-artists and citizen-engineers. These defenders of democracy were serious, dedicated and determined to make a successful place for themselves in civilian life. They gave shape and substance to an entire decade of the college's history.

In fact, their subsequent decline in numbers and influence was noted by *The Standard* editor in 1954 who complained that "college men were being replaced by incompetent boys." The editor grieved the passing of the post-war period of independence when college administrators seemed loath to regulate too heavily the conduct of students who had just fought a war. "These college men," said the editor, "were not tied to parental approval or disapproval, so individual misconduct could be punished only by dismissal from (and usually subsequent re-admission to) school." He cites the mid-term reports to parents, the setting up of faculty advisers, and the close supervision of social organizations' grades as evidence of the lost freedom of the veteran years.

By the early 1950s when veteran enrollments were declining, the war in Korea began to take its toll on growth. There was a loss of nearly 400 students between 1950 and 1952, but by 1953 the growth pattern returned, and at the end of the 1950s the campus population had increased by 37 percent.

This growth rate though, was modest compared to what happened in the 1960s. Veterans' children (baby boomers) began enrolling in colleges, and their numbers were immense. Several other factors contributed as well. A new attitude was developing in America that suggested higher education was a necessity for getting ahead. So a higher percentage of high school graduates began heading for college campuses. In the late 1960s, as the Vietnam war became more unpopular, students sought college enrollment as a means of deferring military service. Thus, when the decade of the 1960s ended, SMS enrollment had increased a record 194 percent. In fact, 1965 was the high-water mark of the decade with a growth of more than 1,000 students in a single year. This increase occurred at a time when the population of the Southwest District was actually less than it was in 1906 when Normal School #4 opened the fall semester with 173 students.

Mary Kilpatric wrote in *The Standard* about the burgeoning enrollment saying, "The traditional joke on campus is that there are more people on probation at SMS than there are students at Drury. She went on to observe that "in this day of (an) elaborately officed administration, it is startling to remember that the Dean of Women once had her desk situated in the girls' restroom."

Accommodating the surge of new students taxed facilities as well as faculty. The college's first attempt at enrollment management was undertaken in the fall of 1966 when only high school students graduating in the upper two-thirds of their class or ranking above the 33rd percentile on the Ohio

SMSU — Tenure system approved for faculty.

Football Bears win conference title, play in Missouri-Kansas Bowl.

Missouri/Springfield

International/USA

Psychological Test were admitted in the fall semester. Remaining applicants were admitted in the spring or summer semester. It was becoming apparent to college officials that higher education was the most common training ground for American adult life. The massification of higher education was under way.

One of the abrupt changes coming with the growth of enrollment was the ratio of women to men on the SMS campus. At the height of the World War II period, the ratio was a pitiful eight women to one man. It took only two years, however, to even the ratio, one to one. By the fall of 1946 the ratio shifted to favor men, two to one. That ratio persisted throughout the 1950s with twice as many men enrolling as women.

Another notable change was seen in the summer enrollment. For 45 years the summer enrollment had always been larger than the fall, winter or spring terms. But in 1951-52, the summer enrollment did not exceed the fall term enrollment, nor has it since that time. Part of the reason could be found in the changes occurring in teacher education. Fewer teachers were coming in the summer to add hours to their transcript to renew their certification since more and more teachers were being graduated with completed degrees.

A more subtle change was occurring in the student mix. While veterans had added maturity to the campus, international students were adding diversity. As early as 1951, 15 foreign students from 13 different countries were studying on the SMS campus. Latin America had a strong contingent of students from countries like Guatemala, Costa Rica and Chile. Five students enrolled from Bolivia, includ-

Doing "wheelies" on a parking lot forbidden to motorcycles was part of the campus scene in 1972.

ing Gaston Zapata, son of the former vice president of that country.

By the middle 1960s the numbers of international students increased to more than 25 representing Panama, Bolivia, Iran, Israel, Cuba, Borneo, Samoa, Brazil, Cyprus, Ecuador, Columbia, Trinidad, Iraq and Costa Rica. International students soon formed their own organization and joined the dozens of other campus groups planning events and contributing to campus life.

Where to Park?

With surges in enrollment came headaches with parking. As early as 1949 the college tried to cope with a deluge of cars, many driven by return-

ing veterans. The college pretended it was a problem of careless drivers, so it appointed a "traffic director" in 1949. Harry Bartlett, a former policeman and city streets commissioner, was introduced to the campus by the announcement that "thoughtless motorists who failed to observe the rules have made it necessary to take action on the situation." He was charged "to assist motorists in getting the maximum use from parking facilities on campus. This includes correct parking and observing parking regulations."

While there was some truth to the fact that "careless drivers" contributed to the parking problem, the larger truth was the college was trying to fit hundreds of cars onto a campus with only

Drury plays first basketball game in Weiser Gym, built from a surplus B-29 hangar.

Harry S. Truman defeats Thomas Dewey for the U.S. presidency.

The board game *Scrabble* marketed.

In November 1954, President Ellis and Librarian Grace Palmer review the plans of the new building going up on the east side of campus. The first free-standing library opened in 1955, but the dedication was deferred until 1956 so it could be included in the Golden Jubilee Homecoming Festivities. The library was named the Memorial Library in memory of the SMS students who had lost their lives in World War II and the Korean Conflict. A War Memorial Book with pictures and other personal information about the 91 students who lost their lives in war-time was placed in the foyer of the library. Dr. Anna Lou Blair of the Foreign Languages department assembled the book displaying the pictures on parchment pages 21 x 25 inches and bound in a Nigerian goatskin cover.

dozens of parking places. Consequently, students were often creative in their quest for a place to park.

In 1950, *The Standard* devoted an entire page to the parking issue calling on the administration to register all faculty and student vehicles, establish and enforce parking rules with warning tickets, and provide verbal scoldings by the Dean, and upon second offense,

suspend all social privileges. A week later *The Standard* reported that the administration had taken no action and the ratio of parking violators to compliant drivers was 10 to 1. It threatened to publish the names of the offenders, including faculty and staff, in the following week's paper.

Student Body President Don Payton sensed the gravity of the issue

and appointed a five-student traffic commission to deal with it. They developed a parking plan, scheduled traffic court each Thursday at 11:00 a.m. in the Board Room, and hired student patrolmen at 45 cents an hour to ticket offenders.

The real problem — lack of spaces — however, was not addressed: The campus was still locked into its original 38 acres and until additional land could be purchased to provide parking, the problem would not go away. In

SMSU
Basketball Bears win conference championship.

Missouri/Springfield

International/USA
North Atlantic Treaty Organization (NATO) founded.
Ireland becomes independent.

December 1950 *The Standard* conceded, "At the present time students can and do park their automobiles in any manner they wish…. We have talked, planned, and read about the parking conditions on this campus for some time now. We have wasted our time and accomplished nothing."

By 1951 novel solutions were being proposed. One person suggested erecting bleachers on the edge of campus where tickets could be sold to spectators to watch "the morning parking race." Profits would be used to build a parking lot. Another suggestion was to redesign cars in a wedge shape "so they could be driven between parked cars more easily." Then someone suggested that cars be built with accordian-like pleats so they could be folded up and occupy less space when they were parked.

By 1955, the parking issue had become a neighborhood problem with student vehicles jamming the residential streets surrounding the campus. The Springfield City Council considered legislation that would restrict parking to one side of the street in residential areas around the campus. President Ellis suggested that the parking problem around the college was no different than the parking problem downtown, the inference being that the city had as much responsibility in solving it as the college did.

With his characteristic flourish, President Ellis concluded by saying, "Incidentally, I know of no subject on which there is more loose thinking and more loose talking than on the matter of parking. No one has an inalienable right to a parking place within a block or so of wherever he is going, wherever that may be. The laws of Missouri do not permit the spending of public

The construction of the Olympic size swimming pool north of the field house started in 1935, but it wasn't finished until 1942. Once completed, it became a popular resort for students, faculty and staff and their families during summer months. This 1952 photo shows a water slide emptying into the shallow end of the pool.

Student Senate replaces Student Council.

Missouri Waltz becomes official state song.

Soviets end blockade of Berlin, but airlift continues.

National Basketball Association (NBA) formed.

THE LEGACY OF
ROY ELLIS

by Arthur Mallory

"Uneasy lies the heads of all who rule. His, worst of all, whose kingdom is a school."
(Holmes)

Roy Ellis used this quote when writing about the presidents of SMS in his book *Shrine of the Ozarks*. My observation of Roy Ellis, third president of the school, was that whatever the situation and however heavy the burden, Dr. Ellis exuded confidence.

From the third year of the establishment of State Normal #4 until his death in 1972, Roy Ellis was one of the best known personalities in southwest Missouri. For more than 60 years, the name Roy Ellis was associated with SMS as a student, faculty member and president.

Born in Wright County of southwest Missouri in 1888, Roy Ellis attended one of the more than 10,000 one room rural schools that dotted the Missouri countryside in those days. He graduated from Hartville High School in 1908, State Normal #4 in 1911, the University of Missouri in 1914, Harvard College in 1917 and completed his Ph.D. at Columbia University. He served as a Sergeant of Infantry in World War I. He taught in the rural schools of Missouri, and he served as elementary principal and superintendent of schools prior to joining the staff of SMS in 1917. Dr. Ellis became president of SMS on January 1, 1927, and held that position until August 31, 1961. He maintained an office on campus until his death in 1972.

A little known fact about Dr. Ellis' leadership was that he was known as the "Dean of Presidents." For 30 years Roy Ellis served as Chairman of the Presidents' Council for the institutions of higher education in Missouri.

President Ellis took a personal interest in students. One late afternoon during the winter term of 1951-52, my freshman year, I was leaving the library, which was located at the North end of the second floor hallway of the Administration Building. At the other end of the hallway President Ellis was coming toward me on his way to his office. I stopped at the large window overlooking the quadrangle pretending to be deep in academic thought. Dr. Ellis stopped, looked directly at me and said, "Mr. Mallory, have you ever heard the story of your great grandpa Zeke Bowman and Bill Starr hunting

possum late one night in the woods near my home place?" He then proceeded to tell me the story, which had a great punch line. He laughed heartily, patted me on the shoulder and went into his office. I knew President Ellis and my paternal grandmother attended school together, but I could hardly believe that he would stop and speak with me as a friend. The president knew my name!

Dr. Ellis was also sensitive and patient when dealing with his colleagues. On one occasion, I called Dr. Ellis at his office in Ellis Hall asking if I could come by for some advice. He stated that he would "be right over." I insisted that I would hop over to his office, to which he replied, "I will come to you." In five minutes Dr. Ellis appeared at my door, hat in hand, ready to discuss whatever I had in mind. I outlined the problem and suggested a couple of possible solutions. His advice was, "on an academic campus, when one contemplates surgery, he must be certain it is worth the shock to the body corporate." We did not commit surgery and things worked out. His wise advice was just right.

Roy Ellis was a visionary. He had guided the college through the Depression, World War II, the return of the veterans, major expansion of the curriculum, the construction of several buildings and the growth of the student body, which in those days was impressive.

One afternoon Dr. Ellis and I were in the lobby of McDonald Arena. I asked for some history of the Arena. Dr. Ellis discussed the controversy that arose when he wanted to build an arena with seating for 3,200 to view a basketball game and other activities. There was a hue and cry that the SMS president was asking for astronomical sums of money to build something the students and people of Springfield would never fill. The president went forward with his plans, and all of southwest Missouri has profited from the vision and intestinal fortitude of a farsighted college president.

Roy Ellis has left a notable legacy. He was not only a strong leader with a firm hand but he was also a friend to every student — and — he knew us by name. ❀

funds to transport elementary school children unless they live more than a half mile from school…. It is assumed that a first or second grader can walk a half mile to school without suffering any ill effects. We adults feel it a hardship to walk three or four blocks."

In November 1955, President Ellis and Board of Regents President Cockrill commissioned the Board to work out a plan for more parking spaces. By February 1956, space for 65 cars was leased from University Heights Baptist Church on the north side of Grand. Again, the administration urged students to "park within the lines, don't block the entry or park on the grass."

By the end of the 1950s a new tack was taken to discourage cars on campus. Studies were cited that demonstrated an association between student car ownership and poor grades. *The Standard* quoted a *Popular Mechanics* article that claimed the expense of keeping a car on campus was nearly equivalent to keeping another student on campus.

The negative publicity did little to discourage cars. Neighborhood streets filled up to the dismay of local residents. A lot west of Greenwood from Harrison to Monroe was opened as well as one on the corner of Grand and Dollison. First and Calvary Church opened its parking lot for students during the day. Realizing the affair with the automobile was not to end soon, the administration set in place parking regulations in the fall of 1967. Faculty and staff were required to buy parking permits for $12 a semester. Students could park free (wherever they could find a legal place). Fines were also initiated. The first offense cost $1, and the second offense $2. All subsequent

offenses cost $3. With parking fees and fines, a whole new era of parking problems and solutions opened extending throughout the 20th and into the 21st century.

Registration was second only to parking on the student complaint list. As the campus grew larger and the machinery for processing student enrollment remained paper, pencils and persons, it became "Excedrin headache number 1621," according to *The Standard*. Despite a number of innovations to speed up the process, students spent hours standing in lines to register for classes, sometimes arriving at the registration table only to learn that the class they sought was closed. There were other hazards as well. An unnamed sophomore in the fall of 1952 had his entire schedule planned when just before time to enroll, he discovered he had been using a winter term class schedule. Some took registration problems as an occasion for entrepreneurship. Two enterprising fellows set up a registration booth for freshman girls. Some girls played along with the gag, and the guys had obtained 44 names before the booth was shut down.

A Revolution in Housing
When State Normal School #4 moved onto its new campus in January 1909, its 400 students had no school residence hall. Housing students had become a cottage industry for enterprising Springfieldians who began developing subdivisions adjacent to the school. Family residences were built with extra rooms which could be rented out to students. In 1914, local entrepreneurs built a three-story facility just west of campus that could house 72 students. The two upper floors were for boys,

and the first floor had a cafeteria and rooms for girls. The facility ultimately became the Lombard Apartments.

In 1910 a group of faculty built two residences which it leased to the school for use as women's residence halls. The arrangement worked well for a while, but as the area around the school built up, patronage declined and the buildings fell into disrepair.

In 1925, the college bought the residences and refurbished them for dormitory use. It also leased a brick building on Madison. The combination of facilities could accommodate 60 girls. But by 1932 the condition of the buildings had deteriorated to the point that they were closed, and ultimately sold.

The college by that time was enrolling more than 1,300 students and housing was becoming a problem. Since the Legislature was reluctant to make capital outlays for college housing, the college decided to rely on local citizens providing "approved housing." Each year the college posted a list of approved housing for students. Owners of the residences approved for college housing were required to enforce college policies on those renting rooms from them. The residences were also subject to periodic college inspections.

The system seemed to work reasonably well. Guidelines developed in 1941 for rooming houses located off campus reflected the college's perception that it held parental responsibility for students enrolled in its classes and living in its approved housing system. Among the regulations to be enforced by those renting rooms included the provision that the house must rent exclusively to male or female residents. All misconduct must be reported to the dean. All illness must be reported to the

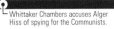
Interfraternity Council established.

Whittaker Chambers accuses Alger
Hiss of spying for the Communists.

People's Republic of China proclaimed
under the leadership of Mao Tse-tung.

college physician. Bed linens were to be changed once a week, and hot water must be available at least three times a week for bathing. The homeowner also was forbidden to evict anyone without notifying the dean of women. In 1952, the homeowner was made responsible for seeing that students were in their rooms "at a reasonable hour," understood to be 10:30 p.m. on weeknights.

The first "on campus" housing was created in 1946. Eight barracks were moved to campus from Alva, Oklahoma, to provide housing for veterans. Two of the barracks were used for single men, while four were adapted for married student housing. Two were located just north of the pool, two just east and two just west. They even featured maid service, much like a motel. By 1950 enrollment was moving toward 2,000, but the amount of available approved housing around campus was not increasing, so the college decided to start its own residential system on campus. A single story res-

idence hall accommodating 64 women was built just north of the Science Building. It would eventually be named Wells Hall in honor of the first Dean of Women.

By 1959 with enrollment reaching almost 3,000, the Women's Residence Hall was expanded to add space for 214 more students. About the same time, the first men's residence hall was built accommodating 230 men. In 1967 it was named Freudenberger Hall in honor of Norman Freudenberger, teacher of Latin and head of the Foreign Language Department for many years.

With the expansion of on-campus housing, policies were put in place requiring all freshman under 21 to live in the dorms unless they were living at home or with relatives. Exceptions were made for those who had served at least two years in the Armed Forces or who had to work elsewhere for their room and board. In 1960 with additional dormitory space available, the policy was revised to require *all* unmarried women and men under 21 to live in campus housing unless they were and living at home or with relatives.

New regulations reflecting issues of the 1960s were added to the "approved housing" guidelines in 1963. All students under 25 years of age were required to live with parents or in approved housing, which was exclusively for men or for women. A place other than the bedroom had to be provided for women to receive their guests.

As growing enrollments pushed the limits of campus space in the 1960s, the parking ticket became an institution at SMS.

The college would no longer certify as approved housing "any arrangement that permits more than one unmarried student to a bed." And finally, there was to be no gambling, drinking, or entertaining members of the opposite sex in their rooms, and women's hours were set at 11:00 p.m. Sunday through Thursday, and 12:30 a.m. Friday and Saturday. Clearly, the homeowner's task of regulating student behavior in rented rooms was becoming formidable.

Campus housing was expanded again in 1965 with an additional story added to both the Men's and Women's Residence Halls bringing the total spaces to 1,338. Campus enrollment had risen to 5,153 in 1965, so another round of residence hall construction was planned for completion in 1966. A high-rise design featuring six-person suites, a unique innovation for the time, was sited just north of the Men's Residence Hall. The men's tower would be eight stories high accommodating

Mary Adams Woods, professor of English, started her college career at SMS in 1913 and served for 45 years. She succeeded Dr. Virginia Craig as head of the English Department in 1946. Professor Woods was a 1912 Drury graduate, completed a master's degree at the University of Missouri in 1918 and did further graduate work at Columbia University. Her distinguished service to the college was recognized in 1970 when a high rise women's residence hall was named Woods House.

SMSU

Mary Lou Billsborough becomes director of social activities.

Boxing introduced as intercollegiate sport.

Missouri/Springfield

Forrest Smith elected governor.

International/USA

1950

343 men while the women's tower would be nine stories high accommodating 392 women. Joining the two towers would be a ground floor food service unit. The following year, the high rise was named Blair-Shannon Residence Hall in honor of long-time faculty members Dr. Anna Lou Blair of the Foreign Language Department and James Shannon of the History Department.

In the meantime, sororities and fraternities were purchasing homes around the college to provide residences for their members. College rules allowed students in good standing who had completed 31 or more hours to reside in Greek houses.

Pressure for housing accommodations had multiple sources. The growing student body was the most obvious. But a deteriorating neighborhood around the college in the 1960s and 1970s exacerbated the problem. Many of the houses built in the area were now more than 50 years old. Their original owners who rented rooms to college students were gone. Increasingly the homes were turned into rental properties, many of which enjoyed little maintenance. So the inventory of "approved housing" shrank, and the neighborhoods in which they were available showed increasing signs of neglect.

By the fall of 1970, 2,092 students were living in campus housing, and the enrollment projections for 1971 suggested at least a 10 percent increase. So the college went to the drawing boards yet another time and developed plans for an additional women's residence hall to be available in 1971. Following the pattern of Blair-Shannon, the new hall would be a high-rise to accommodate 392 women. It was named Woods

The south side of the Student Center as it appeared in 1961.

House in honor of Mary Adams Woods, a long-time professor of English.

So the State College years opened a new dimension of college experience — life in residence halls. In the short span of 20 years, the college undertook eight building projects resulting in five completed residence halls accommodating more than 2,500 men and women. The residence hall dimension of campus life was a unique source of enrichment for students and a substantial challenge to the administration. It forever changed the dynamics of campus life.

Campus Expansion
The growing enrollments literally changed the campus landscape. Throughout the Normal School years

the only building on campus was Academic Hall built in 1909 at a cost of $267,393. The State Teachers College period saw the addition of three new facilities — the Education, Science and Health and Physical Education Buildings. The athletics field, the stadium and the swimming pool also were added during those years. The total outlay for all those improvements was $1,260,521.

Over the next 25 years, though, $27,970,675 would be spent on new campus buildings. The new construction pushed the campus well beyond the original 38 acres deeded to the state in 1905 and initiated a naming process that would last for more than a quarter century.

Silly Putty® invented.

Swimming Curtailed by the Drought

June swimmers were disappointed in 1954 when the SMS pool was not yet filled. The College was waiting for a pump to bring the needed million gallons from a well rather than tax the city water supply, which was at a critically low level due to a drought that began in 1952. In only five of the 27 months between January 1952, and June 1954, did precipitation reach average levels. Precipitation in 1953 was the lowest in the 73 years since records were kept. College officials declared, "We have a moral obligation not to use city water. Local businessmen are losing money daily because of the water restrictions. They would resent the 'waste' of city water to fill the SMS pool." Eventually the pump arrived, the well was tapped and the pool filled.

The start of the State College period saw the portico on Academic Hall deteriorate to the point that large chunks of concrete were falling onto the plaza in front of the building. As an economical move in 1909, the portico and pillars were constructed of concrete rather than the durable Phoenix limestone with which the rest of the building was faced. So at the same time the name of the institution was being changed to SMS, Academic Hall was getting new pillars, a new portico and a new name — the Administration Building, signifying its changing function.

The veteran enrollments in the late 1940s helped make it necessary to add the first new building during the SMS period. In 1948, the Federal Works Agency dismantled a metal building that housed an ordnance repair depot at Camp Crowder near Neosho, Missouri, and shipped it to SMS to provide educational facilities for veterans. The building

was reconstructed on Grand Street at the Administration Building U-drive and was named the Industrial Arts Building. In addition to the industrial arts program, which included courses in general shop, electricity, wood and metals, it also housed the Agriculture Department. Over the years, the building has gone through multiple changes and remodeling and currently houses part of the Art Department.

In 1949 money became available from the state to assist in building either a student center or a men's dorm. President Ellis put the choice to a vote of the students, and the verdict was overwhelmingly in favor of a student center. For almost 50 years, there had been no central gathering place for students between classes or to house recreational functions of various student organizations. Students had created hangouts at cafés and lunch rooms on the edge of campus and experimented with makeshift lounges in the Administration Building. The longing felt for years was for a place students could call their own.

The $554,477 contract for the Student Center was let in July 1949, with completion scheduled for the fall of 1950. Material shortages plagued the proj-

Finding your way through library resources during the SMS period meant having a working knowledge of the card catalog. Those large oak cases with the long drawers are gone now, replaced by computer monitors displaying a feast of information.

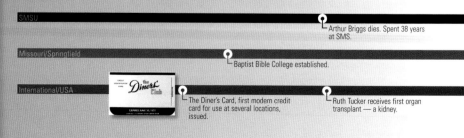

SMSU
Arthur Briggs dies. Spent 38 years at SMS.

Missouri/Springfield
Baptist Bible College established.

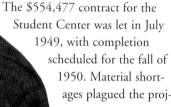
International/USA
The Diner's Card, first modern credit card for use at several locations, issued.
Ruth Tucker receives first organ transplant — a kidney.

The addition of the Student Center building in 1951 at a cost of $700,214 fulfilled a long-deferred dream of campus citizens. This 1954 picture shows students enjoying the first air-conditioned building on campus.

ect, and it wasn't finished until 1951. It was the first air-conditioned building on campus and featured a large, modern cafeteria. Sited just north of the Administration Building and east of the new Women's Residence Hall, it was to become a hub of campus activity.

The home economics program received a boost in 1952 when a residence at 807 S. Kings was purchased for $21,000 and transformed into a Home Economics Practice House. The Practice House allowed students in the vocational home economics program to complete their practice course on campus. Prior to this time, students had to transfer to the University of Missouri or some other campus with a practice facility to complete their practicum.

Aware of the space problems developing on the original 38 acres at SMS, representatives of General Services Administration notified President Ellis

late in 1952 that O'Reilly General Hospital on North Glenstone was closing and the property would be available to local interests. The Board of Regents considered moving the SMS athletics program to the O'Reilly campus, but decided against the idea because of the distance from the main campus. Ultimately, the property became the site for Evangel College.

The Travails of the Library

A college library was to be built in 1941 just north of the Administration Building as a Works Progress Administration project. Plans were approved, materials were on the ground, and some excavation had been completed when word come from Washington that the project was canceled due to the war.

However, in 1947 the library project was revived again. This time the

Andrew McDonald becomes head of Physical Education Department.

U.S. enters the Korean War.

In 1928 the old Greenwood School Building was remodeled to provide a home for the itinerant Music Department, which in earlier years had occupied various nooks and crannies in the Administration Building. When the classroom building was built in 1959, the "bungalow" was demolished to provide room for the new structure. Music took temporary refuge in some barracks buildings north of the Health and Recreation Building until the Fine Arts Building was completed in 1959 where it found a permanent home.

Legislature appropriated funds to construct it. But Governor Donnelly vetoed the bill saying it was "bad business policy to embark on such a large project when labor and material costs are so high." Again in 1948, the Legislature appropriated $900,000 to construct a library. But again Governor Donnelly's pen vetoed the line item along with $5 million in other capital projects while approving a $2 million state office building.

So when the 1953 capital appropriations bill was passed by the Legislature, everyone held their breath until Governor Donnelly had signed it allocating $600,000 for the SMS Library. Construction started in 1954 with opening scheduled for 1955. Sited directly east of the Science Building on National Avenue, the building was faced with Carthage limestone to match its sister buildings across the expanding campus.

Charles Wright, a former student,

wrote a poem on the occasion of the building's dedication, which captured the changing campus scene. Titled "Wistful Retrospect," the poem begins:

the rustic scene
of former years
is now no more…
we've watched
the wooded grounds
retreat…
with each new structure
now complete
to shape
the college there
to be an instrument
more perfect
where
oncoming minds
will be tutored
in the arts of life
efficaciously…
so that perhaps
the problems
of our universe

will pass
on into history
with fewer
great catastrophes
and
in good time.

The college had asked for $1 million for the library, but received only $600,000 from the Legislature, so when the building was opened in 1955, the second and third stories were incomplete. Despite being unfinished, the dedication of the library at Homecoming in 1955 was a particularly moving event. It was dedicated to the memory of former SMS students who lost their lives in World War II and the Korean Conflict. On Friday, November 4, 1955, a hushed crowd of several hundred listened while the Reverend Shrum Burton read the names of those 90 former students. A memorial book with a picture and a brief history of each of the deceased was placed in what was now called the SMS Memorial Library.

Just a month after the dedication of the Memorial Library, the college joined other state institutions in requesting funds for new facilities from a $75 million state bond issue to provide capital improvements. The SMS request was for $5 million to build a fine arts building, a classroom building and two dormitories. By April 1956, the sound of construction equipment could be heard from every corner of the campus. On the southeast side, a fine arts building was taking shape. On the southwest side a classroom building and a practical arts building were emerging. On the northwest side, a men's dorm was going up, and on the northeast side two new wings were being added to the Women's Residence Hall. By 1957-58,

SMSU
First unit of women's residence hall opens.

Missouri/Springfield

International/USA

1951

150   *Daring to Excel: The First 100 Years of Southwest Missouri State University*

First built in 1951, the Student Center became the Student Union in 1965 when a $1.9 million expansion more than doubled the floor space to more than 88,000 square feet. The Union housed food service, recreational and social activities and offices for student organizations and student affairs staff.

six separate buildings were under construction, an unprecedented event in campus history.

On May 1, 1958, a new kind of history was made on campus when four cornerstones were laid on the same day. President Ellis said no such event had been recorded previously by the Masonic Order. By the end of the day historic documents had been sealed in the cornerstones of the men's dorm, the women's dorm, the classroom building and the Fine Arts Building.

The Fine Arts Building was the most elaborate of the new structures. The three-story building was designed to house the Music and Art Departments. The Art Department would have three classrooms for drawing, painting, weaving, crafts, ceramics,

jewelry and sculpture, including an outside terrace area for larger works. The Music Department would have a recital hall seating 300 equipped with a pipe organ, band, orchestra and choral rooms, 11 teaching rooms, 40 practice rooms, a library and a listening room. The $875,000 structure opened a whole new era for the arts on campus.

Naming the Buildings

With an array of new buildings rising on campus, the question of naming them arose. *The Standard* polled students about naming the buildings after prominent faculty and staff members. President Ellis had already voiced his opposition to the idea indicating there would never be enough buildings to recognize all the worthy workers who

had helped shape the institution. But students thought otherwise. Barbara Andrews felt it would be a good idea since "it would give the campus a more dignified air."

Apparently the Board felt differently as well. In the December 1958 Board meeting, President Ellis, for the first time in his 32 years as President, was asked to leave the Board Room. When William Cockrill invited him back into the room, it was to be notified that the Board had voted unanimously to name the new Fine Arts Building in honor of President Roy Ellis. Board President Cockrill explained that "the Board has taken this action after due consideration and feels this token of recognition and appreciation for valuable services and accomplishments by Dr. Ellis is proper and justified under the circumstances." It would be almost a decade before any other buildings would be named in honor of campus leaders, but the tradition had started.

The first of the six new buildings to be completed was the Practical Arts Building, which became home to the Agriculture Department in December 1958. By the fall of 1959 all six buildings were opened "replete with shining floors, spotless windows, new furniture and a rainbow of colorful walls and draperies." A historic, six-building dedication ceremony was held at Homecoming, October 23, 1959. Governor Blair and Dr. Lawrence G. Derthick, U.S. Commissioner of Education, led the list of dignitaries who joined the campus in celebrating its signal achievement.

Just a year after the dedication of Ellis Hall, a Casavant pipe organ was installed in the recital hall at a cost of $40,000. Catherine Crozier, a rising

Dining area and Grand Lounge completed in Student Union.

First telecast of atomic explosion.

22nd amendment ratified — limiting President to two terms.

Julius and Ethel Rosenberg are sentenced to death for espionage.

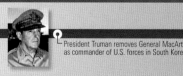
President Truman removes General MacArthur as commander of U.S. forces in South Korea.

star in the music world, was selected to play the dedication concert.

As the college entered the 1960s the pace of growth quickened. Enrollment grew from 3,046 in 1960 to 8,680 in 1970. Sensing itself as a major player in higher education in the state, in 1961 the college purchased a two-story, colonial style home at 736 South National Avenue, and designated it as the president's residence.

Four years later, a $1.9 million addition was completed on the Student Center. The cafeteria was tripled in size. The Bookstore was moved to the Center. Elevators, rooms for student committees and a music area were added. Recreational facilities were also added including bowling alleys and billiard tables. It was only about 50 years earlier that the Normal School *Bulletin* warned students against frequenting

billiard parlors. But now, Dr. David C. Scott, executive officer in charge of business affairs, had the courage to declare, "Pool is a respectable game. We want the girls to play, too." Such a statement would have been unthinkable to W.T. Carrington in 1907.

The two-story wing and basement addition to the Student Center was the first of several additions over the years. At the completion of the 1965 expansion, which doubled its floor space, the building was also renamed the Student Union.

Construction equipment was a perpetual presence on campus throughout the 1960s. "Pardon our Progress" signs could well have been posted from Grand Street to Harrison Street alerting students and visitors to the demands of growth. From 1966 to 1972, when another name change

ushered in a new era, 12 major building projects were completed. A new dedicated facility for Greenwood Lab School on East Harrison, as well as a two-tower high rise residence hall, were finished in 1966. The next year, additions were made to the Memorial Library; the Education Building was renovated, and remodeling was started on the Administration Building. In 1968 a communication arts building was completed on the corner of Grand and National. In 1970 a new residence for the president was purchased at 1515 S. Fairway. In 1971, four building projects were completed, including Morris Hall, which would house the Bookstore and the Health Clinic, a new science classroom building, and a new high-rise women's residence hall. The state college era ended in 1972 with the completion of the third expansion of the Student Union.

A Naming Tradition Established

Nearly $28 million had been invested in campus expansion in the 26 years of the State College period. Eighteen new buildings stood as reminders of the growth. With the vast expansion of facilities, generic functional names would no longer suffice to identify campus buildings. Besides, the whole first generation of faculty and staff who laid the foundations were retiring or passing on, and the value of their work was clearly evident, so the naming began.

It was fitting that the first name to be honored was that of Roy Ellis. When he assumed the presidency of the college in 1926, only three buildings graced the 38 acres. By 1958 when the Fine Arts Building was completed and was designated the Roy Ellis Hall of Fine Arts, the campus was still only 38

On January 9, 1972, President Emeritus Roy Ellis died. Wreaths celebrating his memory and accomplishments were placed at the entrance of the Fine Arts Building, Ellis Hall, the first SMS building to be named for a faculty or staff member. President Meyer described him as "an intelligent, eloquent and efficient college administrator." Commenting on his work style, Meyer said, "He was well organized, rational, and patient; although, he had many opportunities in his job to be otherwise."

SMSU

Missouri/Springfield

International/USA

Bears win conference championships in golf, track and football (shared with Kirksville).

Color television introduced to viewers in the U.S.

Universal Automatic Computer (UNIVAC) installed at U.S. Bureau of Census, becoming the first commercially successful computer.

152 *Daring to Excel: The First 100 Years of Southwest Missouri State University*

Completed in 1967 at a cost of $1.7 million, the classroom building designed to house the Departments of Speech and Theatre, English, and Foreign Languages was named Craig Hall in honor of the legendary English professor and debate coach, Dr. Virginia Craig, who retired in 1952 after completing 46 years of service to the college.

acres, but it had a dozen buildings, nine of which were built under the direction of President Ellis.

It was nearly a decade — 1967 — before the Regents again proceeded with namings. At the July 14, 1967, meeting they authorized the naming of the new high-rise residence hall Blair-Shannon House, in memory of the recently deceased Foreign Languages Department Head Anna Lou Blair and in honor of retired History Department Head James Shannon. Blair and Shannon had both served the college for more than 40 years. The regents also named the new Communication Arts building Craig Hall in honor of Dr. Virginia Craig, another faculty member who served four decades as the venerable debate

coach and former head of the English Department. The first men's residence hall constructed was also named in honor of a four-decade veteran teacher, Norman Freudenberger, former head of the Foreign Languages Department. The first campus dormitory named Women's Residence Hall in 1950 was renamed Wells House in memory of the first Dean of Women, Bertha Wells, who served from 1918-55.

The Regents concluded the 1967 naming spree by renaming the Education Building, Hill Hall, in honor of the institution's second president, Dr. Clyde Milton Hill. Hill actually designed the building during his tenure as president. The Board also renamed The Classroom Building built in 1959 Pummill Hall in recognition of Dr.

Lawrence E. Pummill, a 38-year faculty veteran who headed the Mathematics Department for 17 years.

On December 18, 1970, five more facilities were named by the Board in honor of former faculty members. The Agriculture Building (1958) was named Karls Hall for Dr. Glenn E. Karls, head of the department for more than 20 years. The Health and Recreation Building (1940) was renamed McDonald Arena in honor of Andrew J. McDonald, legendary coach, department head and professor of health and physical education for 40 years. The Stadium was renamed Briggs Stadium for Arthur W. Briggs, a 38-year faculty veteran of the physical education faculty and coach of every intercollegiate sport played during his tenure. The new science building under construction in 1970 was christened Temple Hall in honor of Allen P. Temple, head of the Science Department for almost 40 years, and the new women's residence hall rising on the north side of campus was named Woods Hall in honor of Mary Adams Woods, a professor of English for 45 years and head of the department from 1946-50.

The final naming during the State College years was the re-naming of the Administration Building to Carrington Hall in honor of W.T. Carrington, the first president of the institution who served from 1906 to 1918. The only academic buildings not to carry names honoring institutional pioneers were the Science Building built in 1927 and the newly named Memorial Library built in 1955. Both, however, would be named during the university era.

As the campus expanded and new buildings became dedicated to specific disciplines such as agriculture, math-

Fall enrollment (1,681) exceeds summer enrollment for first time.

Thomas Hennings elected senator from Missouri.

 I Love Lucy debuts.

1946-72 Southwest Missouri State College   153

ematics, music or the sciences, the student experience was significantly altered. One student remembered the "old days" when upon "entering the Science Building the student was greeted by an odiferous conglomeration encountered nowhere else within the confines of the campus. One's nostrils were assailed by the smell of formaldehyde from the biology lab, sulfur from the chemistry lab and supper from the home economics lab." By the end of

the state college period, those memories were fading.

Getting Used to a Student Center
The completion of the Student Center on campus in 1951 also altered the student experience. During an open house in July of that year, a crowd of 2,500 community citizens crowded into the new facility and enjoyed its air-conditioned comfort. No other building on campus was mechanically

cooled. Allan Stallcup, a student, celebrated the event declaring, "We are finally in the Student Center building and it is indeed a wonderful place. The Lounge is a good place to loaf and relax, the snack bar furnishes cokes, ice cream, and the cafeteria serves very good meals…. I just wonder why they couldn't have a public phone here, too." He went on to say, "the games in the Lounge answer a long-standing need for something to do besides sit around in your leisure time, but the practice of charging a deposit on a Ping-Pong™ ball seems rather strange to me." Betty Nelson found it strange that there not a public phone or a pencil sharpener in the Student Center.

Despite the minor glitches in equipping the building, students enthusiastically celebrated the opening of the Student Center on June 28, 1951, with a mixer and dancing in the ballroom to the music of Eddie Ball's Band. Every floor featured events including a Ping-Pong™ tournament, chess games, checker games, bridge and pinochle.

A Student Center Commission was soon appointed to work with Mary Lou Bilsborough to formulate policy and plan events for the building. Charles Strickland, Marion Crenshaw and Don Day were selected to represent the student body on the first Commission. They found themselves struggling with weighty questions. Should the Center stay open during campuswide assembly hours? Would the Greek organizations dominate the use of the facilities? What kind of recreation program should be organized? Should girls be allowed to wear shorts in the building? (Yes, except not in the grand lounge, ballroom or cafeteria.) How do we keep the furniture intact? (At the end of the first year,

The first building to be named for a staff member on campus was started in 1956 and functionally named the Fine Arts Building. As the building was nearing completion, the Board of Regents, in their November 1958 meeting, declared an "executive session" to the surprise of President Ellis who was asked to leave the room. After a brief wait in the hall, Dr. Ellis was summoned to return into the presence of the Board and was told the Fine Arts Building had been named the Roy Ellis Hall of Fine Arts. Knowing the reluctance of the Board to name buildings for people because the number of deserving people far exceeded the number of buildings, President Ellis found himself quite speechless. Upon his retirement from the presidency of the college in 1961, Dr. Ellis was assigned an office in the new building where he took his time-worn desk and chair, and proceeded, among other things, to write the first history of the institution, *Shrine of the Ozarks: A History of Southwest Missouri State College, 1905-1965.*

SMSU

Missouri/Springfield

International/USA

1952

Basketball Bears win NAIA National Tournament in Kansas City.

Dick Button performs first triple jump in figure skating competition.

154   *Daring to Excel: The First 100 Years of Southwest Missouri State University*

The snack bar in the Student Center was popular with both students and faculty in 1956. Professors Robert Hardie of the economics faculty and Oreen Ruedi of the sociology faculty take time out for an afternoon cup of coffee.

one-third of the furniture was so badly damaged it could not be used without repairs.) Why can't music be played in the building, especially in the cafeteria and the snack bar? Why does the snack bar close at 8:30 p.m.? Why can't the grand lounge be open to students? Not all these questions were answered happily for students. They sensed that there were "parents" in the Student Center just like at home. And when they encountered this parental attitude even more strongly in the residence halls, they wondered what being away at college really meant.

By 1958, the Student Center had become an integral part of the campus, a "'home away from home' for SMS students and profs" according to *The Standard*. The writer explored a host of metaphors to describe the role of the new facility on campus, finally ending the celebratory essay saying, "It is the hub of the wheel, the hole in the donut, the core of the apple and the nucleus of the cell. It is the heartbeat of the campus itself." Whatever else it was, the Student Center provided a new center of gravity on campus, anchoring things *on* rather than *off* the campus.

Urban Renewal and Campus Growth

By the middle 1960s the need for more campus land was acute. As late as 1963, the entire campus was squeezed onto the original 38 acres deeded to the state in 1905. Space was needed for Greenwood Lab School, for parking and for additional campus buildings. A master plan developed that year envisioned the campus reaching from National to Dollison, and from Grand to Harrison. But by 1964, only eight additional acres had been acquired, and that was to be used for Greenwood.

With financial assistance from the Legislature, by 1967 the college had been able to acquire 14 additional acres bringing the total to approximately 60 acres. But a new master plan envisioning 12,000 students within 10 years called for additional land.

The college found an ally in

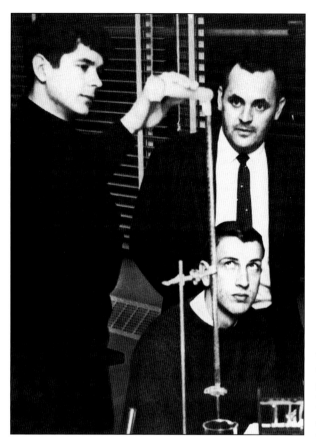

In the fall of 1963, SMS took its first step toward becoming a campus system. The SMS Residence Center in West Plains opened, offering classes in late afternoon and evening in the West Plains High School. Science instructor Loren Denny guides a laboratory experiment at the Center in 1963.

the Springfield Land Clearance for Redevelopment Authority. The city was anxious to clear or rehabilitate deteriorating areas in the city and one such area was north and west of the college. Residential neighborhoods around the college that once housed college students with local families had increasingly become rental neighborhoods with deteriorating structures. The urban renewal plan of the city targeted about 82 acres adjacent to the campus for clearance through assistance given by the federal Housing and Urban Development office. The land could then be purchased by the state at a relatively low cost and be redeveloped as part of the campus.

The confluence of interests on the part of the city of Springfield and the

college proved very beneficial. The new master plan of the college anticipated the need for about 15 square blocks of land north and west of the campus, an area the Springfield Redevelopment Authority was anxious to clear and renew.

In the late years of the state college period and the early years of the state university period, the dilemma of campus space found solution in the need to renew neighborhoods around the college. That is not to suggest that everyone appreciated the college's appetite for land. The discussions about boundaries and directions of growth would continue into the late years of the 20th century.

Expansion into South Central Missouri: West Plains Residence Center

The quickening appetite for higher education in the 1960s produced an unanticipated campus expansion for SMS to West Plains, some 110 miles southeast from Springfield. The West

Plains Campus was not only unanticipated by SMS officials, it became a curious and troubling anomaly to state officials who struggled to understand the state's obligation to support it.

The story begins in February 1963, when newly elected State Representative Granville Vaughn from Howell County was touring state institutions with other newly elected legislators. While visiting the Kansas City area, Vaughn noted the Residence Center in Independence established by Central Missouri State College in Warrensburg. "It occurred to me immediately that we should try to get something like that going in our region. I couldn't help but think of all the boys and girls in our area who would benefit from it."

South central Missouri was included in the service region of SMS, but was more than 100 miles away from the Springfield Campus. Moreover, the area was one of the poorest in the state with family incomes averaging less than $3,000 per year. The prospects of paying board and room on top of semester fees in Springfield was dim at best for most families. The assessed valuation of $62 million in the six-county area was also too low to form the base for a tax-funded junior college.

Higher education, however, was always understood as the most promising solution to the poverty problems of the area. As early as 1890, a two-story brick building financed by public subscription was built to house West Plains College where courses in business, education and stenography were taught. Enrolling more than 100 students, the college was accredited by the North Central Association and had an articulation agreement with the University

SMSU

└ Dr. Virginia Craig retires after 46 years of service. Holt Spicer hired as debate coach.

Missouri/Springfield

└ Lily-Tulip plant opens starting industrial growth in Springfield.

└ Bull Shoals dam completed.

└ O'Reilly Army hospital in Springfield closes.

International/USA

└ Last tram ride in London

└ Eva Peron dies.

└ Mickey Mantle hits his first grand-slammer.

└ Puerto Rico becomes a U.S. commonwealth.

156   *Daring to Excel: The First 100 Years of Southwest Missouri State University*

of Missouri that allowed the transfer of the first two years of work. For 23 years the college served the West Plains area. In 1913 the building was purchased by the Sisters of Charity who opened a Catholic Academy for girls.

The "can do" attitude of the community reasserted itself in 1947 when the West Plains First Baptist Church voted to open its educational facility for the use of a Baptist Junior College. That venture continued into the middle 1950s.

Those early efforts and the continuing need to provide accessible higher education to the south central area led Representative Vaughn in the spring of 1963 to introduce House Bill 665 that would permit "the Board of Regents of Southwest Missouri State College to provide a two-year program of higher education in Howell County

and to confer degrees that are usually granted by junior colleges."

Late that spring when a hearing on the bill was held, 60 residents of Howell, Oregon and Ozark Counties showed up to support the 12 witnesses who were scheduled to testify before the House Committee. Among the witnesses was Dr. Leland Traywick, the newly appointed president of SMS, who read a statement from the Board declaring it "was willing and ready to support and to do whatever the Legislature a sks." Jerry Schroder, president of the West Plains R-VII School Board testified that the Board would give its full support to the enterprise and placed "a million dollar plant" at the disposal of the college for the fall semester.

But Representative Sponslor from Texas County added crippling amendments to Vaughn's bill, which doomed it when a voice vote was taken on June 6, 1963. Before the vote was ever taken, Vaughn, seeing the bill's likely defeat, changed tactics and began talking with Governor John Dalton about establishing a Residence Center in West Plains. The Governor seemed to favor the idea.

By July 1963, the SMS Board of Regents was between a rock and a hard place. The West Plains community was enthusiastic and substantive in its support for the Residence Center. The School Board had voted to provide classroom space, office space and conference rooms for the college within its own buildings. It also pledged the use of its science rooms, facilities and equipment and would pay utilities and maintenance costs for the space used. The Board also pledged to provide a librarian from 4:00 p.m. to 10:00 p.m. through-

St. John's Hospital opened in a new facility.

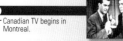

Canadian TV begins in Montreal.

First *American Bandstand* broadcast.

Shoes were "in" in 1954. The *Ozarko* that year built the yearbook around the variety of shoes to be found walking on campus.

out the week as well as give $5,000 for the purchase of additional reference books. The school nurse would be accessible to college students and the school food service department would provide an evening meal.

With that astonishing support from the community but the refusal of the Legislature to approve the establishment of a Residence Center, the SMS Board of Regents was in a difficult position. They were reluctant to offend the Legislature by establishing the Center without its blessing lest the college be punished when appropriation time rolled around again. But local support for the enterprise had built such momentum, the Board was also reluctant to offend the community. It had essentially provided a way the Center could open without an appropriation from the state. As the Board debated the decision in a conference call on July 3, 1963, Regent James Hawkins of

Buffalo told the Board that Governor Dalton was threatening to cut the budget of SMS $200,000 for the coming year if the Board did not open classes in West Plains. The Board decided to give tentative approval to the opening of classes in West Plains in the fall, contingent upon the approval of such action by the six state senators from the southern part of Missouri.

Late in the afternoon of July 3, President Traywick placed a call to Frank Martin II, editor and publisher of the *West Plains Daily Quill,* who had been holding the presses awaiting word from Springfield. "We will be there with classes in fall," declared President Traywick, and Frank Martin spread the word with banner headlines.

In what was clearly the shortest organizational period (71 days) in the annals of higher education, the West Plains Residence Center of SMS opened in West Plains on September 6,

1963. In those 71 days, a campus was organized with a director (Dr. William Bedford), three full-time faculty (Earl J. Nelson, Roy Mayfield and Loren Denny), four adjunct faculty (Neil Pamperien, Christine Bartholet, Owen Worsted and Bette Renfrow), and 45 credit hours of courses scheduled in chemistry, biology, English, history, math, political science and physical education. In those 71 days 115 students were admitted, 111 of whom enrolled. Their average age was 24. Their class day started at 4:00 p.m. when the public school building was vacated, and ended at 10:00 p.m. Most of the students held jobs, working an average of 34 hours a week. Ninety-two of the 111 took a full 15 hour load. They were "can-do students" reflecting the "can-do" attitude of their supportive community.

Dr. Duane Meyer, dean of faculty at SMS at the time, remembers the

Finding answers to dark mysteries has fascinated people throughout the ages. In the middle 1960s the Ouija board was the preferred medium for the Tri Sigs as they took turns asking questions. Some even claimed to get answers!

SMSU — Army ROTC unit established on campus.

Missouri/Springfield

International/USA — General Dwight D. Eisenhower elected President of the U.S. — First hydrogen bomb detonated in a test by the U.S. at Eniwetok Atoll in the Marshall Islands. — Dewey Watson and Francis Crick discover the "double helix" structure of DNA — the basis of heredity.

1953

By the beginning of the 1970s, miniskirts were popular among women on campus, and presumably among the men as well.

breakneck pace required to get things organized to open classes. During those 71 days, in the midst of hiring teachers, preparing a class schedule, finding a director, equipping offices and recruiting students, Representative Vaughn called Dean Meyer and said, "The first thing you have to do is hire a basketball coach." "Well, Granville," replied Dean Meyer, "first we've got to teach English and history and foreign languages and science and math." Basketball had to wait a while.

West Plains was "rather proud of itself for getting a Residence Center and for finding a director with a Ph.D.," recalls Dr. Connie O'Neal, long-time faculty member at West Plains. Indeed, Dr. William Bedford, who was serving as dean at Christian College in Columbia when offered the job at West Plains, was a "find." He had a Ph.D. in American Civilization, as well as both a bachelor's and master's degree in music, enabling him to teach history, American literature, English

and music. Early on he realized it was the community's commitment and cooperation that made the Residence Center possible. "I kept a rather low profile," he said, while spreading the good word to civic groups and clubs in Alton, Ava, Thayer, Willow Springs, Mountain Grove and Mountain View.

"At last the long-held dream for higher education in the heart of the Ozarks had been fulfilled," observed Dr. O'Neal. "But the struggle for survival during the next decade would prove to be even more difficult than the Center's inception." The problem was funding. Without state assistance, the Residence Center had to charge fees in excess of fees on the Springfield campus. Despite continuing efforts on the part of the Board and legislators from the area, the state provided no assistance to the Center throughout the first 10 years.

Dr. George Gleason, president of the Faculty Senate at SMS at the time, characterized the West Plains operation as "long on hope and short on funding." It was hope that kept it alive. As each year closed, the question of re-opening in the fall had to be faced. In 1966, as the uncertainties mounted, Dr. Bedford requested a transfer to the English Department in Springfield, a more stable environment where he could complete his tenure before retirement. Marvin Green, a native to the area, was appointed dean, replacing Bedford.

Green had been a precocious student graduating from high school at age 15, receiving a bachelor's degree at age 18 and a master's before his 20th birthday. He was an experienced administrator, having served as assistant principal at Central High School in

Springfield, principal at Buffalo, superintendent at Bakersfield and counselor at Cabool. Dean Green mirrored the commitment and tenacity of the community in seeing that the noble experiment did not fail. The West Plains media became unofficial recruiters for the campus. The *Quill* carried campus news through the region. Radio station KWPM featured campus personalities and events on a regular basis.

With each challenge, Dean Green, the faculty and the community collaborated to find a solution. The Chamber of Commerce quickly opened a student employment program enabling many students to find work while they studied. The first 35 students applying to the program included a qualified helicopter pilot, a baker, a chauffeur and a stock control clerk.

As early as August 1963, the West Plains Rotary Club announced plans to award a $200 scholarship funding a full year's tuition. Others joined quickly. The First National Bank offered three scholarships. Reed-Harlin Wholesale firm and the Lions Club sponsored scholarships. By the end of the first year, more than $1,800 in scholarship aid had been put together by local businesses. In 1964, the Chamber of Commerce started a scholarship fund drive netting a total of $8,900, and by the time Dean Green assumed the leadership of the campus, a total of 176 scholarships had been granted by the Chamber.

By 1971, contributions to the Scholarship Fund exceeded $50,000. "There were times when the future of the college looked dim," remembers Dean Green, "but the people of this area always have a way of coming through."

Basketball Bears win second consecutive NAIA national title.

KTTS-TV is first Springfield television station to go on the air.

Council-manager form of government approved by Springfield voters.

First west-to-east jet transatlantic non-stop flight is completed.

Edmund Hillary and Tenzing Norgay summit Mt. Everest.

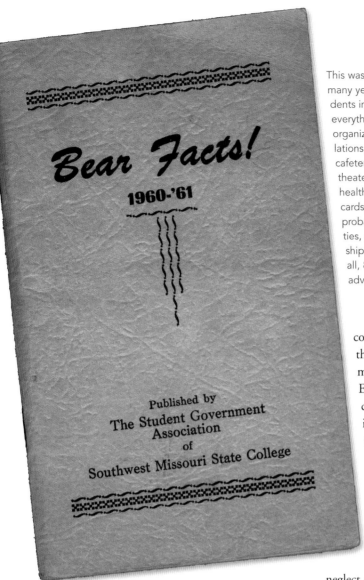

This was the "bible" for many years providing students information about everything from campus organizations, parking regulations, attendance policies, cafeteria service, college theater, course numbers, health services, grade cards, to lost and found, probation, religious activities, school yells, scholarships and study tips — in all, 88 pages of helpful advice.

In 1970 the Residence Center received its first dedicated space. The West Plains School Board made available a portion of a vacated industrial arts building. The Rotary Club volunteered to finance the $7,000 remodeling costs. So in the fall of 1970, 286 students were greeted by a new semi-separate college building with the name of their school "SMS College Residence Center" over the door. By 1970 the curriculum offerings totaled 118 hours each semester compared with 48 the first year. More than 110 courses were offered through 15 departments. Elementary Education majors could earn 90 hours in West Plains toward their B.S. in Education degree. In 1971, the campus produced its first yearbook, *Reflections.* Roots appeared to be going down. The neglect of the Legislature was counter-acted by the commitment of the community to make the brave venture succeed.

The Student Experience
Patterns of Student Conduct

A series of historic events radically reshaped campus life during the State College period. The presence of substantial numbers of World War II veterans in the late 1940s gave the student body an unprecedented maturity that challenged the long-standing parental attitude of college administrators. Students were no longer just girls and boys. There were men and women in their midst who had matured in combat and were not about to be constrained by what seemed to be niggling rules for campus adolescents.

Prior to World War II, a clearly defined *en loco parentis* philosophy prevailed on campus leaving the college free to assert control over virtually everything from lockers, student financial credit and police reports to smoking, alcohol use and behavior at dances. Applying such rules to recent high school graduates was one thing. Trying to apply them to war-seasoned adults created understandable problems.

The problems were not peculiar to SMS. The *United Methodist Student Association Newspaper* in 1949 observed that the toughest problem on campus was the control of student social life, particularly student drinking. *The Southwest Standard* reflected on problems with alcohol occurring at the 1946 Homecoming dance. Apparently some among both alumni and students were imbibing. In an editorial comment reflecting the perception of a substantial change occurring, *The Standard* declared, "Regardless of how shocking the statement may seem to some persons, there is a minority on our campus who would like to have drinking sanctioned at social functions."

Sanctioned or not, drinking became a growing problem into the 1950s. Occasional brawls on or near campus were alcohol-related. Dean Wells's "breathalyzer" test at college dances in the 1930s was becoming a quaint memory as alcohol became increasingly associated with college life. In 1965, upon observing alcohol being consumed at a football game, President Arthur Mallory admonished students

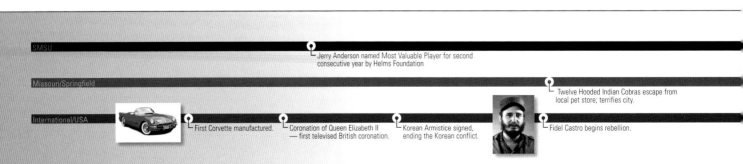

SMSU

Jerry Anderson named Most Valuable Player for second consecutive year by Helms Foundation

Missouri/Springfield

Twelve Hooded Indian Cobras escape from local pet store; terrifies city.

International/USA

First Corvette manufactured.

Coronation of Queen Elizabeth II — first televised British coronation.

Korean Armistice signed, ending the Korean conflict.

Fidel Castro begins rebellion.

The first residence hall built by the college was opened in 1950 and named simply Women's Residence Hall. While intending to continue the tradition of Carthage limestone on campus buildings, the college turned to light colored brick instead when the price of limestone was judged excessive. Several additional wings and stories have been added to the building including a complete refurbishing in 2001.

"to honor the law and practice good sportsmanship" at athletics contests. He encouraged students to be "good personal examples and active in their disapproval" of drinking.

Smoking joined the list of contested policies. As early at 1945, agitation to remove the no-smoking policy was heard. In the spring of 1946, the faculty and Student Council voted to allow smoking on the grounds, but not in buildings. President Ellis, who said, "I have been in favor of smoking for some time," prefaced the new policy with the request to "please toss stubs in receptacles. Should no receptacles be at hand, please scatter the tobacco and roll the paper wrapper into a small pellet. Tobacco will stain walks or stone plazas." It wasn't until 1964 that universities began banning smoking on campus for reasons of health, the University of

Kansas being the first. It removed all cigarette vending machines from campus buildings in that year.

As new trends in student behavior developed, President Ellis maintained his unflagging optimism about the SMS community. "The quality of our present day student," he observed in 1956, "is up to any I've seen in the past. A barrel our size has a few rotten apples in it, but not many. Our students are not angels, but they are serious minded, moral folk."

The 1950s were, of course, a relative quiet period before the storm of the 1960s and 1970s when campus protests and moral challenges to the status quo were ubiquitous across the country. The 1950s were seen as a period in which social conformity was the prevailing norm. The *Ozarko* called students of that period, "the White Duck

generation." Shoes were the markers of conformity. Faculty were described as "leaders in Loafers." Along with wearing White Bucks and suede jackets, students played Canasta, read *Gone with the Wind,* preferred Gregory Peck and June Allyson, drank Coke, listened to *Dragnet,* danced on dates, admired Doris Day and Patti Page, liked to hear "Tenderly, Why Don't You Believe Me?" and bought tickets to *Guys and Dolls.*

They also believed that lots of cheating was going on with exams. At least 55 percent admitted to being part of the problem. More than 70 percent said they were in favor of initiating an honor system, but only one in four said they would be willing to report fellow students they knew to be cheating.

The pressure for change extended to the unwritten campus dress code. Some venturesome students in the

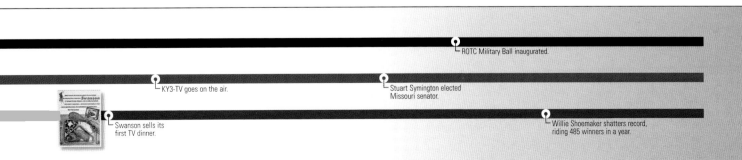

ROTC Military Ball inaugurated.

KY3-TV goes on the air.

Stuart Symington elected Missouri senator.

Swanson sells its first TV dinner.

Willie Shoemaker shatters record, riding 485 winners in a year.

early 1960s experimented with wearing shorts and jeans and slacks to class bringing an official declaration from Dean Bane's office that "shorts are not to be worn to classes by men or women students. Women are not to wear blue jeans, slimjims or slacks to classes."

As early as 1949, a more liberated spirit was detected in cartoons published in *The Standard*. One showed a guy looking at a curvaceous blonde who was saying, "I got an E in math. The professor said I had all the answers in round numbers." By 1952, *The Standard* was complaining about the slowness with which SMS was following campus trends elsewhere.

"But where we really missed the boat and demonstrated our provincialism," opined the editor, "was in not taking part in the nationwide panty raids this spring. Every important university in the country had a panty raid, but SMS males were too slow to recognize the popular form of extra-curricular entertainment and thus lost another notch in the battle for higher education."

By 1966, however, the men were apparently on course, for four of them were put on probation for raiding a women's residence hall. By 1971, SMS women were wanting some of the action. Sitting in the hallway during panty raids didn't seem like much fun, so the women of Woods starting throwing articles of clothing out of their windows nine stories up to the cheers of the men below.

In 1967, Lewd Nude made his appearance streaking across campus sans clothing. By December of that year students were wondering if the Nude Dude or Naked Runner would be discouraged by the cold weather. Detective Jared from the Police Department said no arrest could be made without a description. No one came forth with a clear ID, and streaking continued off and on into the early 1970s.

The campus mood had changed from the compliant 1950s. In the Sixties, the forms of deviance manufactured in collegian's minds were virtually limitless. Their expression tested the limits of college patience and policy. The late 1950s introduced the Elvis craze and with it a host of dances that challenged conventional standards. Church groups began discussing whether rock-and-roll music was morally degrading while campus parties increasingly favored the jitterbug.

Then there was the challenge of feminism and the liberation of the fairer sex. In 1963 *The Standard* reported that Donna Hamilton was expressing her freedom by smoking a petite pipe in the snack bar. "It all started when men gave women the right to vote…in 1920," complained the editor. There was also the issue of obscenity. O.K. Armstrong and his Springfield Citizens Council for Decency sought to ban the showing of the movie *Who's Afraid of Virginia Wolff?* in October 1966. That led to a series of discussions in campus religious groups about the meaning of obscenity and the meaning of censorship. Things were heating up.

By the late 1960s, the challenges to conventionality went quite beyond the trivial. Drug use had become a symbol of emancipation and a defiance of authority for many youth. Surveys on the SMS campus in the late 1960s showed drug use was growing among students and faculty as well. More than one-third of the students surveyed claimed they had used drugs. Thirty-six percent said they had smoked marijuana, while more than 13 percent of the faculty surveyed had used it. The survey also asked whether students thought marijuana was worse than alcohol. Seventy-two percent said "No." When asked if they were given the opportunity to experiment with marijuana, would they do so, more than half of the respondents said they would.

Where once the standards of acceptable conduct were so clear that the *Normal School Bulletin* gave only two sentences to the whole subject, by the 1960s a college without a disciplinary code was a college in jeopardy. The consensus on norms had dissolved. Shared moral principles had increasing-

SMSU
Basketball Bears win third consecutive conference championship.

Missouri/Springfield

International/USA
Groundbreaking begins on Disneyland.
Northland Shopping Mall of Detroit becomes first modern mall.

ly been replaced by a "why not?" attitude. So for the first time in its history, Southwest Missouri State College began to put together a disciplinary code that defined acceptable and unacceptable conduct.

Dean Homer Long remembers the process. "When I arrived on campus in June 1956, I don't recall that a written code of conduct was in existence. Administrative Dean James Bane handled men's disciplinary matters and Dean of Women Jessie Burrell handled women's matters." They apparently operated out of a generalized code of expectations present in the minds of administrators. Sanctions were administered informally. There was no definition of student judicial rights.

In 1957, at the suggestion of Long and others, a student handbook called *Bear Facts!* was published by the Student Government Association. While it gave students advice on coping with college challenges, it contained no formal disciplinary code. In the 1966 *Bear Facts!* a brief outline of student personnel policies was included. The 1967-68 version of *Bear Facts!* stated that "A code of conduct for SMS students containing detailed rules and regulations is being prepared for publication as a separate pamphlet."

By 1969-70, two developments led to the appointment of attorney John Ashcroft as coordinator of judicial affairs. Campus demonstrations and disturbances had accelerated, and students were becoming increasingly rights-conscious. Ashcroft, who had been teaching business courses, was given the task of outlining campus judicial procedures that would assure the enforcement of rules while protecting due process.

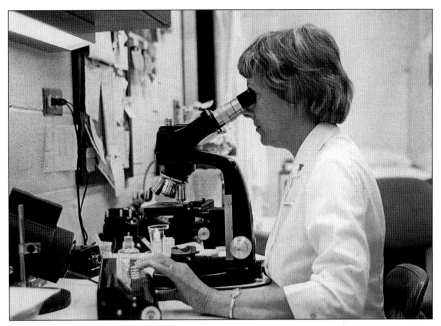

Med Tech Pat Hunt pores over a microscope in the Health Center in the 1960s. Health services to students on the SMS campus have distinguished the institution for more than 75 years.

The development of a code emerged slowly. In 1969-70, *Bear Facts!* contained sections on student personnel policies, grievance procedures, judicial procedure, as well as a President's Statement on openness in relationships. A year later a section on "Expectations and Remedial Action" was added. Finally, in the 1971-72 *Bear Facts!* a section titled "Disciplinary Code" is found, outlining for the first time in the institution's history, a detailed code of conduct expected of students. The struggle to develop stated norms of conduct appropriate to the student community had begun. The struggle would continue into the 21st century.

The Residence Hall Experience

Even before the deluge of student activism in the 1960s and the formation of disciplinary codes in the 1970s, the college was experimenting with a new dynamic in the 1950s. It built its first on-campus residence hall in 1950. While veterans had been temporarily housed in eight barracks moved onto campus in 1946, the first residence hall for traditional students was opened to 64 girls in the fall of 1950. Previous to this time, coping with students' living habits was generally delegated to families in the community who rented rooms or exchanged room and board for student work.

Among the earliest conflicts between students and dormitory officials involved a serenade given by men outside the women's residence hall in 1954. A girl living in the dorm had just become "pinned" to a member of a local fraternity, and his buddies were there to sing her praises. But Dean Bane did not look upon the nocturnal concert with much pleasure and posted a notice saying, "The campus does

"Promenaders," SMS square dance club, appears on Ted Mack's Amateur Hour.

RCA manufactures first color TV set.

Supreme Court rejects "separate but equal" doctrine and orders desegregation of public schools.

While the biology lab in 1948 was a serious learning environment, students could not resist the temptation to "decorate" the skeleton.

not frown on true love. As a matter of fact, the Kewpie doll might be a more representative symbol for our college students than the bear." Nonetheless, the dean declared, "Pinning and other romantic visits to the dormitory after hours must be cleared with the housemother at least three days in advance." The missive ended with a stern warning. "If you love your girl, and want to remain on campus with her, better plan your pinning with the housemother concerned." *The Standard* reported the warning by suggesting that "true love may become official on the SMS campus only with the

consent of the housemother."

While the strictures on romance at the SMS campus may seem harsh, the students here could only be thankful they were not enrolled on the Southeast Missouri State campus. According to the February 8, 1963, *Standard*, kissing on campus had just been banned at Cape Girardeau. "It has been decreed by Dr. Mark Scully, president…that our fellow brethren…can no longer participate in osculation on the Cape Girardeau campus. The decree was the result of objections by 'adult visitors' to overt displays of affection." The report

ended by saying, "It is very regretful that the good night kiss has been replaced by the good night handshake. We wonder what Ann Landers would think of this."

The "parenting" policy of the college struggled (not too successfully) to link dormitory life to academic success. In the fall of 1959 when midterm grades showed that 217 of the 226 men in the dorm had average grades below passing, a new policy was invoked. It required that all men in the dorm must be in their rooms or the study lounge after 8:00 p.m., and that they must be engaged in academic preparation. A similar policy was invoked in the girls' dorm in 1960. Any girl with an M- (C-) in as much as one class received a notice from Dean Burrell that she was required to be in her room from 8:30 to 11:00 p.m. Monday through Thursday. Neither visitors nor phone calls could be received during these hours, and roommates must leave the room to visit with friends.

The consensus developed quickly that you can dictate where students will be at given hours, but you cannot dictate that they will be learning. *The Standard* reported that while some students felt the restrictions were helping them, most "resent the administration's dictatorial tendencies. (They) should realize that coercion of students will accomplish nothing."

Regulations multiplied as college administrators struggled to make dormitory life civil by their standards. There were rules about noise, about visitation, about hours, about chaining doors — all the things that are typical of student behavior massed in a dorm. Similar rules were imposed on students living in "college approved" hous-

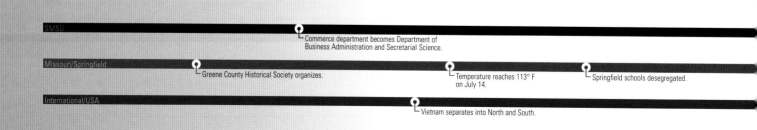

SMSU

Commerce department becomes Department of Business Administration and Secretarial Science.

Missouri/Springfield

Greene County Historical Society organizes.

Temperature reaches 113° F on July 14.

Springfield schools desegregated.

International/USA

Vietnam separates into North and South.

ing in town, except in that case, the homeowner was responsible for their enforcement. Obviously, even though "college approved" households had to "agree to enforce the regulations relative to rooming places for college students," that enforcement varied from home to home. As early as 1955, *The Standard* editor wondered if "townspeople should be used as disciplinary agents, report misconduct and enforce dormitory hours." Furthermore "should responsible students over 21, many of them veterans, be subjected to any regulations covering their private lives?"

Housing headaches multiplied with the growth of the student body and the growth of housing rules. One student in 1966 suggested that since Springfield had become a metropolis, college rules and policies must conform to metropolitan life. "It could have been, a decade ago when Springfield was just a cowpath in the midwest, that the current 11:00 p.m. and 12:30 a.m. curfews were absolutely and correctly taken," he offered. But being situated now in a cosmopolitan community, the college should give up its small town ways. That opinion notwithstanding, Gary Rocca, that same year, was placed on probation for the remainder of the year for "shouting out the window of the men's dorm late at night." According to charges, "Rocca used language of a disturbing and abusive nature, which was heard over a wide area, and which did not reflect the type of responsible citizenship expected of SMS college students." Rocca also had to report to the dean periodically and perform special work under the direction of the dormitory government.

Housing problems of a different sort arose when black students were

entitled to enroll at the college. Local attitudes toward Blacks continued to reflect the racism typical of the Ozarks at that time. Many households offering "college approved housing" refused to rent to black students. A survey done in the summer of 1967 showed black students being told by local homeowners that they had no rooms available, when 30 minutes later they would show available rooms to white housing seekers. The overt discrimination put the college in a difficult position. President Mallory pointed out that all college-approved housing is intended to be non-discriminatory, but "to date the college has not required a signed statement from private homeowners that there will be no discrimination because of race, creed or color." The president went on to say that "the college recognizes that the householders…have the prerogative of determining who will live in their facilities, so long as this is a matter of appraising the fitness of the individual and does not involve discrimination because of race, creed or color." Most homeowners refusing Negro students did so because of their fear of losing white student renters. Students pressured the administration to remove discriminating homeowners from the college-approved housing list. Black students were encouraged to report instances of alleged discrimination. And *The Standard* encouraged "each conscientious student (to) make a personal pledge to confront and challenge damaging prejudice when it appears, rather than merely side-stepping the issue as

most of us are prone to do."

Just a year later in August 1968, 119 placard-carrying protestors marched on the Belmont Apartments for evicting two white students who had invited black students into their apartment. The protestors included students, faculty and two Catholic nuns. Police stood by as the girls' furniture was moved to another apartment.

The housing issue continued to flavor the college atmosphere throughout the SMS years. In the 1960s, other universities were taking bold steps allowing undergraduate women to visit men's dormitory living areas during designated hours. The University of Wisconsin was among the pioneers in this visitation policy. It stated its objective as "an attempt to meet the needs of university women and at the same time, provide opportunities for the development of self-discipline and responsibility." SMS wasn't in the forefront of such experimentation, but it did challenge traditional standards by building a co-ed dorm in 1966. *The Standard* welcomed the innovation but also saw the contrast with previous housing poli-

Student ID in the 1960s containing a photograph, student name and registration number.

Riot breaks out in Missouri State Penitentiary.

First *Miss America* TV broadcast.

Elvis Presley first appears on *The Ed Sullivan Show.*

Alternate Interpretations

In a letter to the editor in 1949, a student called attention to a teacher evaluation project done by a distant college. He pointed out that students were asked to give their evaluations of the performance of their teachers. Faculty pay would subsequently be tied to the evaluations. The student wondered if the Student Council at SMS would sponsor such an evaluation. And furthermore, "Would faculty performance be improved if teachers knew how their students rated them?" The student had overheard one faculty member dismiss the idea because "he had 20 years of experience teaching." The student wondered if it might be more accurately stated that "he had one year's experience twenty times."

cies. "A co-ed dormitory? The class of 1910 would have been shocked. But the new Towers Residence Hall housing 800 students is just that. The men's and women's individual sections are joined by a commons area — cafeteria, study, TV lounge and lobby. The Towers is a progressive part of our expanding campus."

The addition of on-campus housing had a profound impact on campus dynamics. It created new possibilities for a sense of campus community as enrollment rose into the thousands. It also provided additional opportunity for students to struggle with the question of balancing the claims of individual rights with demands for personal responsibility. And certainly, the interaction between the college administration and residence hall students was an invaluable context for constructive policy formation. It had its fits and starts, but generally headed in a responsible direction.

Student Health Services

The history of college health services goes back to 1906 when Dr. D.T. Kizer, M.D. transferred from Springfield Normal School and Business College to the faculty of State Normal School #4. He taught biology, gave eye examinations and provided general medical advice to Normal School students and staff from his faculty office. In 1923 the first actual "health office" was established in the Education Building where Dr. F.T. H'Doubler Sr. worked part time. Two years later, Dr. Ralph V. Ellis was appointed as college physician and part-time biology instructor, and the health office was moved to the second floor of the Administration Building where it was furnished with an examination table, sterilizer and "all the tools of the trade."

A young pre-med student, William E. Taylor, assisted in the health office in the late 1920s and became interested in student health issues. His father, John Taylor, was the founder of Springfield Normal School and Business College in the early 1890s. The young Taylor went on to Rush Medical School completing his training in 1934 and then returned to Springfield to divide his time between the college health office, the varsity athletics office and a private practice in town. By 1936 Taylor had also

Joe Jordan, *Ozarko* photographer for the 1950 edition, carries state-of-the-art equipment for capturing memorable moments of the year.

SMSU

Missouri/Springfield

International/USA

1955

Oregon and Shannon Counties added to southwest service district for a total of 24 counties.

KTTS-TV broadcasts first color picture.

become city physician, but after exhausting work in a typhoid epidemic, 75 home birth deliveries and a 35-pound weight loss, he happily gave up private practice and assumed the full-time role as director of college health in 1937.

Throughout the SMS period, Dr. Taylor pioneered a model college, health care system. The system was funded exclusively through the college leading the 1950 *Ozarko* to observe that "no student or staff member has a vested right to such a service. The students and faculty will be served as time permits and as the physician thinks necessary." By 1956 the enrollment had doubled from the 1937 period when Taylor began his work. He coped by hiring part-time physicians to assist. With the help of volunteers, Taylor gave each entering freshman a complete physical including a dental exam, a chest x-ray, hemoglobin, urinalysis and blood sugar tests. He also instituted a college wide tuberculosis screening program, which has continued into the 21st century.

With the double-digit growth of the campus in the 1960s, the health office, which had moved to the ground floor of the Administration Building, was taxed to the limit. Two classrooms had been converted into three examination rooms, a physician's office, x-ray room, laboratory, sterilization room and a waiting room. By 1962, the staff, which included Dr. Taylor, four part-time physicians, three clinical nurses, two med-techs and three office workers, were handling more than 12,000 patient visits each year as well as giving more than 1,500 freshman physicals.

Plans for a new health center on campus had been developing in Taylor's mind for more than a decade.

Cadets Harold Bengsch (left) and John Rich give their shoes a final shine as Sergeant Neil Gibson adjusts Sergeant Jim Turner's tie in preparation for the 1955 Military Ball.

They became a reality in 1971 at a cost of $659,000. The new health center included a 10-bed hospital open to students while school was in session. Bed care cost was $22 a day, which included general nursing care and catered meals from Broughton Food Service. While neither emergency nor intensive care services were provided, the hospital did care for a wide range of illnesses, communicable diseases and minor injuries. In 1969, a second full-time physician was added to the medical staff, Dr. Sally Hubbard.

The health clinic, like the residence halls, added a new dynamic to student life. Not only were students provided round-the-clock medical care with dorm, rooming house and emergency room visits by Dr. Bill Taylor, they also were provided with medical advice about a whole range of issues. One student in the spring of 1971 complained about the lecture she was given by a clinic staffer when she inquired about birth control pills. Despite the potential for conflicting perspectives on health-related moral issues, the Health Center clearly contributed to the well-being of students throughout the state college years.

Testing, Guidance and Counseling Services

With the enrollment of veterans at the close of World War II, a more systematic set of testing and counseling services was established on campus. Public law mandated that a guidance and testing office be available to veterans studying under the G.I. Bill, so President Ellis established such an office in May 1945.

Dean Bertha Wells retires.

American Airlines crash in Springfield — kills 12, injures 23.

Albert Einstein dies.

Ray Kroc starts McDonald's in Illinois.

Construction begins on Soviet cosmodrome launch facilities.

Supreme Court orders school integration "with all deliberate speed."

The Orchesis Club was established on campus in 1936 to promote the art of modern dance. By the middle 1950s, the group was assisting in musical productions on campus including *Brigadoon* in 1954 and *Oklahoma!* in 1956. Pictured at left, Row 1: Judy Moore, Julia Boehning, Mary Beth Early, Kathryn Buffington, Mary Jane Rambo, and Grace Alsup. Row 2: Irene Tilley, Mary DuBois, Mary Lue Farrar, Pauline Tate, and Karol Knight. Row 3: Donna Maples, Phyllis Young French, Phyllis Ann Frick and Gail Beauman.

While there was a guidance committee established as early as the 1920s to advise students and assist them in adapting to college life, the impetus of heavy veteran enrollments pushed the program toward greater visibility and maturity. Dr. Richard Wilkinson was functioning as campus guidance director in 1947 providing both aptitude testing services as well as student counseling.

In 1950 James Bane was employed as a counselor-trainer and is credited with instituting a student personnel perspective for the campus. Six years later Dr. Homer Long was brought to campus as dean of men and director of guidance. Under his watch, a Counseling Center was established. With the arrival of President Leland Traywick, the Counseling and

Testing Center was officially opened in 1962, with Duane Hartley as the first counselor.

During the first two years of its operation, the Counseling and Testing Center sought input from faculty, housing staff, physicians and student activity leaders in establishing its goals. In those early years, individual interviews with first semester freshmen were held to acquaint them with the services of the center. The focus of those services was to promote students' personal development and psychological wellbeing. Over the years, the center's staff has offered psychological assessments, individual and group counseling, crisis intervention, and educational programs aimed at assisting students in resolving conflicts that interfere with their educational prog-

ress.

As the college grew and matured, its services became formalized and institutionalized. While faculty continued to serve as teachers, counselors, advisers, mentors and friends to students, the institution began to assume increasing responsibility for organizing and delivering the services. Consequently, support staff grew, administrators were added, and the entire educational enterprise became more complex.

Paying Fees, Finding Work and Getting Scholarships

When student fees were set at $6 a term in 1906, they paid for about 9 percent of the costs of the student's education. Fifty years later when fees had gone to $26.50 a term, the share of educational costs borne by the student had increased to 22 percent.

SMSU
Aldo Sebben named athletics director.　　Dr. Duane Meyer joins history faculty.　　New Memorial Library opens. First air-conditioned academic building.

Missouri/Springfield
Flowering dogwood named state tree.

International/USA
Disneyland opens in Anaheim, California.

Campus growth and fee increases seemed to be linked during the SMS years. In 1949, when fees were raised for the first time in 17 years, enrollment had increased almost four fold over the 1944 number. It was only nine years before the next increase that raised fees to $30 a term. Thereafter fees increased almost annually as the college struggled to provide facilities, faculty and services to thousands of students.

College administrators were open with students about how their fee money was used. In 1951, of the $26.50 term fee, $13.90 went to what was called Local Funds. Health care received $1.50; assemblies, forensics, concerts and dramatics received $1.50; social activities received $1; $1.50 went to public relations, Homecoming,

parents day, farm week, agricultural contests, student publications and student guidance; another $1.50 went to intramural and other recreation events; 40 cents went to swimming and physical education; and $6.50 went to debt service on the Student Center building. The remaining $12.60 was used to help pay faculty salaries and cover general educational expenses.

With budget demands growing, in 1958 the college instituted a non-resident fee schedule, which added $25 per quarter to the regular $26.50 term fee for students from outside the state. All the state colleges invoked the non-resident fee structure at the same time so none would have dramatic fee advantages over another. However, the fees at SMS during the 1960s remained the lowest of all the regional state colleges.

When the semester system replaced the term calendar in 1963, fees for a full year went to $150, $30 above the previous term rate for the same period. In 1966, following a year with almost a 25 percent increase in enrollment, fees were hiked $40 with another $50 hike in 1967. College officials identified seven needs dictating the increase: campus expansion, parking, recreational areas, library books, scholarships, convocation programs and the Student Government Association.

Students coped with fee increases in a variety of ways. For veterans, the G.I. Bill paid the bills and provided living expenses. For others, there were scholarships. But in the early 1950s only 5 percent of SMS students were benefiting from scholarships. In 1951, 68 freshmen received full fee Regents

Leon Ward and Sandra Burton watch as Georgia Shipp and Jerry Anderson dance to *Shake, Rattle, and Roll* in the recreation room of the Student Center in 1954. In the background Bill Simmons and Patty Taylor scan the juke box for the next song. The rec room was a popular gathering place for students between classes.

Enrollment exceeds 2,000 for first time.

First graduate program offered in cooperation with the University of Missouri.

Evangel College opens on O'Reilly Hospital grounds.

Fellows Lake, created by Springfield City Water Company, dedicated.

The Honeymooners debuts.

AFL and CIO merge uniting the labor movement.

Montgomery Bus Boycott begins with Rosa Parks refusing to give up her seat to a white passenger.

Sadie Hawkins Day was a favorite event on campus during the 1960s affording women the opportunity to capture the man of their choice.

Scholarships given to top high school graduates from the southwest district. Another 11 students from Latin America and Europe received international scholarships from the college.

By 1966 the Regents Scholarship policy was liberalized to allow it to be given to sophomores, juniors and seniors who were recommended by three faculty and who maintained at least a 3.0, 3.2, or 3.4 grade point average respectively. The previous policy allowed Regents Scholarships to be given only to entering freshmen.

By the 1960s the number of scholarships sponsored by private individuals, businesses, civic groups and academic departments increased the pool of support for students substantially. By the end of the state college period in 1972, the College Catalog listed 10 categories of scholarships totaling well over 200 individual awards. Thirty-three outside organizations were among the sponsors.

The history of the funding of higher education made a radical shift as a result of the Russian launching of the first artificial satellite on October 4, 1957. Sputnik I, as it was called, was about the size of a basketball, weighed only 183 pounds, and took about 98 minutes to orbit the earth on its elliptical path. The successful launch of Sputnik ushered in new political, military, technological and scientific developments, and initiated the space age and a race between the United States and the Soviet Union for scientific and technological pre-eminence. The fact that the first space launch was accomplished by the Soviet Union suggested, among other things, that the United States educational system needed to accelerate its teaching of science and technology. Just one year after the launch of Sputnik, Congress passed the National Defense Act of 1958, which

contained a preamble stating, "The Congress finds that an educational emergency exists and requires action by the federal government. Assistance will come from Washington to help develop as rapidly as possible those skills essential to the national defense."

With that legislation, the first federal student financial aid program of the modern era was born. Congress authorized $47.5 million dollars for the fiscal year 1959. SMS processed its first National Defense Education Act (NDEA) loan in 1959. J.B. Inman was appointed loan officer for the college. With his retirement in 1963, the college organized the SMS Financial Aid Office under the direction of J.C. Bartee.

The National Defense Student Loan (NDSL) program was tailored to assist students who were entering teaching, or occupations in science, math, engineering or foreign languages. They could borrow federal money to finance their education at 3 percent interest with 11 years to pay off the loan. If the teacher taught in a public school, one-tenth of the debt was forgiven for each year of teaching up to five years, amounting to a cancellation of half of the loan.

In 1964, the federal government established the College Work Study program, which allocated money to students who worked on campus or in not-for-profit organizations in the community. In 1965, the Educational Opportunity Grant (EOG) program was added to the mix so that by the middle sixties, federally supported student financial aid had opened the door to higher education for students in the 1960s much as the G.I. Bill had opened the door to veterans at the end of World War II.

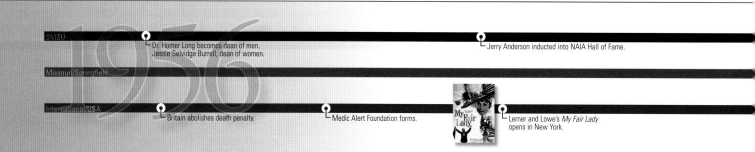

SMSU

Dr. Homer Long becomes dean of men.
Jessie Selvidge Burrell, dean of women.

Jerry Anderson inducted into NAIA Hall of Fame.

Missouri/Springfield

International/USA

Britain abolishes death penalty.

Medic Alert Foundation forms.

Lerner and Lowe's My Fair Lady opens in New York.

By 1966-67, nearly one in five students was receiving federally funded assistance at SMS. Just over $500,000 was distributed to 1,006 students in the form of grants or loans, in addition to the Regents Scholarships and private scholarships that were already in place. By 1969-70, the proportion of students receiving federally funded assistance was one in four, and the total distributed exceeded $1 million.

Although students had an increasing pool of scholarship assistance to draw from, campus and in-town work continued to be important sources of help. While per-hour pay during the SMS period was not exceptional, it was a considerable improvement over the 15 cents an hour paid during the normal school period. In 1947, the going rate was 42 cents. The rate reached $1 an hour by 1967.

In 1949, SMS began paying football players 45 cents an hour for on-campus work. It appears to have been the initial move toward a scholarship-supported athletics program. Central College, at the time, offered room, board and tuition for 16 hours of work by student-athletes each week.

Along with other issues in the 1960s, student pay was a concern. Student workers argued that persons doing skilled work should earn more than those doing unskilled work. They pointed out that other state schools paid freshmen less than they paid seniors who presumably were involved in higher skill tasks. But the argument failed to win any converts in the administration, especially when it turned out that SMS was paying up to 20 cents an hour more for student help than some sister institutions.

In 1965, SMS received its first work-study grant covering 90 percent of the wages earned by low income students who worked at campus jobs or certain off-campus tasks. Under this program over $7,000 in grant money came to the college in the spring semester of 1965.

Student Organizations

From the very beginning, student organizations were an important accessory to classroom learning. In the early years organizational numbers were modest with the literary societies heading the list. But by the state college period, campus organizations had multiplied and taken on a gigantic role in campus life. The 1963 *Ozarko* captures the essence of campus organizational life. "Fall. The time of falling leaves. The time of new faces and new adventures. Rekindling of old times and the creating of new relationships…. It's also a time for organizations…clubs, fraternities, sororities, organizations getting under way. Wheels turn and the cogs move, and school starts rumbling like a newly awakened gargantuan plodding towards its ultimate June hibernation once again."

While there were all kinds of campus organizations — departmental, honorary, political, professional, religious, service and social — none in the state college period equaled the power and prominence of the sororities and fraternities. There was a distinct irony in this since the 1946 *Catalog* introducing the state college era opened the section describing campus organizations with the statement, "The organizations to which the college gives recognition are distinctly democratic. Standards of membership are definitely announced and any student who can meet the

SMS affiliates with National Collegiate Athletic Association (NCAA).

New range of mountains discovered in Antarctica — two over 13,000 feet.

Television remote control device introduced — invented by Dr. R. Adler.

A Request to Representative Marion Bennett

In May 1946, a student petition seeking an extension of the Office of Price Administration in Washington was sent to the Honorable Marion Bennett, former champion debater at SMS and now a congressman from southwest Missouri.

"We, the undersigned," read the petition, "demand that you give full support to the retention of price controls in its present effective form. We feel that greedy business interests are not as important as the welfare of veterans and other small income groups. This is an election year."

~

Enrollment Shifts

In 1952, private colleges and universities in Missouri had 19,423 full-time students. State institutions trailed with only 16,539 enrollments. But when the baby boomers began enrolling in the 1960s, the numbers changed. Public institutions in 1960 enrolled 31,900, a 93 percent increase over 1952. Private colleges and universities enrolled only 24,626 that year, a modest 27 percent gain over 1952.

announced standards is eligible. In no case is membership based on personal or social selection."

Despite the claim about democratic student organizations, the last paragraph of the *Catalog* section on organizations lists at least nine that were clearly sororities and fraternities whose membership was indeed based on personal and social selection criteria.

What was going on was a kind of subterfuge based on the desire to hold on to a past, which was clearly democratic in spirit and in truth in the face of a growing student preference for exclusivity in social life. The first break from the stated democratic club policy occurred as early at 1917 when several male students organized the Knights of the Road Club, which was renamed the Key and Dagger Club in 1921. By 1925, 16 men were living together in a house at 871 Kingshighway and were understood to be a "local social fraternity."

Throughout the state teachers college years, social clubs grew in number and popularity, and several began affiliating with national fraternities and sororities. They remained without "official recognition" by the college until 1949 when the *Catalog* finally dropped the misleading description of campus organizations as "distinctly democratic" and acknowledged that clubs with exclusive membership criteria were part of the family.

The facts of the matter are that even though sororities and fraternities were not officially recognized until the late 1940s, they were clearly regulated and overseen by the college from the beginning. Their social activities were scheduled through Dean Wells's office. By the SMS years, members of fraternities and sororities sat at the planning

'HA! HA! HA!'   By Bob Palmer

R.N.P.

The dismissal of President Traywick in 1964 aroused deep feelings throughout the community. The Springfield newspaper's editorial cartoonist Bob Palmer weighs in on the controversy by calling attention to the fact that President Traywick was quickly hired by the University of Omaha after being asked to resign by the SMS Board.

table when college events were scheduled. Many of their functions were held in college facilities. Their members held the majority of elective offices on campus. Fraternity and sorority news filled *The Standard* as early as the late 1940s. By the 1950s, the college social calendar was dominated by their events. Attempts to organize "independents," as they were called, were sporadic and seldom successful. Greeks had clearly become the central players in the whole college scene. A survey by *The Standard* in 1960 showed almost 42 percent of Greeks were active in various campus organizations, while only 25 percent of the independents were so involved.

SMS was not unique in its embrace of Greek societies. The 1950s

saw fraternities and sororities growing rapidly across the country. The Greek movement began in the United States with the founding of Phi Beta Kappa, an academic honor society, at William and Mary in 1776. Social fraternities and sororities on college campuses grew in popularity after World War II with well over 10,000 chapters by the late years of the 20th century.

Of course, the college community was becoming more diverse as well. While teacher education remained an important magnet drawing students to SMS, an increasing number were interested in business and liberal arts degrees. The economics of the campus were changing too. Fraternity and sorority life assumed a certain affluence on the part of students. SMS Greeks held dances at Riverside, bought corsages and rented tuxedos. The growth of Greek organizations on campus suggested a growing segment of prosperous students.

SMSU

State bond issue approved providing funds for agriculture, fine arts, classroom, and student housing.

Missouri/Springfield

Catholic Diocese of Springfield-Cape Girardeau established.

International/USA   1956Jul

The Andre Doria sinks after colliding with the Stockholm off Nantucket Island.

172   *Daring to Excel: The First 100 Years of Southwest Missouri State University*

Campus elections, like this one in 1968, have traditionally featured innovative ideas for getting out the vote.

As early as 1948, *The Standard* tried to sort out for students the advantages and disadvantages of belonging to one of the Greek societies. It called "misconstrued" the idea that "anyone who does not belong to a social club is null and void." In fact, the paper declared, "Some of the finest and most intelligent people on this campus are unaffiliated with any social group." Cutting the other way, the writer dubbed as "hogwash" the idea that members of Greek organizations "are a bunch of money-mad, feather brained socialites." In reality, the writer declared, "Young people in college fraternities and sororities are level-headed, intelligent young men and women, on the whole, and didn't come to college for the night life alone, as some people are led to believe."

Having disposed of the stereotypes, *The Standard* goes on to advise new students to "look at the situation on the campus thoroughly before deciding whether to join a fraternity or a sorority, or the Independent Student Association, or remain unaffiliated. Some are happier in Greek-Letter clubs. Some are not. Everyone, unfortunately, cannot belong."

And for the person who seeks the exclusivity of a Greek-Letter club but fails to make the grade, the writer advises, "don't come crying on my shoulder. Your life isn't ruined socially, the folks back home won't disinherit you, and your best beau will continue to love you madly. And there's always next term. After all, you'll probably be here for four years, and you're likely to get caught in the 'rush' sooner or later."

Many were indeed caught in "rush." The 1971 *Ozarko* portrayed the significance of the annual ritual this way. "For many, 'rush' was more than a handshake…a favor…a stale smile…a name…a town…cigarette smoke. It was ecstasy. It was heartbreak." Not that social activities were insignificant in earlier years, but throughout the state college years social events gathered a kind of momentum that could define the character of an institution. To be on the inside of that social circle was where most students wanted to be. And "rush" was the route. So as early as 1949, students were being instructed on how to be part of the rush dance. "All men desiring to join a social fraternity, report to Ms. Bilsborough's office and sign a preferential list. Put your first choice, then three others in order of

President Dwight D. Eisenhower re-elected President of the U.S.

The Wizard of Oz makes television debut.

Popular revolt against communist government in Hungary violently suppressed by Soviets.

Work begins on Kennedy Stadium at Parkview High School.

Fidel Castro lands in Cuba with the intent to overthrow dictator Fulgencio Battista.

1946-72 Southwest Missouri State College   173

preference, with which you would consider affiliating," read the instructions.

Prior to signing the preferential ballots, "rushees" had already been entertained by the clubs. "Rush parties" were organized by the sororities while "smokers" were the venue for fraternities. Sigma Tau held their "smoker" in Heer's Garden Room in 1952. "Rushees" were on their most "cool" behavior. Fraternities and sororities portrayed themselves as "cool" as well. When the chemistry was right, your name went on the invitation list.

In 1959, the Greek organizations thought they might help their cause by visiting area towns during the summer to introduce prospective students to campus life at SMS. This Greek Summer Caravan sent out letters to high school seniors advising them of the date when the caravan would visit their town. The first gathering occurred at Roaring River State Park, near Cassville. Only seven girls and two boys came to the display area. On the following Sunday, the Caravan went to Lamar City Park where only four girls and one boy showed up. The Greek Caravan was discontinued after the visit to Lamar.

Part of the rationale for Greek organizations was the promotion of academic development among their members. So the average grades of rival fraternities and sororities were occasionally published in *The Standard*. In 1960, the Sigma Pi men had the highest house grade point average among fraternities with a 1.36 on a three-point scale. Their pledges did less well, however, registering only a .89. The sororities managed better grade point averages overall than the men with the Alpha Delta Pi leading the way with

a 1.77. Three of the fraternity pledge groups had averages below 1.0, which probably accounts for the changes in rush rules in 1960. Called the Rush and Scholarship Improvement Program, it limited fall semester rushing to freshmen who graduated in the upper two-thirds of their high school class. Others must wait until the spring semester and show a 1.2 or better average for their first semester's work. Furthermore, all pledges were required to attend a supervised study hall for two hours every Tuesday, Wednesday and Thursday evening. Pledges would be exempt from further supervised study hall if their midterm grades averaged 1.2 or above. We are not told if this attempt to improve pledge studentship was successful.

Not long after the beginning of the state college era, Greek organizations began buying up residential property in the vicinity of the campus to serve as "houses" where members could live together. In 1951 the Kappa Alpha fraternity bought its own house. It also was the first to retire the Inter-Fraternity Council Scholarship trophy. With the growth of Greek houses around campus, dignitary visits began to occur. In 1952, Stan Kenton visited the TKE house after an appearance at

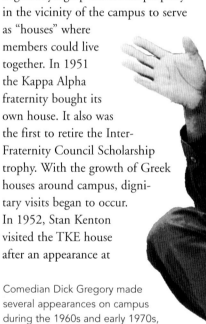

Comedian Dick Gregory made several appearances on campus during the 1960s and early 1970s, sponsored by the Campus Union Board. While humor was his tool, advocacy for civil rights was his message during the turbulent years.

the Shrine Mosque with Sarah Vaughn and Nat "King" Cole. Kenton was a TKE at the University of Illinois. By 1953, five sororities and three fraternities had their own houses adjacent to the campus. As the number of Greek houses grew around campus, so did college regulations. In 1955, the college announced that all fraternities must have a house mother living in the residence effective the summer of '56. The requirement proved a hardship for most of the fraternities who had a difficult time arranging living quarters for a housemother in a residence converted primarily to sleeping rooms.

The problems for which Greek organizations were often remembered were part of the SMS experience as well. In the spring of 1951 an informal "Greek Weekend" occurred, which included a series of unnamed "problem

1957

The European Common Market is formed.

incidents" that led college administrators to request all fraternities and sororities not to participate in any further "Greek Weekends." The ban was a bit ambiguous leading to such questions as "What constitutes a Greek Weekend?" Dean Bane replied simply, "We don't want you to participate in a Greek Weekend, and, if necessary, if you take a belligerent and non-cooperative attitude we will notify your national officers." The conversation ended with the dean saying, "If you want to schedule an outing with faculty chaperones, that's ok."

Greek organizations are credited with adding a creative spark to campus life during the SMS years. In March 1957, the Sigma Pi fraternity decided it wanted to talk with Nikita Khrushchev. They wanted to ask five questions of the Russian Premier. (1) Did the recent visit to the U.S. by Russian agricultural officials benefit the country? (2) Could the West and the East live in peaceful co-existence? (3) Are relations between the U.S. and the Soviet Union improving? (4) Are college students in Russia aware of the world tension? and, (5) Is military training or education of youth of Russia more important? Jack Whitaker and Jack Griffin were chosen to conduct the interview. On the first call, they reached Moscow, but the operator was unable to locate Nikita Khrushchev. On the second call, they reached the Premier's residence, but no one answered. A third effort also proved unsuccessful.

While members of Sigma Pi were trying to reach Moscow, the Alpha Delta Pi members were reaching out to Korea. All of the Greek organizations were involved in service projects of one kind or another. ADP Philanthropy

In the early 1950s, square dancing on the SMS campus was popularized by the Promenaders, a group of SMS students who entered several national contests and were ranked among the best in the nation. In 1954 the group entertained nightly for a month in New Orleans in the Blue Room of the Roosevelt Hotel. Reading clockwise from the bottom, Phyllis Frick, Danny Houser, Jane Lichlyter, Leo Holland, Jean Routh, Jack Webb, Jean Lichlyter, Joe Williams, Pat Cox and Jack Hyde.

Chair Pat Elliot was searching for a new project for her sorority in 1958 when sponsor Dr. Oreen Ruedi came up with a suggestion. "Why don't we adopt a war orphan?" Elliot went to work writing Foster Parents, an international agency assisting war orphans. A nine-year-old Korean orphan, Yoo Keum Soon, was proposed by the agency. Yoo lived in a tent by the River Han in Korea, and was described by Foster Parents as "a cute little girl with a lovely, gentle manner, clever, thoughtful, obedient, helpful to her sister, Bok Soon and her grandmother." Yoo's father disappeared after being seized by communist soldiers in North Korea.

The rest of the family sought refuge in South Korea. The mother died in a refugee camp in Pusan. The grandmother begged on the streets to support the children.

The sorority sisters, compelled by the story, agreed to send $15 a month to provide essentials for Yoo. They sent Christmas gifts, including dresses, warm sweaters and matching skirts, leggings, scarves, a jump rope, Ping-Pong™ balls and paddles, a toy car, candy, puzzles, picture books, blankets and coats for Yoo's brother and sister. It's unclear how long the relationship continued, but it illustrates the enthusiasm with which the Greek community

Bears win MIAA golf tournament.

Missouri Commission on Human Rights established.

Civil Rights Act of 1957 passed by Congress.

grasped opportunities to serve the less fortunate here and abroad.

While members of Alpha Delta Pi were creating a merry Christmas for Yoo in Korea, other brothers and sisters were putting on Christmas parties at Sunshine Acres Rest Home, the Community Training School for the mentally retarded, the Good Samaritan Boys Ranch, and a group of 60 underprivileged children in northwest Springfield. The TKEs gave up their Christmas formal dance to provide a party for children from low income homes in 1959. The children were brought to the Bears Den in a local fire truck. Captain Briny of KTTS-TV fame and his monkey entertained the children before cookies and chocolate milk were served by the TKEs and

their dates. Mike Mulroe played the part of Santa to end the evening for the delighted children.

The SMS period could be called the reign of the Queens. Organizations sponsored a spate of beauty contests, queen contests, and ugly man contests, usually to the benefit of some worthy cause. Beauty pageants and queen contests occupied an ever growing proportion of *Standard* space. There were Hoop Queens, *Ozarko* Queens, Homecoming Queens, Garter Queens, Thanksgiving Queens, Aggie Barnwarming Queens, Military Ball Queens, Tournament Queens, Orchid Queens, White Rose Queens, Queens of Diamonds and a host of organizational sweethearts.

Among the more celebrated royalty

were the Ozarko Queens traditionally chosen by national celebrities. Bing Crosby selected Norene Ruddell in 1948. Arthur Godfrey chose Virginia Pummill in 1949. In 1950 Jack Benny was asked to select both an Ozarko Queen and King. Shirley Carr and Joe Summers were the winners. Other celebrities choosing the queens included Al Capp, the New York cartoonist; Dean Martin and Jerry Lewis; Gary Moore; Pat Boone and Mickey Mantle; Jim Lowe, Natalie Wood and Truman Bradley; Steve Allen and Zsa Zsa Gabor. Were all the judges names to be listed, it would appear to be a Who's Who of the entertainment world at mid-century. The judges were typically sent pictures of the candidates. Occasionally there were also interviews over the phone. One suspects there was as much excitement in selecting the judges as there was getting their verdict.

Of course, social organizations were not the only species on campus. Even at the beginning of the SMS era, only 10 of the 35 organizations listed in the Catalog were social clubs. Departmental clubs had spread throughout virtually every campus discipline enabling students to acquire yet more experience and expertise in their chosen major. Departmental clubs, while primarily educational in focus, also sponsored social events and celebrated achievements with parties and seasonal festivities. Disciplines also organized honorary clubs, many of them sanctioned by national organizations, to recognize their high achieving students. Service clubs multiplied as well giving students first hand experience in philanthropic and community service work.

Religion continued to play a

The Homecoming Parade in 1962 featured golden anniversary classmates driving a 1912 vehicle to the delight of bystanders on St. Louis Street.

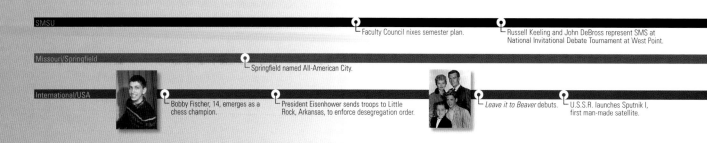

SMSU
Faculty Council nixes semester plan.
Russell Keeling and John DeBross represent SMS at National Invitational Debate Tournament at West Point.

Missouri/Springfield
Springfield named All-American City.

International/USA
Bobby Fischer, 14, emerges as a chess champion.
President Eisenhower sends troops to Little Rock, Arkansas, to enforce desegregation order.
Leave it to Beaver debuts.
U.S.S.R. launches Sputnik I, first man-made satellite.

significant role on campus; however, the organizational structure changed considerably. Throughout the early years, the YWCA and YMCA were the primary sources for religious fellowship and Christian nurture. By definition, they were ecumenical. By the late 1940s, reference to the Y groups had disappeared and in their place had come a variety of groups representing different denominational orientations. The Baptist Student Union, the Wesley Foundation, the Newman Club, Chi Alpha, SMS Christian Fellowship and the Student Christian Association were among the prominent though frequently changing names.

By the end of the SMS era in 1972, the number of organizations had more than doubled from the 35 at the beginning of the era in 1946. While the growth to 95 different organizations is itself impressive, of greater interest is the distribution of organizations according to purpose or background. The largest grouping is social organizations with 26 entries including 16 fraternities and sororities. Following it are honorary organizations with 21 entries representing a host of disciplines. Service organizations numbered 18, which includes student government. There were 15 departmental organizations, six each of religious and professional organizations, and three political groups. What strikes one is the growing diversity on campus. The homogeneity of background, interest and professional aspiration that characterized earlier years was yielding to a diversity that challenged any notion of natural community. While the vast majority of students were still from the Southwest District, and largely from the Greene County area, that did not necessarily guarantee a sense of community. Growth carried with it the new task of making a community of diverse communities on campus.

The Experience of Student Government
Representing and trying to reconcile the differences emerging among groups on campus were high priority issues for student government in the state college period. But student government beginnings were not auspicious. In April 1947 there was only one nominee for student body president, Gordon Foster, who was declared elected though no balloting was conducted. A week later, the decision was reversed, and an election was held with the victory going officially to Foster.

The Student Council concerns in those early post-war years were not profound. In 1947-48 the Council expressed concern about card playing being ended at the College Inn. They also requested a soda machine be installed in the lounge. President Ellis responded by redecorating the lounge and installing a soda machine in the cafeteria. The Council that year also wanted more pencil sharpeners around, and some rules for posting signs. It also protested the high prices charged SMS students to see the Bears play football at Rockhurst. The Council ended the year pleading for a Campus Union to replace the lounge which met student needs so inadequately.

The Student Council the following year addressed more substantive issues. It sought the full disclosure in the *College Catalog* of courses necessary to complete a degree, as well as identifying the term when each course would be taught. The Council also advocated moving from the term to the semester system, a battle that would continue for well over a decade. *The Standard* endorsed the efforts of the student officers declaring, "Past Student Councils have had some success in regulating and promoting pep activities and student mixers, but the Student Council of 1948-49 illustrates that students no longer wish to think and act as babies in knee pants."

By the spring of 1949, *The Standard* became much more aggressive in assessing the effectiveness of student government. The editor called the efforts of the Student Council over the past four years "one grand flop." The fault, according to the editor, lay in the relationship of student government to college officials. "If our Student Council makes a recommendation or desires to take any sort

Drs. Anna Lou Blair and L.E. Pummill retire.

James T. Blair elected governor.   O'Reilly Automotive, Inc. established.

1958

Teamster's Union expelled from AFL-CIO.   Cuban revolutionary forces capture Havana.   First U.S. satellite, Explorer I, launched.

1946-72 Southwest Missouri State College   177

SMS Graduate Selected to Reorganize Japanese Schools

Major Monte Lee Osborne was selected in 1946 by General Douglas McArthur to reorganize Japan's boys' middle schools, girls' high schools and all vocational schools.

~

Golden Anniversary Events

A 500-voice choir from 33 southwest Missouri school districts accompanied by the 125-piece SMS orchestra, all under the direction of Dr. Lara Hoggard, formerly Choral Director with the Fred Waring organization, performed on campus as part of a Music Festival celebrating the 50th anniversary of the founding of the college. A Science Festival on the theme "The Role of Science in Modern Society" was also part of the anniversary celebration. Dr. C. Rogers McCullough of Monsanto Chemical Company lectured on the peaceful applications of atomic energy.

of action on student problems, the President of the Faculty has the power to veto all actions of the Council, and the President of the College has the power to interpret the Constitution. In other words, the faculty advise the Student Council, the President of the Faculty vetoes the Student Council, and the President of the College acts as the Supreme Court. STUDENT GOVERNMENT? It is a farce!"

While there were occasional collisions between student government and college officials in the earlier years, they were generally smoothed over with the student newspaper continuing to praise the integrity and helpfulness of the administration. But as in so many other areas of campus life, a new era was dawning. *The Standard* began unashamedly championing student power and criticizing the administration for its patronizing attitude toward student initiatives. An April 8, 1949, editorial ended by advocating the writing of a new Student Constitution, "one with teeth in it, which delegates (to) the Student Council power to act as legislators as well as an enforcement body." The editor ends the treatise on a high note declaring, "If we fail to see through our blindness and fail to stir from our inactivity, we shall also fail to learn the greatest of all lessons — the lesson of self-government."

Later that month, the Student Council met with President Ellis, Dean Willard Graff and Registrar Guy Thompson to discuss their academic recommendations. President Ellis continued to defend the quarter system "against overwhelming evidence in support of the semester system." The meeting concluded with President Ellis declaring he had both "an open mind

and an open door" but no movement occurred on the semester question.

In December 1949, Don Payton, student body president, proposed a new form of student government. The outline of the plan was approved by Dean Graff. Payton, Don Burrell and Jim Stewart proceeded to draft a new student constitution establishing a Student Senate to replace the Student Council. It would be made up of the student body president, the presidents of the four classes, one elected representative from each of the four classes and four representatives from the All Club Council. Among the Senate's duties would be assisting in the administration of the new Student Union. The new constitution was completed and put to a vote of the students in April 1950. A total of 320 students out of a possible 1,800 voted on the matter, 276 in favor.

The new document lasted only one year. A new constitution was voted on in April 1951. A total of 134 students participated in that election, a bare 7 percent of the enrollment. The document passed 118 to 16. The level of indifference to student elections and particularly constitutional referendums was not peculiar to SMS. In 1951, a revamped student constitution at the University of Oklahoma was approved by 63 votes out of a student body of 8,500.

Despite the tepid endorsement of the new constitution at SMS, the newly formed Student Senate went to work on what it saw as important issues. It called for an investigation of the bookstore and vending machine profits. It talked with the Rolla student body president about disruptive painting done on each campus during the foot-

SMSU
Multiple cornerstone laying ceremonies for agriculture building, fine arts building and classroom building.

Missouri/Springfield

International/USA
Arnold Palmer wins first major golf tournament — Masters.

ball season, arranged the selection of cheerleaders by popular vote, and had weekly conferences with Dean Bane about student-faculty cooperation.

The issue that sparked the most interest in campus elections was the growing power of the Greek community. As early as 1946, despite being a numerical minority, the sororities and fraternities dominated campus politics. The unaffiliated students organized the Independent Students Association late in the year with some 150 members. They planned social events like their Greek rivals, including a "Back-to-School Hop" following Christmas break. But their political clout was negligible. Class elections continued to be dominated by the Greek interests. Half of the available senior class positions for the Student Senate were captured by the TKEs in 1951. The pattern continued throughout the 1950s regardless of the fact that by 1958, only 1 in 6 students was affiliated with a sorority or fraternity. Despite *The Standard* assessment of Greek dominance of campus politics as "an alarming trend," the trend continued throughout the state college period.

One of the lasting benefits of student government initiatives in the 1950s was the publication of a campus Student Directory. Tom Strong headed a committee that prepared the directory, which contained names, addresses and phone numbers of faculty as well as students. "The directories should go like hotcakes with that set of phone numbers," mused President Ellis.

The 1960s brought additional reforms to student government. In 1963 it was recommended that student government move from class-based representation to organization-based repre-

sentation, reflecting the growing clout of organizations on campus. By 1964 a new student constitution was in place providing for three branches of student government — executive, legislative and judicial.

In that same year, the Student Senate flexed its muscles by refusing to endorse the newly designated college president, Dr. Arthur Mallory, until they had an audience with him. The dismissing of President Traywick had aroused considerable reaction against the Board of Regents both on campus and in the community, and the hiring of Mallory was not exactly done through an open process. The concern with the Board's conduct and its failure to have open meetings prompted student government in 1965 to request the Board to allow student representation at Board meetings. Lou Anne Roby, Pat Logue, Don Mann and Ron Link, all student government members, presented a statement to the Board outlining their concerns. "Through the example of our presence, we hope to impress upon the Board a sincere and significant need for proper continuous communication between students, faculty, and Board of Regents, as well as the administration of the college. As students, we have chosen SMS; therefore, it is our belief that the right to question, suggest, or even

maturely criticize does belong to the student; but more important, the right to discuss policies that concern us and to anticipate that our voice will be duly considered by the administration of the college." The Board promised to take the matter under consideration.

President Mallory quickly had his audience with student government officers and initiated a faculty, student and administrative roundtable where issues of mutual concern could be discussed. The first roundtable was held in the fall of 1966, and students voiced their concern about the Junior English Exam, the registration process, a shortage of typewriters for student use and the failure of the cafeteria to be open on weekends. President Mallory assured the students that "there isn't anything we can't accomplish if there exists understanding between faculty, students and the administration."

Mallory held to his promises by inviting the Student Government Association to a weekend retreat at a small resort

Dancing had come a long way since Professor Jim Shannon broke the ice in 1911 gliding across the floor in Academic Hall with his wife in tow. Here, students provide a glimpse of a 1968 version of dancing while they watch the television for news of the presidential election results.

Bears win golf and basketball conference championships.

U.S. and Canada form NORAD.   U.S.S.R. launches Sputnik III.   James Van Allen discovers radiation belts surrounding Earth — first major space discovery.   Charles de Gaulle elected Premier of France.

1946-72 Southwest Missouri State College   179

on Table Rock Lake in the spring of 1967. Present at the retreat were faculty leaders, key members of the administration and student government leaders. The issues outlined earlier were discussed with student government leaders asking, "How can a student pass English 1, 2 and 5 and still fail the Junior English Exam?"" That question plagued both students and administrators until the JEE was dropped several years later.

The volume of letters to the editor in *The Standard* picked up substantially as the interaction between student government and college policy grew. In 1966, the SGA faced its own problem when its president, Gary Dyer, was arrested for driving while intoxicated. Dyer resigned his student government post, but Rod Davis' letter to the editor raised the question as to whether one's private life should be allowed to intrude into his public responsibilities. "Dyer paid for his drunken driving in municipal court," argued Davis. "Why should he be tried and convicted again on campus? We can drink on our own time; we can drive recklessly on our own time; we can watch dirty movies on our own time. Because our own time is precisely that — time of our own and not the college's. So long as it does not interfere with academic standing, what a student does, whether it be legal or illegal, is, or rather should be, out of the realm of the school. Black boards do not a prison make." The spirit of the 1960s was alive and well at SMS!

Assemblies, Convocations and Campus Entertainment

The long festering problem of assembly attendance came to a head with the beginning of the SMS period. Even 20 years earlier students were speculating about what would bring and hold crowds to the weekly programs. *The Standard,* half seriously, suggested that if an admission price were charged, attendance would increase. By 1937 attendance was no better and *The Standard* editor complained about "assembly tasters." "Once upon a time kings employed tasters to sample the royal cuisine and determine whether it was fit for a king…. Some students have formed the habit of coming to assembly with the avowed intent of interrupting the program to leave if it does not prove to be fit for a king," complained the editor.

Indeed, it was a demanding task to produce assembly programs week after week that would catch student interest. The big names were typically saved for commencement addresses such as in 1948 when J.C. Penney, a native Missourian, told the graduates how he borrowed $500 in 1902 to start a clothing store and now, 46 years later, had 1,611 stores nationwide and a business worth $750 million. The assembly programs for 1948 and 1949 featured music, magic, speeches, singing, plays and orations. Much of it was student talent which seemed a partial solution to the campus indifference to assemblies. The innovation worked temporarily, but by the early 1950s a more cynical attitude developed. "Music students can sit back and howl with glee when Mr. Bugle fouls with a blue note, or the string of a fiddle squawks instead of screeching," lamented the editor. Speeches on the Balkans, communism, democracy, Europe and Latin America didn't produce rave reviews either. When *The Standard* asked students how to improve the situation, Marty Shabaz gave an honest answer. "Well, I have no morning classes and I sleep until noon, so it would take an atomic explosion to roust me out of bed."

Rival attractions were also part of the problem. The College Inn and other off-campus gathering places remained open during assembly periods and drew large crowds. Even the Student Center was open and available as a resort for students. So there was a wordy war in the campus paper about whether the college library should continue to remain closed during assembly periods.

Despite the flagging interest for weekly assemblies, there were some distinguished events offered. In the 1950s tennis notables Jack Kramer, Poncho Gonzales, Frankie Parker and Bobby Riggs competed in the arena to the cheers of tennis fans. Hal and Ruby Holbrook presented excerpts from their "Theater of Great Personalities" including Mark Twain, Elizabeth and Essex, and the Brownings. Alex Dreier, NBC news commentator, lectured on "Government is Your Business," and Ruth Bryan Owen Rhode, daughter of William Jennings Bryan, lectured on "Skills of the United Nations."

Anauta, a nomadic Eskimo born on the northern tip of Baffin Island, just 400 miles from the North Pole, told students in 1952 how she became proficient in shooting seal, deer, and polar bear as well as driving dog sleds, building snow houses and making garments from animal skins.

By 1958 there was a conscientious attempt made to revitalize assemblies by bringing important names to lecture and perform in the fieldhouse. Claire Booth Luce was the first of these occasional programs. She presented a series

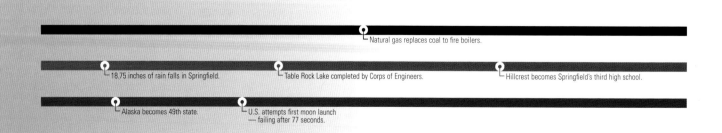

Natural gas replaces coal to fire boilers.

18.75 inches of rain falls in Springfield.   Table Rock Lake completed by Corps of Engineers.   Hillcrest becomes Springfield's third high school.

Alaska becomes 49th state.   U.S. attempts first moon launch — failing after 77 seconds.

A Historical Essay

BY DR. ROBERT FLANDERS

Emeritus Professor of History

Signs seen along the Ozarks road:

Cook wood and slaughtering ■ *For Sale — 10 acers* ■ *Fat Jone's — Apple's* ■ *Sucker Days — This Weekend*
Tomatoes Cukes Hay ■ *VOTE NO!* ■ *Choice Lake Propty $75k up* ■ *Blueberries ½ mile on gravel*
Brush Arbor Revival Sept 13-24 ■ *Trout Ranch* ■ *Sq. Dance Sat. Nite*

Signs like these show maybe we're not quite like everybody else — at least not yet.

Roads are an Ozarks paradox. We're passionate for them, of course. Our roads have been essential in making the Ozarks what it has become. Roads came late to the Ozarks, and we haven't gotten entirely sophisticated about them yet. We face the road squarely and put whatever we have to say right out there, with our own spelling and punctuation. Not everybody hires a big outside ad agency to do their roadside talking for them.

Early settlers into the rough Ozarks country came overland along old Indian trails or buffalo paths, or they paddled or poled up the rivers. Getting around inside the Ozarks was as difficult as getting here. Bad roads, and no roads, was the perennial complaint of citizens against county governments, thought to be the only government rightly concerned with them. I once asked an elderly lady down in Oregon County, Missouri, to name the most important change the modern world brought into the life of a farm family like hers. Telephone? Radio, with market and weather news? Farm machinery? Automobile? "When they built the road to Thayer," she replied. "It was the biggest change. Before that we had to go down the Eleven Point River to trade, clear down to Pocahontas, Arkansas [pronounced po-kee-hon-tus]."

Ozarkers embrace roads and the folks driving on them. In my rural neighborhood, new houses — big and expensive — are built right up near the road so their occupants can stand at the window and look passers-by straight in the eye. The road is the larger neighborhood. Our signs are another way we talk to our neighbors.

Ignoring the signs prepared by big city ad agencies, those remaining — our signs — collectively say that the Ozarks is still a rural and small town region (albeit one in transition), a region of hard working folks, practical and serious, but not too serious. Family and kin, religion, work, neighbors, tradition, are here. Friendly folks, open but skeptical, still provincial, close to the earth (if you've been out there, you know that really means close to the dirt). Men and women now retired from farming or trucking or storekeeping or even the professions grew up pumping water by hand and using a privy, cleaning black soot from kerosene lamp and lantern chimneys, hoeing the garden, chopping sprouts, and hand-picking bugs off potato vines in 100-degree heat. They smelled oak wood smoke and smokehouse ham frying on frosty mornings. They smelled the sweat of horses and humans and walked dusty miles along those precious gravel or dirt roads to one-room schoolhouses in every kind of weather.

The Ozarks is a long-perpetuated frontier region. It still reveals its signature, if you look for it.

When I was a boy in the 1930s Ozarks, we went from our farm up to Springfield some Saturdays when we could get the old Dodge to run. The road was 50, slow winding miles, some of it gravel. Springfield was a big city, it seemed to me, with tall buildings and fancy stores around the square. It fired my imagination. Not far from the square were teams and wagons in front of wholesale houses where farmers traded cream and eggs for feed and blocks of salt and the like.

In Springfield, as in Kansas City, everything seemed up-to-date even at the turn of the 20th century. Boosters named it "Queen City of the Ozarks." Electric lights and streetcars, running water and steam heat, dentists and paved streets (some of them at least), and other paraphernalia of the modern world were here. The first public high school in the Ozarks rose in 1893; and in 1905 Missouri started the fourth state normal school here.

State Normal #4 was another reason to go up to Springfield. It became State Teachers College (STC), then Southwest Missouri State College (SMS), and finally, SMSU. From normal school to comprehensive regional university, SMSU has been integral to the modernization of the Ozarks region. Tens of thousands of its youth have flowed into SMS classes. As graduates they have flowed back, to teach in the region's schools and to function in every other aspect of its economy and society.

Ozarks roads have been paths to modernity, paths to the future. Especially has that been true of the roads that lead to school. As SMSU enters a second century, we can find *our own* sign along the Ozarks road: "Southwest Missouri State University — next right."

of dramatic cuttings titled *Fashions in Love* from Elizabeth Barrett Browning, *Macbeth, Camille, Anthony and Cleopatra, St. Joan* and *Salome*. Weekly assemblies were dropped in favor of a single major event for each term beginning in 1958-59. The Convocations were divided into two groups; "The Master Artists Series," which featured programs with Celeste Holm and the St. Louis Symphony, and "Friday Night on Campus," which included a dozen programs including lectures, films, concerts and travelogues.

Celeste Holm's dramatic program "With Love and Laughter" depicting how relations between men and women have changed, proved very popular. More than 600 people waited an hour and a half for her to arrive after flight problems delayed her arrival until 9:30 p.m. The new format with less frequent programs and more recognizable names seemed to help. Dean Duane Meyer in 1963 observed, "Our students have exhibited a remarkable interest in such diverse topics as contemporary France, Eskimo culture, and new techniques in chemistry."

Indeed the lecture series did bring in notables. Daniel Boorstin of the history faculty at the University of Chicago spoke as did Lester Longman of the art faculty of UCLA, Walter Taylor, anthropologist from Southern Illinois University and social historian Harry Golden. But despite the improved schedule, the crowds, while enthusiastic, were usually small. In 1964 *The Standard* editor wondered about the vitality of intellectual life on campus after reporting the small attendance at forums and panels on controversial issues as well as limited participation in literary opportunities

President Arthur Mallory and his wife Joann enjoy the company of students at the dinner preceding the Christmas Holiday dance and lighting of the luminaria in 1964. Dr. Mallory, a 1954 graduate of SMS, became the college's fifth president just 10 years after he completed his undergraduate work. He was serving as dean of the evening school at the University of Missouri at St. Louis when he was selected to head his alma mater.

and slim attendance at convocations. "Looking at the facts it would seem that intellectualism on this campus is, for all practical purposes, dead. It is buried with apathetic, indifferent students who run home or to the riverbank every weekend, who cannot wait to transfer to another college or leave with a degree, and who would much rather discuss the latest game of hearts than anything resembling an intellectual subject." Deploring apathy seems to be the perennial vocation of college newspaper editors.

By the middle to late 1960s, convocations began to feature controversial civil rights speakers. Dick Gregory, black comedian and artist, accompanied the Mandrell Singers to campus in 1964-65. After the show Gregory dropped his role as social satirist and

talked frankly with students about the civil rights struggle. Later that year John Howard Griffin of *Black Like Me* fame reported to a hushed student audience his experiences walking throughout the south as a white person who had deliberately undergone a skin color transformation to test his thesis that discrimination is based primarily on the appearance of racial difference, and nothing else. Officials at Baptist Bible College reacted to Griffin's appearance at SMS by sending a telegram to Governor Hearnes protesting Griffin's appearance at a state institution and describing his writings as "books of degeneracy."

The 1960s closed out with a variety of lecturers, including Art Buchwald, the columnist and humorist, and Marvin Kalb, the CBS diplomatic

SMSU
└ ROTC Rifle Team wins 5th Army Intercollegiate and Interscholastic Rifle Match.

Missouri/Springfield
└ Springfield Art Museum opens new facility in Phelps Grove.
└ Springfield Civic Symphony celebrates 25th anniversary.

International/USA
└ NASA becomes operational.
└ First transatlantic jet plane service established.

correspondent in Moscow, who told his audience in 1967, "We shouldn't be in Vietnam, but we are there." The Reverend Jesse Jackson addressed racial issues stating, "There is still a chance for survival." Pat Paulson, humorist and presidential candidate in 1968, packed the house with two performances in the fall of 1970. His satirical discussion of the sexual revolution, drugs, astrology, religion, ecology and politics produced a standing ovation by a standing-room-only crowd.

The convocation approach to campus musical entertainment in the 1950s and 1960s reflected the golden era of the 1920s when President Hill brought several world-class artists to the campus. In 1954 Fred Waring brought his "Pleasure Time 1955" to campus featuring an electronic ballet in which his Pennsylvanians merged electronic impulses with musical rhythm to produce "a startling effect — a masterpiece of motion, music and color." The audience was transfixed when the musicians sang the classic favorite, "You'll Never Walk Alone."

Carlos Montoya, the world's foremost Flamenco guitarist at the time, thrilled listeners in 1960 with his personal arrangements of compositions based on the Spanish Gypsy tradition. Roger Williams came to campus in 1961 determined "to build a bridge across the gulf between popular and classical music." His concert went from Bach to Gershwin with an occasional rock-and-roll piece. Summer students were not left out of the convocation series. The Chad Mitchell Trio performed in the summer of 1962 and thrilled the crowd with their latest recording, "The John

Birch Society," which was banned when first released. Considered the top folk group in the country at the time, the Trio "wowed 'em," according to *The Standard.*

The Smothers Brothers entertained in 1963 at a contract cost of $2,000. "The field house is not a great place to entertain," they said, but the crowd didn't seem to mind. The Brothers' parody on "Springfield, the City of Sin" brought the house down. For $3,500 plus 60 percent of the paid admission, the St. Louis Symphony joined with Peter, Paul and Mary in a memorable concert on March 11, 1963.

Throughout the late 1960s a parade of notable performances were staged at SMS, including Jerry Lee Lewis, Dorothy Coulter, Hans Schweiger and the Kansas City Philharmonic, Ray Charles, Jose Feliciano, Al Hirt and Marcel Marceau. Both the campus and the community

were being introduced to some of the best entertainers in the business. That cultural enrichment would become an increasingly important theme of town-college interaction.

Other venues of entertainment included the annual Homecoming celebration with its parades, dances and famous bands. Ted Weems played for several Homecoming dances. Woody Herman made frequent appearances. In 1958, the Crew Cuts, voted the No. 1 vocal group, appeared at Homecoming. In the 1960s, Tommy Dorsey and Helen Reddy entertained Homecoming guests as did Meriam Makeba from Johannesburg. Discovered by Harry Belefonte, Makeba toured the United States singing native songs from South Africa. She was followed in 1961 by Inman and Ira, black folk singers tracing the history of Negroes in America.

Other distinguished visitors came to campus for Religious Emphasis

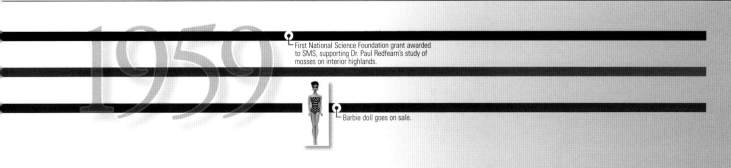

A treasured grade over a prized signature. Ralph Einer Harmon in the spring term of 1949 received a mark of excellence in English 101, fiction, taught by the legendary English instructor and debate coach Virginia J. Craig.

1950

First National Science Foundation grant awarded to SMS, supporting Dr. Paul Redfearn's study of mosses on interior highlands.

Barbie doll goes on sale.

Week, which developed in the 1950s. Dr. Marcus Bach, professor of religion at the University of Iowa, came in 1952 declaring, "Religion is Life's Greatest Adventure." Bach was noted for his outstanding research, which included living with the groups he was studying including Jews and the Doukhabors. In 1957, shortly after the Soviet launching of Sputnik, Religious Emphasis week brought Dr. George Schweitzer, a chemist from the University of Tennessee to lecture on "Research, Reason and Revelation."

Through a variety of venues, the SMS campus was exposed to world affairs, science, politics, the arts and rich variety of entertainment in the 1950s and 1960s. The college was becoming an important cultural asset to the community.

Administrations
Four Presidents in 11 Years
By the late 1950s, there were indications of the imminent retirement of President Roy Ellis who had been at the helm of the college since 1926 and was reputed to be the most senior president of any American college or university. First there was the naming of the Fine Arts Building in honor of President Ellis in 1958.

The next year President Ellis received two awards from the University of Missouri. The College of Education presented him a citation for "Distinguished Service to Education" in March 1959. Three months later in Commencement ceremonies at Columbia, Dr. Ellis was awarded an honorary doctorate.

In October 1959 at the annual SMS Alumni Banquet, Dr. Ellis was given the "Outstanding Alumnus Award." The award was given just one day after six new buildings were dedicated on campus as part of the 1959 Homecoming celebration. Horace Haseltine, president of the Alumni Association said, "No one has made a greater contribution to the college than Dr. Ellis. The selection committee has long felt that he should be so honored,

During the 1960s registration for classes typically occurred in the field house. This bird's-eye view suggests the chaos often associated with that ritual event.

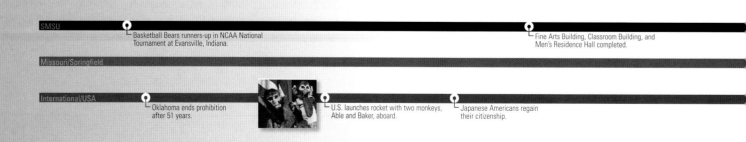

SMSU
Basketball Bears runners-up in NCAA National Tournament at Evansville, Indiana.
Fine Arts Building, Classroom Building, and Men's Residence Hall completed.

Missouri/Springfield

International/USA
Oklahoma ends prohibition after 51 years.
U.S. launches rocket with two monkeys, Able and Baker, aboard.
Japanese Americans regain their citizenship.

but waited until this year's Homecoming which included the dedication of the new buildings on the campus."

The rapid sequence of awards had all the earmarks of honoring a person who was about to end a distinguished career. If so, the anticipations were correct, for in September 1960, Dr. Ellis announced his retirement to the Board of Regents effective August 31, 1961. While at age 72 the president was still a vigorous man, he had already spent more than a half-century nurturing the growth and development of education in southwest Missouri.

Ellis was a "native son." Born and raised on a farm on the Webster-Wright County line, he came to the college when it was State Normal School #4 and graduated with a Bachelor of Pedagogy degree. He returned to the school in 1917 to teach economics and sociology. He was named president of the college in February 1926. Except for six months in the Army during

World War I, Roy Ellis spent the rest of his professional career shaping the growth of SMS. When he became president, there were only two buildings on campus. At his retirement, 14 buildings graced the 38 acres.

In announcing the news of Ellis's retirement, Board President William C. Cockrill said, "It is with deep regret that the Board recognizes plans for the immediate retirement of President Ellis, who, after 35 years as head of this institution, insists that he now step down. To say that he will be sorely missed is, of course, a gross understatement."

When the time of his retirement arrived in 1961, the Board of Regents honored him with the president emeritus title, the first ever given by the college. In the resolution, Ellis was described as having "the longest known tenure of any college president in the nation." He was cited as having "devoted his entire adult life to the intellectual, spiritual and physical growth of SMS."

The search for a new president began immediately. A faculty committee composed of Dr. Duane Meyer, Dr. James Snapp, Dr. Harry Siceluff, Dr. Grace Gardner, Dr. Carl Fronabarger, Dr. George Gleason and Dr. E. Howard Matthews was appointed to advise the Board. They were to compile a list of the "qualifications, talents, virtues and attributes the faculty hopes to find in the new president." They were also asked "to convey to the Board of Regents the names of individuals from whatever source, who seem to best meet those qualifications."

When the sorting and sifting of candidates was finished, the Board took a bold step by offering the presidency to one clearly not a "native

When President Arthur Mallory left SMS in 1971 to become Education Commissioner for the State of Missouri, Dr. Duane G. Meyer was selected as the college's sixth president. He had already served as acting president at the end of both the Ellis and Traywick administrations, so was no stranger to presidential duties. But he came as a classroom teacher of American history and with a teacher's concern for students. He chose to forgo a formal inauguration, dedicating the saved funds to scholarships for students.

son." Dr. Leland Traywick, a professor of economics and assistant dean of the College of Business and Public Service at Michigan State University, was selected as the fourth president. Traywick was a native of Okmulgee, Oklahoma. He was educated, however, at the University of Missouri, and earned his doctorate from the University of Illinois. During the 1960-61 academic year, he was on leave from Michigan State serving with the National Committee for Economic Development in New York City.

In typical Ellis eloquence, the president emeritus, upon hearing of

Louis B. Leakey finds the skull of "Nutcracker Man" in Tanzanyika.

All freshmen under 21 years of age, not living at home, required to live in college residence halls.

Hawaii becomes 50th state.

Bonanza premieres on TV.

Typhoon kills nearly 5,000 in Japan.

Feminism Takes Root on Campus

For more than 46 years Dr. Virginia Craig had encouraged women to take active roles in civic and political affairs. In the spring of 1963 the advocacy seemed to bear some fruit with the organization of the Association of Women Students. The Association made it clear that its subjects were women, not girls, a disputed point on campus for many years. It also set about to discuss the "ideas, aspirations, and questions of women," as well as provide leadership training for women. "We hope to create an awareness of the educated woman's responsibility to contribute her talents in social, political, and intellectual spheres," the announcement declared.

Traywick's appointment, said, "To the new President (Heaven Bless Him!)…. May he have the courage to tread the path of duty though he walk barefooted and alone."

The words were, unwittingly, prophetic. The path of duty was difficult, though short, for Leland Traywick, and there were times he must have felt as though he were walking barefooted and alone. He brought to SMS a mature vision of higher education nurtured in the halls of a major university. He did not arrive critical of the institution he was about to lead. Rather he saw in SMS an opportunity to take a promising college and make it into a leader. He was visionary. He was energetic. But he had never been a president before so had never practiced the art of working with a citizen board.

His dream for the institution was compelling. In his inaugural address titled "On The Razor's Edge of Tomorrow," Traywick argued that "approximately every two centuries there comes a culmination of men and the times which shape the course of destiny 'rough hew it how we will.'" He then declared, "We are on such a crest of events."

That conviction thrust the new president into a frenzy of activity. Within the first two weeks of his presidency, Dr. Traywick established a "Committee on the Future of SMS." The Committee's basic charge was to recommend actions for 15 concerns he had outlined. The concerns covered matters of policy for student life, faculty responsibility and college facilities — areas which essentially opened the door to comprehensive institutional change.

The language in the document containing the charge is significant.

The president opened by saying, "This Committee will be one of the most, if not the most important factor in both the short-run and long-run consideration of SMS that we have had to date. Here in your hands lies the potential of making something even more significant out of Southwest Missouri State College than has been made up to the present time." Of the Committee, the president went on to say that, "only if it has the freedom to investigate, to criticize, and to think and plan creatively, will it succeed. Let it, therefore, be understood that it does have this freedom and likewise this responsibility." His conclusion reiterated the substance of the whole charge saying, "This is to be no paper organization."

The mandate was unprecedented in college history, and when it was revealed that 10 of the 12 members of the Committee were faculty, the campus was amazed. The only two administrators were Dr. Duane Meyer, dean of instruction and admissions and Dr. David Scott, executive officer. The composition of the committee signaled a new philosophy of institutional governance, namely "shared governance," featuring strong faculty input. It also implied discreetly differential roles for administration and faculty, a concept not seen in earlier years when lines of demarcation between administration and faculty were never clear.

On Friday, September 22, 1961, just three weeks after Dr. Traywick arrived on campus, the Committee on the Future of SMS met from 12:45 until 3:00 p.m. Called to order by Chairman Dr. Duane Meyer, Dr. Don Hadwigger was elected secretary. Other members included Drs. Carl Fronabarger, George Gleason, Richard Haswell, Lynn

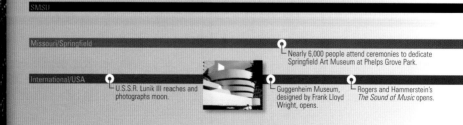

SMSU

Missouri/Springfield

Nearly 6,000 people attend ceremonies to dedicate Springfield Art Museum at Phelps Grove Park.

International/USA

U.S.S.R. Lunik III reaches and photographs moon.

Guggenheim Museum, designed by Frank Lloyd Wright, opens.

Rogers and Hammerstein's *The Sound of Music* opens.

Martin, Howard Matthews, Harold Retallick, Harry Siceluff, David Scott, Mary Rose Sweeney and Mr. Robert Harvey. The Committee looked at its charge and its mandate and immediately set to work.

For 18 consecutive weeks the group worked. They tackled issues that would wilt the resolve of the most seasoned academic. They reached out to knowledgeable groups on campus and capable advisors from national organizations. They organized sub-committees within their group to study individual issues. One wonders how they found time to teach with the weekly preparations necessary for committee deliberations.

The minutes of those meetings are rich in detail revealing informed discussion and valiant struggles to reach consensus. If the original charge was not robust enough, on October 27, President Traywick asked the Committee to also prepare a draft of a college long-range plan that could be submitted to Governor Dalton by December 10.

By early February 1962, the Committee issued its recommendations. The members had taken seriously the president's declaration that "this is to be no paper organization." What

they brought forth was an agenda for change unlike anything that had ever happened before at SMS.

Among their recommendations for the student sector:
- Develop a code of student conduct and a non-academic disciplinary system staffed by a disciplinary officer, students and faculty.
- Establish a judicial system to deal with academic dishonesty.
- Establish a counseling center with professionally qualified staff.
- Create more selective admission standards to manage enrollment growth.
- Establish clear standards for academic probation and suspension.
- Establish an honors program and petition for a Phi Kappa Phi chapter on campus.
- Provide additional scholarships, especially to help students from low-income families.

Recommendations for curricular change were even more dramatic:
- Abandon the quarter system and move to the semester system.
- Rework the entire curriculum to conform to a semester instructional schedule.
- Establish a general education program for all students that includes basic skill instruction in English, mathematics, physical education, science and speech.
- Establish a two-year terminal degree in vocational programs.
- Establish, by 1963, independent graduate programs in education and all the disciplines providing basic skill courses. Hire a director of graduate

studies and organize a faculty Graduate Studies Committee.
- Establish a program in philosophy.
- Establish a Bachelor of Fine Arts program.
- Reorganize academic departments into a divisional structure grouping related disciplines.

Faculty rights and responsibilities were also dramatically redefined by the Committee's recommendations:
- Establish a Faculty Senate with responsibility for curriculum and possessing powers of shared governance. A constitution was created by the Committee.
- Reduce teaching contracts from 11 to nine months with no reduction in salary.
- Encourage faculty research on problems associated with the service area.
- Reduce teaching load from the equivalent of 16 to 12 hours per semester.
- Revise the faculty rank system. The current system "bears no resemblance whatsoever to the accepted practices of American colleges and universities."
- Revise the faculty pay scale assuring equal salaries for men and women.
- Freeze all faculty promotions until a new faculty rank system is devised.

Facility recommendations were similarly challenging:
- Move athletics programs to the O'Reilly General Hospital site where a new stadium, new field house and nine-hole golf course should be built.
- Move Greenwood School from the Education Building to new facilities to be built on the north side of the campus.

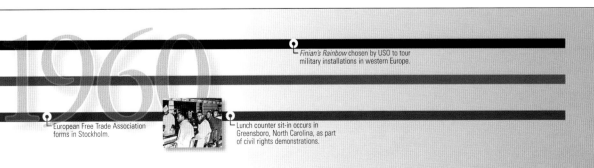

1960

Finian's Rainbow chosen by USO to tour military installations in western Europe.

European Free Trade Association forms in Stockholm.

Lunch counter sit-in occurs in Greensboro, North Carolina, as part of civil rights demonstrations.

- Expand the Student Union.
- Expand the Memorial Library.
- Increase instructional space by 50 classrooms by 1971 in anticipation of a doubling of enrollment. (Enrollment actually tripled by 1971).
- Construct a new dormitory every biennium beginning with a men's dorm accommodating 500.
- Establish parking fees to enable expansion of parking facilities.

Total facility improvements recommended would cost an estimated $15.3 million.

As the recommendations attest, the Committee's five-month assignment was arduous, time consuming, and without reprieve. When its work was completed in February 1962, President Traywick wrote a note to Dean Duane Meyer who had chaired the Committee from its inception, saying, "The quantity of work done was prodigious, but the quality was all that anyone could ever ask." As a matter of fact, the Committee essentially created the magnetic field toward which the institution's compass needle would point for the next 20 years. Two things were driving the speed of change: (1) the rapid growth of the student body, and (2) the aggressive vision of the new president.

The first agent of change was beyond anyone's control. In just two years, the college enrollment had grown by 25 percent. In 1964 the number of 17-year-olds in Missouri would increase by 25 percent over the previous year, and for the succeeding years, it was anticipated that the 17-year-old cohort would grow by 8 to 15 percent each year. Baby boomers were on their way to college like a marching army.

The second agent of change, the president's vision and mode of operation were, however, subject to change.

While the Board did not micro-manage the institution under Dr. Ellis's tenure, they were always informed about major decisions and initiatives. Their sense of control over the institution was never in question. But President Traywick brought a new dynamic to the administration. He interpreted his presidency as a mandate to advance his vision for the college. He was a self-confident man, quick in insight, and action-oriented. Having had no experience in working with public boards, the new president plunged into implementing his vision for the college with minimal consultation with the Regents. The Board grew alarmed at Traywick's ambitious initiatives, some of which were complete surprises to them. After only a few months, the struggle between an aggressive president and a neglected Board became apparent. One Regent allegedly told Dr. Traywick "We don't want to hear anymore about 10-year building plans; we only want to plan two or three months ahead."

President Traywick apparently interpreted the foot-dragging of the Board as their inexperience in higher education governance. So he proceeded to use Board meetings as an occasion to educate the Regents about their role, an unwelcome initiative, to say the least. So things between the president and the Board started badly and grew progressively worse. Dr. Traywick later confessed, "By December, 1961, the honeymoon was over." The honeymoon, if there ever was one, had lasted only four months.

While the honeymoon may have ended, the Traywick reforms were coming in rapid sequence to the Board. A new retirement plan was approved in December as was an immediate

The introduction of ROTC training to SMS in 1952 added a new dimension to both the academic and social life of the campus. Here cadets Green, Johnson, Payne and Tadych form the color guard for the battalion.

fee increase from $35 to $40 a term. The registration process was revised for efficiency. In January 1962, a new faculty sabbatical policy was adopted. Correspondence courses were dropped. Faculty were put on nine-month contracts for the first time in the history of the institution. In February, the Faculty Senate was organized, giving faculty governance powers and responsibilities never spelled out before. The deluge of initiatives continued including moving to the semester system in the fall of 1963. A master's degree in guidance and counseling was started in the summer of 1962.

At the end of his first year as president, *The Standard* reported that "the campus — at all levels — has been in

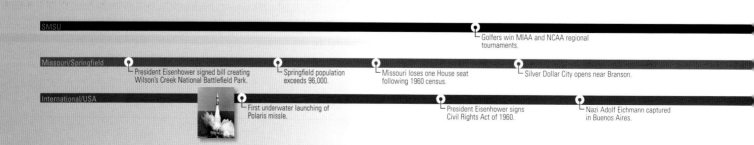

SMSU

Golfers win MIAA and NCAA regional tournaments.

Missouri/Springfield

President Eisenhower signed bill creating Wilson's Creek National Battlefield Park.

Springfield population exceeds 96,000.

Missouri loses one House seat following 1960 census.

Silver Dollar City opens near Branson.

International/USA

First underwater launching of Polaris missle.

President Eisenhower signs Civil Rights Act of 1960.

Nazi Adolf Eichmann captured in Buenos Aires.

constant motion as actual changes and the beginning steps to future innovations were initiated by the dynamic college head." *The Standard* reported, "each one of these innovations has been met with general acceptance as faculty and students alike fall into step behind a vigorous college president who is already confidently striding along — only one year old into his job."

Using every opportunity to recruit public support for his initiatives on campus, President Traywick spoke regularly to civic and community organizations throughout the Southwest District. In October 1962, he addressed the Springfield Rotary Club, telling them that he had just completed a trip to Fort Worth where he personally talked with officials at the regional office of the Housing and Home Finance Agency to arrange a loan for the expansion of dormitories and the Student Center building. When he presented the budget request in Jefferson City for the 1963-65 biennium, which amounted to $6.7 million, legislators were impressed. Representative Paul Canaday observed that this was "a more forward-looking program for the college than we have had for some time." It was part of a set of influences that led Canaday, in March 1963, to co-sponsor a bill introduced simultaneously in the House and Senate that would allow any state college board to change its institutional name to "university when they deem it advantageous."

To all external appearances, the Traywick presidency was moving forward implementing one after another of the Committee's recommendations. But in the Board room, things were not well. At the time, Board meetings were closed to the public and the press,

---

"Suitcase College"

"I suppose there were two reasons for the label ('suitcase college'). One, many students lived in small towns close to Springfield. It was relatively easy to get home. Another was probably due to the unique design of the class schedule. Each class met 60 minutes per class session... four days a week for 12 weeks.... All afternoon classes didn't meet on Fridays. What an invitation to 'pack-up' and go home!"

∽

Dr. Dale Allee remembering his student days in the 1950s

---

so there was little public knowledge of the struggles between the Regents and the new president. As the difficulties mounted, the president's poor interpersonal skills exacerbated the problems. Finally, on June 1, 1964, just three years after assuming the presidency, Traywick announced his resignation.

The story might have ended there, but the president felt compelled to take his case to the public. Shortly after he announced his resignation, he reported that he was forced to resign and said publicly, "I fear for the future of the college. A competent, able Board is needed." His public attacks on the Board continued on almost a daily basis.

The campus and the community were shocked and outraged by the forced resignation of Traywick. Their feelings and his continued public attacks on the Board created a very hostile environment for the Regents. After the local paper came out editorially against the Board's action and urged citizens to contact the Governor, local citizens asked Governor Dalton to conduct an investigation into the matter. But he refused saying, "I have confidence in the Board. They are outstanding citizens of southwest Missouri. They've lived here all their lives, and they're familiar with the situation."

The local chapter of the American Association of University Professors (AAUP) issued a statement on June 8, noting, "with dismay a pattern of secrecy antithetical to any concept of the obligations of a public board." The Faculty Senate met on June 12 and sent a message to the Board reminding them that Leland Traywick had met all 12 guidelines set for the presidential search and should be retained as president. The Student Senate unanimously approved a resolution calling on the Regents for an explanation of their dismissal of Traywick as well as requesting a public explanation of their actions on a half-dozen other matters of campus interest. They concluded their business with a "no confidence" vote for the

---

Starting salaries: elementary teachers, $3,500; secondary teachers, $3,750; business graduates, $4,392.

Ghana becomes a republic.

UFO sighted by three California patrolmen.

Chubby Checker releases *The Twist*.

Flinstones premieres — first prime time animated show.

1946-72 Southwest Missouri State College   189

Board. The Alumni Association, under the leadership of Dr. David Holmes, also called upon the Board to explain its actions.

Through all this, the Board kept a discreet silence, interpreted by many as a lack of accountability. The continual charges of Board incompetence by Traywick finally, on June 8, led to a 24-page statement being read by Board member William O. Russell to representatives of the Alumni Association and others who had rushed to Ellis Hall to hear the discussion. The statement began by saying that the Board demanded "that Dr. Leland Traywick vacate the Presidency immediately because of his conduct before the public." It went on to delineate numerous other concerns with Traywick's administration of college affairs. Upon reading the lengthy statement, Mr. Russell declared the meeting adjourned and entertained no questions. "The Alumni committee and the small audience

were dumbfounded," according to *The Standard.* "The Statement was nice. It was long. And it was prolix with 'documented facts.' But it failed miserably to meet head-on or with finality a single charge made by the fired president." *The Standard* report concluded saying, "Dr. Traywick and his friends have suffered. Undoubtedly the Board and its friends have suffered. But they will get over it eventually. The lasting sufferer is SMS College."

About this time it was learned that Traywick actually resigned in early May at the request of the Board after it had already interviewed a potential replacement, Ross Marshall Robertson, from Indiana University School of Business. He was interviewed between April 30 and May 2.

For a while Leland Traywick may have "walked barefoot and alone" as president of the college. But upon resigning, he mobilized every source of support available to him as he con-

tinued to attack the Board. Students championed his cause with a five block long procession marching through downtown Springfield. Faculty went on record supporting his presidency. The local newspaper endorsed his work and editorially criticized the Board. When it was clear the Board was not going to reverse its decision, calls for its resignation came from the Alumni Association and others in the community. On June 25, six students, Jim Bohannon, Paul McMasters, Cheryl Harmon, Marian Goodman, R.C. Jones and Jackson Harrell traveled to Jefferson City to meet personally with Governor Dalton. After a three-hour discussion with the students, Governor Dalton declared, "As far as I am concerned, I have settled the controversy. This thing will die down if we quit throwing gasoline on it."

As the dust began to settle in July 1964, Dr. George Gleason of the English faculty speaking to the Exchange Club said, "Personally, I'm certain of this about Dr. Traywick: the school, the faculty and the community are all the better for the fact that for the last three years he has worked the hell out of us!" While Traywick's presidency was short, his legacy was long. The agenda from which he worked, created largely by the Committee for the Future of SMS, remained alive through the next two presidencies.

Fortunately, both for SMS and for the agenda Traywick had laid out, Dr. Duane Meyer was named by the Board on June 11, 1964, as acting president. Dr. Meyer had chaired Traywick's Committee for the Future and had taken a leading role in shaping its recommendations. More importantly, he had the complete trust of the campus, particularly the faculty who gave him "a

Local townsfolk cheer as the Drill Squad Cadets from the ROTC battalion parade through downtown in the fall of 1953.

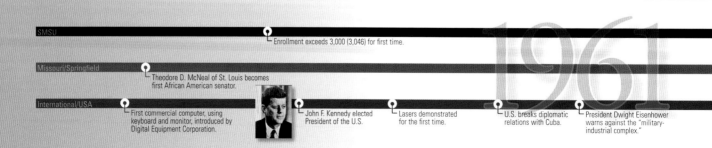

In full military dress, officers of the 1954 Bear Battalion march through the arch of rifles escorting their dates to the second annual Military Ball held March 26 in the Student Center ballroom. Eddie Ball's orchestra provided the music for the festive event.

unanimous vote of confidence."

In the aftermath of the Traywick firing, increasing pressure was put on the Board to open its meetings to the public. *The Standard* editorialized that the distillation of the whole controversy over Traywick was the refusal of the Board to conduct its business in public view. "People who support an institution deserve, and will eventually demand, to know how that institution is run," declared the editor. The Board's response was simply, "No other college holds open meetings."

Shortly after leaving SMS, Leland Traywick was hired as president of the University of Omaha. He lured at least four SMS faculty members to Omaha, but his tenure there was similar to his tenure at SMS — short. His imperious style created immediate problems with the Omaha Board resulting in a second miscarried presidency. Upon leaving

Omaha, Traywick became director of the Bureau of Business Research at the College of William and Mary. No further college or university presidencies were attempted. He died in 1984.

Dr. Arthur Mallory

By early July in 1964, the SMS Board of Regents had selected six faculty to assist them in the search for a new president. The group included Drs. George Gleason, Clarence Ketch, Lynn Martin, R.G. Ruetz, John Shatz and Harry Siceluff. The Board chose to use the same criteria that guided the search in 1961. Only four months later in October 1964, Board President Kenneth Postlethwaite called a faculty meeting to announce the choice of a new president. He prefaced his remarks by saying, "The Board had chosen to limit one of the original criteria — that which excluded from consideration

anyone who had any prior connection with the college." In 1961, faculty concerns over inbreeding and the need to get a fresh perspective, led to its recommendation that the Board find someone who had no previous connection with the college. The era of "native sons" was to end. And it did with the selection of Traywick. But it was not the case with Traywick's successor. Board President Postlethwaite announced that an SMS graduate and native son from the Buffalo area, Dr. Arthur Mallory, would become the fifth president of SMS.

While all of Arthur Mallory's family including his father and mother and several aunts and uncles were SMS graduates, Arthur's choice of SMS had not been automatic. In fact, he had a scholarship to attend Washington University in St. Louis where he planned to study medicine. In the summer of 1951 he came to SMS for summer school in order to strengthen his background in chemistry. "I simply never left at the end of the summer," explained Dr. Mallory.

The selection of Mallory caught the faculty by surprise. While his name had been among other candidates screened by the faculty committee advising the Board, he had not been placed in category A, nor had they had the opportunity to meet or interview him. While it was clear to the Committee that the final decision in appointing a president was the Board's to make, the lack of communication and consultation did little to relieve the faculty's problems with the Regents that had arisen during the Traywick era.

Dr. Mallory began his work on November 9, 1964. The start was not easy. In addition to faculty skepticism,

Dr. Leland Traywick becomes 4th SMSU president.

Dr. Duane Meyer named dean of Instruction and Admissions.

President Kennedy creates Peace Corps.

Ken, boyfriend to Barbie, is introduced.

Yuri Gagarin of the Soviet Union is first man to orbit the earth.

Last journey of the Orient Express train from Paris to Bucharest.

1946-72 Southwest Missouri State College   191

With the beginning of ROTC training in 1952, the Army program quickly produced sharpshooters, drill teams and an ROTC band. Sergeant Venable adds a forceful trumpet part to the 1967 performance.

Paul McMasters' comments in *The Standard* were not reassuring. "With traces of reservation, but quite apparent determination marking his step, Arthur Mallory ascended to the top of a problem heap last week and calmly dug in." As a matter of fact, Mallory had not sought the post. He learned in July that he was being considered, and was invited to visit with the Board. In October he was offered the position, considered it for a week, and declined it. A week later, he was again approached by the Board and this time accepted.

Only 10 years earlier, Arthur Mallory was finishing his senior year at SMS. Thereafter he served two years in the military, returned to take graduate work at the University of Missouri where he received his Ed.D in 1959. Upon finishing his doctorate, Mallory took the position as assistant superintendent of the Parkway School District in St. Louis County. He also taught part-time at the University of Missouri-St. Louis. He was serving as dean of the Evening School at UMSL when invited to take the helm at SMS.

Mallory was the youngest president in the history of the college. He was only 31 when asked to take the helm. Frank Martin, legendary editor of the *West Plains Quill*, reportedly told the new president, "Arthur, you need to grow a mustache. You are too young looking."

Despite his youth, Arthur Mallory "ascended to the top of the problem heap" with sensitivity and grace. With little college administrative experience under his belt, he distinguished himself early on as a good listener. Carefully and methodically he sought to heal a battered campus. His inaugural address on March 26, 1965, was a summons to the future. "My pledge to you is this," declared the president to a crowd of 2,000. "The view is forward. If you will work with me, we will walk and look ahead — together." His audience listened carefully for an agenda, and he did not disappoint them. He disclosed plans for an independent graduate program, the building of a new Greenwood Lab School, improved salaries for faculty and reduced teaching loads. He also reassured faculty that while opportunities for research and publication would be encouraged and supported, the college would not become another "publish or perish" institution. The focus of faculty responsibility would be in the classroom. So the agenda of the Committee on the Future of SMS did not die with the Traywick dismissal. It continued to guide the actions of the new administration and define the aspirations of the burgeoning school.

President Mallory also called on the campus to join him in the quest for

Dr. Donald Nicholson delivers a lecture in his African history class.

SMSU

Excess and diminished grading system dropped in favor of a common plan used by all state colleges.

Missouri/Springfield

Dedication of Wilson's Creek Battlefield.

International/USA

Alan Shepard becomes first American in space.

Berlin Wall is constructed by Soviets to halt defections to the West.

unity. "The administration and faculty, in defense of the freedom of the college, must build an internal cohesion, an internal integrity based upon mutual understanding and respect."

Mallory's words and initiatives resonated well with the campus. *The Standard* editor, reflecting on the Inaugural Address and the first five months of the new administration said, "Perhaps this is the time that the diverse factions and elements of SMS begin to work together. This does not mean that we will not continue to press for greater recognition of the importance of the student, and an increasing role for him in the college. It does mean, however, that by a combined effort much can be done to insure a bright future for SMS."

Dr. Bob Flanders remembers an interview with young President Mallory. "When I was interviewed for the position of (History) Department head in 1968, my final appointment was with President Arthur Mallory. Arthur was then 36, two years younger that I was. At the conclusion of the conversation, he bore a kind of testimony and proffered a sort of call. 'My daddy was a teacher. My mamma was a teacher. Beyond them in the family there were teachers. I'm a teacher. We teach here. Bob, come and join us. Get old and gray with us. Be buried among us.' I related this incident in various academic circles over the years, usually to unappreciative listeners. Said one woman, 'How embarrassing! Didn't you feel terrible?' No, in fact I was moved, almost to tears. The president had got to the nub of things at SMS, as presidents should do. I accepted his call, and 32 years later I am still working out his scenario."

The new president was a consum-

A memorable experience for students in the 1960s was Dr. Duane Meyer's course in American colonial history. With powdered wig and period dress, Dr. Meyer introduced his students to the challenges of the 18th century in America.

mate peace maker. He traveled countless miles throughout the Southwest District speaking to civic clubs, community groups and educators about SMS, its virtues, its growth and its promising future. He worked cooperatively with the Regents and restored trusting relations between the Board Room and the president's office. With his urging, the Board opened its meetings to the press and the public, which helped to rebuild confidence in the Regents. Board actions became regularly reported in the *Nile Green News,* helping overcome the communication problems with students and faculty.

Arthur Mallory proved himself a capable reconciler. The Traywick trauma was sensitively and constructively addressed among faculty and students as well as the public. However, Mallory, like his predecessor, had a relatively short tenure, but for very different reasons. Just six years after tak-

ing the reigns at SMS, Arthur Mallory was invited to take the position of Commissioner of Education for the State of Missouri. In January 1971, he succeeded Hubert Wheeler, himself an SMS graduate.

Throughout his presidency at SMS, Mallory had to deal with campus unrest related to the Civil Rights and the anti-Vietnam War Movements. In November 1970, while he was preparing to leave the college for his new post in Jefferson City, a frantic student rushed into his office declaring that a crowd of students were massing on the steps "threatening to take over the Administration Building." After calling Security, Dr. Mallory rushed down to try to calm the crowd of some 300. When he appeared at the door, the crowd broke out in cheers and applause, and presented him with a plaque "In Appreciation for Devoted Service to Southwest Missouri State

Sabbatical leave policy approved for faculty.

John Dalton elected governor.

Roger Maris ties Babe Ruth's record of 60 homeruns.

from the Panhellenic Council and the Inter-Fraternity Council (I.F.C.), 1970." Thanking the students, President Mallory jokingly said, "I would have been out sooner, but I was hiding in the closet."

Dr. Duane Meyer

When January 1, 1971, came, Mallory had moved to Jefferson City and SMS, for the second time, asked Dr. Duane Meyer to become acting president. A search committee was named which set out qualifications for the new president. He should "display and demand high academic standards, and he should be a leader in his own discipline." Furthermore, his philosophy of administration "should be democratic." Mirroring the disappointment with the Board's unilateral action hiring Arthur Mallory, the search committee added

a final guideline. "The person selected should be acceptable to the administrators, the faculty and the students as represented on the Presidential Search Committee, and to the Board of Regents."

After examining the credentials of more than 100 applicants for the post, it was no surprise when the Board announced in April 1971, that Dr. Duane Meyer would be the new president. With more than 15 years experience on campus, a distinguished record as a historian, an exemplary classroom ability, and twice-experienced as acting president, Meyer began his presidency with a stock of valuable assets. He had chaired the Committee on the Future of SMS 10 years earlier, so he had already had a hand in shaping the aspirations of the college. He could now personally address the goals he had recommended to others. Meyer

began that task with the broad support of faculty colleagues and student leaders. With his coming, SMS was poised to enter its fourth era — becoming a state university.

Academics and Growth

It was clear when the first veterans enrolled on campus under the G.I. Bill that academic adjustments would need to be made to accommodate the new population. The first evident change came with the organization of the Industrial Arts Department in 1947 under the leadership of Doyle Kemper. At the time, only 12 of 128 high schools in the southwest region offered industrial arts courses. So there wasn't a strong, immediate demand for industrial arts teachers, though a curriculum for that purpose was in place. The primary push was from veterans wanting job skills, not degrees. So in addition to degrees in industrial arts, there were also courses designed for non-majors. The program took a leap ahead in 1948 with the erecting of the Industrial Arts Building on the corner of Grand and Carrington Avenue.

In that same year the Missouri Legislature passed Senate Bill No. 4 requiring that any graduate from a state supported college or university "must be given regular courses of instruction in the constitution of the U.S. and of the State of Missouri, and in American History including the study of American institutions." Such courses were not new to the college, but their requirement was.

In 1950, the college began offering professional training in speech therapy. A speech clinic was opened to assist handicapped students and adults throughout the service area. Speech diag-

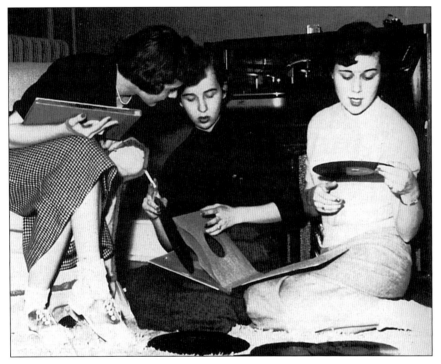

Spinning records at the sorority house were a favorite pastime in the early 1950s. Here Carol Roper, Marianne Squires and Marjorie Brim enjoy their favorite music albums.

SMSU
Faculty put on nine-month contract at 11-month rate.
First Faculty Senate elected by faculty.

Missouri/Springfield

1962

International/USA
NFL prohibits grabbing of face masks.
JFK bans all trade with Cuba except food and drugs.
Eight of nine planets align for first time in 400 years.

194   *Daring to Excel: The First 100 Years of Southwest Missouri State University*

Professor James Shannon, historian, served the college for 47 years. He joined the Normal School faculty in 1908 and served as head of the history department from 1911 to 1955. His classroom lectures became legendary among colleagues and students. An ardent supporter of college athletics programs, Shannon served as president of the MIAA conference for many years.

noses and hearing tests were conducted in a number of area schools as part of the program. Two years later, another health profession affiliated with SMS. St John's School of Nursing students began taking their nursing science courses at SMS.

Perhaps the greatest stimulus to academic change came from the surprising launch of the space vehicle, Sputnik, by the Soviet Union in 1957. Many judged the American educational system to be deficient since the United States had not yet pioneered any space shots. Within a very few years, significant changes were occurring on campus. A general education program with a five-hour requirement in the sciences was adopted, as was the semester system that required all college courses be redesigned. This process got under way in 1963 and drew the editorial attention of the *Springfield News and Leader*. "Southwest Missouri State College is now completing the first thorough revision of its curriculum in its 67-year history…." In the opinion of the editor, this curricular reform "is of greater importance to the young people of this Ozarks area than any of the college's recent programs for improvement of its physical plant." The editorial quoted Dean Duane Meyer as saying that the revision of the 800 course curriculum was akin to "a retooling, such as industry would do for an improved product."

A not-so-popular innovation in the curricular reform was the Junior English Exam imposed by the Faculty Senate in 1963. It required students to demonstrate their proficiency in written communication before they could be certified to graduate. Students did not endorse the idea. Dr. George Gleason was quoted in *The Standard* as saying, "The JEE does not usurp prerogatives of the Almighty as one peeved young lady thought. Instead, the JEE is an effort to help the individual student help himself. When he graduates, he will, it is hoped, be a worthy representative of himself and SMS." Such inventions, no matter how clothed in the language of persuasion, have never been seen by students to be in their interest.

The year 1963 also introduced the first honors program at the college. Coordinated by Dr. William McClure, it was described as "a special program designed for the student of exceptional ability." Special sections of college classes with more individual study and research projects were designed for honors students. Sixty-two freshmen enrolled in the fall of 1963. By 1967 the first graduates were presenting their honors theses. Phyllis Lee Cox evaluated the physical education program and personnel in Missouri public schools. Steven Harlow Mills studied pharmacological effects on blood glucose of the water snake, *natrix sipedon*. Margaret Chase Smith investigated the anxiety level of a selected group of SMS students as indicated by the Taylor Manifest Anxiety Scale. Jim Spindler wrote his thesis on the "Genetic Variants in the Protein Structure of Hemoglobin in the Wild Rabbit." Spindler trapped wild rabbits on an island in Table Rock Lake and compared their hemoglobin with wild rabbits trapped elsewhere.

While the honors program seemed to have great promise, the general edu-

Greenwood Training School renamed Greenwood Lab School.

John Glenn is first American to orbit the earth.

K-Mart opens.

U.S. national debt more than $300,000,000,000.

London trolley buses go out of business.

Thalidomide drug banned in Netherlands.

Southwest Standard staff writers Helen Kristek, Beecher Seeley, Mary Alice Simmons and Herb Branson analyze journalistic style as they prepare to modernize the school paper in 1954. *Standard* editor Tom Reed frequently hosted staff parties at "Club 841," Reed's address on South Weller.

cation program was abandoned for lack of student interest in 1968 and became a departmentally-based effort.

The crown jewel in academic advancement during the SMS years was the achievement of an independent graduate program. As early as 1950, a graduate extension program was offered on the SMS campus by the University of Missouri with classes carrying MU credit taught by Drs. Harry Siceluff, Ray McCoy and James Bane of the SMS faculty. In 1955, it became a cooperative program with half of the classes being taught on the SMS campus by SMS faculty and the other half taught in Columbia with the degree being given by the University of Missouri. In 1960, a Graduate Center was established at SMS allowing all work to be taken in Springfield. Some 43 courses were offered that year

including the complete curriculum for the Guidance and Counseling program. By 1960 there were 176 students enrolled in graduate studies. In 1964 over 50 courses were offered carrying graduate credit. By December 1966 an independent graduate school was authorized by the Board of Regents and scheduled to start in the summer of 1967. Master of Arts degrees would be available in history and English. Master of Science degrees would be available in elementary education, and secondary education in mathematics and theater. The master's in guidance and counseling was also available as an SMS degree. Sandra House was awarded the first SMS graduate degree, a Master of Science, Ed. in Speech and Theater.

Pioneering the Academic Study of Religion in a Public College

Religion has had a prominent place on the college campus from the Normal School days. While no religion courses were formally taught then, religious organizations were part of the core group sponsoring student activities and giving shape to student life. All the school presidents were supportive of the role of faith in the life of the campus. Shortly after Dr. Roy Ellis, son of a Baptist minister, became president in 1926, he wanted to establish formal *Bible* courses on campus. He inquired of other state institutions how *Bible* instruction was carried on their campuses. "Some were conducting such instruction as a part of the regular college program. Others had off-campus units financed by some denomination or religious group," recalled Dr. Ellis.

After several unsuccessful efforts to get local denominations to establish an off-campus center where *Bible* courses would be taught, President Ellis recommended the hiring of Dr. F.W.A. Bosch, pastor of a local Presbyterian church, to teach *Bible* courses part-time on campus beginning in 1938. Ellis recalled that "the Administration and some members of the Board of Regents (were) from the beginning dubious as to the legality of a state financed program of *Bible* teaching." That skepticism proved accurate. In 1950 a group of local pastors challenged the use of state funds for the teaching of religion. The Board solicited an opinion from the State Attorney General who found the college's program of *Bible* teaching unconstitutional. *Bible* teaching on campus was suspended in 1950-51.

There is evidence of denominational rivalry in the story. Allen Bosch,

SMSU

Counseling and Testing Center established.

Missouri/Springfield

International/USA

First active communications satellite, Telstar, goes into orbit.

Marilyn Monroe dies of drug overdose.

son of Dr. F.W.A. Bosch, said of the challenge from the local clergy, "I always had the impression that it was this same group of pastors that founded the Baptist Student Center at about the same time." The Baptist Student Center did begin offering *Bible* courses shortly after the Attorney General's opinion. Academic credit for the courses was provided by William Jewell College, so students wanting credit-earning *Bible* instruction while at SMS could have the credits transferred from William Jewell.

Bosch was stung by the action of the rival group. He never felt he offered a "Presbyterian bias" to any *Bible* courses he taught nor did he attempt any proselytizing in the classroom. In sympathy for his cause, the college retained the services of Dr. Bosch as an instructor of philosophy. The *Ozarko* describes the Philosophy Department as "a department which came into being as the result of a constitutional violation." Bosch continued to teach philosophy courses until his death in January 1955. Interest in teaching religion on campus

revived in 1963 when the Faculty Senate proposed establishing a religion department. Mary Jo Wynn chaired the committee making the proposal, which was reviewed by Attorney General Thomas F. Eagleton. The Attorney General warned that judges' decisions about teaching religion in state supported schools "show a delicate, almost imperceptible line between the permissable and the impermissable practices, between the teaching of religion pedagogically and the teaching of religion for religion's sake, between the teaching of religion as part of the civil morality or history and the teaching of religion as a sectarian doctrine." It would clearly be a delicate task to formulate a proposal to enable teaching religious subjects on a state supported campus without running into separation of church and state issues. However, the campus did not give up on the issue.

The same year the Faculty Senate proposed to establish a religion department, the U.S. Supreme Court in the "Schemp" decision, stated unequivocally that classes promoting one religion could not be taught in public, tax-supported institutions. Ironically, the decision both slammed the door on the teaching of religion, but simultaneously opened another door by the decision's acknowledgement that the objective study of religion was an important part

While having the shortest tenure of any SMS president (1961-64), Dr. Traywick is credited with initiating changes at the college which prepared it to become Missouri's second largest university. Traywick was a graduate of the University of Missouri and completed a doctorate at the University of Illinois. He taught economics and served as assistant dean of the College of Business and Public Service at Michigan State prior to his coming to SMS.

Dr. Robert Stevenson succeeds Dr. Robert Martin as head of Science Department.

U.N. announces population of earth — three billion.

Cuban missile crisis raises the stakes in the Cold War.

Looking Back

Square Dance Promenaders

Square dancing took a leap forward on the SMS campus when the Promenaders, a square dancing group sponsored by Florence Bugg, received national attention. In 1955 the group won second place on Ted Mack's Amateur Hour. The group do-si-doed their way to fame with a profession contract to appear in the Blue Room of the Roosevelt Hotel in New Orleans in March 1955

Dial Phones

In September 1962 the campus made a leap ahead with the installation of dial phone equipment including a dial switchboard accommodating 200 phones.

Apollo 11 Moon Landing

SMS dismissed all classes on July 21, 1969, to enable students, faculty and staff to watch the Apollo 11 moon landing.

Chris Peterson appears on the KWTO show College Town Meeting of the Air in 1963, arguing the need for a tax reduction. The program promoted student interest in civic affairs.

of a liberal arts education. So SMS officials began exploring the possibility of establishing a department that would teach *about* religion. The notion of an academic department where the scholarly analysis of the role of religion in both private and public life would be supported within a public institution was both visionary and daunting.

President Mallory, himself a devout Baptist, knew that the task of establishing a Department of Religious Studies in the college would be controversial. He knew the sentiments of the area. He recognized that Bible Belt folk fully expected that the college would support the faith of their children. From the beginning of his presidency, Mallory had regularly written letters to area ministers advising them of what SMS was doing for their students, including providing encouragement for them to connect with their denominational

organizations on campus. At the time, all religion courses were taught off campus by various groups connected with church related colleges. Those colleges gave academic credit for the courses. Most of the courses were consciously faith-building within a particular denominational framework. Ironically, while SMS could not teach such courses itself, it did accept the credits for such courses from denominational colleges.

The prospect of SMS offering courses on religion was not welcome by many of the churches offering their own courses in their off-campus settings. Charles Johnson, associate director of the Baptist Student Union, which had been teaching some 400 students a year, recalls the feeling. "The Baptists did not take too kindly to the new department initially. Some saw this development as fixing something which wasn't broken, and doing it with tax money. Other Baptists had a more serious question. They saw the new depart-

ment as a blurring of the line, if not an outright violation of the separation of church and state. There was serious talk about taking SMS to court over this constitutional concern."

Clearly, if the new department were to succeed, it would be because it had unique leadership. That leadership had to have both the credentials of scholarship and the attributes of faith. Because the two most powerful denominations in the area were the Baptists and the Church of Christ, one would surely be offended if the other were to capture the leadership of the new department. It was a tightrope President Mallory and Dean Meyer were walking.

Fortunately, the new head of the History Department, Dr. Robert Flanders, had developed a friendship with a colleague teaching immigration history at the Mansfield campus of Ohio State University. He recommended Dr. Gerrit tenZythoff to the administration. Flanders had been

The Bears Den in the new Campus Union was a popular destination for students working their way through a busy registration and orientation process in 1960.

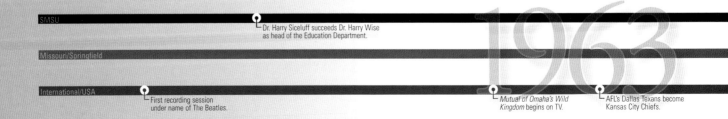

Dr. Harry Siceluff succeeds Dr. Harry Wise as head of the Education Department.

First recording session under name of The Beatles.

Mutual of Omaha's Wild Kingdom begins on TV.

AFL's Dallas Texans become Kansas City Chiefs.

Debaters Tom Strong and Yvonne Ray accompanied by their mentor, Dr. Virginia Craig, traveled to West Point in 1952 to be the first SMS team to qualify for the national championship debate tournament. Strong and Ray made it to the semi-finals placing them among the eight best of the 34 teams entered.

impressed with tenZythoff's skill as a teacher while at Mansfield. He recalled arguing a point of religious doctrine with Dr. tenZythoff. "I said, Gerrit, I could never believe that!" Smiling congenially, tenZythoff replied, "Oh, that's all right. You don't have to believe it for it to be true." Flanders recalls, "I knew instantly not only that he was right, but that the conversation had moved to a higher level. He could state profundities in one sentence that left me pondering. Once I observed, probably at length, that names were very important in the scheme of things. 'Oh, yes,' Gerrit replied, 'The power of naming is the power of God.'"

TenZythoff was invited to visit the campus in 1968. While here, he gave a lecture on the theology of Rudolph Bultmann. A sizeable crowd was on hand to assess the stature of a possible head for the new Religious Studies Department. At the conclusion of the lecture it was time for questions. After a pregnant pause, Dean Robert Gilmore, soon to be Dean of Faculties, rose. "Dr. tenZythoff, which version of the *Bible* do you prefer?" Dr. Flanders remembers the expectant quiet that followed the question — "A quiet crackling with electricity." The subject of the King James Version versus "modern" versions was still a hot topic in some conservative circles. With a big smile, tenZythoff responded, "The Dutch Bible, of course! Dutch is the language of God." After a second or so, the meeting erupted in laughter and applause. "I sensed that Gerrit had just vaulted to the front rank as candidate for head of the Department of Religious Studies," recalls Flanders.

The morning Dr. tenZythoff flew back to Ohio after the Bultmann lecture, President Mallory was flying to Minnesota for a meeting. Weather circumstances put them on the same plane. They sat together. Earlier, President Mallory had worried whether a leader for the department could be found who was both scholar and a Christian. Mallory confided to some on campus that he had doubts whether any person could be both a rigorous scholar and a practicing Christian. But the plane ride to St. Louis settled those questions. He found tenZythoff to be a man of deep religious faith as well as a competent and respected scholar.

The rest is history. Dr. Gerrit tenZythoff came to SMS in the fall of 1969 to head up the Religious Studies Department. He was the only full-time faculty member in the beginning. But campus ministers came rapidly to his assistance. John Wilson, Tom Raber, Jim Robinson, Charles Johnson and Douglas McGlynn all volunteered to teach classes without pay. That continued until 1973-74 when these adjunct instructors were put on the university payroll, and the first two full-time faculty members were hired, Dr. John Wilson and Dr. Robert Cooley.

By the end of the State College period in 1972, the noble experiment of teaching religion in a state supported institution was prospering. Seventeen courses were offered including the first course in world religions titled, The Islamic Faith. Religious Studies courses were counted for elective credit on all SMS degrees as well as meeting the humanities requirement in the general

Baccalaureate services dropped as part of commencement exercises.

St. Louis Symphony and Peter, Paul, and Mary perform together on campus.

Yugoslavia proclaimed a Socialist Republic.

U.S.S.R. launches Luna 4 — misses moon.

education program. A minor in religion was approved by the Faculty Senate. The skillful hands of Dr. tenZythoff were laying the foundations of a program in religious studies which many thought could never be done.

ROTC Introduced in 1952

The Korean War in the early 1950s produced a significant and lasting curricular change on campus — the establishment of a Reserve Officers Training Corps program. By 1951, many students were being drafted for the Korean conflict without being able to finish their college work. An ROTC unit on campus would provide a means for students to finish school and enter the armed forces with a commission. So in 1951, a campus referendum on establishing an ROTC unit showed overwhelming support among students. One thousand and seventy out of 1,087 voted in favor of establishing the unit.

Authorized by Congress in 1916, ROTC units had already trained more than two million cadets on college campuses across the nation. The establishment of the "Bear Battalion" in the fall of 1952 met with enthusiastic response. *The Standard* editorialized that "with the threat of aggression so close, every American male, for several years at least, can look forward to a period of military training of some sort. The ROTC program makes it possible for college students to get at least some of their training without interfering with their college work. Just as this program is a boon to the individual, it is also good for the school in that it will prevent the enrollment from continuing to drop as it has for more than a year."

Two programs were organized at SMS. A mandatory one-credit program for all freshmen and sophomores required two hours of class work and one hour of drill each week. The optional junior-senior program required five hours of class per week and gave six hours credit for each year's work. Upon successful graduation from the upper division program, the student received a commission as a second lieutenant in the Army. Students enrolled in ROTC courses were certified to be "not subject to the jurisdiction of their local draft boards as long as they do satisfactory work in ROTC and college."

Lieutenant Colonel John Killian, a field artillery officer, was assigned to direct the program. Program offices, stockrooms and arsenal were located under the football stadium. Killian greeted 382 new enrollees in the fall of 1952. During the first year, Company "L" of the Pershing Rifles was organized and subsequently chartered by the National Society. In February 1953, the first ROTC ball was held featuring the Grand March under the arch of rifles provided by the crack drill team. Later that spring, after the first Annual Federal Inspection, an ROTC band was organized as part of the Music Department. The first cadets were commissioned in 1955.

Early in its history, the ROTC unit developed several extracurricular organizations in addition to the Band: The Gold Bar, an honorary scholastic fraternity restricted to members of the advanced course sponsored the annual military ball; and The Springfield Rifles, a crack drill team, performed in civic parades, athletics contests and provided military honors for funerals of veterans. Students interested in marksmanship could join the Rifle Club and Corps Rifle Team, which competed with other teams across the country. For those interested in additional training in drill and the manual of arms, there was the Ramrodders.

Between 1955-60, world events stimulated even greater interest in the ROTC. The Cold War intensified with the establishing of the Warsaw Pact by the Soviet Union.

With the Soviet launching of Sputnik I and II and their invention of the first atomic submarine, the race for military superiority accelerated. In 1959, Fidel Castro overthrew

The "Never-Say-Die-Bears," 1953 NAIA National Champions pose before a photomural of the 1952 Bears team, which also won the NAIA National Title. Left to Right: Art Helms, Forrest Hamilton, Bill Thomas, Jerry Anderson, Bill Price, Don Duckworth, John Grimm, Don Anielak and Ray Birdsong. Kneeling: Coach Bob Vanatta and Jim Moulder, team manager.

The class of 1963 was particularly distinguished with four of its graduates becoming General Officers; Major General Fred F. Marty, Lieutenant General John E. Miller, Major General Jarrett J. Robertson and Major General David E. White.

In 1967, the Bear Battalion took on a new look, when the first woman enrolled in Military Science 102. Sheilah Martin, daughter of an Army Lieutenant Colonel, was initially denied admission by the Army officers directing the Battalion at SMS, but they ultimately relented. "I was at first viewed with apprehension by the boys in the class," Martin reported at the end of the year. "They thought it was pretty funny." Earlier that year, *The Standard* carried letters to the editor demanding equal treatment for men and women — if men are required to take ROTC, so should women. Advanced ROTC training and Army commissions were ultimately opened to women in 1973.

the Batista regime in Cuba adding a Communist threat only 90 miles from the U.S. mainland. During this period, the Bear Battalion won both the 5th Army Intercollegiate and the Interscholastic rifle match. They also took first place honors at summer camp in Ft. Riley, Kansas, for compiling the highest average scores of cadets in all competition. Four Bear Battalion graduates from this period went on to become General Officers: Major General Robert Lynn Gordon, '57; Lieutenant General Neal T. Jaco, '59; Major General Robert F. Pennycuick, '59; and Brigadier General William A. West, '59.

ROTC at SMS during the 1960s became controversial as it did on many campuses throughout the country. With the heating up of the Vietnam

War, ROTC was made mandatory for all students enrolled in state-supported institutions. Editorials in *The Standard* attacked the policy. Student petitions against mandatory ROTC were rebuffed for two years by the Faculty Senate. Students, faculty and administrators argued both sides of the issue. In late 1969, the mandatory requirement was lifted by Board action, and ROTC enrollment plummeted from 1,982 in the fall of 1969 to 573 in the spring of 1970, and to 376 in the fall of 1970. While the numbers fell substantially, the quality of cadets who remained was uniformly high leading the Army officers assigned to the Bear Battalion to report that "a voluntary force was more desirable. Those cadets were dedicated to training and to actually accepting an Army commission."

Other Academic Innovations

Accelerated growth led to a number of innovations never considered in earlier years. In 1946, the possibility of night classes was discussed by the Faculty Council for the first time. In the spring term of 1947 the first night classes were scheduled. They met on Tuesday and Thursday evenings for two hours offering courses in English, American literature, salesmanship, accounting, shorthand, and trigonometry.

Academic probation was introduced about this same time. Any student earning below an "M" (C) in three or more subjects was limited to taking a maximum of 7.5 hours the next term. After being on probation for two con-

Bachelor of Music and Bachelor of Fine Arts degrees authorized.

Glendale becomes Springfield's fourth high school.

200,000 African Americans and other supporters of the Civil Rights Movement gather in the capitol for the "March on Washington."

South Africa begins trial of Nelson Mandela on conspiracy.

Looking Ahead in 1957

"What will SMS be like 50 years hence?.... If enrollment increases the second 50 years in proportion to the first 50 years, there will be upwards of 30,000 students searching for parking places, standing in cafeteria lines, seeking a chair in the library and trying...to get a schedule the first four hours of the day. Doubtless, the situation will be somewhat ameliorated by the art of invention. Some may come to school on atomic powered roller skates, some may use helicopters which they could park atop the buildings, and some may even learn to walk to school.... As for library space, surely some unorthodox member of the profession will discover a means of transferring knowledge by a sort of subconscious psychological induction process thus releasing the library space for recreational purposes.... Of one thing we may be sure: the institution must change with the changing times. Biologists tell us that 'the snake which cannot shed its skin will perish.'"

President Roy Ellis, 1957 *Ozarko*

secutive terms, the student was asked to withdraw from school. In 1963, 25 percent of the student body was on probation. By 1968, the number had declined to just over 16 percent.

To help students adjust to the rigors of academic life, an orientation course was added to the curriculum in 1948. The course met weekly for one term with "credit" or "unsatisfactory" entered on the students' record. The purpose of the course was "to acquaint the new student with the college and the opportunities it offers and to encourage the student to systematically analyze himself, his aptitudes and his abilities."

Summer field trips were introduced in the early 1950s by the Science Department. Dr. H.J. Retallick conducted a 5,000-mile geography excursion in the summer of 1952, which included visits to the Mesabi Iron Range, Detroit Lakes Wildlife Station, Paul Bunyan area in Minnesota, Black Hills of South Dakota, Devils Tower, Big Horn Mountains, Yellowstone Park, Salt Lake City, Bingham Canyon copper mines, Garden of the Gods, Royal Gorge and the oil shale at Rifle, Colorado. The course focused on conservation of natural resources.

The grading system also came under scrutiny early in the SMS period. By 1949, the "D" grade was apparently being abused by some faculty. The *Catalog* designated the "D" grade as meaning the credit is delayed because certain parts of the course remain incomplete. Some faculty were assigning the "D" grade to enable students who had failed a course to retake it. During those years, points assigned to grades ranged from 3 for an E (A), to

On October 30, 1948, the Bears traveled to Rolla for the "Game of the Year" against the Miners. A trainload of Bear fans made the trip to Rolla and watched the Bears splash to a 18-0 victory. The *Ozarko* reported that "the rain was falling so hard at times the other side of the stadium was only a dark blot."

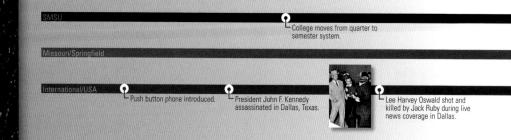

SMSU

College moves from quarter to semester system.

Missouri/Springfield

International/USA
Push button phone introduced. President John F. Kennedy assassinated in Dallas, Texas. Lee Harvey Oswald shot and killed by Jack Ruby during live news coverage in Dallas.

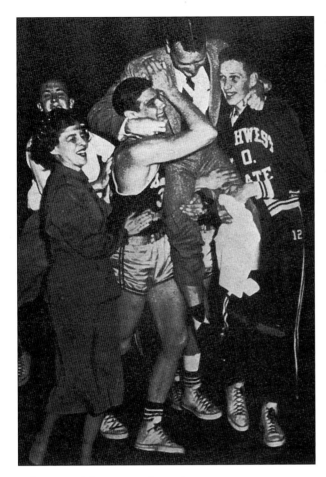

Coach Bob Vanatta is hoisted to the shoulders of Bill Lea and Ray Birdsong as his wife tries to congratulate him on winning the NAIB National Championship in Kansas City in 1952. The Bears went on to win the national title again the following year, the first team to ever win the tournament two years in succession.

1 for an M (C). In 1951 the registrar reported that the school-wide grade point average was 1.52. Women did better than men averaging 1.61 to men's 1.44. Freshmen struggled to achieve a 1.39. By 1956, things had gotten worse for the men who managed only a 1.27 grade point average while women raised their average to 1.73. Finally, in 1961, the grading system changed to a 4 point statewide agreed policy of A, B, C, D and F with I signifying "incomplete." In 1968 a new wrinkle was added to the system enabling the student under certain circumstances to take a course "Pass/Fail." This was intended to encourage students to venture more widely in the curriculum without fear of damaging their grade point average.

Grading systems were always a challenge to faculty. Dr. Tom Stombaugh remembers his first year of teaching at SMS in 1953, and the struggle he had applying the principles he learned in Teacher Training 204. "The first class I walked into at SMS had three people already in it. I talked for a while in hopes that additional people would arrive. They didn't. The ones I had were beginning to get restless, and I surely didn't want to lose them along with my job. It turned out pretty well. I graded on the curve. That's what they said I should do when I took Teacher Training 204. It turned out to be the flattest curve ever seen. The only time someone came close to falling off the back end was when I told them there were three kinds of worms, round, flat and square, and I saw somebody write it down in their notes. I figured that as far along in the term as we were they should have known when I was lying. I decided not to dock them for it. When they were in my class they were Bonnalie (Oetting), John Chapman and Bob Bareis. Two, John Chapman and Bob Bareis, later became distinguished physicians. Not bad for a small class!"

Despite the modest campuswide grade point averages, the 1950s saw individual students receiving distinguished academic awards. Charles Strickland, a championship debater, received a Fulbright Fellowship in 1952 to study at the University of Copenhagen in Denmark. Sally Hoy received a Fulbright Fellowship in 1954 to study art at the University of Oslo in Norway. The following year Jennie Vetrees was named a Fulbright Scholar and attended the University of Mainz in Germany. Bob Irick was awarded the prestigious Woodrow Wilson Fellowship in 1956 to attended Harvard University where he did graduate work in East Asian Regional Studies.

While academic changes were transforming a teacher training institution into a liberal arts college, teacher training remained the focus throughout the early SMS years. With the swelling of public school enrollments by baby boomers in the early 1950s, the demand for teachers grew. In 1951, 248 graduates took the B.S.Ed. degree. By 1960 the number had increased to 388. Throughout the 1950s, almost 75 percent of all degrees granted were teaching degrees. By 1968, however, the percent of teaching degrees awarded had declined to less than half the total and the decline continued into the 1970s.

In 1951, the SMS *Catalog* added a new requirement for the B.S.Ed. degree — "fitness to teach." The earliest diplomas given by the Normal School had carried the assurance that the person

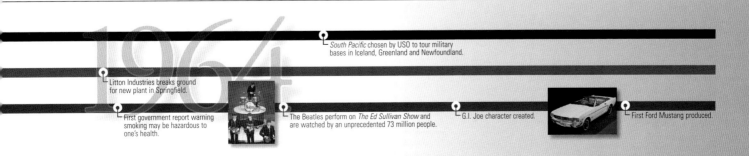

1964

South Pacific chosen by USO to tour military bases in Iceland, Greenland and Newfoundland.

Litton Industries breaks ground for new plant in Springfield.

First government report warning smoking may be hazardous to one's health.

The Beatles perform on *The Ed Sullivan Show* and are watched by an unprecedented 73 million people.

G.I. Joe character created.

First Ford Mustang produced.

Jerry Anderson, the first SMS player to have his basketball jersey retired, provides an autograph for an admiring youngster after leading the Bears to a third-place finish in the NAIA tournament in Kansas City in 1954. Anderson was named to the All Tournament team, the national NAIA squad, and the Helms All America team in addition to being named the tournament Most Valuable Player. Anderson also served as student body president.

certified to teach "has given evidence of good moral character, and ability to teach." The new requirement of "fitness" could be used to weed-out students who may be academically qualified, but judged not to be fit for the classroom. Dr. Dale Allee describes the implications of adopting the "fitness" requirement.

"The fact that a degree in education from the college is, under the law of the state, a direct commission to teach in the public schools of the state, it imposes a strict obligation on the part of the college as to the fitness of the candidate for such a degree for the profession of teaching. More than mere scholastic ability is involved. Physical and mental health, moral ideals and professional attitudes are involved. The right is reserved to restrict the teacher training curriculum to those who measure up to the above criteria."

The name change to Southwest Missouri State College also signaled the emergence of new degrees in the academic inventory. While there had been a Bachelor of Arts degree for some time in addition to the Bachelor of Science in Education, by 1963, a total of five degrees were available. The B.S.Ed. was reserved for prospective teachers. A Bachelor of Science degree was created for studies in vocational and scientific areas. A Bachelor of Music was established for music majors, and a Bachelor of Fine Arts was in place for students in the creative arts area. The shift to B.S. degrees is seen in data comparing degrees awarded in 1958 with those given 10 years later. Nearly 70 percent of all degrees given in 1958 were B.S. in education. By 1968 that proportion had declined to 41.2 percent while the Bachelor of Science degree had grown from 26 percent in 1958 to almost 48 percent in 1969.

The growth of the B.S. degree was fueled by, among other things, the growing interest in the field of business. As early as 1951, the Commerce Department instructed more students than any other department of the college despite the fact that it did not teach any general education or foundation courses. Forty-three courses were listed that year in the department inventory. By 1952, almost 20 percent of the student body were majoring in business, some to teach business in high schools, but most to go into business careers. By 1970, the momentum had clearly shifted away from teacher training with 1,582 students majoring in business while only 932 were in teacher training.

Faculty

Faculty Concerns

Faculty unrest characterized the opening years of the SMS period. In 1949 *The Standard* reported that "certain members of the SMS faculty have been called on the carpet" and told to forget some of their liberal and progressive ideas. From the student viewpoint, "SMS is in need of a great many new and fresh ideas," according to the editor. "We go on record defending those members of the faculty who would be teachers and not stereotypes of patented histories of the past…. It is time we broke away from traditions, fixed standards and methods of the 19th century."

Among the "progressive" ideas quashed by college authorities was the adoption of the semester system.

SMSU

Baseball, wrestling, women's volleyball, field hockey, and tennis added to intercollegiate sports.

Debaters win unprecedented third consecutive Heart of America Tournament championship.

Missouri/Springfield

International/USA

Nelson Mandela sentenced to life in prison in South Africa.

204   *Daring to Excel: The First 100 Years of Southwest Missouri State University*

With the Faculty Council clearly under President Ellis' control, the idea got nowhere until a new president was installed in 1961. Stirrings for a more democratic administrative style continued to surface among faculty. In January 1952, nearly 70 percent of the faculty signed a petition declaring "democracy does not exist at SMS," and asking for a hearing with the Board. Late in January, the Board conducted a six-hour hearing with 19 faculty "to get an unrestricted view of faculty/administration relationships." Each Board member had personally selected three faculty members to attend the hearing. The president of the Board, Roger Taylor, selected the 19th member. The faculty were encouraged to air their complaints, explain their concerns and give suggestions.

On February 15, 1952, the Board announced its findings in two resolutions. In the first, it announced that it "failed to find any lack of democracy." In the second, the Board "instructed President Ellis to call at least one faculty meeting each month with minutes of each meeting to be relayed to the Board."

While faculty salaries did not appear to be part of the agenda at the Board hearing, they were an issue in the early 1950s. The Great Depression had left faculty salaries in a deplorable condition. In 1929, the average faculty salary for 11 months service was $2,513. In 1933 that average had been reduced by 20 percent to cope with budget problems. By 1939, salaries had been restored to the basic rate. While between 1939 and 1950 the average faculty salary had increased 81 percent, the rate of inflation had outpaced the increases, so by the early SMS years,

The second SMS team invited to the West Point Debate Tournament featured Bill Maynard (left) and Irma Jones who won five of eight preliminary rounds in 1955. Maynard was judged second-best speaker in the tournament. Jones received the distinction of being the only woman named to the elimination rounds. Coach Holt V. Spicer, himself a West Point Champion debater in 1952, accompanied his team to the Academy.

faculty had less purchasing power than they had at the end of the Depression.

Some relief came in 1957. With improved state revenues, the Board authorized a 12.5 percent increase for all faculty and staff, the largest increase in more than 10 years. In 1958, the Board again authorized a 12.5 percent increase with a special $200 equity adjustment given to all women faculty. With these adjustments the college claimed "SMS salaries will now compare equally with salaries paid by other colleges of similar size."

Changing of the Guard
The SMS era began in 1946 with only three of the original Normal School faculty still teaching. Clayton Kinsey

and his wife, Lula Padgitt Kinsey, both of the Music Department, retired in 1947, leaving only Dr. Virginia Craig with teaching memories going back to the summer of 1906. Dr. Craig was asked to give the Commencement Address in the spring of 1947, the only time in the history of the institution a faculty member has been so honored. *The Standard* reported that "everyone who heard the address was impressed with two things — the content of the speech and the sincerity of the speaker. Every listener realized that finally here was an address that 'hit home' in every sense of the word, and was given by a woman who meant and practiced everything she advocated." Dr. Craig continued teaching through the spring term of 1952, retiring after 46 years of service.

Another pillar, Norman Freudenberger, who came to the school in 1907 and who had taught Latin for 45 years, also retired in 1952. The college had already lost Arthur Briggs, who pioneered the physical education and athletics program at the school. He died of a stroke in December 1949 while still in service at age 65. Four years earlier, Allen Porter Temple, who had taught physics since 1907, retired. So by the middle 1950s the torch was being passed to a new and younger generation of faculty. Dean Bertha Wells retired in 1955 with 40 years of service. That same year Dr. W.V. Cheek, who had pioneered the business curriculum for 31 years died, as did F.W.A. Bosch, who pioneered the teaching of religion on campus. James Shannon, who had become an institution on campus, also retired in 1955 having taught for 44 years. His American History 53 course had become a campus legend. Shannon had also served as MIAA President for

Dr. Arthur Mallory becomes SMSU's 5th president.

Barry Goldwater visits Springfield.

Civil Rights Act of 1964 signed into law.

FBI finds bodies of three slain civil rights workers in Philadelphia, Mississippi.

23 years guiding the development of athletics policies throughout the state.

In 1957 students saw the retirement of two additional campus leaders. One was Dr. Lawrence E. Pummill, who joined the mathematics faculty in 1920 and headed the department since 1939, retired at age 74 after 37 years of service. While a student at the State Normal School #4 in 1911, Pummill acquired a reputation which followed him for his entire life. Under his picture in the 1911 *Ozarko* this inscription is found, "No one can carry as many subjects, think deeper in mathematics, work harder at debate, or play better on the athletic field." Not only was Pummill respected by his colleagues and students, the Missouri State Legislature recognized his achievements and contributions with a Senate Resolution upon learning of his death on January 26, 1963.

Another SMS pillar retired in 1957 as well — Anna Lou Blair who taught German for 49 years. She joined Virginia Craig, Elizabeth Bragg, Arthur Briggs, Agnes Cowen, Mary Elizabeth David, Joseph Delp, Roy Ellis, W.Y. Foster, Norman Freudenberger, Mary Keith, Henrietta Keller, Clayton and Lula Kinsey, Grace Palmer, Sue Scott Perkins, James Shannon, Bertha Wells and Mary Adams Woods in teaching through three eras of institutional history. They all began their work in the Normal School, continued through the State Teachers College days, and finished their work in the SMS era.

The new leadership cadre began taking shape in the 1940s and 1950s with the coming of Leslie Irene Coger, Duane G. Meyer, George E. Gleason, Jessie Selvidge Burrell, Mary Jo Wynn, Paul Redfearn, Tom Stombaugh,

Byrne Blackwood, Grace Gardner, Bob Gilmore, Aldo Sebben and Holt Spicer. Their numbers were swelled in the 1960s when student numbers grew in double-digit fashion. Forty-one new faculty were added in 1962 alone.

As new faculty were added, the concern for "in-breeding" began to be addressed. At the beginning of the SMS era, nearly 50 percent of the faculty had done their undergraduate work on this campus during the Normal School or STC years. While it was a clear compliment to the institution that it could create that kind of loyalty among its graduates, it was also a liability for an institution that was committed to giving students a broad range of perspectives on issues, a key component of responsible higher education. By 1955, the proportion of SMS graduates on the faculty had dropped to 43 percent and by the end of the era in 1972, the proportion had dropped to just over 26 percent. SMS was reaching out more broadly for academic leadership.

Many of the new leaders built reputations for excellence quickly. Leslie Irene Coger's theater productions quickly caught the attention of drama critics at the national level. In 1952 she became the first person to be designated professor of speech at SMS. In 1955, she was recognized by radio station KGBX as an outstanding educator. Her colleague, Dr. Robert Gilmore, was working on his doctorate in speech at the University of Minnesota in 1958 and was reported to be "having a hilarious time each evening at the Saddle Club in St. Paul where he is appearing in a different melodrama each week." Bob, who was quick with the ad lib, "drew public notice when he turned to a boisterous audience during a perfor-

mance and said, 'Hey! Be quiet, man, we've got a hard scene coming up."

In 1961, only six years after he came to SMS to replace James Shannon in the History Department, Dr. Duane Meyer was appointed as the first dean of faculty by President Leland Traywick. Throughout all previous administrations, the president of the college assumed the role of president of the faculty and there was no academic dean. Traywick saw the need for focused academic leadership and called upon the 34-year-old Meyer to assume the task. At the time the Meyer family already had a full plate at home. In addition to their own four children, Duane and 'Lyn Meyer were caring for Thomas and Riley McClure while Dr. and Mrs. McClure were in Europe for three months. The Meyers remarked at the time that "careful planning must go even into menial tasks now that the family numbers eight. Even the breakfast table must be set the night before in order to facilitate eating and so that Dr. Meyer can be at the college by 8:00 a.m." In addition to managing those chores, Dr. Meyer also managed to publish a book in 1961, *The Highland Scots of North Carolina, 1732-1776,* as well as create a forum for the discussion of research papers written by SMS faculty.

Dr. Meyer not only pioneered the office of academic dean at the college, he also opened the door of senior academic administration to women of the college. In 1965, Dr. Mary Rose Sweeney was named by Meyer as assistant dean of instruction with specific responsibility for academic advising.

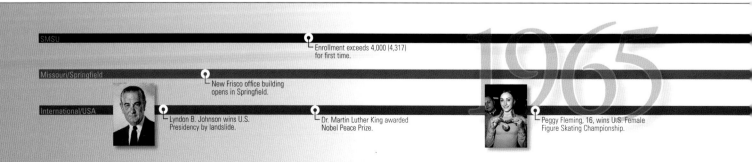

SMSU

Enrollment exceeds 4,000 (4,317) for first time.

Missouri/Springfield

New Frisco office building opens in Springfield.

International/USA

Lyndon B. Johnson wins U.S. Presidency by landslide.

Dr. Martin Luther King awarded Nobel Peace Prize.

Peggy Fleming, 16, wins U.S. Female Figure Skating Championship.

1965

The "Fabulous Four," left to right, Bill Price, Coach Bob Vanatta, Ray Birdsong, Bill "Jinx" Thomas and Don Duckworth. Going to a 2-2 box zone defense in the final three minutes and 10 seconds of a tied game, the "Fabulous Four" scored 12 points to claim the victory over the shocked Sycamores of Indiana State. The Bears went on to win the NAIA Championship beating Hamline University.

Faculty Researchers

While academic research never figured prominently in the hiring of faculty for the first 60 years, there were those who used their research skills very productively. In 1949, Dr. L.V. Whitney, physics instructor, developed several scientific tools including a photoelectric recording device "which records the movement of fish in response to light intensity." He also developed an electric thermometer that measured underwater temperatures in one-fourth the time of regular thermometers. Whitney and his colleagues at the University of Wisconsin in 1951 also developed a sonar device for locating submarines and mines, using high frequency vibrations.

In 1950, Dr. Chauncey Goodchild was invited to join the American Zoological Society in recognition of his research work. He was the first SMS biologist to be recognized by the society. Goodchild had done extensive research at the Marine Biological Laboratory at Woods Hole, Massachusetts, collaborating with others there to write a textbook titled "Selected Invertebrate Types," which was used by a select group of scholars at Woods Hole.

Dr. Paul Redfearn picked up the scholarly tradition in biology after Goodchild went to Emory University. In 1959 Redfearn was awarded the first National Science Foundation grant received by the college. The $7,300 award enabled a two-year study of bryophytes, mosses and liverworts of southwest Missouri. That same year, scholarly research received a boost with the organization of "The Seminar," a forum for the discussion of scholarly papers among faculty. Steering "The Seminar" were Drs. Paul Redfearn, Duane Meyer and William Lane.

During the ensuing year papers were presented by Drs. David Scott, Mary Rose Sweeney, Carl Fronabarger, William McClure, Tom Stombaugh and B.B. Lightfoot.

A grant awarded in 1963 to Stan Vining of the political science faculty enabled a study of the political, social and economic changes in Branson as a consequence of the construction of Table Rock Dam. In 1964, a second NSF grant came to the college. Dr. Jim Wilbur of the chemistry faculty was the principal investigator. He designed a chemotherapy study which involved the use of students in advanced chemistry classes to synthesize compounds useful in the destruction of cancer cells.

In recognition of the growing interest in research by faculty, the Board of Regents authorized a reduced teaching load in 1965 for faculty who did individual research approved by the

Greenwood Lab School moves from Education Building to new facility on Harrison Street.

First U.S. combat troops reach South Vietnam.

R.C. Duncan patents Pampers disposable diapers.

Rolling Stones record *Satisfaction*.

Spaghetti-Os first sold.

Coach Andy McDonald wore many hats during his long and successful SMS coaching and teaching tenure, and he did it in an era when multi-tasked staff members were the rule rather than the highly-specialized professionals who have evolved in many fields in more recent years.

No matter what he did, the one thing that remained constant about "Andy Mac" was the tremendous respect held for him by all who learned under him, played for him or coached with or against him. He was a keen competitor and a man of the highest integrity.

Coach McDonald coached men's basketball at SMS longer than any other man. His tenure began shortly after World War I, survived the Great Depression and extended through World War II. It began when the SMS gymnasium was on the ground floor of the Administration Building and Coach Mac ushered the program in 1940 into a gleaming new arena that was the showplace of the Ozarks. It was a building the SMS Board of Regents in 1970 would rename McDonald Arena, as the Board added its stamp of respect to Andy Mac's legend.

A native of McLouth, Kansas, McDonald saw Army service in World War I in Harry Truman's company and then earned three letters each as a basketball forward and football quarterback/end at the University of Kansas. His KU basketball coach was the legendary Phog Allen. McDonald's teammates included Adolph Rupp, and Andy Mac had classes at KU under Dr. James Naismith, the inventor of basketball.

Coming off the springboard of his play on a Helms national basketball championship team at Kansas, McDonald began at SMS in 1925 as head basketball coach, assistant football coach and a physical education department faculty member. He took over basketball in what was just the second SMS season in the fledgling Missouri Intercollegiate Athletic Association (MIAA). McDonald stayed as basketball coach for a quarter century, setting the tone for a program which enjoyed enduring success under only eight coaches for the last 75 years of the 20th century.

The fortunes of the SMS program were sent soaring with the opening of the new SMS arena in December 1940. Coach McDonald had arranged for the University of Missouri to provide the opposition for the inaugural game in the new arena; an unheard-of arrangement at the time in which the state's land grant university visited a small Teachers College for a game. SMS made the evening an even better occasion with a 35-32 victory over visiting Mizzou.

The seasons immediately following World War II saw the brightest time of McDonald's SMS tenure. Built around a nucleus of four-year performers and led by the first great SMS scorer, Gene Ruble, the Bears, from 1946 to 1950, won 83 of 100 games. They recorded the first two 20-win seasons in SMS history, were ranked consistently among national leaders in team defense and won three straight MIAA championships. SMS made its first appearances in the NAIA national tournament in 1939, 1943 and 1949, and, for McDonald's 23-year tenure, the Bears were 301-166. He became the all-time SMS basketball coaching victory leader. Half a century later, no other Bears' coach has come close to Andy Mac's win total.

His coaching success came at a time when his plate had more on it than basketball. From 1933 to 1937, he served as SMS head football coach, and was a football assistant again from 1938 to 1946. When SMS added men's golf in 1934, McDonald took over the reins of that sport. He took SMS to 14 MIAA golf titles and six NCAA regional championships. It was under his leadership that SMS hosted the first six NCAA Division II golf championships in Springfield, and McDonald guided SMS to a national golf title in 1963. At the death of his long-time friend, A.W. Briggs in December 1949, "Andy Mac" became head of the Physical Education Department. Coach McDonald remained the head of the department until 1965. He coached golf until 1969.

Following the renaming of the SMS Arena as McDonald Arena in 1970, McDonald was inducted into the SMS Athletics Hall of Fame in 1975, the inaugural year for that shrine. He was inducted in 1983 into the National Golf Coaches Association Hall of Fame and went into both the Springfield Area Sports Hall of Fame and the Missouri Sports Hall of Fame in 1988. The Andrew J. McDonald Achievement Award has been given annually since 1969 to the outstanding SMS graduating senior male and female physical education major/varsity student-athletes. Coach McDonald passed away in August 1988, two weeks before his 90th birthday. ❀

college. The first reduced loads were given to Drs. Paul Redfearn, Robert Philibert, Frank Dinka, Lewis Saum and Jim Wilbur.

By 1966, National Science Foundation grants to the college were enabling students to learn the research process. That year Patty Maycock and John Tummons were studying the effects of the thyroid gland in the box turtle. Dave Stickle was sampling blood types of wild rabbits. Frank Bowers was studying the association of specific mosses on particular species of trees.

Dr. Leslie Irene Coger broke new ground in 1967 publishing the first text in the field of Readers Theater. Melvin White of Booklyn College co-authored the work with her. That same year Dr. Gene Logan was elected to the American Academy of Physical Education, an elite group of 100 scholars in the field of physical education. The research achievements of faculty in several disciplines were gaining notoriety for SMS.

Faculty Senate Organized

Among the notable achievements of the faculty during the SMS years was the organization of the Faculty Senate in 1962. It was a watershed event. For the previous 56 years, faculty representation in the work of the college was managed through the Faculty Council. Its name was misleading since the Faculty Council was actually made up of administrators — department heads and the president of the college. Throughout Dr. Ellis's administration, he, with the help of the Council, directed the instructional program of the college. There was no clear distinction between faculty and administration. In 1953 when the American

Association of Colleges for Teacher Education came on campus to make its institutional evaluation, it recommended that an academic dean be appointed to lead the work of the faculty. Dr. Ellis replied, "We don't want to raise an umbrella against constructive criticism, but our Faculty Council does that work. Department heads would resent the intrusion of a single person making these policies."

Faculty sentiments on the matter were undoubtedly reflected in the earlier petition to the Board to examine the health of the democratic process on campus. With the coming of Dr. Leland Traywick and his experience with shared governance at Michigan State University, the interpretation of college by-laws adopted in 1936 took a radical turn. Article VI, Section 5 affirmed that "the President of the College shall, with the advice of the Faculty, adopt a plan of organization whereby the faculty may be enabled to perform in a systematic and thorough way the functions herein assigned to the faculty." To Leland Traywick that meant the organization of a Faculty Senate. He encouraged the Committee on the Future of SMS early in the fall of 1961 to write a constitution for a Faculty Senate. It was largely because of President Traywick's belief in the need for faculty participation in the governance of the institution that the constitution was written and the first Faculty Senate organized in the spring of 1962.

Dr. George Gleason of the English Department was elected to chair the Senate. Dr. Tom Stombaugh of the Science Department was vice chair and Dr. Jack Bush of the Education Department served as first secretary. The mission of the Senate was spelled

out in general terms — "to promote the general welfare of the college, to effect communication between faculty and administration, and to provide a means for collective action of the faculty in the area of academic policy, subject to the approval of the President and the Board." Within six months, that first Faculty Senate had made an impressive record of policy recommendations including curriculum restructuring, course re-numbering, and a faculty rank, tenure and salary schedule. In matters affecting instruction, the Senate recommended hiring a full-time philosophy instructor, expanding psychology offerings to permit a major in the discipline, and developing a B.S. in Nursing. It also developed the requirements for a B.S. in Music degree and approved additions to the science and library science curricula.

The Senate that first year also made several recommendations about student life, including the establishment of an administrative Department of Student Affairs, enlarging the testing service, establishing a counseling service, and revising advisement policies. It also recommended that the administration of student housing be "unified, centralized, and placed in the hands of personnel hired for the purpose."

Clearly, the Faculty Senate had taken its responsibility seriously, and to its credit, the administration and Board of Regents adopted virtually all of its recommendations. A new era in college governance was emerging, and faculty were demonstrating their ability and willingness to tackle substantive problems.

Faculty did not sing in unison on all the issues. Debates were lively; disagreements were frequent; and delays were part of the operating realities.

Student Center expanded and renamed Student Union.

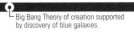
Big Bang Theory of creation supported by discovery of blue galaxies.

Sonny and Cher make first TV appearance on *American Bandstand.*

Medicare, national health insurance for older Americans, established.

Coach Jim Mentis gives instructions to Quarterback Jim Young as the Bears go on in 1966 to defeat the Southeast Missouri State team on their own gridiron for the first time since 1951. The Bears went on to win the MIAA Conference title and a second bid to the Mineral Water Bowl in Excelsior Springs, Missouri.

Student Body President John Ed Miller in 1963 captures some of this in his *Standard* commentary on the struggles between conservatives and liberals on the faculty. "Some want to keep the school education oriented. Others want to make our school one of the finest liberal arts colleges in the Midwest."

In its first 10 years, the SMS Faculty Senate made notable contributions to the development of academic policies. Its curriculum committee supervised the revision of the entire curriculum to accommodate the new semester system adopted in 1963. In 1964 in a landmark action, the Senate established admission criteria to the Teacher Education program. It also established criteria for awarding summa cum laude, magna cum laude and cum laude honors to graduates. In 1966-67, the Senate updated its constitution with a "Statement on Principles of Academic Freedom and Tenure" and a "Statement of Rank and Tenure Policy."

The Faculty Senate responded to campus unrest in the late 1960s adopting a statement on freedoms and responsibilities of all members of the academic community. The Senate also recommended that ROTC be made voluntary "as soon as possible." As the SMS era ended in the early 1970s, the Senate had enacted a "Pass-Fail" grading policy recommended by the Student Government Association, created mini-courses in science giving one hour credit, and established interdisciplinary courses and interdepartmental majors. The first decade of Faculty Senate work corresponded with the period of the college's most rapid growth. This, coupled with administrative crises, student unrest, and complete curricular overhaul provided the faculty an opportunity to demonstrate their commitment and skills to the notion of shared governance. They clearly met the challenge.

Achieving National Recognition

By the early 1950s Southwest Missouri State College had begun to achieve national recognition. Its academic program had already won accreditation by several national organizations, but in 1950 it achieved a long-sought-after goal — to be included in the approved list of the American Association of University Women. The organization's stamp of approval was an endorsement of the college's strengthening liberal arts curriculum since the AAUW was an organization of graduates of liberal arts colleges and universities. Dr. Virginia Craig had long lobbied for the inclusion of SMS, and she was joined in the effort by Dr. Anna Lou Blair, Mary

Gateway Arch completed in St. Louis.

Thirty-four die in Watts Ghetto riot.

"Flower Power" is coined by Allen Ginsberg at a Berkeley, California, antiwar rally.

Adams Woods and Dr. Oreen Ruedi.

In 1951, SMS had its first listings in *Who's Who in American Colleges and Universities.* Fourteen SMS faculty were included in the elite list.

The performing arts at SMS had also gained national recognition by the 1950s. The work of Dr. Leslie Irene Coger in drama had placed SMS among the top 25 drama programs in the country.

Two other programs were gaining national attention as well — forensics and athletics. The climax in these two areas came in 1952 when Tom Strong and Yvonne Ray competed their way into the "Olympics of Debating" — going to West Point to partici- pate in the national debate tourna- ment. Thirty-two teams from across the nation gathered at the Military Academy to match wits. SMS had the smallest enrollment of any school represented in the tournament. Strong and Ray won their way into the quar- terfinals where they lost in a split deci- sion to the University of New Mexico, a team they had defeated earlier in the year. But finishing among the top eight teams at the national tourna- ment confirmed the seriousness with which the debate program at SMS was to be taken. It had been nurtured and developed over 46 years by Dr. Virginia Craig, and while she did not win the 1952 tournament at West Point, she did come away with the winner, a student by the name of Holt Spicer, from Redlands University in California, whose team won the tournament. Spicer was recruited to come to SMS that fall to replace the retiring Virginia Craig as debate coach.

While excitement was develop- ing in forensics in the spring of 1952,

the basketball Bears were winning the MIAA Conference title with a 10-0 mark. They went on to set a school record of 27 victories in 32 games. After beating Central Methodist two of three times in District 16 playoffs, the Bears went on to spacious Municipal Auditorium in Kansas City for the week-long NAIA national tournament. In a six-day run, the Bears knocked off Chadron State, Indiana State, Morningside College, Southwest Texas State and Murray State to bring SMS its first-ever national title in athletics.

The school was on the map with national honors in several areas.

Debate

After a temporary hiatus during the war years, debate picked up again on the campus in 1946. Only 18 months after the dropping of the atomic bomb on Hiroshima, SMS debaters were arguing the proposition "that the U.S., Great Britain, and Canada should, as far as possible, maintain the secrecy of atomic bomb processes until the world government has become stronger than any one nation." The negative prevailed in the Assembly debate program held on January 23, 1946.

Debate tournaments had become the model for forensic competition before the war, and they continued in popularity after the war. Debaters entered as many as 10 tournaments, which expanded beyond team debate to include individual competition in ora- tory, extemporaneous speaking, dramat- ic and humorous declamation, poetry reading, scripture reading and other venues for the display of rhetorical skill. The inclusion of such individual events brought two SMS women of legendary excellence — Dr. Virginia Craig and

First Televised Football Game

Homecoming 1954 provided the first televised football game for SMS fans who watched the contest with Southeast Missouri State (Cape Girardeau) from their homes. KYTV gave full coverage of Homecoming events including the Homecoming Parade, pre-game activities, and half-time events. It had not been a good season for the Bears who stood 2-4 when Cape arrived. Five-thousand fans shiv- ered in the stands as the Bruins took to the field clinging to the hope of a conference upset. It wasn't to be. Cape scored early in the game on a long pass. In the fourth quarter the Indians exploded for three additional touchdowns leaving the Bears on the short end of a 27-0 score — not the TV debut they wanted!

Coach Bill "Junior" Rowe in his second year at SMS in 1964. Rowe was an assistant football coach to Jim Mentis, was SMS's first baseball coach and served as business manager for the Athletics Department.

Dr. Leslie Irene Coger — into a collaborative forensic effort that produced a stream of sweepstakes championships in tournaments throughout the Midwest. Eight consecutive sweepstakes trophies were won by SMS competitors at the Ada, Oklahoma, tournament alone. In 1948, Coger's speakers triumphed at the Savage Forensic Tournament in Durant, Oklahoma. Entering 18 events including poetry, *Bible* reading, storytelling, impromptu speaking, public discussion, book review, dramatic reading, and address reading, the SMS contingent amassed more total points than any other entry.

While there is no public record of her aspiration to qualify an SMS team to compete in the National Debate Tournament at West Point, one can assume that Dr. Craig thought frequently about that possibility. She had

nurtured the program since 1906 teaching argumentation and other debate related courses and conducting on-campus competition between literary societies. She had nurtured the start of intercollegiate debate sending young Roy Ellis and A.M. Cockrell in the spring of 1910 to debate (and lose to) a Cape Girardeau team. In 1914, she listened proudly as the Normal School Band summoned students from their classes to a holiday celebrating debate victories over Cape Girardeau and Kirksville by Lester Thomas and Floyd O'Rear, Bruce Hayes and Lacey Eastburn. In 1932, she pushed the program beyond intercollegiate competition into national tournaments, traveling to Winfield, Kansas. By the start of World War II she had seen her debaters win tournament competition throughout the Midwest and Midsouth.

So in her 46th year of coaching debate, the climactic moment arrived. In 1951-52 her teams competed in 13 tournaments winning 115 out of 162 decision debates. Tom Strong, a brilliant farm lad from Barry County who in 1951 had represented Missouri in the National Oratorical Contest in Evanston, Illinois, and reached the finals with his 17 minute address on

"The Loss of Our Political Integrity," had teamed up with Yvonne Ray, a 21-year-old senior who transferred to SMS from East Central State in Oklahoma because "SMS has the best speech department in the southwest, and I wanted to debate under Dr. Craig." Together they captured the district debate title at Iowa State qualifying them to debate in "the Olympics" — the National Debate Tournament at West Point, the first SMS team ever to qualify for national finals.

A lifetime of debate coaching came to a fitting conclusion as Dr. Craig watched Strong and Ray compete with 31 other schools, moving SMS into the quarter finals after defeating the University of Illinois, George Washington University, Wake Forest, Smith College, Kingsport College and San Diego College. Losing to the University of New Mexico by a split decision left the SMS team among the top eight in the nation, a fitting triumph for a woman who had invested 46 years of her life in training young people to think, assess the thinking of others and articulate conclusions with persuasive artistry. It was a double triumph for Dr. Virginia Craig. Not only had she qualified a team for the National Finals, she also went on to hand-pick her successor from the winning team that year, a senior from the University of Redlands in California, Holt Spicer.

Dr. Craig retired in 1952, bringing a brilliant career to fitting close. But one had to wonder, "How would a young man with a bachelor's degree

from the University of Redlands, still in his 20s with plenty of experience in debate, but none in coaching debate — how would such a person fill the shoes of the venerable Dr. Craig?" The evidence suggests the answer, "Very well." For, as Roy Ellis remembers, "The new debate coach found at his service a smooth-running debating machine with the necessary momentum for a rapid start."

The very next year, Spicer's first as coach, the team continued its winning momentum. At the Novice Tournament at Kansas State, SMS debaters John Tadych and John Pope went undefeated. They repeated the sweep at Arkadelphia, Arkansas, and again at Ada, Oklahoma, where the entire SMS team won Sweepstakes Honors. The wins continued to pile up giving substance to Ellis's description of the program as "a smooth-running debate machine," and credence to Craig's choice of young Holt Spicer to succeed her. The year ended with Kaye Kynion and Richard Thompson qualifying as First Alternate for the 1953 West Point Tournament, and the Missouri Legislature passing a resolution of commendation for the outstanding achievements of the forensic program.

Between 1952 and the end of the SMS era in 1972, the debate program produced no less than 10 teams qualifying for the National Debate Tournament at West Point. While winning the tournament still eluded the SMS program, competing in it during the SMS years had become commonplace. In 1955, Bill Maynard and Erma Jones won the right to compete at West Point. In 1957 John DeBross and Russell Keeling won their way into the national tournament. The follow-

Coach Orville Pottenger watches his 1963 Bears complete an undefeated season. Invited for the first time to the Mineral Water Bowl in Excelsior Springs, Missouri, the Bears lost by a touchdown to Northern Illinois, 21-14.

ing year, they won the alternate spot for the district. In 1959, DeBross and Bob Hartzog won the district title and went on to compete at West Point as did Pat Elliot and Gary Nelms in 1960. In 1964, Kent Keller and Annette Wright carried the SMS banner to the Academy. In both 1969 and 1970, Buford Crites and Ross Eschelman qualified for the nationals. In 1971, the final year of the SMS era, Jim Anderson and Tom Black were given an at-large invitation to West Point.

In 1958-59, after many tournament wins, the SMS debate squad set a record at the Pittsburg, Kansas, competition recording a triple championship in the senior division, the first ever achieved in that tournament. Later that year, SMS hosted an exhibition debate with Harvard University. Pat Elliot and Mary Standefer represented SMS and defeated the Harvard team, even with Harvard alumni as the judges! The year saw the SMS debaters capture 78 percent of its rounds.

In 1964, SMS debaters won an unprecedented third consecutive championship in the prestigious Heart of America Tournament at the University of Kansas. So it was clear that not only was the "debating machine" at SMS well oiled, its young coach was up to the challenge of succeeding the legendary Virginia Craig. Competitors noticed this in 1970-71 when Dr. Holt Spicer received the Air Force Academy Excellence in Coaching trophy recognizing the consistently outstanding quality of debaters sent from SMS to Colorado Springs. That same year, Spicer was given permanent possession of the R.R. Pflaum trophy from Kansas State Teachers College in Emporia.

First courses in speech pathology offered.

St Louis' Busch Stadium opens — Braves lose to Cards 4-3 in 12 innings.

Cesar Chavez's National Farm Workers Union is recognized as the bargaining agent for farm workers.

Miranda Rights established by Supreme Court.

Sniper at the University of Texas tower shoots 45, killing 12 and himself.

Freshman Curtis Perry (54) goes high for the ball in a 1967 contest in McDonald Arena. Perry set a number of school records, including 31 rebounds against University of Texas-Arlington in 1970, and number of field goals (277) in a single season (1969-70). Perry went on to play in the NBA as a starter for the Milwaukee Bucks from 1971-74 and later for the Phoenix Suns (1974-78). His jersey (54) was the second to be retired in SMS history.

During the Spicer era, SMS debating teams reached out beyond the Midwest and Midsouth where they had labored so successfully under Dr. Craig. Transportation was better, program funding was more generous, and there were more staff enabling debaters to travel from coast to coast and participate in 40 or more tournaments a year. Bill Maynard, Pat Kynion, Donal Stanton, Richard Ellis and Richard Stoval all pitched in to move the program forward.

But memories of the earlier days remain vivid. Russell Keeling remembers the late night stops at several motels "until the coach located one that met his standard (cheap!)." Pat Stallings Kruppa was "amused to remember that at the University of Houston we were given a $1 per meal advance — a whopping $9 for the three day event!" A 1950s debater who is now a successful attorney recalls that "The debate trips were very exciting experiences for a teenager from Carthage, Missouri. It was the first time I had stayed in a hotel room, visited the states of Oklahoma, Louisiana and Texas, and eaten meals at a restaurant."

Debate in those days reflected many of the same sexist attitudes that permeated mid-century culture in America. Spicer remembers the segregation of teams. "Mixed teams could compete in the championship division, but teams of two women were segregated." Pat Kruppa recalls, "when I won a watch at West Point in 1957, it was a man's watch. It didn't strike me (or probably anyone else) at the time what a sexist assumption it was to provide only men's watches for the winners!"

Emma Jones Stewart remembers the 1955 West Point tournament. "There were only four girls at the tournament that year…. The first time we walked in to debate before a class of cadets, everyone stood as we entered. We went to the front and put our stuff down, and I noticed everyone else was still standing so I thought maybe we were going to say the Pledge or something. Finally, Bill Maynard whispers to me, 'If you would sit down, so could everyone else.' So I tried it and they did! I guess I really had never had an entire room full of men stand up because I entered the room. As a feminist now I'm not sure about it, but at the time I thought it was really neat!"

When Yvonne Ray transferred to SMS from East Central State in Oklahoma to debate, she experienced a bit of culture shock. "Dress seems to be the thing most different about SMS," she observed. "Down at East Central the girls wear jeans to class and the boys wear boots and cowboy hats all the time. I'm going to wear my squaw boots to school one of these days, and everybody will just die!" Ray did wear her squaw boots and they were noticed, but she was remembered by colleagues not for her natty dress but as one of the most powerful debaters they had ever met.

In March 1962 the SMS debate squad scored two victories that defined the quality of the 56-year-old program. Two freshmen, Charles Collins and Larry Chastain, emerged as champions at the Heart of America Debate Tournament at the University of Kansas. It was the first time a small college had ever won the tournament, and the first time a freshman team had ever triumphed. The freshman duo was matched against such traditional winners as Harvard, Dartmouth, Northwestern and the University of Southern California. In a letter to Bill Maynard, SMS coach that year, Tom Yoe, director of publications at the University of Kansas declared, "The achievement of those two freshmen is nearly beyond comprehension."

Just one week later, on St. Patrick's Day, Annette Wright and Kent Keller defeated the fighting Irish of Notre Dame on NBC's nationally televised Championship Debate. The team, along with Coach Holt Spicer, flew to New York City on Friday where they did last-minute preparation on

SMSU

Dr. Imon Bartley appointed dean of Graduate Studies.

Missouri/Springfield

International/USA

Jerry Lewis' first Muscular Dystrophy telethon.

Star Trek premieres on TV.

National Organization of Women founded.

214   *Daring to Excel: The First 100 Years of Southwest Missouri State University*

the proposition "Resolved: That U.S. agriculture price supports should be drastically reduced." They took the negative position in the debate. Saturday morning saw them rehearsing at the NBC studios next to the set used for the TODAY show. The debate started at 11:30 a.m. Springfield time and lasted 30 minutes. According to Keller, "It felt like about five minutes." The first judge decided for Notre Dame, and Wright said "I sort of felt sick." But after the next two judges decided in favor of the SMS team, Keller "got cold shakes and quivered all over," according to Coach Spicer, who reported that he, as the proud coach, "just sat there and beamed." Keller and Wright had prepared for the debate for over a month. Wright reported that they received valuable assistance from Karl Wickstrom and Jim Reeves of the Producer's Creamery Company in Springfield. Annette remembers, "They explained the technical aspects of the complex resolution and enabled us to understand price supports much better."

By 1966, the strong forensic tradition at SMS had stimulated the organization of the Department of Speech and Theatre with Dr. Robert Gilmore as head. The initial faculty included Dr. Leslie Irene Coger, Dr. Holt Spicer, Byrne Blackwood, Dr. Robert Bradley, Ishmael Gardner and Donald Stowell. The following year, the department offered one of the first independent graduate programs on campus.

While the retirement of Dr. Virginia Craig in 1952 indeed marked the end of an era, it also made clear how strong a foundation she had established in debate. Dr. Richard Haswell, head of the English Department at the time of Craig's retirement, expressed

Bear forward Lou Shepherd (50) battles for the rebound against Southeast Missouri State players in 1967. The Bears captured the conference title in a 10-0 season. Shepherd set a school record single game shooting percentage of 1.000 in 1967 against Northwest Missouri State, making 10 out of 10 shots.

the sentiments of all who had ever worked with her. "Her devotion to debating is well known. For her, it best combined the virtues of reason, integrity, industry and competition. From the early years of literary societies to the

later large intercollegiate tournaments, she spent her energy and enthusiasm lavishly — the only lavish spending a college teacher could afford — on the encouragement and training of her debaters. Those of us who worked with

Football Bears play Adams State in Mineral Water Bowl.

1967

Movie actor Ronald Reagan elected governor of California.

U.S. and U.S.S.R. sign treaty prohibiting nuclear weapons in outer space.

Kwanzaa established as a holiday.

Apollo 1 fire kills astronauts Grissom, White and Chaffee.

1946-72 Southwest Missouri State College   215

Coaches Bill Thomas and Jay Kinser direct their 1968-69 Bears to a fourth straight bid to post-season play. In the national title game, the Bears fell to Kentucky Wesleyan 75-71, completing a 24-5 season.

history. From an 18-4 season in 1946-47, which tied the SMS single season victory mark from the 1927-28 campaign, the Bears logged the school's first 20-win season the following year with a 21-6 record. The 1947-48 Bears claimed their first MIAA Conference championship since 1936. For much of that season, they were the only undefeated team in the nation. The Bears were ranked No. 1 defensively among the smaller colleges of the country allowing their opponents only 36.1 points per game. They also led all colleges in field goal percentages.

The Bears blazed their way to a 25-2 mark in 1948-49 and turned in a 19-5 record the following year to finish the four-year run with 83 wins and 17 losses. The Bears continued to be nationally ranked in defensive genius and twice finished second in MIAA play. The 1949 team beat the MCAU Champions, Missouri Valley twice to advance to the Bear's eventual trip to the second round of the NAIA tourney. In 1950, SMS lost a two-game playoff to MCAU winner Central Methodist College.

Coach McDonald stepped aside from the basketball reins in 1950 to become head of the Physical Education Department upon the untimely death of Arthur Briggs. McDonald had directed his 23 SMS teams to a 301-166 record to become the all-time winningest SMS coach. He continued to coach the golf team for nearly 20 more years.

The search for McDonald's replacement got under way immediately. H.L. Millikan was hired on April 18, 1950, but resigned a few days later to take a better offer from the University of Maryland. On May 5, the Board hired Bob Vanatta, coach at Central

Men's Athletics

While the state college era would be one of profound success for SMS athletics, particularly football and basketball, the post-war transition in sports was a bit bumpy. Air Force cadets marching on the football field had compacted it to near cement-like hardness. Their repeated washing of the floor in the Health and Recreation Building had ruined it for basketball competition.

Furthermore, student interest in athletics contests immediately after the war was lukewarm at best. *The Standard,* in January 1947, described student attendance at basketball and football games as "pitiful." Was there a new era of student-body indifference to

athletics? Or was it that post-war teams were just getting organized? The editor wondered.

The answer was not long in coming. With a new floor installed in the Health and Recreation Building and a nucleus of basketball players that turned in history-making achievements, students were soon complaining that there was not enough room in the 3,200 seat arena.

Coach McDonald's basketball Bears started the first era of sustained success in basketball. He pushed the cage Bears toward the national stage for the first time in what would be the start of an enormous interest in the sport that has sustained itself in southwest Missouri for more than a half century. A nucleus of student-athletes stayed together from the 1946-47 season through 1949-50 and turned in what were then the most significant basketball accomplishments in school

Dr. Craig will gratefully admit that the best of what we try to do today began with her." It remains so at the end of 100 years.

SMSU — Property near Federal Medical Center given to SMSU (125 acres).

Missouri/Springfield — Ned Reynolds hired as sports director for KYTV.

International/USA — Aretha Franklin records *Respect.* — Twiggy, British model, takes U.S. by storm. — First Boeing 737 rolls out.

College who had formerly coached basketball at Springfield High School. Vanatta brought a new brand of basketball to SMS. McDonald's genius was strong defense resulting in low scoring contests. Vanatta preferred hustle tactics. "My teams…have to like to run," he announced. And run they did, as Vanatta scripted an even brighter era for SMS basketball.

While the cagers were flourishing, the SMS footballers were embarking on what was the first five-year winning streak in school history. The field had been restored to a playable surface. New bleachers had been installed on the east side seating 2,700 fans. The class of 1948 donated an automatic scoreboard, which was installed on the field, and in 1949 the Giant Manufacturing Company of Council Bluffs, Iowa, installed a $6,000 lighting system that doubled the illumination on the playing field.

After a 2-6 season in 1946, ailing Coach "Red" Blair surrendered the gridiron reigns to Tommy O'Boyle, who stayed only two seasons but produced the best multiple-year coaching record of any previous coach. The 1947 Bears were 7-2-1 and finished second in the MIAA. In 1948 the team went 9-2, shared the league title, and drew an invitation to the first-ever SMS bowl contest. The Bears played Emporia State in the Mo-Kan Bowl at Rockhurst College in Kansas City and lost 34-20, leaving O'Boyle with a 16-4-1 record.

O'Boyle left for Kansas State and Fred Thomsen, one-time coach at the University of Arkansas, succeeded him in 1949 and logged three straight winning years including a 6-3-1 season in 1951 with SMS sharing the league

Coach "Red" Cross explains the strategy for the 1970 game with Henderson State to sports broadcaster Ned Reynolds. The Bears dropped the contest, 14-12.

title. Thomsen's final SMS team finished 3-6 in 1952.

Thomsen's leaving was not a happy event. The Board dismissed him on December 15. Students circulated a petition advocating his retention. Thomsen asked for an opportunity to appear before the Board "to give my side of the case." The Board replied, "We already have the facts." Thomsen responded, "The move to dismiss me must be based on personal reasons, and I wish to state that this is an unfair stand and not in accordance with ethical standards of NCAA…or with my

understanding of tenure." Students reacted sharply. "I think it was a dirty deal," one said. "Why wasn't he given his requested hearing?" The football Bears would not finish above the .500 mark for another decade.

But the forward momentum in basketball continued. Coach Vanatta wasted no time with the Bears, taking the team to a 22-3 season and a league runner-up spot in 1950-51. The next year the season started with a week-long bus trip to California where the Bears lost two of three games in an NAIA pre-season tourney. But the team blazed back to set a school record with 27 victories in 32 games. The Bears posted a 10-0 season to win the conference championship and whipped Central Methodist two of three times in the District 16 playoff earning the right to go to Kansas City and play in the week-long NAIA Tournament in spacious Municipal Auditorium.

Despite losing Jim Murphy, their leading scorer, who Vanatta dismissed from the team for insubordination, the

Independent graduate program starts.

Galena becomes official mineral of the state.

First successful coronary bypass surgery performed by Rene Favaloro.

Israel defeats Arabs in the six-day war in the Middle East.

Bears, in a six-day run, beat Chadron State, Indiana State, Morningside, Southwest Texas State and Murray State to bring SMS its first national title, the best among 400 colleges. Coach Vanatta's opportunistic basketball shattered the NAIA record by scoring 399 points in five games, averaging 79.8 per game *The Standard* unashamedly declared, "This is the greatest event in the history of this college." When the team returned to Springfield, they were met at the junction of highways 66 and 13 with 3,000 screaming fans creating a colossal traffic jam. President Ellis recalled the event. "It seemed that all Springfield was waiting for them at the city limits. They were surprised, but they liked it. Coach Vanatta was noted for his nonchalance, but on this occasion he smiled in utter abandon. It just started in as a sort of ripple around his mouth and spread all over his face. His glowing countenance was like a headlight on a train of happy thoughts." Another thousand fans were waiting at the Student Center when the team reached the campus.

According to Ellis, "Neither the coach nor team would claim any credit for the victory. Each stubbornly insisted that the other deserved all the credit.

After intense grilling, the boys did finally confess to winning the games but insisted that the coach was responsible. The coach, when hard-pressed by questioning, admitted that he was present at most of the games and did offer some suggestions from time to time as to the tactics to be employed. Such modesty is amusing and most commendable."

The president described the NAIA Championship as "a colossal achievement." But the team wasn't finished. A year later it was more of the same with SMS finishing 24-4, winning the conference title, sweeping two from Missouri Valley in the District 16 match-up, and heading to Kansas City for the national tournament. The 1953 Bears downed Gonzaga, Stetson, Nebraska Wesleyan, Indiana State and Hamline to become the first repeat NAIA winner in the 32-team tournament format.

The highlight of the event and one of the most memorable single events in SMS athletics history came late in the semi-final game with Indiana State. The Bears entered the tournament short on players since Jerry Lumpe had to leave for spring training with the New York Yankees baseball team

the night before the semi-final game. With the game entering its final minutes, four SMS players were already on the bench with five fouls. At the three minute mark, Art Helms committed his fifth personal foul and Vanatta had no one available to substitute. So four players, Bill "Jinx" Thomas, the only starter, Don Duckworth, Bill Price and Ray Birdsong were left to battle an Indiana State team that had scored 100 points or better in each of its previous three games. With the score tied at 72-72, the "Fabulous Four" mounted a four-man zone defense that stymied the Indiana team. Moreover, the four outscored the Sycamores 12-6 in those last three desperate minutes to win 84-78. It put them into the championship bracket against Hamline, which succumbed the following day to the unstoppable Bears, 79-71.

The *Kansas City Times* on March 14, 1953, reported, "The most fabulous game of the National Intercollegiate history was unreeled last night before 8,500 fans in Municipal Auditorium when four Springfield, Missouri State players, all that were left in the whistle-happy contest, beat Indiana State 84-78 to advance to the championship finals."

Jerry Anderson of SMS was named tournament Most Valuable Player, the only sophomore ever to win the award. With a reputation for repeatedly stealing the ball from opposing

Enrollment exceeds 6,000 (6,596).

Zenith opens 697,000 sq. ft. plant to manufacture color television sets.

Thurgood Marshall becomes first African American appointed to the U.S. Supreme Court.

35,000 men and women march on the Pentagon protesting the Vietnam War.

Surveyor 6 is first man-made object to lift off moon.

players, Anderson nearly met his match in the Stetson game. A Stetson player "turned the tables on Anderson, stole the ball from him and took it down court for a Stetson fast-break basket. But in an unbelievable effort, Anderson reversed his direction, tore out down the court at a speed which only he could travel, and not only caught up with the Stetson player, but nimbly and expertly regained the ball from him and started back toward his own basket." By the end of his college career, Jerry Anderson stories would fill a notebook.

The 1953 basketball season ended with Coach Vanatta carrying an SMS record of 73-11, and being recruited by West Point. His replacement was a highly successful high school coach, Eddie Matthews. The Bears' winning tradition continued. They won the 1953-54 MIAA conference title and the District 16 playoff against Central Methodist. They were poised to make their third run at an NAIA title. In the early rounds they disposed of Gustavus Adolphus, East Tennessee State, and East Texas State. In the semi-final round they were dropped by Illinois Western. The Bears came back to defeat Arkansas Tech in the third place game to finish out a three-year 14-1 run in the NAIA national meet.

For the second year in a row, Jerry Anderson was named MVP. He was also named to the All Tournament Team. The Helms Foundation went on to name Anderson the "NAIA Player of the Year," the top honor in small college basketball. "This award is a tribute for Andy's all-out, never-give-up, unselfish attitude he displays on the hardwood floor," declared Coach Matthews. Anderson returned to campus to be elected student body president for his senior year.

During the excitement of the early 1950s, spectators got more than a little "into" games on campus. The MIAA conference regularly rated coaches, players and crowds on their sportsmanship during athletics contests. In a report issued in May 1954, SMS coaches were given high marks, players were rated at 92 percent, four points below the conference average, and the SMS crowd was rated at 77 percent, well below the conference average of 89 percent. It was a concern to college officials. President Ellis said, "The intent of the crowd may be in general, good. But, I believe persons visiting our basketball games, and in turn visiting games at other schools in our conference, would say that our fans are more boisterous and at times more belligerent in their criticism of players and officials, than they would obtain at comparable contests at other member institutions." *The Standard* laid the blame on "townsfolk who encourage students to be outrageous at games."

Some of the spectator excesses were attributable to deepening rivalry between SMS and Rolla, which had become the successor to Drury once athletics contests were suspended between the Bears and the Panthers. In the fall of 1952, a week before the SMS-Rolla football game, thousands of dollars in damage was done to buildings defaced with black paint including the Student Center, the Women's Residence Hall and the Field House. Student leaders immediately responded. Bill Patterson, president of the Rolla Student Council said, "It seems the best approach to the problem would be an attempt to sublimate rather than quell the emotional displays resulting from the rivalry between our athletics teams. What I have in mind is a traditional trophy, such as an 'old oaken bucket'

In the spring of 1954, the College Players put on Arthur Miller's *Death of a Salesman*. Director Irene Coger briefs the cast, which included Bill Price as Willy Loman and Sue Graves as Linda.

First Xerox photocopier available in library.

Frisco railroad ends passenger service to Springfield.

GRADUATE

The Graduate, starring Dustin Hoffman and Anne Bancroft, premieres.

First heart transplant is performed by South African surgeon Dr. Christiaan Barnard.

1968

Jacques Cousteau's first undersea special on TV.

Vince Lombardi resigns as coach of Green Bay Packers.

A 1950 Football Memory

Many will remember the Pittsburg State football game of 1950. Joe Stevens of the Bears intercepted a Gorilla pass and raced down the field toward pay dirt. As he streaked past the Gorilla bench, an over-eager Gorilla sub dashed out onto the field and tackled Stevens. But officials would have nothing of the kind. They awarded a touchdown to the Bears who finished the contest with a 20-7 win.

~

Mythical Faculty Basketball Team

In January 1954, a letter from Illinois State arrived on campus inviting SMS to participate in a men's faculty basketball tournament in February. "At stake," the letter declared, "will be the World's Men's Faculty Basketball Championship for Small Colleges."

The Standard editor immediately went to work to name the SMS team. "At Center will be 'Bevo' Cralle, beanie-capped phenom of the hardwoods. Forwards will be 'Handy-Andy' McDonald and 'Blazing Ben' Koeppel. At the guard positions we would have two streaks of lightning — Holt 'Spike' Spicer and 'Driving Dave' Scott." To our knowledge the game was never played. The Bruin team was just too formidable.

"...and in the middle will be a large tree for Harry to climb." Dr. Coger describes the scene from the 1954 production of *Brigadoon* while Sam Anderson and Sue Graves listen intently.

which would belong to the victor of each SMS-MSM football game each season." SMS Student Body President Don Dedmon agreed, and in 1954, "Ye Olde Powder Keg" rivalry started. The trophy was awarded at the end of each football game and would be retained by the victor until its team was defeated. President Ellis said in 1965, "'Ye Olde Powder Keg' has, oddly enough, restrained explosive enthusiasm in the student groups." It did, at least, until 1968 when a near-riot occurred in Rolla after an SMS-Rolla basketball game.

While "'Ye Olde Powder Keg" was being put in place, a new face was seen on the SMS campus. Aldo Sebben was hired as track coach and assistant football coach. Sebben became athletics director in 1955 and held that position for 27 years, the longest in SMS history. Sebben was head football coach from 1956 through 1961 during which time tackle Bill Kaczmarek was drafted

by the San Francisco '49ers, one of the first SMS football players to go on to professional play. "Best tackle I have ever coached," declared Sebben. His coaching chores included track and cross country until 1972 when athletics director duties required his full attention.

SMS made a significant move in its national affiliation in 1956, switching from the NAIA to join the NCAA when the latter added a college division to its major college team membership listings. SMS made an almost immediate impact with its NCAA affiliation by reaching its first College Division Basketball championship in March 1958. Coach Eddie Matthews' Bears posted a gaudy 22-2 record that included an MIAA title, victories over Centenary and Regis College in the regional tournament at SMS, and a loss to the University of South Dakota in the national quarterfinals in Evansville, Indiana.

A year later, Matthews again had the Bears in high gear. They turned

SMSU
└ Basketball Bears ranked 4th in the nation.

Missouri/Springfield
└ Race riots occur in Kansas City in response to the death of Dr. Martin Luther King.

International/USA
└ Rev. Dr. Martin Luther King assassinated in Memphis, Tennessee.

in a 23-3 season in 1958-59, as well as another MIAA crown, and regional tournament wins over Centenary and Abilene. Advancing to the national quarterfinals in Evansville, the Bears bested Hope College and Los Angeles State, but then suffered an 83-67 setback at the hands of the University of Evansville playing on its home floor.

It was in these years that the Bears started seeing their earliest rankings in national small college polls. SMS ran off lengthy winning streaks at the start of each of the 1958 and 1959 seasons to capture national attention, the situation further enhanced by a school record 41-game home-court winning streak from 1956-60.

In 1961, former U.S. Marine Corps Colonel Orville Pottenger came to SMS from Parkview High School to take over football coaching chores. He produced the team's first winning season in a decade in 1962. In 1963 he fielded a team that would capture the imagination of the entire region. The Bears raced through the regular season undefeated at 9-0, including a perfect 5-0 MIAA title run. The season included non-league wins over potent foes Drake and Akron. Then the Bears faced off against Northern Illinois in the Mineral Water Bowl in Excelsior Springs, Missouri. NIU won, 21-14.

Pottenger stayed with the gridiron Bears one more season and then turned the club over to Jim Mentis in 1965. Mentis had the Bears back in the MIAA title spotlight with a 5-0 record in 1966 and took them to another Mineral Water Bowl game where they fell to Adams State, 14-8.

By the end of the 1965-66 season SMS was competing in nine intercollegiate men's sports including wrestling, swimming, baseball, football, basketball, track, cross-country, golf and tennis.

The Bears' basketball team was shocked when Coach Eddie Matthews suffered a fatal heart attack in the spring of 1964 after 11 successful seasons with the college. The baton passed to Assistant Coach Bill Thomas, one of the "Fabulous Four" of 1953 fame. Thomas quickly made his own mark. In a five-year run from 1966 through 1970, Thomas took the cage Bears to five straight MIAA titles and five straight NCAA College Division Tournament appearances. SMS followed its league titles with regional championships in 1967 and 1969, and advanced to the finals in Evansville. The 1967 Bears got past Valparaiso in the quarterfinals and Illinois State in the semifinals before losing to Winston-Salem 77-74 in the national title game. In 1969, SMS defeated Montclair State and Ashland to set up a championship game with Kentucky Wesleyan. Wesleyan ran up a big lead before the Bears staged a strong comeback in the second half, only to lose 75-71. The Bears were ousted in regional play in 1966 by Abilene Christian, by Evansville in 1968 and South Dakota State in 1970.

Two long-time SMS athletics pioneers were honored by the Board of Regents in 1970 with the renaming of the football facility Briggs Stadium in honor of Arthur Briggs who coached, taught and administered athletics programs from 1912 to 1950. The basketball facility became McDonald Arena in honor of A.J. McDonald who played on the 1922 national championship team from the University of Kansas along with Adolph Rupp, and then came to SMS in 1925 to begin what

A campus pioneer in women's athletics, Florence Baker Bugg came to SMS in 1930 and taught physical education classes for 32 years. Bugg choreographed Dr. Irene Coger's campus production of *Oklahoma!* in 1956 to rave reviews.

was to become the most successful basketball coaching career in the history of the school.

The SMS era opened athletics competition to black student-athletes. When the school desegregation order was issued in 1954, all Missouri state colleges and universities opened their doors to black students. By 1957 black student-athletes were contributing to the growing strength of SMS teams. Chester Shipps played basketball under Coach Bill Thomas in 1956-57. "Dopey" Huddleston played in the backfield for the football Bears. LeRoy Johnson made the track squad. By 1960, black student-athletes began making names for themselves in intercollegiate competition. Eldo Perry, playing guard for the football Bears, was named to the All-Conference Team. Ron Golden, Bill Boylton and

Theater group presents *Wonderful Town*, and a variety show to troops in the Pacific Command.

Robert F. Kennedy assassinated by Sirhan Sirhan in California.

1946-72 Southwest Missouri State College 221

Charles Marshall were all members of the "S" club as football lettermen. In 1965 Cornelius Perry was named to the All-Conference Team. By the late 1960s, All-American honors went to black basketball players Danny Bolden and Curtis Perry. Perry went on to play in the NBA.

Shortly before his death in February 2002, Max Gee, who played SMS basketball in the late 1960s, wrote in his own obituary about the achievements of his basketball team during a period when race relations on campus were very tense. "Our 1968-69 Bear's team was arguably the best Division II team in school history. While our second place finish in the NCAA tournament was a big accomplishment, I'm most proud of the breakthroughs we made in racial harmony. At a potentially explosive time in history, we were able to take a few white kids from racist backgrounds, blend them together with a few black kids from inner-city Washington, D.C., and St. Louis, and learn that skin color means nothing, and form true friendships that extend far beyond the basketball court."

With the beginning of the SMS era, financial aid began to be available to promising student-athletes. *The Standard* reported in 1949 that football players were being paid 45 cents an hour for a variety of tasks around campus. In the 1950s, a Work-Aid Program was developed that paid student-athletes by the hour for ushering at games, cleaning up the stadium or arena after games, and working high school track meets and basketball tournaments. There were no conference regulations or policies governing financial aid for student-athletes at the time. In the late 1940s colleges like Central Methodist were offering board, room and tuition for 16 hours of work by student-athletes, an attractive option for a promising player.

In 1958, MIAA officials approved a policy allowing conference schools to provide financial aid (room, board, and fees) to student-athletes. The aid must be paid from athletics revenues or alumni or business gifts. No state funds could be used to assist student-athletes. The ruling went into effect in the fall of 1959 and SMS was granted 35 such "grants-in-aid."

About the same time football players were receiving 45 cents an hour for campus work, football coach "Red" Blair was working on an idea that would provide an added incentive for promising student-athletes to choose SMS. In the late 1930s, he had envisioned an athletics dormitory built with outside funds that would provide housing for student-athletes. The idea fell dormant during the war years but was revived in 1946. The dorm notion caught the attention of several supporters of Bear athletics and by October 1949, the "Southwest State College Educational Foundation" composed of interested businessmen and alumni was formed to raise money to build a $60,000 athletics dormitory just east of National on the north side of Grand. Plans were to have the dorm open by August 1950.

Despite 60 percent of the faculty pledging to give to the project, and $639 being raised among students by November 1949, 10 years later only $24,000 had been gathered. Nonetheless, construction began in the spring of 1959 and by the fall, 36 men were living in the partially completed facility. The college's first effort at television fund-raising occurred on February 16, 1959, when a telethon for the dorm was conducted during the SMS-St. Michaels basketball game. Six hundred dollars were pledged.

Living in the athletics dorm was

Mike Dowdy and Janice Duley starred in the popular 1960 theater production *Little Foxes*.

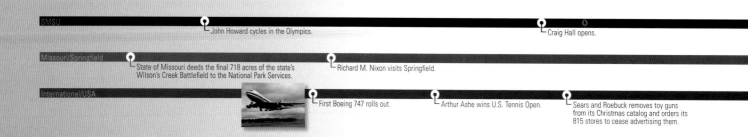

organized on a cooperative basis. Residents would pay rent equivalent to the cost of operating the building, estimated to be between $7 and $10 per month. The building was eventually completed and served student-athletes through the remainder of the SMS era.

Women's Athletics

Despite the fact that a women's basketball team was among the first athletics teams to compete for State Normal School #4, the achievement of respect and recognition for women's athletics has been a long and difficult struggle. The women's basketball team in 1908 defied the gender division so typical of American life at the turn of the 20th century. Alfred Lord Tennyson had laid out the parameters of that division in his poem "The Princess."

> *Man for the field and women for the hearth*
> *Man for the sword and for the needle she*
> *Man with the head and woman with the heart*
> *Man to command and woman to obey*
> *All else, confusion.*

Tennyson had articulated what was presumed by most to be "the natural order of the universe." If it were disrupted, chaos and confusion were sure to follow. So the introduction of gender equality into education, and ultimately into athletics, was seen by some to threaten the very foundation of the social order.

The ideology of separate spheres based on gender constituted a virtually invincible barrier to the development of women's athletics. Teddy Roosevelt complained at the end of the 19th century that "males in our society had

Finian's Rainbow, co-produced by Dr. Irene Coger and Elton Burgstahler of the Music Department in the spring of 1960 was subsequently chosen to go on a seven-week tour of Europe during the spring of 1961. The overseas tour of military bases was organized by the Defense Department and co-sponsored by the USO and the Educational Theater Association. This was the first Missouri theatrical group to be chosen for a USO tour. Taking time out from tobacco picking to sing a happy song are Kay Fraker, Linda Fay, Gwen Theis and Janet Simmons.

become too soft and effeminate because frontiers and battlefields no longer existed to test manly courage and perseverance." According to Roosevelt, only sports could create "the brawn, the spirit, the self-confidence and the quickness of men." The football field "is the only place where masculine supremacy is incontestable," he declared.

While it was clear to lots of people at the time that athletics competition was a distinctly male enterprise, the opinion was not unanimous. Throughout the early years of the 20th century there were pioneers who not only advocated education for women, but also physical education, and, more radically, athletics competition. There is a fascinating story here we haven't time to tell, but which shaped the context

in which women's athletics slowly but then dramatically developed at SMS.

For years prior to the state college era, women's sports were restricted to "Play Day" programs in which women from several schools would travel to a host institution, choose up teams from among all players, and engage in a variety of competitive games. By 1949, Margaret Putnam reported that the St. Louis Physical Education Convention leaders were "highly in favor of competitive sports for women." But about the same time, the *Springfield Leader and Press* went on record against competitive athletics for women. "For years our girls have not entered sports on a competitive basis. We have no objection to Play Day, but our policy has been against competition in girls' sports

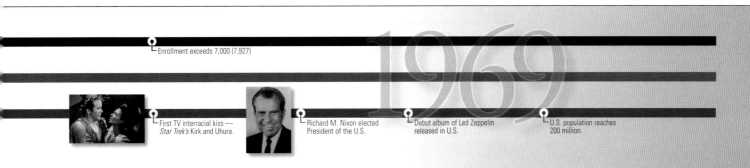

Enrollment exceeds 7,000 (7,927)

1969

First TV interracial kiss — *Star Trek's* Kirk and Uhura.

Richard M. Nixon elected President of the U.S.

Debut album of Led Zeppelin released in U.S.

U.S. population reaches 200 million.

Mike Ferguson points an accusing finger at a sprawling Leland Gannaway as Lynn Skaggs looks on with consternation. Skaggs took the title role in the 1960 play *Matchmaker* with Ferguson and Gannaway playing supporting roles.

— except for tennis."

The bias against competitive sports for women was present on the SMS campus as well. In 1948, *The Standard* reported that "most girls on campus are aware that competitive sports are taboo. The Women's Athletic Organization here not only refrains from competitive sports but also forbids any of its members to take part in any competitive game with any outside-of-school organization such as the YWCA or others." The editor closed his piece asking, "How can colleges and high schools defend their stand on no competition for women?"

The answer was "with increasing difficulty." The momentum was building to challenge the stereotypical understanding that athletics competition was a singularly male enterprise. By the late 1950s on the SMS campus, female competition was limited to intramural sports and Play Days. But by 1960, "Sports Days" had emerged to compete with Play Days for women. Sports Days featured competition between schools, and while SMS continued to sponsor both Sports Days and Play Days, the trend was clearly in the direction of intercollegiate competition.

These early women student-ath-

letes chipped in to buy gas for drivers taking them to contests at rival schools. They paid for their own meals. Their uniforms consisted of physical education T-shirts with numbers taped or sewn on by students. Sometimes faculty sponsors volunteered their own vehicles. There was no institutional budget to support women's athletics.

In the early years, women's competition was held in swimming, tennis, basketball, volleyball, softball and some running events in track. Often a student would compete in several sports. Schools competing against SMS included the University of Missouri; Central, Northeast, Northwest and Southeast state colleges; and Drury, Central Methodist, Stephens and William Jewell colleges. The first women's team to be formally organized was in tennis in 1958.

Things took a decided turn for the better in 1964. Dr. Wayne McKinney came from California to head the Physical Education Department. He saw the need for women's competitive sports. He also believed all physical education majors should have some experience in competitive sports. McKinney started providing some funds from his departmental budget to buy gas for women's team travel. Student-athletes continued to pay for their own meals and sported T-shirts for uniforms.

National sponsorship for women's sports came from the Division of Girls' and Women's Sports, a section of the American Association for Health, Physical Education and Recreation (AAHPER). With McKinney's encouragement and support, SMS women reached out for greater opportunities competing in U.S. Volleyball

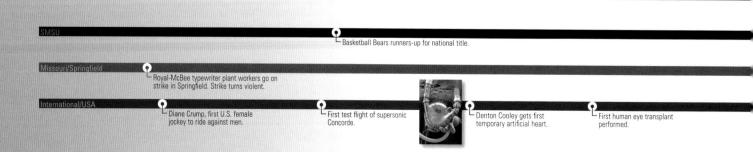

SMSU

Basketball Bears runners-up for national title.

Missouri/Springfield

Royal-McBee typewriter plant workers go on strike in Springfield. Strike turns violent.

International/USA

Diane Crump, first U.S. female jockey to ride against men.

First test flight of supersonic Concorde.

Denton Cooley gets first temporary artificial heart.

First human eye transplant performed.

Association tournaments, U.S. Tennis Association contests, and Amateur Athletic Union (AAU) basketball. By the end of the 1960s, SMS women's teams were competing in basketball, cross country, field hockey, softball, tennis, track and field, volleyball and gymnastics. The 1970 *Ozarko* was the first yearbook to carry accounts of women's basketball, coached by Reba Sims, and volleyball, coached by Dr. Mary Jo Wynn. The volleyball team included Linda Dollar and Sue Schuble and went on to take top honors at the State Collegiate Volleyball tournament at Bolivar.

During the 1969-70 school year, a group of college women, including Dr. Mary Jo Wynn from SMS, approached the NCAA asking it to include women's sports in the organization. The NCAA was uninterested. On four separate occasions the NCAA voted against the inclusion of women's sports. Spurned by the NCAA, the women formed the Association for Intercollegiate Athletics for Women (AIAW) in 1971. It became the official national organization for all collegiate sports for women. SMS was a charter member of the AIAW and began state competition as part of the Missouri Association of Intercollegiate Athletics for Women. The AIAW organized women's competition on a state, regional and national basis enabling teams to qualify for national tournaments and win national championships. Competition was divided between small colleges (less than 3,000 students) and large colleges. SMS competed in the large college section of Region VI, which included Missouri, Nebraska, Kansas, Minnesota, Iowa, North Dakota and South Dakota. The first national competition for SMS was in volleyball

where they surprised many larger schools by placing ninth in the nation.

By 1971-72, SMS women's athletics were beginning to be recognized. The sports section of the *Ozarko* carried pictures of Kay Hunter's softball team, Dr. Rhonda Ridinger's field hockey team, Dr. Mary Jo Wynn's volleyball team, and Reba Sims' basketball team, as well as the tennis and gymnastic teams.

So by the end of the state college era, women's athletics competition was established at SMS and was beginning to be acknowledged as a viable presence in the larger athletics program. But the big changes pushing SMS women's athletics into national prominence was to come after 1972 when Title IX of the Education Act became law and required gender equality in college athletics. That revolutionary force and its consequences for athletics at SMS will be explored later in the State University section.

Theatre and Music and National Attention

While forensics, basketball and football were gathering national headlines for SMS, the performing arts were climbing into national view as well.

When Leslie Irene Coger came to State Teachers College in Springfield in the fall of 1943, the campus was struggling with declining enrollments and a badly skewed male/female student ratio. The campus was under virtual siege by World War II. But that did not deter the ambitious, young dramatics coach from announcing try-outs for her first STC production, *Letters to Lucerne*. The play had just completed a successful Broadway run and provided parts for 11 women and four men — about the right ratio for the existing campus population.

Dr. Elton Burgstahler came to the SMS Music Department in 1956 serving as music theory coordinator. Burgstahler taught composition, bassoon, instrument repair, as well as conducting the band and orchestra on occasion. He was described by his colleagues as "a man who can do anything." Many of his compositions are still performed by high school ensembles and solos. Burgstahler retired in 1986.

The SMS drama program did not begin with Coger, but it certainly thrived under her leadership. The first course in play production was offered in 1915, but it was not the first instance of theater on the campus. From 1911 to 1914, the Coburn Players made regular stops during the summer to put on a series of Shakespearean plays. The senior class traditionally put on a play in the spring. The *Ozarko* also sponsored an annual play to help raise money for the yearbook. Miss Christiana Hyatt taught the coursework and directed the plays in those early years.

Drama on campus took a leap ahead in 1940 with the organization of College

Baseball Bears runners-up for national title.

Concert Chorale tours Europe for 10 weeks.

Noble and Associates advertising agency established in Springfield.

Hee Haw premieres on TV.

First color images of Earth from space — transmitted from Apollo 10.

Neil A. Armstrong becomes first man to walk on the moon.

1946-72 Southwest Missouri State College   225

On June 1, 1963, a tent appeared west of the Administration building between the field house and the football field. It was an experiment by the theater folk to escape the sweltering heat of the indoor auditorium for summer theater productions. The Coglizer Tent and Awning Company of Joplin produced a 55 foot circular green and tangerine tent to house the experiment. Forty years later Tent Theatre remains a thriving tradition on campus.

Theater under the leadership of Miss Dorothy Richey. In addition to "Folio Follies," a stunt night entirely written, produced and directed by College Theater members, the group also put on a major production each term.

So by the beginning of the SMS era, theater had established itself as a major player in campus life — so much so in fact that *The Standard* commenced a long investigation into the inadequacies of the auditorium stage for theater productions. In its July 9, 1948, issue it reported "SMS ranks at the bottom of a list of three state colleges in stage space that can actually be

used for producing a play. Maryville College reports they have 400 square feet; Kirksville, 864 square feet; while SMS has 252 square feet."

The auditorium stage actually measured slightly more than 500 square feet, but over half of it was occupied by the pipe organ. The rumor had floated about for some time that some very conservative influences in the early years had argued for the installation of a pipe organ on the stage in hopes of discouraging the production of plays, which were seen as morally degrading. Whatever the original circumstances, by 1948 *The Standard* declared that

"throughout the history of the present stage, selection of plays and settings have been hampered by the space-consuming organ."

But space limitations, outmoded curtains weighted down with brick bats, an excess wattage load on the dimmer switch, and hazardous stage conditions did not deter Miss Coger. In the spring of 1948, with all those limitations, she presented Moliere's famous comedy, *Tartuffe,* a satirical attack on religious hypocrisy. Maybe it was just this that the organ advocates feared. First played in France in 1664, *Tartuffe* was promptly banned after the first

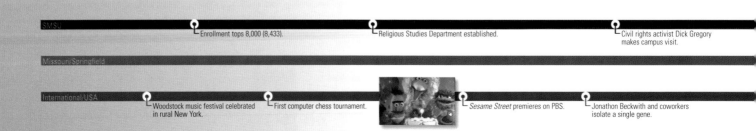

performance following an outcry from the priestly class. The ban was lifted in 1668 and the play has been staged continuously for more than 300 years.

Coger was courageous to present such a play in the Bible Belt, but she was also serious about exposing her students to the best in theater. "There is no more brilliant comedy than Moliere's *Tartuffe*," she declared. "It is the only play ever written in which the appearance of the chief character is delayed until the third act. If the hypocrite, Tartuffe, appeared too early, the audience, like the characters in the play, might be deceived by his pretended saintliness." Coger added, "To know this great play is an important part of a liberal education."

It would not be the last time such an argument would be invoked to defend a controversial theater production at the college.

The Coger legend began building quickly. In the spring of 1953 she directed *Romeo and Juliet,* a production she called "one of the most ambitious projects ever undertaken by College Theater because of its numerous difficulties both in dramatic interpretation and technical arrangement." The difficulties notwithstanding, Bill Kelsay as Romeo and Bettilou Goza as Juliet, under the guiding hand of Irene Coger, turned in stellar performances. That fall she turned to comedy, producing *See How They Run,* noting that the show "will not solve any earthshaking problems, but should provide two hours of riotous entertainment."

In 1954, Coger's production of *Brigadoon* received plaudits from a theater alumnus, Kenneth Cantril, who attended SMS from 1938 to 1940 and went on to a professional acting career

including performing in *Brigadoon* in Australia for 14 months in 1951-52.

Demanding productions became the norm for the young director. In 1955 Dr. Coger tackled *Death of a Salesman,* coaching Bill Price as Willy Loman and Sue Graves as Linda into brilliant performances. "Dr. Coger has caught the significance of the playwrights meaning," observed a critic.

Irene Coger had an insatiable appetite for theater productions. During Christmas break in 1953, she and Mary Adams Woods went to New York where they saw 18 plays in 12 days. "We were only run out of four theaters," she said. "That's a pretty good average considering the fact that we went backstage after every play to observe the settings and how they were equipped for quick scene changes." During the 1956 Christmas break, Dr. Coger and Elizabeth Mills of the English Department did another marathon of play watching including in their itinerary *Inherit the Wind, Red Roses for Me,* and *Damn Yankees.* "Many new trends were noticeable," reported Coger. "Symbolic and suggestive sets were used extensively and several of the theaters had the new curved stage projection idea."

The annual Christmas-break trips to New York became standard fare for the ambitious drama coach. In 1958, she went on stage herself in New York and walked off with $800 in prizes and merchandise as a winner on the daytime TV quiz show, *The Price is Right.*

In the spring of 1956, Dr. Coger collaborated with the Music Department, the Physical Education Department, and the Art Department to produce five sell-out performances of the musical extravaganza *Oklahoma!*

Looking Back

Sportsmanship at a Cost

It was 1941. Coach Howard "Red" Blair's football team had set a national record with 18 consecutive wins. Playing Northeastern Oklahoma, the Bears had fought back from a two-touchdown deficit to tie the Indians 14-all with only three minutes remaining. Coach Blair told the team to attempt an onside kick and try to recover the ball and score again to claim the game and extend the winning streak.

The play was executed and Bear end Russ Kaminsky recovered the ball on the Indian 49 yard line. Following a mild protest from the Indian bench, Coach Blair walked out onto the field and told the officials that Kaminsky had in fact touched the ball before it had traveled the mandatory 10 yards. The officials reversed their decision and required the Bears to kick again. This time the energized Indians fought their way to a touchdown with 45 seconds left, ending the Bears 18 game winning streak but elevating their coach to celebrity status for his sportsmanship. The event was featured in *Esquire* magazine under the headline, "A Coach and His Code."

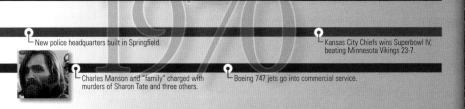

New police headquarters built in Springfield.

Kansas City Chiefs wins Superbowl IV, beating Minnesota Vikings 23-7.

Charles Manson and "family" charged with murders of Sharon Tate and three others.

Boeing 747 jets go into commercial service.

Graduating from SMS in 1949, Dr. Robert Gilmore returned to teach speech in 1959. He took a leading role in developing Tent Theatre in 1963. In 1968, he became dean of the Division of Arts and Humanities and later served as dean of faculty and provost under President Duane Meyer. He retired in 1993 and died in 1997.

One hundred-thirty students were involved in the production. Dr. Kenneth Dustman conducted the 30-piece orchestra and Florence Bugg did the choreography. *The Standard* reported, "Student interest and enthusiasm reached a new high in entertainment circles," with the production of *Oklahoma!*

In her first 13 years on campus, Dr. Coger directed 36 plays, including a hilarious 1956 summer production of *The Four Poster* in which faculty picked up the leading roles. Dr. Coger herself played the part of Agnes and Thomas Hicks of the English Department played Michael. The comedy was staged "under the stars" on the third-floor terrace of the Student Center.

By 1959 the theater program at SMS had attracted national attention and was among 25 schools invited to submit samples of their work from which eight schools would be chosen by the Defense Department to entertain troops overseas. "I am extremely pleased that our dramatics program has been rated among the top 25 among many leading colleges and universities in the nation," Dr. Coger said when notified that SMS was chosen as an alternate for the 1960 tour.

Invited again in 1960 to compete, Coger's group was chosen to present the wacky musical *Finian's Rainbow* to armed forces throughout Europe in the spring of 1961. *Finian* received an enthusiastic welcome on campus. Dr. Coger predicted that "the wacky, delightful, charming and vitally alive musical will draw people back to see a second and third performance." It did, and before going on the USO tour, the cast of 40 and a full orchestra traveled to Jefferson City on March 8, 1961, to perform in the Capitol Rotunda where Governor Dalton welcomed them saying, "This represents the first time that a Missouri College or University has been asked to present a play overseas for our armed forces."

Before leaving for Europe, the cast also staged *Finian* for USO officials and American Educational Theater Association personnel. Last-minute preparations for the trip abroad were hectic. Dr. Coger was asked to reduce the cast of 40 to 15, which she did by eliminating the orchestra and bringing a portable celesta and tape recorder for the music. Scenery had to be broken down into 30 segments to fit into footlockers. The 2-hour and 30-minute

original version had to be compacted into 1-hour and 45-minutes. With all that completed, the excited troupe departed on March 20 from McGuire Air Force Base aboard a Military Air Transport plane and headed for France, Germany and Italy where they would stage the production 35 times. Coger's productions were chosen again in 1964 and 1968 to go on the USO tours signalling an established reputation for excellence.

Tent Theatre

A new wrinkle in the theater program appeared in 1963. Summer productions in the Auditorium were becoming difficult. "The Auditorium was just unbearable in the summer," Dr. Robert Gilmore recalled. "It was bad enough to rehearse in, but it was too much for an audience. They were simply not coming." Gilmore and Coger considered several alternatives for the summer including moving into the air-conditioned Student Union Building where productions would be done in the round, or air-conditioning the Auditorium, or moving into a tent outdoors. After conversations with Dr. Richard Haswell, head of the English and Speech Department, a fourth possibility emerged — going to Branson to produce in a theater used earlier by the Southern Illinois University summer program.

While tent theaters were used extensively in the summer in the East, not many were found in the Midwest. But after weighing all the alternatives, the tent idea prevailed with Gilmore and Coger. The Coglizer Tent and Awning Company in Joplin was consulted about the project. They created a 55-foot, circular, green and tangerine,

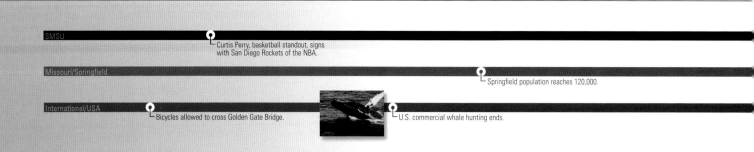

circus type tent for the summer productions at a cost of $2,100. By June 1, 1963, the colorful tent made its appearance west of the Administration Building and between the stadium and the Field House. With the tent up, Ishmael Gardner designed a stage to fit into it. Built in the college carpenter shop, the stage was assembled and erected in the tent just before the first production scheduled for June 26.

Twenty-six theater company members and 10 associates met with Managing Director Robert Gilmore who told them, "This time it was more than just another opening of another show." Rather, "It was the opening of a new season in a new theater, the feeling and spirit of which is unlikely to be recaptured."

On the evening of June 26, Irene Coger directed the young company in *Come Blow Your Horn* to a capacity crowd. Unsuspected at the time, a

tradition was born that night on the SMS campus. What was intended to be a bridge between the oppressive heat of the Administration Building auditorium and the emergence of a new Communication Arts Building with an air-conditioned theater, Tent Theatre established itself as a continuing tradition. For the ensuing 40 years, Tent Theatre has encouraged and celebrated young talent, challenged the best in directors, and entertained thousands of patrons from near and far.

By the end of the first season, 7,494 patrons had seen four shows. Coger called the experience, "Thrilling." Gilmore felt that the initial season had gone amazingly well but guessed that luck had played a big part in the initial success. "Had it not been for Mel Gardner, we wouldn't have had Tent at all," recalled Gilmore. "None of us knew anything about tents, except Mel. A physical giant 55 feet in diameter is a

huge piece of canvas and rope, and the know-how and where-with-all to keep the thing up itself is something of a fantastic achievement."

With no formal budget allotment, Tent Theatre in its opening season was clearly a financial experiment. Its expenses that year totaled $6,446.97. Income was $6,985.95. So it remained in the black.

During the summer of 1963, Tent Theatre was the talk of the town at dinner parties. The *News and Leader* and *The Standard* gave glowing reviews of the tent innovation. The novelty of setting was matched by the excellence of performance. Tent Theatre directors over the years constitute a virtual Who's Who of drama at SMS — names that have also become recognized nationally.

The genius of Tent over the years has been the excellence of its learning experience for young actors. Bob Gilmore and Irene Coger understood from the beginning that undergraduate students needed the opportunity to work with graduate students in summer productions. Working against all odds in 1963, Gilmore and Coger succeeded in getting a graduate course approved by the University of Missouri to be offered during the summer. It was a six credit hour Theater Practicum. Coger, Gilmore and Gardner would teach it. This allowed more seasoned actors to participate in Tent productions providing role models for younger undergraduate actors. The work was relentless. Sixteen hour days were common. But Gilmore lauded the company saying "They were people who can learn without being taught."

At the end of the opening season, the experiment was clearly a success. So a 32-foot section was added to the

The first building added to the campus at the end of World War II was initially an ordnance repair depot at Camp Crowder near Neosho, Missouri. It was disassembled and moved to campus in 1948 by the Federal government at a cost of $61,966 as part of a plan to provide educational facilities for veterans enrolling in the nation's colleges. It was reassembled on the SMS campus and a second floor was added. Originally named the vocational building, the structure housed both the Industrial Education and Agriculture Departments and was renamed the Industrial Education Building.

Judge Don Burrell named Alumni Association President.

General Electric takes over Royal-McBee plant.

Little Theatre acquires Landers Theatre.

The Beatles break up.

Four students killed at Kent State University when National Guard troops open fire on demonstrators.

Catch 22 opens in movie theaters.

An Added Trauma in the 1960s

In December 1966, Dr. Richard Wilkinson's Psychology 121 class was studying the effects of fear, conflict and emotion on individual behavior. During one class period a man burst loudly into the classroom interrupting the lecture and demanded that Dr. Wilkinson talk to him about his grades. With lips quivering with anger, the student struggled with Dr. Wilkinson, drew a gun, fired and fled.

Three students responded. One came to the aid of Professor Wilkinson. Two others chased down the assailant who turned out to be Bob Zay, a drama student. Wilkinson and Zay had planned the event as an experiment to test the class's response to emotional stress.

Some were immediately reminded of the Kennedy assassination. One girl fled the room fearing a mass murder. The majority reported clammy hands, heart palpitations and shaking of the body.

center of the Coglizer tent to expand seating for the 1964 season. Chairs were put on risers for better viewing. Dr. Robert Bradley joined the directing staff. But the second season brought new challenges. Construction elsewhere at the college cut off power several nights and a military generator was pressed into service to allow productions to go on. Then vandals cut 13 of the ropes nearly collapsing the entire tent. Nonetheless, the second season exceeded the first in tickets sold and patrons' praise.

In 1966, the Missouri Council on the Arts took note of Tent Theatre and provided a $3,000 grant to hire three professional actors to augment the staff and enhance the learning experience of students. More than 8,000 patrons attended the four productions.

During the 1963-64 year when the coffee-house craze was sweeping the country, students at SMS initiated their own night club with checkered tablecloths and candles. The Purple Onion became a showcase for campus talent including folk musicians, satirists, vocalists and poets. Jane Murdock is remembered for her folk music performances in the 1960s.

The plan for the summer of 1967 was to move the tent to the patio area just north of the new Communication Arts Building, but construction delays forbade that, so Tent went into its fifth season on the familiar site west of the Administration Building. By the end of the season Gilmore reported to the Board of Regents that the green and tangerine tent "had more patches than original material." He intimated that the department would not ask for a new tent but would open the 1968 season in the air-conditioned comfort of the theater in the new Communication Arts Building. After all, that was the original plan. The Tent was simply a bridge between the insufferable auditorium and the promise of air-conditioned comfort in the new building. But *The Standard* absolutely erupted at the news declaring in an editorial, "OK — So Scrap the Tent, But Not the Idea!"

The summer of 1968 saw the old patched tent erected for the last time, but in the new patio outside the Communication Arts Building. The charm and intimacy of the Tent prevailed over the upholstered seats and the air-conditioned comfort of the new theater inside the building. In 1969, a new tent was ordered from Coglizer, and the Tent Theatre tradition has continued to delight audiences and challenge actors into the 21st century.

Proud and Sassy Bands

Adding to the excitement of the performing arts on campus was the growth of bands — a concert band, a marching band, and an ROTC band. The band tradition was nearly as old as the school going back at least to 1908 when a 16-member all-male band was pictured in the *Normal School Bulletin.* By the State

SMSU
President Arthur Mallory appointed Commissioner of Education for the State of Missouri.

Missouri/Springfield
Battlefield Mall opens.

International/USA
Building begins of Amsterdam metro.

The Mary Tyler Moore Show premieres.

College period the band had grown to more than 75 members under the leadership of Winston Lynes.

By 1964, Elton Burgstahler was declaring "A band should be proud and sassy." His vision was that "the band is not just a musical but also a show organization." So on October 16 that year, Burgstahler led his band onto the field "with a panoramic view of American sports including stock car racing, fishing, archery, horse racing, hunting, football, baseball and basketball." Ninety high stepping marchers produced a sassy review to the delight of the crowd, and Burgstahler promised that the band's numbers would soon swell to 140 or 150. In 1966 scholarship assistance was available for the first time for band members. Fifty-four new freshmen swelled the ranks to 120, delighting Howard Liva, director.

The big break came in 1967 when the marching band was invited to represent Missouri in the Mardi Gras parade in New Orleans. NBC-TV gave coast-to-coast exposure to the Bruin Band as it marched through the French Quarter.

A decade earlier, the concert band went on a trip to three area high schools for concert performances. While enroute to Lockwood, the two chartered busses were stopped by the Highway Patrol for speeding and $25 fines were imposed on both drivers. To the surprise and delight of the drivers, band members came to the rescue ponying up $15 to assist in paying their fines. Generosity was added to their proud and sassy tradition.

Campus Unrest in the 1960s

Marian Goodman, *Standard* editor in 1966-67, summarized her experience on the SMS campus during the middle 1960s as she prepared to graduate in May of 1967. "If these past four years

have done anything for us, it is that the gloss has been removed from our youthful idealism and taught us that rose-colored glasses are not a good thing to see the world through. College has taught us that the world is often nasty, sometimes tasteless. Idealism dies a little when friends are reviled, when bastards win, when liars get by, when shallow people are listened to, when stupid people graduate. And it happens here."

Her assessment of her college experience mirrors some of the turmoil of the 1960s when some college campuses and the nation as a whole were convulsed by political assassinations, peace demonstrations, draft card burning, race-riots, police violence and general social unrest. A cultural revolution was under way that would leave the United States forever changed.

From 1954 through the middle 1960s, the civil rights revolution swept the nation. Starting in the South with protest movements against long-standing policies of discrimination, a new generation of heroes emerged including Rosa Parks, Medgar Evers, and Dr. Martin Luther King, who in August 1963 delivered an impassioned

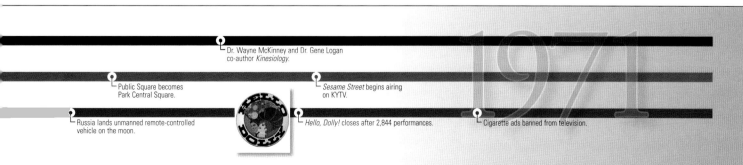

Dr. Wayne McKinney and Dr. Gene Logan co-author *Kinesiology*.

Public Square becomes Park Central Square.

Sesame Street begins airing on KYTV.

Russia lands unmanned remote-controlled vehicle on the moon.

Hello, Dolly! closes after 2,844 performances.

Cigarette ads banned from television.

Students in the 1960s were anything but passive. Civil rights, free speech, feminism, the war in Vietnam all created occasions for celebrating the First Amendment. The Student Union facilitated the debate with a "soap box" in 1965.

speech in Washington, D.C., that is still considered as one of the high points of American political oratory. Three months later, President John F.

Kennedy was assassinated in Dallas, Texas, adding to the trauma of the times.

By 1964, the civil rights issue had moved from the South to northern cities where urban riots contributed to the summer heat. Watts, Newark and Detroit became the new loci of upheaval joining Montgomery, Birmingham and Selma in creating a geography of racial dissent. In 1968, an assassin's bullet claimed the life of Dr. Martin Luther King.

Then it was Black Power, the Black Panthers, and prison riots, still in search of racial justice. Add to the mix an undeclared war that had placed a half-million American troops in Vietnam suffering 58,000 casualties. Domestic opposition to the war was reaching a fevered pitch as the draft reached increasingly into middle-class families as well as the homes of the poor and minorities. Baby boomers were coming of age with no interest in going to Vietnam. An explosive youth culture was emerging that would remove many of them from the social mainstream into alternative and dissenting lifestyles. New forms of political and religious thought were emerging as well as radical experimentation in music, dress, and personal appearance abetted by an extensive use of illegal drugs.

The mix of events and trends was lethal. By 1967 when Marian Goodman wrote of her new perspective on the world, hippie culture had become a mass movement. As the drug culture grew, vast numbers of youth were brought into conflict with the law and established institutions. Political tensions reached a climax in the 1968 Democratic Convention in Chicago where anti-war protesters demonstrat-

ing outside the convention were broken up by a "police riot." The rhetoric of dissent escalated. Police and government officials were called "pigs." It came to a climax on a college campus in April 1970 when Ohio National Guardsmen fired on demonstrating Kent State students, killing four. One historian concludes that "the convergence of political and racial violence between 1967 and 1971 resembled some of the bloodiest years of American history including the mid-1870s and 1919-20."

This was the context for campus life at SMS in the 1960s. Our concern here is to discover how deeply involved the campus was in the churning events of the decade. Was isolation in the Ozarks tantamount to insulation from the events of the time? Not entirely.

In the early 1950s when the McCarthy hearings were under way ferreting out communists in government, education, the arts and nearly every other sector of American life, *The Standard* editor said, "It's surprising to find out how little some college students know or care about the important events taking place in the world around them." That complaint had surfaced repeatedly since the founding of Normal School #4.

Again in 1964 *The Standard* editor poked fun at SMS students by observing that "around the world college and university campuses are in turmoil — students are constantly on the alert for opportunities to establish a precedent…. They realize they must do something to acquire or preserve their freedoms. But closer to home, what do SMS students consider worthy of protest? Three hour finals? No place to play cards? Only a week between semesters? What will be the next real

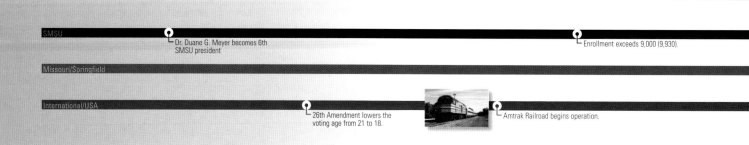

crisis SMS students will have to face?"

A year later a new *Standard* editor observed that "on campuses across the nation these days, there's a lot of hell-raising going on under the banner of 'a struggle for academic freedom.'" The editor goes on to point out that the "protesting" minority on the SMS campus have many detractors in the local community "who mistakenly interpret the 'struggle' on this campus as one of academic freedom because they are unaware of the points at stake." The struggle here, the editor observes, is not for academic freedom. "We are struggling for survival." Whereas students at Berkeley and elsewhere were demonstrating for "free speech," the right to smoke marijuana, or the right to buy contraceptives in the university bookstore, the editor asks, "Can you imagine SMS students asking for such as these? No. SMS students merely ask the right to know, to learn, to think, and to be able to consider such things as what the college governors envision for the college for the future. To consider why these things are envisioned. To know why student opinions are invalid. To know why they have no right to say what they think."

So at SMS, campus activism, in large part, was addressed to local issues — issues still lingering after the Leland Traywick debacle, not free speech, drug use or the Vietnam War.

The comparisons continued into 1966 when a new editor cited Berkeley's Free Speech movement and then asked, "Is academic freedom dead on the SMS campus, or has it ever been born? One way to measure is to view its convocation speakers. How controversial can a speaker be and still be permitted to speak? State colleges nationwide

Parents' Day remained a popular event throughout the 1960s and 1970s. Here, Mr. and Mrs. Will J. Hill share the spotlight as Parents of the Day with their daughter, Susan Drake.

ranked 3.5 on a 5-point scale of permissability of controversial speakers. The survey showed 80 percent would welcome Earl Warren, Barry Goldwater and Martin Luther King. Sixty percent would welcome James Hoffa, Robert Welch, George C. Wallace, Barry Sheppard and Robert Moses. How many controversial speakers have we had? John Howard Griffin, O.K. Armstrong, and a Vietnam speaker."

The editor ends with a telling observation. "It's not that there has been no controversy. Rather it is that, to some extent, there can be no controversy here.... We're not asking for a Berkeley type campus, but we are asking the opportunity to hear both sides

in order to make a mature decision."

To be sure, there were issues beyond the arbitrariness of the Board and the seeming indifference of the administration to student perspectives. Early in November 1965, Len Grannemann announced, "It's time SMS students stand up for their convictions!" A march was planned in support of the Vietnam War. Several fraternities and sororities joined in planning the event. However, *The Standard* reported "the student rally and march in support of the U.S. Vietnam policy was canceled. Student apathy was cited as the reason."

However, as the Vietnam War dragged on and more students became

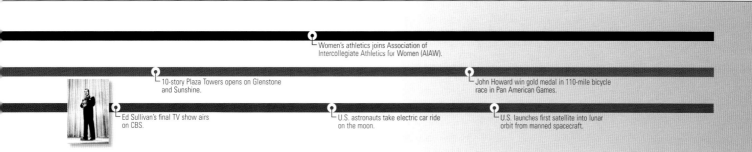

Women's athletics joins Association of Intercollegiate Athletics for Women (AIAW).

10-story Plaza Towers opens on Glenstone and Sunshine.

John Howard win gold medal in 110-mile bicycle race in Pan American Games.

Ed Sullivan's final TV show airs on CBS.

U.S. astronauts take electric car ride on the moon.

U.S. launches first satellite into lunar orbit from manned spacecraft.

"Powder Puff Football" was a hit with intramural set in the late 1960s. Here, Jane Agers of the Bonebreaks streaks for a "first and 10" as Bearcat defenders Alice Wilhoit and Kathi Goff close in.

eligible for the draft, campus interest increased. In February 1967, a "how to" article on draft-dodging to Canada by Rick Robertson appeared in *The Standard.* An editorial three weeks later declared, "You. The peaceniks, the socialist, the intellectual, the idealist. Whatever name you go by. You're the guy who says the Vietnam War is 'immoral.' You're the one who becomes angry when a few Vietnamese citizens are bombed…. You're the one who knocks our President and our country. Buddy, you are out of it. You have sat back in the safety of your college campus and read a lot of inane, naïve trash. Written by people like you — people who wouldn't know how to make a living if they didn't have some campus to set [sic] around and 'philosophize' on. Reading their asinine junk has made an authority on the world out of you.

Here's hoping that you have a spark of patriotism left and that you will wake up in time to see what's really happening."

Dave Dunlap, Ed Brookshire and Ted Wells responded, "It will take more than 'TW's' editorial to dissuade me from my opposition to the Vietnam War." Demonstrations against the war were spreading across the country, particularly on college and university campuses where the draft had become an important issue. National polls were reporting that a majority of Americans "disapprove of student and faculty demonstrations associated with civil rights and the Vietnam War." Such demonstrations were seen as harmful to the country.

As early as 1964, SMS had invoked a zero tolerance policy on campus disturbances. "Any student who participates in disturbances either on

or off campus, or who lingers in the immediate area of such a disturbance is subject to suspension or dismissal from college." In December 1968, the administration reported, "Last week we experienced two unauthorized demonstrations in which students congregated in front of the residence halls on campus and caused some minor damage. Fortunately, no one was hurt. We are most appreciative of the positive attitude and cooperation shown by the vast majority of students in not only refusing to participate in these demonstrations, but also in discouraging others from participation. We commend you for your maturity and responsibility."

In 1969 the State Legislature was considering a bill that would make it illegal to participate in demonstrations on state college campuses. RESIST, an SMS student group, planned a march on the Capitol to protest proposed legislation.

In May 1971, an "End the War" Symposium was held on campus drawing more than 200 students. Folk singers Tony Flacco and John Ehlers opened the symposium. Members of Vietnam Veterans Against the War showed slides of Vietnam, held an anti-war panel discussion and answered questions. Dr. Denny Pilant of the political science faculty also addressed the symposium stating, "We can only be afraid of Vietnamese Communism on the theory that it is an extension of Chinese Communism. I think that theory is a fallacy."

As public sentiment against the war mounted, another anti-war rally was held on campus on May 11, 1972. Three SMS department heads, spoke at the event. Ed Albin of the Art Department deplored "the apathy

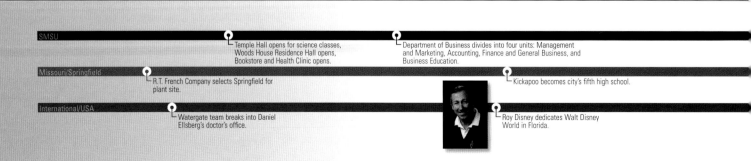

SMSU

Temple Hall opens for science classes, Woods House Residence Hall opens, Bookstore and Health Clinic opens.

Department of Business divides into four units: Management and Marketing, Accounting, Finance and General Business, and Business Education.

Missouri/Springfield

R.T. French Company selects Springfield for plant site.

Kickapoo becomes city's fifth high school.

International/USA

Watergate team breaks into Daniel Ellsberg's doctor's office.

Roy Disney dedicates Walt Disney World in Florida.

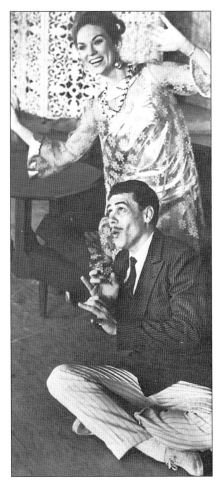

Neil Simon's *Barefoot in the Park* was a feature of the 1967 Tent Theatre series. The summer series featured 34 performances including George Bernard Shaw's classic *Misalliance*, and two musicals, *Once Upon a Mattress* and *Oh, What a Lovely War*.

indicated by the number of students here." Albin went on to say, "Unified and working together, youth can make change through elections, but you'll have to stand up and fight for your democratic rights." Dr. Max Skidmore of the Political Science Department said, "Coming to a rally and blowing off steam makes you feel good, but it doesn't accomplish anything."

Skidmore went on to suggest, "Make your feelings known. Go to the Young Democrats or Young Republicans meetings." Dr. Gerrit tenZythoff of the Religious Studies Department joined Albin and Skidmore in denouncing President Nixon's mining and blockading of North Vietnamese ports.

College officials notified local police and the Highway Patrol of the scheduled rally in 1972. But many on campus deplored the action of law enforcement officers who took many photographs of rally participants. Captain Swackhammer of the Highway Patrol defended the picture taking saying, "The photographs taken will be filed for future use. In case anyone there becomes an antagonizer or ringleader, then we can better identify him and take him out. These people will tell you themselves that if you remove their leaders…they've got a lost cause."

But Dr. Lloyd Young, head of the Sociology Department, had serious reservations. "It seems clear to me that the police or highway patrol have a legal right to observe or photograph events happening in public places. However, the function of these agencies is to deal with crime. That they should be so concerned with political activities is an ominous sign in an open society. Someone needs to re-read Jefferson's first inaugural: 'If there be any among us who wish to dissolve this Union, or to change its republican form, let them stand as undisturbed as monuments of the safety with which error of opinion may be tolerated, where reason is left free to combat it.'"

While the Vietnam War stimulated some activity on campus during the 1960s, it was mild compared to campuses elsewhere in the country. A

Town Meeting on the Air on KWTO

From the Grand Lounge of the Student Center, radio station KWTO broadcast a 12 program series in 1963 with Paul McMasters, Student Chairman of the Radio Committee, as host. The series ranged from "The People's Right to Know," a discussion of news coverage by newspapers, to "Meanings in Modern Art" featuring Max Tyndale and Ellen Curley, art majors. The Political Economy Club discussed "Labor Unions and National Defense" while sociology majors John Spurlin and Melinda Field discussed "Marriage and the College Student."

Regents approve constructing an FM radio station.

Woods House Residence Hall opens

Communist China admitted to the United Nations.

Golden Gate Bridge lights out all night due to power failure

The Homecoming parade was always a festival of fun and creativity. In 1967, the PiKAs swept up first prize with their flying machine and a friendly wave from the aviator.

more powerful issue at SMS during this period was race and civil rights. As early as 1948 discussions about civil rights were occurring in SMS classes. Helen Watson spoke to the Sociology Club in February that year calling attention to the local theater designated for colored people. "We want to be punished for our crime, but not for our skin color," she said. A year later Alvin Tidlund speaking on "Equal Rights for Negroes" won the Annual Interschool Oratorical Contest.

But in April 1950, a Negro singer was barred from appearing at a fraternity formal dance. Four years later, Etta Moten, Broadway star of *Porgy and Bess*, and a highlight feature of the 1954 Homecoming celebration, received one of the greatest ovations given in SMS Lyceum history but was denied service at a restaurant adjacent to campus because of her race. The affront outraged *The Standard* editor who

called for a boycott of the restaurant.

Negroes were admitted to campus in the fall of 1954, but little mention was made of their presence in student publications. Students continued to talk about civil rights in oratorical contests, but on-campus acceptance of black students developed slowly. As late as 1956, the Delta Sigma Epsilon sorority was still featuring its "Delta Darkey Minstrel Show…as one of the biggest events of the year."

In 1965, civil rights workers Otis Flournoy and the Reverend George McClain who helped organize the Selma, Alabama march, visited campus at the invitation of the Wesley Foundation. They characterized the SMS campus as "a large white ghetto and a small Negro ghetto with very few people forming a community in between where race is a secondary thing." They were puzzled by the fact that whereas civil rights was "the great historical movement of our

day, there was no dialogue on this campus about race issues." One student from New York commented, "The situation here is odd. If the race issue is broached, people just freeze."

When the urban riots started, letters to the editor in *The Standard* portrayed polarized views. Some saw the riots as the only way Blacks had for gaining access to the benefits of American society. If blame was to be placed it should be on white prejudice and discrimination, not on black rebellion. Another letter asserted, "There is a divine order in the universe…. God's marker for man to follow is color. Through color men can see the right order of the world. The white clouds are above the brown dirt. Were there blue people they would be better than the white, but the white must always be above the black…. Unless this order is maintained, our merciful God will destroy us in atomic fire."

In April 1968, a three-hour memorial service was held on campus for Dr. Martin Luther King, attended by some 1,500 students. Curtis Perry delivered the eulogy. Willie Jenkins called upon everyone to stand up for human rights

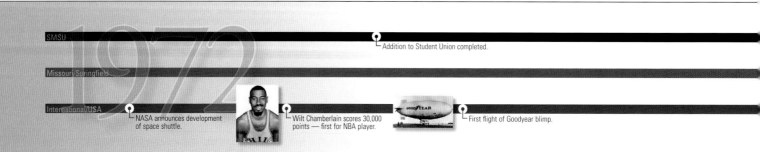

SMSU — Addition to Student Union completed.

Missouri/Springfield

International/USA — NASA announces development of space shuttle. — Wilt Chamberlain scores 30,000 points — first for NBA player. — First flight of Goodyear blimp.

and freedom. Anderson McCullough climaxed the occasion with a moving speech on the need for unity. But despite the show of solidarity at the assassination of Dr. King, the campus continued to face charges of discrimination against black students.

As early as 1967, black students were speaking out about their experiences at SMS. The Ecumenical Center hosted a discussion in April that year in which several black students gave their perspective on the "two ghetto" experience on campus. "A white student has nothing to gain by associating with us," declared Danny Bolden, "but the apathy is on both sides. It creates the segregation." Steve Barksdale, referring to recent racial incidents near the dorms, said, "Whites expect us to get excited. They're shocked when a Negro doesn't retaliate. If students were really afraid, they'd have guns in the dorms."

Gwen Taylor, a black dorm resident, was asked about prejudice in the residence halls. "It's definitely there," she said, "but people are hiding their prejudices. Tension builds up and I think it is harder on girls." Taylor went on to point out that most Negroes are judged by the standards of the poorer, underprivileged ones, and she scorned "the tendency of the white men to judge all Negroes just because of one bad one." The evening concluded with agreement that racial problems on campus would not be solved until there was more communication between Blacks and whites.

In 1968, the Black Student Union was established on campus to give black students a voice in campus policy. According to chairman Ronald Johnson from St. Louis, the BSU also would work for racial equality, help

to introduce black culture into SMS life, and assist black students scholastically and socially. Fifty students were present at the organizational meeting. Some on campus interpreted BSU as part of a Black Power initiative on campus. Tensions increased under that perception.

But efforts continued to be made to foster understanding. In October 1969, Jesse Knight and Udo Gallop of the Black Student Union met with the Sigma Phi Epsilon fraternity to try to break down communication barriers and "tell it like it is." No fraternities had admitted any black students to this point and when asked about his interest in joining a fraternity, Knight replied, "If being accepted into a fraternity meant being a mere token, not real brotherhood, then neither me nor the fraternity would receive anything from the membership." Responding to the same question, Gallop replied, "Let's face it, fellows. You have your mind made up as to who you are going to accept, and right now it just isn't a black person. If you had a sorority over for some kind of function, just what would we do? Let's work together instead of against one another."

In May 1969, Student Senate leaders tried to respond to the black feeling of exclusion by adding two black cheerleaders to the existing squad of 10 white cheerleaders. Two days later at the regular Student Senate meeting, the action was rescinded because some felt it was taken "under duress." The Senate appointed a committee to review the cheerleader selection process. In response to the Senate action, fights broke out between white and black students on campus, and a firebomb was thrown into the powerhouse.

Black student grievances escalated in the spring of 1970 including calls for the dismissal of Dean Rives. Charges of discrimination were also hurled at Dean Bowman, Dean Meyer, Coach Bill Thomas and Dean Wienzral. Cheerleader selection rules were revised, but no special spots were given to Blacks. The Board of Regents called for an end to the racial discrimination debate, to no avail. By March tensions were high. The Black Student Union called for a protest boycott of classes, declaring, "It is not a feudal question of sub-sociality that exists here, rather it is the urgent need to 'do something now' about the ethical problem confronting the SMS campus." On May 15, 500 students, primarily Greeks, gathered in front of the Union in response to a rumor that black students intended to raid Wells Dormitory. The campus was in uproar. Fights broke out. The Industrial Education Building was firebombed. Finally about 1:00 a.m. the crowd began to disperse as rain pelted the scene.

While the unrest and disturbances on the SMS campus were mild compared to other campuses elsewhere in the country, the isolation of the Ozarks did not insulate the institution from the upheavals of the era. As on most campuses, a few with militant purposes could create dramatic confrontations and historic spectacles. On the race issue at SMS, it is noteworthy that in November 1971, the campus selected a black woman, Sheila Bowie, to reign as Homecoming Queen. Robbyn Warrick, another black woman, was named captain of the varsity cheerleading squad that same year.

The 1960s were not simply about civil rights and the Vietnam War. With

West Plains Residence Center given a "recognized candidate for accreditation" status.

Administration Building renamed Carrington Hall.

Two giant pandas arrive in U.S. from China.

U.S. Supreme Court bans the death penalty.

Break-in occurs at Democratic Headquarters in Watergate Building in Washington, D.C.

First women FBI agents sworn in.

1946-72 Southwest Missouri State College 237

As enrollments grew rapidly in the late 1960s, innovative methods for teaching large numbers of students were developed. Dr. Clarence Ketch, a sociologist, experimented with teaching the introductory sociology course by television. Monitors were located in several classrooms. Here, Dr. Ketch helps a student grasp the sociological perspective.

The ecology movement also emerged in the late 1960s. With pictures taken from an Apollo spacecraft portraying the pristine beauty of the planet earth, attention was called to the rampant pollution of the atmosphere by industrial plants and auto emissions.

During those turbulent years, many latent issues became manifest, supported by the momentum of protest and change. Its cumulative character unleashed a virtual revolution in traditional values.

The counter-cultural revolution that touched on values long endorsed but often ignored, received special attention on college campuses where experimental lifestyles thrived and open discussion of sex, religion, drugs and situational ethics were commonplace. On the SMS campus, such discussions were often sponsored by campus religious organizations. O.K. Armstrong, a conservative spokesman in the Ozarks and former Congressman from the the 7th District, was a frequent visitor to campus counteracting what he considered to be the moral decline of America. In October 1966, Armstrong addressed a campus group on "The Crisis in the Spiritual Life of This Nation." Citing the screening of the movie *Who's Afraid of Virginia Wolff,* Armstrong identified "three sicknesses causing the spiritual crisis: materialism, lawlessness and immorality." Christened "decency police," conservatives such as Armstrong made regular forays onto both the Drury and SMS campuses to champion values perceived to be under attack.

Religious groups on campus were particularly active in examining the fault lines in American culture. In 1966 the Wesley Foundation invited Dr.

the publication of *The Feminine Mystique* by Betty Freidan in 1963, the feminist movement was reborn carrying the cultural revolution into family life, gender relations and language conventions. The founding of the National Organization for Women (NOW) and the publication of Kate Millett's *Sexual Politics* pushed the revolution even deeper into American life.

The emerging discontent with traditional concepts of gender and sexuality gave birth to the "gay rights" movement which asserted that homosexuality was a natural and acceptable lifestyle. The movement gained particular notoriety in 1969 when gay citizens rioted at Stonewall Bar in New York City protesting the long-standing pattern of police brutality and harassment.

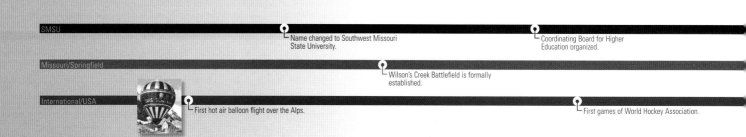

SMSU
└ Name changed to Southwest Missouri State University.

└ Coordinating Board for Higher Education organized.

Missouri/Springfield
└ Wilson's Creek Battlefield is formally established.

International/USA
└ First hot air balloon flight over the Alps.

└ First games of World Hockey Association.

By 1970, the war in Vietnam was heating up as were student opinions on the matter. Peace marches and demonstrations were part of campus life in the early 1970s.

Alan Pickering, university pastor at the University of Nebraska, to lecture on "*Playboy*: Pornography or Audio-Visual Hot Line?" He told a packed house that "*Playboy* is right. Puritan prudery has had its day, and piety based on touch-me-not sex is almost as extinct as the dodo bird." Dr. Oreen Ruedi of the sociology faculty responded to Pickering's lecture on *Playboy* saying, "…like 100 ice-cream cones, it's too much, even two copies." Ed Albin of the Art Department observed, "I see no equation between 'The Sleeping Venus' and *Playboy* foldouts." Gary Wolfe closed the commentary asking, "How do we define pornography? Where do we draw the line?"

Religious ferment was also part of the scene. In October 1966, the Ecumenical Center sponsored a discussion of Bishop John A.T. Robinson's *Honest to God*. The Center invited "anyone who, like the book's author, is

tired of religion's outmoded symbols, its traditional formulations and its irrelevance to the modern world," to participate. Bernard Cooney, Frank Jones and James Robinson led the discussion. A few weeks later the Center showed the film *The Parable* portraying Jesus as a clown traveling with a circus. The film had been shown at the World's Fair and was widely discussed for its role in provoking religious exploration. In February 1967, the Center continued its examination of controversial issues by scheduling a discussion of Joseph Fletcher's provocative best-seller, *Situational Ethics*. The discussion examined the character of the so-called "new morality" and asked if it indeed did relativize everything. In April 1967, the Center renewed its focus on countercultural themes with a discussion of LSD and drugs on campus.

While SMS was impacted by the 1960s, reflecting its themes and issues, it was hardly a center for cultural change. Midwest conservatism made Berkeley look surreal during those years. But students at SMS grasped clearly the nature of the counter culture developing around them. The crassly materialistic, secular culture that had shaped American society for years was being over-hauled. But the danger was, as Irving Kristol pointed out, that the counter-culture's attack on secular materialism could bring down or discredit "human things of permanent importance. A spiritual rebellion against the constrictions of secular humanism could end up…in a celebration of irrationalism and a derogation of reason itself."

Now, we are nearly a half-century past the 1960s and still asking what the decade means to America. Roger

Kimball suggests it means "sexual liberation, rock music, (and) chemically induced euphoria…. Some would inscribe a plus sign, others a minus sign beside that famous triumvirate." He goes on to say, "The Sixties also mean free floating protest and political activism, a 'youth culture' that never ages, a new permissiveness together with a new affluence: Dionysius with a credit card and a college education."

Evaluations of the effects of the Age of Aquarius on contemporary life are numerous and often contradictory indicating that the Age "did not end when the last electric guitar was unplugged at Woodstock." "It lives on in our habits and values, in our tastes, pleasures and aspirations," according to Kimball.

The counter-cultural movement escorted SMS into its fourth era. While the Purple Onion was still playing in the Student Center, while End-The-War rallies were still occurring under the watchful eye and clicking cameras of law enforcement, and while the black and white ghettos were still trying to figure out how to break down the walls of separation on campus, movements were also afoot to bring to fruition a dream first articulated 65 years before — becoming a state university. To that story we turn next. ■

Three commencement tradition begins with first winter graduation program.

Mary Gant becomes Missouri's first female state senator.

Richard M. Nixon re-elected President of the U.S.

LIFE The Year in PICTURES 1972

Life magazine ceases publication.

President Harry S. Truman dies.

Southwest Missouri St

upon the nomination of the facul

authority of the Board of Governors

Margeaux Elizabeth

the degree of

Bachelor of Fine A

Musical Theatre

summa cum laude

in the Honors College

Given under the Seal of the University at

State of Missouri, on the seventeenth

the year Two Thousand and

Barbara Burns

President, Board of Governors

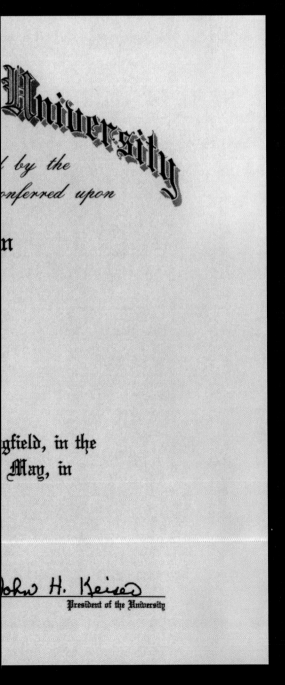

1972-2005
Southwest Missouri
State University

Contents

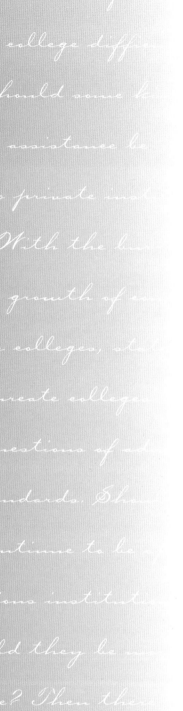

1972-2005

Southwest Missouri State University

Despite the daunting challenges of rapid growth and a tight budget in 1975, President Duane Meyer greeted his task with a buoyant smile. The *Ozarko* described him as "leading the institution from the last remnants of the Puritanism and rigidity of a teacher's college to the tolerance and flexibility demanded of a true university." Under the weight of his presidency, Meyer, according to the *Ozarko* editor, "developed a certain grace which complemented the accessibility, and above all, the humanity which he never lost in the transition from history professor to dean to university president."

Although the timing was not particularly propitious, on April 1, 1971, the Board of Regents appointed Dr. Duane G. Meyer as sixth president of Southwest Missouri State College. Some time later the *Ozarko* editor asked President Meyer, "Is there any truth to the rumor that you were appointed president of SMSU on April Fool's Day?" "Yes," replied the president, "Unfortunately, that was the case. I have attempted to get the Board of Regents to explain that date and the reason for having made the choice at that particular time. They have refused to say anything about it, indicating that only time would answer that question."

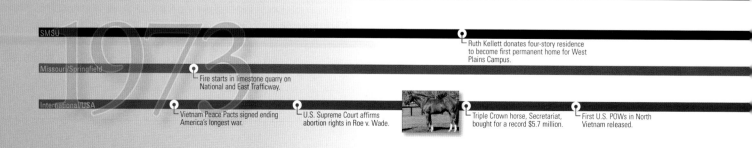

SMSU

Ruth Kellett donates four-story residence to become first permanent home for West Plains Campus.

Missouri/Springfield

Fire starts in limestone quarry on National and East Trafficway.

International/USA

Vietnam Peace Pacts signed ending America's longest war.

U.S. Supreme Court affirms abortion rights in Roe v. Wade.

Triple Crown horse, Secretariat, bought for a record $5.7 million.

First U.S. POWs in North Vietnam released.

While the timing may have not been propitious, the appointment certainly was. The history professor who had already served as acting president twice, and served as the first dean of faculty, was warmly welcomed to his new responsibilities by faculty, staff, students and the community.

Challenges of the 1970s

Not long after his appointment as president, Dr. Meyer was asked to be the keynote speaker at the first annual Higher Education Conference in Jefferson City. Looking out over a crowd of 300 college and university administrators, board members, legislators and community leaders, the president, employing his quick wit, declared that the task ahead for higher education was difficult. He reminded the listeners of the ad the Pony Express Company had placed in the St. Joseph newspaper in 1860:

Wanted: Young, skinny, wiry fellows, not over 18. Must be expert riders willing to risk death daily…. Wages: $25 per week…orphans preferred.

"Some tasks are more difficult than others," he said dryly while inviting the audience to join him in the challenging venture of guiding higher education through what appeared to be dangerous and turbulent times.

Dr. Meyer continued by reminding his listeners that Samuel Johnson wrote that he started out in life to be a philosopher, but had to give it up when cheerful thoughts kept creeping into his mind. With a smile on his face, the president declared, "In many ways, college and university administrators might seem to need a similarly pessimistic kind of training."

By this time the audience was giving rapt attention as the young president ticked off the circumstances that challenged the most optimistic and provided daily brushes with death for every administrator. "We find higher expectations among students and parents," Dr. Meyer declared. "They want us to meet the educational needs of a rapidly changing society and to do a better job of it than we did a few years ago."

Coupled with rising expectations was declining financial support. "We also find, to our chagrin, that we are no longer the favorite state agency. There may be more concern among our state legislators and citizens for drainage and disposal systems, better health care, environmental regulations or improved transportation systems," he warned.

Furthermore, "The fuse of tolerance is not as long as it once was. We're subject to more and closer scrutiny by the public, by the Legislature, the news media and by the very students who populate our classrooms," the president added. "We may not have as much public confidence as we did 10 years ago."

As he continued to sketch the environment in which colleges and universities would be working throughout the years ahead, the Samuel Johnson story took on added meaning. The president outlined a variety of issues facing public higher education in Missouri.

There was the challenge of statewide coordination of higher education. How could the new Department of Higher Education oversee the increasingly complex state system of colleges and universities? Tax-supported institutions were less costly than private colleges and universities with the result that public institutions were overcrowded while private institutions had surplus space. Should the state continue to subsidize higher education in the face of private college difficulties? Should some kind of state assistance be given to private institutions? With the burgeoning growth of community colleges, state baccalaureate colleges faced questions of admission standards. Should they continue to be open admissions institutions, or should they be more selective? Then there was collective bargaining. Faculties in many institutions across the country were voting for union representation. Should this be encouraged, or even permitted in Missouri? What about duplication of services in state colleges? When funds are limited can the state afford to support computer science programs or agriculture programs in each of its institutions, or should institutions focus on specialties? Would such specialization change their role as regional institutions?

After listing the challenges facing higher education in the 1970s, President Meyer ended his keynote reminding the audience that Thomas Hart Benton, the great Missouri Senator of the last century, "had certain rituals of life that he honored. He arose

Last U.S. combat troops leave Vietnam.

Japan allows its citizens to own gold.

Gold hits record $102.50 per ounce in London.

R.T. French plant dedicated.

NCAA makes urine testing mandatory for participants.

each morning at four, took an invigo-rating bath, and then had a servant rub his body with a horsehair brush. When asked why he went through this somewhat painful process, the Senator replied that he found it 'stimulating.'" Dr. Meyer closed his keynote saying, "I hope that these remarks regarding...the present environment in which we work, and the key issues facing us will be stimulating to you as you think about Missouri higher education."

Whether the conferees went home thinking about Pony Express riders, grim philosophers or rubdowns with a horse-hair brush, we do not know. What we do know is that President Duane Meyer aptly described the challenges he was per-sonally taking on as the sixth president of Southwest Missouri State College.

Achieving the Coveted Title of State University

President Meyer presided over Southwest Missouri State College for only 16 months. On July 28, 1972, the Board of Regents officially renamed the college Southwest Missouri State University. In a brief ceremony in front of Carrington Hall, the Board announced publicly the action they had just taken in the board room where Regent Edison Kaderly had moved approval of Resolution No. 26-72. Representatives of the administration, faculty, students and alumni gathered to hear the announcement and sign the official scroll changing the name.

Among the dignitaries was Dr. Virginia Craig, at 94, the only faculty member to witness all four eras of the institution's history.

Authorization to change the name had been given by the Missouri General Assembly, which passed Senate

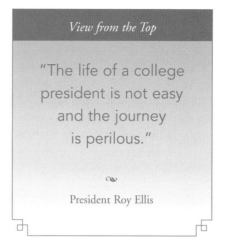

Bill 427 on April 21, 1972, and sent it to Governor Hearnes for signing. The dream of university status went back nearly 50 years. In 1924, Board President J. Glaser, enumerating the accomplishments of the college to that point, declared, "It will be but a question of a few years until 'The University of the Southwest' will be an accomplished thing." The *Ozarko* of 1924 also made its assessment of the school's progress noting that "in the past 25 years we have seen the phenom-enal growth of the future 'University of the Ozarks.'" In the early 1960s, stimulated by the aggressive agenda laid out by President Leland Traywick, a bill was introduced in the House to allow the college to be renamed university. In 1967 the *Ozarko* editor observed, "We seem to be bulging at the seams: more students, a new classroom building, a new dormitory, expanded library facili-ties. Where will all this lead us? Perhaps to new academic programs and univer-sity status."

So the dream was realized in the summer of 1972. But it would not be the last time we would hear about a name change. As early as 1985, momentum was building to rename

SMSU "Missouri State University." That story comes later.

Becoming a university in 1972 was simply an acknowledgement of what had been happening to the institution over a number of years. Its enrollment had reached nearly 10,000. Its curricu-lum had expanded to embrace a wide variety of disciplines and programs. Graduate studies were producing more than 100 master's degrees each year. Faculty had grown to more than 500, the vast majority of whom had termi-nal degrees, and many of whom were engaging in research.

The new status did nothing to ease the burdens of the president. Dr. Meyer saw that the new status required more accountability, more planning, additional program development and further accommodation of ever-growing enrollments. His sensitivity to the tasks before the university led him to forgo a formal inauguration ceremony, opt-ing instead to use the funds to provide scholarships for SMSU students. The gesture signaled his commitment to the welfare of the institution over any personal interests that may have been served by an inaugural celebration.

The Situation of the 1970s

While President Meyer had outlined many of the challenges facing him and other college presidents in his keynote address in Jefferson City, there were other perspectives on the situation as well. The *Ozarko* editor in 1973 assessed the new president's leadership by saying, "In two years, Dr. Meyer proved capable of continuing the tradi-tion of effective leadership with which SMSU has been blessed, leading the institution from the last remnants of Puritanism and the rigidity of a 'teach-

SMSU

Enrollment exceeds 10,000 (10,471).

Missouri/Springfield

International/USA

First all-U.S. Women's Wimbledon — Billie Jean King beats Chris Evert.

President Nixon refusses to release Watergate tapes of conversations.

Monster Mash and *Smoke on the Water* go gold.

How Craig Hall was numbered...

"Just draw a number and place it on the nearest door."

Not a few have wondered about the room numbering system in Craig Hall. A 1976 *Standard* cartoonist provides the answer.

ers college' to the tolerance and flexibility demanded of a true university."

Providing leadership "from the last remnants of Puritanism" was essentially a matter of steering a vehicle already in motion. The counter-cultural movement of the 1960s and early 1970s had already dispatched Puritanism and created the momentum toward a more liberated view of virtually everything. Steering the momentum of social change into constructive policies was the challenge. And apparently, the new president was managing that task well. The *Ozarko* editor continued his assessment of the new administration by saying, "In his second year especially, (President Meyer) developed a certain grace which complemented the accessibility, and above all, the humanity which he never lost in the transition from history professor to dean to university president."

But a new moral compass wasn't the only challenge at the beginning of

the university period. In a report published by the Office of Institutional Research, Larry Gates claimed that, "In no other period in the last 50 years has higher education experienced such numerous and substantive pressures from outside its ivy-covered walls." He cited 20 areas where outside influences were impacting the university, beginning with the crisis of confidence in higher education itself created by campus unrest in the late 1960s. Fluctuations in the job market left hordes of college graduates without employment. OPEC oil prices in the mid and late 1970s wreaked havoc with institutional budgets. Increased government regulations, including affirmative action, privacy rights, sex and age discrimination, and copyright regulation, absorbed administrative time and attention. Declining freshman aptitudes were impacting the curriculum, often requiring remedial instruction. Verbal scores on college entrance exams declined 11 percent during the 1970s. Quantitative scores declined 7 percent. Paradoxically, while aptitude scores were declining, college grade point averages were climbing. Grade inflation has continued unabated throughout the university period. Student interest grew

increasingly vocational in the 1970s pushing the curriculum to greater and greater specialization while focusing on job-market opportunities. These were among the challenges facing the newly-established university.

Coping with the Problems of Growth

Growth at SMSU during the 1970s contradicted patterns at many of the other state universities. The enrollment had declined at Central Missouri State during the 1970s 21.5 percent. Northeast also experienced steep declines. At SMSU, enrollments *increased* over the decade by 64 percent.

Growth had been the norm for the university for 29 consecutive years beginning in 1953. The local newspaper observed, "It took exactly 50 years for Southwest Missouri State College to reach the 2,000 figure in enrollment, but since 1955 it's much like hitching a ride on the tail of a comet." Fueling the enrollment growth was the increasing number of part-time students. In 1970, part-timers constituted only 18 percent of the student body. By 1979 they accounted for 31 percent. Students were increasingly taking advantage of evening classes, and a growing number of non-traditional students were beginning college studies.

Growth slowed during the 1980s to a 22 percent rate for the decade. But over the two decades the university more than doubled in size from 8,964 students in 1970 to 19,377 in 1989. Crowding became a serious problem with some business school classes enrolling more than 230 students. For much of that period, the university operated under an open enrollment system, requiring only a high school

62 foreign students enrolled from 23 countries.

Vice President Spiro Agnew resigns under tax evasion scandal.

Pirates of the Caribbean ride opens at Disneyland.

What It Meant to Work
on *The Standard*

"At the practical level, toiling for the paper meant struggling to arrange interviews between classes and long nights. We were a fairly stereotypical representation of the Gen X demographic — we weren't looking to start revolutions or striving to flaunt high ideals. Not many of us came to SMSU as aspiring journalists. (If that had been our goal, we probably would have attended the J-School up near the state capitol.) A fair number of us, however, did discover journalism in Springfield.

There were those who maintained that it was just a job: i.e. a paycheck every two weeks, and a blurb on the resume at the end of it all. In reality, though, no sane person would do the work just for the paycheck and the few perks we enjoyed. In Greek mythology, Sisyphus was doomed in the afterworld to continuously roll a boulder up a hill. We actually had to sculpt the boulder we were rolling up that hill. Unlike Sisyphus' rock, ours came to rest on the crest of the hill where we could catch our breath for a bit and examine it for rough patches and fissures. Then, however, it was time to begin the sculpting anew and the ascent up the next incline, and then the next, and the next until the semester came mercifully to an end. There were easier ways to put beer in the fridge and stockpile caseloads of ramen noodles.

(continued on next page)

diploma for admission. The need for a more selective admissions policy was apparent, but without a community college present in Springfield, the university was the only option open for students who wanted the benefit of a state supported education.

The open admissions policy, however, was not a particularly good investment for state tax dollars. While it accommodated all students who wanted a college education, it resulted in relatively low retention rates and lower than expected graduation rates. In response, the state Coordinating Board for Higher Education mandated that students admitted in the fall of 1989 must have ACT scores of at least 17. This was intended to improve retention rates and graduation rates.

In 1990, Ozarks Technical Community College was established in Springfield, providing a second post-secondary education option for area students. About the same time, the Coordinating Board for Higher Education was encouraging state universities to select from an array of admission characteristics that suited their regions and resources. Northeast Missouri State University opted for the most restrictive policy and became a "Highly Selective" institution. The University of Missouri chose the second category and became a "Selective" institution.

In 1992, the University Planning Advisory Council, under the Chairmanship of Dr. Denny Pilant, recommended that SMSU join MU as a "Selective" admissions campus. Acting President Russell Keeling passed the recommendation on to the Board of Regents which approved it. Other state institutions selected more liberal admission policies — "Moderately Selective" or "Open."

Because the "Selective" admissions standard raised the bar to an ACT score of 24 or equivalent points based on class rank and other factors, called the "Selection Index," the consequence of implementing the standard immediately could have been catastrophic. It had to be phased in.

The whole idea of setting restrictions on enrollment created tension among patrons of the university. Many understood the university as the point of access to a better life through education, and to be denied admission because of low aptitude scores seemed undemocratic to many. In 1995,

Jean Maneke, news editor for the 1972-73 *Standard* checks out story details with a news source in *The Standard* office.

SMSU

State Fruit Experiment Station in Mountain Grove becomes part of SMSU.

Missouri/Springfield

International/USA

President Nixon imposes 55-mph speed limit.

Barbara Streisand's first No. 1 hit — *The Way We Were.*

President Keiser negotiated with the Coordinating Board a phasing-in of the "Selective" admissions standard with its full implementation to occur in the fall of 2005. While the "Selective" admissions message was being publicized and discussed in the early 1990s, enrollment declined at the university from 1992 through 1995. Thereafter it regained its historic pattern of growth carrying it into the 21st century. In terms of ACT scores, there has been a steady improvement from the minimum of 17 imposed in 1989. By 1994 the average freshman ACT score was 21.7. By 2003 it had risen to above 23.6.

Attracting the Best

For decades, encouragement to enroll at the university had been given to academically promising students by granting them Regents Scholarships. In 1983-84, under the leadership of President Marshall Gordon, the effort to attract academically superior students was accelerated through the Presidential and University Scholarship programs. The Presidential Scholarship granted the student a "full ride" — fees, room and board, and books. To be eligible for the award, students had to be in the top 3 percent of their class, score 28 or above on the ACT test, or be in the top 10 percent of their class and score 30 or better on the ACT. All eligible candidates are interviewed and their leadership skills assessed by a campus committee. In 1983-84, 15 Presidential Scholarships were awarded. The following year, 25 awards were made. By 1987, 65 Presidential Scholarships had been awarded.

About the same time, President Gordon initiated a program to recruit National Merit Finalists to the university. They represented the cream of the crop of high school graduates across the nation. In 1986, more than one million high school juniors took the Preliminary Scholastic Aptitude Test/ National Merit Scholarship Qualifying Test to enter the competition. About 5,500 were selected as National Merit Finalists representing the upper one-half of 1 percent of high school students taking the test. In 1986, 19 National Merit Finalists enrolled at SMSU. Twenty-three more enrolled the following year, and 30 additional Merit Finalists enrolled in 1988. By 1987, SMSU had more National Merit Finalists enrolled than any of the 372 institutions in the American Association of State Colleges and Universities.

The effort to create a critical mass of academically gifted students at the university enabled the re-establishment of the honors program (first opened in 1963 but soon after disbanded) demonstrated that the institution could attract and hold highly qualified students, and it provided support to the policy decision to become a "Selective" admissions institution.

With the steady growth in enrollment came problems of accommodating students. Enrollment peaked in 1991 with 20,419 students on campus, at a time when facilities and faculty were prepared for 17,000. Student reaction to "bigness" was not always positive. Student Bob Miller suggested that the university "should set a limit on the number of students until they can provide parking, housing and classroom space." Linda Bogad took a more cynical view. "They're only worried about how many ways to accumulate money to keep the university going and not

(continued from previous page)

Why did we do it then? As I said, The *Standard* was a microcosm of professional journalism. How many college students get paid to put something into print? Even fewer are blessed with the chance to decide what goes to print. The story you wrote or layout you designed wasn't handed in to a professor but it appeared in black and white before the whole campus. We were a student-run paper. Every ad sold, piece of copy written and edited, photo cropped, and layout designed was done by students. We have to report finances to a Publication Board and had a faculty advisor, but every week the resulting blame or praise belonged solely to us.

Granted, our achievements may have been less than monumental. We didn't run any scoundrels out of office or win any landmark legal cases. We did let some embarrassing (but non-libelous, mind you) gaffes show up in print. However, we turned a profit, were never sued, sparked a debate or two by correspondence, kept the student body informed and even entertained — and we learned. Occasionally, The *Standard* (a weekly paper run by part-time student journalists) even managed to honestly scoop the *Springfield News-Leader* (a daily, professional newspaper). Moments like that cannot be cashed at the bursar's office or encapsulated into a bullet comment on a resume."

Randy Arndt,
Standard editor, 1994-95

Junior English exam abolished.

Last Japanese soldier, operating in Phillipines, surrenders — 29 years after World War II ended.

Barbara Walters becomes news co-anchor of *Today Show.*

Patricia Hearst announces she has decided to join her captors, the Symbionese Liberation Army.

"Eugene, he says he's claiming our living room in the name of "King Meyer" and the expanding colonies of SMSU."

With a burgeoning student enrollment in the 1970s, a *Standard* cartoonist pokes fun at the rapid expansion of the university into residential neighborhoods.

Changing Gender Ratio in Enrollment

At the beginning of the university period in 1972, male students constituted 53 percent of the student body while females accounted for only 47 percent. But by the fall of 1977, for the first time since World War II, females outnumbered males in the student body, and by the end of the 1985, women accounted for 55 percent of the enrollment. That dramatic change in college enrollment patterns remained steady at SMSU through the beginning of the 21st century.

A *Standard* cartoonist laments the failure of the General Assembly to provide funding for handicap access in 1977.

worried about the needs of students." SMSU had the largest undergraduate class in the state that year. Students came from 110 of the 114 Missouri counties, 49 of 50 states and 46 foreign countries. Five hundred valedictorians and salutatorians were on campus in 1991 along with 120 National Merit Finalists.

In fall of 2001, the enrollment exceeded 20,000 again, and in the fall of 2003 a record 20,671 students were enrolled. By this time classroom space had increased and faculty numbers had grown to make accommodating that many students a bit easier.

The full enrollment, however, also included more than 11,000 additional students who are taking life-long learning work at the university outside its degree-granting programs. Continuing education has put a new edge on the university's service to the area and added a significant increase to the student population.

The experience at SMSU is consistent with national data showing men as the campus minority throughout the country for more than 20 years. Graduation data make the gender disparity even more striking. Nationwide in 1998, male students were awarded only 44 percent of the baccalaureate degrees. At SMSU, the disparity was even greater with men earning only 40 percent of all the undergraduate degrees granted.

The consequences of this startling reversal in roles have become a concern to educators and employers across the nation. The implications include the changing nature of the workforce as well as the changing male role in society. From the women's perspective, campus social life becomes more complex as well with fewer men available.

While gender ratios were changing during the university years, the geographical distribution of students on campus moved steadily toward a statewide representation. As early as 1985, nearly 40 percent of SMSU students were coming from outside the 24-county service area, although Greene County continued to be the primary source for enrollments, and accounted for approximately one-third of the student body. The St. Louis area is the second largest contributor to the student body accounting for more than 15 percent.

Campus Expands to Accommodate Growth

Campus development since 1905, when 38 acres of land at Grand and National valued at $15,000 was given to the Board of Regents to begin building State Normal School #4, has been dramatic. By 2002, the campus had grown to 225 acres, spreading northwest to include substantial sections of

SMSU

— Dr. Mary Jo Wynn named director of women's athletics.

— Van Cliburn performs in McDonald Arena.

— Student Volunteer Services program established.

Missouri/Springfield

International/USA

— Soviet dancer, Mikhail Baryshnikov, defects to the West.

— President Nixon resigns during Watergate investigation; Gerald Ford becomes President and grants Nixon full pardon.

248   *A Centennial History of SMSU*

A Historical Essay

BY DR. JON MORAN

Professor of Philosophy

ETHICAL CHALLENGES AND THE UNIVERSITY

As the university enters its second century of existence, it is challenged by a series of ethical dilemmas that confront the new millennium. Why, you might ask, is a university challenged by ethical dilemmas? Is it not the case that ethical guidance is more likely to be found in churches and in the regulations of professional licensing agencies? In a sense, of course, this is the case. But these efforts are not sufficient. As citizens in a pluralistic society we must reach some agreement about the life we share together. To do this we need to search for a common language in which we can debate issues from the perspectives of our various traditions.

Unfortunately, one way of dealing with value diversity is a relativistic form of skepticism. We assume that no view can be seen as true. We resign ourselves to accepting the idea that ways of life are lifestyles, none of which is better or truer than the others. Such an attitude is likely to rob discussions of their seriousness. We may come to see our interactions with one another as cynical jockeying to fulfill our self-interested goals.

One motive for embracing value relativism is the fear that the alternative is a totalitarian imposition of one value perspective on all. This, of course, is possible, but by no means necessary. We can accept the fact that reasonable people can fail to reach agreement on fundamental issues. We can continue to pursue the truth in our various religious and philosophical perspectives. But there remains a public sphere in which public decisions must be made. There are no private policies on the death penalty or the demands of social justice. It is in this public area that we need ethical discussion in which we can interpret our differing traditions to one another in the

hopes of finding common ground.

Consider some of the ethical dilemmas that face us. With the growth in medical technology, the allotment of health services becomes more complicated. Given our ever increasing ability to keep ourselves alive for longer periods of time, and given the inevitable scarcity of resources, how should we decide who shall receive valuable medical care? In most areas of life our society lets the market decide. Those who receive services are those who can pay for them. Yet, wisely it seems, we always have hesitated to leave the preservation of our lives to the vagaries of the market. Medical personnel have traditionally given free care to those unable to pay, and we have resisted the selling of body parts (although recent proposals advocating the latter policy raise issues about the morality of encouraging the poor to sell body parts).

Coupled with general health concerns are the problems resulting from an older population. A few years ago a prominent medical ethicist suggested that we should begin to think in terms of a normal lifespan. After we reach a certain age, preference would be given to young people who have yet to live a normal life span. Is this common sense or age discrimination?

Disputes over physician-assisted suicide can make us think carefully about our attitude toward death and the responsibilities of medical personnel to preserve life and "do no harm." On this issue, in particular, public discussion often seems to suffer from a general lack of information. Few of us are clear about the circumstances surrounding death, about the activities of hospice and about provisions for pain care. We need a clearer grasp of the

options available in order to advocate a rational policy.

It is still difficult to predict how the results of the human genome project will impact our conduct. How should we use the information we are gaining about our genetic makeup? Should we adopt the notion that we should engineer ourselves to be whatever we wish? Surely ridding life of dreaded diseases is a good, but how far should we go?

Other issues, no doubt, will continue to plague us. Environmental concerns raise ethical issues. Questions about social and economic justice are likely to take a variety of new forms.

What resources can universities provide to meet these challenges? I would suggest two.

First, universities can supply factual information. Most of the issues we find most troubling are troubling precisely because they are complicated. To make intelligent decisions we must be aware of the factual complications.

Second, universities can provide their students with philosophical models for carrying on rational, ethical discussion. These are not simple formulae that will yield mechanically calculated, ethical truths; rather, they are ways of shaping discussion in publicly accessible ways.

In the final analysis one can only hope that these contributions will enhance the interpretive dialogue, allowing us to build a common community composed of genuinely different individuals whose lives are shaped by varied systems of belief. ✦

the downtown area. The first building, Academic Hall, completed in 1909, was valued at $225,000. In 1992, the university's assets in land, buildings and improvements, equipment and library holdings amounted to $260,430,431. Over the next decade those assets grew more than 80 percent to a total net worth of $465,515,228 in 2001.

In the university period from 1972 to 2002, more than 70 building projects, including new construction, renovations and purchases, were made to keep pace with the growing demands of an expanding student body, a rapidly developing curriculum and accelerating services to the area. More than 2 million square feet of space are dedicated to the educational enterprise itself.

Fueling this robust growth of facilities during the university period was a variety of factors, including the doubling of enrollment from 10,000 to more than 20,000 students, the addition of new programs, particularly in health and business, student recreation facilities and practice facilities for the burgeoning band program. With the passage of the Americans with Disabilities Act also came the need for extensive remodeling of all campus buildings to accommodate disabled students.

The plight of disabled students was graphically portrayed in a 1977 *Standard* cartoon showing three wheelchair occupants sitting at the base of myriad stairways, formidably reaching up to all kinds of campus destinations. A sign read, "Welcome to SMSU." Throughout the middle 1970s the university struggled with the ADA task: ramps were built to circumvent steps, elevators were installed in inaccessible older buildings and restrooms were remodeled to access wheelchairs.

Part of the celebration of the 75th anniversary of SMSU in 1980 was the unveiling of the cornerstone of the first Springfield Normal School and Business College built by John Taylor in 1894 east of Pickwick and North of Cherry street. The cornerstone was donated by Mr. and Mrs. Thomas O'Day Smith. Student body president Gary Osredker and Faculty Senate Chair Dr. Bruno Schmidt unveil the historic cornerstone.

Students joined President Meyer in handicap exercises to acquaint the campus with the problems faced by blind students, those with hearing loss, and those confined to wheel chairs.

By 1993 significant progress had been made in accommodating the disabled, but at least $6 million in additional remodeling was needed to be in full compliance with ADA mandates. All barriers were to be removed by January 26, 1995. That deadline was not met at SMSU, nor at many other public institutions, since funding was dependent on state appropriations. But the work continued so that by the turn of the century, every campus program was accessible to the disabled.

Campus Expansion and Urban Renewal
It had been clear for some time that the campus had to have access to new land in order to accommodate

the growth that was occurring in the 1970s. Purchases north of the campus in the late 1960s increased the space to 53 acres. But it was Urban Renewal through Springfield's Land Clearance for Redevelopment Authority under the leadership of Floyd Mattlage that opened the door to significant expansion. The Authority, created in 1962, quickly established plans to redevelop some 350 acres near downtown and SMSU. In May 1972, the Authority approved the redevelopment of an area bound by National on the east, Grand on the south, Kimbrough and Holland on the west and Cherry on the north. Within this general area, 34 acres would be sold to SMSU where master plans called for the construction of a classroom building, a new library, and a physical education complex which would include playing fields, an arena, exercise fields and parking.

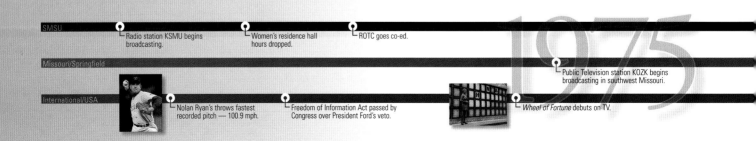

SMSU

Radio station KSMU begins broadcasting.

Women's residence hall hours dropped.

ROTC goes co-ed.

Missouri/Springfield

Public Television station KOZK begins broadcasting in southwest Missouri.

International/USA

Nolan Ryan's throws fastest recorded pitch — 100.9 mph.

Freedom of Information Act passed by Congress over President Ford's veto.

Wheel of Fortune debuts on TV.

1975

At one time, the private homes in the redevelopment area served the housing needs of SMSU. Until 1950, the college had relied on local residents to supply housing for students near the college. That had resulted in a substantial build-up of subdivisions around the university, which provided rented rooms to students. By the 1970s, parts of the area were clearly blighted and the razing resulted in the demolition of landmarks such as the Kingsbard Apartments, which had played a prominent role in college life in earlier years.

In addition to the land acquired through urban renewal, the university also purchased homes south of Grand and other locations to enable the development of parking lots and green space. Things didn't always go as they were planned. President Meyer insisted that all his co-workers keep him thoroughly advised about developments in their areas of responsibility. He had made a similar commitment to the Board of Regents promising that they would never be blindsided by a campus development. Former Regent Ramona McQueary remembers receiving a late evening call from President Meyer. He told her that something he was afraid would happed, actually did happen. "My heart started pounding," she recalls. "What is it?" she asked Meyer. "We've mistakenly torn down a house we didn't own," he replied. The home was south of the campus on Normal Street where demolition of other purchased houses was already under way. Fortunately, the resident was not at home at the time of the demolition. She returned home later in the day to find her house and furnishings pushed into the basement. The university quickly bought the demolished house and the furnishings.

While most property acquisitions to accommodate growth went smoothly, the Ebbet's Field episode in 1993 was otherwise. Nick Russo operated the Ebbet's Field restaurant, a popular campus hangout just west of the Juanita K. Hammons Hall for the Performing Arts, the only business left on the north side of Cherry between Kimbrough and John Q. Hammons Parkway; and, according to the university, it would constitute a significant design problem for the parking garage if it remained. Russo rejected all offers from the university, which finally went to court to exercise the right of eminent domain to obtain the property. Perceived as a David and Goliath story, many on campus supported Russo, but ultimately the property was obtained for $289,000, and the building was razed, solving the design problem for the parking garage.

Capital Projects in the University Era

Capital expansion started in the 1960s to accommodate burgeoning enrollment which continued into the early 1970s. Temple Hall, housing the sciences, was completed in 1971; as were Woods House, a new high-rise residence hall; Taylor Health Center; Baker Bookstore; and a warehouse on Grand. From 1970 through 1973 capital funding was granted only for maintenance. Then in 1974-75, after seven consecutive years of rejected requests, $2.8 million was appropriated for the construction of Kemper Hall to house the Industrial Education program. It was sited on urban renewal land west of the stadium.

Another building placed on urban renewal land northwest of the campus

Kemper Hall opens for industrial education programs.

Center for Archeological Research established.

Aristotle Onasis dies.

was the student recreation building. The idea originated in the Student Government Association where it was discussed for several years. The building would include a new basketball arena planned to seat 10,000, swimming facilities and a variety of recreational and university sports activities. The $5.5 million dollar facility would be funded primarily through a student fee assessment, beginning in the fall of 1974. The proposal had a mixed reception among students. Some claimed existing recreation facilities were seldom used. Others wondered why they would be assessed for something that wouldn't be built until after they were gone. Others felt that if the students were going to pay for it, they should have the right to vote for or against it. Jim Porter, SGA president in 1974, said a campus statistics class had done a survey and found that 60 per-

cent of the student body was in favor of the building.

In March 1974, President Meyer declared, "The die is cast." The Board approved plans on March 17 and solicited bids. In June when the bids came in, they were $2 million over the $5.5 million budget. The Regents revised the plans, cutting down the size of the building. In September, acceptable bids were received, and preparations were made to let contracts. In October, President Meyer and Dean Tom Wyrick scheduled a meeting with students hoping to address their concerns about accessibility of the building in light of the Athletics Department's use of the facility, and whether or not student organizations sponsoring concerts there might have to pay a fee for maintenance. When the president and the dean appeared, they were greeted by no more than 20 students.

Ground was broken January 21, 1975, and $4 million in revenue bonds were sold to finance construction. The new plan called for an arena seating 9,200 fans, an eight-lane swimming pool, six handball courts, a rifle range, weight training facilities, multiple basketball courts and volleyball and tennis areas. While the building was being built, local civic leader and entrepreneur John Q. Hammons, himself a student at the university in the State

Teachers College days, came forward with a plan to assist in the recreation building project. He pledged $1 million to support maintenance and operation costs of the building. His substantial gift was recognized by naming the building Hammons Student Center, the first building on the university campus to be named for someone other than a faculty or staff member. That naming initiated a trend that gained substantial momentum as the institution moved toward the end of the 20th century.

Another 1970s addition to the campus came without a university request, similar to the establishment of the West Plains Campus in 1963. In 1899 the state established the State Fruit Experiment Station at Mountain Grove. It operated under state supervision for three-quarters of a century. In 1974, under an Omnibus State Reorganization Act, the Fruit Experiment Station was given to the University to operate. It has since developed into the third campus in the SMSU system housing the Department of Fruit Science and offering classes from the West Plains Campus.

A High-Rise Apartment Added to the Inventory of Residence Halls

Despite the heavy investment in student housing during the 1960s, the continued growth of the student

John Q. Hammons, an alumnus of SMSU, provided the first major private gift to the university in 1975. He donated $1 million to support the maintenance and operation of the student recreation building that was already under construction. In appreciation of this gift, the building was named Hammons Student Center, the first building on campus to be named for a private donor. Since that time Mr. Hammons, a successful entrepreneur and civic leader, has built two fountains and a residence hall on campus, which was later sold to the university, as well as contributing to the completion of a performing arts facility on campus that bears the name of his wife, Juanita K. Hammons. In addition, Mr. Hammons built a $32 million baseball stadium, Hammons Field, located at the corner of John Q. Hammons Parkway and Trafficway, which is being used by the SMS Bears baseball team. Opening Day for Hammons Field was April 2, 2004.

SMSU
Campus size grows to 125 acres.

Missouri/Springfield
Catholic Diocese sets up refugee office for Vietnamese immigrants.

International/USA
Oldest animal fossils found in U.S. — found in North Carolina.
Jaws, by Steven Spielberg, opens.
Suez Canal reopened — had been closed since 1967.

John Q. Hammons Student Center opened in 1976 as the largest indoor arena in southwest Missouri. With a main arena seating capacity of almost 9,000 and as home for SMS basketball, volleyball and swimming, Hammons Student Center saw men's basketball teams total more than 2.5 million fans in the facility's first 27 years of operation, while the women's team was among the top 10 in average attendance 10 years in a row at the turn of the 21st century.

body in the 1970s left the university still struggling to enforce its policy of requiring freshmen and sophomores to live in university residence halls. Dean Wyrick reported to the Board in November 1975 that residence hall occupancy was at 98.4 percent of capacity with 892 freshmen and sophomores still living off campus because there was insufficient space in university housing. By January 1976, President Meyer had developed a plan for building an apartment complex to ease the shortage. He presented the plan to the Board, which in turn authorized the administration to seek bids. In the meantime, Dr. Meyer learned that Sunvilla, a 19-story apartment facility at 833 E. Elm, was for sale. The build-

ing contained 89 apartments, 39 more than were in the university plan. The purchase price for Sunvilla was less than construction costs of the new complex. Two acres of land adjacent to the tower had parking for 138 cars. Each apartment was equipped with a full kitchen, including refrigerator, stove, garbage disposal and dishwasher.

It was a dream solution and the Board quickly passed a resolution approving the $1.7 million purchase price. It also approved a resolution allowing all existing leases for current occupants to be honored. Most of the current residents were senior adults. When it was built it was known as a luxury apartment building with a penthouse apartment. What wasn't known

was who lived in the penthouse.

President Meyer recalls the circumstances. "Unknown to university officials, State Senator Paul Bradshaw and his wife lived in the penthouse apartment on the 19th floor. Senator Bradshaw was a very influential member of the Senate Appropriations Committee, a committee with nearly life or death power over the university. The senator could have complained over the loss of his home, but he didn't," recalls Dr. Meyer. "He recognized that the purchase of Sunvilla was a great help to SMSU in relieving the housing problem. Senator and Mrs. Bradshaw cheerfully moved out when their lease expired."

When college students began moving in later in the year, an 80-year-old resident said she enjoyed her new neighbors. "College students are my kind of people," she said. "I hope to stay even after my lease expires."

While Sunvilla took some of the pressure off the housing crisis, in the fall of 1977 the university had to do what it hadn't done since the summer of 1906 — send students to live in Fairbanks Hall on the Drury College campus.

Residence hall additions in the 1970s concluded with the purchase of the Dogwood Apartments on Cherry Street for $535,000 in 1979, accommodating 98 students. But as the decade ended, the on-campus housing policy was still unable to be fully implemented. The growth of the student body was simply outpacing every effort to accommodate it.

Growing Toward Downtown in the 1980s
As Urban Renewal enabled the university to expand north and west, opportunities to acquire older buildings near downtown pushed campus boundaries

Enrollment exceeds 12,000 (12,153).

A three-acre burial site with 6,000 clay statues of warriors found dating as early as 221 B.C. discovered by Chinese archaeologists.

Jimmy Hoffa disappears.

into the city center which provided a new dimension to university life and made the institution a partner in downtown renewal. The Kentwood Arms Hotel, long a Springfield landmark with its celebrated Crystal Room, came on the market in 1984. The university was still struggling to house students and the prospects of refurbishing the hotel into a residence hall looked promising. Purchased in 1984 for $850,000, the site provided a five-story hotel, an attached motel wing, and five acres of land between St. Louis and Walnut streets. A $3.5 million renovation enabled 200 students to move into the newly named Kentwood Hall in the fall of 1988. To provide additional space for parking, the Lohmeyer-Windle Funeral Home, just west of the Kentwood, was purchased and razed.

A year after the Kentwood purchase, a medical office building on the corner of Kimbrough and Cherry became available. Purchased for $1,575,000, the Professional Building was ideally suited to provide classrooms and office space. By the turn of the century, it had been thoroughly renovated and became the home of the College of Health and Human Services.

Another purchase near downtown provided the students with an art gallery to display their work. The Sorosis Women's Club building on the corner of Walnut and Hammons Parkway was part of the historic district on Walnut Street. Wyrick Funds made the purchase possible and the university agreed that, "the historical integrity of the house be maintained." After some renovation to accommodate climate requirements for art work, the Student Exhibition Center opened on April 18, 1986.

As the 1980s ended, the university

The Duane G. Meyer Library, constructed at a cost of $6.8 million and dedicated in 1980, provided students with an attractive and functional setting for research and study. At its opening the library contained more than 350,000 volumes and 388,000 microform units, overseen by 17 professional librarians and a staff of 20. It was named for retiring President Duane G. Meyer in 1982, the last building named in honor of a university faculty or staff member.

reached even further into the downtown area with the SMSU Foundation purchasing a six-story bank building on the corner of Jefferson and McDaniel, one of the newest buildings downtown. It would house the SMSU Alumni Association and the SMSU Foundation, and by the turn of the century, through a lease agreement between the University and the Foundation, the building also provided space for University Relations, University Communications, Publications, Photographic Services, Continuing Education, Academic Outreach and the Centennial Project.

Renewed Building on Campus
The 1980s began with renewed building on the west side of the campus. In anticipation of Division I athletics

competition, a new athletics facility for men's sports was built just northwest of McDonald Arena. Female student-athletes were not thrilled with the new training and locker facility for men's sports. Female student-athletes "are in dire need of such facilities," declared Dr. Mary Jo Wynn. In 1985, the facility was renamed the Forsythe Athletics Center, in appreciation for a substantial contribution toward its cost by Ray and Susie Forsythe. Forsythe was a stand-out football player in the late 1940s and served on the Board of Regents from 1977-83.

At the same time the new library was being constructed immediately west of McDonald Arena, an impressive array of fountains were under construction in the mall area between Temple Hall and the library. John Q. Hammons had indicated an interest

SMSU

Business programs have 1,759 majors, Teacher Education, 718.

Missouri/Springfield

Progressive Farmers Association (PFA) begins retail activities in Springfield.

International/USA

Martina Navratilova, tennis star, asks for U.S. political asylum.

Elizabeth Taylor remarries Richard Burton — her sixth marriage.

Saturday Night Live premiers.

254 *A Centennial History of SMSU*

in building an impressive fountain on campus shortly after he contributed to the student recreation building. On August 18, 1980, the $360,000, 80-foot by 140-foot John Q. Hammons Fountains were dedicated, continuing a campus fountain tradition going back almost 70 years. As the spacious water display erupted, Mr. Hammons declared, "I've never seen a fountain display noteworthy of intrinsic value. This fountain is what I wanted it to be. It is very stimulating and motivating."

Just a month later, marking the 75th anniversary of the university, the $5.5 million Duane G. Meyer Library was dedicated at ceremonies featuring Governor Joe Teasdale. Twenty-five years earlier a new $600,000 library had been dedicated on the east side of campus. The Meyer Library virtually doubled the space of the earlier Memorial Library. An annex to house closed-stack books was also built north of Forsythe Athletics Center. It would house lesser-used items and could be constructed more cheaply. The old Memorial Library building was renamed Cheek Hall in 1981 and after renovation provided space for Business, Mathematics, and Computer Science Departments.

Finding a Way Across Grand Avenue

Troubled by the dangerous situation of 3,000 pedestrians crossing Grand from Parking Lot 24 each day while 15,639 autos sped down the street, the Board explored building an overpass to give students and staff a safer passage to and from campus. In 1980, the overpass idea was scrapped as too expensive and too obtrusive. Instead, students, regents and faculty decided to build an underpass eight feet high, 12 feet wide and

60 feet long, 14 feet under the street, with stairs at each end. The passageway was opened in September 1981. Early use patterns were not encouraging since pedestrians were preferring the dangers of the street to the inconvenience of the steps. Finally, fences were built corralling pedestrians into the underpass. Even that was not fully successful. Athletic youth could be seen leaping the fence throughout the day. But the underpass remains, providing safer passage to thousands every day.

Star Gazing Near Marshfield

In 1976, Dr. George Wolf of the Physics Department persuaded the administration of the need for an off-campus, dark-sky astronomical observatory. That began a year-long search for suitable land, and a multi-year search for funding for the facility. In early 1977, William and Retha Baker donated 10 acres of land in Webster County for the observatory site and later in the same year increased the gift to 39.5 acres to include a nature area and trail. It was an ideal location — away from city lights and traffic. The land was donated in memory of Mrs. Baker's parents, Harry W. and Ida Stone. Harry had delivered mail along the route adjacent to the observatory for 44 years.

In September 1978, the Bakers raised funds from Marshfield residents to help construct an observing pad at the site. Members of the Physics Department and the Society of Physics Students held an "observatory raising party" and placed 12 steel piers in concrete to serve as bases for the department's many eight-inch telescopes. Later that month electricity was brought to the piers and Rost Ready Mix of Marshfield poured the concrete

ROTC Produces Nine General Officers

During its 50th anniversary celebration in October 2002, the SMSU Bear Battalion reflected on its achievements since 1952. Among the notable accomplishments was the commissioning of nine graduates who eventually became General Officers in the U.S. Army. From the class of 1957 were Major General Robert Lynn Gordon; Lieutenant General Neal T. Jaco, Major General Robert F. Pennycuick and Brigadier General William A. West were from the class of 1959.

The class of 1963 also produced four general officers: Major General Fred F. Marty, Lieutenant General John E. Miller, Major General David E. White and Major General Jarrett J. Robertson who died in a helicopter crash in Germany in 1993. The ninth member of the Bear Battalion to achieve the rank of General Officer is Brigadier General Tony L. Stansberry, class of 1967.

In its first 50 years, the Bear Battalion commissioned 1,620 officers.

Godspell selected for USO tour in European Command.

Liberty Bell moved to new home behind Independence Hall.

Looking Back

Broadcasting More Than 80 Years

While university broadcasting is generally thought to have started on May 7, 1974, when KSMU went on the air, broadcast history actually goes back to the State Teachers College days. On December 2, 1922, station WQAB at 834 kilocycles on the AM band sent its first broadcast to the campus and the city of Springfield. Science Department students under the leadership of Professor A.P. Temple operated the station.

At the time only one other radio station was broadcasting in Springfield, WIAI, operated by Pearson Ward from Heer's Tower on the public square. Both local stations were considered by the federal government as experimental stations. By 1923, WQAB ceased broadcasting because it was interfering with the reception of high-powered stations from elsewhere in the state. But in 1924, the college was back on the air. With the assistance of Pearson Ward, station KFNH was licensed to operate at 1270 kilocycles on January 24. The new station's single purpose was education and various STC departments contributed programming, but quarrels over time allotments among the departments and the lack of operating funds doomed the enterprise. On May 24, 1924, the station was deleted from the list of federal broadcast assignments.

pad at cost to complete that section of the observatory.

In June 1980, Rost Ready Mix, again at cost and funded by the university, constructed a 14-foot by 38-foot concrete building designed by Dr. Wolf to house telescopes and equipment. During the next two years several donors, including alumnus Dr. Stephen Bodanske, the Bakers and the SMSU Alumni Association, funded the construction of two steel telescope domes to complete the facility.

In January 1983, Dr. Wolf obtained a 16-inch professional grade telescope on a permanent loan from Cerro Tololo Inter-American Observatory in Chile to mount in the larger dome. A 14-inch telescope obtained earlier through federal grants was mounted in the smaller dome. In April 1983, a completed Baker Observatory was dedicated. Since that time the observatory has continued to provide astronomy students and faculty many opportunities for observation and scientific research. Twice each year citizens from around the area and members of the university community attend the observatory open houses to look through the telescopes and see light years into the past.

An Elegant Residence Hall Opens
The struggle to provide housing continued into the middle 1980s with the university seeking to interest local builders to erect a major dormitory to be paid off by student residence hall fees. Again, SMSU benefactor John Q. Hammons stepped to the plate and built an $11 million hall to house 6l6 students, the largest residence hall on campus. In addition to its size, its amenities made it clearly an upscale addition to

In September 1978, students and faculty from the Society for Physics Students took part in an "observatory raising party." Dr. John Northrip is aiding the efficiency of the auger as the group placed 12 steel piers in concrete footings to serve as telescope bases. The site for the observatory is near Marshfield, Missouri on land donated by William and Retha Baker. In April 1983 the finished Observatory was dedicated.

the university housing inventory. The suites contained a kitchenette with refrigerator, counter-top stove, sink and microwave; phone; computer; moveable oak furniture; and carpet. They were quite elegant compared to more modest residence halls elsewhere on campus. But, as Mr. Hammons pointed out, students were becoming more affluent, and coming from more affluent homes they expect more in their university quarters.

In addition to the suite furnishings, the hall provided cable hookups, study rooms, typing rooms, meeting rooms, a fitness center, tanning beds, a convenience store, deli, video rental store and parking spaces for 500

SMSU

Dr. Virginia Craig dies.

Missouri/Springfield

International/USA

Jockey Bill Shoemaker wins his 7,000th race.

cars. While the building wasn't quite finished in the fall of 1986, students moved in, paying $285 a month for two-person suites, and $235 a month for four-person suites. Marie Casey, a resident assistant, moved in a week early declaring, "It's not finished yet, but I love it to death!"

Instead of leasing the building from Mr. Hammons, the university purchased it using tax-free bond money. It was named Hammons House in honor of the contribution of the generous benefactor.

The Business School Gets a New Home

While Hammons House was under construction on the north side of the campus, there was also intense building activity going on at a southwest location. The largest building on campus at the time was rising out of the ground across the street, west of the new library. It would have 131 offices,

180 study spaces, 220 lab stations and 21 graduate assistant stations. The $15 million, four-story, 165,000-square foot classroom building for the College of Business Administration was to be named David D. Glass Hall in recognition of a substantial gift by the Wal-Mart President and CEO and SMSU

William and Retha Stone Baker donated the land for the astronomical observatory and helped raise funds to insure that the project would be a success. Seen here in the April 1983 dedication, both were graduates of SMSU, he in 1927 and she in 1928.

graduate. Classroom space in the building accommodates 1,800 business students an hour and would enable the College of Business Administration to consolidate all its programs into a single building.

Glass grew up in Mountain View, Missouri, graduating from SMSU in 1960 with a bachelor's degree in business accounting, joined Wal-Mart in 1976, and became president and CEO in 1984. When it came time to dedicate the new building on April 6, 1988, an auspicious crowd was on hand. The venerable Sam Walton, founder of Wal-Mart, was there as was his brother, James L. "Bud" Walton. Governor John Ashcroft remembered the days in the late 1960s when he taught business law at SMSU in much more modest surroundings, and David Glass declared, "In business, we give high marks for excellence, so my decision to invest in SMSU was based on that. This is a university on the move!" As he concluded his address he said, "I am truly impressed — almost overwhelmed, in fact — with the progress that Southwest Missouri State University has made.... We have a quality of education here that is as good as young people can get any-

Dedicated in April 1983, the Baker Observatory in Webster County provides students with a new perspective on the universe through the eyes of a 16-inch, a 14-inch and several eight-inch telescopes. The 12 piers on the concrete observing pad allow entire classes or other large groups to use the eight-inch portable telescopes during observing sessions.

Hammons Student Center opens with an appearance by Bob Hope.

President Gerald Ford visits Springfield.

President Ronald Reagan visits Springfield.

Fourth of July parade in Springfield celebrates nation's 200th anniversary.

Reverend Sun Myung Moon ends U.S. ministry with rallies in New York and Washington D.C.

Mysterious illness takes 34 lives at American Legion Convention in Philadelphia; 151 others stricken with "Legionnaires Disease."

where…. I've never been in a facility housing a business school that exceeds this one."

A Hall for the Performing Arts

As far back as the 1950s, there was talk in Springfield about the need for a performing arts center. The community had developed a symphony orchestra, a community theater, numerous choral groups, a ballet, and a regional opera, among other groups. In 1968, Springfield voters were asked to support a $13.5 million civic center complex that would include a performing arts center. Voters turned it down. In 1983, John Q. Hammons proposed building a 2,000-seat performing arts center on property he would donate. The estimated cost was $9 million. City Council asked the voters to fund the proposed facility through a 1 percent restaurant tax on the retail sale of food and bever-

ages. That proposal was also defeated at the polls.

Not until 1985 did a performance center appear feasible. That year the Missouri General Assembly appropriated $5 million toward the construction of a performing arts center in Springfield on the condition that the university and the community raise the remaining $5.8 million. By the end of the 1989-90 school year, $5.6 million had been raised or committed. John Q. Hammons had donated the site for the structure in 1988. In December 1989, at a surprise reception, Juanita K. Hammons learned the new facility would be named for her in recognition of the gift that she and Mr. Hammons had donated to the project.

In October 1989, the Board of Regents authorized the sale of revenue bonds to provide interim financing, letting bids in late 1989. Construction started in April 1990 and was scheduled for completion in 24 months. The building would be magnificent in appearance — 11 stories tall at the rear, five stories in the front, with a gracefully curved glass front. Not only would it showcase local performing arts groups including university groups, but it would also provide a venue for traveling Broadway shows and concert artists.

In February 1988, the Board of Regents had approved a $10.8 million budget for the building. To its chagrin, the Board was told by President Gordon in September 1991 that the

total cost for the building would be $6 million above the budget. A series of conflicting explanations of how the budget had been exceeded led to an extremely tense relationship between the Board and the president. In October 1991, President Gordon told the Board that the total cost of the performing arts center would be $17.3 million. Board President Jack Miller announced that the $6.5 million in additional funds would come from three sources: (1) the SMSU Foundation agreed to provide $1.5 million in cash; (2) the SMSU Foundation agreed to borrow $2 million from local banks and repay the principal and interest on this loan over the next five to seven years; and (3) the SMSU Board of Regents agreed to use $3 million from unrestricted reserve funds.

Since university funds were being used for the facility, the building design had to be changed to provide academic space justifying the investment of university dollars. A rehearsal hall was modified for use by SMSU music groups. Faculty offices and specialty studios for music students were added to the design.

The budget fiasco sufficiently undermined the Board's confidence in the university administration that it asked Missouri State Auditor Margaret Kelly to conduct an audit of the university which commenced in November 1991.

Despite the chaotic events surrounding the planning, funding

In 1988, the new College of Business Administration Building was named David D. Glass Hall in honor of the president of Wal-Mart and a distinguished graduate of SMSU. Glass is a native of Mountain View, Missouri and graduated with a bachelor's degree in Business Accounting in 1960. His business career started with Consumer's Markets and Crank Drug Stores in Springfield. In 1976, he joined Wal-Mart, becoming president in 1984. Glass has served on the SMSU Foundation and contributed generously to the university's advancement.

SMSU

Coordinating Board for Higher Education authorizes eight associate degrees in 19 academic areas.

Sunvilla apartments purchased for campus housing.

Specialist degree added to graduate program.

Missouri/Springfield

Ritter Springs Park dedicated.

International/USA

North and South Vietnam reunited after 22 years of separation.

Jimmy Carter elected President of the U.S.

Winnie Mandela banished from South Africa.

Juanita K. Hammons Hall for the Performing Arts, completed in 1992, has become a cultural center for southwest Missouri, providing a venue for university music, drama and dance programs, community opera, ballet and symphony performances, university convocations, community assemblies, and a year-long schedule of Broadway shows, recording artists and a wide range of professional entertainers.

and building of the Hall, Enoch C. Morris Jr., who was hired in September 1989 as executive director of the new facility, continued to plan for the gala opening of the building. In September 1991, Carol Channing came as guest of honor to the first Juanita K. Hammons Hall for the Performing Arts gala held at Highland Springs Country Club. In August 1992, construction was completed and the first concert was performed — a "Hard Hat" concert for workers involved in the construction of the building and their families. Country singer Merle Haggard was the featured artist. He donated his time and talent for the event. In September, the new facility was formally dedicated and the entire month featured free performances by university and community arts groups.

In the years since the opening of the Hall, the outstanding talent shown in Broadway shows such as *Cats, Oklahoma!, Madame Butterfly, Camelot,* and *Fiddler on the Roof,* as well as the stellar performances of such artists as Tony Bennett, Robert Goulet, Bob Dylan, Victor Borge, Wynton Marsalis, Carol Channing and Ray Charles have done much to dispel the cloud that hung over the project at its beginning. But the mistakes were costly. A president lost his job, and the university had to scramble to find funding to support the facility. However, within a few seasons it was hard to find anyone who didn't think that the Juanita K. Hammons Hall for the Performing Arts was one of the best things that ever happened to Springfield. Even at $17.3 million, it was a bargain.

Improvements in the 1990s

Throughout the 1990s, more than $70 million in new construction occurred on campus. In 1991, a twin to the new Hammons House was added providing on-campus living space for more than 600 additional students. Campus parking problems were addressed in 1995 with a Park-N-Ride facility sited just west of the Juanita K. Hammons Hall for the Performing Arts. Coupled with the parking garage was an elaborate system of shuttle bus routes that reached the heart of the campus and into the downtown area. In 1996, C. Robert Wehr and James R. Wehr donated $2 million for a building for the Band program and the facility was named Wehr Band Hall. It was the largest gift to the university and the SMSU Foundation at that time. In 1998, the campus' largest classroom building was completed at the west end of the mall. The $20.25 million Public Affairs Classroom building housed the College of Humanities and Public Affairs as well as radio station KSMU and the Ozarks Public Television station KOZK. The facility was renamed Strong Hall in 2002 in recognition of a major gift from the Tom Strong family. In 1999, a $3 million physical therapy classroom building was added to the allied health complex on the corner of Kimbrough and Cherry.

The 1990s also saw $56 million in renovations improve campus facilities. The Professional Building, housing allied health programs, was completely refurbished as was the Forsythe Athletics Center. Karls Hall, headquarters for the Agriculture Department, celebrated a $4.9 million renovation in 1998, the 50th anniversary of the establishment of the department. A 24,000-

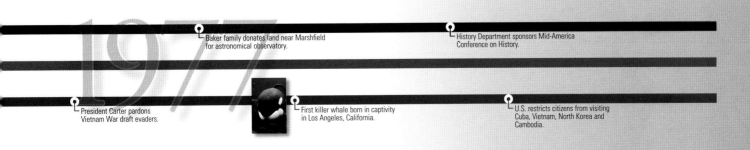

Baker family donates land near Marshfield for astronomical observatory.

History Department sponsors Mid-America Conference on History.

President Carter pardons Vietnam War draft evaders.

First killer whale born in captivity in Los Angeles, California.

U.S. restricts citizens from visiting Cuba, Vietnam, North Korea and Cambodia.

square-foot addition to the building includes newly equipped classrooms and a third-level greenhouse complex.

The largest renovation project of the decade was the $13.1 million reworking and expansion of the Student Union completed in 1999. A gift from Robert W. Plaster resulted in the change of name to Robert W. Plaster Student Union. The Student Union has undergone two major additions since it was built in 1951. The latest addition was "The Mall in the Middle," a project which included the renovation of Wells House, the Baker Bookstore and the Taylor Health and Wellness Center, all clustered near the middle of the campus.

The Renaming of Briggs Stadium

One of the more controversial improvements of campus facilities occurred in 1991 when Briggs Stadium was renovated and expanded to accommodate more football fans. The stadium, originally built in 1930 when Arthur Briggs was in his 18th year as head of the Physical Education Department, was named Briggs Stadium in 1970 in honor of the man who had served the institution for 38 years, founded the physical education program, coached every sport played during his tenure and was the winningest football coach in the institution's history.

The renovation of the facility doubled the seating capacity to 16,600, added 24 skybox suites, a press box, six classrooms, 12 racquetball courts, snack bar areas, administrative offices, and a weight and aerobics room among other improvements. The cost for the project was $7.6 million. Inarguably, it was a major improvement to the facility. Robert W. Plaster made a major gift in support of the project and was honored by having the facility renamed the Robert W. Plaster Sports Complex.

While the new facility was a hit with the fans, the new name did not set well. The 1992 *Ozarko* description of the event read, "In trade for the luxury of expanded bleachers, skyboxes, a new press box, and the expansion of a new sports complex, SMSU lost a name that had proudly adorned the stadium for the past 50 years — Arthur W. Briggs." *The Standard* editorial headline shouted, "Sold! To the highest bidder." It went on to declare that *The Standard* would not honor the new name. It would continue to refer to the complex as Briggs Stadium. The *Ozarko* joined the name boycott saying, "More than a few people balked at the sudden name change on the eve of the 50th anniversary of Briggs Stadium, calling it a blatant sell-out, destruction of a tradition and a disgrace to the name SMSU. *The Southwest Standard* and the *Ozarko* will continue to refer to the sports complex as Briggs Stadium, in accordance with the wishes of the student body and in honor of a man who may not have contributed $1.5 million cash, but instead dedicated millions of hours and his career to the betterment of the university and its program." The boycott lasted only two years.

The fact that the SMSU Foundation announced that it would establish a $100,000 scholarship program in memory of A.W. Briggs, rename the remaining fragment of Belmont street Briggs Street, and install a bust of Arthur Briggs outside the new complex with a description of his contribution and achievements, did little to assuage the outrage. Briggs' grandsons said the university had sold out. Ed McClung, a 1973 graduate and owner of W.F. Cody's restaurant on East Sunshine, commented on the issue by running a radio spot that offered a name change for his restaurant to anyone offering a few million dollars.

Facility Naming Tradition Changes

The Briggs Stadium name change introduced the public to some new realities in institutional financing. True, private funding was the key to establishing the institution in Springfield initially. Land valued at $15,000 plus $25,000 in cash were the only assets available as State Normal School #4 opened in the summer of 1906. Thereafter, however, any capital improvements were funded by the state, and the institution continued to be clearly "state supported." There is no record of generous private gifts until 1976 when John Q. Hammons agreed to assist in the construction of the student recreation building after the state had made it clear it would not fund it. Until that time, all buildings on campus had been named in honor of faculty or staff who had contributed years of dedicated labor to the institution's success. Hammons Student Center, however, pointed a new direction.

During the 1970s and 1980s, no facility names were changed to honor private donors. In 1972, the Administration Building was renamed Carrington Hall to honor the first president. In 1975, the new industrial arts building was named Kemper Hall in honor of the pioneer industrial arts educator, and the science building surrendered its generic name to honor the contribution of long-time educator Dr. Harry Siceluff. The Board continued the naming tradition in 1975 by nam-

ing the renovated home economics house Burgess House in honor of Floy Burgess who spent 38 years developing the program, 37 as department head.

The Board continued the naming tradition in 1981 by renaming the renovated library building Cheek Hall in honor of Virgil Cheek, long-time head of the Commerce Department. A new building housing the bookstore and the health clinic was named for Lee H. Morris, college business manager and treasurer for the Board of Regents. Morris was the first staff member to be honored in the naming process. Two other staff members were honored that same year. The bookstore was named the Baker Bookstore in recognition of the service of Walter I. Baker, university auditor and secretary to the Board for four decades. The health clinic was named the Taylor Health

Center in honor of the service of Dr. William E. Taylor, college physician and director of the Health Center. The last university building to be named for a faculty or staff member recognizing their contribution to the institution occurred in 1983 when the new library was named the Duane G. Meyer Library.

Wall of Fame Established

Will there ever be faculty, staff or administrators names on new facilities at SMSU? It doesn't appear likely. President Marshall Gordon, as part of his termination agreement, asked for a building to be named for him. The Board declined. However, in 2002, a Wall of Fame was established in Plaster Student Union that will contain names of former faculty and staff who "have continuously demonstrated character and integrity, whose service resulted in meaningful change at the university, and who had a notable impact on students." The first class of inductees to the "Wall of Fame" included Dr. Byrne Blackwood who directed Tent Theatre for 20 years; Arthur Briggs, first full-time director of athletics (1912-38); Margaret Crighton who served as reference librarian from 1942-1972; Dr. Robert

Thirteen faculty and staff members were included in the first Wall of Fame induction class in 2002. Plaques honoring each member were mounted on the Wall of Fame in Plaster Student Union.

Dr. Gerrit tenZythoff
1969-92

Gerrit tenZythoff founded the SMSU religious studies department and served as department head. The first religious studies department at a public institution in Missouri, it became one of the largest in the Midwest under tenZythoff's leadership.

Induction Class 2002

Office of Grants opens to assist faculty research.

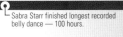

Sabra Starr finished longest recorded belly dance — 100 hours.

Elvis Presley dies.

President Carter signs Panama Canal Treaty returning control of Panama Canal to Panama in 2000.

The Public Affairs Classroom Building became Strong Hall in 2002 when the Board of Governors accepted a $3 million gift from the Tom Strong family. The College of Humanities and Public Affairs is housed in Strong Hall along with radio station KSMU and Ozarks Public Television.

retrieval, remote document access, collaborative work areas and a host of new communications and research technologies. Several technology-supported classrooms, remote media distribution and a multi-media production center will bring digitally enhanced learning to the entire campus.

Associated with the library is the Jane A. Meyer Carillon, providing the university with an outstanding example of the world's largest musical instrument. A gift from the Kenneth E. and Jane A. Meyer Foundation, the Carillon was dedicated to the memory of Jane A. Meyer who died just over two months prior to its dedication. Jane's enthusiasm and support for the university was legendary. In the dedicatory address, President John H. Keiser observed, "Although it is new, the Carillon represents the focused traditional voice of SMSU, enriched by Jane's presence. Every day on campus the Carillon will break into self-centered thought patterns, into selfish specialization and require all to contemplate the same music at the same time. In her business, Jane knew that many people feel inconvenienced when they have to hear about such topics as transportation, clean air, foreign policy, public safety, or political issues when their minds are elsewhere. But she also knew that great societies are built when everyone hears the universal, to some the angelic language of the Carillon, the same music at the same time."

It seems fitting that the Carillon was sited on the corner of the library. Summoning all who hear it to a great repository of knowledge, the instrument

Gilmore who served the university for more than 30 years in Tent Theatre and the Speech and Theatre Department, as well as dean of faculties and provost during the Meyer administration; Dr. George Gleason, long-time head of the English Department; Wilda Looney, who spent 31 years in the Residence Life and Services Department; Dr. E. Howard Matthews, mathematics teacher and assistant to the president in the Meyer administration; Don Payton, public relations officer from 1956-86; Aldo Sebben, director of athletics from 1955-82; Dr. Holt Spicer, successor to Dr. Virginia Craig as debate coach in 1952; Dr. Gerrit tenZythoff, founder of the Religious Studies Department; Dr. Cliff Whipple, first head of the Psychology Department; and Dr. Richard Wilkinson, first full-time psychologist at SMSU. So the recognition of faculty, staff and administrators who have "made a difference" at SMSU

will continue on the "Wall of Fame," if not a building.

New Facilities 2000 and Beyond

As the new century opened, major building projects were under way to improve facilities and accommodate rising expectations from students. Wells House, the first university built dormitory, underwent a major renovation after 50 years. The structure was gutted and thoroughly refurbished at a cost of $10.1 million. A dramatic change also occurred at the Meyer Library which was expanded and renovated and a carillon added to the existing building at a total cost of $27.6 million. The new Meyer Library now provides space to house electronic document

Commemorative Medallion struck for the dedication of the Public Affairs Classroom Building (Strong Hall) on October 13, 1998.

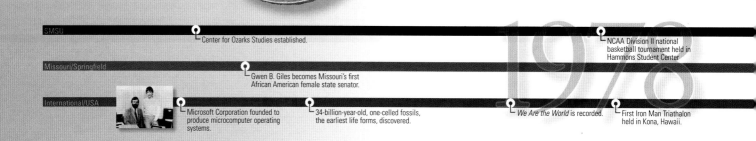

reminds one of the mission of the university — to develop educated persons.

Campus Beyond the Walls

To suggest that the aggressive building program during the university period adequately describes campus development for the period is to miss the genius of the 21st century: the creation of distance learning. In 1907, outreach and distance learning was Dr. Virginia Craig taking a train to Marshfield to teach English composition techniques to public school teachers on a Saturday morning. Nearly a century later, outreach was still a policy of the university, but the means had changed and the reach had lengthened.

The digital revolution had enabled the university to promise "anytime, anyplace learning opportunities." Distance learning technologies today enable the university to extend its curriculum and academic programs to learners well beyond the walls of the Springfield campus. Those technologies include audioconferencing, radio, television (interactive video, telecourses, microwave), satellite transmission, audiocassette and videocassette programs and a variety of computer-based systems including synchronous and asynchronous computer conferencing.

The distance learning strategy of the "Extended Campus," as it is called, centers on three major delivery systems: interactive video, Internet-based instruction, and telecourses. Interactive video is illustrated in BearNet, which reaches throughout the 24-county service area. It is able to link classrooms in West Plains or Lebanon with classroom sites in Springfield, other states, and international locations. SMSU Online provides Internet-based instruction

anytime, anyplace in the world. An asynchronous system, SMSU Online enables students to access their courses anytime and anyplace via the Internet. The system enables students to study and participate in discussions whenever and wherever they choose. SMSU Online also offers a "virtual high school" program called Missouri Virtual School. The program focuses on math, science and foreign languages.

The third major delivery system, telecourses, enables learners with the opportunity to take classes in their own homes, according to their own schedule.

While the Extended University is in its infancy as far as technology and services are concerned, the years ahead promise information delivery systems to sophisticate rapidly and enable bold new programs of outreach that would startle Dr. Craig. But the intent is the same — to provide educational opportunities to as many people as possible. In 1907, the numbers were dozens. At the turn of the 21st century, the numbers are thousands.

The University System

When Dr. John H. Keiser became president of the university in July 1993, it was apparent to him that the university, with its branch campus in West Plains and the Fruit Experiment Station in Mountain Grove, provided an opportunity to develop an integrated, multi-campus system that could deliver educational services in an efficient and systematic way. So he set as his goals, (1) to improve the focus of the university mission, (2) to increase standards for both teaching and learning, and (3) to operate in a systematic fashion.

What he saw was the possibility of Springfield becoming a truly selec-

Computer History at SMSU

1963 — First computer purchased and assigned to Enrollment Services Department.

1967 — Computer Center Department created with staff of five and $90,000 budget.

1971 — Gene Ellis hired to administer Computer Center. A 1401 punch system with manual processing in use.

1972 — First on-line system, IBM 360-25, purchased for academic use with a computer lab located on 4th floor of Carrington Hall.

1979 — On-line registration begins.

1984 — 4341 system installed. Computer Center employs 30 with $2 million budget. SMSU programmers and analysts write university's mission critical application systems.

1986 — 100 personal computers installed in Hammons House. An AT&T Information Systems Network (ISN) installed providing a campuswide data network. NOTIS, an automated library system, introduced to campus.

1991 — SMSU connected to the Internet via MOREnet. E-mail services made available to student population.

1997 — BearNet established, enabling distance learning initiatives.

1998 — Computer Services grows to 56 staff members and a budget more than $3 million.

2000 — First electronic imaging system comes on line. Y2K comes and goes without major incident.

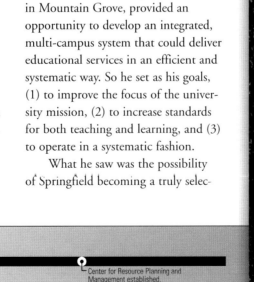

Graduate programs in education and business approved for offering in Joplin.

Center for Resource Planning and Management established.

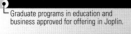
Dallas first broadcast on TV.

Betty Ford enters treatment hospital for addiction.

tive admissions campus with a growing graduate program. West Plains would be a two-year open-admissions campus and Mountain Grove could become a research campus. It was a bold vision, but he saw the system delivering education to both urban and rural environments with the opportunity for students in West Plains to migrate to Springfield when they had completed their associate degree.

Part of the plan for achieving systematic operation was to connect all three campuses electronically. So by 1994, Springfield and West Plains were connected with two-way interactive video using both voice and video transmission. This allowed an instructor in a Springfield classroom simultaneously to teach in both Springfield and West Plains, with students hearing and participating in discussion from both campuses. A challenge to the instructor, to be sure, but efficient and productive for the student.

Three other components of the system include the Baker Observatory in Webster County, the Graduate Residence Center in Joplin and the Bull Shoals Field Station.

Developments in West Plains, 1972-2002

Growth on the West Plains Campus was gradual. By 1972, the Residence Center was beginning its second decade with an enrollment of 243, more than twice the enrollment when it opened in 1963. By 1982, 564 students were taking courses. But by the turn of the century, the campus was brimming with more than 1,500 students.

Until 1973, the West Plains Campus operated on a year-to-year basis, depending on student fees, private gifts, and assistance from the West Plains School District and SMSU in Springfield. But on May 8, 1973, the Legislature acknowledged its obligation to support the Residence Center and appropriated $50,000 for operational expenses. That same year Ruth Kellett donated her four-story Gregorian style home to the Board of Regents "as part of the institution's Residence Center." The Kellett home was the first permanent facility for the campus. After renovation, the first classes were held in Kellett Hall in the spring of 1974. The new facility opened the possibility of scheduling classes during the day, rather than only in late afternoon and evening hours when classes were held in the local high school.

Clarity about funding the West Plains Campus came in 1975 when the Legislature designated the Residence Center as part of the university, and funds for its operation would be included in the university's budget on the same basis as the Springfield Campus. That freed the North Central Association to determine that West Plains should share any accreditation given at Springfield "since they are clearly an effective branch of that institution and operationally dependent upon it."

By 1977, the name West Plains Residence Center was dropped and the Regents declared the campus to be SMSU-West Plains. The Legislature gave its first capital appropriation to West Plains that year providing funds to asphalt a parking lot at Kellett Hall,

West Plains students gather in front their first campus building, Kellett Hall, in 1982. The West Plains enrollment that year was 564.

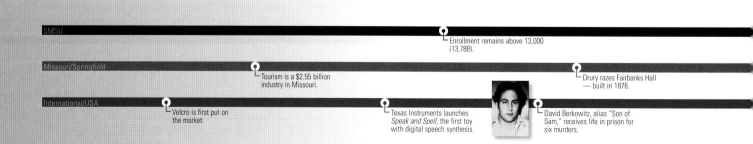

SMSU

Enrollment remains above 13,000 (13,788).

Missouri/Springfield

Tourism is a $2.55 billion industry in Missouri.

Drury razes Fairbanks Hall — built in 1876.

International/USA

Velcro is first put on the market.

Texas Instruments launches *Speak and Spell*, the first toy with digital speech synthesis.

David Berkowitz, alias "Son of Sam," receives life in prison for six murders.

The Lybyer Enhanced Technology Center brought new opportunities for students at the West Plains Campus. Featuring an open computer lab with 54 workstations and four computer classrooms with 24 student stations, the new facility provides state-of-the-art equipment for data processing. A CAD classroom and two distance learning classrooms enable participation in classes taught on the Springfield campus. The facility also houses the innovative Center for Business and Industry Training providing on-site training to area workforces.

insulate Kellett Annex and paint the exterior of the renovated home.

The funding question for the West Plains Campus was further clarified in 1981 when the Legislature passed a Permanent Status Bill stating, "The Board of Regents of Southwest Missouri State University is authorized to continue the program of higher education at West Plains, Missouri, which was begun in 1963 and which shall be known as the West Plains Campus of Southwest Missouri State University. Southwest Missouri State University may include appropriate requests for the branch facility at West Plains in its operating budget." The campus was no longer on a year-to-year basis.

With its status as a branch campus clarified, efforts began in earnest to develop facilities. In 1984, the Regents purchased the vacated Central Complex

from the West Plains School Board for $225,000, providing the campus with a three-story complex with classrooms, a gymnasium and an administration building. By this time the curriculum had increased to approximately 100 courses being offered each semester and students seeking degrees in 46 different academic areas. Accreditations came in 1985 with both the North Central providing joint accreditation through 1995 and the Missouri Board of Nursing granting full accreditation to the Associate Degree in Nursing with a five-year site approval. While the full-time faculty had increased by 225 percent since 1975, nearly half of the classes

Dean Marvin Green served as dean of the West Plains Campus from 1966-86.

were still taught by adjunct faculty.

Dean Marvin Green, who had administered the campus since 1966, retired as dean of West Plains in 1986. He continued teaching until 1997. Under his leadership, the West Plains Campus had gone from a dream in the eye of local supporters, fearful at the end of each year that the tenuous experiment might not survive to the next year, to an established branch of the university with more than 700 students studying their way into new possibilities. The campus covered 20 lots, 13 buildings and 18 full-time faculty. Dr. Richard Brauhn, vice president of Academic Affairs at Mount Marty College in Yankton, South Dakota, succeeded Dean Green and served as dean until 1990. On July 1 of that year, Dr. Marvin Looney began a seven-year period of leadership that saw the facilities of the campus improve remarkably.

In 1991, the first phase of the Garnett Library was completed. In 1994, the first Residence Hall was built on campus. In 1995, the Legislature approved a $2.8 million appropriation

Louise Brown, first so-called "test tube" baby conceived through in vitro fertilization process, born in England.

Tailgate parties begin before Bears' home football games.

John Paul I elected pope by College of Cardinals — dies 34 days later.

Camp David Accords signed by Egyptian President Anwar Sadat and Israeli Prime Minister Menachem Begin.

Looking Back

Second Class of Wall of Fame Inductees Selected

Eight former faculty and staff members were selected as the second class of inductees into SMSU's Wall of Fame, one of the highest honors a faculty or staff member can receive from the university. They are Edgar Albin, head of the Art Department from 1962 to 1974; Dr. Vincel Bixler, former head of the Finance and General Business Department who served on the faculty from 1963 to 1995; Maurice "Gene" Edwards who retired as Bursar and Secretary to the Board of Regents in 1990 completing 40 years of service; the late Judy Geisler, who served 15 years in both faculty and student affairs roles between 1973 and 1995; Dr. Roar Irgens an award winning teacher and microbiologist researcher who completed 25 years at SMSU in 1990; Mildred Wilcox who retired as secretary to Provost Robert Gilmore in 1979 and has continued to work part-time at the university since, stretching her service to over 40 years; Dr. Mary Jo Wynn, a 41-year stalwart who retired in 1998 as director of Women's Athletics; and Dr. Robert Martin, professor of chemistry and head of the Science Department who served the university for 41 years between 1921 and 1962.

to build a new classroom building, which the Board of Governors named Emory L. Melton Hall in honor of the state senator from Cassville who, over the years, supported the fledgling effort. In 1996, the Legislature again looked with favor upon the West Plains Campus providing $4.3 million for the construction of an Enhanced Technology Center, which was named for Senator Michael J. Lybyer of Huggins, Missouri.

Entering the 21st century, the West Plains Campus was outfitted with state-of-the-art facilities. It had also established a national reputation in community college sports. Its basketball team and volleyball team took the floor in 1993 and each ended the year with a winning season. Chelsea Taylor was an All-America Honorable Mention Volleyball player that first year. Just three years later the men's basketball team had players named to All-America teams, and the volleyball team broke into the Top 10 of the NJCAA national poll. Every year since 1997, Grizzly Volleyball players have been named to the All-America teams.

Academic excitement was building as well. In 1994, the North Central Association granted separate accreditation to the West Plains Campus, freeing it to develop its associate degree programs. In June of that year the nursing program was granted an additional eight-year accreditation and learned that its graduates had a pass rate of 93.7 percent on their Board exams, the highest in the nation.

So by the time President John H. Keiser viewed the SMSU landscape in the middle 1990s, he saw "system" possibilities inherent in what 30 years earlier was but a tenuous operation at best. A similar story of development was occurring in Mountain Grove.

Grapes have been an important part of the development of the Fruit Experiment Station in Mountain Grove since the 1930s. When the Station became part of the SMSU campus in 1974, grape research accelerated. In 1985, a major grant enabled the establishment of a viticulture and enology advisory program. Research opportunities at Mountain Grove now support a master's program in Plant Science. Its first graduate was Lilly Boppuri in 1998.

SMSU

Missouri/Springfield

International/USA

Susan B. Anthony dollar issued.

First game of Women's Pro Basketball (WBL) — Chicago Hustle vs. Milwakee Does.

The Experiment at Mountain Grove

By the end of the 19th century, the Ozarks had become a major fruit growing area in the United States. But fruit diseases were also becoming a major limiting factor in commercial production. The Missouri Legislature responded to the situation in 1899 by establishing the Fruit Experiment Station at Mountain Grove. Its mission was to "experiment with the different kinds of fruits, to wit: Apples, peaches, berries of all kinds, grapes and small fruits of all kinds, and to ascertain the varieties that are the best adapted to this state...."

J.T. Stinson was the first director and is credited with the saying, "An apple a day keeps the doctor away." During his two-year tenure, 265 varieties of apples, peaches, grapes and strawberries were planted on the 190-acre site. Stinson resigned in 1902 to become Superintendent of Horticulture at the World Exhibition in St. Louis. Experiments with fruit varieties resulted in advisory publications for growers throughout the state. By the 1920s, the peach industry had nearly disappeared in the Ozarks, but grape growing was increasing in popularity and profitability and Station Director Frederick Faurot accelerated research to support the grape industry. Over the next 20 years, new fruit varieties were developed including the Loring peach released to the public in 1946.

In 1974, under an omnibus reorganization plan for state government, the Fruit Experiment Station was assigned to Southwest Missouri State University. The Missouri fruit crop industry has continued to rely upon the research bulletins and industry advisory programs generated for more than a century. Current research, both basic

and applied, is focused on pomology, enology, viticulture, plant pathology, entomology, molecular genetics and plant physiology.

In 1994, the Fruit Experiment Station took on a new identity with an expanded mission. It became the Mountain Grove Campus of the university and home of the Department of Fruit Science. Two years later a master's degree in fruit science was offered through a collaborative program between the Agriculture, Biology, Chemistry and Fruit Science Departments.

In 1999, the Mid-America Viticulture and Enology Center was established on the Mountain Grove Campus. It is dedicated to improving product quality and profitability of the grape and wine industry through research, advisement, education and service. The Center's goals include the development of an interstate research consortium to better serve the industry throughout the Midwest.

Under the stimulus of becoming part of the SMSU system, Dr. James P. Baker was appointed Chancellor of the Mountain Grove Campus in October 1998. The campus also began developing multiple functions in addition to fruit development. Its advisory program for fruit producers is accomplished through traditional on-site advisory classes and workshops coupled with interactive video and Internet-based training through VineNet, a sub-network of the SMSU-Extended Campus BearNet. The Mountain Grove Campus also serves as an extended campus for SMSU-West Plains offering courses leading to the Associate of Arts in General Studies degree to residents in the Mountain Grove area.

Undergraduate and graduate courses originating in Springfield are also available on BearNet.

The Bull Shoals Field Station

The most recent addition to the campus system is the Bull Shoals Field Station, which provides a location for faculty, students and visiting scientists to conduct research and educational programs that promote the understanding of southwest Missouri ecosystems. The Field Station is sited on five acres of land owned by the Corps of Engineers, adjacent to Bull Shoals Lake. It has access to 5,600 acres of the Drury-Mince Wildlife area owned by the Missouri Department of Conservation. The Field Station opened in 1999 through a cooperative agreement between the university, the Corps of Engineers and the Missouri Department of Conservation. Research at the Field Station will provide answers to questions about organisms in their native habitats and solutions to problems resulting from rapidly changing environments in the Ozarks region.

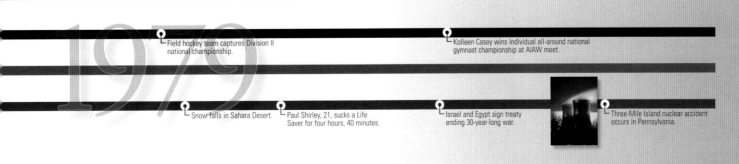

1979

Field hockey team captures Division II national championship.

Kolleen Casey wins individual all-around national gymnast championship at AIAW meet.

Snow falls in Sahara Desert.

Paul Shirley, 21, sucks a Life Saver for four hours, 40 minutes.

Israel and Egypt sign treaty ending 30-year-long war.

Three-Mile Island nuclear accident occurs in Pennsylvania.

The multiple campus system is administered by the SMSU System Coordinating Council composed of representatives from all campuses. The Council ensures that the campuses operate cooperatively, efficiently and economically.

What began in 1963 as a rather onerous burden in West Plains, whose survival remained a question for many years, has led to the development of a sophisticated system for delivering quality educational services to citizens of southwest Missouri in multiple locations. Opportunities are being seized and developed providing growing evidence of a maturing university.

Academic Development in the University Period

Soon after SMSU became a university in name as well as in fact, President Meyer appointed an 18-member academic planning commission "to prepare a broad academic master plan focused on a 10 year span." The president emphasized the priority of academics.

Music instructor Jeremy Chesman at the keyboard of the Jane A. Meyer Carillon. The instrument contains 48 bronze bells ranging in weight from 29.35 pounds to 5,894 pounds. The bells were manufactured by Royal Eijsbouts in Aston, Netherlands.

"Other kinds of planning will follow the development of our academic goals," the president said. "As a tax supported institution, we exist to serve the people, and this academic planning procedure is to determine what the people need."

Dr. James Pollard was selected to chair the commission. Thirteen faculty and staff, four students and an alumnus rounded out the blue-ribbon group. In September 1972 the commission held hearings in Lamar. Subsequent meetings were held in Springfield, West Plains, Monett, Neosho and Lebanon.

The benefits of planning became apparent by the middle 1970s when the university offered several new health programs including degrees in nursing, nurse anesthesia, radiologic technology and medical technology. Anticipating the emergence of the computer age, a major in computer science and data processing was added. When it was introduced, only three computer terminals were available to students. By 2002, it had become one of the most popular majors in the university, enrolling more than 1,000 students.

Such planning became crucial to the institution. It opened the door to curriculum expansion, the addition of new programs and increasing support from the Legislature. From 1984 through 1990 when the planning process bogged down, not a single new program was approved by the Coordinating Board for Higher Education (CBHE). Institutional planning got back on track in 1992 when Acting President Russell Keeling appointed a University Planning Advisory Council. With the arrival of Dr. John H. Keiser as president in 1993, the planning process accelerated

The Jane A. Meyer Carillon was dedicated on April 13, 2002. Jane Meyer served on the SMSU Foundation Board, the Music Department's advisory committee, the SMSU Athletics Advisory Board, the Fast Break Council for women's sports, and the Advisory Committee for the Juanita K. Hammons Hall for the Performing Arts. The idea for a carillon first emerged in the spring of 1999 when Wesley Wilson, Student Government Association president, suggested to President Keiser that a tower with a carillon would be a fitting way to celebrate the university's centennial. That same year the Board of Governors voted to make the stair tower in the new library into a tower for a carillon. In March 2000, the Kenneth E. and Jane A. Meyer Foundation donated the funds to purchase the 48 bronze carillon bells.

greatly. With institutional planning back on track, the door of opportunity opened. Between 1993 and the turn of the century, 37 new programs were approved by the CBHE, including 18 at the master's level.

Academic growth during the

SMSU

Dr. Ralph Williams named dean of the school of business.

Missouri/Springfield

Dewey Short named to Ozark Hall of Fame.

International/USA

Longest doubles table tennis match — lasted 101 hours.

Margaret Thatcher becomes first woman prime minister of England.

Elton John first pop star to perform in Israel.

268 *A Centennial History of SMSU*

university years can be seen through increases in academic departments from 23 in 1972 to 41 in 2002. At the beginning of the university era, 68 fields of study were available to students. In 2002, it had more than doubled to 140. The number of undergraduate courses had increased from 1,177 in 1972 to more than 1,800 in 2002. Graduate courses had increased nearly 10-fold, from 129 to 1,285.

This robust growth occurred despite the elimination of many programs beginning in the early 1980s. The entire array of two-year programs on the Springfield campus was eliminated by 1991 when Ozarks Technical Community College opened its doors to 1,179 students. The arrival of OTC enabled SMSU to focus its mission. The cooperative relationship between the two institutions proved to be a boon to higher education in southwest Missouri. In the fall of 2001, SMSU-Springfield and OTC had a combined headcount enrollment of 25,823. That represented an increase of 32.6 percent over 1990. Statewide headcount enrollment over the same period increased only 3.3 percent, indicating that public higher education opportunities in Springfield grew at 10 times the state rate.

Beginning in 1993, the academic planning process focused on five themes central to metropolitan life — professional education, health care, business and economic development, the performing arts and public affairs. In 2000, the university changed "performing arts" to "creative arts" and "health care" to "health," and also added "science and the environment" to the themes. That focused framework defined for the institution the direction of academic development into the 21st century.

Innovations in Academic Programs

About the same time university status was granted to SMSU, serious experimentation with teaching and learning was under way. Trying to cope with large enrollments, the Art, Religious Studies and Sociology Departments experimented with using multi-media instruction and classroom television to multiple class settings. The Economics Department began using a computer terminal for instructional purposes. Professors in the Political Science and Philosophy Departments were using the telelecture system to bring outside experts into the classroom.

In 1973, courses by newspaper were featured. The *Springfield News-Leader* ran articles in its Sunday paper as part of a course called "America and the Future of Man." It was a modest attempt at asynchronous teaching and learning. Only two contact sessions in a classroom were scheduled for those taking the course for credit.

As computers became more highly developed, a virtual avalanche of innovations in teaching and learning occurred. Computer labs proliferated over campus, and PowerPoint lectures characterized the classroom. Homework increasingly involved the Internet and class assignments and reports were transmitted by e-mail. By 1995, computer literacy became a general education requirement.

Cooperative Education Comes of Age

While cooperative education was not new, making its appearance at the University of Cincinnati in 1906, it didn't arrive at SMSU until 1980. Cooperative education integrates classroom studies with supervised work assignments in business, industrial, organizational and corporate settings. It gives students a "real world" experience and enables them to make good choices

Opportunities to work directly with patients and clients in many campus clinical settings have been a valuable asset to students. Here Tonya McKinney, a speech therapy major, works with a young client in the 1980s.

Enrollment exceeds 14,000 (14,891).

Three women's sports (volleyball, softball, gymnastics) move to Division I competition.

Gold hits record $303.85 an ounce in London.

Rainbow seen in Northern Wales for a three-hour duration.

Jerry Lewis' 14th Muscular Dystrophy Marathon raises $30 million.

Mother Teresa of India awarded Nobel Peace Prize.

1972-2005 Southwest Missouri State University   269

Jane A. Meyer Carillon

Dedicated in 2002, the 48 bells in the Jane A. Meyer Carillon were cast at Royal Eijsbouts in Asten, Netherlands. Covering four octaves, the largest bell measures 5 feet 1.5 inches in diameter and weighs 5,894 pounds. The smallest bell is 8 inches in diameter and weighs 29.5 pounds. The total bell weight of the Carillon is 32,660 pounds. The bronze bells contain a minimum of 20 percent tin, with the smaller bells having a larger (24 percent) amount of tin to increase their brilliance of tone. Each bell is inscribed with "Eijsbouts Astensis me Fecif anno MMI" (Eijsbouts at Asten made me in the year 2001.) The 10 largest bells also contain inscriptions requested by the donor. The Carillon is complete with a tower keyboard and an electronic keyboard located in Ellis Hall.

in career opportunities. The idea of "experiential education" has been around for a long time but it became increasingly relevant as students saw college education as career preparation.

A Title VIII grant written by Dean Ralph Williams of the College of Business Administration funded the beginnings of cooperative education at SMSU. That first year, 76 students from 17 different academic departments were placed in 44 organizations. The placements ranged broadly from marketing support assistant at IBM, soil conservation trainee for the U.S. Conservation Service, media intern at Dayco, marketing intern for the St. Louis Cardinals to legislative interns at the state capitol in Jefferson City.

Marketing major Darren Schilling worked in the Walt Disney World Fellowship Program, spending a full year at EPCOT Center. As a fellow in the program, Darren promoted cultural exchange. He shared an apartment with two other World Fellows, a Moroccan and a Japanese. According to Darren, exchanging ideas with his roommates and entertaining foreign dignitaries at EPCOT were "not-to-be-forgotten experiences."

Agriculture majors Sherri Hedgpeth and Emma Woods spent two co-op summers with the Raptor Rehabilitation and Propagation Project in St. Louis where they worked with injured birds, raised raptor chicks and toured with the project's show "Traveling Talons."

In the first 18 years, more than 6,000 students participated in cooperative education placements earning $30 million to assist with their college expenses and racking up 12,000 credit hours toward their graduation

requirements. The program became part of the Career Services office in 1998, and includes computer accessibility, allowing organizations to post their own internships and students to enroll themselves in co-op programs. By 2002, 2,500 students were participating in some kind of "experiential education" annually. Nearly 85 percent of graduating seniors now have work experience in their major area of study.

Citizenship and Service Learning

A unique variation on the "experiential learning" theme was added to the curriculum in 1996. Students were given the opportunity to apply their classroom learning in a not-for-profit setting. The Citizenship and Service Learning program provides students an additional hour of academic credit in exchange for 40 hours of volunteer work in a charitable agency. The public affairs theme incubated the idea with some outstanding results. Dr. Tim Knapp's social inequality class applied their classroom learning to problems of poverty in the community. In the process students learned first-hand what it meant to be "at risk" or "abused" in homeless shelters, soup kitchens and the Family Violence Center. Dr. Peter Sanderson's computer science class was introduced to the problems that organizations face in a highly technical world. They built databases and web sites for several not-for-profit organizations in the community. Tara Tyler worked with the Interagency Task Force on Gang and Youth Violence as the service-learning component of her crime and society course. She educated young people about the dangers of drug use, and their parents about peer pressures on Springfield youth.

SMSU

Missouri/Springfield

International/USA

Iranian students seize U.S. embassy in Teheran taking 63 U.S. citizens hostage.

Kramer vs. Kramer opens.

Eleven trampled to death in Cincinnati concert by The Who.

"Public affairs education is based on the belief that academic disciplinarians must consciously add 'citizen' to their designation. It is based on the belief that we can and must educate for what students are as well as for what they do…. We must consciously become 'citizen historians,' 'citizen biologists,' 'citizen nurses,' 'citizen teachers' and 'citizen computer scientists.'"

∽

President John H. Keiser
State of the University Address
January 11, 1996

Dr. Robert Norton's students created a television program called *Salsa* featuring authentic models of diversity, held interviews with Latinos from several South American countries and educated both Hispanic and American audiences about Hispanic culture. The program was the first regular Spanish-language program produced locally. It was targeted to upper-level Spanish students in area high schools and colleges.

More than 200 community partners have joined the Citizenship and Service Learning program, providing settings in which students practice both the skills and insights they are developing in the classroom as well as the virtues of citizenship as they contribute their time and expertise to public schools, the Red Cross, social service programs and other not-for-profit organizations. More than 80 courses on campus now have service learning components with nearly 200 students enrolled each semester

President Keiser describes the service learning program by recalling the African proverb, "When you pray, move your feet."

"To make a difference, an intellectual commitment or a strong belief requires action," observes Dr. Keiser. "The involvement that comes with service-learning is a major advantage to students who wish to see how their academic discipline can be applied."

Honors Program Renewed

While the number of superior students coming to the university in the 1980s was small relative to the total campus population of almost 20,000, it was sufficiently large to enable the honors program to be reconstituted after an absence of nearly 20 years. The new program, developed under the leadership of Dean Curtis Lawrence and approved by the Faculty Senate in 1985, received its first students in 1986.

The program provides high-achieving students the opportunity to pursue an enhanced, advanced course of study leading to special recognition at the time of graduation. In 1991, the program was strengthened and renamed Honors College. By the year 2000, 749 students were pursuing studies in the Honors College. Their average ACT score was 29, and their cumulative grade point average was 3.76.

Honors College graduates have majored in every department at the university. Many enroll in pre-professional programs and have gone on to graduate study at Harvard, Georgetown, Emory, Stanford, Washington University, Duke, Rice, Temple, University of Chicago and other elite institutions. Honors students have also won prestigious scholarships and fellowships from the National Science Foundation, the Department of Defense, Howard Hughes Medical Institute, Southern Medical Association and the Fulbright program.

In the fall of 1987, Honors House at 912 E. Elm was opened as a residence hall, accommodating 24 honors students. In the fall of 2000, a new Scholars House was opened at 1116 E. Cherry accommodating an additional 112 Honors College students.

Academic Majors Shift Toward Business

As the university era began in 1972, teacher education remained a primary focus. Forty-two percent of the graduates that year received B.S.Ed. degrees. However, almost one-fourth of the degrees that year were awarded to business majors, and by the end of the 1970s, business majors outnumbered education majors.

By the beginning of the 21st century, the College of Business Administration enrolled more than 4,000 students, almost twice as many as the College of Education. Not only was it

Ralph Abernathy speaks on campus.

General Assembly appropriates $2.4 million to remodel Memorial Library into a classroom facility.

Gold hits $1,000 an ounce.

Israel and Egypt exchange ambassadors for first time.

President Carter organizes 65-country boycott of Moscow Summer Olympic Games.

Post-it® Notes introduced.

THE LEGACY OF
DR. DUANE G. MEYER

by Donald R. Payton

D r. Duane G. Meyer — historian, author, humanitarian and academician — served on the SMSU faculty and staff 40 years, including 12 as president.

When the Board of Regents appointed him president in 1971, they selected an educator/administrator familiar with virtually all aspects of the institution. He joined the faculty as a history professor in 1955, played a key role in formulating the school's first Faculty Senate, served as academic dean under two presidents and had been acting president twice.

During the dozen years of his presidency, SMSU experienced a period of unparalleled growth, expansion and development. The steady enrollment growth provided an impetus that led inexorably to more classrooms, more faculty, more campus acreage and more academic programs. Library facilities grew commensurately, spurred by interest in business and technology. By the mid-1970s, as enrollments declined nationally, student numbers continued to grow at SMSU, topping 12,000 in 1975. During this eventful period the academic structure of the University evolved, with the establishment of schools (i.e., School of Business, School of Education, School of Arts and Humanities, and Graduate School); the graduate programs flourished, with courses for the most part, taught by professors, not graduate assistants; a key decision was made to expand evening classes, thus changing significantly the services provided to the City of Springfield and the surrounding area. In addition, work began on a $5.5 million recreation building (Hammons Student Center, which opened in 1976); a campus radio station (KSMU) began operation; federal funding provided a 34-acre SMSU urban renewal project; and a decision was made to retain Greenwood, the Laboratory School, which became the only on-campus training school in the state.

During the ensuing years of Dr. Meyer's presidency, enrollment continued to grow annually; new buildings were added and old buildings remodeled; size of the campus grew to 125 acres; research centers were added in archaeology, urban planning and economic research; construction started on a new library (which would later bear his name); the school's West Plains Campus was officially placed under authority of the university; SMSU athletics programs attained NCAA Division I status; and the SMSU Foundation, the fund-raising arm of the institution, was established. By the end of the 1970s enrollment was approaching 16,000 and still rising, enrollment in the School of Business topped 3,500, and a financial impact study revealed university-related spending contributed more than $147 million annually to the economy of Springfield and Greene County.

Dr. Meyer was a visible and highly respected spokesman for higher education, locally and throughout the state. He was president of the Missouri Intercollegiate Athletic Association, 1966-71; served on the Missouri Commission of Higher Education; and was president of the Missouri Council on Public Higher Education. His credibility with the State General Assembly and his peers throughout the state was widely recognized; and, prior to state reorganization, he played a key role in unifying the various sectors of higher education, which led directly to beneficial legislation, including university status for SMSU. The State Fruit Experiment Station was also assigned to SMSU when state government was reorganized.

A devout Presbyterian and Sunday school teacher, he maintained a calm and ever-patient demeanor when dealing with the institution's problems and diverse publics. Throughout his presidency he maintained cordial rapport with the Board of Regents, faculty, staff, students, media and the general public. Recognized for his wit and keen sense of humor, he enjoyed addressing civic clubs on such topics as *I Dreamt I Was Walking Down St. Louis Street in My Academic Regalia.*

A noted author as well as historian, he wrote *The Heritage of Missouri,* a popular textbook, and *The Highland Scots of North Carolina – 1732-1775.*

He retired from the SMSU presidency in June 1983, for reasons of health, and spent the last 12 years of his 40-year SMSU tenure in the classroom. He received the university's esteemed Bronze Bear Award in August 2000. ❖

the largest college in the university, it was the largest business program in the state and among the largest in the country.

Students have increasingly taken a practical attitude toward higher education. The job market has become a compelling reality as students take on considerable debt in the quest for a degree. It comes as no surprise that the department whose graduates command the highest beginning salaries, computer information systems, also enrolls the highest number of majors in the College of Business Administration.

But despite the popularity of business majors, there has also been a dramatic increase in the total number of majors from which current students can choose. More than 140 programs of study are offered in 82 different disciplines recognized in eight different bachelor's degrees at the undergraduate level. At the master's level, 39 disciplines offer programs. There are also pre-professional programs in dentistry, medicine, engineering, journalism, law and theology.

In addition to the numerous degrees offered, the university now also offers certificates to students who complete a core of prescribed courses designed to increase competency in a stated discipline area. Graduate Certificate Programs include instructional technology specialist, post-master's nurse educator, post-master's family nurse practitioner, sports management and project management.

At the spring 2002 graduation, President Keiser announced that a total of 77,881 baccalaureate degrees had been awarded since 1906, 9,270 master's degrees since 1968, and 666 specialist degrees since 1977 — an impressive measure of institutional performance.

Graduate Programs Multiply

The growth of graduate programs over the United States has been phenomenal. In 1900, only 1,583 master's degrees and 382 Ph.D. degrees were awarded throughout the entire nation. A century later the numbers had swelled to more than 410,000 master's degrees and 45,500 Ph.D. degrees awarded in 1999.

While graduate courses had been offered at SMSU since 1967, it was only in the spring of 1972 that the North Central Association granted the university full accreditation to offer graduate degrees. Five-hundred graduate students were enrolled in courses at that time, most part-time.

The majority of graduate students in the 1970s and 1980s were teachers in the public schools seeking master's degrees. In 1976, the specialist's degree was added to the graduate inventory to facilitate the development of school administrators.

It wasn't until the 1990s that graduate education became a priority for the institution. At the beginning of the decade, there were 19 graduate programs enrolling more than 1,500 students. By the end of the decade, the number of programs had more than doubled to 41. Enrollment had more than doubled to over 3,000, making graduate students almost 19 percent of the student body. SMSU had become the third largest provider of graduate education in the state, and the prospects for graduate education remain bright — 60 percent of the entering freshmen in 2001 indicated they planned on doing graduate study.

Many new graduate programs have been added in health care, articulating the work of the university with the regional health centers in Springfield. The establishment of the Ozarks Public Health Institute in 2001 further enhances this relationship.

Graduate student enrollments reflect the same sex ratio as the undergraduate figures — females predominate 64 percent to 36 percent. More than two-thirds of graduate students are part-time, and well over half are over the age of 30. Seven percent are international students.

Innovation remains a key component in developing graduate programs, particularly in those areas where students wish to do graduate work while they remain on the job. The Master of Science in Computer Information Systems illustrates the principle. It is essentially an on-line program enabling information technology workers to complete the program in just 23 months without interrupting their careers. The program gained national recognition for being one of the first accredited graduate programs designed exclusively for information technology professionals, combining classroom and distance learning. *The Philadelphia Enquirer*, reporting on the program said, "Harvard and Stanford observe: Southwest Missouri State University's on-line graduate program is on the cutting edge." Students from companies around the world including Allied Signal, AT&T, Caterpillar, DuPont, Federal Express, Microsoft, Pratt Whitney, United Technologies, and Wal-Mart have enrolled in the program.

Pioneering is going on in another area as well. The Communication Sciences and Disorders Department enrolled its first class into its doctorate in audiology program in August 2002. The program is the first free-standing

New Library and Hammons Fountains completed.

Forsythe Athletics Center opens.

Judge Russell Clark orders the desegregation of Missouri schools to alleviate the isolation of black students.

Mount St. Helens erupts, killing 34 in fires, mudslides and floods.

World Health Organization announces eradication of small pox.

Cable News Network (CNN) debuts.

Jean-Claude Droyer climbs Eiffel Tower in two hours, 18 minutes.

Endowed Chairs Established

Through the generosity of William G. and Retha Stone Baker, David D. Glass, and the Tom Strong family, four endowed chairs have been established at SMSU. The first chair was the Baker Chair of Insurance, established in 1982 in honor of Joseph Daniel Delp, first SMSU faculty member to teach business courses. Associate Professor John E. Patton holds that chair. The chair provides a salary supplement for the holder as well as scholarships for students.

In July 1998, the David D. Glass Distinguished Leadership Chair was established in the College of Business Administration. The chair is specified to be held by the dean of the College of Business Administration. Funds supporting the chair also provide faculty development grants, student leadership scholarships and supplemental funds for the maintenance of Glass Hall.

The Blanche Gorman Strong Chair of Protestant Studies was established in 2002. The chair is held in the Department of Religious Studies and honors the memory of Tom Strong's mother, a 1924 alumnus. The chair will enable the department to hire a specialist in Protestant Studies.

A fourth chair will be established by 2005, also funded by the $3 million Strong family gift. The Strong Chair in Public Affairs will reside in the College of Humanities and Public Affairs and will be used to attract an outstanding scholar in public affairs.

doctoral program offered by the university. Dr. Neal DiSarno, department head, explains, "With the increased technologies in cochlear implants, newborn hearing testing and balance rehabilitation and assessment, the ASHA truly believes that it is not possible to get all the information presented, synthesized and to be an adequately trained practitioner with two years of training." So all graduate audiologists are required to have doctoral-level training in the future. Again, the program is tied to health realities including longer life expectancy and universal newborn hearing screening mandated by the state.

Graduate education clearly appears to be the growth sector at SMSU for the years ahead. Not only do career expertise demands of most disciplines exceed what can be provided at the bachelor's level, but professional opportunities and earning capacity for people who hold graduate degrees, are improved as well.

Academic Structure Changes

In the beginning, things were simple. The summer session of 1906 was organized around two departments, the Normal department and the Sub-Normal or high school department. That was enough to get started. But by the fall session, six academic departments were operating — Pedagogy, English, Mathematics, History and Civics, Science, and Foreign Languages. Three years later a conservatory was added to the academic structure. By the end of the State Teachers College period in 1945, 13 academic departments were listed in the bulletin.

As the institution grew in enrollment and academic complexity, more

elaborate structures were created to organize and administer programs of study. A new layer of organization was put in place in 1968. Disciplines and departments were grouped into four divisions each presided over by a director. Dr. Robert Gilmore administered the Arts and Humanities Division. Dr. Imon Bartley headed the Graduate Division, while Dr. Carl Fronabarger and Dr. Patrick Copley headed the Science and Technology and the Teacher Education Divisions, respectively. These directors reported to the dean of faculties, a position created in 1961 and held by Dr. Duane Meyer.

At the beginning of the university period in 1972, the four divisions were renamed schools, and the School of Business was added. Another major academic reorganization occurred in 1985 when the division nomenclature was dropped and six separate colleges were set up, administered by deans. The adoption of the "college" terminology asserts that the institution is truly a multi-faceted university. Deans provide academic leadership, and throughout

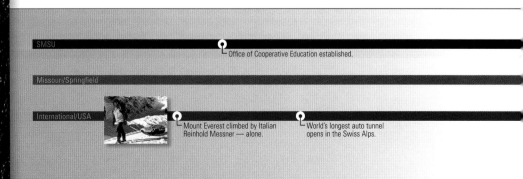

SMSU
Office of Cooperative Education established.

Missouri/Springfield

International/USA
Mount Everest climbed by Italian Reinhold Messner — alone.
World's longest auto tunnel opens in the Swiss Alps.

academia, the term implies a structure devoted to high standards of teaching and scholarship.

In 1994, another academic reorganization occurred increasing the number of colleges to eight. In 1995, a new wrinkle was added to the academic structure. The Department of Accounting was renamed the School of Accountancy. The enhancement provided by the new title was added to other departments and collections of departments early in the 21st century. The School of Teacher Education, the School of Communication Studies and the School of Agricultural Sciences brought added integration of discipline specialties and provided opportunity for synergistic effects as closely related departments worked together.

The vocabulary of academic organization itself is witness to a maturing institution. The term that described the entire institution in 1905, "school," now describes a combination of disciplines. In 1919, the institution was called a college; that term now describes nine separate units within the institution. Six departments provided the full academic offerings of the Normal School in 1906-07. By the time the institution entered the university era in 1972, it had 23 departments. By 2002, 44 separate academic departments organized into nine colleges presented the 140 programs of study offered by the university. The academic vocabulary and its accompanying numbers tell a story of rapid and compelling change.

Accreditations: The Mark of Academic Excellence

As higher education has grown and institutions have multiplied into the thousands, the issue of quality

has become increasingly important. Accreditation has become a device for quality assurance at both the program and institutional level. SMSU received its first quality endorsement through accreditation in 1927 when it was among a select group of Teachers Colleges that were admitted into full standing by the North Central Association.

Over the years, institutional accreditation became supplemented by program accreditation which identified academic excellence within a disciplinary or program area. By 1985, in addition to institutional accreditation through North Central, programs in teacher education, music, nursing, chemistry and social work were all individually accredited by national agencies. As the university entered the 21st century, 21 specialized accrediting agencies had placed their quality stamp of approval on no less than 57 different programs at SMSU.

Some surprising things can happen on the way to accreditation. In 1991-92, the Missouri Department of Elementary and Secondary Education (DESE) came to the university to evaluate and accredit its 52 separate teacher education programs. After a four-day site visit by a team of 18 evaluators from DESE, the university was awarded eight No. 1 ratings, the highest number awarded to any institution to date by DESE. The previous record high No. 1 ratings was three. In addition to the eight outstanding programs, the accreditation team identified three additional programs as "exemplary," providing models for the rest of the teacher education programs in Missouri.

Four years later, the College of Education stood for evaluation and reaccreditation by the National Council for the Accreditation of Teacher Education (NCATE), which had put its seal of approval for quality on SMSU teacher education programs for many years. To the shock and surprise of everyone, when the site visit was

Internships have played an important role in introducing students to the world of work. Steve Settles was a graduate student intern with the National Geographic Society in 1985.

Enrollment exceeds 15,000 (15,845).

Burlington Northern acquires Frisco railroad.

Cosmonauts Popov and Ryumin set space endurance record — 184 days.

Ronald Reagan elected President of the U.S.

Congress establishes "Superfund" to clean up hazardous waste sites.

1972-2005 Southwest Missouri State University   275

By the 1970s the infamous Junior English Exam was taking its toll on aspiring college graduates.

"I was on my way to success... Then I failed the J.E.E."

completed, NCATE announced that it would not reaccredit the SMSU program. It cited three problems: (1) lack of diversity in recruiting both students and faculty; (2) lack of adequate communication with program graduates; and (3) inadequately organized professional education unit within the university.

The university appealed its case to NCATE and lost. To lose NCATE accreditation would not affect any student's certification to teach in Missouri; the DESE accreditation just four years earlier guaranteed continuing certification. But the loss of NCATE was a stinging blow since it was the premier national accrediting body that identified the best from the rest. It threatened to be a public relations disaster. But the university mobilized itself to address the problems. Four years later, in 1999, NCATE revisited the campus and found the problems corrected.

Reaccreditation by NCATE was given unconditionally, and the university took deserved pride in meeting the challenges of an elite national agency.

As the College of Business Administration grew rapidly in the 1980s, it set its sights on being among the premier business schools in the country. To achieve that, it would have to be accredited by the American Assembly of Collegiate Schools of Business. The AACSB accredits only about 20 percent of the 1,200 business schools in the country, including Harvard, Stanford, MIT and the Wharton School of Business at the University of Pennsylvania. To achieve that lofty goal amounted to an enormous challenge not only to the College of Business Administration, but also to the entire campus.

AACSB standards included evidence of substantive research by the faculty attesting to their competence and ability to advance the frontiers of business research. While there were some College of Business Administration faculty who were doing research and publishing in respectable journals, most were under the crush of heavy teaching loads. Every year the

enrollments increased and the teaching burden became heavier, leaving little time for research. It became clear very quickly that senior people with strong research credentials would have to be hired in order to meet accreditation standards. The market for such people in the 1980s was very tight. Faculty with demonstrated research skills could command salaries twice what was currently being paid at SMSU. Moreover, they could negotiate half the teaching load that existing faculty enjoyed. Clearly, to enter the elite market would be costly and would take time.

Gearing up for AACSB accreditation took nearly a decade. The coveted award was announced on April 15, 1992, and included undergraduate and graduate programs in the College of Business Administration as well as the undergraduate and graduate programs in accounting. Accreditation meant that the business program had met national standards in such areas as faculty resources and qualifications, student abilities, intellectual climate, admission policies, degree requirements, library resources, computer facilities and financial resources. "Graduation from an AACSB-accredited institution is highly regarded by employers and graduate schools," declared Dean Ron Bottin. "Some employers restrict their recruiting efforts to AACSB-accredited schools."

The benefit to students and the reputation of the institution is unquestioned. But the cost to achieve and sustain the accreditation has been a sore point with some faculty in other departments across campus whose operations are not as generously funded. The accreditation process convinced everyone that market principles oper-

SMSU
— Dr. Leslie Irene Coger retires from Speech and Theatre Department.
— SMSU Foundation established.

Missouri/Springfield
— Car wash explosion kills two, injures 15 in Springfield.

International/USA
— Dynasty and Hill Street Blues premiere on TV.
— Jean Harris convicted of killing Scarsdale Diet doctor, Tarnower.
— Walter Cronkite signs off as anchorman of CBS Evening News.
— John Hinckley attempts to assassinate President Reagan.

ate in the academic world as they do elsewhere. An unspoken tradition over scores of previous years suggested that a doctorate in physics was of equal value to a doctorate in marketing or accounting. And a doctorate in economics or sociology was of equal value to the one in physics. But during the 1980s when the School of Business Administration was having to "buy" its research credentials, often at twice the salary of other disciplines, the solidarity once characteristic of faculty collapsed. Innocence had been banished and the vagaries of the academic marketplace took up residence on campus. Morale in non-business disciplines continued to suffer as resentment of those who perceived themselves as underpaid lingered.

Junior English Exam Dropped

Ask any student in the 1960s and early 1970s what they despised most in their

academic program at SMSU and the reply would probably be, "the Junior English Exam." University *Bulletins* in the 1950s declared that proficiency in English was a graduation requirement, but apparently at that time it was assumed that the proficiency required would be achieved in the required freshmen composition courses. By the early 1960s, an anomaly was being observed. Students who passed freshmen composition often proved unable to write comprehensible papers and exams in upper division courses in all disciplines across campus.

The Faculty Senate proposed a cure. Passing a written English proficiency exam during the junior year would be required for graduation. The exam would have to be passed before the students could register for their 60th hour of academic credit. So beginning in the fall of 1963, the Junior

During the summer of 1979, 23 students in the Industrial Education Department built a full-size two-seater experimental aircraft modeled after the 1948 Piper Vagabond. Built in 20 days under the leadership of Bill Ghan (right), an industrial education teacher at Mansfield High School, the "Wag-a-Bond," as it was called, was assembled for Tom O'Loughlin (left) from Jackson, Missouri, who invested $12,000 in the craft. The workshop, the first of its kind at SMSU, was coordinated by Dr. Houston Taylor (center).

College of Business Administration Creates International Linkages

Students and faculty from the College of Business Administration have two additional linkages with the global community as of September 2002. The Board of Governors approved an agreement setting up exchanges between the Universidad de Las Americas in Santiago, Chile, and IBMEC in Rio de Janeiro, Brazil. This brings the total number of exchange agreements between COBA and international institutions to 11. Nine previous agreements have been signed with universities in France, Germany, Belgium, The Netherlands and Finland. The exchange programs develop student's linguistic skills and their international competency. More than 80 SMSU students have already studied in Europe, and 70 European students have studied at SMSU.

All SMS athletics teams join Division I competition.

Raiders of the Lost Ark premieres.

English Exam became a particularly stubborn hurdle for students to clear.

The exam was unpopular with those who constructed it, those who took it, and those who graded it. Students disparaged it for a decade, complaining that the topics chosen were dumb and the grading unfair. How many students were kept from graduating because of not passing the exam is unknown, but finally in 1974, the Faculty Senate, at the request of the Student Government Association, passed a resolution abolishing the exam. President Meyer signed the resolution, probably with a sigh of relief. Dr. George Gleason of the English Department said, "It will be much easier for the English Department if we don't have to fool around with this kind of thing!"

However, the problems the Junior English Exam sought to solve remain unsolved, according to most faculty. Students are still passing English com-position courses but failing to write proficient papers and exam essays. But instead of a coercive exam to screen out failures, today there is a Writing Center to assist students in developing compositional skills.

Reforming General Education

One wit has said that reforming the curriculum is about as easy as moving a cemetery. The history of the general education curriculum at the university would support that notion. The idea that a student ought to have a broadly based education at the undergraduate level has been agreed upon in principle for a century. How to achieve that when the student's primary interest lies in his field of major study has challenged faculty for decades. One solution has been the creation of a general education requirement that mandates exposure to a variety of disciplines. Students at SMSU have dealt with that reality for more than a half-century.

But the philosophy undergirding general education continues to be debated, and university faculties continue to struggle with the question of what a sound general education requirement should look like. During the university period, several attempts to reform general education were attempted with only modest success. Turf-battles over courses to be included in a program always led to political alliances that protected departmental interests.

But in 1993, with the encouragement of President John H. Keiser, the Faculty Senate organized itself to develop a more efficient and coherent general education program. Concurrent with the effort in the Faculty Senate, President Keiser sought to achieve a statewide mission in public affairs for the university. The coupling of the General Education Program with the public affairs mission follows a pattern that goes back almost a half-century to the Harvard University *Redbook* study, which concluded that the function of general education "was to prepare students for the duties of citizenship in the modern world."

The university's new public affairs mission approved in 1995 provided general education reform with a substantive challenge. The new program would need to integrate the more traditional general education goals of numeracy, literacy and critical thinking with those inherent in the new public affairs mission. The student would not only be equipped with the basic skills, but the program would assist in producing "citizens of enhanced character, more sensitive to the needs of community, more competent and committed in their ability to contribute to

In the 1980s students in Human Anatomy Lab became familiar with cats as they mastered the principles of vertebrate anatomy. Today, human cadavers greet the anatomy students.

SMSU

Missouri/Springfield

International/USA

Grand Street underpass opens.

Prince Charles of England marries Lady Diana Spencer.

IBM personal computer introduced.

278 *A Centennial History of SMSU*

society and more civil in their habits of thought, speech, and action."

The committee struggled mightily with its assignment and ultimately provided a coherent framework on which to hang the details of general education. The achievements included: (1) reducing course options from more than 350 to less than 100; (2) articulating a more precise and clearly defined set of goals; (3) creating a more prescriptive organization of the general education categories; and (4) providing for a junior level capstone course linked explicitly with the university's public affairs mission.

The capstone course is clearly the most radical reform of the program and the most challenging to implement. A student must have completed 60 hours before taking the capstone course. A variable topics course, the capstone provides an integrative and interdisciplinary experience that addresses public affairs issues and choices of broad importance from the perspective and interaction of multiple fields. Each capstone course is developed by two or more professors from different disciplines. Examples of current capstone courses include: "Animal Rights Movement and the Social Construction of Reality," taught by a sociologist and a veterinarian; "The Cold War and Its End in Theory and Practice," taught by a sociologist and a defense and strategic studies professor; "Education and the Seduction of Modern Culture," taught by education professors from early childhood and secondary settings; and "The Legacy of Prometheus: Exploring the Interface of Science and Culture," taught by a physicist and a foreign language professor.

In addition to providing an opportunity for the student to explore an

Dr. John Northrip explains the intricacies of the atom to his physics class in the 1980s.

important public issue in depth, the course also integrates all the earlier general education courses by requiring the student to demonstrate creativity; the ability to reason, to analyze materials not keyed specifically to their academic major; and to synthesize diverse viewpoints. The course serves to remind students that as they function in an occupational role, they retain their responsibilities as citizens to promote the general interests of the community

The capstone course is in its early years, but initial reports indicate that it provides an excellent opportunity to confront students with policy issues that have wide-ranging effects in everyday life. To reflect on such issues is part of the task of an educated person and an obligation of a responsible citizen.

A second innovation in the General Education Program reform was the development of the Introduction to University Life course. Piloted in the fall of 1994, the course focused on increasing retention rates and helping freshmen maximize their potential to succeed in college. Early data suggested both goals were being met, and the course was added to the General Education Program by the Faculty Senate in 1995. A unique feature of IDS 110 is the peer leadership component. Selected sophomores, juniors, and seniors serve as liaisons to the instructors of IDS 110. They facilitate class discussions, provide resource information, and serve as role models for appropriate academic, personal and leadership behaviors. Dr. Mona Casady played the leading role in developing the course and monitoring its development. Staff members, as well as faculty, volunteered to have IDS 110 added to their regular teaching load.

The Mystery of Grade Inflation
It wasn't until 1940 that any SMSU student graduated from the institution with a perfect "A" or 4.0 grade

Center for Business and Economic Development established in School of Business.

Sandra Day O'Connor becomes first female to be named to the U.S. Supreme Court.

U.S. national debt tops $1 trillion.

Muhammad Ali's 61st, and last, fight.

Scientists identify acquired immune deficiency syndrome (AIDS), a previously unknown disease.

Graduate Program Growth

Between 1995 and 2002, SMSU has added 23 new graduate programs, many in health care to support the health care industry and health needs in southwest Missouri. Included in the 23 new programs is a cooperative doctorate in education with the University of Missouri, and SMSU's first stand-alone doctorate — a professional doctorate in audiology. Between 1989 and 2002, graduate enrollment has grown from 1,390 to 3,270, placing SMSU third behind the University of Missouri-Columbia and the University of Missouri-Kansas City in number of graduate students.

~

Reaching Out

SMSU is one of only two campuses in the state that has students from every county in Missouri. Students from 45 other states and 91 foreign countries are among the 20,000 plus students enrolled in credit courses. Additionally, 10,000 enrollments are expected in various continuing education and professional development program courses during the 2002-03 year. Some 48,000 children ages 2-11 are reached each week through programming on the university's public television station KOZK/KOZJ.

point average. The first to do so was Dorothy Martin Simon, daughter of Science Department Head Dr. Robert W. Martin. Twenty-four more years elapsed before a second student achieved that perfect record. In 1964 Lyna Lee Montgomery entered the elite circle. The current records system does not enable identifying a graduate's GPA between 1965 and 1978. However in 1979, six of the 1,657 graduates had straight "A's" and there has not been a year since 1979 when there weren't several 4.0 graduating seniors. In 1979, less than 1 percent (.36) of the graduates had only "A's" on their record, but by 1998, 45 graduated with that distinction, representing more than 2 percent of the class.

The phenomenon is commonly called "grade inflation." It is a nationwide occurrence. It caught the attention of the Faculty Senate at SMSU in

Brother Tobias, a Trappist Monk from Assumption Abbey near Ava, Missouri, provided insight into world religions in his visit to campus in October 1979.

Dr. Paul Redfearn, professor of biology, received the first National Science Foundation grant for the university in 1959. His study, "Mosses in the Interior Highlands of North America," led to a major publication in the *Annals of The Missouri Botanical Gardens*. Redfearn's career at the university spanned 31 years during which time he also served as a Springfield city councilman and mayor.

1976. A Senate Committee reported 15 factors associated with the worrisome trend. In that decade alone, the percentage of "A" grades rose 6.6 percent. "C" grades dropped 6.3 percent. In 1970, the business school gave "A's" to 11.5 percent of their students; a decade later, the number nearly doubled to 22.3 percent. Education and psychology gave 28.2 percent "A's" in 1970; at the end of the decade they were giving 37.8 percent of their students "A" grades.

What makes the whole process mysterious is that during the time students were earning better grades in their university courses, their performance on ACT and SAT college entrance exams was declining.

There seems to be no end in sight. In the 20 years between 1982 and 2001 the average GPA for graduating seniors has risen from 2.92 to 3.14. The spring 2002 graduating class had a GPA aver-

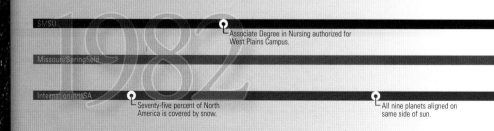

SMSU — Associate Degree in Nursing authorized for West Plains Campus.

Missouri/Springfield

1982

International/USA — Seventy-five percent of North America is covered by snow.

— All nine planets aligned on same side of sun.

age of 3.18. A full 34 percent of the class graduated "with honors"; in 1984, only 16 percent gained that distinction. Linda Johnson, degree analyst in the Degree Check Office wonders where it will all end. "I fear that the average GPA may overtake the minimum GPA for honors!" she said.

Faculty

As the university period opened in 1972, the institution lost several of its key links to the past. President Roy Ellis, whose association with the school went back to 1909, died on January 9, 1972, at 83 years of age. Doyle Kemper, industrial education pioneer, died a month later at age 66. And the venerable Dean Bertha Wells died on April 1, 1972. None of those pioneers witnessed the transition of SMSU to a state university. But Dr. Virginia Craig, at 94, joined in the celebration of the new status in the summer of 1972. She was associated with the institution over its entire life and she had witnessed four different names, State Normal School #4, Southwest Missouri State Teachers College, Southwest Missouri State College and Southwest Missouri State University marking the path of institutional development. She died in March 1976.

Faculty Growth

By the beginning of the university period, SMSU employed more than 400 faculty, making it increasingly difficult to connect with colleagues across campus. Friendships and associations were increasingly formed within departments and schools, as opposed to earlier years when one could expect to know people from many different disciplines. Commencement time broke

Underground instruction for speleology students at Tumbling Creek Cave was provided by Tom Aley, a water specialist and owner of Ozark Underground Laboratory.

the solidarity of departmental ties as the faculty procession was organized by seniority, arranging participants by the year of their hire. Ultimately, that tradition was abandoned as unworkable as faculty numbers continued to grow.

By fall 2001, SMSU employed 719 full time faculty, two-thirds of whom were tenured. As has been the case over several decades, female faculty are underrepresented in the mix, constituting only 37 percent of the tenure-track staff in 2002.

During the 1970s, faculty salaries were a perennial concern. While average nine-month faculty salaries increased from $10,556 to $18,624 over the decade, there was actually a net loss in purchasing power. The Consumer Price Index for that same period increased 95.4 percent while salaries increased only 76.3 percent. In real dollars, full professors experienced a 15.6 percent loss of purchasing power

over the decade. Associate professors saw a 17.5 percent decline.

By the early 1980s, concern over the salary issues stirred faculty to talk about creating a collective bargaining unit on campus to negotiate salary matters. In February 1983, about 25 percent of the faculty signed a petition urging the establishment of union representation. While the state constitution forbade state employees from striking, some faculty felt that the American Federation of Teachers could effectively represent their interests in salary matters. The compensation issue was felt by all faculty, but there was less consensus about how to deal with it. Many faculty were reluctant to go the union route, despite the growing popularity of faculty unions at the time.

President Gordon was faced with the problem immediately upon his assuming office in 1983. Not only was there concern about salaries in

Ozarks Labor Union Archives established.

Missouri London Program opens.

Dr. Michall E. DeBakey performs first successful heart transplant.

Surfer Colin Wilson rides surfboard for 2.94 miles.

ET: The Extra Terrestrial released.

Coca-Cola launches Diet Coke.

1972-2005 Southwest Missouri State University   281

general, there were also salary dispari-
ties between male and female faculty.
Female full professors in 1984 were
earning, on average, $609 less than
their male counterparts. A faculty task
force on gender-related issues reported
in November 1985 that female faculty
earned $768 less than male faculty with
the same rank, degree, education and
experience.

Beginning in the fall of 1984, the
Board voted a 10 percent increase in
faculty salaries, which encouraged the
instructional staff. The whole issue of
faculty rewards became a high-profile
matter during the 1980s. A merit program was introduced that resulted in
differential increases in pay for faculty
based on performance. The program
created enough unhappiness among
most faculty that its differentiating
qualities declined toward the end of
the 1980s. Faculty merit evaluations
increasingly aggregated at the higher
levels. By the early 1990s, the system
was virtually bankrupt
since the universi-
ty had not given
merit increases
for several
years.

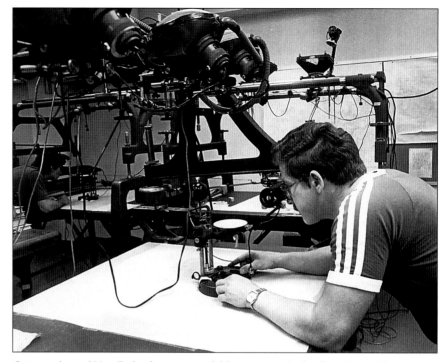

Cartography and Map Technology was available as a major in the Geosciences Department
in the middle 1970s. Dr. Vincent Kurtz headed the program, which provided students such
as Ed Whitmore (above) with opportunities to practice the science of map making in the
cartography lab.

Faculty Awards

While difficulties with keeping salaries
abreast of inflationary trends continued,
the 1980s did see a significant increase
in faculty recognition and rewards.
In 1983-84, the SMSU Foundation
awarded its first Excellence in Teaching
Awards to Dr. Alice Bartee, Dr. James
Layton, Dr. Rhonda Ridinger and Mr.
John Schatz. Since that time more
than 50 faculty have been honored
with the award. The following year,
1984-85, Burlington Northern established a Faculty Achievement Award

for Teaching Excellence, which was
won by Dr. James Moyer, and a Faculty
Achievement Award for Outstanding
Scholarship was won by Dr. Dominic
Capeci. Fifteen Burlington Northern
Faculty Achievement Awards were
granted between 1984-93.

Giving evidence to the growing
scholarly and research accomplishments
of the faculty, the SMSU Foundation
established an Excellence in Research
Award in 1986 and honored Dr. Jim
Giglio, Dr. Harry Hom and Dr. Juris
Zarins in its first year. Thirty-two
faculty have received the Foundation's
Excellence in Research Award.

A new Distinguished Scholars
Award was added to the list of honors
and recognition in 1987. It recognizes
exceptional scholarly achievement and

Dr. Andrew Lewis of the History Department was awarded
a prestigious McArthur Foundation Fellowship grant in
1984, the first ever awarded to an SMSU faculty member. The grant, in excess of $200,000, supported
Lewis' research into French medieval history.

SMSU

SMSU official flag adopted by
Board of Regents.

Missouri/Springfield

International/USA

TYLENOL

Seven Americans die when cyanide is
placed in bottles of Tylenol leading to the
introduction of tamper-proof packaging.

EPCOT Center opens in Orlando, Florida.

Internationally acclaimed artist Zhi Lin of the SMSU Art Department worked in 2000 on one of his monumental 12x7 paintings in the series "Five Capital Executions in China." The uprising at Tiananmen Square in 1989 convinced Lin that art must be more than beautiful. It had to speak to reality. These five epic paintings, under way since 1992, picture the centuries-old practice of public execution in his homeland. Calling attention to the horrific as well as the "civilized" spectacle of death by starvation, flaying, decapitation, firing squad, and drawing and quartering, Lin evokes reflection on the "taken-for-grantedness" public executions and other forms of inhumanity.

faculty have carried the distinction of Distinguished Scholar.

In 1990-91 the SMSU Foundation established the Faculty Achievement Award for Outstanding Scholarship, granting the first award to Dr. Patrick Sullivan. Five additional awards have been made.

With the university's statewide mission in public affairs came a new award in 1994-95 honoring both faculty and staff, the Excellence in Community Service Awards, also funded by the SMSU Foundation. The first staff persons honored with the award were Mike Jungers in Student Life and Development, and Patsy D. Corbett, Center for Archaeological Research. Dr. Doris Ewing of the Sociology and Anthropology Department and Dr. Peggy Pearl of the Child Development Center received the first faculty awards.

Two new recognitions have been added to the list of distinguished awards. In 1998, the Distinguished Professor award was established, creating an ongoing faculty rank beyond professor, to recognize extraordinary accomplishment. A Distinguished Professor designation is available annually if there is a candidate worthy. To date, Dr. Dominic Capeci, Dr. James Giglio, Dr. Charles Hedrick, Dr. Paula M. Kemp and Dr. James O'Brien hold the distinction. The second award is University Fellow. It provides a reduced teaching load for three years enabling holders of the status to further their work in teaching, research or service. The initial awards went to Dr. Jan Squires in teaching; Dr. James Giglio, Dr. Dennis Hickey, and Dr. Victor Matthews in research; and Dr. Rhonda Ridinger in service.

The current array of awards and

grants the faculty member a reduced teaching load to continue their scholarly pursuits. The first recipient of this award was Dr. Dominic Capeci. Dr. Capeci was honored with the award again in 1991-92. Fourteen other

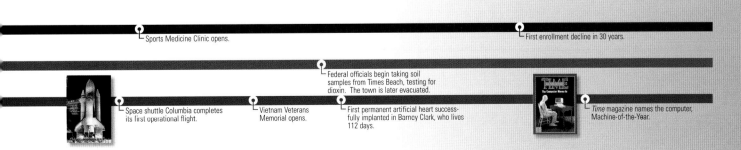

Sports Medicine Clinic opens.

First enrollment decline in 30 years.

Federal officials begin taking soil samples from Times Beach, testing for dioxin. The town is later evacuated.

Space shuttle Columbia completes its first operational flight.

Vietnam Veterans Memorial opens.

First permanent artificial heart successfully implanted in Barney Clark, who lives 112 days.

Time magazine names the computer, Machine-of-the-Year.

Three Faculty Inventions Patented

"We see this as a transition in university life," declared Dr. Frank Einhellig, dean of the Graduate College. The event was the announcement in January 2003 that the university holds three patents for inventions developed by its faculty. Dr. Ryan Giedd of the Physics and Astronomy Department developed a microsensor capable of detecting harmful chemicals or biological elements in the air or water supply. Dr. Reza Sedaghat-Herati of the Chemistry Department developed a process known as PE-Gylation that allows more efficient delivery of compounds to human cells and plants. Commercial applications can be made in the chemical and pharmaceutical industries. A faculty team of Drs. Klass Bakker, Richard Biagioni, Mary Byrne, Thomas Byrne and Ron Netsall developed a device and method for sensing and assessing abdominal and thoracic breathing behaviors of patients with speech-motor impairments, hearing impairments, and persons with voice or speech fluency difficulties.

recognitions for outstanding faculty and staff cover three pages in the current *Undergraduate Catalog*. Nearly 250 persons are identified there as distinguished achievers.

Selected Evidences of Excellence

The growing excellence of the university's faculty drew attention from prestigious national sources as well. In 1984, the McArthur Foundation awarded a $204,000 fellowship to Dr. Andrew Lewis of the History Department to support his work in French medieval history. Lewis also won the John Nicholas Brown prize from the Medieval Academy of America.

Dr. Juris Zarins's discovery of the lost city of Ubar in Oman in December 1991 was listed by *Time* magazine as No. 3 in the top 10 scientific discoveries of 1992. *Discover* magazine listed Zarins's TransArabia expedition as one of the top 50 stories in 1992. The *New York Times*, the Cable News Network,

Associated Press, network television stations and nearly every major newspaper carried the story. Ubar was the financial center of the lucrative frankincense trade as early as 3500 B.C. Ubar's wealth prompted T.E. Lawrence (Lawrence of Arabia) to call the city "The Atlantis of the Sands." Lawrence and his colleague Bertram Thomas searched unsuccessfully for Ubar earlier in the century.

In 1997, Dr. Ron Netsall, professor of communication sciences and disorders, was granted the highest award attainable in his field by the American Speech Language Hearing Association — the Honors of the Association award. The distinction recognizes Netsall's scholarly achievements over a lifetime. In the 53-year history of the award, only 108 persons have received it. Netsall's work has centered on neurological speech disorders. The body of his work "has forever altered the course of clinical diagnosis and treatment of

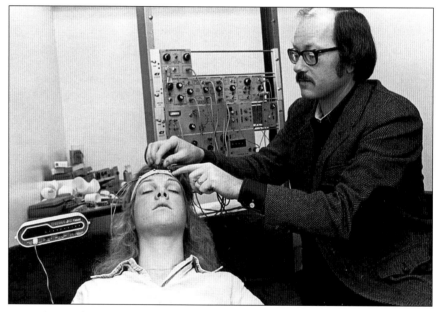

Dr. Fred Maxwell works with student Janice Davenport in the bio-feedback lab in the Psychology Department in 1980.

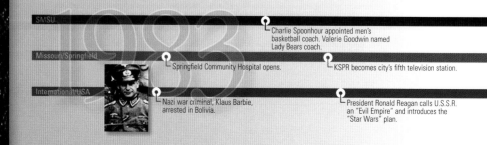

SMSU

Charlie Spoonhour appointed men's basketball coach. Valerie Goodwin named Lady Bears coach.

Missouri/Springfield

Springfield Community Hospital opens.

KSPR becomes city's fifth television station.

International/USA

Nazi war criminal, Klaus Barbie, arrested in Bolivia.

President Ronald Reagan calls U.S.S.R. an "Evil Empire" and introduces the "Star Wars" plan.

neurogenic speech disorders," according to Dr. Fred Minifie from the University of Washington.

Research traditions have been established in the arts and letters as well. Dr. Ed Carawan of the Modern and Classical Languages Department has been doing extensive work on Athenian legal procedures. His work promises to chart a new approach to the entire field. A departmental colleague, Dr. Carol Anne Costabile-Heming, is breaking new ground in understanding the impact of German reunification on literature and film.

Professor John Prescott of the Music Department has established a national reputation in composition. His *Prelude and Toccata* was performed in 1990 by the United States Army Band in a concert on the steps of the U.S. capitol.

Professor Tita Baumlin of the English Department has served as editor of the internationally acclaimed scholarly journal *Explorations in Renaissance Culture* since 1994. Her colleagues in the English Department publish, on average, 20 books every three years. A colleague, Dr. Michael Ellis, is doing pioneering work in preparing electronic glossaries. He created the *Glossary for the Electronic Beowulf*, the first such scholarly effort of its kind. It contains 3,000 entries and 5,000 hyperlinks, a massive resource for researchers.

Dr. Charles Hedrick of the Religious Studies Department has been working with a vanguard group of international scholars researching the Jesus tradition. In addition to publishing *The Gospel of the Savior*, a new gospel manuscript in Coptic dating back to the second century, Hedrick also has published a challenging new

In the spring of 1981, five students accompanied Dr. Juris Zarins to Arabia where they documented artifacts collected at Taima and Nejran, ancient cities excavated from beneath desert sands. From left, Majid Khan, Zarins and Larry Ayres are shown tracing ancient drawings from a desert cliff.

title, *Parables as Poetic Fictions: The Creative Voice of Jesus.* The book raises significant issues for the study of gospel parables.

Zhi Lin, professor of art, won the prestigious Lila Wallace-Reader's Digest Artist-at-Giverny award, allow-

ing him to paint for three months in 1998 in the studios of Claude Monet, founding father of Impressionism, in Giverny, France. Lin lived and worked in the Monet estate painting landscapes inspired by the unique scenery of Giverny and the original landscaping

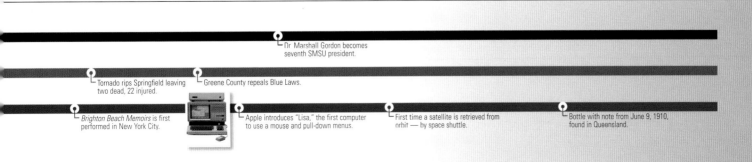

Dr. Marshall Gordon becomes seventh SMSU president.

Tornado rips Springfield leaving two dead, 22 injured.

Greene County repeals Blue Laws.

Brighton Beach Memoirs is first performed in New York City.

Apple introduces "Lisa," the first computer to use a mouse and pull-down menus.

First time a satellite is retrieved from orbit — by space shuttle.

Bottle with note from June 9, 1910, found in Queensland.

Dr. Wayne McKinney succeeded Coach "Andy" McDonald as head of the Health and Physical Education Department in 1964. McKinney became a campus leader in scientific research as well as giving strong support and encouragement to the development of women's athletics. McKinney retired in 1989.

and gardens designed by Monet.

Distinguished Professor Dominic Capeci has maintained a research interest in issues of race for more than 25 years, publishing five books. His 1991 book, *Layered Violence: The Detroit Riots of 1943,* co-authored with Dr. Martha Wilkerson, was selected as an Outstanding Book by the Gustavus Myers Center for Human Rights in the United States, and was anthologized in John Hollitz, ed. *Thinking Through the Past: A Critical Thinking Approach to U.S. History.*

Eight faculty in the College of Business Administration were granted the Distinguished Faculty Research Award in 2002, the most prestigious research honor granted by the col-

lege. The award is presented annually to professors who have published 15 or more articles in refereed journals over the past five years. Those honored in 2002 include Drs. Chung Kim, John Satzinger, Randy Sexton, Keith Denton, John Kent, Steve Parker, Charlie Pettijohn and Dane Peterson.

Professor J.D. Crouch, associate professor of Defense and Strategic Studies, was appointed by President George W. Bush to be assistant secretary of defense for international security policy in 2001. Crouch was formerly a principal deputy secretary of defense in the first Bush administration prior to his coming to the university in 1992.

Jerry Hoover, director of Bands, was presented with an honorary doctorate of music while in London with the Bruin Pride Marching Band. The degree was issued from the National Conservatory of Music in Mexico City where Hoover's Jazz Band performed in 1990.

These are but random examples of the growing national and international reputation of SMSU faculty.

Faculty Senate

With the beginning of the university era in 1972, the Faculty Senate celebrated its 10th anniversary. It had taken seriously the responsibility for curriculum development and had demonstrated effective leadership in that role. It had also begun to experiment with advisory resolutions to the administration on a variety of matters ranging from student welfare to communication channels between the administration and the faculty. On all Faculty Senate actions, the president of the university has veto power, and while most curricular actions were approved by the president, the resolutions dealing with non-curricular matters had a considerably lower success rate.

In 1972-73, for example, Senate resolutions concerning communication channels with the administration, evaluation of department heads and administrators, and a resolution seeking a change in summer school were all disapproved by the administration. In 1977-78, all 40 curricular actions by the Faculty Senate were approved, but the administration "received," but did not approve, resolutions regarding salary inequities, promotion and tenure, credit by examination and advanced placement. The principle of "shared governance," always difficult to understand by business-types who typically operate out of a "one-in-charge" model, was being shaped in the interaction between the administration and the Faculty Senate. It was clear that faculty expertise granted it authority in curricular matters, but even there it was not

SMSU

Dr. Robert Gilmore resigns as provost and dean of faculties.

New Library named for Duane G. Meyer.

Missouri/Springfield

International/USA

First non-human primate (baboon) conceived in a lab dish in San Antonio.

Supreme Court rules retirement plans can not pay women less than men.

Ira Gershwin dies.

U.S. invades Grenada.

absolute. What was not clear was the extent of faculty authority in non-curricular matters. But that did not deter the Senate from advising the administration regularly on how to improve the institution.

When the state withheld 10 percent of the university's funding because of revenue shortfalls in 1982-83, the whole issue of budgeting became a concern for the Senate. Realizing that those whom the decisions affect should have some voice in shaping policy, the administration set up the President's Council to assist in planning the budget. The Council included members of the faculty and the Student Government Association, as well as administrators. It served as an illustration of how "shared governance" was working out in practice. The administration still had the ultimate responsibility for developing the budget, but the advice of the faculty would be sought.

In the latter years of President Gordon's administration, faculty morale became a salient issue. Surveys identified several factors, the merit pay plan being central. Again, the Senate was included in a group charged by the administration to develop a new plan responsive to faculty interests.

Reviewing the Faculty Senate minutes of the university period, one gets a clear picture of two separate agendas. First, there was the struggle over curricular development. What new programs should have priority? How should general education be strengthened? Typically, those curricular matters occupied the Senate during the fall semester. Then in the spring came a cascade of resolutions and their accompanying debates over general matters of concern to the faculty. The resolutions were like a barometer registering the atmospheric pressure among the professoriate. They constituted the footprint of prevailing sentiments, wishes and concerns of the faculty. They also mirrored the year's experience and the cumulative effect of administrative performance. There were times when the Senate gave unqualified support to the decisions of the president and the Board as in the decision not to interfere with the *The Normal Heart* production in the fall of 1989. There were other times when the Senate felt the Board was getting a biased picture of the state of the university and asked to have a faculty representative appointed to the Board. And then there was the memorable Senate meeting in November 1991 in which it declared it "no longer retains confidence in the ability of President Gordon to lead this institution." The

Among the visitors to campus in the 1970s was Admiral Grace Hopper, one of the first computer software engineers and one of the most incisive "futurists" in the world of computing. Hopper invented the compiler, the intermediate program that translates English language instructions into the language of the target computer. She told SMSU students that she did this "because I was lazy, and hoped that the programmer could return to being a mathematician." Her work foreshadowed enormous numbers of developments which are now the bones of digital computing.

First education specialist degrees granted

Average freshman ACT score 18.7.

University Plaza Hotel opens.

1984

Heathrow Airport robbed of 6,800 gold bars worth $38.7 million.

U.S.S.R. leaves weapon disarmament talks.

Court orders breakup of AT&T.

"no confidence" vote was the first ever passed by a Faculty Senate.

As guardians of curricular integrity, the Senate has given careful attention to the emerging distance learning technologies. Debates over whether programs delivered primarily by media are as effective as programs with the professor present have occurred from the late 1990s and into the 21st century.

The Senate also has been concerned with conditions of employment for faculty. It has defined and refined standards for hiring at each rank, standards for granting or denying academic tenure and standards for promotion. These concerns finally led to the publication of a *Faculty Handbook* in 1986, which outlined the procedures for hiring and retaining the most qualified instructors.

Matters of due process and academic freedom have also been a concern of the Senate and policies governing these matters have made their way into the *Faculty Handbook* and the Faculty Senate Constitution and By-Laws.

Leadership in the Faculty Senate appears to have been a male prerogative for the first 19 years. Dr. Linda Park-Fuller broke that tradition in 1988-89 when she was elected to serve as Chair of the Faculty Senate. In the 14 years since that time, women have served as chair of the Senate seven times.

With more than 30 years of accumulated experience, the Faculty Senate has established itself as an important actor in the life of the university. It provides a forum in which competing and sometimes conflicting visions of the institution are voiced. Tensions between preserving the heritage of the past and meeting the challenges of the future are often aired in Senate debate.

The Will to Include

"The history of human enlightenment and ethical enhancement is the history of increasing inclusivity."

∾

President John H. Keiser
State of the University Address
August 20, 1998

Each year brings a new agenda of concerns. On occasion the Senate disagrees with decisions made by the administration. At times they have urged action the administration has been unable or unwilling to take. On occasion the Senate has advocated changes students have welcomed, and there have been times when students resisted changes created by the faculty. The Senate has sometimes led, sometimes followed in shaping university policy, but it's clear that one cannot understand the development of the institution since the early 1960s without taking the role of the Faculty Senate into account.

Teaching into the 21st Century

Immense changes in teaching loads characterized the 20th century. In the summer of 1906, Dr. Virginia Craig taught seven 50-minute classes each day, as did most of the rest of the Normal School faculty. By 1910 the class hours were reduced to 45 minutes, and each instructor typically taught six classes each day. The Missouri Educational Conference in 1916 agreed

to limit college level teaching to 18 clock hours per week, a dramatic reduction in light of the earlier loads. Along with many other reforms in 1963, teaching loads were reduced to 14 hours per week. Since that time teaching loads have continued to spiral down with the current *Faculty Handbook* setting a goal of a nine-hour teaching load. Many instructors with research agendas are granted even lighter teaching loads to enable them to develop their research interests.

The love of teaching has characterized many of the university's outstanding faculty. On the occasion of his retirement in 1995, Dr. Duane Meyer observed, "Teaching is a psychologically fulfilling vocation. In many ways one is helping intelligent, inquisitive young people enjoy their lives more and enrich their children's lives." After serving as president of the university for 12 years, Meyer went back to the classroom in 1983 to take up again the task he loved so much. Two years later, he received the university's Excellence in Teaching Award. In 1986, Meyer was honored by the Missouri Committee for the Humanities with the title, Lorberg Lecturer.

Dr. Meyer's students remember his legendary lectures on American and Missouri history. With his glasses folded in one hand he worked the room walking back and forth, painting a picture of the historical event with words and gestures. He brought history alive by weaving personal experiences and modern day events into his lectures. Part of his genius lies in his belief in people. "I basically like people, and I feel that most people, students or staff, will do the best they can," he said.

Another in the "great teacher"

SMSU

Central High School in West Plains purchased to provide classroom space.

Baker Astronomical Observatory becomes fully operational.

Missouri/Springfield

Two Springfield councilmen recalled.

International/USA

More than 10 million computers are in use in the U.S.

Kareem Abdul-Jabbar breaks Wilt Chamberlain's all-time career scoring record with 31,421 points.

A Historical Essay

BY DR. ALBERT R. GORDON

Professor of Biomedical Sciences

100 YEARS OF PROGRESS IN THE BIOLOGICAL SCIENCES AT SMSU

Since 1905, the nature and status of biological studies at Southwest Missouri State University have been determined primarily by evolving institutional goals, a changing educational philosophy for biological education, and the explosion in biological knowledge, particularly during the last 50 years.

Initial instruction in biology at SMSU was the result of the demand for teachers of biology in area high schools. By 1900, specialized courses in botany, zoology and human physiology, and later in general biology, had become popular in high school curriculums. A general biology book by Thomas Huxley and Henry Martin, noted biologists of the time, was used by most teacher education colleges through the 1930s. Biologists of the early 20th century were involved in the discovery, identification, description, and classification of life forms with which we humans share the planet. There was so much to know that many early biologists spent their careers attempting to distinguish, catalog, and group the forms of life. Much of what professional research biologists were accomplishing became the emphasis of biological education in our nation's schools and colleges. Not only had biologists become more specialized, but the education of biologists had become more specialized. General biology at the university was no longer a single subject in the teacher education curriculum; it now became an introduction to the specific fields of biological specialization. By the 1960s those who were hired at SMSU or elsewhere could no longer be expected to be able to teach everything in the biology curriculum, as had been the case in previous decades. Specializations led to questions of how

a biologist is defined and what specific knowledge base defines the biologist. Was one who defined himself as a zoologist, anatomist, physiologist, or botanist also a biologist? In name, yes, but according to the older definitions, no. The problem of subject area identity has always been a problem more for biologists than for other scientists.

By the 1950s and 1960s biological education was undergoing significant change. The impetus behind this change was the the Cold War, and a national need for more scientists and engineers. Consequently, science, including biology, flourished and witnessed unparalleled growth during this period. To meet the educational expectations of a comprehensive university, new graduate programs appeared, biology among the first. Later, in an environment of great scientific advancement and environmental awareness, the social unrest of the 1960s suggested the need for a shift from the knowledge theme to an emphasis on personal and social needs of students. In response to these new themes, the Biology Department at SMSU developed strong environmental education emphasis, one that continues to contribute to the preservation and well-being of our Ozarks region.

Overall, the most important changes in biology during this period were the rapid acceleration of existing knowledge and the initiation of new biological fields. Whole new biological areas such as cell biology, developmental biology, molecular biology, the new genetics, and immunology arose.

As a result of the burgeoning field of biology, a departmental reorganization occurred in 1984 which established a separate biological unit called the Department of Biomedical

Sciences. Conceptually, the new department differed from its sister Biology Department in the much the same way that physics differs from chemistry. The new department focused on the cellular and subcellular levels of biological organization and the unity, rather than diversity, of biological process at these levels. Since knowledge in cellular and molecular biology provided new approaches to the problems of health and disease, a human focus of biological expression for the department was natural, and human biology became the unifying theme of the department. Since 1984, there has been a rapid development of the applications of cell and molecular biology in our society. Along with programs in dietetics and medical technology, the program in cell and molecular biology supports the needs of new industries such as biotechnology and genomics, and the subject matter is the basis for unparalleled progress in biomedical research. Whereas announcements of new discoveries in the biomedical sciences once came weekly, they now come nearly daily. Since the mid-1980s knowledge has been doubling in less than a five year period.

Today, biology at SMSU, as expressed by two strong complementary departments, has come to represent envious models for other educational institutions that seek to best meet the needs of biology students and society in today's world. At 100 years, the present is a tribute to the legacy of a rich history. With such firm foundation, the next 100 years will find the biological sciences at SMSU playing a significant role in serving the mission of a mature university in a new time. ❀

tradition was the late Howard Orms who came to SMSU in 1966 to teach in the Theatre and Dance Department. He retired in 1993 and died in 2001 at age 80. He is remembered by Sterling Macer, an SMSU graduate and a successful movie actor and producer. Macer came to SMSU in 1983 and was in a communications class that featured guest lecturers from all the disciplines in the college of arts and letters. "It was all very mundane," remembers Macer. "And then Howard Orms started talking about theater and what life in the theater was all about. But Howard wasn't just talking about it, he was performing. It was strange because Howard has an emotional arc. One thing I can see is him almost on the verge of tears talking about theater. And the girls down in the row from me almost cried along with him. He totally controlled his surroundings. And then he cut it off, and that was the perfect illustration of what it was all about. Afterwards, I walked up to him and said, 'I'd like to be a theater major.'"

On the occasion of his retirement, Orms observed, "I believe that there is so much we have to experience, and if I could lead someone to discovering themselves [sic], then it is all worth it."

While the advances in teaching technologies may promise more efficient modes of instruction and greater flexibility in learning, it's doubtful if any will replace the master teacher.

Establishing a Research and Public Service Tradition

Throughout SMSU history, there have been faculty whose interest in research has been part of their self-understanding. While not living under the "publish or perish" mandate, many, none-

theless, made names for themselves in significant scholarly achievement.

The pace of research and service quickened as the university era began. Dr. Wayne McKinney came to SMSU in 1965 having already established a personal reputation for blending research and teaching in physical education. As the newly appointed head of the Physical Education Department, McKinney set his sights on recruiting faculty who had enthusiasm and competence in the discipline, and the ability to contribute scholarship to the field. As early as 1969, his department had become noteworthy for its achievements. Three department members, Dr. Gene Logan, Dr. Harold Falls and Dr. McKinney himself had been elected to membership in the prestigious Research Council of the American Association of Health, Physical Education and Recreation. The Research Council at the time had members from 61 colleges and universities, only 13 of which had more than three members from any one Department of Physical Education, establishing a ranking for SMSU as 14th in the nation.

The impetus to scholarly activity increased when the institution acquired university status. Three years into the era, Dean Robert Gilmore began publishing an annual report of professional achievement documenting the growth of research and scholarship throughout the campus.

In 1977, the first office of grants

After a long and successful career in community theatre, Howard Orms spent 27 years mentoring theatre and drama students, including Kathleen Turner, John Goodman and Jack Laufer. He retired from the Theatre and Dance Department faculty in 1993. He died in 2001.

was established with Dr. Stan Burgess as director. Burgess assisted faculty in obtaining external grants to support their research as well as alerting faculty to external funding opportunities in their disciplines.

The university had already received National Science Foundation Grants, but in 1978, Dr. Robert Flanders, head of the History Department, received a $266,000 National Endowment for the Humanities grant for the production of two documentary movies dealing with Ozark life as it exists in Shannon County. The films were to focus on the history, culture and changing circumstances of Shannon County, termed "an exemplary county of the Ozarks," by Dr. Flanders. The project was completed in 1982. "I wanted to produce a humanistic film," Flanders said, "the type that treats people as persons, not as a population. It reflects their dignity

History Professor Andrew Lewis receives McArthur Foundation Fellowship.

Margaret B. Kelly becomes first female to hold statewide elective office when she is elected state auditor.

Lisa Rose (then Richardson) joins KY3.

Chemical companies agree to $180 million compensation for U.S. Vietnam veterans with health problems associated with "Agent Orange."

DNA is successfully cloned from an extinct animal — the quagga.

Government orders airbags or seatbelts would be required in cars by 1989.

Japan beats U.S. for Olympic gold medal in baseball.

and simple humanity. Their love for life, the value they place on where they live, and their very being, is enormous." The films, *Shannon County Home* and *The Hearts of the Children* show how the people of Shannon County define themselves as human beings, how they relate to their environment, and focus on their religion, history and literature, both oral and written.

The Beginning of Research Centers: Center for Archeological Research

The 1970s also saw the establishment of centers for research and public service. The first of these was the Center for Archaeological Research (CAR) created in 1975 by the Sociology Department. Dr. Robert Cooley was the founding director. CAR was established in response to the growing and urgent demand for contract archaeology programs to perform cultural resource assessments mandated by federal and state legislation. Proposed power lines, highways, dam sites and other major construction projects in areas sensitive because of their potential cultural resource value were the immediate focus of research and assessment.

Over time, the CAR has also provided educational services within the academic community, providing anthropology students and others with first hand experience in archaeological excavation. Since 1975, the Center has completed more than 700 projects, funded primarily by external grants and contracts. The projects have included all phases of archaeological investigation including document and record searches, literature reviews, reconnaissance and intensive surveys, test excavations, mitigative or intensive excavations, monitoring and site preservation. CAR staff have also produced large-scale overviews, predictive models, National Register and National Historic Landmark nominations and management plans.

Agencies for which the Center works include the U.S. Forest Service, the Missouri Department of Transportation, the Arkansas Highway and Transportation Department, the Missouri Department of Natural Resources and the U.S. Corps of Engineers.

Grants and contracts to the Center between 1975-99 amounted to nearly $6 million. During the early years of the Center's work, clients were typically private companies and municipalities scattered through the Ozarks. Between 1978-81, 278 such projects were completed. In recent years, the number of projects has been fewer, but the scale has been typically larger.

In addition to the extensive contract archaeological work, the CAR has traditionally operated the SMSU Summer Field School in Archaeology for six to eight weeks. In recent years, two field schools have been operating, one in southwest Missouri and the other in North Carolina, offering both prehistoric and historic archaeology.

The Center has been actively involved with both public and professional communities sponsoring monthly meetings of the Ozarks Chapter of the Missouri Archeological Society, and an annual Artifact Identification Day, regional efforts for Missouri Archaeology Awareness Month and volunteer excavations of threatened sites.

Staffed by six full-time professional archaeologists, a laboratory supervisor and an administrative secretary, the Center is under the direction of

Center for Applied Science and Engineering Established

In an effort to increase the development of advanced technology industries in Missouri, the Board of Governors on February 21, 2003, approved the establishment of a Center for Applied Science and Engineering (CASE). The center provides engineering and technical support and conduct "high risk" research and development to advance the competitiveness of Missouri-based industries.

The university is already working on developing products for extremely low cost night and smoke vision cameras, biosensor instruments for homeland security, plastic materials that can light up and, most recently, products for hydrogen fuel cells that can be used in the automotive industry.

The university will be working collaboratively with Missouri industries on research and development projects that can have a positive economic impact on southwest Missouri. The Springfield Business and Development Corporation, a subsidiary of the Springfield Area Chamber of Commerce, is a collaborator in the initiative.

First Presidential Scholarships awarded.

John Ashcroft elected governor.

Cosby Show premieres on TV.

McDonalds makes its 50-billionth hamburger.

Ronald Reagan re-elected with greatest electoral landslide in history.

Looking Back

National Geographic Magazine Visits Big Eddy Site

A photographer from the *National Geographic Magazine* spent two weeks in the summer of 2002 taking about 5,000 pictures of the striking Big Eddy archeological site in Cedar County. The site is being excavated by archeologists from the Center for Archaeological Research who report that its stratified layers of artifacts provide one of the richest chronological records of prehistoric habitation the Center has worked on in its more than 25-year history. Dr. Neal Lopinot, Director of the Center, indicates it is possible that the earliest residents of North America inhabited the site.

~

Capital Improvements

Expenditures for capital improvements on the SMSU campus from 1906 to 2002 total $258,429,493.

Normal School Period
(1905-1919)
$267,393

State Teachers College Period
(1919-1946)
$1,260,521

State College Period
(1946-1972)
$27,970,675

State University Period
(1972-2002)
$228,930,904

Dr. Neal Lopinot who has conducted archaeological investigations in the Midwest for more than 28 years.

Center for Ozarks Studies

About the same time the Center for Archaeological Research was being formed, a National Endowment for the Humanities Grant enabled the establishment of the Center for Ozarks Studies. Conceived by Dr. Robert Flanders, head of the History Department, the Center focused on understanding regional culture and history. A pilot grant of $30,000 supported planning efforts in the summer of 1976. Included in the planning group were Dr. Flanders, Dr. Donald Holiday of the English Department, Carol Mock, linguist and sociology instructor, Dr. Robert Cooley, professor of religious studies and archaeology, and Dr. Milton Rafferty, head of the Department of Geography and Geology.

During the 1976-77 school year, a course titled "History and Culture of the Ozarks" was taught. It was the first non-departmental, interdisciplinary course offered by the university. The course was research-oriented. Students pored over their own Ozarks family histories seeking to discover patterns of culture, geographical movements, places and types of settlement, attitudes toward the land and family work. According to Dr. Flanders, "The students have added greatly to our understanding of the history and culture of the Ozarks."

During the summer of 1977 a "Festival of Ozarks Studies" was held which included three one-week programs of Ozarks studies for graduate and undergraduate credit and for the public on a non-credit basis.

A memorable product of the Center's work was the multi-media program *Sassafras: An Ozarks Odyssey,* developed at the end of the 1970s. By the early 1980s more than 20,000 people had seen the program as it was shown throughout the region.

The Center for Ozarks Studies and the Center for Archeological Research emerged in the 1970s under a growing awareness that the culture and traditions of the area were undergoing enormous change. The capturing and archiving of the cultural and historical resources of the area became a passion that has continued into the 21st century.

Center for Resource Planning and Management

A third center for research and service was established in 1978. An academic support and applied research unit of the Department of Geography, Geology and Planning, the Center for Resource Planning and Management (CRPM) in its early years focused on cartographic projects and research on Native American tribes.

As the Center developed, it defined its mission as (1) enhancing the Geography, Geology and Planning Department's academic programs by providing opportunities for student research and practical learning through participation in community research projects, (2) providing outreach services to local, regional, state, and federal governments, organizations and public agencies, to advance knowledge and to assist in the development of public policy on resource utilization and community development, and (3) supporting and creating opportunities for faculty applied research and publication.

SMSU — Kentwood Residence Hall opens.

Missouri/Springfield

International/USA — Thirty-three unknown Bach works found in Yale library. — Sony launches first 8-mm compact camcorder.

1985

For more than 25 years the Center for Archaeological Research (CAR) has done contract archaeology throughout the Midwest. The Big Eddy site on the Sac River near Stockton Lake was opened in 1997. The site is particularly valuable because it includes evidence of human habitation going back 13,500 years, and the prehistoric artifacts are stratified providing a detailed chronology of the prehistoric period. CAR Director Neal Lopinot, left, and research archaeologist Jack Ray stand in one of the excavation pits at Big Eddy in 2001.

Since 1989, the CRPM staff, students and associated faculty have conducted more than 120 community projects. More than 280 students have had experience working on local planning and development projects. More than $1.5 million in external grants from local, state and federal sources have supported the work of the Center.

A major catalyst to the Center's public service mission is its administration of the Southwest Missouri Council of Governments (SMCOG), a voluntary organization of local governments in a 10-county area in southwest Missouri and one of 19 active regional planning commissions in the state. Diane May, Center director, has served as executive director of SMCOG since its organization in 1990.

Among the many projects completed by the Center include planning documents for many southwest Missouri cities including Aurora, Billings, Clever, Fair Grove, Hollister, Indian Point, Nixa, Ozark, Rogersville, Republic, Washburn and Willard. County plans have been completed for Christian and Taney Counties. The Center has also completed health needs assessments in Barry, Cedar, Dade, Dallas, Laclede, Lawrence, Lincoln, Pettis, Stone and Taney Counties.

Grant writing assistance is also offered by the Center to local governments. Between 1993-2000, the Center successfully generated more than $4.7 million in state and federal grants, loans and tax credits with total project investments of more than $13 million.

Center for Economic Research

In 1971, an economic data base was generated in the Economics Department by Larry Cox and Dr. David Lages as a service to area businesses. Local area economic and social data derived from federal and state agencies provided insight into the growth patterns in the area.

In the early 1980s the project became part of the Center for Economic Research, another in the developing array of research and outreach centers in the university. Under the leadership of Dr. Joe Bell, the function of the Center changed in 1986. Two publications were started. *Southwest Missouri Economic Indicators* is published quarterly. It contains data related to employment, banking and retail sales. Reporting on retail sales was curtailed in 1993 because of the State Legislature's decision to restrict such reporting to affected governments only. An annual publication, *Southwest Missouri Economic Review*, contains articles by economics and sociology faculty of the university.

In the spring of 1999 the Center changed its name to the Bureau for Economic Research. The annual data reports of the Bureau have assisted the local banking and business communities as well as local governments in understanding the local economy, and they have assisted in their planning for economic development.

Missouri General Assembly appropriates $5 million for a performing arts facility.

First nursing class graduates at West Plains.

Cox Medical Center South opens.

Queen City drive-in movie closes.

Ban on leaded gas ordered by EPA.

Michael Jordan named NBA Rookie-of-the-Year.

Center for Business and Economic Development

The research and service role of the university developed rapidly in the 1980s and 1990s. In 1981, the College of Business Administration opened a Center for Business and Economic Development, its outreach arm designed to help public and private business entities improve their management abilities and retain job opportunities for American workers. Three programs within the Center provide specialized expertise. The Small Business Development Center, in addition to giving management and technical assistance to small enterprises in southwest Missouri, also provides statewide service for international business as a satellite office of the World Trade Center of St. Louis. Center personnel offer assistance in strategic planning, market research, cash flow analysis, procurement and exporting. A satellite office is located on the West Plains Campus as well. More than 2,000 clients are assisted each year.

The Management and Development Institute is the training arm of the Center for Business and Economic Development. Offering a broad base of non-credit programs and seminars in such areas as management, supervision, human resources, and strategic planning, the Institute provides professional certification programs and in-house training programs for a variety of public and private organizations. It typically serves more than 5,000 persons annually.

The WIN Innovation Program is the third outreach tool of the Center for Business and Economic Development. A novel cooperative venture with Wal-Mart Stores, Inc., the Innovation Institute provides innova-

tion evaluation and referral assistance to independent inventors throughout the United States and Canada.

Center for Scientific Research and Education

In 1985, the Center for Scientific Research was established. Its early work centered on polymer chemistry with Dr. Sanjiv Mohite as principal investigator. By the late 1980s, additional faculty from departments in the College of Science and Mathematics were conducting research in the Center. Between 1987-97, 15 scientists from biology, biomedical sciences, chemistry, computer science, geosciences, physics and technology had generated more than $1 million in external funding and produced more than 30 publications in scientific journals, as well as technical reports, to funding agencies sponsoring research.

In 1997, the Center was reorganized around an expanded mission "to promote and support scientific research opportunities, further the education and expertise of current and future science educators, and to work cooperatively with area schools to enhance science education." The Center also seeks to assist private firms, not-for-profit organizations, governmental agencies and educational institutions in the solution of scientific problems. In recent years the Center has received more than $2 million in outside funding.

Center for Social Sciences and Public Policy Research

In 1986, the Department of Sociology, Anthropology and Social Work established the Center for Social Research. Dr. David Hartmann directed the Center from 1986-94, focusing on

survey research for a variety of external clients including local government agencies and private organizations. Conceived initially as both an outreach tool and an educational center for students interested in the design and execution of social research, the Center was reorganized in 1999 as an interdisciplinary center in which both faculty and students in the College of Humanities and Public Affairs could conduct both theoretical and applied research. The Center continues to conduct research for community and governmental organizations on a variety of issues of local, state and national concern. Recent clients include the city of Springfield, Ozarks Literacy Council, Missouri Catholic Conference, University of Missouri Extension Office in Jasper County, University of Health Sciences in Kansas City, and the cities of West Plains, Festus, St. Robert and Bates City.

Center for Industrial Productivity

The year 1998 saw the establishment of yet another outreach center. Focused on assisting business and industry develop new manufacturing technologies, the Center for Industrial Productivity also provides training for professionals in manufacturing. Supporting area businesses and industries in the pursuit of manufacturing excellence, the Center also co-sponsors the "Excellence in Manufacturing Series," which provides workshops and seminars aimed at improving management practices, applying new technologies, and remaining competitive in the global economy. Faculty in the Industrial Management Department provide the expertise.

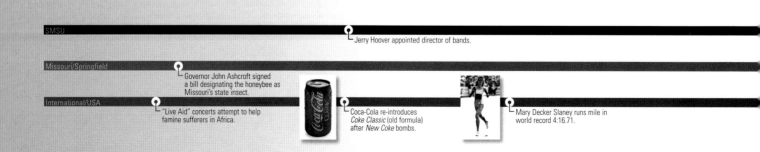

SMSU

Jerry Hoover appointed director of bands.

Missouri/Springfield

Governor John Ashcroft signed a bill designating the honeybee as Missouri's state insect.

International/USA

"Live Aid" concerts attempt to help famine sufferers in Africa.

Coca-Cola re-introduces *Coke Classic* (old formula) after *New Coke* bombs.

Mary Decker Slaney runs mile in world record 4:16.71.

Institute for School Improvement

The College of Education in 1998 established the Institute for School Improvement, which provides oversight for a number of professional development programs for area teachers. Project investigators also conduct research to examine the impact of programs on teaching and learning, linking theory to practice. Professional development activities include direct assistance to public school teachers, administrators and university faculty through several outreach units.

The institute also has oversight responsibilities in community/school partnerships including the Springfield R-12 Storefront School, the SMSU Literacy Center and the Outreach Coordinator for Continuing Education. The institute conducts research and program evaluation activities utilizing both quantitative and qualitative methods. Research focuses on curricular and instructional processes as they relate to classroom practice and student achievement.

At the end of the 2000-01 year, 15 different on-campus centers for research and public service were operating, utilizing faculty expertise, enabling student learning through participating in research projects, and solving problems for area organizations, businesses and governmental units.

Ozarks Public Health Institute

A new outreach arm of the university developed in 2001-02 is the Ozarks Public Health Institute. Beginning with an examination of the state of personal, community and environmental health issues in southwest Missouri, the vision for the Institute soon expanded to provide a fully integrated approach to

addressing health issues in the Ozarks by combining university resources and partnerships with community, health and educational organizations. The approach addresses near-term needs while recognizing that the greatest impact for the long term will come from an informed citizenry who set a high priority on personal and community health. The Institute will serve as a resource base for local communities by developing educational materials and distributing them to community organizations, and by producing public service programs offered to communities through the campus radio station, KSMU, KOZK Ozarks Public Television and distance learning methods.

Five central themes provide focus to its work.

- Education, training and public advocacy programs will reduce substance abuse with an initial emphasis on reducing the use of tobacco among young people and adults throughout the Ozarks.
- Professional development of public health practitioners and health care providers will be improved by traditional classroom-based and distance-learning education and training programs.
- Education of all citizens in the areas of science and technology will enable wise decisions concerning personal, community and environmental health.
- The application of scientific knowledge will improve public health and the environment through the identification, monitoring and amelioration of chemical and biological hazards.
- The university itself will become a model for health and wellness through programs that serve as the

Student wages increase from $2.85 to $3.35 per hour.

Enrollment exceeds 16,000 (16,030).

The wreck of the RMS Titanic discovered.

A hole in the ozone layer over Antarctica is detected.

Microsoft Windows 1.0 is introduced and sells for $100.

Archaeology students at SMSU have had opportunities to work at a variety of sites in the United States and abroad learning the techniques of excavation, artifact identification and report writing. Dr. Burt Purrington is working with students in a 1992 field school.

basis for training programs and replication in health care, business and educational institutions throughout the Ozarks.

The Institute was authorized by the Board of Governors in February 2001. Dr. Dalen Duitsman was named director with an advisory board co-chaired by Harold Bengsch, director of the Springfield-Greene County Department of Health, and Dr. Cynthia Pemberton, dean of the College of Health and Human Services.

Faculty/Student Collaboration on Research Grows

As faculty capability for scholarly research developed during university years, so did their commitment to include students in the exciting enterprise. In 1982, Dr. John Wilson of the Religious Studies Department took 11 students as members of a 35-person archaeological dig in Capernaum. They uncovered 286 gold dinar coins, the largest discovery of its kind in Israel. In the same year Dr. Larry Banks of the Physics Department was assisting students doing energy experiments on an old Springfield house. The study was funded by a $50,000 grant from the U.S. Department of Energy.

In 1983, President Marshall Gordon allocated an additional $25,000 to the faculty research budget to assist faculty in getting started in the research enterprise. "I don't think we're going to tilt ourselves into a research-oriented university," observed Graduate School Dean Russell Barnekow, "but research is a very valuable learning and teaching tool." A research committee composed of two faculty from each of the university's schools was established in 1983 to examine research proposals and requests for funding and reassigned time. In 1989, after receiving the Distinguished Scholar status for his accomplishments in research, Dr. Harold Falls said that the growth in research was good news, especially for students. "Undergraduate students who are interested have the opportunity to get involved in research in many departments across campus," Falls observed, "At SMSU students can have direct contact with research professors here…. These opportunities, especially at the undergraduate level, certainly aren't available at the larger research universities."

In 1989 three university professors and two students were involved in a research process involving polymers. Looking for new materials that could be used for automotive components, Drs. Clif Thompson, James Wilbur and Sanjiv Mohite of the Center for Scientific Research, and chemistry majors Rex Whitfield and Raafat Shaltout used Styrofoam beads under high temperature in their experiments. They were seeking a strong, energy- and sound-absorbent material (polymer) that would be both a good insulator and could be easily coated with surface materials. The project was a collaborative effort with Diversified Plastics in Nixa.

Other faculty in the 1980s were stoking the research fires in their disciplines as well. In 1987, Dr. Chris Field in the Biomedical Sciences Department began working with Walter Reed Army Institute and NASA to study why human cell tissues deteriorate during space travel. Understanding the effects of weightlessness on body tissues is critical to prolonged space travel and the establishing of space stations. Field's expertise in viruses, DNA work and genetic engineering equipped him to contribute to the team of 100 scientists

SMSU
Eighty-three faculty involved in $1 million of funded research.

Missouri/Springfield
Tom Dye joins KY3.

International/USA
Largest swearing-in ceremony — 38,648 immigrants become U.S. citizens.

Marvin Green retires as dean of West Plains Campus after 20 years. Dr. Richard Braun appointed to succeed him.

U.S. Space Shuttle Challenger explodes shortly after takeoff killing seven astronauts.

1986

Dr. Chris Field at work in his lab in the Biomedical Sciences Department.

working on the issue. In March 1992, Field traveled to Kennedy Space Center to examine myoblast cultures he had prepared to go on the shuttle flight. Field analyzed the effects of the flight on the cultures after they returned from space.

Dr. Roar Irgens, from the Biology Department, traveled literally "to the ends of the earth" to study biological life in polar regions. He drilled through ice glaciers, studied habits of whales and dolphins, and rubbed shoulders with seals and penguins in his quest for understanding.

In the early 1980s, Dr. Juris Zarins, professor of archaeology, was comparing the Genesis account of the Garden of Eden with other primitive folk stories about creation that were passed down for thousands of years

before the book of Genesis was included in the *Bible*. Intrigued by the similarities, Zarins set out to find the Garden of Eden, the cradle of civilization. He believed the story of Adam and Eve in the Garden of Eden is actually a condensed account of the greatest revolution in the history of mankind: the shift from hunting-gathering to agriculture, which occurred about 10,000 years ago. Using the sciences of geology, hydrology and linguistics in addition to LANDSAT space images, he located what he believes to be the mythical Garden of Eden under the waters of the Persian Gulf between Iraq and Iran. The scholarly community immediately took notice when he published his findings in 1986. *Smithsonian* magazine ran a nine-page article in May of that year. *Newsweek* reported his work in its June 22 issue. National Public Radio and the Canadian Broadcasting Company also interviewed Zarins while NBC-TV explored the possibility of making a documentary in the fall of 1988.

The focus of Zarins' scholarly work has been on pastoral nomads — people who herd animals for a living — in Saudi Arabia. On the relationship between teaching and research, Zarins

is resolute. "I don't think you can find a gifted teacher who's not doing research, Zarins said. "In a university setting, research and teaching go hand in hand. You have to try to do both well. I can't imagine myself teaching 12 hours a semester until the day I die without doing research."

The developing research capacity at the university caught the attention of Dr. Jim Broerman in 1991 while he was still chief scientist for solid-state sciences at McDonnell Douglas Research Laboratories. He was leading a team of eight Ph.D.s developing lasers and infrared detectors for space and military use when he decided to come to SMSU in 1991 and help build a materials science program. He assisted the university in acquiring the molecular beam epitaxy and microlithography labs from McDonnell Douglas. The $1.5 million equipment enabled scientists to layer materials at the thickness of an atom. The companion piece is capable of producing features a minimum of 1/200ths the thickness of a human hair. The equipment led to the development of new courses in solid states physics and semi-conductor devices, as well as a master's program in materials science. According to Broerman, "The equipment gives students the same advantages they would have at any of the top 10 schools in the country. This is a unique facility in Missouri. There is no other molecular beam epitaxy laboratory in either industries or universities in the state. The equipment gives students training and experience in a technology that is at the forefront of modern opto-electronics."

Faculty expertise is increasingly being tapped by government agencies. In 1990, the Missouri Department of

Volunteer Service to the Community

During 2002-03, the faculty, students and staff at SMSU contributed 143,678 hours of volunteer services to various organizations in the community. Since 1997-98 when statistics were first kept, the campus community has averaged more than 100,000 hours of service per year, the equivalent of 50 employees working full-time for a year.

~

Economic Impact

SMSU has an economic impact of about $664 million per year in the local economy or about $1.82 million per day. Its $183 million budget is similar to the R-12 School District or the City of Springfield. With its 2,000 full-time employees, SMSU ranks among the top five employers in the Springfield area. An estimated 10,000 of the 20,000 enrolled students work part-time in the community or on campus.

Alcohol and Drug Abuse contracted with Drs. Jim Wolk, Patrick Sullivan and David Hartmann to develop and implement a follow-up evaluation of state-funded clients who have completed outpatient and residential alcohol and drug abuse treatment. The $312,000 contract provided opportunities for students working in the Center for Social Research to do telephone interviews and data assessment. Drs. Wolk and Sullivan served on the social work faculty. Dr. Hartmann, from the sociology faculty, directed the Center for Social Research.

Another faculty member became a leading expert in artificial insemination of elephants. Beginning in 1987, Dr. Dennis Schmitt, associate professor of veterinary medicine in the Agriculture Department, worked with Dickerson Park Zoo in Springfield in its elephant breeding program. Using ultrasound technology to detect ovulation in elephants, Schmitt had exceptional success in elephant breeding. In 2000, he worked on a breeding project with the Toledo, Ohio Zoo.

While much of the research effort at the university is problem-solving or applied research, theoretical or pure research has begun to develop as well. In 1997 Dr. Dean Cuebas of the Chemistry Department received a National Science Foundation grant of $207,503 for a project t itled, "The beta-oxidative biosynthesis of bile acids." The research resulted in three publications in refereed scientific journals.

The Growth of Sponsored Research

In the 30 years since SMSU began to call itself a university, faculty, staff, administration and students have mobilized themselves in remarkably creative ways to conduct basic and applied research. The evidence of faculty research capability, the emergence of research and service centers, and the collaboration of faculty and students in providing technical assistance to area industries and organizations all point to a maturing institution.

The acknowledgement of institutional capability can, to a degree, be measured by the extent to which outside organizations and agencies contract for services to be rendered, problems to be solved, and investigations to be conducted. As early as the 1950s, individual grants were being made to faculty to conduct scientific studies. By the early 1970s an Office of Grants was established to facilitate the research and service function of the university. Systematic records of grants and contracts began to be kept in the early 1980s. Dr. William A. Alter III, director of the office of sponsored research since 1996, reports that between 1983-2002, the university received more than $86 million in grants and contracts, reaching an all-time high of $11.1 million in 2002-03. More than 200 separate grants and contracts were awarded to the university in 2002. The scale of the grants has continued to rise with 200 over the past 19 years exceeding $100,000. Six of the 200 exceeded $1 million. The Office of Naval Research awarded the largest single grant of $1.875 million in 2002 to Dr. Ryan Giedd, head of the Physics Department and his team for "Biosensors made from Carbon and Polymer Based Micro-electromechanical Systems."

In the 18 years since 1983, 36 percent of all the external grant funds have supported projects focusing on education either at the K-12 or higher

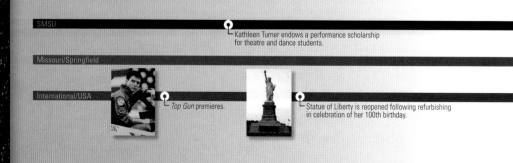

SMSU
Kathleen Turner endows a performance scholarship for theatre and dance students.

Missouri/Springfield

International/USA
Top Gun premieres.

Statue of Liberty is reopened following refurbishing in celebration of her 100th birthday.

education level, attesting to the continuing leadership the university shows in its teacher education programs. Another 36 percent supported projects that provided services to the local or regional communities. A full 24 percent of the grants supported basic and applied research projects. The remaining 4 percent purchased equipment for education and research projects.

The growth of Centers and Institutes across campus is clearly related to sponsored projects. By 2001, 15 centers were receiving external funding for research, education and service projects. Almost half of all grants, both in numbers and dollar amounts, have been received by university centers.

A substantial number of grants involve partnerships with other organizations including school districts, state agencies, businesses and not-for-profit organizations. A recent $890,000 grant from the National Science Foundation titled "Opening the Horizon: Strengthening Science Education for Middle School Girls" is intended to increase the interest of middle school girls in pursuing higher education and careers in mathematics, science and engineering. The grant involves a partnership among the three campuses of SMSU at Springfield, West Plains, and Mountain Grove, and four other institutions of higher education.

Indicative of the quality of work being done, the university revised its Intellectual Property Policy in fiscal year 2001 to protect the intellectual investment of faculty and staff and the potential for commercial value coming from laboratory creations. In 2001, three patent applications were filed with the U.S. Patent and Trademark office.

The First Ozark Mountain Outhouse Race to benefit the Special Olympics and United Cerebral Palsy of Southwest Missouri in 1982 had students pushing and laughing in Phelps Grove Park.

The Office of Sponsored Research and Programs assists faculty and staff in the acquisition of external support for university-based projects. It identifies opportunities and helps develop competitive proposals, coordinates their submission, provides training to enhance competitiveness, and reviews proposals to ensure compliance with sponsor's regulations and university policies. It has become an important facilitator of the research and service components of the university's mission.

Town/Gown Trials and Triumphs

The March 21, 1965, edition of the *Springfield News-Leader* carried an article by Larry Hazelrigg celebrating the mutually beneficial relationship between SMSU and Springfield. He identified SMSU as "an educational, cultural and economic asset that is increasing in value with each passing year."

Hazelrigg documented the cultural contributions by listing national and international artists and performers who visited campus in previous years.

Center for Social Research established by department of sociology, anthropology and social work.

President Reagan visits Springfield.

Volcanic eruption in Cameroon releases poison gas killing 1,734.

Federal health officials announce AZT will be available to AIDS patients.

He recognized the cultural contributions of the Theatre Department and the Music Department. He cited the civic contributions of faculty who serve as church organists, chair persons of the Springfield Arts Festival and members of Community Betterment Councils. He noted that the Agriculture Department under the leadership of Dr. Glenn Karls had responded to 1,100 phone calls in the past year seeking advice on agriculture problems, prepared 1,625 letters dispensing valuable information and held more than 550 personal conferences on farm issues in the Ozarks.

"The college is contributing more and more to the life of the community while at the same time pumping millions of dollars into the economy," declared Hazelrigg. Citing the building projects on the horizon, the article concluded with Robert Peace's observation that "SMSU is one of the best tax dollar investments people of the area can make."

But by the 1970s and the beginning of the university period, *Springfield News-Leader* articles were more likely to report neighborhood noise problems, parking violations, student/police encounters and growing tension between residents of neighborhoods around the university and students. The continuing growth of the university had pushed students into residential neighborhoods adjacent to the university. Dormitories could not be built fast enough to accommodate housing needs, so increasing numbers of students were renting rooms and entire houses in neighborhoods close to the university. Fraternities and sororities were buying homes in residential neighborhoods to serve as houses for their members.

Coupled with the increasing presence of students in family residential neighborhoods were lifestyle differences. In 1973, three fraternities were cited by neighbors for excessive noise, vandalism and parking violations. Representatives from the Greek organizations and the neighborhood met to try to work out solutions. Occasionally, accommodations were made, but often the life habits of students and families in the neighborhoods were so dramatically different, that compromises were difficult to achieve.

City Ordinances Passed

By 1978, the problems had become acute enough that the City Council took action. It passed an ordinance changing the definition of a family from five unrelated individuals to three. Citing problems of the fire department reaching fires because of so many cars parked on the street and on lawns, the Council said it was acting in the interest of safety and protecting the stability of property values throughout the city. But it was clear to students that restricting the number of unrelated individuals living in a house in a residential neighborhood was directed primarily at them. *The Standard* carried a cartoon in its March 3, 1978, issue showing a police officer forcing the tearful 4th Keebler Elf from his treehouse home. While the provisions of the ordinance applied first to the Rountree neighborhood east of the campus, it was also applied to areas around Drury that were experiencing the same problems. Ultimately its provisions applied city-wide.

But the problems did not abate. Some residents were outraged at student behavior when parties occurred

in neighborhoods. In September 1978, the Sigma Pi fraternity sued two of its neighbors for harassment, citing repeated phone calls to the police, brandishing a firearm, shining flashlights to frighten girls and threatening fraternity members. On the other hand the Lambda Chi fraternity tried to establish a "good neighbor" policy with families near its house. Several neighbors accepted its offer to assist with yard work.

Alcohol and parties became the sore point. Police were called repeatedly to some Greek houses where things got out of hand. Students were arrested for indecent exposure and resisting arrest. The Interfraternity Council disciplined unruly houses.

By 1979, with more city ordinances being considered to create "responsible agents" in rental property and Greek houses, the university began considering the development of a "Greek Row" where all fraternities and sororities would be grouped together near campus and out of residential neighborhoods. While advocates of the idea cited a host of reasons for bringing the Greek community together, opponents warned that "Greeks will fight or prank each other to death."

Jeff Carter, SGA president in 1979, suggested that students should make their positions known to the City Council. He advocated students registering to vote in city elections, as well as having neighbors who had no problems with students contact their council representatives to indicate that the perception that students in residential neighborhoods are all problems was simply not true.

Politics did seem to mix into the situation. Dr. Paul Redfearn of the

SMSU

Missouri/Springfield

Vice President Bush makes stop at Hickory Hills Junior High.

International/USA

1987

Surrogate Baby M case begins in Hackensack, New Jersey.

Biology Department lived in one of the heavily impacted neighborhoods east of the campus. He ran for city council and was elected in 1973. He served as mayor from 1979-81 and took an active role in shaping city ordinances to deal with neighborhood problems. In 1979, a noise ordinance was passed that made it a misdemeanor to create excessive (heard beyond property boundaries) noise between 10:00 p.m. and 8:00 a.m. Mayor Redfearn supported the ordinance, which caused some students to accuse him of a conflict-of-interest. The Student Government Association sought, unsuccessfully, to pursue the conflict-of-interest question. The excessive noise ordinance required no citizen complaint for police to investigate. The city assigned a special police task force to curb noise in the SMSU area, resulting in yet more intense interaction between police and students.

Under considerable pressure from city officials, the university proposed a "rowdy house" designation for residences that are the repeated object of neighborhood complaints. The designation would give students 30 days to vacate the premises or be expelled from school. Students responded saying if the university wants to solve the noise problem, it should provide more on-campus housing for students, not invoke penalties on "rowdy houses."

The excessive noise ordinance did seem to reduce citizen complaints, at least about noise. However, parking remained a sore point in the early 1980s. Again, the problem was the university's inability to accommodate student vehicles on university parking lots. So students' cars filled the streets around the school, often parking illegally. City police typically wrote 20-30

The Normal Heart
COGER THEATRE

parking tickets a day, but on August 24, 1980, they issued nearly 150 tickets when a citizen's complaint to the mayor resulted in the city manager getting a call about stepped up enforcement.

Parties and alcohol became the focus of concern in the 1980s. The university directed Greeks not to serve or consume alcohol in their front yards. But the problems worsened. The *Springfield Leader and Press* reported student behavior before and after parties included fraternity men urinating on neighbors' lawns, exposing themselves to children, breaking into homes, stealing, jumping on cars and throwing rocks at neighbors. Police surveillance of parties on Greek Row increased with students charging harassment. In November 1984, a fraternity party

got out of control. Police were pushed, tripped and had beer thrown in their faces. Seventeen youth were arraigned on peace disturbance charges. The Sigma Phi Epsilon fraternity was placed on a two-year suspension. As party patrols by the police increased, fewer warnings were given and more citations were issued. Party hosts were held responsible for party behavior. Students felt police were unfairly targeting SMSU, but police replied, "We have to put the water where the fire is."

In 1991, the university contracted with the city to establish a police substation on the north side of campus to provide for around-the-clock security. The proposal came in the wake of community reaction to the so-called "riot" on Elm Street in July 1991. The substation operated on a trial basis for the first 10 weekends of the fall semester. In January 1992, the substation

No smoking rules take effect in federal buildings.

PTL leader, Jim Bakker, resigns after sex scandal with Jessica Hahn.

Texaco files for bankruptcy.

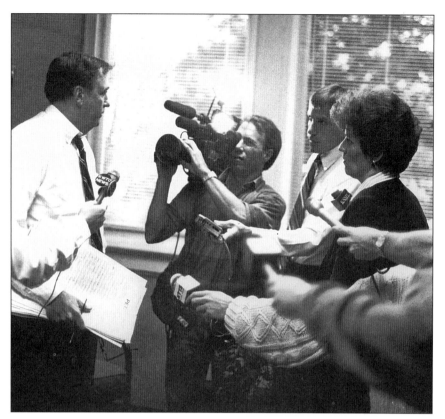

President Marshall Gordon is presented with a petition to cancel the student theatre's presentation of *The Normal Heart* by State Representative Jean Dixon in the fall of 1989. Representative Dixon arrived unannounced at the president's office with an entourage of news media.

was made fully operational providing a police presence on campus 24 hours a day, seven days a week. A generally positive response from students greeted the officers as they rode their bicycles over campus and practiced a campus version of "community policing."

The Normal Heart *Production*

In the fall of 1989, community attention shifted from noisy parties on Greek Row to Coger Theatre where rehearsals for Larry Kramer's play *The Normal Heart* were under way.

The play had been presented across the country more than 600 times without incident. But when it came to southwest Missouri, things went differently. *The Normal Heart* deals with the early years of the AIDS epidemic. The play focuses on the toll of human suffering occasioned by the refusal of society to acknowledge the seriousness of AIDS. Set in New York City among the homosexual community in the early 1980s, the play had received rave reviews across the country because of its frankness and honesty. Considered one of the most powerful contemporary dramas, the play has had a positive impact on AIDS awareness and research.

Despite the enthusiasm elsewhere, in Springfield the play created a firestorm of criticism.

At the October 1989, Board of Regents meeting, state Representative Jean Dixon, R-Springfield, demanded that President Gordon and the Regents cancel the play. Dixon and her supporters in the Citizens Demanding Standards group accused SMSU of using tax dollars to put on a play that "promotes the homosexual lifestyle."

Based on legal counsel's opinion, President Gordon and the Regents refused to cancel the play. "We will not be blackmailed into breaking the law," Gordon said. "To cancel the play would violate the First Amendment rights of our students, faculty and staff, as well as First Amendment rights of the citizens of Missouri. The play will go on."

Between October and the opening night in November, local media featured the issue with stories, letters to the editor and editorials. There were letter-writing campaigns, petition drives, resolutions passed, demonstrations mounted, sermons preached, speeches given and coffee shop debates organized both for and against the production. Not only did local and state media cover the story daily, but NBC-TV, CNN and CBS all sent crews to Springfield to cover the drama of the drama. Radio talk shows took up the issue. Media interviews from Los Angeles to Boston focused on the Ozarks phenomenon. Media in Paris, France, even featured the story.

With tension mounting as the day of the opening neared, security for the six days and eight performances of the play was increased. SMSU security and local police worked together to provide a safe environment for cast and crew. Mark Joslyn and Tim Casto held the leading roles.

Tickets for the eight performances

sold out in three and one-half hours, a record according to Dr. Robert Bradley, head of the Theatre and Dance Department. John McElhaney, who directed the play, assumed the media attention did much to sell it to patrons. SMSU theatre alums Kathleen Turner, Tess Harper and John Goodman all voiced support for the university's decision that "the play must go on." Harper came to Springfield for the dress rehearsal and Turner came to campus the week following the play. Legislators, including Representative Doug Harpool, D-Springfield, also defended the play and the university's right to put it on.

The play went on as scheduled, but not without incident. On November 15, the opening night of the play, fire completely destroyed the home of SMSU senior Brad Evans, president of a campus group supporting the play. Fire investigators determined the fire was deliberately set. A reward fund of $10,000 was established to help solve what was perceived by the community to be a "hate crime." The Citizens Demanding Standards group who objected to the play, condemned the violence and contributed nearly half the reward money. The crime was never solved.

Two months later, the university won two awards from the American College Theater Festival Midwest Conference. Members of the Theatre and Dance Department won a special meritorious achievement award for performing *The Normal Heart* in the face of adversity. President Gordon was also recognized for his support of the play.

Later in the year in an interview with the *Ozarko*, President Gordon said of the "Normal Heart" event, "I think we all realize there were no clear winners — or losers — in a situation as sensitive and complex as this one became. Nevertheless, it remains to be seen what long-term effect, if any, all the controversy will have on the university and the performing arts and the teaching of humanities in this state in general. Individuals on all sides have benefited in at least some small way from the many opportunities for discussion, information, sharing and debate."

That assessment was modest. *The Normal Heart* was one of those singular occasions when an institution comes of age. The event was unplanned, unanticipated, and uncontrollable, but nonetheless pivotal to the stature of a maturing university.

Faculty in Service to City Government

Dr. Paul Redfearn was not the first faculty or staff member to serve in city government. In 1959, Dr. David Scott of the Political Science Department was elected mayor of Springfield. He served until 1962. There is no record of others from the university who served on the city council in earlier years, but in more recent times, local government has benefited frequently from university expertise. Dr. Redfearn served two full terms on the Springfield City Council, from 1973-81. Larry Cox of the Economics Department served as mayor of neighboring Republic from 1974-79.

Other faculty have served on the Springfield city council since the 1970s including Lynn Livingston, Dr. Mary Alice Owen Cantrell, Ralph Manley, Dr. Russell Rhodes and Dr. Bob Jones. Drs. David Lages and Mary Jo Wynn served on the City Utilities Board. A number of faculty and staff have served on city boards and commissions ⊞

The Foreigner, directed by Howard Orms, selected for regional American College Theater Festival.

Hammons Tower, tallest building in the city, opens.

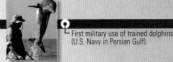

First military use of trained dolphins (U.S. Navy in Persian Gulf).

TV reports rescue of 18-month-old Jessica McClure 58 hours after she fell into a 22-foot well.

Part of the joy of being a biology major in 1983-84 was working in the animal research lab. Senior Carla Senter displays a friend from the lab.

recent years. Charlotte Hardin, coordinator of Minority Student Services, was elected to the Springfield R-XII School Board in 1990.

John Ashcroft was serving as coordinator of judicial affairs as well as teaching business law as the university era began in 1972. In the fall of that year, Ashcroft was appointed state auditor and left for Jefferson City. He was subsequently elected Missouri Attorney General, Governor of the State of Missouri, Senator from Missouri and in 2002 was appointed Attorney General in the George W. Bush administration.

Partners in Progress

As the university's inventory of expertise grew, opportunities to partner with area businesses, industries and organizations developed. As early as 1976, the Physical Science Department collaborated with the Springfield Police Department to obtain a $28,000 x-ray

analyzer that could be used with the scanning electron microscope already owned by the university. Using the two instruments together, it was possible to do crime lab work in 24 hours, which otherwise would take the police department several days to complete. The analyzer had a computer that identified minute particles and produced a readout of chemical elements within the particles. Police had 24-hour access to Temple Hall to use the equipment.

Collaboration with health care providers also has become a tradition. In 1990, St. John's Regional Health Center was sending tumor tissue samples to the University of Missouri-Columbia for diagnosis of certain cancers and diseases. In cooperation with SMSU, the hospital purchased an electron microscopy lab and located it on the SMSU campus where university faculty and students could use it in teaching and research. The lab was

the only one of its kind in southwest Missouri at the time. It had the capacity to analyze tissue samples three-millionths of an inch thick. It produced a positive print of the tissue called a micrograph. The print assisted the physician in diagnosing cancer or other diseases. By using the electron microscopy lab at SMSU, processing time for physicians was reduced from two weeks to 24 hours.

A year later, St. John's and SMSU cooperated in establishing a Sports Medicine Center on the St. John's campus. Staff and students from the sports medicine program at SMSU continue to work in the Center providing rehabilitation services to patients with sports-related injuries.

Partnering with the health care industry has meant establishing an array of health care programs at the university including physical therapy, physician assistant, nursing, nurse practitioner, respiratory therapy, sports medicine and athletics training, medical technology, radiography, dietetics, therapeutic recreation, nurse anesthesia, communication sciences and disorders, social work, gerontology and psychology.

In November 2000, SMSU and The Forest Institute of Professional Psychology signed an agreement to explore the possibility of establishing a long-term partnership. The Forest Institute, founded in 1979, provides professional training and degrees, including the Doctor of Clinical Psychology. Among several areas of mutual interest, the two institutions have agreed to explore the development of joint and cooperative programs in psychology and related areas, and to collaborate with the use of facilities including libraries. According to

SMSU

Missouri/Springfield

Ann K. Covington becomes first woman named to Missouri Supreme Court.

International/USA

Van Gogh's *Irises* sells for record $53.6 million.

Digging begins to link England and France under English Channel.

Australia's 200th anniversary-parade of tall ships in Sydney Harbor.

1988

President Keiser, "One of the goals of our new long-range plan is to 'establish partnerships with other institutions and entities to achieve the university mission.' With SMSU's emphasis on health programs, primarily at the graduate level, this appears to be a partnership worth pursuing."

Long-standing partnerships with the public schools in southwest Missouri have contributed to the professional development of teachers, curriculum development and expansion of course offerings through distance learning technologies. The university's six-year plan published in 2000 indicates that a new focus for the institution will be the expansion of partnering, "a key ingredient to succeeding in the 21st century." The plan identifies the public schools as among the institutions with whom SMSU "has enjoyed mutually beneficial partnerships for many years."

Economic Impact of the University

As early as 1905 when the committee on locating State Normal School #4 visited Springfield, it was clear that such an institution in any city would bring economic benefits. When local businesses volunteered 37.5 acres of select land on the corner of Grand and National, plus $25,000 cash as an enticement to locate the school here, they were aware they were making a long-term investment. However, it is doubtful that they had any idea of how liberally that investment would pay off.

Larry Hazelrigg's 1965 story in the *Springfield News-Leader* identified the college as "one of Springfield's, and the area's, fastest growing industries. It's impact, economically, is almost impossible to measure." Professor Rex Ebrite, instructor of business, made one of the first attempts to measure the economic impact of the school in 1965. He surveyed 129 business management students and discovered they spent an average of $711 a semester for food, lodging, clothing, transportation and entertainment. Multiplying that number by the total enrollment of 4,100, student spending per semester amounted to $2.9 million.

More sophisticated studies began in the 1980s through the Economics Department's Center for Economic Research. Center economists estimated that $147 million had been contributed

Instructional Program Expenditures 1910-2000

Fiscal Year	Constant 2000 Dollars — Total Education and General Expenditures	Revenue from State Appropriations — Constant 2000 Dollars	Revenue from State Appropriations — Percentage of Total	Revenue from Student Fees and Other Income — Constant 2000 Dollars	Revenue from Student Fees and Other Income — Percentage of Total	Total Headcount Enrollment	Constant 2000 Dollars — Total Expenditures Per Student*
1910	$ 1,366,787	$ 1,080,175	79.03%	$ 286,611	20.97%	405	$ 3,375
1920	$ 1,504,554	$ 1,142,547	75.94%	$ 362,007	24.06%	500	$ 3,009
1930	$ 3,578,099	$ 2,665,491	74.49%	$ 912,608	25.51%	1,083	$ 3,304
1940	$ 4,464,900	$ 3,234,900	72.45%	$ 1,230,000	27.55%	1,508	$ 2,961
1950	$ 5,860,087	$ 5,091,239	86.88%	$ 768,848	13.12%	1,795	$ 3,265
1960	$ 8,830,230	$ 7,979,411	90.36%	$ 850,819	9.64%	3,004	$ 2,939
1970	$ 41,292,109	$ 31,517,273	76.33%	$ 9,776,788	23.68%	8,964	$ 4,606
1980	$ 61,266,361	$ 50,078,738	81.74%	$ 11,193,836	18.27%	15,845	$ 3,867
1990	$ 108,371,189	$ 70,971,206	65.49%	$ 37,409,325	34.52%	20,652	$ 5,248
2000	$ 137,166,189	$ 84,701,776	61.75%	$ 52,592,470	38.34%	19,371	$ 7,081

* Student expenditures include fees, books, room and board for a full year.

In 1910, students were paying approximately 21 percent of the cost of their education at SMSU. By 2003, that percentage had doubled to more than 40 percent. Data from the Coordinating Board for Higher Education in 2003 show that between 1980 and 2002, the proportion of the state budget going to higher education had dropped from 16 percent to 11 percent, a decline of more than 31 percent. In 1980, the tax base in Missouri enabled it to rank as high as 15th in support of higher education. The 16 percent of the state budget given to higher education that year placed it 50th among all states.

Basketball Bears to NCAA tournament for second consecutive year.

David D. Glass Hall, home of the College of Business Administration, opens.

Barbara Bush visits Springfield.

Bobby Allison, at 50, becomes oldest driver to win Daytona 500.

NASA reports accelerated breakdown of ozone layer by CFK.

It is reported that nicotine is as addictive as heroin.

THE LEGACY OF
LESLIE IRENE COGER

by Dr. Robert H. Bradley

Leslie Irene Coger arrived at Southwest Missouri State Teachers College in the fall of 1943 and taught and directed theatre productions there until her retirement at the end of the summer term in 1981. She was a highly energetic, outgoing and warm individual and quickly became a familiar figure on campus. While theatre activities had long been a part of the campus scene, she established a theatre program of courses and activities.

Born January 18, 1912, in Huntsville, Arkansas, Coger received her B.A. degree from College of the Ozarks (Arkansas) and M.A. from University of Arkansas. In the 1930s she attended the Curry School of Expression in Boston. A.S. Curry, the founder of the school, wrote a series of textbooks based on his classroom practices that might be summed up in his often-used phrase, "To think the thought, hold the thought, and share the thought." Coger taught that basic axiom for the rest of her career. Her doctoral dissertation in the mid-1950s at Northwestern University was *A Comparison of the Methods of Curry and Stanislavski.* She had chosen Northwestern because it was the academic center for the emerging field of oral interpretation that was to be her area of expertise. Devoting the rest of her teaching career to melding theories of performance into the developing field of oral interpretation, she became a national authority in 1967 when she and co-author Melvin White published *Readers Theatre Handbook: A Dramatic Approach to Literature,* the first textbook in the field. It went through three editions and is still referred to throughout this country and abroad including a translation into Japanese.

At SMSU Irene was a dynamic force. She initiated a summer theatre program. In 1963, she established a national festival, the Ozarks Spring Interpretation Festival, the first in the nation to focus on group performance, and she continued to host it every year until her retirement. In summer 1963 on the SMSU campus, she founded with Robert Gilmore the Tent Theatre. In that first summer she directed two productions, a comedy and a musical. In all she would direct 14 productions in Tent with her final official activity at SMSU being a production in the summer of 1981. She was one of the first women to direct and tour overseas for the United States Organization (USO) to military bases with musicals originating with SMSU students and to do so four times between 1961 and 1973.

She is always remebered first as a teacher. Irene loved teaching, loved the classroom — after all, it was a mini-theatre event as far as she was concerned. The students learned through her excitement and enthusiasm. She entertained. At a time when she taught acting, students remembered her arriving on the first day, standing on the desk and doing a tumble to the floor. She would get up, brush herself and inform them that they would be able to do the same kind of actor's fall by the end of the semester. While she stimulated students in her classroom, she also demanded work. She gave extensive reading assignments. In her course on performing in period drama students had to read about customs, manners, and everyday life in Greece, Rome and Elizabethan London. Actors were supposed to know wherein they performed.

Irene never stopped learning. Through her retirement years she still attended the national conferences for theatre and interpretation. She wanted to stay abreast of what was developing in her fields. While Irene had always been a traveler, during her retirement, she became an avid world traveler. Upon her return to Springfield, she then eagerly presented slide talks on her adventures to exotic locations.

Coger received many local, state and national commendations, honors and awards. The USO recognized her several times for the excellence of her USO shows. The Speech and Theatre Association of Missouri recognized her as an Outstanding Teacher for the Year and bestowed on her the Emeritus Teacher Award, and she was declared "Pioneer of Education" by Arthur Mallory, Missouri Commissioner of Education. The Missouri Council of the Arts recognized her for her quality of contributions to the arts of Missouri. At the John F. Kennedy Center for Performing Arts in Washington she was inducted into the College of Fellows of the American Theatre. Perhaps no recognition pleased her more than the theatre in Craig Hall being named in her honor following her retirement.

Irene died April 16, 1999, in Springfield. On May 8 in the theatre named to honor her, friends and former students from New York to Florida to California gathered to remember and celebrate her life. It was a gorgeous, sunny spring day. All those attending knew that she had arranged it that way.

to the local economy by university spending in 1980. By 1984, the estimate had increased to $365 million, or a $1 million per day. At the time, SMSU was the largest employer in Springfield with more than 3,000 on its payroll. The estimate was based on $152 million in direct spending by SMSU students and employees. That amount had a multiplier effect of $213 million, bringing the total economic impact to $365 million. By 1990, the economic impact had increased to $1.7 million a day or a total of $618.4 million for the year. The report also indicated that the university accounts for approximately 23,000 jobs in the city.

An update of the 1984 study was done for the year 2001 by Professor Emeritus of Economics Larry Cox. He reports the economic impact of the university in 2001 was approximately $664 million, or $1.82 million a day.

The university period has seen relationships with the community both strained and cordial. The growth of the institution has created a positive impact economically and culturally. The completion of the Juanita K. Hammons Hall for the Performing Arts has multiplied the artistic benefits to the community, while the growth of academic programs has brought an ever larger number of scholars and notable public figures to campus. But the growth also created strains in neighborhoods around the university as student lifestyles conflicted with area residents. Growth also created anxieties for traditional family residential areas such as Rountree and Phelps Grove Park until long range plans for the university expansion pointed toward downtown. That proved to be a relief to property owners east and south of the university,

and a boon to the redevelopment of the downtown area.

Athletics forged strong ties between the university and the local community as men's and women's teams had successful seasons and gained national attention. The adoption of the public affairs mission stimulated a "strongly interactive relationship with the surrounding community" as well. Linkages with local civic organizations multiplied as students, faculty, and staff explored new citizenship roles. On balance, the era has been one of mutual enrichment between university and community.

Funding the University

Funding of higher education is not a mark of distinction in the state of Missouri. Conservative in orientation, the state has been reluctant to increase the tax burden for the benefit of higher education. The University of Missouri was authorized in 1839 and began operations in 1841, but it wasn't until 1867 that it began receiving annual appropriations from the State Legislature. When the state authorized the establishment of State Normal School #4 in Springfield in 1905, it provided no budgetary support. The school started operation with tuition income and $25,000 in private gifts.

In the 1980s, Missouri had a sufficient tax base to rank 15th in the country in its support of higher education. It actually ranked 50th. By 1984-85, it raised its ranking to 46th of 50 states.

Less than a year after President Keiser took office in 1993, the state was asked to vote on a constitutional amendment, known as "Hancock II," which proposed tightening further the provisions of Hancock I, passed by

Missouri voters in 1980, restricting the State Legislature's ability to raise taxes. In 1994, Mel Hancock was serving in Congress from the 7th Congressional District, which includes much of southwest Missouri. After studying the proposed amendment, President Keiser concluded that its passage could further weaken the financial status of higher education in Missouri. He led the higher education charge against "Hancock II," including a heated debate with Congressman Hancock in which he claimed passage of the amendment would strangle higher education funds by 32 percent. Hancock countered that the amendment "would return tax control to the people," as well as bringing more business into the state, "which would be good for everyone."

To the relief of educators and others across the state, the amendment failed in the November 1994 general election by a 68 to 32 percent margin. However, it did not change the conservative funding tradition with which the university had been contending for years. SMSU occupied a particularly vulnerable position in state funding throughout the 1990s because of its rapid growth during a time when legislative appropriations were not based on enrollment changes. In 1994, the state spent an average of $6,024 per student enrolled in state colleges and universities. The University of Missouri received $8,453 per student from the Legislature. SMSU received $3,741.

That funding inequity has continued into the 21st century. In 2001-2002 the Legislature appropriated an average of $8,482 for every student enrolled in a four-year state college or university. SMSU received $5,778, the lowest per-student allocation of

Dean Franklin Kenworthy killed in auto accident in Springfield.

Enrollment exceeds 17,000 (17,885).

Missouri Supreme Court rules in the Nancy Cruzan "right to life" case.

New York City's Rockefeller Center declared as a national landmark.

1972-2005 Southwest Missouri State University 307

Standard cartoonist R. Weber pictures President Marshall Gordon tip-toeing past the Student Government Association office on his way to a Board meeting in 1987 to request a student fee increase. By 1990, the proportion of educational expenses borne by the student had increased to over 30 percent.

all seven state universities. Put differently, SMSU, in 2001-02, enrolled 16.1 percent of all the students enrolled in four-year public institutions, but received only 11 percent of the state appropriation for public higher education. Funding continued to lag behind enrollment — by 31.2 percent in 2001-02.

Despite the inequity in funding, the university has been able to distinguish itself among its sister institutions. In the fall of 2001, SMSU ranked first among the five regional universities in numbers of graduate students, standing just below the University of Missouri-Columbia and UMKC. The fact that the SMSU has struggled (successfully) over the years with the handicap of under-funding has been used as a legislative argument for not correcting the inequity.

The Student Burden

Historically, state supported higher education was a means of providing access to the benefits of advanced learning to all citizens. The subsidizing of higher education not only gave families of modest and limited means access to college, but it also enabled the state to have a better trained workforce with benefits accruing to the state's economy as well as businesses and industries locating here.

But over the years, what was once understood as state *supported* higher education has evolved into state *assisted* higher education as the proportion of the cost of educating a student borne by the state has steadily declined. In 1907, the student share was about 9 percent of the total cost. By 1963, student fees covered 17.2 percent of the cost of education at SMSU; the state provided the remaining 82.8 percent.

By the beginning of the university period, the proportion paid by students had increased 20.8 percent. Ten years later in 1983, the student proportion had increased to 22.1 percent. More dramatic increases in the student financial load came in the 1990s. In 1998, more than one-third of the total cost of their SMSU education was borne by students, and as the economic downturn reduced state revenues in 2002, students were paying 43 percent of the cost of their education in 2002-03.

The increasing burden on students can be seen by expressing basic fees from 1906 to 2002 in constant 2000 dollars. The per-hour cost of instruction to students in 1906 (in constant 2000 dollars) was $17.01. When state support was added in 1907, the cost per-hour dropped to $12.34. It did not exceed that number until 1918-19, the end of the normal school period, when the per-hour cost increased to $13.45. At the end of the state teachers college era in 1945, the per-hour cost had increased to $21.26. At the end of the state college era in 1972, per-hour costs stood at $42.52. During the university period, per-hour costs have increased from $41.20 in 1972-73 to $128 in the fall of 2002. These figures represent basic fees for in-state, undergraduate students. Out-of-state fees are typically twice the resident fee.

A student entering the university in the fall of 2002 with a 12-hour semester load would expect to pay $1,596 in basic fees, $115 in supplemental course fees, $217 in student services fees, for a total fee assessment of $1,928. Housing and board expenses would be additional.

SMSU

516 minority students enrolled.

Library purchases first CD-Rom for selected reference sources.

Missouri/Springfield

International/USA

Britain bans broadcast interviews with IRA members.

308 *A Centennial History of SMSU*

Strategies for Financing a College Education

As the cost of a college education has increased over the years, the strategies for managing the cost have changed. A large proportion of students still work 20 or more hours a week either on campus or in area businesses, and families still invest savings in their children's education. But neither of those strategies typically provides a complete solution to the cost problem. Consequently, all of higher education has had to develop financial aid plans to assist students.

As early as the State College period, federal assistance became available through both loans and grants. The growth of federal assistance over the past 35 years is a complex story we will not detail here, but without that significant supplement to existing institutional resources, the majority of students who have attended SMSU in the past 30 years would probably not have been able to manage.

Compared to the dollars currently provided through the financial aid office, the scale in the late 1970s was modest: 2,496 grants and scholarships were given totaling nearly $1.6 million; 1,432 loans totaling $1.3 million were made; and student employment and federal work-study programs added another $1.1 million bringing the total student aid package in 1977-78 to $3.9 million.

A second important factor in providing financial assistance has been the establishment of the SMSU Foundation in 1981. It gave academic departments a vehicle for establishing scholarships to honor alumni, faculty members and other causes. The annual telephone campaign sponsored by the Foundation has added substantially to the scholarship resources available to students.

At the beginning of President Gordon's tenure in 1983, scholarship programs were expanded significantly in an attempt to attract additional academically gifted students. With 15,233 students enrolled in 1987-88, total financial aid had exploded to $20.3 million, an increase of more than 420 percent in 10 years. More than two-thirds of the total amount given was based on financial need.

Ten years later with 16,794 students enrolled, total financial aid dispensed by the university had increased another 215 percent to $64 million. Whereas in earlier years the amount awarded as grants and scholarships and the amount taken out in loans were nearly equal, by 1997-98, grants and scholarships amounted to $21.3 million while loans totaled $36.2 million.

It is this increase in loans that concerns university administrators. Billie Jo Hamilton, director of financial aid, reported that the class of 2001 carried an average debt of $19,429 as they graduated. She estimated that parents probably borrowed an additional $10,000 to finance the nine semesters it typically takes to complete an undergraduate degree. Handing that kind of debt load along with a diploma to a graduating senior takes a bit of the celebrating out of commencement.

By 2001-02, the university was distributing $77.7 million in financial aid to 12,357 students; more dollars than were appropriated for the entire nation in 1960 through the National Defense Education Act.

Todd Morris, director emeritus of financial aid, recalls that the entire financial aid program operated in the 1960s with just a full-time director and a part-time student worker. The full-time staff in 2002 numbered 26, assisted by five graduate students, a half-time professional and several student workers. "In the beginning, the student's financial aid record was limited to the 80 characters that could be punched into an IBM card," recalls Morris. "By the time we reach the Centennial Year, financial aid will be using a state-of-the-art server-based financial aid system that is fully integrated with systems in admissions, records and financial services."

In the early 1990s when the Financial Aid Office was struggling to keep abreast of the growing work load and students were waiting in long lines to be helped, *The Standard* ran an editorial cartoon entitled "Line of the Living Dead." It showed skeletal, emaciated students standing in line at the financial aid office. A sign in the window said, "Waiting Time — Infinity." Acting President Russell Keeling responded, authorizing six additional staff members.

There is a unique division of labor in the SMSU financial aid program, which is typical of most universities; institutional scholarships and fellowships are all merit based; federal grants and loans are need based. So in 2002, a total of $11.2 million of institutional funds were distributed to 4,249 students. Of that number, 271 were athletics scholarships amounting to $853,634. More than $10 million was given in merit-based scholarships to an additional 3,978 students.

Deciding to Seek Private Funds

As noted previously, the goal of publicly funded colleges and universities making higher education essentially "free"

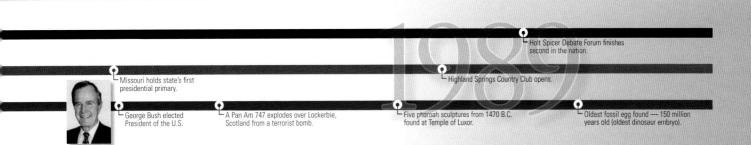

Missouri holds state's first presidential primary.

George Bush elected President of the U.S.

A Pan Am 747 explodes over Lockerbie, Scotland from a terrorist bomb.

Five pharoah sculptures from 1470 B.C. found at Temple of Luxor.

Holt Spicer Debate Forum finishes second in the nation.

Highland Springs Country Club opens.

Oldest fossil egg found — 150 million years old (oldest dinosaur embryo).

to any person wanting it has become an unrealized dream. But the vocabulary has remained intact. "Tuition" has been charged at SMSU only in 1906-07 when no state funds we available to cover educational costs. After that time, fee charges were considered to cover "incidental" costs rather than educational costs such as faculty salaries, etc. So to this day, students pay "incidental fees," not tuition. But the reality is that "incidental fees" in 2002-03 covered more than 40 percent of the educational costs.

As the university era opened in the 1970s, significant changes began in the funding of higher education in Missouri. Up to that time, few public institutions like SMSU pursued private donations. But late in the 1970s, the effects of spiraling inflation and a stagnant economy pushed state higher education officials to invoke two new policies: (1) Each Missouri public institution must set student fees at a level that would equal 28 percent of the respective institution's "educational costs"; and (2) Institutions that could acquire private donations for a portion of new construction costs would be given priority for available matching state funds.

The effect of these policy changes by the Missouri Coordinating Board for Higher Education was to transform "incidental fees" into "tuition," and to guarantee that student fees would increase on virtually an annual basis. The policy also sent a signal to all the public institutions that their future prosperity would depend in large part upon their ability to raise funds from private sources.

Understandably, SMSU officials were reluctant to ask individuals to pro-

vide financial support for services that for almost three-quarters of a century had been financed by tax dollars. Their reluctance is reflected in the fact that SMSU was the last of the five original "regional" institutions to enter the private fund-raising arena.

The precipitating event that pushed the Board of Regents into private fund-raising was the controversial decision in 1980 to move the SMS intercollegiate athletics program into Division I of the NCAA. For the most part, the faculty opposed the move, feeling that Division I competition would drain scarce resources away from academic excellence. On the other hand, the Springfield community generally applauded the idea, seeing the possibility for athletics preeminence at SMSU. The Regents promised that the additional athletics funding necessary to participate in Division I competition would come from gate receipts and private donations. The irony here is that athletics became the precipitating cause that led to an aggressive charitable program which benefited not only athletics, but also academics.

With the decision to go Division I in athletics, the Board proceeded to hire the institution's first fundraisers. Ralph Manley, a well-known

Springfield businessman, was named director of development. Bill Maynard, an SMSU alumnus and champion debater, was named athletics development officer. These two fundraisers reported to a new assistant to the president, Kenneth Brown, who had been hired to assist with the transition to Division I athletics.

Establishing the SMSU Foundation
Quickly after commencing their work, the development staff saw the need for an educational foundation through which the university could operate its fund-raising program. Kenneth Brown appeared before the Regents in November 1980 to report the administration's view that a Foundation should be established. The Regents concurred, and 60 days later, on January 13, 1981, a certificate of incorporation was issued by the Missouri Secretary of State to the SMSU Foundation, Inc., showing President Duane Meyer, Board of Regents Treasurer Maurice E. Edwards, and Presidential Secretary Wilma Tolbert, as incorporators.

The Board of Regents served for six months as the first Foundation Board of Directors. In May 1981, Kenneth Brown was appointed by President Meyer as the first executive director of the Foundation. By July 1981, 12 area citizens were appointed to replace the Regents as the Foundation's first permanent Board. They included three former Regents: Dr. Joseph F. Johnston, Ramona McQueary and Howard Randall. Eight additional directors were named, including Dr. Stephen Bodanske, R. Dwain Hammons, Georgia Calton, Gene Ruble, Darrel Love, R. Wagner Love, Virginia Dailey and Dr. Glenn Johnston.

SMSU
Enrollment exceeds 19,000 (19,377).
Library catalog goes online.

Missouri/Springfield
An 18-inch snowfall shuts down the Ozarks.

International/USA
Tanker *Exxon Valdez* spills 11 million barrels of oil off Alaskan coast.

In the fall of 1981, the Foundation conducted its first annual national phone campaign under the direction of Julie Ebersold. Dozens of faculty, staff and students gathered in a specially equipped room in the basement of the Campus Union to call thousands of alumni across the country. That first event raised $50,000, an incredibly encouraging start.

In early 1982, the university hired Greg Onstot, a highly successful director of alumni relations at Central Missouri State, to become director of development and alumni relations. Shortly after his arrival, Onstot was named executive director of the SMSU Foundation, replacing Brown.

Immediately, Onstot began a systematic study of the most successful university foundations, which might serve as a model for the SMSU effort. The careful approach proved successful. The Founders Club was established to encourage gifts for academics and capital projects. This effort has brought in millions of dollars for academic needs as well as funds for capital projects such as the Juanita K. Hammons Hall for the Performing Arts, David D. Glass Hall, Robert W. Plaster Sports Complex, Duane G. Meyer Library, Forsythe Athletics Center, William H. Darr Agricultural Center, Wehr Band Hall and Strong Hall.

The focus of the Foundation's effort under Onstot's leadership has been both "friend-raising" and "fund-raising." The approach has been signally successful. In the 23 years since its establishment, the Foundation has raised more than $89 million, with an additional $26 million in deferred gifts, making a total of $115 million in gifts to the university. In 2002-03,

the SMSU Foundation received a record 34,992 gifts totaling more than $7 million.

The gifts have been as large as $3 million, and as small as a few dollars, but collectively they have created a community of support that is vital to the university's future. Brown, who went on to teach accounting at the university after establishing the Foundation, remembers some poignant stories of giving. Hazel Belle Scott, a widow and long-time cleaning lady in Springfield, sent her only son, Robert Lee Scott, to SMSU in the 1940s. Like many other students at the time, Robert was called away to World War II before his studies were completed. A theatre major, Robert wrote his mother from New York on his way to the European war zone, that he had been able to attend a Broadway show in the city. This was the last time Mrs. Scott heard from her son. Robert went down with his crew on a bombing mission over Germany. Hazel Belle's final days were lonely. Heart-broken over her loss, she resolved to leave a memorial for her son at the university. Those who knew her said she deprived herself to save money for the fund. When she died in 1980, she left her modest home on the north side of Springfield and her savings to the university to establish the Robert Lee Scott Memorial Scholarship, which continues to this day to benefit needy students.

At this writing, a major comprehensive fund-raising initiative, "*The Campaign for SMS: Imagine the Possibilities,*" is under way. Planned to conclude in 2005, the campaign covers a wide range of opportunities from supporting the student body, promoting faculty development, enhancing the learning environment, assuring contin

Among the many competitive activities open to students in 1980s were rodeo events. Lisa Williams cuts a corner in the barrel racing event at the Ozark Empire Fairgrounds.

ued program support and growth of the endowment as major areas of emphasis. The campaign goal is $50 million.

Athletics Fund-Raising

The decision to go Division I in athletics competition involved significant investments in facilities and programs. By the year 2000, the budget for intercollegiate athletics stood at more than $8 million. The university's education and general budget provides approximately half of the $8 million, covering salaries and fringe benefits for the majority of athletics personnel, plus out-of-state fee waivers for student-athletes. The remaining $4 million is raised through gate receipts, radio and television programs, NCAA grants, concession profits and gifts to The Bears Fund.

While there was some modest

The Normal Heart production controversy receives nationwide attention.

One million Chinese dissidents, led by students, demonstrate for democracy in Beijing.

First test flight of U.S. stealth-bomber.

Pete Rose is suspended from baseball for life for gambling.

fund-raising for athletics as early at the 1960s, the first comprehensive effort came in 1982 with the establishment of the SMSU Foundation and The Bears Fund. That first year, more than $100,000 was raised. In 1983, the amount doubled. In 1988, The Bears Fund had its first $1 million year. Going into the 21st century, gifts to The Bears Fund had grown to nearly $1.5 million annually.

By 2000, The Bears Fund, along with other athletics revenues, paid for all 240 scholarships for nearly 400 male and female student-athletes participating in 21 intercollegiate sports. It was also providing monies to fund the operational budgets of all the sports.

In 1984, donors to The Bears Fund numbered just over 1,000 individuals. By 2001, there were more than 2,500. Donors have had the option of designating their gifts to go to either women's or men's sports since 1983. In that year $500 was given to women's programs. By the next year, more than $17,000 was given to women's programs, and by 1989 the $100,000 mark had been reached. While contributions to men's sports have been consistently larger over the years, the growth of contributions to women's sports has been phenomenal. In the decade between 1990 and 2000, contributions to women's programs increased almost 300 percent to more than $375,000. The entire Bears Fund, over the same period, increased just 28 percent.

The university period has been one in which new partners in education have been sought by the institution. Private funding for capital projects, shifting educational costs to students through regularly increasing fees, and supporting academic and athletics

Matt Cepicky demonstrates his power-swing against Arkansas in the 1999 Fayetteville Regional Tournament. Named MVP for the tournament even though SMS didn't win, Cepicky went on to lead Division I with 30 homers in 1999 and signed a professional baseball contract upon leaving SMS.

enterprises through charitable gifts represent the new environment in which the university lives. In some ways it resembles the beginnings of the institution when the grant of a choice plot of land, charitable gifts of $25,000, and tuition from 573 summer school students launched State Normal School #4 in 1906.

Student Life and Achievements

The university years have witnessed not only a student body growing in numbers, but also in individual and team achievements. Programs such as debate and athletics, which had already gained national attention, continued their winning ways. Theatre and music featured outstanding productions. Individual students brought distinction to the university by winning distinguished fellowships for graduate study at the best universities

in the country. In a word, achievement had become the norm.

Debate Thrives

Debate teams during the 1970s continued the winning tradition, which had characterized forensics at SMSU for decades. In 1974, the team set a school record winning four major tournaments. In 1977 the university was chosen for the first time to host the 31st National Collegiate Debate Tournament, a blue-ribbon achievement in itself.

By the 1980s, two different styles of debate were competing for collegiate attention. The traditional National Debate Tournament style featuring factual presentation found a rival in the Cross-Examination Debate Association (CEDA) style emphasizing a value-oriented, emotional approach to persuasion. SMSU began competing in CEDA tournaments, and as early as 1983 was quickly ranked in the Top 10 nationally. In the fall of 1983, SMSU debaters won the Berkeley Invitational Tournament, considered one of the best in the country, with 40 teams from 25 leading schools matching wits. In 1987, SMSU finished ninth of 326 colleges in CEDA competition, winning four first place sweepstakes awards and a total of 79 trophies. The following year, the team finished eighth in the nation with a third-place finish at the CEDA national tournament at the United State Air Force Academy. Dr. Candy Clark, forensics director that year said, "The basketball team tries to make it to the Final Four in the NCAA Tournament. We made it to the Final Four in debate."

Being ranked in the Top 10 debate programs nationally had become a tra-

SMSU

Campus grows to 190 acres.

Missouri/Springfield

International/USA

Earthquake measuring 7.1 on the Richter scale strikes San Francisco just minutes before the World Series begins as millions watch on television.

The Berlin Wall falls as the border opens between East and West Germany, and the Soviet Empire begins to collapse.

312 *A Centennial History of SMSU*

dition by the late 1980s. On October 21, 1988, the debate program was named the Holt V. Spicer Forum in honor of Dr. Holt Spicer who had succeeded Dr. Virginia Craig in 1952. The momentum in the SMSU program by the end of the decade had pushed it to a second-place finish in the CEDA national tournament held at SMSU in the spring of 1990. Competing against 238 teams from 119 schools, SMSU actually placed three of its teams in the top 64. Robert Olson and Eric Morris were defeated in the final round.

The moment of destiny came in the spring of 1992. CEDA's national tournament was held in Arlington, Texas, with 237 teams and 129 colleges competing. Dr. Holt Spicer was back

The campus is forever a place of creative entertainment. Mike Tyler, Cindy Ash, Fred Lines and Roy Waddell helped raise more than $2,000 for the Cerebral Palsy Weekend with the Stars Telethon by going underwater for a "pool poker" game in Hammons Student Center in January 1982.

in the coaching chair as interim forensics director. Forty years earlier at West Point, N.Y., he had become the first debater to win the national tournament two consecutive years. On March 30, 1992, he won his third national title, this time as coach. According to those who were present, it wasn't even close. Jef Jarman and T.J. Wolfe simply blew away all comers to win the national championship, the first in the history of SMSU. Coach Spicer was delivered an unforgettable going-away present — his first national title as a coach. He retired from the university that spring. Later that year the Holt Spicer Debate Forum would be featured on ABC's "Good Morning America" show.

In 1995, the debate team changed

back from CEDA competition to the National Debate Tournament competition exclusively. For three years the team had competed in both tournaments, but the cost in travel and the splitting up of the team into two different styles did not prove effective. In 1996, SMSU, ranked 15th in the nation, and qualified two debate teams for the National Debate Tournament at Wake Forest University. Again in 2000, two SMSU teams qualified for the NDT held this time in Kansas City. It was the third consecutive year two SMSU teams had been awarded slots in the national tournament. Matt Vega and Troy Payne were the first team in the 96-year history of SMSU debate to qualify for four consecutive National Debate Tournaments. The honors continued in 2002 with SMSU being awarded the hosting of the NDT, only the second time in the 56-year history of the NDT that its championship tournament was awarded to the school.

The debate tradition in Springfield is a long and distinguished one. In its November 10, 1996, issue, the *Springfield News-Leader* noted that 18 Springfieldians have won the National Forensic League All-American award since it was established in 1986, more than any other city in the nation, and more than many states. "The university program is at least partly responsible for strong programs throughout southwest Missouri, particularly Springfield," the paper reported. "Here, good debating is more a tradition than a trend."

Honorary Societies Grow
By the time the university era began in 1972, there were already more than 20 national honorary societies on campus recognizing the academic excel-

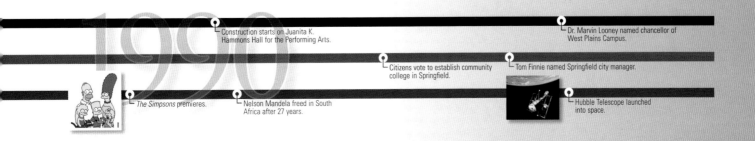

1990

Construction starts on Juanita K. Hammons Hall for the Performing Arts.

Dr. Marvin Looney named chancellor of West Plains Campus.

Citizens vote to establish community college in Springfield.

Tom Finnie named Springfield city manager.

The Simpsons premieres.

Nelson Mandela freed in South Africa after 27 years.

Hubble Telescope launched into space.

Part of the fun of Derby Days in 1989 was "water bombing." Here Shelley White, an Alpha Chi Omegan, is "bombed" by Dave Schwarz of the Sigma Chi fraternity.

lence, character and leadership qualities of students. Individual students were winning national recognition for their achievements as well. Denise Fenimore won a 1985-86 Emmy Award from the Academy of Television Arts and Sciences in Hollywood for her news feature dealing with marketing research, the only Emmy winner from an 11-state region and only one of nine nationwide.

In 1986-87, the American Marketing Association student chapter received the first place award in national AMA competition among 140 colleges and universities. The SMSU Dairy Cattle Judging Team placed first in the nation in competition at El Reno, Oklahoma.

That same year, the SMSU Advertising Team, in its first year of existence, finished second in American Advertising Federation competition in District 9, just one-half point behind the winner, Iowa State University. The five-member team of Terri Wilson Hall, Cindy Hughes, Monique Valleroy, Vicki Newman and Kyla Edwards, received the same assignment as all other entries — use $12 million in the best way possible to market the Chevrolet Cavalier. The teams began their planning in September and made their presentations in March. The presentations included a 50-page marketing plan book and a 20-minute team presentation. Hall and her teammates decided to focus on the 18- to 24-year-old target group, using light humor, an original jingle and distinctive graphics. By the end of February, the team knew the entire script for the 20-minute presentation, and were the only team to make its presentation without notes. They had practiced the script more

than 100 times. "Back in September, all of us were leery of the competition and how we would do," admitted Hall. "But (sponsor) Dr. Steve Greene kept telling us he wouldn't send us to the competition with something that was stupid. I'm glad now that I stuck with it," she said. "It was worth all the hard work."

National Merit Scholars were doing well also. In the late 1980s, Tom Bough was SMSU's first applicant for a Rhodes Scholarship. He was accepted at Arizona State to do graduate study in music. Harvard Law School accepted two SMSU applicants from among 8,500 applications for an incoming class of 560. David B. Pointer, a Presidential Scholar and Merit Finalist, received a Phi Kappa Phi Fellowship for graduate study at Harvard. Paul Carver was a winner of the Curl Political Science Scholarship at SMSU.

In 1989, Allen Kerkeslager, an antiquities major, won one of the most distinguished awards ever given

At some point in nearly every fraternity/sorority competition, the "wheelbarrow race" is run to the delight of spectators who watch the men trying to keep up with their pushers.

to an SMSU student. He was given a William Penn Fellowship to do doctoral studies on Christian origins at the University of Pennsylvania. Other SMSU students were winning places in professional schools. In 1990, 11 of 15 SMSU applicants to medical school at the University of Missouri and the University of Kansas were accepted. In 1991, eight graduates were accepted into law school, nine into medical school, three into veterinary medicine, and six into dentistry. The following year, six were accepted into law school, 12 into medical school and five each into dentistry and veterinary medicine.

Southwest Standard *Awards*

Over the years since 1912 when the first edition of *The Southwest Standard* was published, editors have increasingly focused on achieving the excellence the paper's name implies. In the 1930s *The Standard* joined state and national associations and started entering contests for college journalists. From that time forward, the paper and its writers have garnered dozens of awards.

The April 25, 1975, issue reported the newspaper was rated "average" in Missouri Collegiate Newspaper Association competition. While *The Standard* had won four awards, the judges were candid in their critique: "If you could get away from childish writing, your paper would dramatically improve. You have a lot of imagination and energy, but you also have obvious problems." Two years later, six individual awards were made, but "the judge said the reporters and editors do not go out of the office enough."

By the 1980s, things were getting better. In 1984, *The Standard* was named the best newspaper in the state,

the only time to this writing. After the paper became a broadsheet, it was judged best in the state in 1985. In that same year *The Standard* received a first place with special merit award from the American Scholastic Press Association, scoring 970 out of a possible 1,000 points. From 1984-1989, the paper won five-star All American awards, and a regional Pacemaker Award in 1990.

In 1990, Editor Traci Bauer won a first amendment award from the Society of Professional Journalists for her actions to protect first amendment rights. Bauer successfully sued the university in federal court to obtain access to campus crime records.

Between 1996-2001, the paper won a total of 21 first place awards in state competition. Overall, the paper

Stuffing 10 students into a telephone booth celebrated the raising of over $10,000 by Alpha Phi Omega and Gamma Sigma Sigma for victims of muscular dystrophy in 1975. Rod Reed added a special touch to the dance marathon celebration by swallowing a gold fish for every $1,000 raised.

has won from 13 to 18 awards each year. In 1998, the paper was named a finalist for a Pacemaker award in a national contest of the American Collegiate Press. The Pacemaker is one of the highest honors for collegiate journalism, and the second time in the history of *The Standard* to be recognized. In 2002 the photo staff swept the awards given in the photo page category.

As early as 1912, the editor described the aspirations of *The Standard*. "To it," he said, "all other schools would do well to refer in case they desire properly to construct, test, or regulate their own official organs as regards the extent of their influence, the quantity and quality of their contents, and their permanent value to the subscriber." It took a while, but those lofty goals are being reached.

"Greek Row" Develops

The Greek scene at the beginning of the university era included five sororities and 11 fraternities. Despite being

Dr. Katherine Lederer presents *Many Thousand Gone.*

Defense and Strategic Studies department hosts national conference on security strategies for the 1990s.

Iraq invades Kuwait.

Tim Berners-Lee writes program for World Wide Web to make the Internet more accessible for physicists at CERN in Geneva.

East Germany and West Germany merge to become Germany.

1972-2005 Southwest Missouri State University   315

Democracy

"The quality of democracy depends on the quality of its citizens rather than on its leaders or laws... democracy is ordinary men and women doing extraordinary things on a regular and constant basis."

∽

President John H. Keiser
State of the University Address
August 17, 1995

a numerical minority, the Greeks had established themselves as the dominant political and social faction on campus. Their organizational skills carried most campus elections. Their penchant for parties and celebrations dominated the social calendar.

Throughout the 1970s, fraternity and sorority chapter houses were primarily renovated residences. Judith Payton, a 1978 graduate and Alpha Delta Pi alumna, remembers their house on historic Walnut Street. "Between 25 and 29 girls lived in the house," she said. "We shared three bathrooms and had an open-door policy. Back then we were only served five meals a week."

Nathan Carlson, Sigma Pi fraterni-

ty alumnus, remembers living with his fraternity brothers. "At that time, we didn't have a house," he said. "Several of us rented an older house together and it seemed more like apartments."

As the Greek community grew and began to build new houses, the university encouraged them to relocate away from residential neighborhoods and congregate north of campus along Cherry and Elm streets in what has been called "Greek Row." The move not only helped solve neighborhood problems, but it also created the opportunity for closer cooperation among Greek houses. In 1988, the first "new" fraternity house, Sigma Phi Epsilon, was constructed at 1043 E. Cherry. Since then more than 23 chapters with houses have built new facilities or renovated existing houses on Greek Row.

The architecture of Greek Row is traditionally Greek with Federal and Jeffersonian touches. Almost all include Greek columns and pediments. "The columns dimensions are figured by an historical formula that follows the proportions of the human body," explains Jill Burton, project architect at Casey and Associates, who designed the Kappa Alpha house renovation in 1994. There is a notable exception, however. The Alpha Delta Pi house on Elm Street carries a Prairie style design providing a striking contrast to its columned neighbors.

While the Greek system nationally has experienced a decline in numbers, the SMSU experience has remained steady with approximately 12 percent of the campus holding membership in fraternities and sororities.

Black and Latino Greek Organizations Established

In 1984, the first black fraternity, Kappa Alpha Psi, was established on campus. The national fraternity was started at Indiana University, according to Michael Chatman, the first president of the SMSU chapter. Although the fraternity is predominately populated by African Americans across the country, according to Chatman, "We do have white brothers." Chatman added, "By next year, I fully expect to have white members." The chapter received its charter from the national organization in 1985, and acquired its own residence in 1989-90. It had 10 members by the spring of 1990. Beginning in 1989, three additional black fraternities had been established. Phi Beta Sigmas organized in 1989, Alpha Phi Alpha in 1991 and Iota Phi Theta in 1998.

According to the February 8, 1991, *Standard,* two black sororities joined the Greek community. Delta Sigma Theta was organized in December 1989 and Alpha Kappa Alpha was established in May 1990. Sigma Gamma Rho was established in 1992, and a Latino sorority, Sigma Alpha Chi, was established in 1997.

Hazing and Alcohol Problems

Hazing abuses occurred in the middle 1980s among SMSU Greeks, but they appear to be in decline. In 1985, a male pledge was tied to a flagpole and stripped. He sued the fraternity and settled out of court. Another fraternity used a "hot box" where pledges were required to do physical exercises in a steam room. While hazing activities were often "off the wall," by the end of the 1980s many of the Greek organizations were eliminating haz-

SMSU

Missouri/Springfield

International/USA

Judge Russell Clark rules in favor of *Standard* in Bauer vs. Kincaid et al. lawsuit.

Charlotte Hardin elected to School Board, first African American citizen to win a Springfield election since 1906.

First Night New Year's celebration begins.

Mary Robinson elected as first female President of Ireland.

Shoeless Joe Jackson's signature is sold for $23,100.

Operation "Desert Storm" liberates Kuwait.

1991

Traci Bauer, *Southwest Standard* editor and her attorney Douglas Greene walk away from the Federal Court House in Springfield in 1991 after testifying in the case involving access to campus security records. U.S. District Judge Russell Clark ruled in Bauer's favor in March 1991, carrying important implications for the Department of Education's interpretation of the Family Education Rights and Privacy Act.

ing from the pledge ordeal. TKEs abolished the two-tiered system all together in 1989. New recruits were initiated immediately to avoid hazing abuses. Scott Williams, a senior TKE denounced hazing as "creating feelings of inferiority, incompetency, hatred, and low self-esteem."

While hazing went into decline, alcohol problems did not. The 1981 *Ozarko* characterized "beer chugging" as "a favorite pastime for many college students." It carried a picture of "chugging" at a Sigma Chi Derby Day event. In 1988, three fraternities scheduled an annual "chug-off" where fraternities were to compete to consume the largest amount of beer in the shortest time. The "chug-off" was canceled when the university warned of disciplinary

action and threatened to report the organizations to their national offices.

Alcohol has continued to be a problem among college students, and not just the Greek community. Binge-drinking has become commonplace on college campuses across the nation, and recent research suggests that the increase in alcohol consumption among college women is alarming. A survey by Harvard University's School of Public Health in 2001 reported that about 44.4 percent of college students are binge drinkers — men who have had five or more drinks and women who have had four or more drinks at least once during the two weeks in which the survey was taken. "Fraternity and sorority houses remain a bastion of binge drinking," according to the survey. The survey indicates 75.4 percent of students living in fraternity or sorority houses reported themselves as binge

drinkers in 2001, down from 83.4 percent in 1993.

In May 1989, a Social Responsibility Policy was passed by the Board of Regents, which banned "open Greek parties." All parties were required to be registered with the university and a guest list supplied. Drinking games or themes were banned, and if alcohol was to be served, alternate food and drink also had to be served. Response to the policy has varied. Tim Hofer said, "It shows that Greeks are willing to accept responsibility...it teaches us to govern ourselves." An unhappy sorority sister said, "I remember when I was a freshman, we would pay two dollars and drink off the keg all night."

Over the years Greek organizations on the SMSU campus have lost their national charters after being involved in liquor law violations and peace disturbance complaints. Conflicts with police were commonplace during warm-weather seasons when parties spilled outdoors and planners lost control. Some of the journalistic accounts of parties-gone-crazy give the impression that such an event was a mark of distinction. The 1985 *Ozarko* headlined a story about a Sigma Phi Epsilon extravaganza as "A Party to End All Parties." The event brought 11 police cars and a paddy wagon to the house where a melee erupted as police sought to arrest 14, several of whom were charged with "breaking custody." The 1992 *Ozarko* carried an account about a similar event, characterized by some as a "riot," which occurred during the Greek summer meeting. After Britches Bar on National Avenue was closed by the fire marshal, droves of students marched noisily down Elm Street and congregated in front of the Phi Delta

Briggs stadium renovated, becomes Robert W. Plaster Sports Complex.

Dr. Juris Zarins discovers the Lost City of Ubar in Oman.

Hammons School of Architecture opens at Drury.

Four white Los Angeles police officers indicted for beating motorist Rodney King.

U.S. minimum wage goes up from $3.80 to $4.25 per hour.

Oldest bride, Minnie Munro, 102, weds Dudley Reid, 83, in Australia.

Student Affairs deans in 1982 included (left to right) Earle Doman, Dr. Tom Wyrick, Sarah Bickel and Dr. Homer Long.

Theta fraternity house where things went from bad to worse. Complaints brought the police and in the confrontation, police used pepper mace to control the crowd. That event led to the cancellation of the 1992 Greek summer meeting by university officials. Acting President Russell Keeling later reversed the decision, giving the Greek community a second chance to conduct an orderly summer meeting. Cliff Davis, assistant to Dr. Keeling, was given the responsibility of overseeing the planning of the 1992 event, and to the credit of the students, the event went off without a complaint.

Not all Greek parties turned sour. Sigma Chi "Derby Days" was a popular party event throughout the 1980s. The fraternity invited sororities, women's residence halls, and all off-campus women to participate in the week-long event leading up to the crowning of the "Derby Days Queen." House decora-

tions were judged. Skits ranging from "Izod Cowgirls" to "Slick Dancers" were presented. It was the one event where Greek and independents mixed together in fun and competition.

Greek Week also provided memorable events with games and competition between houses. Entertainment included wheelbarrow races, building human pyramids, pizza and taco eating contests and bat races. Carnival booths featured dart throwing, pie throwing, jail break, kissing booths (always busy) and dunking booths. Contests included the annual tug-of-war, horseshoes, keg toss and an obstacle course.

Sadie Hawkins Week was another favorite Greek event in the 1980s. Sigma Nu fraternity established "Dog Patch, U.S.A." By Sigma Nu accounts, "women flocked to their house to chase the men of their dreams." A Daisy Mae look-a-like contest was held. Kathy Taylor, a Sigma Kappa, was crowned in 1981.

Alcohol remains a problem on the SMSU campus as it does on college campuses across the nation. SMSU officials report a decline in residence hall drinking violations in recent years brought on, in part, by the parental notification policies and the presence of the Police Substation.

Greek Philanthropy

Greek philanthropic achievements can be overshadowed by headlines about parties-out-of-control, encounters with police and "chugging contests." But the fact remains that a substantial part of Greek life involves philanthropy. While the Derby Days event was going on, sororities often set up booths to sell cold drinks and earn money for their philanthropy. In 1990, 10 percent of their earnings went to the sponsoring Sigma Chi fraternity who sent the money to the Cleo Wallace Center in Colorado, a home for retarded children. The local Ozark Food Harvest is often a beneficiary of Greek philanthropy. In 1977, the Lambda Chi Alphas had a "Teeter-Totter-A-Thon" to raise money for the American Cancer Society. President Meyer and performer Tom Jones rode the board for a spell to help the effort. In 1990, the event went for 149 hours without stopping resulting in $750 for The Ronald McDonald House.

Over the years the Greeks have raised money for favorite individual charities. During the 1990s, Gamma Phi Beta sponsored camp Sechelt in Canada for underprivileged girls. Tri Sigs donated to the Robbie Page Foundation. Phi Delta Theta donated to a former member's fund, the Lou Gehrig's foundation. Sigma Kappa sponsored a farm school in Greece,

SMSU

Molecular beam epitaxy laboratory purchased
for research in materials science.

Missouri/Springfield

President George Bush visits Marshfield
for Fourth of July celebration.

Andy Williams breaks ground for his
own theater in Branson.

Ozarks Technical Community College opens.

International/USA

Jeffrey Dahmer arrested
for multiple slayings and
cannibalism.

President Bush declares recession
is near an end.

Monice Seles, 17, defeats Martina
Navratilova, 34, to win U.S. Open.

318 *A Centennial History of SMSU*

donated to the Alzheimer's Foundation and provided staples to the Maine Seacoast Mission.

On February 3, 1990, Greek organizations banded together to sweep and pick up trash in the downtown area of Springfield. Earlier, they had washed windows and planted trees in central Springfield. "The project is not only an opportunity to work for the good of the downtown area, but (it) lets the community know that we're here to stay and plan on making Springfield a better place," reported Greg Lauman, a Phi Delta Theta member and coordinator of the downtown-cleanup effort.

In 2001-02, the Greek community completed 9,518 hours of community service and donated more than $45,000 to various charities. During the campuswide philanthropy event, "Relay for Life" the Greek community had 500 participating and raised $37,000.

By 2002, the Greek community had grown to 10 sororities and 18 fraternities claiming a total membership of 1,304, about 12 percent of the full time undergraduate population. In the fall of 2001, fraternity grade point average was 2.71 as compared to 2.77 for all males on campus. Sororities showed a 3.0 GPA, while all campus females showed a 3.09 GPA.

Greek members typically put on several educational programs for the entire campus. In 2001-02, 19 such programs were presented, including Alcohol 101, AIDS Awareness, Party Drugs, Sexual Awareness, Depression and its Signs, Defend Yourself and Mothers Against Drunk Drivers.

Coping with alcohol problems has been a focus for Greeks in recent years. Several houses voluntarily pledged themselves "alcohol free." In 2001-02,

five of the 12 fraternities had become "alcohol free." Of the remaining seven, only four actually had social events in their house.

Crime on Campus and the Landmark Bauer Suit

Crime statistics on campus have reflected trends in the country as a whole. As the 20th century was winding down, crime was winding up. While earlier eras may not be accurately represented by their occasional reports of theft and brawls with friends across Jordan Creek, it is clear that campus crime became a serious issue during the university era.

By 1973, 50 percent of all the rapes reported in Springfield occurred within a few blocks of the campus. By 1976, Tom Wyrick, dean of students, ordered a survey of campus lighting to establish a system of illumination that would deter assaults. Judy Geisler, dean of women, organized a program on rape prevention with films, panel discussions and question and answer forums. Ken Nobles, director of security, reminded female students that escorts are available from his office for night walks to parking lots or residence halls.

As the campus grew, the problem worsened. The November 2, 1984 *Standard* reported two additional rapes bringing the semester total to 15. Calls for campus security escorts tripled. On October 22, 1986, Daryl Decker tackled an assailant holding a three-inch knife on a female student outside Woods House on campus. The assailant was attempting to force the student into his car. Decker, an ROTC student, was presented with the ROTC Heroism Medal on March 25, 1987, by

Dr. Ken Rutherford Honored

Dr. Kenneth Rutherford of the Political Science Department and co-founder of the Landmine Survivors Network, received a humanitarian award at the Benefit Gala for the United

Nations Association's Adopt-A-Minefield Campaign held in Los Angeles in 2002. Joined by his wife, Kim, Rutherford was presented the award by Sir Paul McCartney and Heather Mills McCartney.

Looking Back

Midwest Sports Medicine Center established, a joint effort between SMS and St. John's Health Center.

Tornado hits metro Springfield.

Bass Pro buys K-Mart shopping center.

Anita Hill testifies that Clarence Thomas sexually harassed her.

Magic Johnson, NBA star announces he is HIV positive.

The Soviet Union disintegrates and Russia becomes one of many autonomous states.

Brigadier General Jerry A. White.

By the late 1980s, bomb threats had been added to the inventory of campus worries. In the spring of 1988, seven bomb threats were received. In the wake of increasing concern about campus safety, the university, in 1989, established a policy to deny news media access to campus security records, defining these records as educational records protected by the federal Family Educational Rights and Privacy Act (FERPA). The policy was established after *The Standard* questioned the inconsistency with which reports were being made available to the paper. Traci Bauer, editor of *The Standard* at the time, felt that information contained in the security reports was pertinent

Uninvited guests Brother Jed and his wife, Sister Cindy, appeared at the North Mall in the fall of 1983 where they badgered students about their immorality. Referring to SMSU as "a three-dimensional cesspool." Brother Jed continued his preaching in the midst of cat-calls and verbal abuse from students. Though they were escorted off campus by university security, they vowed to return. And they have...many times.

to the student body and should be available for publication. She also believed that there were legal issues involved, so on January 17, 1990, Bauer filed a lawsuit against the university in federal court. The suit became known as Bauer V. Kincaid, et al.

Joining Bauer in the suit was a retired court of appeals judge, Douglas W. Greene, who said he joined the suit "because of his great belief in freedom of information and his support of students' rights." In 1991, President Marshall Gordon explained the university's position saying, "We cannot in good conscience release such personal, identifiable information, with the possibility that such information may be harmful to an individual's name and career." The university also cited the American Civil Liberties Union position, which maintained that arrest records should not be made available to

the press and/or public, while conviction records could.

Bauer's position was that *The Standard* was willing to withhold from publication the names, addresses and personal information of a rape or assault victim, and would not print the names of suspects who have not been charged. She also believed the ACLU policy did not apply since the security office keeps neither arrest nor conviction records.

In the hearing before Federal District Judge Russell Clark, the university argued it could lose its federal funding if it were to release the records since they were protected by the Family Education Rights and Privacy Act (FERPA). By this time, college newspapers all over the nation had taken notice of the case realizing it could set a precedent for similar cases in process in other locations. On March 13, 1991, Judge Clark ruled in favor of Bauer. He stated that withholding the campus crime reports violated the First Amendment freedom to gather and publish information. He also stated the threat to withhold federal funds under FERPA was unconstitutional.

The Board of Regents held its monthly meeting just two days after the ruling was given. They voted unanimously not to appeal the judge's decision, and agreed to make security reports available upon request. They also agreed to pay $8,000 toward Bauer's legal expenses and the $1 in damages awarded to her by the court.

Because the ruling has implications for the FERPA policy, the U.S. Department of Education decided it would appeal Judge Clark's decision. It later withdrew its appeal. The Bauer suit changed the way the FERPA regu-

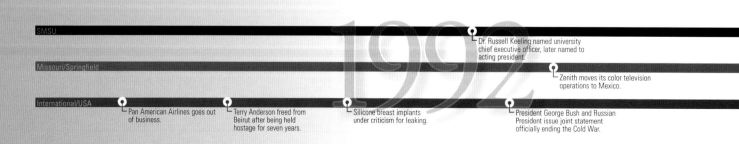

SMSU

1992

Dr. Russell Keeling named university chief executive officer, later named to acting president.

Missouri/Springfield

Zenith moves its color television operations to Mexico.

International/USA

Pan American Airlines goes out of business.

Terry Anderson freed from Beirut after being held hostage for seven years.

Silicone breast implants under criticism for leaking.

President George Bush and Russian President issue joint statement officially ending the Cold War.

lations were practiced nationwide.

Sean Kliethermes, *Standard* editor in 1993-94, was a reporter on the staff when the court judgment was announced. He recalls, "I'll never forget the day the lawsuit ruling was announced. The blackboards at *The Standard* seldom got erased, so there was usually a semester's worth of stuff up there. The day of the announcement, I remember walking in and noticing that a portion had been wiped clean and someone had written 'WE WON!' in big letters using the sides of the chalk instead of the points. For me, that sight cemented the feeling that I was part of something big."

Residence Hall Life

Finding a place to live was among the challenges faced by students coming to SMSU in the 1970s. In 1975, the campus housing shortage was so acute that the coordinator of off-campus housing appealed to local landlords through radio, television and newspapers to assist in providing places for students to live. It was reminiscent of the State Teachers College days when students scrambled to find rooms to rent and apartments to lease in adjacent neighborhoods. In fact, in the fall of 1972, things went back to the Normal School days. Seventy-three students were housed (not happily) in Drury's Fairbanks Hall. The housing problem continued throughout the decade. In 1979, some 80 students were housed temporarily in residence hall study lounges and game rooms.

Among other things, the housing crisis created co-ed dorms. There were no long debates about its appropriateness. In the fall of 1972, there were simply more women to be housed

than the women's dorms could accommodate, so they were moved into Freudenberger occupying the west side of the first floor, north wing. The problem persisted into the fall of 1973. This time, women were assigned to the seventh and eighth floors of Shannon, another men's residence hall.

Women's dorm hours were an issue in the early 1970s as well, but that issue wasn't solved as quickly as the co-ed dorm dilemma. Men had never been subject to "hours" in university residence halls, and to many, this was blatant discrimination. In the fall of 1973, Sandy Brown, Blair House Judicial vice president, sent a letter to the Department of Health Education and Welfare (HEW) in Washington, complaining about the injustice imposed

on women who were disciplined for dorm hours violations. "I have reached the point where the insult of 'hours' is unbearable," wrote Ms. Brown. "I feel as if I am guilty of a greater crime than the violators of the regulations every time we pass sentence."

Early in 1974, HEW officials toured the campus inquiring, among other things, about dorm hours. Two months later, Dr. Tom Wyrick, dean of students, announced the women's dorm hours would end on April 16. For security purposes, women's residence hall doors would be locked at 11:00 p.m., but a night attendant would be stationed at the entrance to allow entry to residents after 11:00 p.m.

With the lifting of women's hours, the university took one more step in

In the fall of 1983, Michael Chatman and several friends decided to form the first black fraternity on the SMSU campus. Founding members of Kappa Alpha Psi included (front) James Houston, Darren Johnson, Wayne Evans, and (back) Dave Alpough, Bobby Macer, Mike Chatman and Cornelius Blow. Not pictured, Johnny Longstreet.

Lady Bears advance to Final Four for first time.

Debate team wins national tournament.

Founders Park idea is proposed.

Three Springfield women, Sherrill Levitt, Suzie Streeter and Stacy McCall, disappear.

John Gotti convicted of racketeering.

U.S. Dream Team beats Cuba in first exhibition basketball game, 133-57.

An early snow becomes an occasion for snow football in Briggs Stadium on a winter evening in 1989.

the direction of gender equality. It would not be the last, but it was significant. Its significance was not lost on residence hall committee chairmen who had traditionally held their meetings shortly after 11:00 p.m. After April 16, it was difficult to get a quorum at the regular hour. One resident noticed a change in the dorm atmosphere after women's hours were dropped. "The residence hall has become more like an apartment. We have lost some of the meaning of dormitory life." No one agitated to get "hours" reinstated, however.

Visitation Hours Change
Once women's dorm hours were dropped and co-ed dorms had become a fact of life, dorm visitation policies became the salient issue. A *Standard* article in February 1973 declared that university policies governing visitation of the opposite sex in residence halls was "way out of date." In the spring

of 1975, an "experimental visitation policy" was adopted that allowed open visitation from 7:00-11:00 p.m. on Friday, and from 1:00 p.m.-11:00 p.m. on Saturday and Sunday. By 1984, visitation hours had been expanded in Blair-Shannon — Sunday through Thursday, opposite sex visitations could occur between 10:00 a.m. and midnight; Friday and Saturday, visitation hours were extended to 1:00 a.m.

Over time, the visitation policy was further liberalized so that by 2002-03, students who had previously lived in university housing for at least one semester, or students who had completed 24 or more credit hours, or any student 20 years of age or older who wished to live in an environment with a 24/7 (anytime) visitation policy, could request such housing in Kentwood Hall, Sunvilla Tower, New Residence Hall or Shannon House. Students preferring to live in a more restrictive environment with no 24-hour visitation privileges could request to live in an area of refurbished Wells House.

Residence Hall Social Events
Despite the student habit of referring to their housing as "dorms," Arnold Townsend, director of housing in the 1980s, insisted, "We are not housing people in 'dorms.' We are living in residence halls where things happen. The important thing is not just space, but how it is used." Residence hall life, according to the 1985 *Ozarko*, included "empty pizza boxes, panty raids, dirty clothes, new friendships, loud music, oh…and studying." Freshman Suzie Famuliner from Lee's Summit included among her memorable experiences in the residence hall "finals food, and a Christmas Party with a root beer kegger

in Wells Lounge."

Residence hall-sponsored social events in the 1980s included dances, movies and float trips. One January, Freddy residents sponsored a get-together to combat the freezing weather with an "I Hate Winter" theme party. Throughout the year, intramural competition occurred between residence halls with soccer, volleyball, basketball, water polo, softball, track and weight-lifting leading the list of popular events.

Residence hall rooms were typically quite bare, providing an open invitation for ingenious decorating schemes. In 1981, Carlton Davis, Perry Key and Phil Barker decorated their walls with a collage of music album covers. Scott Klemel and Dean Ferrell "built a loft" which "saved a lot of floor space." Chip Morgan, a resident assistant in Freudenberger, used a "play-room" approach. He put a Coke machine in his closet, along with a gumball machine and a sunflower seed machine. He added a sofa, chair, refrigerator and, beside his phone, a "Public Telephone" sign.

Residence hall rituals were also a part of dorm life. The 1982 *Ozarko* captured one. "The room is dark. A group of women sit in a circle and softly hum a tune. A single candle is lit and passed around the circle. Suspense reigns as the participants await that revealing moment when the flickering candle flame is blown out." The candlelight ceremony is a way of announcing a romantic happening in a woman's life. If the candle passes around only one time, the girl is announcing she has been "lavaliered" — received a fraternity necklace. If the candle passes around two times, the girl is announcing she is "pinned" — received a fraternity pin. If the candle goes three rounds, the

SMSU

Juanita K. Hammons Hall for the Performing Arts opens.

Missouri/Springfield

International/USA

Barcelona, Spain hosts 25th Olympic Summer Games.

The world's largest shopping center, Mall of America, opens in Minneapolis.

FCC votes to allow competition for local phone companies.

322   *A Centennial History of SMSU*

assembly goes wild! She is engaged!

There were some down-sides to living in residence halls, no matter what period. The noise level and the lack of privacy were the most frequent complaints during the university era. Then there was phone sharing, and people pulling the fire alarms in the middle of the night sending everyone outside in the freezing weather. Susan Roberts said, "They did it for fun, but it was no fun standing out in the cold waiting to get back into your room to go to sleep." Visitation hours and escort policies were a hassle, too. In the 1980s each hall had its own policy about escorting visitors to resident hall rooms. Some eliminated escorts, to the aggravation of others. "It was a little shocking to come out of the shower room with a towel on and finding a guy standing in the hall," observed Ann Shetland.

Residence hall life in the 21st century carries many of the same themes as earlier years, but there are some differences too. Entering the new millennium there were more than 3,800 students housed in campus residence halls, just over 20 percent of the student population. Specialized living environments have come to characterize campus housing. Those preferring to live in a quiet environment can find it on special floors in Blair-Shannon and Hammons House. Those interested in a "wellness" environment can live

in Woods House where comprehensive wellness activities are part of the residential experience. Students wanting an international experience can sign up at Sunvilla where four floors are designated for a culturally broadening experience. Those interested in a public affairs focus in residence life are welcomed to Kentwood. Honor students who wish to live together are grouped in the new Scholars House. Those wanting an environment emphasizing academic preparation are welcomed to the Academic Bridges floor at Freudenberger. There's even a place for those experiencing transitions in their lives.

So residence life is showing the impact of personal-preference marketing. One size no longer fits all.

Poet Laureate Gwendolyn Books inspired the campus on her visit during Black History Month in February 1986.

Looking Back

SMSU Student Makes Presentation to the United Nations

Scott Waddle, political science major, stood before the United Nations on September 30, 2002 to defend the human rights of those around the world living with disabilities. He presented a plan for the United Nations to establish a treaty protecting the rights of the disabled. Estimates are that up to 15 percent of the world's population is living with disabilities which often leads to a denial of basic rights such as education, healthcare, and protection from discrimination in employment resulting in further poverty, morbidity and mortality. Waddle spent two summers working for the Center for International Rehabilitation and has interned with the U. S. Army's Humanitarian De-mining Center teaching the observance of humanitarian de-mining operations in foreign countries.

Bill Clinton campaigns at Hillcrest High School.

Mel Carnahan elected governor.

William Jefferson Clinton elected President of the U.S.

Student Organizations

Accommodating an array of personal preferences and interests summarizes the history of university-recognized organizations on campus. By the beginning of the university era in 1972, there were just over 100 organizations, but their variety was sufficient to require their listing in the *Catalog* to be under several different headings. Ten years later, 155 organizations presented themselves to the student as associational possibilities. In 1992, the number had grown to 230 and by 2002, the inventory of clubs, organizations and associations had reached more than 250.

The 1981 *Ozarko*, commenting on the growth of associational possibilities, said, "There's something for everybody," and went on to prove it by citing two new organizations that year — the SPIFs, Students with a Professional Interest in Food, and the Fantasy Club, for those who like to play Dungeons and Dragons.

In April 1980, a National Day of Concern for the hostages in Iran was celebrated on campus. Students wore yellow ribbons to commemorate the occasion.

Some organizations, like the Black Student Union, continued, but under a new name. In 1977, BSU became Harambee, a Swahili word for "togetherness." By 1982, its membership had grown to 40. New organizations appeared emphasizing the democratic approach to organizational recognition. The Gay and Lesbian Alliance was formed in 1985, under a mood of cautious optimism. Letters-to-the-editor in *The Standard* showed respectful acceptance, but stopped short of endorsing GALA at the time. The organization has lobbied for the inclusion of "sexual orientation" in the university non-discrimination policy. The group has been supported in their efforts in recent years by the Student Government Association and the Faculty Senate, but the proposal has failed to gain approval by the Board of Governors.

Statement of Community Principles

As the student body grew, organizations proliferated, and individual interests demanded accommodation, it became apparent that the glue that held the campus together was weakening. The best that could be said of a campus of almost 20,000 students populating 250 different organizations and majoring in more than 140 different fields of study was that it had become "a community of communities." In the middle years of the 1990s, several faculty, student leaders and student affairs staff members met to assess this loss of community. They realized that the claims of uniqueness were an inevitable part of growth. But they also affirmed that a fundamental central purpose guided the institution in all its expressions. That purpose was to develop educated persons, and the common vocation of

students, staff and faculty was to foster the conditions under which learning could occur. Out of that conviction grew a document titled "Community Principles," developed and endorsed by students, staff and faculty in 1998. It represented the core values that undergird an authentic learning community. It reads:

"The community of scholars that is Southwest Missouri State University is committed to developing educated persons. It is believed that educated persons will accept responsibility to act in accordance with the following principles:

- Practicing personal and academic integrity.
- Being a full participant in the educational process, and respecting the rights of all to contribute to the 'Marketplace of Ideas.'
- Treating others with civility, while understanding that tolerating an idea is not the same as supporting it.
- Being a steward of the shared resources of the community of scholars.

Choosing to accept these principles suggests that each participant of the community refrains from and discourages behavior that threatens the freedom and respect each member deserves."

The statement reflects some of the challenges being faced by the academic community in the closing years of the 20th century. Other challenges are reflected in the regularly expanding student disciplinary code. The normative consensus was sufficient in 1906 to allow the institution to have no disciplinary code, only a reminder in the *Bulletin* that students should behave themselves. But by the end of the 20th century many of the social

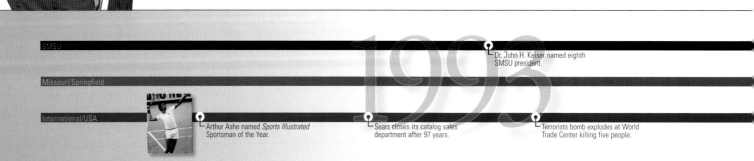

SMSU

Missouri/Springfield

International/USA

Arthur Ashe named *Sports Illustrated* Sportsman of the Year.

Sears closes its catalog sales department after 97 years.

Dr. John H. Keiser named eighth SMSU president.

Terrorists bomb explodes at World Trade Center killing five people.

1993

The capture of 53 Americans in the U.S. Embassy in Tehran, Iran, by a group of Iranian students led to a campus demonstration on December 13, 1979, at the North Mall. The Ayatollah Khomeini was burned in effigy along with a makeshift Iranian flag during the otherwise peaceful demonstration displaying solidarity with the hostages.

reporting and adjudicating academic dishonesty, and the responsibility of the faculty to include in their course syllabi the sanctions to be administered for cheating. The policy established an Academic Integrity Council composed of 10 students and 10 faculty to hear cases under the chairmanship of the vice president for Academic Affairs. Included among the sanctions for dishonesty is the issuing of an "XF" grade, which indicates on the transcript that the student's failure in the course was due to academic dishonesty. Additional sanctions include denial of privilege to hold office in any student organization, denial of privilege to represent the university in any intercollegiate activity, required service to the university and/or the community, and suspension or expulsion.

This proliferation of documents defining appropriate student behavior reflects the problems encountered in managing an enormously varied student body of more than 20,000 with contrasting backgrounds and traditions. The homogeneity celebrated by earlier administrators has given way to a cosmopolitan campus, and one courageous enough to try to define for itself the essentials for living together.

Smoking Banned
The long-smoldering smoking issue was ultimately dealt with during the university period. Some will remember in 1974 when Winston cigarettes were given away on campus. A few were offended by the action, but by the 1980s non-smokers' interests were clearly on the ascent. In 1984, a nonsmoking section was set aside in the Bears Den. In the spring of 1988, the use of smokeless tobacco was forbid-

agreements had dissolved. In their place came written rules, a campus disciplinary code devoting a full 12 pages to outlining the behaviors that would put one's good standing in jeopardy and the judicial procedures and penalties invoked for violations. The policies are outlined in *The Code of Student Rights and Responsibilities.*

As the 20th century came to a close, other documents were developed setting forth the values and ideals guiding university life. Greek Governance and Greek Relationships documents were developed as diagnostic tools to assist the Greek community in evaluating their campus citizenship. These documents encouraged Greeks to focus their efforts on academic success, lead-

ership, philanthropy and fellowship.

As the new century got under way, student leaders, in cooperation with university staff, developed a Code of Student Rights and Responsibilities to assist in shaping student conduct. A Social Event Risk Management Policy for student groups was also developed reflecting the university's expectations for organizational events on campus.

The growth of academic dishonesty resulted in the creation of a nine-page Student Academic Integrity Policy and Procedures paper approved by the Faculty Senate in December 1999, and by the Board of Governors in 2000. Put in operation in the fall of 2000, the policy outlines the expectations for academic integrity, the process of

Park & Ride Facility designed.

Hancock II proposal debated throughout Missouri

Gerald Moseman hired as education officer for public schools.

Internet use becomes widespread with the creation of the browser Mosaic by University of Illinois graduate students.

Branch Davidian compound attacked by federal agents near Waco, Texas.

Trials using gene therapy to treat cystic fibrosis begin in the U.S.

To a sellout crowd of 9,466 in Hammons Student Center, John Denver provided a memorable evening on November 13, 1978, with many of his well known songs including *Rocky Mountain High* and *Sunshine on My Shoulders*.

den in campus buildings and smoking could occur only in designated areas. The momentum in the direction of a smoke-free campus picked up in 1990 when cigarette machines were removed from all buildings. In 1993, a total ban on smoking in university classroom buildings was passed by the Board of Regents. In outdoor events, smoking was restricted to designated areas. The era of presidential cigars was over. In 2000, smoking was banned in residence halls, and in 2002 the smoking room in Plaster Student Union was eliminated, making all campus buildings smoke-free.

Student Concerns: Parking

Parking has been a problem on campus from the time President Carrington drove his surrey to the circle drive and tied up the sorrel horse. But by the 1970s, student ire peaked. At issue was the problem of fairness. Nancy Taylor summed it up in 1975, "I don't think it is fair for the school not to provide parking lots and then give students tickets." In the mid-1970s, more than 6,000 tickets a year were issued for parking violations. In 1978, students formed the STOP committee, "Students Together on Parking." They carefully researched the problem and reported that between July 1976 and the end of June 1977, 10,500 parking

tickets were issued on campus, and an additional 1,900 were issued by city police on streets around the university. Their study showed there were 4,670 parking spaces on campus to accommodate 11,458 registered vehicles. There were more than 7,000 commuters coming to campus daily. The STOP committee recommended building a high rise parking facility across the street from Craig Hall containing 2,400 spaces which would cost between $55 and $75 per space.

In January 1979, the Regents approved a paid parking plan which would generate $100,000 a year, the money earmarked for parking facility construction. But it would be 15 years before a high rise parking structure would actually appear on campus.

Race and International Issues

Race, like parking, became a perennial concern during the university period. In the early 1970s, Dora Kensey's column in *The Standard* titled "Soul Talk" called attention to the miniscule number of black students on campus as well as the virtual absence of any black faculty. Moreover, she said, there are no activities of interest to Blacks. With fewer than 50 African American students, international students were more numerous in the 1970s. "Soul Talk" often accused campus officials of recruiting only black male student-athletes. But there was some movement on the part of the university to recognize the role of Blacks in American life. In 1973, from February 8-16, the university held its first Black History Week, featuring a number of guest lecturers, music performances, a teach-in and career counseling for Blacks.

Political scientists Drs. Denny

SMSU

SMSU has 16 percent of state's students enrollment in state colleges and universities, but receives only 11 percent of state's higher education budget.

Missouri/Springfield

International/USA

Mattel and Fisher Price Toys merge.

326 *A Centennial History of SMSU*

Pilant, Frank Mazella and Frank Dinka conducted a campus survey in 1974 dealing with race on campus. Pilant concluded that black/white relationships on campus were not hostile or even discourteous. The problem is invisibility: "Blacks often feel they just don't exist on this campus," he said.

By 1983, the black student population had reached 105, still a miniscule group in relation to the 14,400 other students. There were still no black fraternities, few black entertainers, and most students assumed Blacks were mostly student-athletes. Black students criticized the caution and apologetic approach of many faculty. Racial separation remained the rule with Blacks sitting together for meals and grouping in a common area in the classroom.

In the spring of 1992 when the Rodney King verdict was announced in California, SMSU students staged a peaceful march and demonstration in protest. What began as a march ended up as a five-hour rally and sit-in on the front steps of Carrington Hall. University administrators, including Acting President Russell Keeling, as well as local news media, listened as students, black and white, vented their frustrations and what seemed to be pent-up anger. "No human should be treated the way African American students are treated on this campus," declared Shannon Campbell of Waynesville. "Are we invisible?" asked Toni Gates. "Can you not see me?"

On Friday, September 17, 1976, Bob Hope gave the opening show in the newly-opened Hammons Student Center. Barbara Mandrell warmed the crowd up with country music, and then gave the stage to Hope who displayed his easy-going manner throughout a monologue that even included Wilson's Creek. His satirical jokes delighted the audience. He sang the trademark "Thanks for the Memories" to the accompaniment of the SMSU Jazz Band. After the show, SMSU Vets made a special presentation to Hope "in appreciation of the memories he has give us."

Enrollment drops to 19,438.

Flood 1993 devastates areas in Missouri and throughout the Midwest.

Myst becomes the first commercially successful CD-Rom

PLO and Israel reach historic peace accord.

Germany unemployment hits country record of 3.5 million.

Bears No. 2?

In October 1992, Doug Humphries, a junior, noticed pencils in the bookstore with a disturbing message. "...Who's behind the dark-red pencils for sale in the SMSU Bookstore that proclaim 'Southwest Missouri State University Bears No. 2?' How can this institution's athletes be expected to excel if their efforts are unremittingly being subliminally undermined by these ubiquitous implements?"

~

First Truman Scholar

Marie Steinwachs, a graduating sociology major, was named a 1999 Truman Scholar, the first SMSU student to receive the prestigious scholarship. Elected on the basis of her leadership potential, intellectual ability, and likelihood to "make a difference," Steinwachs was notified of the award in a surprise visit to President Keiser's office.

Rally leader Emmanuel Seals spoke of making a difference, putting a stop to discrimination instead of just voicing concern about it. "It is time for us to turn this mess around," declared Seals. "It's time for us to come together and have that theoretical idea of the human race become a reality."

Among the complaints voiced at the sit-in was the lack of an African American studies program, the few black faculty, and perceived discrimination in hiring residence hall assistants. Acting President Keeling told the crowd that he hoped he could find solutions to the problems they raised, and hoped his administration could build a trust with the students so "they will know it is not my intent to exclude them or anyone else."

By 1992, the African American population on campus was just under 400, just 2 percent of the student body.

Demonstrations and sit-ins became of part of university life across the country during the last third of the 20th century. Late in 1979, when Iranian students crashed the American Embassy in Teheran and took 53 hostages, immediate anti-Iranian demonstrations broke out across the country. While Rolla and Columbia campuses had demonstrations, about 400 SMSU students staged a peaceful rally on the North Mall on December 13. It was called "pro-American," not "anti-Iranian." Speeches were given by Rich Graney and Greg Sarensen encouraging campus support for the United States and asking students not to blame the Iranian students on the SMSU campus. At the end of the rally, Ayatollah Khomeini in effigy was held up before the crowd with a target on him. The effigy was later burned. Iranian stu-

At Homecoming in 1991, John Goodman was given the football jersey he never earned as a student at SMSU. Goodman transferred from a junior college in St. Louis to SMSU to play football in 1973. "I came down here to see if I could walk-on the football team. I was ineligible, so I wound up in the Theatre Department. I had always been interested in acting. I was the class clown in high school, which kept me out of more serious trouble," says Goodman, "but I never really considered making a living as an actor until I left SMSU." Since graduating from SMSU in 1975, Goodman co-starred for nine seasons in the television series *Roseanne* as well as starring in a host of movies and stage productions.

dents on campus reported no problems.

In January 1991, a candlelight vigil was held at the North Mall protesting the Gulf War. It was organized by Students for Social Change. The group asked Dr. Burt Purrington of the anthropology faculty to speak at the vigil. His speech was interrupted several times by hecklers shouting from dorms while others ran by the vigil carrying patriotic signs and flags. But free

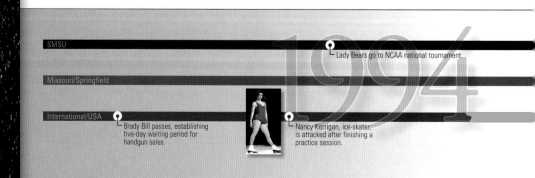

SMSU

Lady Bears go to NCAA national tournament.

Missouri/Springfield

International/USA

Brady Bill passes, establishing five-day waiting period for handgun sales.

Nancy Kerrigan, ice-skater, is attacked after finishing a practice session.

1994

speech prevailed with both supporters and objectors to the Gulf War expressing their convictions.

Entertainment on Campus

During the early years of the university period, most scheduled entertainment was given in McDonald Arena. Lily Tomlin, star of the memorable TV show *Laugh In* was among the 1973 performers. That same year, students paid $1.50 to hear Jim Croce. One of the most popular programs of the early 1970s was the Ozark Mountain Daredevils, a local band which developed a love-affair with the SMSU students treating them to repeated encores. Another popular group was the Nitty Gritty Dirt Band, which played on campus in October 1974. John McEuen did Stephen Vincent Benet's "Mountain Whippoorwill," that night bringing the cheering audience to its feet. The band joined with the local Daredevils to close the program with "Will the Circle Be Unbroken?"

With the completion of Hammons Student Center in 1976, a new venue was available for entertainment and the first few years were filled with star-studded performances. Bob Hope and Barbara Mandrell opened the Center on September 17, 1976, with 9,000 people in attendance. Students, of course, immediately asked "Why Hope? Why Mandrell? Isn't this supposed to be *our* student center with programs for us? Why are there no rock concerts on the schedule?" Hammons' staff had to walk a fine line to accommodate both student and community interests. But during the first year, Black Sabbath did come with a memorable rock concert along with Johnny Cash, ZZ Top, Mac Davis and Dolly Parton, Captain

and Tenile, REO Speedwagon, Helen Reddy, and the Emmitt Kelly Jr. Circus — a little for every taste.

In October 1977, Red Skelton performed for a near-capacity crowd. Before the show, Skelton went out among the crowd, visiting and signing autographs, giving impromptu interviews. "I come in early," Skelton said, "because it is often hard to convince them that my act is what they want to see." Skelton ended up endearing himself to skeptical students. He drove around Springfield, stopping his car to take pictures, getting his own food and shopping for props for his show.

Elvis was also part of the 1977 schedule. Fans waited for days outside Hammons Student Center to purchase tickets. Floor seats were pricey — $15, the highest yet for any HSC event, but the show sold out in five hours. Reviews of his performance included words like "fat, pitiful, tired, voice and belly sagging, seen better days," but despite the obvious decline of the rock-and-roll genius, he worked his magic on the sell-out crowd.

When Black Sabbath played on February 18, 1977, the decibel level went off the charts. They "launched into a barrage of acid rock," declared the *Ozarko* in its description of the event. "The most talked about aspects of the concert were the drug and alcohol related arrests, along with damage done to the dressing room prior to the show by the group's bizarre shooting of fireworks and a total misuse of facilities." A few years later Ozzy Osbourne was scheduled to perform but was summarily canceled by HSC staff over growing concern that he had bit off the head of a bat at an earlier concert.

In the late 1970s, HSC hosted

England Dan and John Coley, Debbie and Pat Boone, and the ever-popular John Denver who returned to SMSU after a Homecoming appearance in 1968. Other names rounding out the 1970s series included Genesis, Arlo Guthrie, the Allman Brothers Band and The Lettermen.

While the discussion continued about who should decide what programs would be presented in HSC, the train of outstanding talent continued to come to Springfield. The Oak Ridge Boys with Ray Stevens opened the 1980s along with Bob Seeger, the Statler Brothers and The Beach Boys. Willie Nelson performed for 7,000 in May 1980. He continued until after midnight, one of the longest performances on record. Country music stars Larry Gatlin, Hank Williams Jr., Waylon Jennings, and Mickey Gilley joined with Blue Oyster Cult, Henry Mancini, Englebert Humperdink, the

The "Tug of War" has been around as long as fraternities and sororities have competed on campus. Cheerleaders on the sidelines shout encouragement to the pulling team.

West Plains Campus granted five-year independent accreditation by North Central Association.

Enrollment drops to 18,333.

"Whitewater" investigation of Clintons started by a special prosecutor.

Supreme Court outlaws excluding people from juries because of gender.

Paula Jones files sexual harassment suit against President Bill Clinton.

1972-2005 Southwest Missouri State University   329

Not for the faint-hearted were the bridge jumps at Springfield Lake. Scott McFarland, Roger MacBride, Nicki Lumkle, David Lowman, Lance Hall and Rick Latham show how it is done.

Pointer Sisters, Huey Lewis and the News, and the Imperials to provide a cross-section of popular culture new to Springfield.

Barry Manilow flattered SMSU musicians in 1983 by asking the Concert Chorale and the SMSU Express to join him on stage. A record crowd of 9,369 packed HSC to hear Manilow's only Missouri concert. Another 1983 sell-out was Alabama with Janie Fricke. Tina Turner returned to the campus in 1985 and gave what was described as "the outstanding performance event of the year."

President Ronald Reagan appeared at HSC in 1986 to support the senatorial candidacy of Christopher Bond. He brought the audience to its feet when his first words were, "It's good to be here in Spoon's Temple of Doom." Two years later George W. Bush visited SMSU. At the time, his father, President George Bush, was defending himself against charges of lying in the Iran-Contra Affair. "You can disagree with him on taxes or defense," the younger Bush said, "but don't question this man's integrity."

Hammons Student Center hosted an eclectic series of entertainment events over the years. From the Denver Nuggets of the NBA playing exhibition basketball to George Carlin providing a laugh-a-minute, fans saw some of the best in the nation. Kenny Rogers captivated more than 9,000 fans in 1979, while Mikhail Baryshnikov fascinated 3,000 fans in 1991. The largest concert performance occurred on November 13, 1978, when John Denver entertained 9,466 fans. Repeat performances have been frequent with the Harlem Globetrotters returning 15 times. George Strait, Alabama and Barry Manilow returned four times.

By 1992, Juanita K. Hammons Hall for the Performing Arts had opened and soon it became the primary venue for entertainment. One of the last big concerts in HSC was Garth Brooks, who played on September 17. More than 14,000 fans camped out to buy the 9,000 tickets allocated in a unique lottery system. Randy Blackwood, director of Hammons Student Center, calls it "one of the most challenging and meaningful times in the history of Hammons Student Center."

Convocation Events

There were never any lottery systems required to distribute tickets to convocation events. Despite the stature of convocation speakers and programs, attendance has typically been small. Those who did take advantage of convocation programs were put in touch with some of the best minds discussing the most challenging problems and issues of the day. Norman Cousins, editor of *Saturday Review* and author of a proposed World Constitution, addressed students and faculty in 1974. The then young Tchaikovsky competition champion Van Cliburn thrilled fans with his piano mastery in a memorable McDonald Arena concert in April 1974. Joan Fontaine, Oscar-winning actress, spoke to students and faculty on three centuries of women poets in 1976. In a prescient event in 1978, author Ted Howard, lectured on "Who Should Play God?" The presentation examined the (very early) possibilities

Mountain Grove Campus opens at Fruit Experiment station.

Nelson Mandela elected President of South Africa in first non-racial election in South African history.

Channel tunnel between Britain and France is opened.

Disney's *The Lion King* opens in theaters.

Crayola announces the introduction of scented crayons.

of genetic engineering and cloning.

Leonard Nimoy included SMSU in his last tour speaking on "Spock and I" in 1978. His rights to portray the famous space traveler, Spock, were expiring. Another famous actor, John Houseman, who starred in the 1973 movie *Paper Chase*, portraying a demanding law professor, came to campus with The Acting Company performing both *Antigone* and *Romeo and Juliet*. Houseman, despite his 76 years, gave brilliant lectures to speech and drama students in Craig Hall.

In 1985, 25 years after their counter-cultural activities, Abbie Hoffman and Jerry Rubin came to campus in a "Yippie versus Yuppie" debate.

Rubin, an ex-political activist turned Yuppie, said, "Students were hostile to the system in the 1960s. Now they want to be effective in the system."

In 1988, Dr. Edward Teller, who convinced President Franklin Roosevelt to allow him to begin work on the atomic bomb during World War II, spoke to a group of students and faculty in Carrington Auditorium about strategic defense. The same year, a standing-room-only crowd heard Dr. Arthur M. Schlesinger Jr., historian and author, describe the 1980s as "the age of apathy." Speaking about campus responses to important issues, Schlesinger told the audience, "I just wish American students could find some middle ground between hysteria and apathy."

In 1995, the Reverend Jesse Jackson told students, "Young America can get things accomplished. We have the power right now on this campus to stop racism and violence." Four years later, F.W. de Klerk, South Africa's Prime Minister during the transition from apartheid to the election of Nelson Mandella, spoke about the courage and perseverance required to achieve social change. In August 1999, Nobel Prize Winner and Nazi concentration camp survivor Elie Wiesel encouraged students to tear down the walls of separation.

Convocation events leading into the 21st century continued the tradition of bringing varied viewpoints and timely issues to campus. Among those traveling to campus in 2001-02 were Kevin Klose, CEO of National

In the spring of 1978, Kurt Anderson found that riding his unicycle, Sylvester, was a quick and agile way to get to classes.

Public Radio, internationally acclaimed photographer and filmmaker Gordon Parks, Democratic vice presidential candidate Joseph Lieberman, civil rights advocate Ted Kennedy Jr., author Neil Postman, and U.S.-China relations expert Dr. Xuecheng Liu.

Fads and Fashions on Campus
"Streaking," running nude through the campus, ushered in the university period of student creativity. While "streaking" provided a carnival-like atmosphere on campus, it also drew "outsiders," which according to *The Standard*, "spoiled the fun." By the middle 1970s, enthusiasm for the "sport" waned as did police patience. In March 1975, *The Standard* reported that "the only attempt that has been made near SMSU garnered a $154 fine

By the 1980s, T-shirts with messages were becoming the rage. Glenda Beauman models one the English Department would love to hate.

Grizzly House, first West Plains Campus residence hall opens.

Executive-in-Residence program opens in College of Business Administration.

Hancock II defeated at the polls by Missouri voters.

First telephone link between Israel and Jordan established.

Cessna crashes into front yard of White House.

The "World Wide Web" (WWW) makes Internet more accessible to general users.

for the student-athlete. He shot across National at Cherry in full view of a policeman."

Wet T-shirt contests at area bars picked up where "streaking" left off. Males proposed wet gym shorts contests to provide gender equity.

Backpacks became part of the campus uniform in the 1970s. The appropriateness of wearing slacks was re-debated. As the disco craze spread, rolled-to-the-ankle jeans with high heels, shiny blouses, leather slacks, and slinky, flowing dresses were picked up by the women. Men wore goose down jackets or vests with hiking boots and backpacks. Both sexes went for curly hair. Digital watches, pocket calcula-

tors, citizen-band radios, pop rocks, body painting, MIA bracelets, hot pants, pet rocks, leisure suits and toga parties were all a part of pop culture. Favorite hang-outs on a Saturday night included Amador Mining Co., Wicker Works disco, Drury Inn, Fire and Ice and the Spaghetti Factory.

The "kissing bandit" enlivened residence hall life in the 1980s. Wearing a black cape and white mask, the bold kisser ran down the halls of Woods and Wells singing, "I'm the kissing bandit," grabbing girls, kissing them and then presenting them with a lollipop. (The victims reported him to be a good kisser.)

Costly fads in the 1980s included plastic milk crates being stolen from

grocery stores and eating places and turning up in dorm rooms as book shelves, trash receptacles, foot rests, storage bins and coffee tables. Local dairies were not amused by the fad. The crates cost $3 each. Local hospitals were not amused either when "scrubs" began turning up on campus as the preferred student uniform. Those who didn't have access to "scrubs" found used clothing a suitable substitute. Then T-shirts with pictures and slogans added to the variety of looks on campus. "You can put whatever you want on them," observed Dan Sullivant.

The 1981 *Ozarko* observed that the diversity and uniqueness of clothing styles in the 1980s "make it possible for any college student to pick the look and action that fit his tastes." When *Urban Cowboy* was released in theaters across the country, everything seemed to turn western. Cowboy hats and boots of every design were worn with boot-cut Levi or Lee jeans. Blouses featured yoked collars and string ties. A suede or leather vest was chic. Others went the "preppy" direction with Izod pants, belts and shirts. Other popular designer fashions were Jordache, Gloria Vanderbilt and Calvin Klein.

You were clearly fitting into the 1980s if you called out for pizza, had a portable stereo, wore wayfarer sunglasses with shrink-to-fit button-fly jeans, ate frozen yogurt while watching music videos, played hacky-sack, and preferred things pink, purple and turquoise. Single dating was giving way to group dating in the 1980s, and *General Hospital* at 2:00 p.m. was a "must." Not just a few college students were hooked on soaps. Sharon Patterson of Kansas City admitted she scheduled her classes around the soaps. Then there

Erecting the green and tangerine tent outside Craig Hall signaled the start of Tent Theatre Rehearsals in the summer of 1981. It took the entire Tent Theatre crew to man the ropes and raise the tent.

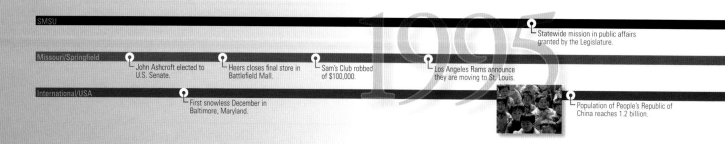

SMSU

Statewide mission in public affairs granted by the Legislature.

Missouri/Springfield

John Ashcroft elected to U.S. Senate.

Heers closes final store in Battlefield Mall.

Sam's Club robbed of $100,000.

Los Angeles Rams announce they are moving to St. Louis.

International/USA

First snowless December in Baltimore, Maryland.

Population of People's Republic of China reaches 1.2 billion.

With the coming of Jerry Hoover as director of Bands in 1985, the Marching Band increased from 63 to 210 members by the fall of 1987. That year the band was invited by the Denver Broncos to perform for the Broncos-Chicago Bears Monday Night Football game.

While modest in size (70) in 1976 compared to what it would become a decade later, the Marching Band provided proud moments for spectators and marchers alike.

was Valley Lingo or Valspeak that swept across the campus in the early 1980s. Originating in the San Fernando Valley in California, Valley Lingo punctuates conversation with "awesome," "I'm sure," "You know," and "I mean." Speech pathologists diagnosed the use of Valley Lingo as an "unhealthy addiction." Dr. Lillian Glass, a speech pathologist in Beverly Hills who ran a deprogramming center for what she called Valley speech, said, "If kids don't outgrow the addiction, they will enter adulthood sounding like people with sub-normal intelligence."

Popular hangouts in the 1980s included Bombay Bicycle Club, W.F. Cody's, Merlin's, Murphy's, Beethoven's,

Ebenenzer's, Lucy's, Jonathon's, Harlow's, The Regency, McSalty's and The Hangar. Creative entertainment could often be found in fraternity or sorority houses. The Sigma Chi's tried each year to put on a "record breaking" event. In 1981 it was "lapsitting." With help from Drury and local high school students, the fraternity attempted to break the record of 5,147 people "lapsitting" for 2 minutes and 17 seconds. The attempt failed.

Wyrick Fund Established

In the midst of changing tastes and passing fads, SMSU students have made a lasting contribution to the campus through the Wyrick Commission established in 1982. The original idea was to provide students an opportunity to identify campus needs and then to fund projects to meet those needs. Established under the leadership of Dr. Tom Wyrick, dean of students, students

design and submit projects for campus improvement, which are then put on a ballot for student approval. The winning project(s) are funded through a $5 per student fee assessed each semester. Through 2002, nearly $4 million in campus improvements had been funded by the Wyrick Commission. The Commission is made up of eight students and five faculty members who review campus improvement projects before presenting them to the student body for a vote.

Projects in the early years included such things as typewriters accessible to students in the library. The typing lab was opened in 1984 by President Gordon. Twenty-nine IBM Selectric III correcting typewriters were installed in rooms on the second and third floors of the Meyer Library. Students quickly lined up to use them. Linda Richmond said, "I had to wait in line 30 minutes to use one. They need to make the labs

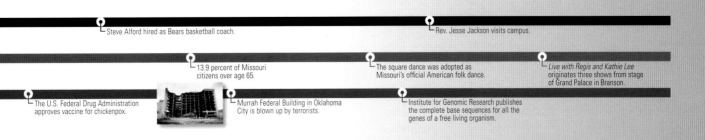

Steve Alford hired as Bears basketball coach.

Rev. Jesse Jackson visits campus.

13.9 percent of Missouri citizens over age 65.

The square dance was adopted as Missouri's official American folk dance.

Live with Regis and Kathie Lee originates three shows from stage of Grand Palace in Branson.

The U.S. Federal Drug Administration approves vaccine for chickenpox.

Murrah Federal Building in Oklahoma City is blown up by terrorists.

Institute for Genomic Research publishes the complete base sequences for all the genes of a free living organism.

Pride Band Facts

The SMSU Pride Marching Band has been thrilling audiences for years. It has appeared three times in Macy's Thanksgiving Day Parade in New York City since 1988. It performed in the 106th Tournament of Roses Parade in Pasadena, California, the Lord High Mayor of Westminster's New Year's Day Parade in London, the Orange Bowl Parade in Miami, and at the Magic Kingdom in Walt Disney World.

Approximately 380 students participate in the Band program, which includes the marching band, concert bands, jazz bands and entertainment ensembles, totaling 18 separate bands.

In a typical year, the SMSU Bands perform 180 times. How far does each bandsman march in a year? About 180 miles. Remember seeing the Pride Band's Sousaphone (tuba) line? The eye-catching group carries a pricey instrument at $5,600 each.

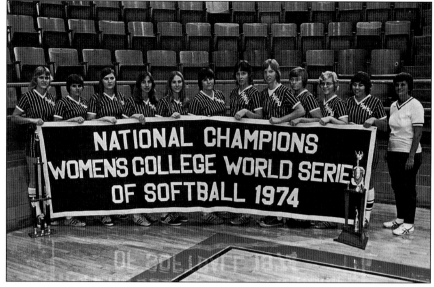

The first women's national athletics championship was won by the women's softball team in 1974. With a 19-4 season record and a 9-0 record in post-season play, the women captured the MAIAW state championship and went on to win the National Championship in Omaha. From left to right: Janet Cutbirth, Susan Alley, Dianne Gaehle, Dee Bratcher, Janis Morgan, Debbie Dace, Cindy Henderson, Pam Mangrum, Irene Barnes, Robbie Johnson, Becky Goad and Coach Kay Hunter. Not pictured: Karen Bethurem, Mary Doyen, Glenda Bond and Brenda Guinier.

larger." Dean Wyrick reported that the machines were under heavy use. "We can't keep ribbons in them," he said.

Typewriter labs quickly gave way to computer labs on the Wyrick Commission list. Other improvements over the years include an all-weather track in Plaster Sports Complex, an indoor jogging track in McDonald Arena, a Student Exhibition Center, a campus lighting project, a multi-cultural resource center, softball field, intramural sports fields and training equipment in Plaster Sports Complex. Forty separate projects had been completed by 2002.

Ozarko *Tradition Ends*

After 80 years of publication, the *Ozarko* yearbook ended with the publication of the 1991-92 edition. Declining student interest in yearbooks contributed to its demise. For several years fewer than 200 of the books had been purchased by students for about $25 each. Production costs averaged about $50,000, which left the university with a substantial deficit to cover.

According to Paul Kincaid, director of university relations and the administrator overseeing the production of the yearbook, "The only place where yearbooks are succeeding are private colleges where each student is charged a fee and is given an opportunity for a yearbook."

Will the *Ozarko* return? It could, but the form may not be the same. It could be a magazine instead of a book, or even a CD. If it should return, a student fee would likely be assessed to pay for it, making it available to all graduates.

SMSU
Selective admissions policy implemented.
Enrollment drops to 17,442.

Missouri/Springfield

International/USA
The Hale-Bopp comet is discovered.

Other Traditions Prosper: Choral Music, Tent, and Bruin Pride Band

Choral music traditions at SMSU are as old as the institution. During the Normal School period, a variety of glee clubs and choral groups entertained both on and off campus. Prior to World War II, Horatio Farrar was entertaining Dad's Day guests with the Choral Club. The group broadcast their Christmas Chapel service.

With the coming of Sam Gordon as director of choral activities in 1965, choral music became a campus feature. The first of the Elizabethan Christmas Dinners was held that year, a tradition that celebrated its 38th anniversary in 2002. In 1972, the Concert Chorale

Senior Chris Dufner tallied 69 of the 127 goals scored by Coach Rhonda Ridinger's SMS Field Hockey Team as it won its way to the AIAW Division II National Championship in 1979. The season record of 28-2-1 included 23 shutouts. Dufner also played shortstop on the SMS Softball team and was awarded the opportunity to compete in the 1979 Pan American Game trials in Colorado Springs, Colorado.

was touring Europe while the college was becoming a university.

By the 1980s, four choral ensembles were performing under the direction of Dr. Guy B. Webb. When Webb first arrived in 1980, the Concert Chorale had four basses, a few more tenors, and an abundance of sopranos and altos. At the first rehearsal, Webb announced that five rehearsals a week would be necessary to adequately prepare the group for the concerts and tours scheduled. The four basses walked out after the rehearsal never to be seen again. Hasty recruitment brought the Chorale up to 65 voices and the program began to grow. By the middle 1980s, the Chorale was giving 20 concerts a year.

In 1985, the group made its first trip abroad under Webb's direction. Concerts were scheduled in England, France, Belgium and Germany, including one in Springfield's Sister City, Tours, France. In 2002, the group toured Iceland, Denmark and Sweden singing in the native languages to rave reviews from local musicians.

Tent Theatre

Tent Theatre remains a popular tradition as it entered its 40th year in 2002. In 1988, it celebrated its 25th anniversary with a special show featuring 50 former and present tent performers. The show titled *Five-by-Five Follies* featured songs and sketches in five-year segments from the 25-year history of Tent. It was directed by Dr. Robert Gilmore. An alumni reunion, including Oscar-nominated actress Tess Harper, actor John Goodman, TV star Gracie Harrison, soap opera actress Pam Kristian, off-Broadway director Dr. Judith Midyett, multitalented

Curtis Perry (#54) played for the basketball Bears of Coach Bill Thomas from 1966-70 in one of the brightest eras of Bear success ever. The teams won four straight MIAA championships and advanced to the NCAA Division II tournament each year, with national runner-up finishes in 1967 and 1969. Perry went on to a seven-year NBA career after becoming the Bears' all-time scoring leader (1,835 points) and all-time rebounding leader (1,424 rebounds).

Christopher Coaley who produced a Michael Jackson video, and Bruce Morrow, Voice of America announcer, accompanied the special show. By the 35th anniversary of Tent in 1987, more than 1,200 people had been in acting or technical roles in the summer productions creating a highly visible Tent alumni association.

BearNet ITV system operates between Springfield and West Plains enrolling 103 students.

The Red House, written by SMSU student Brett Christopherson and directed by Jack Parkhurst, selected for Regional American College Theater Festival.

A newly renovated Vandivort Theatre fills a void in the Springfield arts community.

New York City reinstates the death penalty.

Prime Minister Yitzhak Rabin assassinated by religious extremists.

1972-2005 Southwest Missouri State University   335

William Fauntleroy of SMS drives on guard William Avery of Duke in the 1999 NCAA Division I East Regional semi-finals in East Rutherford, New Jersey. In making the most successful SMS NCAA tournament appearance, the 1998-99 Bears of Coach Steve Alford upset Wisconsin and Tennessee in the first two rounds of the national meet to reach the Sweet Sixteen and then lost 78-61 to Duke, a team with four NBA first-round draft choices in its starting lineup.

Bruin Pride Band

According to Willard Scott, NBC commentator, "It doesn't get any better than this," referring to the Bruin Pride Marching Band's performance in the 1988 Macy's Thanksgiving Day Parade in New York City. Jerry Hoover's band was given the prime location, leading Santa Claus in the nationally televised parade. The band also performed at the Orange Bowl a few weeks later. "It's just one big roller coaster ride that just keeps going," declared Hoover.

With 90 seconds to perform before the grandstand at Macy's parade, Hoover said proudly, "We hit it on the money. We had to go to extremes to make it work," he added, noting the intricate movements of drums, flags, trombones and Sugar Bears. "Throughout the parade, we were stopping, marking time," said Linda Dixon, one of the 281 band members. "We were exhausted by the time we got to the grandstand." But when the lights of the cameras struck their eyes, the energy came surging back "I just blew hard," recalls Dixon. "I can't describe the emotion we had."

National television opportunities opened for the band shortly after Jerry Hoover came in 1985. When he arrived, the band numbered 99. Two years later it had surpassed Hoover's goal of 200, and was drawing players from both coasts as well as the Midwest.

"I wanted to build an outstanding band program — with enthusiastic kids who were strong in character and would take a lot of pride in the group," Hoover said. Hoover's own enthusiasm and drive is obviously contagious. Former Band secretary Linda Kearbey affectionately calls him "a little tornado."

Hoover has made a point of knowing all of his band members by their first name, even when the numbers exceed 300 as they recently have. "The band is a social organization — a big family," according to Hoover. "You feel like you know a lot of people, and that you belong."

To instill discipline, Hoover had required band members to report to "boot camp" a week before the start of fall semester classes. There they master the basics such as the glide step, pivots, and flanking movements. They attempt the dreaded 32-count Box of Death drill, which features several different steps, lateral slides and horn lifts. Once fall semester begins, band members practice eight or more hours a week, including Saturday mornings before home football games.

For Hoover, the marching band is an art form. "It's difficult to do well because it combines the physical and the aesthetic — the sensory and the fine motor skills. Band members must function in complete, precise harmony

Coach Charlie Spoonhour made his first appearance at SMS as assistant basketball coach from 1968 to 1972. He returned in 1983 as head coach and led the Bears for nine seasons, winning four regular season conference championships, three conference tournament championships and leading the Bears to seven post-season tournament appearances. "Spoon's Temple of Doom" characterized the home court advantage during those early Division I years.

while putting out music."

What does the "little tornado" think of the challenge? "Where else can you stage every performance in front of thousands of people, and play everything from jazz to classics? It's show biz on a 100-yard stage!"

Athletics

As the university period opened, intercollegiate athletics was poised to make sports headlines. Looking for improved competitive challenges, several women's sports moved to the large college division of the Association for Intercollegiate Athletics for Women (AIAW) as early as 1971. By 1976, women's volleyball, softball and gymnastics had pioneered the move to Division I competition. By 1982, all men's and women's programs were competing in NCAA Division I athletics.

By the mid-1980s, the men's basketball team was playing in national post-season tournaments, first the National Invitational Tournament (NIT), and then successive appearances in the NCAA. In 1999, the Bears made it to the Sweet Sixteen. In 1991, the Lady Bears joined the men in post-season play making it to the NCAA Final Four in 1992 and again in 2001, as well as a Sweet Sixteen appearance in 1993. Sports announcers across the country were learning that a regionally-named university had its eye on a national goal.

The Growth of Women's Programs
Women's athletics lay virtually dormant until the 1960s. Women's tennis kicked things off in 1959. Volleyball followed quickly in 1964, softball in 1965, basketball, indoor and outdoor track, field hockey, cross country and gymnastics in 1969, and golf in 1970.

Coach Linda Dollar acknowledges congratulations on the SMS 1993 Missouri Valley Conference volleyball championship. Dollar coached SMS volleyball from 1972 through 1995, and her career dual match record of 758-266-21 (.735) made her the first women's coach ever to reach the 700-win plateau. She retired with the second best all-time win total in women's volleyball history. Her teams won 16 AIAW state or Gateway/MVC conference titles with a total of 13 appearances in national tournament play.

The surge in women's athletics can be traced to some significant trailblazers. Florence Bugg and Margaret Putnam pushed the envelope in the early years when the appropriateness of women's athletics was questioned by many. Dr. Wayne McKinney provided moral and financial support in the late 1960s when women's teams had no travel budgets. Then in 1974, Dr. Mary Jo Wynn, who had played on and later coached women's teams in the formative years, was named director of women's athletics, giving the whole enterprise a recognized spot in the university's athletics program. Men's and women's sports gradually merged into a single Athletics Department in the 1990s.

Division I competition actually began with women's sports. The early success of volleyball and softball elevated those two sports to the large

The First Visit to the Final Four

While it wasn't an auspicious beginning, a 76-64 loss to Texas, by the end of the season the Lady Bears became the first NCAA Division I program in the state of Missouri to reach intercollegiate basketball's most coveted spot — a place in the Final Four.

Along the way there were signs, including a 17-1 conference record and a conference tournament championship. The first tournament hurdle was Kansas, Coach Cheryl Burnett's alma mater. The Jayhawks were quickly dispatched 75-59. Then to Iowa City to meet Iowa, the top seed in the Midwest Regional, at their home. With 1,000 cheering Lady Bear fans in the stands, the team fought to a six-point lead at half-time only to fall behind by three points with 33 seconds left. A three-pointer by Melody Howard put the game into overtime. The Lady Bears trailed by one point as the final seconds ticked away. With the ball loose on the floor, Secelia Winkfield grabbed it and threw up what would be THE shot of the year giving the Lady Bears a 61-60 stunning victory over Iowa.

The Lady Bears romped through the next two rounds outscoring their opponents Mississippi State and UCLA, 177-128. Suddenly, the Lady Bears were in the coveted spot, The Final Four, the lowest seed ever to advance to the final round. Matched against the Lady Toppers from Western Kentucky who played flawless basketball, the Lady Bears ended their historic journey, 84-72.

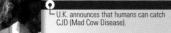

Lady Bears reach NCAA tournament for 6th consecutive year.

Jon Feeney acquitted in triple murder case.

U.K. announces that humans can catch CJD (Mad Cow Disease).

Sotheby auction of Jackie Onasis items brings $34.5 million in four days.

Baseball Bears Go to College World Series

The SMS baseball Bears made their first-ever appearance in the NCAA Division I College World Series in Omaha, Nebraska, in June 2003, with more than 38,000 in the stands and a live national TV audience (ESPN) watching the two games. The Bears performed well, losing a narrow 4-2 decision June 14 to Rice University team which went on to win the national title nine days later.

In the elimination game of the series, SMS faced four-time College World Series champion Miami (Florida). The Bears got a three-run homer to pull within 6-5 in the eighth inning, but lost 7-5 to end the season 40-26.

SMS qualified for the CWS by winning two of three from Nebraska to win the Lincoln Regional, then took two straight from Ohio State to win the Columbus Super Regional. It was the first SMS Regional title and the first Super Regional appearance for the Bears.

The Bears captured the regular Missouri Valley Conference title earlier in the season. A record seven members of the SMS Team were ready to begin professional baseball careers after being selected in the 2003 Major League Baseball First-Year Player Draft.

In 1974, the Bear's Cross Country team won the Division II National Championship, the first MIAA team ever to win a national title in cross country. Coach Chuck Hunsaker said of his team's record, "To reign as national champions in the world's greatest track nation is a great honor — the dream of a lifetime." (Bottom Row, Left to Right) Scott Brown, Mike Jones, Captain Calvin Brous, Tim Kuhman. (Row 2) Ron DeClue, Mike Werner, All-American and MVP John Prasuhn, All-American Dan Dwyer, All-American Rick Garver, Rick Callison, Steve Murphy. (Top Row) Coach Hunsaker, Assisstant Coach Ken Norton, John Tideman, Gary Vipperman, Howie Orndoff and Mike McCorkele.

college division in the Association of Intercollegiate Athletics for Women (AIAW) as early as 1971, 11 years before men's teams moved to Division I competition in the NCAA. The women's softball team played in the AIAW large college national softball tournament every year from 1969 through 1974, and again in 1977, 1978, 1980 and 1982. Kay Hunter's Bears finished third nationally in 1969, 1971 and 1973, and finished as national runner-up in 1970. The coveted national championship came in 1974 when the Bears beat Massachusetts, Luther, Eastern Illinois, Wayne State and Northern Colorado in the national tournament.

In 1976, the AIAW moved from large college/small college division competition to Division I, II, and III competition; Division III was reserved for non-scholarship-granting schools. President Meyer asked Dr. Wynn to present her proposal for moving all women's sports to Division I in the AIAW to the Board of Regents. Dr. Wynn remembers one Board member inquiring if this would not make SMSU men second-class citizens since they were competing in NCAA Division II. The proposal was tabled, but it was taken up at the next Board of Regents meeting. Then it was decided to permit women's volleyball, softball and gymnastics to compete in Division I and all other women's sports to compete in Division II. The Board also authorized a study of the possibility of moving all men's and the remain-

SMSU — Seventh member added to Board of Governors.

Missouri/Springfield

International/USA — Bomb explodes in the Centennial Olympic Park in Atlanta, killing two. — Dolly, a sheep successfully cloned by Ian Widmut at the Roslin Institute in Edinburgh, Scotland, is born.

ing women's sports to Division I status, but that did not happen until 1982.

One of the early success stories in women's athletics was in the field of gymnastics. Under Coach Chic Johnson, the women's gymnastics teams had won state and regional championships four years in a row and placed second, sixth, third, and fifth nationally in the late 1970s. SMS gymnast Kolleen Casey won the AIAW National Division I All-Around Award in 1979.

Dr. Rhonda Ridinger led the field hockey team through 18 years of outstanding success. Between 1971-90, the team captured seven conference championships, three regional championships, and a Division II national championship in 1979.

Volleyball was the first women's sport to gain national recognition. In 1971, the team, coached by Mary Jo Wynn and Linda Dollar, traveled to

Newscaster Terry Moore from KOLR interviews Coach Andy McDonald in 1980. McDonald was a daily visitor to campus after his retirement in 1969. He died in 1988, just two weeks short of his 90th birthday.

Long Beach, California, to compete in the AIAW national tournament. Most of the powerhouse teams had never heard of Southwest Missouri State and were surprised at its ninth place finish. Since moving into Hammons Student Center in 1976, the volleyball team amassed a 252-76-2 record through the 2000 season. Linda Dollar coached the team until 1995, amassing a record 758 wins in her coaching career. She was the first coach in NCAA history to win 700 matches.

Until 1976, women's athletics operated without the benefit of scholarships for student-athletes. Even in 1976, the scholarships were modest, essentially covering books. The total grant money that first year was $18,862, while men's sports received $67,683 that year. By the end of the decade, the grants-in-aid to women had increased to $49,526.

Since the first AIAW national championships in 1972 until the AIAW dissolved and women's athletics joined the men in the NCAA, SMS women won 18 state championships, 14 regional crowns, and two national championships in Division I softball and Division II field hockey.

Basketball in a New Facility

The first major athletics facility addition in more than 35 years came on the scene in the fall of 1976 with the opening of John Q. Hammons Student Center. Funded by a substantial naming gift and an annual student fee allocation, the facility provided almost 9,000 seats for basketball in what was the largest indoor arena in southwest Missouri. It also provided facilities for swimming and volleyball. The building was also a focus for student activity

Tony Piazza (14) greets Shaun Marcum (10) at home plate after Marcum's three-run home run in the 8th inning June 16 against Miami in the 2003 NCAA Division I College World Series. SMS lost two-run decisions to Miami and eventual national champion Rice University in the Bears' first visit to the College World Series in Omaha, Nebraska.

with racquetball courts, five full-sized basketball courts, which could be used for a variety of activities, and other recreational features.

SMS moved into the facility in grand fashion. After making an NCAA basketball tournament appearance in 1974, in which the team won a regional title and defeated St. Joseph's and New Orleans in Evansville before a 67-52 championship game loss to Morgan State, the Bears won their 19th and final MIAA title in Hammons Student Center in 1978. SMS hosted an NCAA regional tournament and dropped a one-point decision to Lincoln University in the championship game, a loss that cost Coach Bill Thomas' Bears a chance to win the national championship on their home

Missouri Fine Arts Academy opens.

Dr. Robert Bellah gives first Public Affairs Convocation, "The Moral Crisis in American Public Life."

City Council turns down proposal by Kickapoo Indians for resort and casino.

TWA jumbo jet explodes over the Atlantic soon after takeoff from JFK, claiming 230 lives.

Prince Charles and Princess Diana divorce.

Baltimore Orioles end season with record 257 home runs.

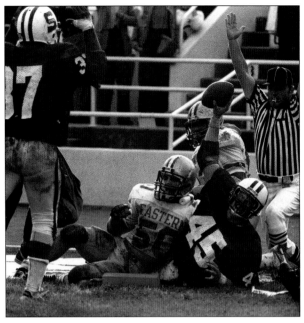

In the closing minutes of the 1984 Homecoming game, Terry Cummings plunges across the goal line for a game-winning two-point conversion to beat Eastern Illinois 29-28.

floor. SMS had been selected as the host site for the NCAA Division II (the successor to the College Division) national semifinals and finals for both 1978 and 1979. The Bears just missed being able to play in the event.

While basketball was closing out the 1960s with five straight league titles, the baseball Bears of Coach Bill Rowe became the newest athletics success. From a stand-

Homecoming buttons have been popular over the years.

ing start in 1964, the Bears had their first winning season in 1968, and then were selected to host the NCAA Division II World Series on their home field, Springfield's Meador Park, in a four-year run from 1968-71. SMS won regional championships, which enabled it to also play in the World Series it hosted in 1969 and 1970, finishing as the national runner-up in 1969 and in third place in 1970.

The last few years of the Bears' Division II life saw SMS host both regional tournament and national tournament competition in each of four sports: basketball, baseball, cross country and golf. The university hosted and won an NCAA Division II golf championship in 1963 under coach McDonald, and the Bears hosted and won an NCAA Division II cross country title in 1974 under coach Chuck Hunsaker.

In its new Hammons Student Center home, with notable Division II successes piling up and with a rapidly-climbing enrollment, sentiment

grew toward moving SMS athletics in the direction of a Division I program. Women's athletics had already moved some of its competition into AIAW Division I in 1976. The issue came under close scrutiny by administrators and the Board as the 1970s wound down. The university made public in 1980 its intention to upgrade to major college competition, and the 1982-83 year saw all university sports upgraded to Division I status, with football competing on the I-AA level. That coincided with the inclusion of women's sports under the NCAA banner as the AIAW dissolved. Aldo Sebben stepped aside as director of athletics and former baseball coach and athletics business manager Bill Rowe became the school's first Division I director of athletics. With the move to Division I, the university needed a new league affiliation. SMS left the MIAA in 1981, spent a year as a Division II independent, and then joined the four-school Mid-Continent Conference for football. In 1982, other men's sports became charter members of the Association of Mid-Continent Universities (AMCU), which included Cleveland State, Eastern Illinois, Illinois-Chicago, Northern Iowa, Valparaiso, Western Illinois and Wisconsin-Green Bay. The same year, the women's programs also joined a new league — the Gateway Collegiate Athletic Conference, which included 10 schools: SMS, Bradley, Drake, Eastern Illinois, Illinois State, Indiana State, Northern Iowa, Southern Illinois, Western Illinois and Wichita State.

The four-team Mid-Continent Conference football league dissolved after the 1984 season and SMS, Northern Iowa, Eastern Illinois and Western Illinois added new members

SMSU

$72.8 million in construction projects planned for 3 campus system.

Dr. Marvin Looney retires as West Plains Chancellor.

Missouri/Springfield

House Speaker Bob Griffin indicted on public corruption charges.

Governor Mel Carnahan re-elected.

International/USA

Cornerstone dedication for Holocaust Museum in New York City.

William Jefferson Clinton re-elected President of the U.S.

Dow Corning provides $295 billion to settle breast implant suits.

1997

SMS football has been played on the same site since 1930. The original stadium was built in the center of the campus in 1940, and underwent many improvements over the years. Most notable was a four-stage renovation in 1987-1991 which saw the stadium receive a new artificial playing surface, a new upper deck and press box on the west side, and many other enhancements. Named Briggs Stadium in 1970, the facility became the Robert W. Plaster Sports Complex with the 1991 renovation. A new artificial playing surface was added in 2000.

Valley Conference (MVC), long one of the best-known major college leagues and a good geographic and philosophical fit for the university athletics program. After some deliberations and a number of visits, MVC members voted unanimously early in 1990 to invite SMS to join what is the oldest athletics conference west of the Mississippi River. SMS left the AMCU that spring and began play in the MVC the following fall. The MVC added women's programs two years later as the Gateway dissolved for women's sports. For the first time in school history, all men and women's teams were under the same conference umbrella. The Gateway had been in existence since 1985 as a football home for the eight schools competing in that I-AA organization, and the women's field hockey team became affiliated with one of the most far-flung leagues in college athletics when it joined in the formation of the Northern Pacific Field Hockey Conference, which included schools on both the east and west coasts.

Illinois State and Southern Illinois, as football became the only men's sport in the Gateway Conference. It marked the first time in Division I annals that football would be played in a women's conference.

The Bears enjoyed a marked run of success in its new digs in the AMCU. Bear teams closed out the 1980s with an unprecedented run of accomplishment, winning league championships in basketball in 1987, 1988, 1989 and 1990; baseball in 1984, 1985, 1986, 1987, 1988 and 1989; swimming in 1983, 1984, 1987, 1988, 1989 and 1990; cross country in 1984, 1985, 1986, 1987, 1988 and 1989; golf in 1987 and 1988; tennis in 1984, 1985, 1986, 1987, 1988, 1989 and 1990; and the league all-sports championship in 1987, 1988, 1989 and 1990. SMS was the runaway league leader in average

home basketball attendance each year, and Coach Rowe was named league Executive of the Year four times as the university closed out its AMCU stay solidly at the top of the heap in the still-young conference.

The SMS men's sports dominance of the AMCU had administrators and supporters looking for bigger mountains to climb as the 1980s wound down. A consideration for a number of years had been the Missouri

With affiliation changes, the structure of SMS programs was also fluid. Women's gymnastics was discontinued in 1979. Men's soccer was added in 1981; wrestling was discontinued in 1994; women's soccer was added in 1996, and women's swimming came onto the scene in 1998.

After a 10-year run as head football coach from 1976-85, former SMS All-American player Rich Johanningmeier turned the coaching reins over to Jesse Branch. Johanningmeier's tenure saw his teams post a 58-44-5 record and win the last SMS MIAA title in the 1970 season. It was

First issue of *SMSU Journal of Public Affairs* published.

Wehr Band Hall opens.

In a civil trial, O.J. Simpson found guilty of causing the death of his wife, Nicole Brown Simpson, and her friend Ronald Goldman.

Ashes of *Star Trek* creator, Gene Roddenberry, are launched into space.

Microsoft releases Internet Explorer 4.0.

Russia and Chechnya sign peace deal after 400 years of conflict.

Jackie Stiles Inducted into the Missouri Sports Hall of Fame

Only a year after completing her last season as a Lady Bear, Jackie Stiles was inducted in the Missouri Sports Hall of Fame. The statue of Jackie at Highland Springs captures her legendary jump shot. Her achievements include:

MVC Player of the Year, 1999, 2000, 2001

2001 AP First Team All-American

2001 Kodak First Team All-American

NCAA leading scorer in Women's Basketball history, 3,393 points, 1998-2001

2001 Wade Trophy Recipient, Women's Collegiate Player of the Year

2001 WNBA Rookie of the Year

Missouri Sports Hall of Fame Inductee, 2002

Johanningmeier who ushered SMS football into the NCAA I-AA era in 1982. Branch stayed at the helm for nine seasons in which he produced a 55-44-1 mark from 1986-94. That included a string of five successive winning seasons from 1989 through 1993. The 1989 Bears were one of the highest-scoring teams in America and won the school's first Gateway Conference football title as they became the first SMS football team to advance to post-season national play. The Bears scored a home win over Maine in the first round of the 1989 I-AA playoffs before losing at Stephen F. Austin in the second round. In 1990, SMS again won a league crown to gain the league's automatic playoff berth. The 1990 Bears lost at home to Idaho in the first round of the playoffs to finish 9-3. Coupled with a 10-3 record from 1989, those two seasons produced the highest two-year win total in SMS football history.

That era, in which the Bears were also 27-3 on their home field over a five-year period, saw that home field gain new stature. A four-year renovation of Briggs Stadium saw the facility get an artificial playing surface in 1987, a new all-weather running track in 1988, enhanced seating and other improvements on the east (student) side in 1990, and an upper deck and new press box on the west side in 1991 which boosted the seating capacity of the stadium to 16,300. Renamed the Robert W. Plaster Sports Complex, the facility would put the SMS stadium on a par with the top I-AA football facilities in the country.

The move to Division I brought heightened acclaim when SMS teams achieved athletics success, and the earliest sources of that success were the men's

Melody Howard played professionally for two seasons with the ABL Colorado Explosion. Howard played for four straight SMS regular season conference championships, conference tournament championships, and NCAA tournament teams including the 1992 SMS NCAA Final Four team. She graduated in 1994 as the then SMS women's basketball career scoring leader with 1,944 points.

and women's basketball teams, largely through the efforts of two new head coaches who arrived in the late 1980s.

Charlie Spoonhour had been an assistant to Bill Thomas on the men's basketball staff from 1968-72, and, after stints at two junior colleges and two Big Eight Conference schools, Spoonhour returned in 1983-84 as

University named to *John Templeton Foundation Honor Roll for Character Building Colleges.*

Murney and Associates real estate firm established.

Diana, Princess of Wales, dies in a Paris car crash.

the Bears' head coach in the second SMS year in both Division I and the AMCU. In an all-too-short nine-year run, Spoonhour put SMS men's basketball on the national map. His teams closed out the 1980s with the best winning record in the country for any new Division I school for the decade of the 1980s, winning 20 or more games and making post-season national tournament appearances in his last seven years in a row.

Spoonhour's run of success began in 1985-86 when the unheralded Bears finished as AMCU runner-up, drew an invitation to play in the prestigious National Invitation Tournament and scored home upset wins over Pittsburgh and Marquette in the NIT's first two rounds. A one-point setback at Florida in the quarterfinals was all that stood

Cheryl Burnett is the winningest coach in SMS women's basketball history compiling a 319-136 record from 1987 to 2002. Her teams made 10 NCAA and one WNIT tournament appearances her last 11 years with the Lady Bears, and she guided SMS to NCAA Final Four appearances in 1992 and 2001.

between SMS and a trip to the NIT semifinals in New York's Madison Square Garden as SMS finished with a 24-8 record.

The next year the Bears claimed their first AMCU crown, hosted and won the league tourney and gained selection for the first time to the NCAA Division I Championship Tournament. SMS drew a 13th seed in the Southeast Regional and scored an upset win over Clemson before losing by four points to Kansas in the second round. The 1987 Bears finished with an all-time SMS record victory total in a 28-6 campaign. SMS repeated its league crown in 1988 and earned the league's automatic berth into the NCAA in the first year the AMCU had automatic qualification. The Bears dropped a four-point decision in the first round to Jerry Tarkanian's Nevada-Las Vegas team.

SMS followed its regular season title with another AMCU tourney crown in 1988-89 and lost to eventual national runner-up Seton Hall in the NCAA first round. The Bears gained an at-large NCAA bid in 1990 and dropped a first-round decision to perennial power North Carolina. SMS lost in the finals of the MVC tournament in its first year in the new league and wound up back in the NIT where the Bears beat Coppin State and then lost to Southern Illinois in the 1991 second round. In 1992, SMS closed out Spoonhour's tenure by winning the MVC tourney title for the first time, returning with the MVC automatic bid to the NCAA, and losing in the first round to Michigan State.

Spoonhour's coaching successor, Mark Bernsen, guided the Bears to the quarterfinals of the NIT in 1993, and,

Jackie Stiles drives upcourt against Purdue University in the 2001 National Semifinals in St. Louis. A four-time all-Missouri Valley selection, three-time league Player of the Year, and consensus All-America, Stiles led the nation in scoring as both a junior and senior. Her career total of 3,393 points set an all-time NCAA women's basketball career scoring record. She went on to play professionally and was the WNBA Rookie of the Year in 2001.

in 1995, SMS plucked a well-known name from the Division III coaching ranks when former Indiana All-America Steve Alford became the new head coach. Alford had the Bears back in the NIT in 1996-97, in a 24-win campaign, and, in 1999 took the men's team deeper into NCAA play than ever before. The Bears that year drew a 12th seed after their at-large NCAA selection, where they knocked off fifth-seeded Wisconsin and fourth-seeded Tennessee in the first two rounds of the national tourney. Down to the Sweet Sixteen teams remaining in the regional semifinals, the Bears were paired against top-seeded and top-ranked Duke, and finally bowed out

BearNet links Springfield, West Plains, Lebanon, Joplin and Nevada.

First cooperative doctoral program offered at SMSU.

House Speaker Bob Griffin pleads guilty to taking $4,000 bribe.

Bill Clinton becomes first President to use the line-item veto.

Mother Teresa dies in India after years of devoting her life to the poor.

U.S. releases a redesigned $50 bill.

of the tournament in a 17-point loss to a Blue Devil team, which sent four players into the National Basketball Association the next year. Alford left in the spring of 1999 to become head coach at the University of Iowa and his successor Barry Hinson produced a 23-win season and a trip to the second round of the NIT in his first season at the SMS helm.

Lady Bear Basketball

The Lady Bears gained even greater acclaim. In its Division II days, SMS made two trips to AIAW Division II regional tournament play under coach Reba Sims in the 1970s, and had earned an at-large spot in the AIAW national tournament in 1981 in a 25-10 season under coach Marty Gasser. The Lady Bears had, however, only enjoyed three winning seasons in the 12 years before former SMS assistant Cheryl Burnett became SMS

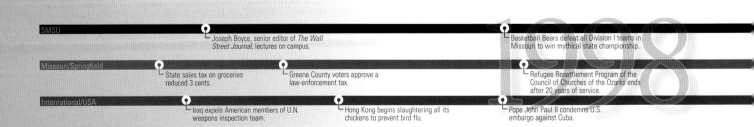

head coach in 1987-88. After two sub-.500 seasons, Burnett took her third SMS team to 19 wins and then broke through in a 26-5 campaign in 1990-91 after which SMS made its first NCAA tournament appearance, beating Tennessee Tech at home before losing to the eventual national champion, Tennessee.

The following year produced a season by which all future SMS campaigns would be judged. The Lady Bears ran off a 21-game win streak from mid-January and captured Gateway Conference regular season and tourney titles to march in the NCAA on a roll. SMS whipped Kansas at home, upset regional top seed Iowa on the road in the second round and advanced to regional play. There the Lady Bears rolled over UCLA and Mississippi to put SMS into the elite of college basketball, the NCAA Women's Final Four in Los Angeles with a field including Stanford, Virginia and Western Kentucky. SMS drew Western Kentucky in the national semifinals and dropped an 84-72 decision but still ended with a remarkable 31-3 season record.

Burnett's Lady Bears moved into the Missouri Valley Conference the next year, won the league regular season and tourney titles, and scored NCAA tourney wins over Oklahoma State and

Former Michigan State University Associate Head Coach Katie Abrahamson-Henderson was named May 14, 2002, to be head coach of the SMS Lady Bears. In her first season she led the Lady Bears to a Missouri Valley Conference Tournament Championship and to an appearance in the NCAA tournament where they fell to Texas Tech. In 2004, the Lady Bears again won the Conference tournament and met Notre Dame in the NCAA, losing in overtime.

at Maryland before a loss to Louisiana Tech in the Sweet Sixteen. SMS followed its league crown with a tourney runner-up spot and took its NCAA at-large bid in 1994 to a first round win over Northern Illinois and a four-point loss at Virginia in the second round.

The Lady Bears made it four straight NCAA appearances in 1995 by winning the regular season MVC crown and then knocking off Utah in the NCAA first round before being eliminated by Colorado. The 1996 SMS team won a seventh straight conference regular season crown, won the league tourney, but, for the first time, failed to win its NCAA opener, losing in the first round to Texas to wind up the season at 25-5.

SMS missed the 1997 NCAA tournament, but came back in 1998, after second place regular season and league tourney finishes, to gain an at-large NCAA spot where the Lady Bears fell to Notre Dame in the first round as SMS finished 24-6. Burnett's 1999 team again won 25 games and a regular season Valley crown. The NCAA tourney included a first-round win over California-Santa Barbara and a second-round loss to Colorado State. SMS in 2000 was again second in both league regular season and tourney play and lost in the first-round of the NCAA to Auburn.

The 2000-01 Lady Bear team again achieved the pinnacle of the women's college game, advancing to the NCAA Final Four. The Lady Bears won both the Valley regular season and tourney crowns and drew a fifth seed into the NCAA West Regional. SMS knocked off Toledo in the first round, won at fourth seeded Rutgers in the second round, upset regional top seed

SMSU
Joseph Boyce, senior editor of *The Wall Street Journal*, lectures on campus.

Basketball Bears defeat all Division I teams in Missouri to win mythical state championship.

Missouri/Springfield
State sales tax on groceries reduced 3 cents.

Greene County voters approve a law-enforcement tax.

Refugee Resettlement Program of the Council of Churches of the Ozarks ends after 20 years of service.

International/USA
Iraq expels American members of U.N. weapons inspection team.

Hong Kong begins slaughtering all its chickens to prevent bird flu.

Pope John Paul II condemns U.S. embargo against Cuba.

1998

Duke in the regional semifinals, and rolled past Washington for the regional championship. SMS advanced to the Final Four in nearby St. Louis and fell to Purdue in the national semifinals, closing out Burnett's 14th SMS season with a 25-6 record.

The explosion of interest in SMS women's basketball had the Lady Bears generating huge crowds in Hammons Student Center as SMS women's attendance ranked among the Top 10 schools in the nation 10 years in a row and led NCAA Division I in average attendance in 1992-93.

The 2000-01 year will be remembered for the records achieved by four-year starter Jackie Stiles. The 5-foot-8 Stiles, from Claflin, Kansas, was named the top women's college basketball player for 2000-01 by the Honda Awards program. Stiles set an all-time NCAA scoring record with 3,393 points, a single season scoring record with 1,062 points, and led the nation in scoring for two consecutive years. By the end of the season Stiles had accumulated almost a dozen awards including being selected for the Associated Press All-America first team.

Stiles and teammate Tara Mitchem became the first Lady Bear basketball players ever to be drafted

The Bears' first Division I post-season appearance came in 1986 when victories over Pittsburgh and Marquette gave the team a quarter-finalist match with Florida where they lost 54-53.

by the Women's National Basketball Association. Stiles was selected in the first round by the Portland Fire as the fourth overall choice, and in her first year of play with the Fire was named WNBA "Rookie of the Year." Mitchem was selected in the fourth round by New York Liberty.

At the end of the 2001-02 season, Coach Cheryl Burnett surprised athletics officials by resigning as Lady Bear coach after 15 years. She had amassed a 319-136 record. Burnett noted that "philosophical differences" between herself and the administration reached a point of no return. She described her resignation as taking a "huge leap of faith." Katie Abrahamson-Henderson, "Coach Abe," Michigan State associate head coach, was named to succeed Burnett.

Division I Achievements

The move to Division I competition raised the bar significantly for SMS student-athletes and teams. But 20 years after the first full season of Division I competition in all sports, the move appears to have been a stimulus to achievement. Twenty-eight individual student-athletes have been named All-Americans. In men's competition, 13 regular

Grizzly Athletics Celebrate 10 Years

Under Coach Trish Kissiar-Knight, Lady Grizzly Volleyball on the West Plains Campus owns an enviable 384-99-3 record in its first 10 years. Annually contenders for the regional championship, the Lady Grizzlies have won three consecutive Region 16 titles and made three consecutive appearances at the NJCAA Division I Women's Volleyball Championship Tournament. Knight has coached nine NJCAA All-Americans, one Distinguished Academic All-American and one Academic All-American.

Tom Barr coached the Grizzly basketball team to a 214-77 record in his 10 years as head coach. Barr quickly took the Grizzlies to post-season play. From 1995 to 2001 the cagers competed for the Region 16 championship, winning it in 1998 and 1999. Barr has coached six All-Americans, and two Distinguished Academic All-Americans.

A Grizzly Hall of Fame was established on the West Plains Campus in 2001.

First Bronze Bear awarded to John Q. Hammons.

Oprah Winfrey beats Texas cattlemen in beef trial.

The FDA approves Viagra, a drug for erectile dysfunction.

U.S. trade deficit biggest in decade.

African American Slate Heads Student Government

Rafiel Warfield and Andrea Smith were elected in the spring of 2003 to head student government at SMSU for the 2003-04 academic year. It is the first time in the history of the school that an African American ticket has been elected to the top student government posts. Warfield, from Springfield, was elected Student Body president, while Smith, from St. Louis, was elected vice president.

"Being African American is not going to be a deciding or defining factor for us," Smith said. "We didn't run on that. We will be addressing all students' needs." The two met initially in a high school debate tournament in Springfield. Their political ambitions were apparent even then. "We always had decided we were going to run," Smith said, "but we didn't know if at the time we would both be in school. We were, so we ran," Smith said.

Warfield has a political master plan for which the campus job is a first step. Next is law school and then…"I plan to be mayor of Springfield and then Governor of Missouri," he declared to Steve Koehler, *Springfield News-Leader* education reporter.

season championships have been won, while women's teams have won 21 conference championships. In conference tournament championships, the school has amassed a total of 59 — 35 for men's teams and 24 for women's teams. Post-season appearances total 44, with men's and women's teams each having 22.

While a part of the Mid-Continent Conference, SMS teams won 30 conference titles, more than twice as many as any other league school. It also won the all-sports crown five times. In the Missouri Valley Conference, the Bears continued their winning ways with the all-sports trophy in 1999-2000 and again in 2001-02 and 2002-03.

For men's sports, baseball, basketball, swimming and tennis have been the big winners, while for the women, the successes have come in basketball, softball and volleyball.

In addition to the 44 post-season team appearances, there have also been 48 individuals who have participated in post-season competition in golf, swimming, tennis, and indoor and outdoor track.

Student Characteristics at the Turn of the Century

Since 1966, an annual survey of college freshmen has been conducted by the Graduate School of Education and Information Studies at the University of California at Los Angeles. It provides a profile of beginning college students each year in the United States and enables the tracking of trends in their attitudes, experiences and outlooks.

Clearly, college students at the beginning of the 21st century are quite different than those who commenced their higher education during the Cold War or the Vietnam War, and they are dramatically different from those who attended classes in Academic Hall in the spring of 1909.

Of interest to us are trends that are being shown in the longitudinal data. The survey, completed in 1999, provides evidence of several trends in college freshmen outlooks, experience, attitudes and aspirations. Freshmen, nationwide, reported feeling increasingly "overwhelmed by all I have to do." Levels of stress are nearly twice as large for women as they are for men. Entering freshman are also increasingly "disengaged academically." They reported increasing levels of boredom in class. Frequency of oversleeping and missing a class or an appointment continues to rise. Further evidence of the disengagement is seen in the declining number of hours freshmen spend studying in their last year in high school. Ironically, at a time when academic disengagement is growing, student high school grades have reached record heights. This grade inflation finds its counterpart in college grade point averages.

The national data also show a declining commitment to social activism. While the vast majority of high school students performed volunteer work during their final high school year, their long-term interest in "influencing social values," participating in community action programs, or becoming a community leader is in decline, as is their interest in "helping others who are in difficulty." Beginning freshmen are increasingly inclined to think "that racial discrimination is no longer a major problem in America."

National freshmen data showed smoking and drinking on the decline. While more than 50 percent still

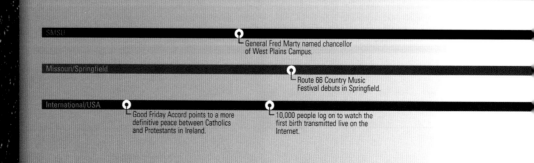

SMSU
General Fred Marty named chancellor of West Plains Campus.

Missouri/Springfield
Route 66 Country Music Festival debuts in Springfield.

International/USA
Good Friday Accord points to a more definitive peace between Catholics and Protestants in Ireland.

10,000 people log on to watch the first birth transmitted live on the Internet.

On the evening of April 2, 2004, SMS Bear pitcher Derek Drage threw the first pitch of a new era in baseball history at SMS. For the first time in the 41 years of SMS baseball, the team had a home field just blocks away from the university. An opening game crowd of 8,000 at the new Hammons Field built by Springfield entrepreneur John Q. Hammons, celebrated the opportunity to watch Bear baseball in one of the finest college ball parks in the country. The opening night crowd watched the Bears take Southern Illinois into extra innings, dropping the contest 3-2 in the 10th.

reported they drank beer frequently or occasionally during the last year, it is considerably down from the 75.2 percent who reported doing so in 1981. A decline in partying is also indicated as is a modest decline in smoking.

The data showed increasing interest in teaching careers, as well as a growing interest in careers in the arts.

The Center for Assessment and Institutional Support, under the direction of Dr. Martha Kirker, has been supervising the collection of data from SMSU for the national report. While SMSU data does not go back far enough to provide clear evidence of any trends, SMSU does have 2001 data, which provides a valuable profile of entering freshmen. Seventy percent of the men and 67.3 percent of the women think of themselves as above average or in the highest 10 percent academically. However, when they reported their high school grades, only 41.5 percent of the men and 57.7 percent of the women reported grade averages of A- or better. Apparently, the students felt their academic ability exceeds their high school achievements. Nearly one in five felt they would need tutoring in math in college, and one in 10 felt they would need tutoring in writing.

While about one-third felt that developing a meaningful philosophy of life while in college was essential

Exchange program with Qingdao University in China opens.

First Internet-based graduate program, Master of Science in Computer Information Systems, begins.

Russia buries Tsar Nicholas II and family, 80 years after they died.

Terrorists bomb two U.S. Embassies in Africa leaving 258 dead and more than 5,000 injured.

or very important, a much higher percentage (73.4 percent) considered being well-off financially to be essential or important, and that college was an important factor in making more money and getting a good job. Economic interests appeared to be the most powerful factor motivating the pursuit of a college degree. While that is not news to most people, it is a change from earlier generations.

Comparing SMSU freshmen in 2001 with freshmen at other public four-year institutions across the nation provides some interesting contrasts. SMSU freshmen were more likely to be frequent smokers (13.3 percent), beer drinkers (54.3 percent), and wine or liquor drinkers (54.9 percent). SMSU freshmen were also more likely to show signs of "academic disengagement."

More than half reported being frequently bored in class and more than 40 percent reported frequently or occasionally oversleeping and missing a class.

But SMSU freshmen were also more likely than their national cohorts to attend a religious service (84.4 percent), perform volunteer work (81.8 percent), attend a public recital or concert (81.7 percent), and visit a gallery or museum (58.6 percent). They were also more likely to communicate frequently with e-mail (70.4 percent), use the Internet for research or homework (74.4 percent), and frequently use a personal computer (83.3 percent).

While SMSU freshmen were more likely to spend two hours or less a week doing homework (39.8 percent), they were also more likely to spend 11 or more hours a week working (62.1 percent). More than three-fourths said they spend five hours or less per week watching TV. Just over 40 percent

expect to help pay college expenses by working, and more than 50 percent expect to earn at least a B average in their college courses.

SMSU students were less likely to be on either extreme politically. Only 23.4 percent reported themselves on the liberal or far-left side of the political spectrum, and an equal number reported themselves on the conservative or far right side. SMSU freshmen were less likely to agree that the death penalty should be abolished (25.4 percent), than their national peers (32.2 percent). About one-third felt strongly that marijuana should be legalized. Politics, overall, did not rank as very important to SMSU freshmen as only 15 percent reported themselves as frequently discussing politics, and only one in five thought it is very important to keep up to date with political affairs.

While SMSU freshmen appeared only modestly interested in political

affairs, almost half reported themselves as participating in organized demonstrations in the past year, about the same frequency as their national cohorts. Nearly three out of four did volunteer work, but more than half reported that volunteer work was part of a high school class requirement.

The survey covered a number of indicators of active citizenship and civic engagement as a means of providing a "before" and "after" measure of the impact of the public affairs mission at the university. While SMSU seniors were more likely than entering freshmen to vote in national elections, write a letter to the editor about an issue of concern, work with individuals in a homeless shelter, lead a community discussion group on an issue of concern or work with individuals of a different race, religion or culture, they were less likely than the freshmen to volunteer time to civic organizations like the Red Cross or United Way, or donate blood or contribute money to charitable causes. So while seniors were somewhat more civically engaged than freshmen, the difference is marginal.

Comparing SMSU seniors in 2001 with incoming freshmen, seniors were somewhat more likely to see cheating on an exam as harmful (48.5 percent). Each group was persuaded that buying a research paper and turning it in as one of your own was quite harmful (58 percent). Almost 60 percent of each group saw telling a joke that contains an ethnic or racial slur as harmful. Seniors were more likely to see keeping the extra money given to you by clerk by mistake as harmful (45.6 percent) than were freshmen (37 percent). Nearly one in five freshmen considered drinking alcohol when you are under

SMSU
Enrollment reaches 18,207.
Average freshman ATC score, 23.5.

Missouri/Springfield
Mark McGwire hits 70th homerun for the St. Louis Cardinals setting a major league record.

International/USA
John Glenn at 77 accompanies space shuttle Discovery in flight.
More than 10,000 die in Central American Huricane, Mitch.
President Clinton admits "an inappropriate relationship" with intern Monica Lewinsky and is impeached by the House of Representatives.

age as not at all harmful. Only 12.1 percent of seniors saw it as not harmful. Seniors were more likely (62.7 percent) to see harm in speaking disrespectfully to someone you disagree with than were freshmen (51.8 percent).

A variety of conclusions may be drawn from such data, but it is clear that a university that is deliberate in its effort to shape character and promote responsible citizenship among students is in touch with current reality.

Globalization of the University

When President Roy Ellis lauded the college's homogeneity, the world had not yet become a global community. To be sure, the college was aware of countries abroad and had even developed scholarships to assist students from far places to attend here. In fact, the first year the school opened it had several students from outside the literal United States. Admittedly, Indian Territory wasn't far from Springfield, but it was outside the boundaries of any state.

It wasn't long before occasional students from Central America found their way to the Ozarks. By the end of the State College period, a small, but significant number of foreign students were a regular part of the campus. They came from Latin America, Europe, the Pacific Islands, the Caribbean, Hong Kong, Japan, Africa, Saudi Arabia and Taiwan. In the fall of 1973, foreign students numbered 62 and represented 23 different countries.

By 1981, the foreign student population had grown to 84 from 30 countries, with large contingents from Iran, Cameroon and Nigeria. The visitors were often amazed at the stereotypes carried in the heads of local students. Mehia Fathi of Iran said, "I never saw

even one camel in Iran. The first camel I ever saw was in the Springfield zoo!" By 2002, international students numbered more than 500 and represented 85 different countries.

But the internationalization of the campus was not to depend on an influx of students from abroad. A multifaceted approach began in the 1980s which included more guest speakers and convocation addresses by people with differing cultural backgrounds. It also included study/scholarship packages to assist SMSU students to study abroad, as well as development seminars and global research opportunities for faculty. "We are making an educational and financial commitment to the development of priorities that will help our graduates in the 21st century," explained Dr. Curt Lawrence, director of special academic programs. In 1990, the university hosted two guest speakers from abroad. Sir Fergus Montgomery, a member of the British Parliament and an advisor to former Prime Minister Margaret Thatcher, spoke on campus, as did Slovak Artist Martin Kellenberger, a children's book illustrator.

"The world is changing. Barriers are coming down. Countries are emerging. The world is changing at a phenomenal rate," observed President Marshall Gordon in 1990. "We have expanded our exchange agreements with a variety of countries."

The International Studies Committee offered opportunities to study abroad in 40 different countries in the 1990s. An intensive Spanish program was offered in the summer in Costa Rica involving 16 SMSU students. An exchange program with Moscow State University began in

Looking Back

Bronze Bear Award Established

The Bronze Bear Award, established in 1998, honors "extraordinary achievement and/or outstanding support" for SMSU. The award includes a framed resolution and a 45-pound, 18-inch bronze bear patterned after the 2,500-pound, 14-foot bronze bear designed by Dr. James Hill and erected in front of Plaster Student Union.

Four persons have received the Bronze Bear Award. The first was given to John Q. Hammons, Springfield international developer and philanthropist, in 1998. In 1999 David D. Glass, former president and CEO of Wal-Mart Stores, Inc., and owner of the Kansas City Royals baseball team received the award.

The first Bronze Bear to be awarded to a faculty member was presented to Dr. Duane G. Meyer, president emeritus and emeritus history professor in 2000. In 2003, Springfieldians William H. "Bill" Darr and his wife Virginia were honored with the award. The Darrs have supported students through scholarships and graduate assistantships in agriculture, broadcast journalism and piano.

Groundbreaking for $27.9 million expansion of Meyer Library and Information center.

Gerontology program receives nations first Program of Merit award.

Pope John Paul II visits St. Louis.

Miss USA Pageant is televised from Branson.

Senate acquits President Clinton on both counts of impeachment.

NATO bombs Serbia to halt atrocities in Kosovo.

1991. An exchange program for faculty and students in the People's Republic of China added to the mix of opportunities.

Branching Out to China

By the turn of the century, the momentum had increased and the strategy had enlarged to include the idea of branch campuses abroad. President Keiser had negotiated an agreement with Liaoning Normal University (LNU) in the People's Republic of China to establish a branch campus of SMSU-West Plains there. Through the agreement, Chinese students can enroll in freshman and sophomore level courses offered at West Plains at LNU in Dalian, China. Teachers who teach in the program at LNU are hired by the West Plains Campus and teach in English. Courses there may lead to an Associate of Arts in General Studies degree from West Plains. Students may then transfer to SMSU, or elsewhere in the United States, or continue toward a bachelor's degree in China. The SMSU-LNU agreement is designed to lead to a cultural exchange between the two universities and promote friendship and understanding between the two countries.

President Keiser had already negotiated an exchange program for students and faculty with Qingdao University in the Peoples Republic. SMSU faculty go regularly to Qingdao to teach English and Qingdao faculty come to SMSU to teach Chinese. "It's an opportunity for our land-locked students here to experience life and education in China, in a port city with an absolutely beautiful beach beside the campus," Dr. Curt Lawrence observed. Professor Shouquan "Sam" Wang

The 1991-92 school year made the Regents' task seem like a job from hell. Board President Jack Miller (left) and Regent Jim Craig ponder the implications of cost over-runs on the construction of the Juanita K. Hammons Hall for the Performing Arts and the future of President Marshall Gordon.

arrived in Springfield in August 2000 to teach Chinese. "It helps me find similarities and differences in working as a faculty member in two different kinds of universities," said Wang.

Another cooperative venture exists in India. The Madras School of Social Work offers its students an MBA program as a joint effort with the SMSU College of Business Administration.

Will there be more SMSU campuses in countries abroad in the future? The new planning document, *Countdown to the Centennial: A Long-Range Vision and Six-Year Plan (2000-2006),* suggests that possibility. It asserts that the university "will assess the desirability or feasibility of opening new education centers and campuses based on demonstrated need. These centers and/or campuses could be local — i.e., within the university's historic

24-county service area in southwest Missouri — or they could be international."

The importance of international education is also emphasized in that document. "International programs are becoming increasingly important in aiding students in better understanding the world in which they live and the global issues that they will confront in the future. In order for students to have a greater understanding and appreciation for their role in the world community, SMSU will explore the feasibility/desirability of requiring that students have academic experience with a foreign language or foreign culture before graduating."

Stay tuned!

Governance and Administrative Transitions

Board of Regents Changes

By the beginning of the 21st century more than 80 citizens of the state had served on the SMSU Board of Regents, or Board of Governors, as it was renamed in 1995. Their service has been instrumental in guiding the institution through its various stages of development. For most Board members, the experience was a mixture of gratification and vexation. Policy decisions are never easy to make; pressures are always present and applause is rare. But these folk have a perspective on the institution shared by no others. They witness its trials, debate its policies, decide its direction and hire its presidents.

Six years of service involving at least 72 separate meetings is enough for most, although several have served multiple terms. W.S. Candler from Mountain Grove holds the record, serving 22 years, from 1913-35. S.E. Trimble of Springfield and W.J. Sewell of Carthage both served 18 years, ending in the 1940s. T.H. Douglas of Bolivar was the last Regent to serve more than two terms — he completed 17 years in 1959.

It's easy to notice the prevalence of male pronouns to this point. The first woman appointed to the Board was Mrs. W.B. Linney of Springfield, wife of a prominent physician. It took 20 years to get the first woman appointed to the Board, and it took almost 50 more years to get the second appointed. Ramona McQueary was added to the Board in 1973, followed by June Hamra, Carol Robinson, Barbara Burns, Allison Smith, Janice Dye, and, in 2002, Mary Sheid. Since 1973, there

were only four years (1989-93) when women were not present on the Board.

Agitation to have a student on the Board came early in the university era. In 1976, the Student Government Association petitioned the Regents to include a student representative. They argued that they should have a voice in decisions that affected their lives. President Meyer replied to the SGA that the Board should be made up of independent folk, people without a vested interest. The Board rejected the student petition arguing that they had no authority to change the system. Moreover, they were responsible to the citizens of the state, not the students on campus. They felt that communication with the students was already adequate.

There was pressure for student representation on university boards elsewhere in the state as well. In 1984, the Missouri General Assembly passed House Bill 998 authorizing all state universities to include Governor-appointed student members to their Boards. The student representatives would have voice, but not vote in Board meetings. Michele Nahon was appointed first Student Regent at SMSU and attended her first meeting September 21, 1984. Women have had an easier time being Student Regents than men. By 2002, eight different women had served in that role, while only three men had been appointed.

In 1995, the Board of Regents officially became the Board of Governors as a result of Senate Bill 340, which

authorized a statewide mission for the university. It became the third Missouri institution to be governed by Governors. The Senate bill also increased the number of voting members to seven. SMSU Alumnus Dan Behlmann, of St. Louis, was the first "seventh" voting member. His first meeting came on May 17, 1996.

Administrations in the University Era

The university era has been characterized by visionary presidents. Their tenures, even when added together, don't reach the 35 years served by Dr. Roy Ellis. But the 30 years embraced by this writing do reflect the work of forward-looking leaders who grasped the potential of the institution as well as the opportunities of the times.

In the fall of 1984, the Board of Regents welcomed the first student regent, Michelle Nahon of Springfield. House Bill 998, passed by the General Assembly in the spring of 1984, mandated the appointment of a student regent to each of the State University Boards. The student regent serves with voice, but not voting privileges.

Public Affairs Classroom building and Physical Therapy Classroom Building open.

"Mall-in-the-Middle" includes expanded Student Union.

Payne Stewart wins U.S. Open.

Ozark Mountain Ducks' home opener.

Nelson Mandela retires as President of South Africa.

John F. Kennedy Jr., his wife and sister-in-law, die after their plane crashes off Martha's Vineyard.

Attorney General Janet Reno reopens investigation of 1993 Waco, Texas standoff.

Dozens of people exposed to radiation in Japan's worst nuclear accident.

A team of 300 Bears fans unfurl a larger-than-life American flag which covered Plaster Field during the halftime festivities at Homecoming, 2002.

Duane G. Meyer, 1971-1983

The hallmark of the Duane G. Meyer era was growth. During the 12 years of his presidency, the university enrollment grew from 9,663 to 15,653, becoming the second largest public four-year institution in the state. President Meyer reported annual increases while most of his colleagues on other campuses in the state reported static or declining enrollments. Coping with enrollment increases and very tight state resources challenged the history professor turned administrator. "The question is, how to grow…and grow prudently…," the president remarked. "Perhaps our conservatism will help."

It seemed important to President Meyer to remember who he was. He kept an ear of corn on his desk from the family farm where he was raised in Iowa. "I just keep it on my desk as a symbol of my rural origins," he explained. "Besides, it goes with the color scheme," he added. But those who knew him knew that the corn stood for the kind of accessibility and hospitality typical of rural families. "He never lost his humanity in the transition from professor to president," observed the 1973 *Ozarko*.

President Meyer faced the challenge of creating a university mentality on campus while introducing eight associate degrees in 19 academic areas.

It was a stretch to provide both a community college experience and a university experience in the same institution. But he saw clearly where the future lay as he pushed graduate learning beyond the master's level to the specialist level, as well as seeing the establishment of the first research and service centers.

He pointed the institution forward as he inaugurated Division I athletics competition, established the SMSU Foundation, launched the campus radio station KSMU, and initiated public-private partnerships in building Hammons Student Center.

When President Meyer announced his retirement from the presidency in December 1982, effective June

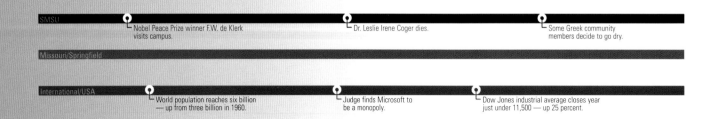

SMSU
Nobel Peace Prize winner F.W. de Klerk visits campus.
Dr. Leslie Irene Coger dies.
Some Greek community members decide to go dry.

Missouri/Springfield

International/USA
World population reaches six billion — up from three billion in 1960.
Judge finds Microsoft to be a monopoly.
Dow Jones industrial average closes year just under 11,500 — up 25 percent.

A Historical Essay

BY DR. JOHN H. KEISER

President, 1993-Present

CHALLENGES OF THE SECOND CENTURY

As SMSU enters its second century, its fortunes will depend on how well it keeps its basic commitments. Its identity and substance must remain clear and focused. Building on the strengths and traditions of the 20th century, alumni, students, administrators, faculty, as well as state decisionmakers, must understand and support the basic concepts — the metropolitan university, the multi-campus system, the comprehensive public affairs mission, and the single purpose, i.e., developing educated persons. Of course, change will occur, but it will be positive only if it takes into account the university's location, its stewardship of place, and its proven strengths; only if there is system-wide consensus on its broader ideals; and only if its acknowledged ultimate reason for being is to create opportunity for citizen-students.

SMSU must define, regularly discuss and insist upon the highest academic standards for and from every member of its community. Because of competition for qualified students from a variety of sources, there will be pressures to "commodify" the university which, if yielded to, will guarantee its decline as it finds that it cannot and should not compete primarily as a business enterprise. The university owes its students the highest quality education in their majors as well as in citizenship because their competition in life will come from Beijing, New Delhi, Moscow and Mexico City more than from St. Louis or Kansas City. Their careers and ultimately their country will depend on the quality of their education.

SMSU must recognize itself and be recognized as a public good and constantly demonstrate what that means. Teaching must be established as life's ultimate profession, and nurturing progeny must be recognized as life's ultimate responsibility. The faculty, staff and students at SMSU who recognize that each is a professor of moral philosophy inasmuch as their behavior is observed by others, and, the citizen-professor and the citizen-student who demonstrate that individually and collegially they represent an essential active part of a sustained democracy, will keep public higher education at the forefront of the Ozarks, and central to American society. It has been that way since 1776, and SMSU has understood the essence of that since 1905. It must continue to do so.

In each of the three traditional activities SMSU engages in, i.e. teaching, research and service, it must consciously establish partnerships with those whose interests are similar. It must be publicly engaged. The relationship with the public schools, particularly as SMSU trains teachers, must be close and strong. Both research and service must be related to the public affairs mission and done in conjunction with related industrial, public and philanthropic agencies in order to make their products focused and efficient. Broadcast services must be seen as high-quality, reasonably-priced teaching and public affairs tools that, when supplemented by the Internet, can effectively deliver the university's as well as the public's message. Utilizing its many resources, first-response capacity to environmental and health-related terrorism in the region should be coordinated by the university.

SMSU must emphasize accountability to the groups whose money it is spending by acknowledging that those constituencies define accountability as a combination of focused productivity, standard-based relevance and equitable per-student support from the state of Missouri for those it serves. While accountable decisionmaking on or off campus recognizes politics, it emphasizes the need to make educational decisions for educational reasons rather than for special-interest, regional or politically-correct purposes. Consistent with its metropolitan university classification, the cities in which the SMSU system's campuses are located must be shown that there has never been a great city without a great university.

The recognition that the SMSU system stands for a set of basic principles for each of its members must be honored and not crippled by the creation of increasingly independent and unrelated administrative units, unrelated social or political groups, or factions that use the university for special cause. SMSU must continue to find ways to emphasize that it values good people and their ideas over anything else, i.e., equipment, buildings or amenities. If it is not "a privilege to be a Bear," fewer people will seek affiliation, and collegial pride will be impossible.

Just as an individual cannot function with loss of memory, SMSU will not prosper if it forgets its history. The challenges of the 21st century are great, but recalling the challenges presented to individuals by the wars and depression of the 20th century and the way SMSU helped individuals meet them, should build confidence in the university's capacity to deal with the future. ⚜

Study abroad has become commonplace for SMSU students in recent years, enabling them to be immersed in the different cultures they are studying. Political science major Richard Jones participated in the university's study-away program by traveling to the People's Republic of China and teaching conversational English to Chinese students at Qingdao University.

30, 1983, he also declared his intention to return to the classroom. "It's a great personal time for me," he declared, "because I am able to study the discipline I love." When he left the president's office, Dr. Meyer had spent six years in the classroom, nine years as academic dean, one year as acting president, and 12 years as president. His presidency remains at this writing the second longest in the history of the university.

Marshall Gordon, 1983-1992

The choice of Dr. Duane Meyer to lead the college in 1971 was clearly a conservative choice on the part of the Board. Meyer was a known quantity having already distinguished himself on campus as a history professor, dean of faculty, and then serving twice as acting president. He was no stranger to the Board. But at his retirement in

1983, for only the second time in the institution's history, the Board stepped boldly outside the university family to find a high-profile, aggressive president who could build on the solid foundations already laid.

After more than 100 applications had been screened and winnowed down to finalists, Dr. Marshall Gordon, an organic chemist and administrator with an 18-year service record at Murray State University in Kentucky, was named SMSU's seventh president in 1983. The 46-year-old Kentuckian had received his Ph.D. at Vanderbilt and taught at Murray State for 13 years. He was appointed dean of the College of Environmental Sciences there in 1975, vice president of university services in 1977, and became acting president at Murray State in 1981.

With the backing of the Board, Dr. Gordon set four objectives for his

administration: (1) to create financial stability at a time of declining state support; (2) to improve and expand campus facilities; (3) to attract quality personnel "who can do the job," and (4) to "provide the leadership necessary to accomplish our mission." The objectives were laudable, but some on campus interpreted them as implicit criticisms of the existing quality of faculty and leadership, especially when colleagues from Murray State were brought to SMSU to fill key staff positions.

Nevertheless, the possibilities at SMSU were clear to President Gordon. He sought to inspire a yet greater vision for the institution. He frequently spoke of "transcending the average," "stretching for higher levels of achievement," and often described SMSU as "an institution on the move" and "the scholar's choice." In talking about its place in the Missouri system of higher education, President Gordon said, "Challenges that were once left for other Missouri institutions are becoming fewer and fewer in number because SMSU is becoming more and more aware of its potential to be a more active force in the state's system of higher education." The new president had high expectations. "Given the forces and the directions that are in place now, the only answer is more. You can expect SMSU to do more tomorrow than it is doing today," he declared.

The vision of the aggressive new president was bold. He set out to enhance the university's reputation by growing its enrollment, attracting academically gifted students, expanding its facilities, and beautifying its campus. While the vision was compelling, some faculty and staff were slow to embrace the enterprise. The president's manage-

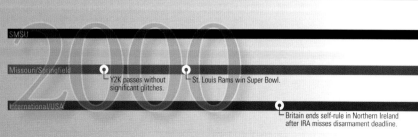

The Missouri-London program has given SMSU students an opportunity to study abroad and travel to tourist destinations on the continent. Heather Buffington, Jennifer Naeger and Elizabeth Leighninger pose before the Eiffel Tower in Paris.

ment style was a problem to many. They experienced it as closed and secretive, making it difficult to establish the trust necessary to mobilize the troops. Students had problems as well. Accustomed to an open and accessible previous administration, a *Standard* editorial in September 1983 inquired, "Does Marshall Gordon Exist?"

Despite these handicaps, President Gordon pushed intently for an institution with greater credibility. He set

about early to improve facilities. New residence halls were built. Academic facilities were upgraded with the acquisition and refurbishing of the Professional Building, and the building of David D. Glass Hall to house the College of Business Administration. The president pushed the business faculty to achieve accreditation with the AACSB, and thus be numbered among the elite business schools in the country. Faculty in all the colleges were encouraged to add research to their teaching and service functions. Achievers were given recognition and rewards for their accomplishments. Gordon pressed to get Greek Row established north of the campus. He saw the promise of Division I athletics and expanded and refurbished Briggs Stadium into Plaster Sports Complex to accommodate 10,000 additional fans. The president worked hard to improve the quality of students by offering a new array of scholarships. National Merit Finalists, for example, became more commonplace on campus.

While the vision articulated by the president was ambitious, his administrative style proved a handicap even in Jefferson City where his efforts to achieve a name change to "Missouri State University" failed twice. During this time the Coordinating Board for Higher Education was asking all public universities to prepare planning documents that would focus their missions. President Gordon saw the planning process as outlined by the CBHE as more constrictive than constructive, and consequently lost the support of the Coordinating Board as he continued to procrastinate developing a plan.

Confidence in the president declined sharply in 1986 when he

Student Fulbright Fellow

Elizabeth Taglauer, a 2002 graduate of SMSU, was selected as a 2002-03 Fulbright Research Fellow. She traveled to France in October 2002 to begin conducting cell adhesion protein research at the Marie Curie Institute in Paris. These proteins are important in the prevention of certain cancers. Taglauer graduated magna cum laude with a major in cell and molecular biology and a minor in French. Upon the completion of her work in France, Taglauer plans to attend medical school.

~

$837,000 Grant to SMSU Biologist

In July 2003, Dr. Paul Durham of the Biology Department won a four-year $837,000 grant from the National Institute of Dental and Craniofacial Research in the U. S. Department of Health and Human Services to study causes and possible therapies for temporomandular joint disorders. The disorder affecting an estimated 12 million people causes pain and deterioration in the jaw point near the ear. Durham has previously done research on migraine headaches. "The nerve that causes migraine headaches is also linked to tooth pain, sinus headaches and jaw pain," Durham said. "We want to identify the pathway and find a clinical application to block it, maybe with an injection."

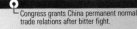
More than 40 graduate programs operating on campus.

Missouri population reaches 5,595,211.

Congress grants China permanent normal trade relations after bitter fight.

Elian Gonzales returned to his father in Cuba after court order is enforced by armed federal agents in Miami.

Honorary Doctorate Awarded to Sister Lorraine Biebel

Breaking a long-established tradition of not awarding honorary degrees, the Faculty Senate in 2002 recommended to the administration that the university award honorary doctorates to recognize extraordinary achievements of distinguished citizens.

The first honorary doctorate in public affairs was awarded to Sr. Lorraine Biebel on May 16, 2003. Sister Lorraine, as she is affectionately known throughout southwest Missouri, retired in 2002 after 54 years of public service, including the founding of The Kitchen and its associated services to homeless and indigent people. The services emerging from her pioneering work involve 750 volunteers and over 54,000 hours of service each year.

"Without fanfare and with humility, Sister Lorraine has addressed a dire need in Springfield — the caring of the poor and homeless," said Dr. James Giglio, Faculty Senate committee chair who established the award and nominated Sister Lorraine as its first recipient.

The west mall showing the most recent additions including the Duane G. Meyer Library and the Jane A. Meyer Carillon, John Q. Hammons Fountains, Glass Hall and Strong Hall.

asked for the resignation of Dr. Tom Wyrick, vice president for Student Affairs, with 17 years of distinguished service at SMSU. Wyrick was considered by students to be a highly effective and trusted advocate for their interests. He was respected by faculty, staff and alumni as well. His dismissal stunned the campus.

The deterioration in trust began to seriously hamper the work of the administration. Faculty morale sagged. Rumors floated about contract irregularities and scholarship abuses. The SMSU Foundation came under criticism. Cutbacks in Regents Scholarships created a negative reaction. The renaming of Briggs Stadium was an outrage to many. But the ultimate unraveling of the administration was brought on by the discovery in September 1991 that there were substantial cost overruns in the construction of the Juanita K. Hammons Hall for the Performing Arts. By October 1991, Board of Regents President Jack Miller

announced publicly that the total cost of Hammons Hall would be $17.3 million, well above the projected cost of $10.8 million. He indicated that the additional funds would come from the SMSU Foundation — $1.5 million in cash and $2 million in borrowed funds, which the Foundation would pay back to area banks over the succeeding five to seven years. An additional $3 million would come from university reserves. Because university funds were being used to finance the building, its design had to be changed to add academic space. A rehearsal hall was added as well as faculty offices and specialty studios for music students.

As concerns over finances deepened, Board President Miller also announced that the Regents would ask State Auditor Margaret Kelly to conduct an audit of the university. She began her work in November.

By then the media had begun pumping out regular reports of alleged irregularities at the university. For the

SMSU — Lybyer Enhanced Technology Center opens at West Plains. — Branch campus established at Liaoning Teachers University in Dalian, China.

Missouri/Springfield — July floods rip through southwest Springfield. — Governor Mel Carnahan, son Randy and Chris Sifford killed in plane crash near Cape Girardeau.

International/USA — Tobacco settlement promises states $206 billion over next 25 years. — Federal elections in Yugoslavia end autocratic rule of President Milosevik.

first time in its history, the Faculty Senate passed a "no confidence" resolution on the president. The vote was 29-17. It was followed by a faculty-wide "no confidence" vote of 339-199. The non-academic staff also passed a "no confidence" resolution, 349-128. The Student Senate, however, voted in support of the president's leadership, 35-9.

Gordon, allowing Gordon to retain the title of president until June 30, 1993.

In July 1992, State Auditor Margaret Kelly released the 103-page audit report on SMSU during a public meeting on campus. While Kelly said no laws had been broken, the document revealed serious problems in administrative practice and over-

administrative council received letters of reprimand.

Unfortunately, the concluding drama of President Gordon's administration tends to overshadow its substantial achievements, most of which were accomplished in the face of rising criticism and declining support. Student enrollment took a substantial turn toward academic excellence with the recruitment of National Merit Scholars. A new era in student housing opened with the addition of Hammons House, New Hall and Kentwood Hall. Athletics achievements, particularly in men and women's basketball, were groundbreaking. Faculty research was encouraged and supported as never before. Unique programs such as defense and strategic studies were established drawing national attention. The College of Business Administration was impressively housed in David D. Glass Hall and successfully examined for accreditation by the prestigious AACSB. Moreover, what would eventually become an affirmed achievement, the university and community now had a hall for the performing arts. The Gordon era may have been short by SMSU standards, but it was not without its valued contributions.

With the completion of the $27.6 million addition to the Duane G. Meyer Library in 2002, the facility was rededicated on September 21, 2002.

In late December, President Gordon hired an attorney to represent his interests. The Board reciprocated. After more than seven hours of negotiations lasting through the night, the Board of Regents reached a settlement with Dr. Gordon on February 11, 1992. Dr. Gordon agreed to relinquish power but to retain the title of president until June 30, 1993, with his current salary and benefits. In June 1991, President Gordon's five-year roll-over contract had been renewed and he had been granted tenure in the Chemistry Department. As part of the agreement, Dr. Russell Keeling, acting dean of the College of Arts and Letters, was appointed by the Board to assume the president's duties. He was given the title chief executive officer to accommodate the Board's initial settlement with Dr.

sight and gave recommendations for improvements in 20 separate areas.

After receiving the Auditor's report, the Board of Regents reconsidered the settlement with Dr. Gordon approved in February. On September 14, Board President Jack Miller announced that the Board of Regents had modified the settlement made earlier with Dr. Gordon. Under the terms of the new agreement, Dr. Gordon agreed to give up the title of president as of September 30, 1992, with his various other benefits to be phased out by February 1, 1993. Dr. Gordon also agreed to surrender his tenure in the Chemistry Department.

In other action, the Board accepted letters of resignation from three of the six members of the administrative council. Two other members of the

Acting President Russell M. Keeling, 1992-1993

The Gordon era ended as Dr. Russell Keeling was named acting president effective October 1, 1992. The Board also announced that a national search for a new president would begin immediately.

Enrollment reaches 19,371.

Physician Assistant graduate program opens.

Smoking banned in residence halls.

Mel Carnahan's name remains on election ballot — Defeats John Ashcroft in Senate race. Jean Carnahan appointed to U.S. Senate and becomes first woman senator from Missouri.

Bob Holden elected governor.

Jack Merritt elected Greene County Sheriff.

Global warming talks collapse at Hague Conference.

In a hotly disputed process, George W. Bush is declared winner of the presidential election in the United States.

1972-2005 Southwest Missouri State University   357

The 14-foot, 2,500 pound Bronze Bear was placed on a three-foot concrete base in front of the Plaster Student Union on April 9, 1999. The Bronze Bear had its origin in 1997 when Professor James Hill of the Art and Design Department was commissioned to create an 18-inch statue of a bear to be awarded to individuals who had made extraordinary achievements and/or given outstanding support to SMSU. The 14-foot Bronze Bear replicated the 18-inch statue. Donated by Bill and Virginia Darr, the massive statue was cast in the Sante Fe bronze foundry, requiring more than six months to pour.

The Purpose

"The single purpose of SMSU is to develop educated persons as responsible citizens in a changing world."

∾

President John H. Keiser
State of the University Address
August 22, 1996

Only Russell Keeling could describe the experience of holding the institution on course while a hurricane was crashing over the administration. But he captured the essence of the effort in the 1991-92 Annual Report, titled *Turmoil and Triumph.* There Keeling said, "It seems to me the real story from last year is that, in spite of the ordinary hardships and distractions, the highly professional and dedicated faculty of the university continued to do an excellent job of teaching their students, doing their research, and providing service to the university, the region and the world. As long as that happened, no matter what else happened, it was a good year."

It was indeed remarkable that for all the distractions, the year under Keeling's watch produced some important achievements for the institution. On April 15, 1992, the long coveted AACSB accreditation was given to both undergraduate and graduate programs in the College of Business

Administration. The teacher education program was reaccredited by the Missouri Department of Elementary and Secondary Education with the highest overall rating ever awarded by DESE. The university also was recognized as ranking first among American Association of State Colleges and Universities members and among the 10 Missouri Valley Conference schools in number of National Merit Scholars enrolled. The debate squad won its first national tournament championship, and the Lady Bears went to their first Final Four in the NCAA tourna-

ment. The institution remained focused through the storm in Carrington Hall.

Dr. Keeling brought a wealth of experience to his leadership role. He was a championship debater at SMSU and returned as a faculty member in 1968. He served as an assistant dean throughout the Meyer administration. He subsequently served as assistant to President Gordon, acting dean of the College of Arts and Letters, and acting vice president of Academic Affairs.

Assuming the CEO responsibility, Dr. Keeling found the university facing a $2 million deficit. He cut administrative costs by $250,000 and made fee adjustments that pointed toward

2001

SMSU
Jackie Stiles named collegiate woman athlete of the year, sets national scoring record.

Missouri/Springfield
After special elections in January, Republicans win control of the Missouri Senate for the first time in more than 50 years.

John Ashcroft confirmed as U.S. Attorney General.

International/USA
U.S. submarine, Greenville, sinks Japanese fishing boat — killing nine.

British livestock epidemic, foot-and-mouth disease, reaches crisis levels.

U.S. spy plane and Chinese jet collide.

On February 22, 2003, the SMSU Chapter of Habitat for Humanity dedicated its fifth house in four years. The "Blitz Build" on campus took just 96 hours, thanks to many volunteers.

a more stable financial future. Where growth and expansion that had been the hallmarks of the Gordon administration, Keeling promised to focus on academics, open communication, establish a collegial approach to decision-making and restore confidence in the university. He also promised to slow the pace of change and reign-in ambitions that were beyond budgetary feasibility. Hoping to have a long tenure to work on the important goals he outlined, Dr. Keeling became a candidate for the president's position, but the Board elected, for the first time in the history of the institution, to appoint as president a person with previous presidential experience.

John H. Keiser, 1993-Present

With the coming of Dr. John H. Keiser, SMSU acquired a president who had already been around the block. Both President Meyer and President Gordon had short stints as acting president, as did John H. Keiser at the University of Illinois at Springfield. But Keiser also had 13 years of experience as president of one of the fastest-growing universities in the inter-mountain region — Boise State in Idaho.

Some on campus and in the community were concerned about the hiring of Dr. Keiser since he had been fired at Boise State. The search committee and the Board of Regents, however, determined that Dr. Keiser was fired "for the right reasons" — advocating for Boise State to Idaho's single statewide governing board and for raising substantive, but difficult educational issues. His courage was seen as a significant asset.

Dr. Keiser earned a Ph.D. in history from Northwestern University in 1964 and began his academic career at Westminster College in Fulton, Missouri. He served as vice president

The 2,500 Pound Bear

Towering 14 feet above the ground just north of the Robert W. Plaster Student Union stands the latest version of the SMSU Bear. Designed by Dr. Jim Hill of the Art and Design Department and contributed to the university by Bill and Virginia Darr, the bear is the model from which 18-inch, 45-pound Bronze Bear Awards are given by the university.

Hill, who had never sculpted animals before, found the bear too big a challenge to turn down. To prepare for the project, Hill went to the Tulsa zoo and then spent a day sketching bears at Bass Pro Shops in Springfield. He discovered that live bears and stuffed bears are quite different. "Live bears have tight, hard lips, and their lower lips are like liver so they can scoop up berries." He also observed that live bears are "toed in" when they walk on all fours. To discover how the hind feet are set in a standing bear, Hill went to Dickerson Park Zoo in Springfield where he had a quick and startling lesson in the movement of an angry 400 lb. bear. "At that point I knew that I wanted to inject that force and that energy into the bear I was creating," Hill recalled.

After all the preliminary sketches, photographs, and models, Hill completed the sculpture in 10 days. Perhaps better than anyone, Jim Hill knows what President Keiser means when he says, "It's privilege to be a Bear."

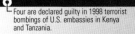
SMSU hosts Missouri Campus Compact.

Four are declared guilty in 1998 terrorist bombings of U.S. embassies in Kenya and Tanzania.

Slobodan Milosevic extradited to The Hague to stand trial for war crimes.

Bear Logos

Over the years, several bear logos have been designed for the university. In 1997, a new logo was approved by the Athletics Department. The stylized bear head was created by Kevin Prejean. It replaced the 1984 logo of a bear walking through a "U." That bear, according to athletics officials, "never caught on."

1997

1984

for Academic Affairs at the University of Illinois at Springfield from 1971-78 and was appointed president at Boise State in 1978.

In his inaugural address at SMSU on January 29, 1994, President Keiser gave some immediate clues about his agenda. He defined his situation by describing a university president as "someone who is temporarily in a position to do something about issues which he could otherwise have the luxury to be cynical about or rise above." His would clearly be an activist administration. Addressing issues would be primary. He went on to place the student at the center of institutional effort. Education for what students are was given priority over education for what they do. "American higher education suffers from succumbing to social, economic and political pressures, which have caused us to emphasize — to educate for — what we and our students *do* and to forget the importance of who and what we and they *are*," the president said. "The true character of our students, regardless of culture or origin, will be formed more by exposure to the best that has been thought and said about inescapable timeless questions than by computer competence, as important as that is," he declared.

A New Vocabulary

Along with his vision and idealism, Keiser brought a new vocabulary to SMSU that quickened a new institutional self-understanding. While SMSU had operated branch campuses in West Plains and Mountain Grove for many years, President Keiser broke new ground by defining the institution as a "system." The inference was that the university was a multiple-

Elevating the Bear

"It's a privilege to be a Bear."

∽

President John H. Keiser

campus entity with distinct but closely articulated functions. West Plains was defined as the open admissions campus. Springfield was the selective admissions campus, and Mountain Grove was the research campus. To begin operating "in a systematic fashion" gave notice of an institution on the move.

Complementing the "system" approach was the early focus on integrating the campuses electronically. "Information technology" emerged as an institutional priority. Connecting West Plains and Mountain Grove electronically with the Springfield Campus became an immediate priority. "Distance learning" entered the vocabulary as electronic voice, video and data connections were established. So comprehensive was the thrust into electronic connectivity and Internet-based learning that a fourth "virtual campus" became a reality.

President Keiser also saw the metropolitan setting of the university significantly defining its role in teaching, research and service. Frequent references to the "metropolitan conversation" helped the institution understand the significance of its five themes first introduced in 1994. The administration defined the institution as a "three campus metropolitan university whose single purpose is to develop educated

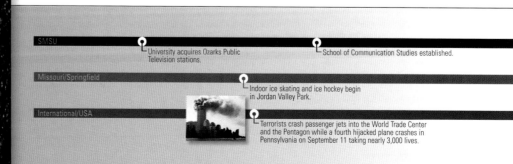

SMSU — University acquires Ozarks Public Television stations. — School of Communication Studies established.

Missouri/Springfield — Indoor ice skating and ice hockey begin in Jordan Valley Park.

International/USA — Terrorists crash passenger jets into the World Trade Center and the Pentagon while a fourth hijacked plane crashes in Pennsylvania on September 11 taking nearly 3,000 lives.

During President Keiser's administration the university developed a succinct and challenging mission statement centered on public affairs and focusing on five themes. The five themes were identified by President Keiser as the substantive issues of contemporary metropolitan life.

persons while focusing on five themes: professional education, health care, business and economic development and the performing arts, with special statewide emphasis on public affairs." Those five themes were understood to be "at the heart of that metropolitan conversation."

While colleges and universities often publish mission statements that fill several pages in their catalogs, President Keiser focused the issue by saying, "SMSU has a single purpose: to develop educated persons." He went on to say, "The characteristics of an educated person are clear, measurable, and recognizable. An educated person is someone who is literate in the broadest sense, has an appreciation for the beauties and complexities of citizenship in his or her community and in the world, has the skills and motivation to continue to learn after leaving the uni-

versity, and can solve problems through the mastery and use of one or more academic disciplines." That definition has become classic among faculty, staff and students, and continues to focus the task of the university.

Perhaps the most compelling phrase in the new institutional vocabulary is "public affairs." It focuses attention on the classic role of higher education — to prepare people to be responsible citizens and leaders. It stands at the heart of President Keiser's vision for the university.

The Statewide Public Affairs Mission

By the time John H. Keiser arrived at SMSU, more than 40 percent of its Missouri students were coming from outside the southwest service region. Over the years the university had built a large clientele from the St. Louis and Kansas City areas as well other sec-

tions of the state. It was already reaching statewide. Some years earlier, Northeast Missouri State University in Kirksville had persuaded the state Coordinating Board for Higher Education that it should pursue a statewide specialized mission in liberal arts, differentiating it from other regional universities. With the precedent already set, and with President Keiser's long-held conviction that the truly educated person has "an appreciation for the beauties and complexities of citizenship," work began on a comprehensive institutional plan that would have public affairs as its integrating and distinguishing theme.

A Case Statement was prepared in 1994 arguing that, "public affairs is about taking values seriously.... (It) involves cultivating civic virtues, strengthening the bonds that unite people, and provoking reflection about and commitment to the collective sources of our individual rights." The statement continued saying, "When

Ozark Public Health Institute established.

Enrollment exceeds 20,000 again.

National Fish and Wildlife Museum opens in Springfield.

U.S. launches war against Al Queda and the Taliban in Afghanistan.

Deadly anthrax mailings kill six in the U.S.

Looking Back

92,113 Degrees Awarded Since 1906

With a recording-breaking 1,953 diplomas awarded at the spring commencement of 2003, a total of 92,113 degrees have been issued since the first graduating class in 1906. Three separate graduation ceremonies were scheduled May 16, 2003, to accommodate the largest graduating class in SMSU history.

Of the 1,501 baccalaureate degrees awarded, 112 were from the Honors College, the university's most rigorous curriculum. Scholastic honors were given to 425 graduates whose grade point averages were 3.4 or above.

Since 1906, the university has awarded 966 associate degrees, 80,452 baccalaureate degrees, 9,987 master's degrees and 708 specialist's degrees.

the public affairs theme is successfully implemented into the life experience of students it should produce 'individuals of character more sensitive to the needs of the community, more competent in their ability to contribute to society and more civil in their habits of thought, speech and action.'"

The Case Statement argued that "our society needs more than workplace competence or critical thinking skills from higher education. It needs the recovery of core values that sustain social order, create responsible public leadership and promote community in the midst of diversity."

The document with its lofty goals and specific reasons why SMSU was equipped to launch the distinctive thrust was sent to the Coordinating Board for Higher Education in the fall of 1994. It was a bold move. But the Coordinating Board saw the genius in the proposal and on January 13, 1995, approved the idea of granting SMSU a statewide mission with public affairs as its distinguishing contribution. The next hurdle was the General Assembly. During the spring of 1995 the proposal was debated in both the House and Senate. It had an uphill battle. Some legislators remembered earlier attempts to obtain a name change for SMSU that failed. Others trivialized the concept by claiming it was only a thinly veiled excuse for training hordes of government bureaucrats or gaining additional state funds.

University representatives fought back. They pointed out that public affairs at SMSU would not be a new curriculum in the formal sense. "It is not a new discipline," administrators pointed out, "nor is it likely to create new majors or new academic programs.

It is primarily a perspective that will be built into the content of existing programs." Point-for-point, criticisms were answered as university leaders spoke at hearings in Jefferson City. Clarifying the intent of the proposal, one administrator testified, "The public affairs theme suggests the creation of a learning environment where civic virtue is celebrated and practiced, where citizenship obligations are explored and encouraged, where the capacity and the commitment to think about the public implications of private behavior is cultivated, and where the capacity to recognize and reflect on public issues is nurtured."

By the end of the session, Senate Bill 340 had passed the House 110-48 granting the statewide mission. The Senate affirmed the idea 23-11. Governor Mel Carnahan signed the enabling legislation at Kentwood Hall in Springfield in June 1995. The statewide mission in public affairs acknowledged SMSU as a major educational resource for the state, as well as defining a unique and important niche for the university in meeting the state's educational needs.

Implementing the Public Affairs Mission
Implementing the public affairs mission proved to be a challenge to leadership in all sectors of the university. As early as the fall of 1995, the university held the first Public Affairs Convocation at Juanita K. Hammons Hall where a near capacity crowd of 1,700 heard renowned author and teacher Dr. Robert Bellah speak on "The Moral Crisis in American Public Life." He challenged the audience to overcome class divisions and to understand freedom as the opportunity "to do what we

SMSU — Photographer Gordon Parks launches College of Arts and Letters Lecture Series.

Missouri/Springfield — Shady Inn, landmark restaurant, closes.

International/USA — Enron Corporation, one of world's largest energy companies, files bankruptcy. — President Bush singles out Iraq, Iran and North Korea as the "axis of evil" in his State of the Union Address to Congress

2002

During a memorial service in 2003, students remember the nearly 3,000 lives lost during the September 11, 2001 terrorist attacks in New York, Washington, D.C. and Pennsylvania.

ought, rather than what we like."

The public affairs mission quickly established linkages with local citizens as they explored the vision of civic responsibility under the auspices of The Good Community Committee. The Committee, under the leadership of university faculty, spent the entire month of October 1995 examining the attributes of the "good community." News media joined the enterprise contributing 80 feature stories, four weekend editorials, and numerous radio and television interviews. The notion of responsible citizenship and civic virtue resonated well throughout the community.

In November 1995, more than 100 faculty gathered in roundtable discussions across campus sharing insights about the problems and prospects for

integrating the public affairs theme in to the existing curriculum. The process of making constructive citizenship a pervasive element in the experience of students was under way. The General Education Program made provisions for the inclusion of a Capstone Course where public problems and discipline-specific public challenges were explored in depth. The Faculty Senate adopted the Citizenship and Service Learning Program enabling students to apply their classroom learning in assisting not-for-profit community agencies and organizations solve real-life problems in the city. Public affairs scholarship awards were initiated to recognize outstanding student contributions to civic life.

Students began catching the vision. Tera Williams worked with Alzheimer's

patients at an extended care facility in Springfield as part of her service learning experience. Observing the dilemma of patients struggling with dressing themselves and eating meals, Tera saw the progressive loss of dignity attendant with the disabling effects of the disease. Keeping the patients' clothes clean was a practical need, but more to the point was the need to protect their dignity. Tera designed a prototype terry cloth cover-up including pockets Alzheimer's patients could wear during mealtime. The cover-up could tolerate heavy bleaching and constant tugging and protected the colorful regular clothes the patients wore. Tera's invention was voted the most creative project at the National Society for Experimental Education Conference. But more importantly, for her, it made life easier

University attempt to change name to "Missouri State University" stalled by a filibuster in the Senate.

Colonel Kent Thomas named chancellor of West Plains Campus.

Evangel University wins NAIA Division II men's basketball national championship.

Daniel Pearl, reporter for the *Wall Street Journal,* killed in Pakistan.

Pedophilia scandals rock Catholic church.

East Timor becomes a new nation.

The women behind the men who served as presidents of the university since 1964 include (left to right) Dr. Annette Gordon, Joann Mallory, 'Lyn Meyer and Nancy Keiser.

for people struggling with hardships. It was about caring.

Faculty work for public benefit reflects the public affairs focus as well. Dr. Ken Rutherford, a political scientist, brought his passion for humanitarian concern to his students. Dr. Rutherford lost both legs as a result of a landmine while serving as a United Nations humanitarian aide in Somalia. He and a fellow-amputee friend founded the Landmine Survivors Network (LSN). That organization became part of the International Campaign to Ban Landmines, which won a 1997 Nobel Peace Prize. Rutherford had served earlier in the Peace Corps and says his goal is "to have four or five students join the Peace Corps every year."

The Public Affairs mission elevated community service to higher visibility. A survey done in 2002-03 showed that more than 143,000 hours of community service had been given by SMSU faculty, staff and students during that academic year.

Institutional initiatives embraced the public affairs mission as well. In February 2001, the university announced the establishment of the Ozarks Public Health Institute to address public health issues through collaboration with business, community, educational and governmental organizations. The emphasis will be on education, training, public service and research programs. An initial focus will be to reduce substance abuse in youth and adult populations.

In 2000, the university held its first Public Affairs Academy, a week-long summer experience for high school students cultivating a better understanding of their role as citizens. The Missouri Public Affairs Academy involves students in on-site observations of government as well as exposing them to state politicians, lawyers, media representatives and others who share their insights about the meaning of responsible citizenship.

A vocabulary change is occur-

ring on campus as well. Increasingly, students are identified by a "hyphenated major." The university no longer graduates just chemists, teachers, artists, accountants or nurses. Rather, the focus has turned to citizen-chemists, citizen-teachers, citizen-artists, citizen-accountants and citizen-nurses. Citizenship has become understood as a life-long vocation, making unique claims upon whatever else we are.

Institutional Plans and Accountability
During the 1980s and early 1990s, the university struggled to put together an institutional plan that the Coordinating Board for Higher Education would approve. The lack of such a plan had stalled the approval of new academic programs. President Keiser saw planning as the key to institutional success. Throughout 1993-94, campuswide input was sought on appropriate goals for the institution. By the end of that academic year, a comprehensive 76-page document titled *Welcoming the 21st Century: A Long-Range Vision and Five Year Plan (1995-2000)* was published. It contained the key elements of the institution's long-range vision, which included focusing the university mission, increasing standards in both teaching and learning, and operating in a systematic fashion.

Five themes that cut across all disciplines were given as part of the new focus and defined the institution's areas of strength. A diagram showing the relationship of the themes to the curriculum emphasized their role in creating the educated person.

At the unveiling of the plan, President Keiser announced, "This is more than a plan — it is our promise to the Coordinating Board for Higher

SMSU

Tent Theatre celebrates 40th anniversary.

Public Affairs Classroom Building renamed Strong Hall.

As of summer 2002, 78,086 baccalaureate degrees, 9,379 master's degrees, and 683 specialist's degrees have been awarded by the university since 1906.

Missouri/Springfield

Dominic James, age two, dies from abuse while in foster care, focusing attention on child welfare system in the state.

International/USA

President Bush announces intention to form a Homeland Security Department.

Accounting scandals at Enron, Arthur Anderson, WorldCom and other major corporations reveal deceptive business practices.

Pennsylvania miners rescued after spending 77 hours in a dark, flooded mine shaft.

364 *A Centennial History of SMSU*

A Historical Essay

BY ANDREA MOSTYN

Office of University Communications

THE FIRST LADIES

There is a saying, "behind every great man is a woman." And while not everyone may agree, Southwest Missouri State University's past four presidents have all had supportive women standing behind them. SMSU's current and past three first ladies share similar philosophies on their roles as the wives of a college or university president.

"I saw my role as being a hostess for the university and a support for my husband," said Marlyn ('Lyn) Meyer, whose husband, Dr. Duane Meyer, served as president from 1971-83. This sentiment was common for the other first ladies.

The first ladies served as advocates for the university — "raising friends." They were hostesses for many official and unofficial university functions and attended many events with their husbands. Serving as a hostess for university functions was the primary role mentioned by the first ladies. They hosted legislators, students, faculty, staff, members of the Board of Governors or Board of Regents, friends of the university, potential donors, visiting dignitaries and others.

Each first lady has favorite memories of functions they hosted. Meyer fondly remembers the BBQ they hosted for new faculty each fall. She also enjoyed hosting the retirement brunch for women who retired from the university each year.

Dr. Annette Gordon, whose husband, Dr. Marshall Gordon, was president from 1983-92, said she and her husband became known for hosting Founders Club members at their home before Tent Theatre and having other university friends over after Tent Theatre.

Joann Mallory, whose husband, Dr. Arthur Mallory, was president from 1964-71, particularly enjoyed hosting the faculty wives. "You knew everyone on the faculty," she said. "You knew their wives, their children. It was small enough in those days that it was just a great atmosphere with the faculty."

Nancy Keiser, whose husband, Dr. John H. Keiser, became president in 1993, described a memorable student picnic. "One of the most successful parties was when 125 high school students from the Missouri Fine Arts Academy had gathered in the back yard," said Keiser. "A torrential rain storm came just when it was time to sit down to eat. When the potato salad began to float, I decided it was time to bring the guests inside. It was a fine group of ladies and gentlemen. They wiped their feet; they sat on the floor; they took turns performing — lining up at the piano. Exposure to a home is good for young people away from home."

Mallory and Keiser mentioned the challenge they faced of being a hostess when they were more comfortable in the background. "I had never been an outgoing person like that," said Mallory. "I had to become a more professional person."

All of the first ladies said they supported their husbands, but they were not involved in university business. Mallory said her husband insulated her from any problems that he might have been facing on the job. Gordon, although she had been a colleague of her husband's when they were both chemistry professors, said she also did not become involved at all in university decisions.

Another role they all saw as very important was providing stability at home.

"My first priority has been the family," said Keiser. "I hope that a stable and predictable home environment after the challenges on the job contributed to John's 33-year career as a central administrator." All the ladies agreed providing a stable homefront was important. Meyer and Gordon were both working when their husbands were hired as presidents, but resigned their positions so they could support their husbands.

"I was teaching at Central High School when Duane became president and I did resign at the end of that semester, because I realized that I would have responsibilities associated with his job and I still had two children at home," said Meyer. "So I felt in order to do a good job, I wouldn't be able to do both."

Gordon was a full professor at Murray State when her husband was hired. "And I did not teach again full time until 1993," said Gordon. "I did teach, for a few semesters, a course at Drury. I eventually stopped doing that because there were just too many conflicts."

The four first ladies were involved in the SMSU Dames, which originally included the wives of faculty members. As more women were hired as faculty members, the group expanded to include female faculty and staff members. The Dames allowed the women who are involved with the university to get to know each other and provide support for their families.

"It's just a different life for younger people now," said Mallory. "When we were younger it was very important that you had these gatherings. Now everyone has their own life and the wife works and the husband works." All four first ladies enjoyed the Dames and were disappointed that it is no longer active.

The first ladies agreed that the traditional role each of them held is changing as more women are hired as presidents and more women work outside the home. It's not the same today, said Keiser. "The younger women have their own careers." ❁

"Public affairs is primarily a perspective and, therefore is intended to be pervasive in the experience of students.... (It) is about cultivating civic virtues, (and) strengthening the bonds that unite people. Public affairs demands the creation of a learning environment...where citizenship obligations are explored and encouraged, where the capacity and the commitment to think about the public implications of private behavior is cultivated, and where the capacity to recognize and reflect on public issues is nurtured."

∾

President John H. Keiser
State of the University Address
January 12, 1995

Education, the Missouri General Assembly, and the citizens of the state of Missouri." A provision for accountability accompanied the plan. An Annual Performance Report was promised, which would document progress along 30 dimensions outlined in the plan. The Performance Reports were filed regularly and by the turn of the century, more than 80 percent of the goals outlined in the plan had been achieved.

A second plan was prepared in 1999-2000, titled *Countdown to the Centennial: A Long-Range Vision and Six-Year Plan (2000-2006)*. It retained the emphasis on focusing the mission, increasing standards in teaching, scholarship and learning, and operating in a systematic fashion. It added a fourth goal, "to establish partnerships with other institutions and entities to achieve the university mission." Science and the environment was added as an institutional theme. The second plan continued the bold confidence in the institution's ability to mature as one of Missouri's leading public universities.

The Templeton Foundation Award

Only two years after the public affairs mission had been granted and the university had begun its immediate implementation, the John Templeton Foundation took note of the unique focus and announced that SMSU would be added to the 1997-98 Honor Roll for Character-Building Colleges. That elite list contained only 135 schools, just 6 percent of the nation's four year institutions. "One of the primary goals of education is the development of moral character — those habits of heart, mind and spirit that help students know, love and do what

is good," said John M. Templeton Jr., president of the John Templeton Foundation. "Because of Southwest Missouri State University's efforts to develop moral character in students, the John Templeton Foundation is pleased to name SMSU to our Honor Roll for Character Building Colleges."

SMSU was one of fewer than 10 public institutions nationwide to be named to the Honor Roll for Character Building Colleges in 1997. The John Templeton Foundation distributes 65,000 copies of each issue of its *Honor Roll for Character-Building Colleges Reference Guide* to public libraries, high school guidance counselors and interested parents across the country.

In 1999, the Templeton Foundation again named SMSU to the *Templeton Guide: Colleges That Encourage Character Development*. SMSU was one of only four public institutions to be named to both the Honor Roll and the Presidential Leadership section. Additionally, four university programs were featured as exemplary in character development — the Introduction to University Life course, the capstone general education course, the Natural High Club in substance abuse prevention and the Citizenship and Service Learning initiative.

Campus Compact Leadership

In December 2000, SMSU was named as the host institution for Missouri Campus Compact, a statewide organization of college and university presidents committed to helping students develop the values and skills of citizenship through public and community service. Twenty-seven Missouri colleges and universities joined together under the leadership of SMSU to form the 23rd state

SMSU
Jane A. Meyer Carillon dedicated.
First class enrolls in audiology doctoral program.
Campus made smoke-free with closing of smoking room in Plaster Student Union.

Missouri/Springfield
UMR graduate Aaron Buerge is *The Bachelor* for the second season of ABC's new hit show.
Jim Talent defeats Jean Carnahan for Senate seat.

International/USA
Five Al Qaeda terrorist suspects arrested in New York.
Jimmy Carter wins Nobel Peace Prize.
Car bomb linked to Al Qaeda kills 180 in Bali, Indonesia.
Ten killed and three wounded in deadly sniper shootings around Washington, D.C.

President John H. Keiser delivers his 20th State of the University Address on January 9, 2003, in Plaster Student Union Theater.

Campus Compact organization.

Campus Compact is a national organization whose objectives articulate particularly well with the SMSU public affairs mission. In 1999, its Presidents' Declaration on the Civic Responsibility of Higher Education declared, "This country cannot afford to educate a generation that acquires knowledge without ever understanding how that knowledge can benefit society or how to influence democratic decision making. We must teach the skills of democracy, creating innumerable opportunities for our students to practice and reap the results of the real, hard work of citizenship."

The Ewing Marion Kauffman Foundation, recognizing the enhancement of higher education by Campus

Compact, gave $100,000 to fund the first year of the program in Missouri. Grants to individual faculty members of $1,500 to $3,000 were available to start or strengthen service learning courses. Several were earned by SMSU faculty.

Missouri Fine Arts Academy

Other endorsements of the quality of SMSU academic programs came as well.

In the spring of 1995, the Missouri General Assembly appropriated $150,000 to support a three-week, intensive summer program for the most talented high school students of dance, music, theatre and the visual arts in Missouri. Thirty Missouri institutions were interested in hosting the program. Applicants were eventually reduced to four, all of which underwent site visits by the Department of Elementary and Secondary Education. SMSU was chosen to host the first Missouri Fine Arts Academy, held in the summer of 1996.

One-hundred-fifteen students from across the state attended the first Academy, engaging in interdisciplinary study as well as advanced study in their own area of the arts. The public affairs

Graphic Design Program Honored

"It may be the best design program I've ever seen." This was the way well-known graphic designer Art Chantry described the SMSU graphic design program in the fall 2002 issue of _Print_, a national magazine dedicated to graphic design professionals.

The sentiments were echoed when participants were announced for the prestigious international poster competition held in Mexico City in October 2002. The competition enables students to compete with professional designers. Just 200 professional winning designs are selected from over 5,000 entries worldwide. Of the winners, 20 came from the United States, and of those 20, nine were entries submitted by SMSU faculty and students in the graphic design program.

Honored in the 2002 competition were SMSU Professor Cedomir Kostovic and his students Nickie Bowers, Jennifer Buso, Philip Cheaney, Eli Hall, Jenny Hardie, Ryan Jones and Laura Thompson.

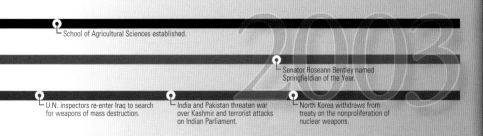

School of Agricultural Sciences established.

Senator Roseann Bentley named Springfieldian of the Year.

U.N. inspectors re-enter Iraq to search for weapons of mass destruction.

India and Pakistan threaten war over Kashmir and terrorist attacks on Indian Parliament.

North Korea withdraws from treaty on the nonproliferation of nuclear weapons.

On July 1, 2001, Ozarks Public Television joined the university's broadcasting program providing both radio and television services to the region. Students such as Amber Lancaster, shown above, now have the opportunity to work in developing programming for KOZK and KOZJ, which provide coverage for 57 counties in four states reaching 500,000 households each week.

mission played a role here as well. Students spent time in local agencies learning about the role of the arts in a variety of rehabilitation programs and sharing their artistic knowledge with local youngsters.

State support of the program has grown to more than $300,000 a year. Students selected for the Academy now number more than 200 annually. SMSU remains the host institution. The interdisciplinary nature of the Academy is its genius. Susan Cole, coordinator of state programs for DESE explains, "A student may be accepted to the Academy because of how well she plays the flute, but she is not here to play the flute. This is not band camp." The Academy has been designed to encourage young artists to break through personal barriers and stretch their comfort zones. Creating art, on canvas or on stage, can be a

messy, uncomfortable experience. But focusing on the creative process, its joys and its woes, is the opportunity of the Academy. A student summed it up saying, "My experience has been life-changing. It has confirmed my belief that I can make it in the arts. It has renewed my passion."

Public Radio and Public Television

As the 21st century opened, a new opportunity in broadcasting presented itself to the university. The Board and management of Ozarks Public Television (KOZK-TV, Springfield/ KOZJ-TV, Joplin) approached President Keiser proposing a partnership that would enable the stations to make the capital investments necessary to comply with the federally mandated digital television broadcast standard. Seeing the potential public television had for distributing educational ser-

vices to the region, Dr. Keiser ordered a careful analysis of the stations' assets, liabilities and potential, which was completed in January 2001. An agreement was reached later that month that Ozarks Public Television's licenses and other assets would be transferred to SMSU pending approval of the FCC. The station commenced operating as a university service on July 1, 2001.

Broadcasting was not new to the university. As early as 1922, WQAB, an experimental station at 834 kilocycles, broadcast from campus. In 1924, KFNH at 1270 kilocycles, opened broadcasts on campus. Both of these stations were short-lived, and broadcasting remained dormant on campus until May 26, 1972, when the university filed FCC Form 340 to apply for a license for a frequency modulation (FM) station. Dr. Clifford House, Dean Holt Spicer and Alumni Director Jim Allwood collaborated on the application, which they submitted on August 15, 1972, the very time when the college was becoming a university.

The case for the assignment of a broadcast license to the university in 1972 included the assertion that, "the station is necessary to implement the new curriculum in communication and persuasion with an emphasis on broadcasting offered by the Speech and Theatre Department." The case statement went on to say, "the station would enrich the educational experience of students who would perform in musical and dramatic programs as well as those who would write scripts and news copy. Student government and departmental organizations will use the facility to develop student oriented programs in public affairs and campus problems." The public benefit was noted as well.

SMSU
— Name change bills for SMSU filed in both House and Senate.
— Lady Bears capture MVC basketball tournament, go on to NCAA and lose to Texas Tech in first round.

Missouri/Springfield
— Two tornadoes on May 4 tore long paths across southwest Missouri, killing 18 people.

International/USA
— Space Shuttle Columbia disintegrates on re-entry with loss of entire crew.
— United Nations Security Council refuses to endorse war against Iraq.
— U.S. and Britain launch war against Iraq.
— U.S. declares official end to combat operations in Iraq.

"The general public will be exposed to educational programming not available through commercial stations."

The FCC acted favorably on the application, assigned the station the 91.1 megaHertz location on the FM dial, and granted the requested call letters, KSMU. The station signed on the air May 7, 1974, from its studios in a charming white stucco house at 1015 S. National. Rick Billington, a student announcer, introduced Dr. Robert Gilmore who welcomed listeners to the station which at the time was radiating 5,800 watts from a 250 foot tower located at the university's agricultural demonstration station in southwest Springfield. The early program schedule focused on classical music and jazz.

A big boost came in 1976 when KSMU was certified by the Corporation for Public Broadcasting (CPB) as eligible to receive funds appropriated to the Corporation by Congress. KSMU also became an affiliate of National Public Radio (NPR) that same year. *All Things Considered,* NPR's groundbreaking news program, became a fixture on KSMU and has remained one of the station's most popular programs. NPR programs were fed to affiliated stations by telephone line until 1980 when NPR became the first radio network in the country to distribute its programs by satellite.

Construction and equipment to get KSMU on the air cost $52,765. The SMSU Alumni Association contributed $10,000 to help fund equipment. An unsolicited donation to the station from Mrs. Andalafte came in February 1975, the first listener contribution. By 1976 the university provided $68,612 in direct support to the station. By 2001, the university support

had expanded to $464,488. Listener and corporate support had grown from $6 in 1977 to $459,000 in 2001. Direct grants from the Corporation for Public Broadcasting increased from $13,346 in 1977 to $184,328 in 2001.

Audience grew slowly during the first decade. In 1978, Arbitron Corporation estimated an audience of 7,800 persons. But when power and coverage were increased, audience size grew rapidly to 40,000 per week in 2001. As a feature of the university, KSMU's total yearly "attendance" exceeds that of the university's athletics events, art events and all campus visitors combined — some 2 million people "attend" this university production each year.

Expanded coverage for KSMU began in Joplin in 1981 where a low-power transmitter was placed into service. By the turn of the century, KSMU was broadcasting in the Branson area, Joplin, West Plains, Mountain Grove and Neosho in addition to the Springfield area. Long-range plans point to transmitters in Lebanon, Fort Leonard Wood, Lamar and Shannon County areas, as the station seeks its goal of serving 95 percent of the 24 county university service area by 2006, with special emphasis on service to rural areas.

When KSMU moved from its stucco house on South National to the new Public Affairs Classroom Building in August 1998, the C.W. Titus Foundation gave a $480,000 grant to equip the state-of-the-art studio complex. As the station opened a new era in its new facility, President Keiser asked the station to create a vision statement that reflected its goals and objectives. He suggested a decep-

First Honorary Doctorate to be awarded to Sister Lorraine Biebel.

First Commencement ceremonies for students receiving SMSU-West Plains' Associate of Arts degree on Liaoning Normal University campus in China.

Springfield opens its new Exposition Center and nearby parking garage in Jordan Valley Park.

Supreme Court decisively upholds the right of affirmative action in higher education.

Mutinous troops attempt unsuccessful coup in Philippines.

NATO assumes control of peacekeeping force in Afghanistan.

tively simple vision, "To be the best university radio station in the country." Arlen Diamond, director of broadcasting services, says, "We're pursuing that vision."

Broadcasting at SMSU is closely tied to the public affairs mission. It seeks "to encourage the exploration of ideas and their application to citizenship." With the addition of the public television station, university broadcasting is reaching more than 300,000 people throughout southwest Missouri. As the move to digital broadcasting occurs, the opportunity to divide the main channel into four discrete standard-definition channels means virtual quadrupling the number of program streams that can be broadcast simultaneously. The broadcast educational possibilities are enormous.

Will It Ever Be Missouri State University?

The idea that Southwest Missouri State University should be renamed "Missouri State University" has been around for a long time. As early as 1979, students were circulating petitions advocating the name change to Missouri State.

Shortly after President Gordon arrived on campus, Dr. James Fisher, a higher education consultant, was hired to appraise the institution. "I'll tell you this," he said, "with your present name, you're going to stay regional and provincial." Many challenged the accuracy of that statement because SMSU had already begun attracting a substantial proportion of its students from outside its service region. As to the provincial part, not many friends were made by that assessment, either.

Whether Fisher's statement was accurate or not, it served to stimulate the push for a name change. In the fall of 1985, petitions were circulated on campus by students supporting the name change. The Board of Regents was persuaded it should happen. In January 1986, Senate Bill 662 was introduced on the first day of the session to change the name to Missouri State University. The January 16 issue of the *Springfield News-Leader* quoted President Gordon giving a dozen reasons why SMSU deserved a name change. It became clear early on that resistance from other state universities would have to be overcome before the bill had a chance at passage. President Julio Leon of Missouri Southern State College said, "Until I see what the effects might be, I'm uncommitted. I'm not in favor of it and I'm not against it."

Early in the discussion of the proposal, a controversy arose over a remark President Gordon allegedly made to President Leon. According to reports, President Gordon told President Leon that he would give him the West Plains Campus and the Fruit Experiment Station in exchange for his support for Senate Bill 662. The report of the offer spread quickly throughout the legislative offices in Jefferson City and lead to heated discussions in the Senate Education Committee. President Gordon claimed he made the comment only jokingly and never expected Leon to take him seriously. But serious were the effects on the bill's prospects in the Senate Education Committee. It died there on February 11, 1986.

A second attempt was made in 1988. Separate bills were introduced in both the House (1611) and the Senate (815). Again arguments were presented including the fact that SMSU was the state's second largest institution, and as President Gordon pointed out, "We are not a regional university. We are anything but that, and I think it's time we got that recognition." But the decision was going to be political, and legislators from other areas of the state felt their institutions were being ignored. Representative Everett Brown of Maryville offered an amendment to the House bill providing that all regional universities become "Missouri State University." They would be distinguished from each other by adding their cities after the name. So under that amendment, SMSU would become "Missouri State University-Springfield." But again, the proposal suffered defeat. The House defeated the bill on a floor vote, and the Senate Bill was never voted out of committee.

The 2002 Effort to Become Missouri State University

When President Keiser took the reigns in 1993, he persuaded the Board of Regents to set the name change issue to a much lower priority. He argued that if the university did its work well and pursued its vision faithfully, the name change would come eventually in recognition of what the university had become. Following that lead, the university made no effort to seek a name change for the next eight years.

In 2002, the idea of changing the university's name originated with SMSU area legislators, not the university. The legislative initiative was endorsed by the Board of Governors, the Faculty Senate and the Student Government Association. The House bill provided that in addition to SMSU becoming Missouri State University, it would change Missouri Western,

SMSU

Three patents issued to SMSU based
on innovative work by faculty.

Missouri/Springfield

International/USA

California governor Gray Davis
ousted in recall vote — actor Arnold
Schwarzenegger elected in his place.

Archbishop Bernard Law resigns in the
midst of sexual abuse scandal in the
Roman Catholic Church.

Saddam Hussein is captured
by American troops.

The university's first attempt at becoming Missouri State University occurred in 1985-86. The kickoff for the campaign was held at the University Plaza Hotel where President Marshall Gordon displayed the new T-shirt and banner carrying the hoped-for name. Representative Bob Holden, Board President Bill Barclay and Senator Dennis Smith look on appreciatively.

Missouri Southern and Harris-Stowe from colleges to universities. The case presented for the passage of the bill was persuasive. Broad support developed in the House and it passed the measure in late March by 100-53. In mid-April, the House Bill came out of the Senate Education Committee with a 7-3 favorable vote. Only a Senate floor vote remained. While the sentiment was building in the Legislature that SMSU had indeed earned the new name, the Senator from Columbia representing the University of Missouri, Senator Ken Jacob, was threatening a filibuster against the bill, ostensibly to protect the University of Missouri's interests as the state's flagship institution. Interestingly, even the MU student newspaper, *The Maneater,* editorially supported the name change for SMSU. Acknowledging that the grant of a new name would accelerate the already palpable competition between MU

and SMSU, the competition, argued the editor, would be good for students. "In theory," argued the editorial, "MU would now have an impetus to improve those areas where SMSU has it trumped, including our desperately lacking fine arts program." The editorial concluded saying, "The students of Missouri would benefit because they would have a viable, much cheaper alternative to the MU system with a similar statewide legitimacy. Concerns for MU's top-dog position in Missouri are natural, but a little competition never hurt anyone. And it might just be a godsend to students."

When the Bill was reported out to the Senate floor for debate, there were more than 22 votes committed to it. Only 18 were needed to pass it. But the Senator from Columbia was determined to frustrate the will of his colleagues in the interests of the University of Missouri. He prevented a vote on

the bill by filibuster.

President Keiser expressed disappointment over the lost opportunity for the State. "Name changes for the four institutions included in the bill would have enhanced the state's higher education system and allowed the state to be more competitive with surrounding states," Dr. Keiser declared. "Since the MU Senator killed the bill, we can chalk it up as another 'missed opportunity' for the State of Missouri."

The president concluded his comments to the faculty and staff in the May 2002 *Focus* saying, "While they have withheld the name, they cannot hold us back. And that is a promise. The jealousy and insecurity that those opposed to the name change showed during the legislative session have nothing to do with the name change itself, but rather with existing factual analysis. It was while we were riding for the 'SMSU' brand that the university clearly distinguished itself on the way to becoming the best metropolitan uni-

2004

President John H. Keiser announces his retirement from the presidency of SMSU to be June 30, 2005.

Third five-year, long-range plan titled *Daring to Excel: A Long-Range Vision and Five-Year Plan (2005-2010)* under development through the president's office.

State Auditor Claire McCaskill challenges Governor Bob Holden in Democratic primary.

Low-carbohydrate diets become the rage across the country — it is alleged that one in three Americans are overweight.

Intelligence reports justifying the war in Iraq discredited by Senate Intelligence Committee report.

Hooray! Graduation time, May 2002.

versity in the United States."

Bills proposing a name change to Missouri State University were filed again in 2003 by legislators from southwest Missouri. Again, the proposal was held hostage by the threat of a filibuster by Senator Jacob. Supporters from the southwest district wondered when "the label would describe what was in the can." With a stand-alone doctoral program, students from every county in the state, enrollment surpassing 20,000 and graduate programs growing more rapidly than in any other state institution, the label clearly needed to say Missouri State University. At the end of the 2003 legislative session, even the opponents acknowledged that the name change was inevitable. With the overwhelming evidence of benefits to both the institution and the state, most agreed that the question was no longer "if" but "when."

President John H. Keiser is scheduled to retire June 30, 2005. He remained in the president's office two

years beyond his original plan in order to participate in the centennial celebration. His 12 years as president places him third behind Dr. Roy Ellis who served 35 years and Dr. Duane Meyer who served 12 years and three months.

Forward to the Centennial

Institutional momentum is palpable as SMSU moves toward the beginning of its second century. Enrollment exceeds 20,000. Another 10,000 are enrolled in continuing education programs. Graduate enrollment is third largest in the state. Two doctoral programs are offered along with more than 40 master's and specialist's programs, 19 of which have been added since 1995.

A statewide mission in public affairs granted by the General Assembly in 1995 has invigorated the educational program bringing national recognition as a character-building institution. Extending educational opportunities throughout the region by a variety of distance learning technologies has

been strengthened by the acquisition of Ozarks Public Television. Courses on the Internet, a cooperative degree with an Indian university and a campus in China, have pushed the internationalization of the university to new heights. The United Nations approval of Meyer Library as the 43rd United Nations depository in the United States provides students with U.N. documents spanning a half-century, and further accentuates the global reach of the Ozarks institution.

Establishment of the Ozarks Public Health Institute expands the service the institution provides to southwest Missouri. A grant of $282,000 for a service project to reduce tobacco use throughout Missouri endorses the Institute's promise as a major player in area health enhancement. Other sponsored programs through university centers and faculty initiatives drew more than $8 million to the institution in 2001-02. A $3 million grant in 2002 to SMSU physicist Dr. Ryan Giedd to continue development of solid-state sensors able to detect chemical and biological agents in the environment illustrates the growing capability of the institution to contribute to national defense research. The appointment of Dr. J.D. Crouch of the Defense and Strategic Studies faculty to be assistant secretary of defense for international security policy in the George W. Bush administration illustrates the growing quality of faculty expertise. More than 70,000 SMSU alumni contributing citizen and professional skills and talents to communities across Missouri, the United States and more than 50 countries abroad are part of the legacy the university is building.

While recent achievements are

SMSU

Name change to Missouri State University again frustrated by political maneuvering in the Missouri General Assembly.

Search process for a new president started under the leadership of Michael Franks, vice president of the Board of Governors.

Missouri/Springfield

Second *Vison 20/20* report submitted to the City.

Springfield voters approve school levy increase.

International/USA

Photos released of Iraqi prisoners abused by U.S. forces at Abu Ghraib prison.

Former U.S. Senator John Danforth of Missouri, appointed as Ambassador to the United Nations.

Saddam Hussein indicted by Iraqi court.

noteworthy, the vision of the institution is decidedly forward. The most recent institutional plan, *Countdown to the Centennial: A Long-Range Vision and Six-Year Plan (2000-2006),* spells out a striking future. The 90- page document spells out the priority goals for the immediate future. They include further focusing of the institutional mission around five themes at the heart of every metropolitan conversation. Raising the bar another notch to improve teaching, scholarship and learning, and continuing to operate as system remain important. Establishing partnerships with business, industry, schools, government, and universities both here and abroad becomes a fourth goal.

Watch for collaboration with the City of Springfield in further renewing the downtown area by expanding the SMSU footprint there. The "extended campus" will be extending further through additional on-line courses, expansion of electronic networks connecting classrooms on all campuses, and additional telecourse offerings. Look for further expansion of international opportunities for students, including additional cooperative campuses abroad.

Capital investment between 1994 and 2000 totaled more than $60 million. Planned investment to 2006 is targeted at $185.83 million. New facilities envisioned include Ozarks Public Health Institute, a new library at West Plains, a new Art and Design building, a new Support Services facility, a Science Complex, a Craig Hall renovation and addition and a Professional Building addition.

Watch for the completion of a $50 million comprehensive fund-raising campaign in celebration of the Centennial, and increasing reliance on external grants, contracts, federal appropriations and private gifts to fuel the drive to excellence.

Program maturation will replace program growth that characterized the 1995-2000 period, although a bachelor's degree in e-Business, and a Bachelor of Science in Education-Dance are scheduled for development. New graduate degrees planned include an Education Specialist degree in Guidance and Counseling, master's degrees in Agricultural Economics and Public Archaeology, a post-professional master's degree in Physical Therapy, and a joint doctorate with the University of Missouri in public administration.

Look for the public affairs focus to be enriched with a Leader-in-Residence program in which a national or international luminary will be housed at SMSU for a limited period of time during which a body of work will be conducted significant to public affairs. Look for students and faculty to be invited to participate in the project with the guest. The Public Affairs Academy will expand to three weeks and include students from all Missouri counties, mirroring the success of the Fine Arts Academy. Don't be surprised if all students are required to have a foreign language or experience in a foreign culture as part of their graduation requirement.

Graduate certificate programs will be developed for those seeking focused expertise beyond the undergraduate level. While not as extensive as a master's degree program, the certificate programs will provide students with a focused, coherent group of courses designed to develop expertise in a particular area of study.

To keep faculty current in a rapidly evolving teaching environment, an Academic Development Center was created. The Center provides on-going faculty development programs linked to the rising standards for teaching, research and scholarship.

Continuing education programs on the Springfield Campus are expected to expand to 12,000 students, while the West Plains program will grow from 450 to 1,900. Lifelong learning will continue to push the development of continuing education.

Accountability will continue to be key. Sixty-seven system performance measures are published at the end of the *Countdown to the SMSU Centennial* holding the institution's feet to the fire.

The hyperbole found in State Normal School #4 *Bulletins* nearly a century ago has become the substance of the 21st century university. It has "Dared to Excel" from the beginning, it has more than met that dare and it won't be changing that tradition. ■

Harold Bengsch, who served as director of the Springfield-Greene County Health Department for 19 years, receives honorary Doctor of Public Affairs degree at spring commencement.

Center for Applied Science and Engineering established research and development in downtown Springfield.

Missouri voters asked to decide if the state constitution should be amended "so that to be valid and recognized in the state, a marriage shall exist only between a man and a woman."

Rockaway Beach, Missouri seeks constitutional amendment to permit building a casino riverboat on the White River.

A $21 million federal grant received to turn MFA milling site into Jordan Valley Innovation Center in downtown Springfield.

Ronald Reagan dies at age 93.

Senator John Kerry of Massachusetts wins Democratic primary race for President. Senator John Edwards of North Carolina selected as his running mate.

Don Gorske of Fond du Lac, Wisconsin, eats his 20,000th Big Mac.

182-carat diamond found by 25-year-old miner in Guinea.

Centennial Celebration Events

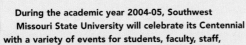

During the academic year 2004-05, Southwest Missouri State University will celebrate its Centennial with a variety of events for students, faculty, staff, alumni and the region — all guided by the Centennial theme "Daring to Excel." Many annual events will incorporate a Centennial flavor and new events will celebrate the accomplishments of the past 100 years.

Members of campus colleges, departments, offices and organizations will contribute to the events — each providing their unique strengths and interests. Athletics, the arts, academia and many others have planned events to meet a wide variety of interests.

A new event for the university, the Public Affairs Conference, will occur for the first time in April of the Centennial year. This annual event will bring many distinguished individuals to campus each year. The Centennial year will also see the continuation of long-time traditions on the university, such as Homecoming.

SMSU-West Plains and SMSU-Mountain Grove also plan to celebrate the Centennial with a variety of special events.

For more information about all these events and for a complete list of Centennial events, visit http://calendar.smsu.edu/centennial.asp

2004

August 22

The **New Student Convocation, the Campus Kickoff for the Centennial Celebration,** will be held at 2 p.m. in Hammons Student Center. For more information, call 417-836-5527.

September 7-May 3

■ **Tales to Celebrate Our Multicultural Heritage**, presented by Meyer Library, will be held from 7-8 p.m. Sept. 7, Oct. 5, Nov. 9 and Dec. 7 in 2004 and Jan. 11, Feb. 1, March 1, April 5 and May 3 in 2005 in Plaster Student Union, Room 313. For more information, call 417-836-4525.

September 10-12

■ The **Community Kickoff for the Centennial Celebration** will begin with the **Ozarks Celebration Festival Concert and Ice Cream Social,** featuring "Hogmolly" and "Big Smith," at 7 p.m. Sept. 10 at the Strong Hall Amphitheater. The **Ozarks Celebration Festival: A Centennial Celebration**, featuring traditional Ozarks arts, crafts and performers, will be held all day Sept. 11-12. For more information, call 417-836-6605.

■ **Bearfest Village**, featuring food, games and entertainment for the whole family, will be held from 2-6 p.m. Sept. 11 on the parking lots south of Plaster Sports Complex. For more information, call 417-836-4143.

■ **The SMS football Bears will take on Sam Houston State University** at 6 p.m. Sept. 11 at Plaster Sports Complex. Tickets can be purchased by calling the SMSU box office at 836-SMSU or (toll free) 1-888-4-SMS-TIX. For more information, call 417-836-5402 or visit *www.smsbears.net*

■ "Jeremy Chesman and Friends: **A Centennial Carillon Concert,**" will begin at 7:30 p.m. Sept. 12 on the lawn adjacent to Meyer Library. For more information, call 417-836-3028.

September 13-16

■ SMSU will present the second annual **Public Affairs Week**, including events which celebrate and promote SMSU's statewide mission in public affairs. For more information, call 417-836-3010.

■ The Staff Senate Public Affairs Committee presents Dr. Don Landon speaking on **"State Normal School to SMSU: Where We've Been and Where We're Going."** The brown-bag lunch presentation will be held from noon-1 p.m. Sept. 14 at Plaster Student Union, Room 313. For more information, call 417-836-8580 or visit *www.smsu.edu/staffsenate/PublicAffairs/PAW*

September 26

■ A **Centennial Concert**, presented by SMSU's music department, will begin at 2 p.m. at Juanita K. Hammons Hall for the Performing Arts. For more information, call 417-836-5648.

October 4

■ The **College of Health and Human Services Multidisciplinary Forum**, highlighting 100 years of progress in the treatment of diabetes, will begin at 5 p.m. in Plaster Student Union Theater. Campus and community groups will provide informational exhibits in the PSU Atrium from 3-5 p.m. For more information, call 417-836-6981 or visit *www.smsu.edu/chhs*

October 22-23

■ **Centennial Homecoming: 100 Years of Magical Milestones** will include an alumni dinner, parade, football game and other special activities. For more information, call 417-836-5654.

■ The **Alumni Dinner** will begin at 7 p.m. Oct. 22 at the University Plaza Hotel Convention Center. A social hour begins at 6 p.m. Reservations are required. For more information or to purchase tickets, call 417-836-5654.

■ The **Homecoming 5K Run**, which begins and ends in Phelps Grove Park, will begin at 8 a.m. Oct. 23. For registration information, call 417-836-5791.

■ The **Homecoming Parade** will begin at 9 a.m. Oct. 23 at John Q. Hammons Parkway and St. Louis St. and end at Madison Ave. For more information, call 417-836-4386.

■ **Bearfest Village**, featuring food, games and entertainment for the whole family, will be held from 9 a.m.-1:30 p.m. Oct. 23 on the parking lots south of Plaster Sports Complex. For more information, call 417-836-4143.

■ **The SMS football Bears will take on Southern Illinois University** for its Homecoming game at 1:30 p.m. at Plaster Sports Complex. Tickets can be purchased by calling the SMSU box office at 836-SMSU or (toll free) 1-888-4-SMS-TIX. For more information, call 417-836-5402 or visit *www.smsbears.net*

November 19

■ The **Wall of Fame Induction Ceremony**, recognizing retired faculty and staff who have contributed greatly to the university, including a special Centennial group of retirees from the first half of SMSU's history, will begin at 1:30 p.m. in the Plaster Student Union Ballroom. For more information, call 417-836-5886.

2005

February 18-March 13

■ A **Centennial Exhibition**, featuring artwork in juried exhibition as well as archival material relating to the university, will be held at the Springfield Art Museum. For more information, call 417-836-4143.

March 17-18

■ The **Founders' Day Celebration**, marking the university's founding on March 17, 1905, will include events scheduled throughout the weekend. For more information, call 417-836-5654.

■ The **Centennial Gala and Art Auction** will be held on March 18. For more information or to purchase tickets, call 417-836-4143.

■ A **Centennial Concert**, featuring **Mannheim Steamroller,** will be held at 7:30 p.m. April 17 at Juanita K. Hammons Hall for the Performing Arts. For more information, call 417-836-6776. Tickets can be purchased by calling the SMSU box office at 836-SMSU or (toll free) 1-888-4-SMS-TIX.

April 13-15

■ The university's inaugural **Public Affairs Conference** will bring prominent people from a variety of disciplines and backgrounds and from public, private and academic arenas to several locations on campus. For more information, call 417-836-8501.

❀ Presidents, Deans and Chancellors ❀

Springfield Campus

1906-18
William Thomas Carrington, President
Normal School #4

1918-26
Clyde Milton Hill, President
Normal School #4
Southwest Missouri State Teachers College

1926-61
Roy Ellis, President
Southwest Missouri State Teachers College
Southwest Missouri State College

1961-64
Leland Eldridge Traywick, President
Southwest Missouri State College

1964-71
Arthur Lee Mallory, President
Southwest Missouri State College

1971-83
Duane G. Meyer, President
Southwest Missouri State College
Southwest Missouri State University

1983-92
Marshall Gordon, President
Southwest Missouri State University

1992-93
Russell Keeling, Acting President
Southwest Missouri State University

1993-present
John H. Keiser, President
Southwest Missouri State University

West Plains Campus

1963-66
William Bedford, Dean
West Plains Residence Center

1966-86
Marvin Green, Dean
West Plains Residence Center

1986-90
Richard Brauhn, Dean
West Plains Residence Center

1990-97
Marvin Looney, Chancellor
West Plains Residence Center
Southwest Missouri State University-West Plains

1997-2001
Fred Marty, Chancellor
Southwest Missouri State University-West Plains

2001-present
Kent Thomas, Chancellor
Southwest Missouri State University-West Plains

Mountain Grove Campus

1974-84
Dr. Kenneth Hanson, Director
State Fruit Experiment Station

1984-2004
Dr. James F. Moore, Director
State Fruit Experiment Station

1998-present
James P. Baker, Chancellor
SMSU Research Campus at Mountain Grove

❀ Board of Regents/Governors ❀

❀ Foundation Board of Directors ❀

The Board of Regents established the Southwest Missouri State University Foundation in 1980. It was recognized as a 501(c)(3) not-for-profit organization in January 1981. The purpose of the Foundation is to develop an environment which promotes giving and therein seek, receive, manage and distribute resources appropriate to support programs of instruction, research and public service of the university.

W. Stephen Bodanske
1981-84

Georgia Calton
1981-84

Virginia P. Dailey
1981-93

Dwight Douglas
1981

Ray L. Forsythe*
1981, 1984-93

R. Dwain Hammons
1981-88

June S. Hamra
1981

John L. Harlin
1981-87

Glenn W. Johnston Jr.
1981-87

Joseph L. Johnston*
1981-84

Harry B. Kelly Jr.
1981

Max W. Lilley
1981

Darrel L. Love
1981-85

R. Wagner Love*
1981-93

Thomas M. Macdonnell
1981

Ramona F. McQueary*
1981-94

Howard F. Randall
1981-87

Gene H. Ruble
1981-88

Edward F. Stracke
1981

William G. Baker
1982-84

Ora Dale Ryan Gillette
1982-85

Robert B. Noble*
1982-85

Ruth K. Palmer
1982-85

W.W. Morris
1984-85

Basil J. Boritzki
1985

Juanita K. Hammons
1985-95

Robert E. Stufflebam
1985-94

John D. Whittington*
1985-94

Robert W. Bitter
1986-1995

James H. Cooper
1986-92

David D. Glass
1986-95

Kenneth E. Meyer*
1986-95

Thomas M. O'Sullivan Sr.
1986-89

Ransom A. Ellis Jr.
1987-91

T. Edward Pinegar Jr.
2000-2005

Bill R. Foster*
1988-93

Jeffrey C. Hutchens
1988-93

Robert L. Price
1988-93

William E. Barclay Sr.
1989-90, 1995-97

Jack K. Hood*
1989-94

Daniel F. O'Sullivan
1990-95

Wm. Terry Fuldner*
1991-97

Robert W. Plaster*
1992-97

Kenneth W. Brown
1993-95

Rose Marie Boone
1994-99

Jay D. Burchfield
1994-95

Clay Cantwell*
1994-99

Cynthia F. Hollander*
1994-99

Wm. Wayne Miller
1994-99

David A. Trottier
1994-95

Virginia C. Bussey
1995-2000

George W. Johnston Jr.*
1995-2000

Joyce Mahoney
1995-97

Leslie Irene Coger
1996-98

William H. Darr*
1996-99

Vivian H. Drago
1996-2001

John Q. Hammons
1996-2001

W. Bryan Magers*
1996-2001

Robert E. Roundtree
1996-2001

Marion L. Wolf
1996-2001

Grant W. Lawson*
1997-2002

Alvin L. Clifton
1998-2003

Jacquie A. Dowdy*
1998-2003

William V. Turner
1998-2000

Jane A. Meyer
1999-2001

Thomas L. Black
2000-05

James R. Craig
2000-05

Alva R. Ellison
2000-05

James P. Ferguson
2000-05

Fred M. McQueary
2000-05

Robert M. Garst
2001-06

Thomas G. Strong
2001-06

Bernice S. Warren
2001-06

W. Wayne Bischler
2002-04

Gregory L. Curl
2002-04

Jay R. Padgett
2002-04

Christopher T. Fuldner
2002-04

Richard A. Seagrave Jr.
2002-04

Pat L. Sechler
2003-06

Joseph W. Turner
2003-06

Ex-Officio Members of the SMSU Foundation

William E. Barclay Sr.
1981-86

Duane G. Meyer
1981-83

Marshall Gordon
1983-91

T. Edward Pinegar Jr.
1987

Clay Cantwell
1988-90

Jerry L. Hall
1991-92

Russell M. Keeling
1992

John H. Keiser
1993-2005

James R. Craig
1994, 1996

Joseph W. Turner
1997-99

William H. Darr
2000-

Officers of the SMSU Foundation

Thomas E. Allen
1981-2003

Maurice E. Edwards
1981-89

Kenneth W. Brown
1981-82

Gregory P. Onstot
1982-

Daniel W. Wiser
1990-98

Cindy R. Busby
1998-

Kent Kay
2003-

*served as president

❀ Student Government Association Presidents ❀

Student government did not arrive on the SMS campus until 1921 when three students, Robert W. Martin, William V. Cheek and Freda Marshall sat down with President Ellis and drafted the first student government constitution. In the early years student government was called the Student Council. Over the years new constitutions were written, each more elaborate than their predecessors. The Constitution of 1958 designated the body as The Student Government Association, and its legislative arm as the Student Senate. Presidents of the student body have been elected continuously since 1920-21.

1920-21 R.W. Martin	1935-36 Leon Lapp	1950-51 Don Burrell	1965-66 Pat Logue	1980-81 Gary Osredker	1995-96 Kendal L. Orr
1921-22 James Althouse	1936-37 Louis Sharp	1951-52 Ron Downing	1966-67 Michael Mitchell	1981-82 Randy Carter	1997-97 Chris Steines
1922-23 R.W. Anderson	1937-38 Marguerite Noble	1952-53 Don Dedmon	1967-68 Rich Anderson	1982-83 Mike McCoy	1997-98 Jeremy Robinett
1923-24 R.W. Anderson	1938-39 Warren Bennett	1953-54 Jerry Sweaney	1968-69 Len Hall	1983-84 Doug Jameson	1998-99 Wesley D. Wilson
1924-25 Aaron Botts	1939-40 Walter Bailey	1954-55 Jerry Anderson	1969-70 Mike Compton	1984-85 Bruce Law	1999-00 Theresa Streckfuss
1925-26 Elton Moon	1940-41 Jack Wommack	1955-56 William Thomas	1970-71 Jeff Schaeperkoetter	1985-86 John Sullivan	2000-01 Sam Garman
1926-27 Guy Thompson	1941-42 Eddie Michael	1956-57 William Fugitt	1971-72 Dan Slais	1986-87 Julie Simpson	2001-02 Adam Warren
1927-28 Maynard Willis	1942-43 William Perkins	1957-58 John Rich	1972-73 Ralph Stubblefield	1987-88 JoDonn Chaney	2002-03 Jacob Wyrick
1928-29 Meekie Wright	1943-44 Mary Burns	1958-59 Robert Hartzog	1973-74 Jim Porter	1988-89 Mark Parrish	2003-04 Rafiel Warfield
1929-30 Tom Welsh	1944-45 Steve Forrest	1959-60 James Bacon	1974-75 Mike Franks	1989-90 Jim Bornemann	2004-05 Chris Curtis
1930-31 James Moore	1945-46 Leonard Ernstman	1960-61 Joe Rich	1975-76 Rodney Sell	1990-91 David Kellett	
1931-32 Buford Thomas	1946-47 Emmett Davis	1961-62 Xavier Baron	1976-77 Doug Harpool	1991-92 Scott Austin	
1932-33 Don Owensby	1947-48 Gordon Foster Wes Pelsue	1962-63 Edward Miller	1977-78 S.M. (Mark) Seaman	1992-93 James R. "Rob" Swafford	
1933-34 Joe Nickle	1948-49 Paul Anderson	1963-64 Mike Hannigan	1978-79 Jeff Carter	1993-94 Antonio "Tony" Rice	
1934-35 Dwight Darby	1949-50 Don Payton	1964-65 Ken Burchett Wayne Link	1979-80 Gary Osredker	1994-95 Benjamin "Ben" Stringer	

❀ Joseph N. Boyce/*Wall Street Journal* Award ❀

The Joseph N. Boyce/*Wall Street Journal* Award was established in 1997 to recognize students whose lives illustrate the values associated with the public affairs mission of the university. Joseph N. Boyce, a senior editor of the *Wall Street Journal*, gave a public affairs convocation address on the campus in 1996. He refused an honorarium for his appearance and the public affairs steering committee dedicated it to establishing an award for students who have a "demonstrated record of service and leadership qualities consistent with the goal of the public affairs mission." The award is presented annually during the new student convocation at the beginning of the fall semester. The winners include:

1998	1999	2000	2001	2003
Christie Wolfe, Education	Emily Ann Johnston, Business	Erika L. Horton, Communication	Kevin Lotz, Social Work	Abigail M. Hagy, History

❀ Pepsi-Cola Public Affairs Scholarship ❀

Scholarships in the amount of $1,000 (or more) are awarded each spring for the following school year. A committee of faculty, staff and one student was originally established in 1997, and chaired by Dr. David Belcher, Dean of the College of Arts and Letters. Dr. Pauline Nugent, Department of Modern and Classical Languages, has chaired this committee since 1998. Awards have been presented to the following students in the years indicated:

1998-99	1999-2000	2000-01	2001-02	2002-03	2003-04
Aimee M Lubbers	Dwight M. Alden	Kellie Branson	Kelsi E.Ervin	Claudia Garman	Benjamin Mertens
Wesley D. Wilson	Teri D. Buell	Teri Buell	Wendy K. Parker	Becky Rotert	Stuart Miller
Christie L. Wolf	Monica L. Giles	Erin Chindlund	Kelli M. Hall		Sarah Pinnell
Kristopher J. Wolfe	Erika L. Horton	Michelle Doering			Brianna Reitzner
	Jaime B. Nejdlik	Amanda Hall			Kimberly VanLeer
	Kendra R. Thomas				

❀ Faculty Senate ❀

The first Faculty Senate was organized in 1962 under the administration of President Leland Traywick. As early as 1927, President Roy Ellis organized the Faculty Council, made up primarily of academic department heads. This group served as a cabinet to the president who served both as president of the faculty and of the college. James W. Shannon of the history department served as chair in 1927. President Ellis served continuously as chair from 1928 until retiring in 1961, with the exception of a brief period in 1929 when M.A. O'Rear chaired the group.

With the organization of the Faculty Senate in 1962, for the first time in the history of the institution the faculty had a defined role in the governance of the college.

1962-63 & 1963-64
George D. Gleason
Arts & Letters
English

1964-65 & 1965-66
Tom A. Stombaugh
Science & Math
Biology

1966-67
L.T. Shiflett
Science & Math
Mathematics

1967-68 & 1968-69
Paul L. Redfearn Jr.
Science & Math
Biology

1969-70 & 1970-71
Charles Tegeler
Arts & Letters
English

1971-72
David L. Heinlein
Humanities & Social
    Sciences
Political Science

1972-73
J.N. Smith
Health & Applied
    Sciences
Agriculture

1973-74 & 1974-75
Robert Beach
Health & Applied
    Sciences
Technology

1975-76
Donald McInnis
Science & Math
Geosciences

1976-77 & 1977-78
Jack W. Bush
Education &
    Psychology
Lab School

1978-79
Frank L. Clark
Business Administration
Finance & General
    Business

1979-80
Robert L. Norton
Arts & Letters
Foreign Languages

1980-81
Bruno Schmidt
Science & Math
Computer Science

1981-82 & 1982-83
Robert D. Beckett
Arts & Letters
English

1983-84
Vernon Thielmann
Science & Math
Chemistry

1984-85
Charles Stufflebeam
Health & Applied
    Sciences
Agriculture

1985-86
Ron Pope
Education &
    Psychology
Curriculum &
    Instruction

1986-87
John Catau
Science & Math
Geosciences

1987-88
M. Michael Awad
Science & Math
Mathematics

1988-89
Linda Park-Fuller
Arts & Letters
Theatre & Dance

1989-90
Stefan Broidy
Education &
    Psychology
Curriculum & Inst

1990-91
Larry George
Arts & Letters
Foreign Languages

1991-92
Lois M. Shufeldt
Business Administration
Computer Information
    Systems

1992-93
Bert P. Helm
Humanities & Social
    Sciences
Philosophy

1993-94
Mona J. Casady
Business Administration
Administrative Office
    Systems

1994-95
Rhonda R. Ridinger
Health & Human
    Services
Health, P.E., &
    Recreation

1995-96
Charlene A. Berquist
Arts & Letters
Communications

1996-97
Jon R. Nance
Business Administration
School of Accountancy

1997-98
Steven L. Jensen
Natural & Applied
    Sciences
Biology

1998-99
David M. Quick
Arts & Letters
Art & Design

1999-00
Genevieve R. Cramer
Education
Reading & Special
    Education

2000-01
Paula A. Kemp
Natural & Applied
    Sciences
Mathematics

2001-02
Thomas G. Plymate
Natural & Applied
    Sciences
Geography, Geology &
    Planning

2002-03
Lois M. Shufeldt
Business Administration
Marketing

2003-04
James N. Giglio
Humanities & Public
    Affairs
History

2004-05
Lois M. Shufeldt
Business Administration
Marketing

❀ Staff Senate ❀

The first organization of SMS staff members was established in November 1988 under the administration of President Marshall Gordon. Named the Staff Advisory Council, the group consisted of eleven staff members from a variety of job classifications.

In 2001 the Council refined its purpose, objective and mission and changed its name to Staff Senate. Its mission statement declares that the Staff Senate strives to enhance the university purpose of developing educated persons and the university's mission in public affairs as well as promoting the highest standards of personal and professional development, productivity and social responsibility. The welfare and growth of the staff is maintained through a fact-finding, deliberative and consultative group of representatives who conduct studies and make reports and recommendations to the administration

1988 Mark Stillwell	1993 Shirley Randall	1996 Randy Blackwood	1999 Sharon Lopinot	2002 Mary Lynne Golden
1989 Mark Stillwell Mike Murphy	1994 Marilyn Erhardt Shirley Randall	1997 Dale Moore	2000 Darren Young	2003 Lisa McEowen-LeVangie
1990-1992 Mike Murphy	1995 Shirley Randall Randy Blackwood	1998 Debbie Thomas	2001 Sara Clark	2004 Phil Nichols

❧ Outstanding Alumni Award ❧

Established in 1956, the Outstanding Alumni Award recognizes significant personal and professional achievement on the part of SMSU graduates. Criteria include noteworthy success in business, industry or profession, loyalty to the university and exceptional contributions to society.

1956
Hubert Wheeler*

1957
Finis Engleman*
Dr. Dorothy Martin Simon
  Pittsboro, North Carolina

1958
Frances Hamilton*
Brig. Gen. Ralph Snavely
  Pebble Beach, California

1959
Dr. Roy Ellis*

1960
Dr. William E. Smith*

1961
Dr. Clyde Hill*
Morris Stephens
  Lake Bluff, Illinois

1962
Dr. Charles C. Killingsworth*
Dr. Robert J. Moon*

1963
Dr. Arthur Smith*

1964
Hon. Marion T. Bennett*

1965
Hon. Jack A. Powell*
Dr. Virginia Garton Young
  Columbia, Missouri

1966
Dr. Keith Baker*
Dr. Everett Keith*

1967
Dr. Harold Haswell
  San Antonio, Texas

1968
David R. Kennedy*
Dr. Frank R. Kennedy
  Ann Arbor, Michigan
Dr. Hall Kennedy*
Harold A. Kennedy
  Walnut Creek, California
Ralph E. Kennedy
  Northridge, California

1969
Howard A. Cowden*
Dr. Herbert W. Schooling*

1970
Dr. Eugene E. Garbee*
Dr. Frank L. Padgitt*
Dr. Frederick M. Raubinger*
Hon. A. P. Stone Jr.*

1971
Maj. Gen. Warren K. Bennett*
Dr. Charles K. Martin Jr.*
Dr. Edwin L. Martin*

1972
Dr. Kirk L. Denmark*
Dr. Harry H. Knight*
Dr. Glenn O. Turner
  Springfield, Missouri

1973
Dr. James R. Amos*
Capt. Edward D. Estes
  Virginia Beach. Virginia
Kate Frank*
Dr. Jesse B. Johnson*

1974
Daisy Sifferman Cook*
Dr. John L. Lounsbury*
Dr. Lyle Owen
  Lubbock, Texas
Raymond A. Young*

1975
William G. Baker*
Retha Stone Baker*
Clarence C. Burnett*
Ernest H. Newcomb*

1976
Dr. Willard J. Graff*
Blunt H. Martin*
Admiral Max K. Morris
  Jacksonville, Florida
Dr. Frederic St. Aubyn*

1977
Dr. Leon Billingsly*
Dr. M.O. Looney
  Pontiac, Missouri
Dr. Charles J. McClain
  Columbia, Missouri
Dr. Donald D. Shook
  Overland Park, Kansas

1978
Hon. Don E. Burrell*
Dr. Joe E. House*
Ellis C. Rainey Sr.*

1979
Paul R. Brackley
  Metairie, La.
Dr. Donald N. Dedmon
  *Pawleys Island,
  South Carolina*
Dr. Byron W. Hansford*
Dr. J.L. Johnston*
W.W. "Webb" Morris*

1980
Dr. Bonnalie Oetting Campbell
  Houston, Texas
Dr. Arlene Crosby Mazzone
  Easton, Connecticut
Eugene T. Scafe*
Dr. Ronald K. Wright
  Ft. Lauderdale, Florida

1981
Dr. Harlan Bryant*
Dr. William R. Cheek
  Houston, Texas
John Q. Hammons
  Springfield, Missouri
E.E. "Johnny" Johnson*

1982
Basil J. Boritzki
  Naples, Florida
Dr. John E. Chapman
  Brentwood, Tennessee
Dr. Horace C. Dudley*
Dr. Quentin D. Ponder
  Ft. Wayne. Indiana
Champ M. Reese*

1983
Dr. Lois Peterson Callahan
  San Mateo, California
Don C. Dailey
  Springfield, Missouri
Dr. Joe E. Kuklenski Jr.*
Neil C. Wortley
  Springfield, Missouri

1984
Woodrow W. Denney*
David D. Glass
  Bentonville, Arkansas
Dr. Raymond W. Lansford
  Columbia, Missouri
Clyde W. McConnell*
Robert B. Noble
  Springfield, Missouri
Gene H. Ruble
  Nixa, Missouri

1985
Dr. David B. Kesterson
  Denton, Texas
Kenneth E. Meyer
  Springfield, Missouri
Winnie Faulkenberry Weber
  Tavernier, Florida

1986
Ray Forsythe*
Ramona Frazier McQueary
  Springfield, Missouri

1987
Dr. Harold D. McAninch
  Naperville, Illinois
William Tillotson
  Palos Verdes, California
Thomas Strong
  Springfield, Missouri

1988
James O. Glauser*
William L. Rowe Jr.
  Springfield, Missouri
Dr. C. William Young*

1989
R. Dwain Hammons
  Stockton, Missouri
Maj. Gen. Fred Marty
  Springfield, Missouri
Amanda Linkous Mahr*

1990
Burl Henderson*
John D. Whittington
  Springfield, Missouri

1991
Dr. S. Gaylen Bradley
  Hershey, Pennsylvania
Maj. Gen. Robert L. Gordon
  Williamsburg, Virginia

1992
Nancy Maschino Dornan
  Springfield, Missouri
Lt. Gen. Neal T. Jaco
  San Antonio, Texas

1993
Lt. Gen. John E. Miller
  Oakton, Virginia

1994
Dr. Wanda R. Gray
  Springfield, Missouri
Marvin W. Ozley
  Leawood, Kansas
Dr. Bernice S. Warren
  Springfield, Missouri

1995
William H. Darr
  Springfield, Missouri
John L. Harlin
  Gainesville, Missouri
Maj. Gen. David E. White
  Huntsville, Alabama
Dr. Mary Jo Wynn
  Springfield, Missouri

1996
Dr. Jerry L. Atwood
  Columbia, Missouri
Dr. Jim D. Atwood
  Amherst, New York
Hon. John C. Holstein
  Springfield, Missouri

1997
Jim R. Craig
  Springfield, Missouri
Dr. Peggy Tuter Pearl
  Springfield, Missouri

1998
W. Wayne Bischler
  Sunrise Beach, Missouri
Dr. Barbara D. Burns
  Lamar, Missouri

1999
Ethel Farrell Curbow
  Springfield, Missouri
Tom Black
  Nashville, Tennessee

2000
Hon. Roy D. Blunt
  Strafford, Missouri
William A. Lacy*

2001
James B. Anderson
  Springfield, Missouri
Terry W. Thompson
  Monett, Missouri

2002
James E. Smith
  Clinton, Missouri
Brig. Gen. William A. West
  Leavenworth, Kansas

2003
Marla J. Calico
  Fair Grove, Missouri
Grant W. Lawson
  Nixa, Missouri

* deceased (as of April 2004)

❀ Award of Appreciation ❀

In 1965 the Alumni Association established the Award of Appreciation in recognition of distinguished achievement by retired faculty members. Criteria for selection include noteworthy success in professional life and loyalty to the university. The Alumni Association Board of Directors amended the award in 2001 to include retired staff members who had distinguished themselves in service to the university.

1965
Dr. Virginia J. Craig*
James W. Shannon*

1966
Mary Adams Woods*
Dr. Harry A. Wise*

1967
Mayme Candler Hamilton*
Dr. Walter O. Cralle*

1968
Floy T. Burgess*
Dr. R.W. Martin*

1969
N. Bertha Wells*

1970
Elda E. Robins*
Jesse H. Collins*

1971
Esther M. Hennicke*
Dora M. Hennicke*

1972
Dr. Richard E. Haswell*
Iva M. Ray*

1973
Florence Compton*
Dr. Donald H. Nicholson*

1974
Mareta Williams Pons*
Dr. Glenn E. Karls*

1975
Dr. O. P. Trentham*
Dr. Oreen M. Ruedi*

1976
Laura Roman Dodd*
Horatio M. Farrar*

1977
James E. Bane*
Margaret S. Crighton*

1978
Dr. Efton R. Henderson*
Marie Content Wise*

1979
Estle Funkhouser*

1980
Dr. James C. Snapp*

1981
Florence Baker Bugg*

1982
Dr. Don L. Calame*

1983
Dr. Mary Rose Sweeney*

1984
Andrew J. McDonald*
Dr. Leslie Irene Coger*

1985
Dr. James R. Pollard
    Springfield, Missouri

1986
Elizabeth A. Mills*

1987
Dr. Grace Gardner*

1988
Wilfred H. Adler*

1989
Dr. L. Thomas Shiflett*

1990
Dr. Richard Wilkinson
    Springfield, Missouri

1991
Dr. David Heinlein*

1992
Dr. Max. H. McCullough*

1993
Neva P. Johnson
    Springfield, Missouri
Dr. Gerrit J. tenZythoff*

1994
Aldo A. Sebben*

1995
Dr. Duane G. Meyer
    Springfield, Missouri
Howard R. Orms*

1996
Dr. Violet Harrington Krischel
    Springfield, Missouri
Dr. Holt V. Spicer
    Springfield, Missouri

1997
Ilah M. Dixon*
Dr. Robert K. Gilmore*

1998
Dr. Ivan D. Calton
    Springfield, Missouri
Dorothy F. Padron
    Springfield, Missouri

1999
Dr. Tom A. Stombaugh*
William J. Thomas
    Springfield, Missouri

2000
Leo E. Huff*
Dr. Mollie Autry Molnar
    Springfield, Missouri
Dr. Vernon E. Renner
    Springfield, Missouri

2001
Dr. Byrne D. Blackwood
    Springfield, Missouri
Dr. Mary Alice Cantrell
    Springfield, Missouri
Dr. Paul L. Redfearn Jr.
    Springfield, Missouri

2002
Maurice E. Edwards
    Springfield, Missouri
Robert M. Scott
    Springfield, Missouri
Dr. Peggy Stone Thomas
    Ozark, Missouri
Mildred D. Wilcox
    Springfield, Missouri

2003
Dr. Vencil J. Bixler
    Springfield, Missouri
Wilda F. Looney
    Springfield, Missouri
Donald R. Payton
    Springfield, Missouri
Patricia R. Pierce
    Springfield, Missouri

deceased (as of April 2004)

❀ Outstanding Young Alumni Award ❀

Established in 1985, the Outstanding Young Alumni Award recognizes an alumna or alumnus 45 years of age or younger whose endeavors in business, the professions, civic life, philanthropic leadership, the arts, public service, volunteerism and related avenues of distinguished service have brought honor to the university. The award acknowledges the rapid growth of the university in the 1970s and 1980s.

1985
Kathleen Turner
New York, New York

1987
Linda Dollar
Springfield, Missouri

1988
Hon. Karen Mason See
Kansas City, Missouri

1990
Gordon L. Kinne
Springfield, Missouri

1991
Michael H. Ingram
Springfield, Missouri

1992
William J. Noonan, III
Kenner, Louisiana

1993
Gregory L. Curl
Charlotte, North Carolina

1994
Charles H. Armstrong
Houston, Texas
Dr. Kim Skeeters Finch
Springfield, Missouri
Hon. Bob L. Holden
Jefferson City, Missouri

1996
Becky Geers Oakes
Columbia, Missouri

1997
Sterling R. Macer Jr.
Studio City, California

1998
Richard H. McClure
Kirkwood, Missouri
Gary M. Tompkins
Eldon, Missouri

1999
Pam Hicks Holmes
Nixa, Missouri
Bill Mueller Jr.
Mesa, Arizona

2000
Denise Wells Fredrick
Springfield, Missouri
Doug M. Pitt
Springfield, Missouri

2001
Dr. David W. Osborne
Santa Rosa, California

2002
Robin E. Melton
Ozark, Missouri

2003
Dr. Barry S. Arbuckle
Aliso Viejo, California
Kimberly George Carlos
Kansas City, Missouri

❀ Lifetime Achievement Award ❀

The Lifetime Achievement Award was created in 1999 to honor university graduates who have distinguished themselves in professional achievement and community service over a lifetime. The award recognizes alumni whose life and accomplishments have earned the respect of their professional colleagues and their community.

1999	2000	2001	2002	2003
Harold K. Bengsch	John Q. Hammons	Paul J. Connery	Dr. M.O. Looney	Dr. Robert J. Huckshorn
Springfield, Missouri	*Springfield, Missouri*	*North Haven, Connecticut*	*Pontiac, Missouri*	*Boca Raton, Florida*

❀ Alumni Association Presidents ❀

Throughout the history of the institution, the SMSU Alumni Association has been the principal organization through which graduates and former students continue affiliation with their alma mater. Formally organized in 1907-08, the mission of the Alumni Association solidly remains the same — to promote and encourage continued interest, involvement and pride in SMSU.

1908 D.W. Clayton	1927 Myrtle Teter	1959 Horace Haseltine	1977 Darrel Love	1995 Margery Laker Bates
1909 P.P. Callaway	1941 Virgil Cheek	1960 Joseph Johnston	1978 Don Simmons	1996 Malcolm Decker
1910 E.C. Wilson	1942 Virgil Cheek	1961 Don Dailey	1979 Peggy Tuter Pearl	1997 Voncille Megarian Elmer
1912 M.R. Floyd	1944 Jack Powell	1962 Fred Rains	1980 LeRoy Mitchell	1998 Teresa Williams Carroll
1913 Shelton J. Phelps	1945 Jack Powell	1963 Jerry Sweaney	1981 Georgia York Calton	1999 Glenna Hanks Frazier
1914 T.J. Walker	1946 Leon Miller	1964 David Holmes	1982 Willard Graff	2000 T.J. Siebenman
1915 John Boyd	1947 Howard Potter	1965 Herb Bockhorst	1983 Sharon Armstrong Nahon	2001 T.J. Siebenman
1916 Roy Ellis	1948 W. Ray Daniel	1966 Tom Strong	1984 E.E. "Johnny" Johnson	2002 Stan Curbow
1917 W.Y. Foster	1949 Gordon Wardell	1967 Charles Harrison	1985 Gordon L. Kinne	2003 Stan Curbow
1918 Anna L. Blair	1950 Ransom Ellis Jr.	1968 Forrest Lambeth	1986 William E. Kirkman	2004 Bill Thomas
1919 Grace Palmer	1951 John Robinette	1969 James Glauser	1987 Gib Adkins Jr.	
1920 George Ryan	1952 John Flummerfelt	1970 Don Burrell	1988 Paul Silkwood	
1921 W.R. Rice	1953 Jessie Burrell	1971 Ronald Conn	1989 Bill Rabourn	
1922 O.P. Keller	1954 James R. Craig	1972 Kerry Montgomery	1990 Lesley Fleenor Trottier	
1923 H.E. Detherage	1955 Charles Shrum Burton	1973 Sandra Lyle House	1991 T. Wesley Dunn	
1924 Elizabeth Peiffer	1956 Carl Fox	1974 Glenn Johnston	1992 David McQueary	
1925 Finis Engleman	1957 Roy Litle	1975 Jeanne Craig Stinson	1993 Jan Bischoff Carroll	
1926 W.T. Clopton	1958 J. Harold Skelton	1976 Wayne Graham	1994 Faunlee Breeding Harle	

❀ Wall of Fame Recognition ❀

The Wall of Fame in Plaster Student Union is the designated location to recognize and honor faculty and staff who have excelled at SMSU and made significant contributions to the positive college experience of students. The Wall of Fame recognition was established in 2001 with the first class inducted in 2002. Eligibility requirements include full-time employment with the university for at least 10 years, service that has resulted in meaningful change at SMSU, continuous demonstration of character and integrity, respect by the larger community, and positive influence on students. Individuals who have been previously honored in the naming of a campus facility and those who have previously received the Bronze Bear award are excluded from eligibility for Wall of Fame recognition.

2002 Inductees

Dr. Byrne Blackwood

Arthur Briggs

Margaret Susan "Maggie" Crighton

Dr. Robert Gilmore

Dr. George Gleason

Wilda Looney

Dr. E. Howard Matthews

Don Payton

Aldo Sebben

Dr. Holt Spicer

Dr. Gerrit tenZythoff

Dr. Cliff Whipple

Dr. Richard Wilkinson

2003 Inductees

Edgar Albin

Dr. Vencil Bixler

Gene Edwards

Judy Geisler

Dr. Roar Irgens

Dr. Robert Martin

Mildred Wilcox

Dr. Mary Jo Wynn

2004 Inductees

Dr. James Bane

Dr. John "Bill" Northrip

Dr. Paul Redfearn

Dr. Thomas "Tom" Stombaugh

William "Bill" Thomas

Dr. Thomas "Tom" Wyrick

Centennial Inductees (1905-50)

Florence Baker Bugg

Dr. Walter O. Cralle

Joseph Daniel Delp

Hiland D. Kelley

Clayton P. Kinsey

M.A. O'Rear

Margaret Julietta Putnam

Deborah D. Weisel

Dr. Harry Arthur Wise

❀ Faculty and Staff Recognition Awards ❀

Recipients of SMSU Foundation Excellence in Teaching Award

Dr. Alice F. Bartee
Political Science
1983-84

Dr. James R. Layton
Reading
1983-84

Dr. Rhonda R. Ridinger
Health and Physical
Education
1983-84

Mr. John D. Schatz
Agriculture
1983-84

Dr. M. Michael Awad
Mathematics
1984-85

Dr. R. Thomas Fullerton
Foreign Languages
1984-85

Dr. Duane G. Meyer
History
1984-85

Dr. Clifford I. Whipple
Psychology
1984-85

Dr. R.G. Amonker
Sociology
1985-86

Dr. Genevieve R. Cramer
Reading
1985-86

Dr. Max H. McCullough
Educational Administration
1985-86

Dr. Martha F. Wilkerson
Sociology
1985-86

Dr. Steven L. Jensen
Biology
1986-87

Dr. Robert E. Thurman
Physics
1986-87

Dr. Nancy Walker
English
1986-87

Dr. E. Dale Wasson
Economics
1986-87

Mr. Jim A. Escalante
Design
1987-88

Dr. John W. Northrip
Astronomy
1987-88

Mr. Howard R. Orms
Theatre
1987-88

Dr. Peggy S. Pearl
Child and Family
Development
1987-88

Dr. Jack C. Knight
Philosophy
1988-89

Dr. Burton L. Purrington
Anthropology
1988-89

Mr. Dennis H. Rexroad
Art and Design
1988-89

Dr. Charles E. Stufflebeam
Agriculture
1988-89

Dr. Betty L. Bitner
Secondary Education
1989-90

Dr. David A. Daly
Communications
1989-90

Dr. Lyndon N. Irwin
Agriculture
1989-90

Dr. Vera B. Stanojevic
Mathematics
1989-90

Dr. Michael L. Bell
Secondary Education
1990-91

Dr. Joseph J. Hughes
Foreign Languages
1990-91

Dr. Nancy K. Keith
Computer Information
Systems
1990-91

Dr. Vernon J. Thielmann
Chemistry
1990-91

Dr. N. June Brown
Reading
1991-92

Ms. Joanne M. Gordon
Nursing
1991-92

Dr. David J. Lutz
Psychology
1991-92

Dr. James F. O'Brien
Chemistry
1991-92

Dr. Wayne L. Anderson
Business Law
1992-93

Dr. Gloria J. Galanes
Communications
1992-93

Dr. Russell G. Rhodes
Biology
1992-93

Dr. Woodrow Sun
Mathematics
1992-93

Dr. John S. Bourhis
Communications
1993-94

Dr. Mary K. Coulter
Management
1993-94

Dr. Peter Richardson
Management
1993-94

Dr. Leonila P. Rivera
Special Education
1993-94

Dr. Kurt E. Chaloupecky
Accounting
1994-95

Dr. Donald H. McInnis
Atmospheric Science
1994-95

Dr. Richard L. Myers
Biology
1994-95

Dr. Belva W. Prather
Music
1994-95

Dr. W. D. Blackmon
English
1995-96

Dr. Chris Bersted
Psychology
1995-96

Ms. Sharon Ellis
Theatre and Dance
1995-96

Dr. Shahin Gerami
Sociology and Anthropology
1995-96

Recipients of SMSU Foundation Excellence in Research Award

Dr. James N. Giglio
History
1986-87

Dr. Harry L. Hom Jr.
Psychology
1986-87

Dr. Juris Zarins
Anthropology
1986-87

Dr. Russel L. Gerlach
Geography
1987-88

Dr. Charles W. Hedrick
Religious Studies
1987-88

Mr. Wade S. Thompson
Art
1987-88

Dr. James T. Jones
English
1988-89

Dr. Victor H. Matthews
Religious Studies
1988-89

Dr. Carol J. Miller
Business Law
1988-89

Dr. Katherine G. Lederer
English
1989-90

Dr. George J. Selement
History
1989-90

Dr. William A. Wedenoja
Anthropology
1989-90

Dr. Shouchuan Hu
Mathematics
1990-91

Dr. Arden T. Miller
Psychology
1990-91

Dr. Ronald L. Coulter
Marketing
1990-91

Dr. Allen J. Edwards
Psychology
1991-92

Dr. Worth Robert Miller
History
1991-92

Mr. Bill B. Senter
Art
1991-92

Dr. William J. Burling
English
1992-93

Dr. Michael J. Cerullo
Accounting
1992-93

Dr. David J. Hartmann
Sociology
1992-93

Mr. Dwaine L. Crigger
Art
1993-94

Dr. Ryan E. Giedd
Physics
1993-94

Dr. James F. O'Brien
Chemistry
1993-94

Dr. Martha F. Wilkerson
Sociology
1993-94

Dr. David W. Gutzke
History
1994-95

Dr. Shouchuan Hu
Mathematics
1994-95

Dr. Karl W. Luckert
Religious Studies
1994-95

Dr. John Havel
Biology
1995-96

Dr. Kishor Shah
Mathematics
1995-96

Dr. Logan Skelton
Music
1995-96

Dr. Xingping Sun
Mathematics
1995-96

Recipients of Burlington Northern Foundation Faculty Achievement Award for Outstanding Scholarship

Dr. Dominic J. Capeci Jr.
History
1984-85

Dr. Bertrand P. Helm
Philosophy
1985-86

Dr. Paul L. Redfearn Jr.
Biology
1986-87

Dr. Karl W. Luckert
Religious Studies
1987-88

Dr. J. Ramsey Michaels
Religious Studies
1988-89

Dr. Mark E. Rushefsky
Political Science
1989-90

Recipients of Burlington Northern Foundation Faculty Achievement Award for Teaching Excellence

Dr. James C. Moyer
Religious Studies
1984-85

Dr. Mona J. Casady
Administrative Office
Systems
1985-86

Dr. L. Dale Allee
Secondary Education
1986-87

Dr. V. Andree Bayliss
Reading
1987-88

Dr. Stanley M. Burgess
Religious Studies
1988-89

Dr. L. Dennis Humphrey
Biomedical Sciences
1989-90

Dr. Roar L. Irgens
Biology
1990-91

Dr. Donal J. Stanton
Communications
1991-92

Ms. Dorothy F. Padron
Elementary Education
1992-93

Recipients of SMSU Foundation Excellence in Community Service Awards

Faculty

Dr. Doris W. Ewing
Sociology
1994-95

Dr. Peggy S. Pearl
Consumer and Family
Studies
1994-95

Dr. Ruth V. Burgess
Curriculum and Instruction
1995-96

Dr. Lloyd R. Young
Sociology
1995-96

Mr. Edward J. DeLong
Library Science
1996-97

Dr. Richard L. Nichols
School of Accountancy
1996-97

Dr. Lynd on N. Irwin
Agriculture
1997-98

Ms. Janice Reynolds
Greenwood Laboratory
School
1997-98

Dr. Katherine G. Lederer
English
1998-99

Dr. Pauline Nugent
Modern and Classical
Languages
1998-99

Dr. Janice Schnake Greene
Biology
1999-2000

Dr. Paula A. Kemp
Mathematics
1999-2000

Dr. Dalen M. Duitsman
Health, Physical Education
and Recreation
2000-01

Dr. Bruton L. Purrington
Sociology and Anthropology
2000-01

Dr. Judith A. John
English
2001-02

Dr. Amy F. Muchnick
Music
2001-02

Staff

Mr. Mike J. Jungers
Student Life and
Development
1994-95

Ms. Patsy D. Corbett
Center for Archeological
Research
1994-95

Ms. Charlotte C. Hardin
Minority Student Services
1995-96

Ms. Linda A. Lock
Music
1995-96

Ms. Tina C. Stillwell
News Services
1996-97

Dr. Ann M. Orzek
Counseling and Testing
1996-97

Ms. Deborah A. Gallion
Juanita K. Hammons Hall for
the Performing Arts
1997-98

Dr. Frederick D. Muegge
Taylor Health and Wellness
Center
1997-98

Ms. Barbara L. Helvey
Citizenship and Service
Learning
1998-99

Dr. Cecil A. Poe
Printing Services
1998-99

Mr. Mark A. Johnson
Residence Life and Services
1999-2000

Ms. Polly B. Laurie
Communication Sciences
and Disorders
1999-2000

Ms. Carol B. Silvey
West Plains Development
2000-01

Ms. Dana D. Carroll
University College
2000-01

Mr. Clinton D. Copeland
Career Services
2001-02

Mrs. Jean Ann Percy
College of Business
Administration
2001-02

Ms. SuzAnn A. Ferguson
Career Services
2002-03

Ms. Catherine Hawkins
School of Social Work
2002-03

Recipients of SMSU Foundation Faculty Achievement Award for Outstanding Scholarship

Dr. W. Patrick Sullivan
Social Work
1990-91

Dr. James S. Baumlin
English
1991-92

Dr. Victor H. Matthews
Religious Studies
1992-93

Dr. Paula A. Kemp
Mathematics
1993-94

Dr. Peggy S. Pearl
Consumer and Family
Studies
1994-95

Dr. Phyllis Bixler
English
1995-96

Recipients of SMSU Foundation Faculty Achievement Award for Teaching Excellence

Dr. Carter M. Cramer
Secondary Education
1993-94

Dr. Olen L. Greer
Accounting
1994-95

Ms. Irene Francka
Computer Information
Systems
1995-96

Distinguished Scholars

Dr. Dominic J. Capeci Jr.
History
1987-88, 1991-92

Dr. Russel L. Gerlach
Geography
1988-89, 1992-93

Dr. James N. Giglio
History
1988-89, 1992-93

Dr. James F. Miller
Geology
1988-89, 1992-93

Dr. Harold B. Falls Jr.
Biomedical Sciences
1989-90, 1993-94

Dr. Bertrand P. Helm
Philosophy
1989-90, 1993-94

Dr. Charles W. Hedrick
Religious Studies
1991-92, 1995-96

Dr. James F. O'Brien
Chemistry
1991-92, 1995-96

Dr. Dominic J. Capeci Jr.
History
1992-93, 1996-97

Mr. Wade S. Thompson
Art
1992-93, 1996-97

Dr. James N. Giglio
History
1993-94, 1997-98

Dr. D. Keith Denton
Management
1994-95, 1998-99

Dr. James F. Miller
Geology
1994-95, 1998-99

Dr. Charles W. Hedrick
Religious Studies
1996-97, 2000-01

Dr. James F. O'Brien
Chemistry
1996-97, 2000-01

Mr. Mark M. Biggs
Media Journalism and Film
2001-02, 2005-06

Recipients of SMSU Foundation Award

Teaching

Dr. Pauline Nugent
1996-97

Dr. Kishor Shah
1996-97

Dr. Carol J. Miller
Finance and General
Business
1997-98

Dr. Anthony D. Simones
Political Science
1997-98

Dr. James S. Baumlin
English
1998-99

Dr. Cedomir Kostovic
Art and Design
1998-99

Dr. Richard L. Myers
Biology
1999-2000

Ms. Vonda K. Yarberry
Art and Design
1999-2000

Dr. James F. O'Brien
Chemistry
2000-01

Dr. Joseph J. Hughes
Modern and Classical
Languages
2000-01

Mr. Mark M. Biggs
Media Journalism and Film
2001-02

Mr. Roman Z. Duszek
Art and Design
2001-02

Research

Dr. John T. Pardeck
1996-97

Mr. Zhi Lin
1996-97

Dr. Dean A. Cuebas
Chemistry
1997-98

Dr. S. Alicia Mathis
Biology
1997-98

Dr. Michael D. Burns
English
1998-99

Dr. Wenxiong Chen
Mathematics
1998-99

Dr. Don L. Moll
Biology
1999-2000

Dr. Lynn W. Robbins
Biology
1999-2000

Dr. Robert A. Mayanovic
Physics, Astronomy and
Materials Science
2000-01

Mr. Cedomir Kostovic
Art and Design
2000-01

Dr. Dennis V. Hickey
Political Science
2001-02

Dr. Mark M. Richter
Chemistry
2001-02

**Recipients of SMSU
University Award**

Teaching

Dr. Tita French Baumlin
1996-97

Dr. Christina Biava
1996-97

Dr. Charles W. Boyd
1996-97

Dr. C. Edward Chang
1996-97

Dr. Jean M. Delaney
1996-97

Dr. Jane E. Doelling
1996-97

Dr. Erwin J. Mantei
1996-97

Ms. Phyllis R. Shoemaker
1996-97

Dr. Carol F. Shoptaugh
1996-97

Dr. William E. Thomas
1996-97

Dr. Pearl M. Yeadon-Erny
1996-97

Dr. Yongwei Zhang
1996-97

Dr. Carey H. Adams
Communication and Mass
Media
1997-98

Dr. Larry N. Campbell
Mathematics
1997-98

Dr. Joel D. Chaston
English
1997-98

Dr. Randy K. Dillon
Communication and Mass
Media
1997-98

Dr. Janice S. Greene
Biology
1997-98

Dr. Lyndon N. Irwin
Agriculture
1997-98

Dr. Harry R. James
Agriculture
1997-98

Dr. Janis L. King
Communication and Mass
Media
1997-98

Dr. Karl R. Kunkel
Sociology and Anthropology
1997-98

Dr. George Mathew
Mathematics
1997-98

Ms. Evelyn S. Maxwell
Greenwood Laboratory
School
1997-98

Dr. Jan R. Squires
Finance and General
Business
1997-98

Dr. Linda G. Benson
English
1998-99

Dr. Genevieve R. Cramer
Reading, Special Education
and Instructional Technology
1998-99

Dr. John B. Harms
Sociology and Anthropology
1998-99

Dr. Donald R. Holliday
English
1998-99

Dr. Kathryn L. Hope
Nursing
1998-99

Dr. Beth Hurst
Reading, Special Education
and Instructional Technology
1998-99

Dr. Katherine G. Lederer
English
1998-99

Dr. David J. Lutz
Psychology
1998-99

Dr. S. Alicia Mathis
Biology
1998-99

Dr. Norma D. McClellan
Music
1998-99

Dr. Heidi Perreault
Computer Information
Systems
1998-99

Dr. Woodrow Sun
Mathematics
1998-99

Dr. Wayne L. Anderson
Finance and General
Business
1999-2000

Dr. Isabelle Bauman
Communication and Mass
Media
1999-2000

Dr. Phyllis Bixler
English
1999-2000

Dr. W.D. Blackmon
English
1999-2000

Dr. Margaret L. Buckner
Sociology and Anthropology
1999-2000

Mr. Michael D. Burns
English
1999-2000

Dr. John S. Heywood
Biology
1999-2000

Dr. James B. Hutter
Agriculture
1999-2000

Dr. Nancy K. Keith
Marketing
1999-2000

Dr. Roseanne G. Killion
Mathematics
1999-2000

Dr. David B. Mcinert
Computer Information
Systems
1999-2000

Dr. Cynthia K. Wilson
School of Teacher Education
1999-2000

Dr. William J. Burling
English
2000-01

Dr. J. Clark Closser
English
2000-01

Mr. Dwaine L. Crigger
Art and Design
2000-01

Dr. Samuel C. Dyer Jr.
Communication and Mass
Media
2000-01

Dr. Lyndon N. Irwin
Agriculture
2000-01

Dr. George H. Jensen
English
2000-01

Dr. Marianthe Karanikas
English
2000-01

Dr. John L. Kent
Marketing
2000-01

Ms. Maria Michalczyk-Lillich
Art and Design
2000-01

Dr. D. Wayne Mitchell
Psychology
2000-01

Dr. Sarah B. Nixon
School of Teacher Education
2000-01

Dr. Margaret E. Weaver
English
2000-01

Dr. Michael E. Ellis
English
2001-02

Ms. Candace D. Fisk
Greenwood Laboratory
School
2001-02

Dr. Erwin J. Mantei
Geography, Geology and
Planning
2001-02

Dr. George Mathew
Mathematics
2001-02

Dr. S. Alicia Mathis
Biology
2001-02

Dr. James C. Moyer
Religious Studies
2001-02

Dr. Mark A. Paxton
Media, Journalism and Film
2001-02

Dr. Peter Richardson
Management
2001-02

Dr. Elizabeth J. Rozell
Management
2001-02

Dr. Eric D. Shade
Computer Science
2001-02

Dr. Thomas L. Wyrick
Economics
2001-02

Dr. Pearl M. Yeadon-Erny
Music
2001-02

Research

Dr. M. Christopher Barnhart
Biology
1996-97

Mr. Mark M. Biggs
Media, Journalism and Film
1996-97

Dr. Dominic J. Capeci
History
1996-97

Dr. Joel D. Chaston
English
1996-97

Dr. James O. Davis
Psychology
1996-97

Dr. Dennis V. Hickey
Political Science
1996-97

Dr. Corinne M. Karuppan
Management
1996-97

Dr. Jiang-Kai Zuo
Physics, Astronomy and
Materials Science
1996-97

Dr. David J. Dixon
Psychology
1997-98

Dr. James N. Giglio
History
1997-98

Dr. Charles W. Hedrick
Religious Studies
1997-98

Dr. Victor H. Matthews
Religious Studies
1997-98

Ms. Sarah E. Perkins
Art and Design
1997-98

Dr. Mark E. Rushefsky
Political Science
1997-98

Mr. Wade S. Thompson
Art and Design
1997-98

Dr. Bobby C. Vaught
Management
1997-98

Dr. M. Christopher Barnhart
Biology
1998-99

Dr. Thomas V. Dickson
Communication and Mass
Media
1998-99

Dr. LiYing Li
Sociology and Anthropology
1998-99

Dr. Julie J. Masterson
Communication Sciences
and Disorders
1998-99

Dr. Kevin L. Mickus
Geography, Geology and
Planning
1998-99

Dr. Carol J. Miller
Finance and General
Business
1998-99

Dr. Linda Park-Fuller
Theatre and Dance
1998-99

Dr. Liang-Cheng Zhang
Mathematics
1998-99

Mr. Mark M. Biggs
Communication and Mass
Media
1999-2000

Dr. Charles W. Hedrick
Religious Studies
1999-2000

Dr. George H. Jensen
English
1999-2000

Dr. James T. Jones
English
1999-2000

Dr. Paula A. Kemp
Mathematics
1999-2000

Dr. William Garrett Piston
History
1999-2000

Dr. Dennis L. Schmitt
Agriculture
1999-2000

Dr. Michael M. Sheng
History
1999-2000

Dr. Wayne C. Bartee
History
2000-01

Dr. Mark C. Ellickson
Political Science
2000-01

Dr. James N. Giglio
History
2000-01

Dr. Dimitri Ioannides
Geography, Geology and
Planning
2000-01

Dr. Chung S. Kim
Computer Information
Systems
2000-01

Dr. Kant B. Patel
Political Science
2000-01

Dr. Robert T. Pavlowsky
Geography, Geology and
Planning
2000-01

Dr. Charles E. Pettijohn
Marketing
2000-01

Dr. James S. Baumlin
English
2001-02

Dr. William J. Burling
English
2001-02

Dr. Joel D. Chaston
English
2001-02

Ms. Sharon R. Harper
Art and Design
2001-02

Dr. John E. Havel
Biology
2001-02

Dr. Paula A. Kemp
Mathematics
2001-02

Dr. John E. Llewellyn
Religious Studies
2001-02

Dr. Randall S. Sexton
Computer Information
Systems
2001-02

Service

Dr. Genevieve R. Cramer
Teacher Education
1996-97

Dr. David J. Dixon
Psychology
1996-97

Dr. Bradley J. Fisher
Gerontology
1996-97

Dr. John W. Northrip
Physics, Astronomy and
Materials Science
1996-97

Dr. Paula A. Kemp
Mathematics
1997-98

Dr. Katherine G. Lederer
English
1997-98

Dr. John T. Pardeck
Social Work
1997-98

Dr. Rhonda R. Ridinger
Health, Physical Education
and Recreation
1997-98

Dr. Judith A. John
English
1998-99

Dr. Lynda M. Plymate
Mathematics
1998-99

Dr. Lois M. Shufeldt
Marketing
1998-99

Dr. Ralph R. Smith
Communication and Mass
Media
1998-99

Dr. Genevieve R. Cramer
School of Teacher Education
1999-2000

Dr. Janice Schnake Greene
Biology
1999-2000

Dr. Mary Ann Jennings
School of Social Work
1999-2000

Ms. Virginia Fay Mee
Management Development
Institute
1999-2000

Dr. R. Bruce Johnson
Agriculture
2000-01

Dr. Paula A. Kemp
Mathematics
2000-01

Mr. Gary L. Ward
Sports Medicine and Athletic
Training
2000-01

Ms. Vonda K. Yarberry
Art and Design
2000-01

Dr. Lyndon N. Irwin
Agriculture
2001-02

Dr. David M. Quick
Art and Design
2001-02

Dr. Kristene S. Sutliff
English
2001-02

Dr. Vernon J. Thielmann
Chemistry
2001-02

Distinguished Professor

Dr. Dominic J. Capeci
History

Dr. James N. Giglio
History

Dr. Charles W. Hedrick
Religious Studies

Dr. James F. O'Brien
Chemistry

Dr. Paula A. Kemp
Mathematics

University Fellow

Teaching

Dr. Jan R. Squires
Finance and General
Business
1999-2002

Dr. Heidi R. Perreault
Computer Information
Systems
2000-03

Dr. Phyllis Bixler
English
2001-04

Dr. Nancy K. Keith
Marketing
2001-04

Dr. Larry N. Campbell
Mathematics
2002-05

Dr. Heidi R. Perreault
Computer Information
Systems
2003-06

Research

Dr. James N. Giglio
History
1999-2002

Dr. Dennis V. Hickey
Political Science
1999-2002

Dr. Victor H. Matthews
Religious Studies
1999-2002

Dr. M. Christopher Barnhart
Biology
2000-03

Dr. Carol J. Miller
Finance and General
Business
2000-03

Dr. John T. Pardeck
Social Work
2001-04

Dr. Dennis V. Hickey
Political Science
2002-05

Dr. Robert T. Pavlowsky
Geography, Geology and
Planning
2002-05

Dr. Dominic J. Capeci
History
2003-06

Dr. Carol Anne Costabile-
Heming
Modern and Classical
Languages
2003-06

Service

Dr. Rhonda R. Ridinger
Health, Physical Education
and Recreation
1999-2002

Dr. Lois M. Shufeldt
Marketing
2000-03

Dr. Paula A. Kemp
Mathematics
2001-04

Dr. Peggy S. Pearl
Consumer and Family
Studies
2001-04

Dr. Lyndon N. Irwin
Agriculture
2002-05

Dr. Rhonda R. Ridinger
Health, Physical Education
and Recreation
2002-05

❀ Athletics Hall of Fame ❀

The SMS Athletics Hall of Fame was established in 1975 by athletics director Aldo Sebben. The Women's Athletics Hall of Fame was founded in 1981 by women's athletics director Dr. Mary Jo Wynn. The two shrines merged and had their first joint induction in February 1999. The original Hall of Fame was a joint endeavor of the SMS Letterman Alumni Association and intercollegiate athletics. The first 22 years of the men's hall saw 179 people enshrined, while 70 went into the first 18 induction classes of the women's hall. The 2003 induction class brings the total membership of the combined Hall of Fame to 281 former student-athletes, coaches and administrators.

1975-76 Induction

Jerry Anderson
basketball
1951-55

Howard Blair
football coach
athletics director
1938-47

Dwight Bumpus
football
track
1938-41

Virgil Cheek
football
basketball
track
1919-22

Max Cherry
football
track
1918-23

J. H. Collins
football
basketball
track
1920-24
track coach
1924-64

Finis Engleman
football
track
1918-23

Harold Harmon
football
1938-40

Russ Kaminsky
football
basketball
golf
1939-42

A. L. McDonald
football
basketball
golf coach
1925-69

Gerald Perry
tennis
1937-40

Victor Reaves
football
track
1919-22

Gene Ruble
basketball
1946-50

Bob Vanatta
basketball coach
1950-53

1976-77 Induction

Ray Forsythe
football
basketball
track
1946-50

Henry Kilburn
football
basketball
track
1928-32

Ben Koeneman
football
1951-56

Ed Lechner
football
basketball
1938-41
football assistant coach
1956-61

Cornelius Perry
football
track
1963-66

Orville Pottenger
football
track
1938-42
football coach
1961-64

Walter Reynaud
football
track
1922-26

Morris Stephens
football
basketball
tennis
1933-37

1977-78 Induction

Chester Barnard
football
basketball
track
1914-18

John Batten
football
1948-52

Victor Fite
track
1926-29

Jim Gant
basketball
1962-66

Ray Haley
football
1947-51

Edwin Matthews
basketball coach
1953-64

Louis Stark
football
basketball
track
1926-30

Gordon Wardell
football
track
1927-30

1978-79 Induction

Arthur Briggs
football
basketball coach
athletics director
1912-33

Carl Davis
football
basketball
track
1922-26

Carl Fox
basketball
1926-29

Mark Frye
basketball
1933-36

Efton Henderson
football
1920-23

Duke Hiett
football
basketball
1925-27

Clyde James
football
basketball
1920-24

Bill Kaczmarek
football
1954-57

Paul Matthews
football
basketball
track
1919-23

Webb Morris
football
basketball
1933-34

Joe Nickle
football
basketball
1931-34

Eldo Perry
football
1961-64

1979-80 Induction

Thomas Dodd
football
basketball
1924-28

Harold Eberhart
basketball
1930-34

Burl Henderson
football
1922-25

Jack Israel
basketball
1957-59

Henry May
football
1948-50

Charles McCallister
football
1942-47

Max Oldham
basketball
1954-58

Dell Scroggins
basketball
1931-35

Gene Webb
golf
1940-42

Jeff Wise
football
track
1925-29

1980-81 Induction

Jim Ball
basketball
1940-43

Willis Bass
track
1936-39

Florence Baker Bugg
administration
1930-62

Erwin Busiek
tennis
1948-50

Tom Clopton
football
baseball
track
1910-14

Mary Phyl Dwight
softball
volleyball
cross country
track
basketball
1970-74
softball coach
1985

Cindy Henderson Snead
softball
basketball
1972-75

Curtis Perry
basketball
1966-70

Margaret Putnam
field hockey
basketball
tennis
softball
swimming coach
1930-63

Jack Russell
football
basketball
1936-39

George Sample
football
1959-62

John Stater
football
1925-28

Bill Stewart
football
basketball
golf
1939-41

Bill Thomas
basketball
1950-53
basketball coach
1956-80

John Tindall
football
basketball
track
26-31

Jim Toler
football
1955-56

1981-82 Induction

Clayton Abbott
football
track
1920-24

Lonnie Adams
football
basketball
track
29-33

Jim Althouse
football
track
1920-22

Lester Barnard
football
basketball
track
1913-17

Marion Donald
track
1935-39

Charles Finley
football
basketball
track
1956-60

Hal Hillhouse
football
track
1929-33

Mary Kay Hunter
softball coach
1972-82

Jim Julian
football
basketball
track
1950-52

Carlos Maze
football
track
1931-34

Dr. Wayne McKinney
administration
1964-80

Carol Nations Gledhill
volleyball
basketball
field hockey
swimming
gymnastics
track
1963-66

Preston Ward
basketball
1945-49

Virginia Wilcox
game official

1982-83 Induction

Bill Baker
basketball
track
1936-39

Herbert Bench
track
1936-39

Marion Berry
football
basketball
track
1933-37

Danny Cook
baseball
1966-69

Linda Dollar
volleyball coach
1972-95

Dr. Mildred Evans
volleyball
field hockey
track
tennis coach
1966-74

Forrest Hamilton
basketball
1951-53

Dick Kerin
football
1942-48

Bill Lamberson
track
1967-70

Jim Mentis
football
1946-50
football coach
1962-68

Cecile Reynaud
volleyball
field hockey
1972-75

1983-84 Induction

Danny Bolden
basketball
1963-67

Cheryl Diamond Murray
gymnastics
1973-77

Howard Elliott
football
track
1938-41

Art Giacomin
football
1957-60

Dr. Charles Johnson
gymnastics coach
1969-79

Carol Meyer
basketball
softball
field hockey
1969-72

Tom Mullen
football
1970-73

Gene Rimmer
football
track
1938-41

Nora Sousley Greenwade
softball
field hockey
volleyball
1970-73

Bill Stringer
football
1963-66

Fred Thomsen
football coach
1949-52

Ken Watkins
basketball
baseball
1966-70

1984-85 Induction

Karen Bethurem
volleyball
basketball
softball
1970-74

Kolleen Casey
gymnastics
1977-80

Dr. Nancy Curry
coach
administration
1967-96

Ralph Colby
football
1952-54

Ralph Harrison
football
basketball
golf
1945-51

Bruce Hollowell
golf
1962-66

Bill Lea
basketball
1948-52

Homer Martin
football
1946-48

Leon Miller
tennis
1938-40

Sue Schuble
volleyball
basketball
softball
golf
track
1966-70

Jim Somers
football
1947-49

Tom Tipton
swimming
1970-74

Carl Wilks
basketball
1958-62

Chuck Williams
basketball
1967-71

1985-86 Induction

Denny Burrows
basketball
1936-40

Jack Clingan
football
1945-52

Chris Dufner
field hockey
1976-79

Joanie French
volleyball
basketball
softball
track
1974-78

Daryel Garrison
basketball
1971-75

Ben Green
swimming
1969-73

Vern Hawkins
basketball
1945-47
play-by-play broadcaster
1950-85

Bill Helfrecht
football
baseball
1967-71

Jay Kinser
basketball
1956-60
basketball
golf
tennis coach
1964-85

Marilyn Moore
volleyball
basketball
softball
field hockey
track
swimming
tennis
1958-62

Lou Shepherd
basketball
1964-68

Cindy Wilson
golf
basketball
1977-79

1986-87 Induction

Mary Ellen Cloninger
volleyball
basketball
softball
1966-69

Phil Crawford
football
basketball
track
1938-42

Bill Douglass
football
track
1963-67

Carl Durham
football
1928-31

Becky Geers Oakes
field hockey
1972-75

Bill Lucas
golf
1961-64

Eleanor Jones Pitts
volleyball
softball
track
1970-74

Randy Magers
basketball
baseball
1970-74

Charles Marshall
basketball
1960-64

Don Provance
football
1946-49

Dr. Rhonda Ridinger
field hockey coach
1971-90

George Simpson
football
track
1955-57

1987-88 Induction

Jodie Adams
tennis
1975-79

Penny Clayton
softball
1978-80

Ed Cook
basketball
1946-50

Susan Cooper
volleyball
1977-78

John Garcia
track
1941-47

Bob Grider
football
1937-40

Rich Johanningmeier
football
1960-63
football coach
1976-85

Andy Newton
basketball
baseball
1973-76

Glenda Rauch Climer
volleyball
field hockey
track
1963-67

Aldo Sebben
football
track
cross country
coach
athletics director
1952-82

1988-89 Induction

Don Anielak
basketball
1952-54

Tom Coil
wrestling
1971-73

Walton Harmon
football
1931-34

Pat Hogan
football
baseball
1963-66

Dick Jones
baseball
1969-72

Tanya Muentefering
field hockey
track
1974-77

John Prasuhn
track
cross country
1973-77

Reba Sims
basketball
softball
field hockey coach
1969-79

Debbie Dace Swyers
volleyball
softball
1973-75

Sharman Paine Walker
tennis
1971-74

Bill Welch
golf
1957-60

1989-90 Induction

Tom Adams
tennis
1966-69
tennis coach
1975-77

Bob Blakley
football
baseball
1973-77

Diane Cline
softball
1978-80

Wally Dawson
football
1962-65

William Doolittle
basketball
1970-74

Dan Dwyer
track
cross country
1974-76

Tommy O'Boyle
football coach
athletics director
1947-48

Kathy Pace Major
volleyball
1967-68

Fran Salsman
tennis
volleyball
basketball
field hockey
track
1960-64

Jennifer Seveland Box
volleyball
1979-82

Kent Stringer
football
1972-75

Gino Travline
football
1973-76

1990-91 Induction

Jeanne Calhoun
field hockey
softball
1965-68

Don Carlson
basketball
1963-67

Becky Duffin
softball
1981-83

Jimmie Dull
basketball
1974-78

Russell Orms
golf
1968-71

Vicki Richardson Schutzler
track
gymnastics
field hockey
1973-76

Gayle Runke
golf coach
1974-92

Steve Seal
baseball
1969-70

Fred Tabron
football
track
1970-73

Dale Williams
swimming coach
1965-79

1991-92 Induction

Bob Dees
football
1948-51

Stephanie Dutton
field hockey
1978-81

Trish Kissiar Gilliam
volleyball
1976-79

Mary Slater Gunn
track
cross country
1969-73

Dennis Hill
basketball
1973-75
basketball assistant coach
1978-89

Jim Murdock
track
1962-64

Russ Robinson
basketball
1955-59

Phil Shannahan
basketball
1963-67

Jeanette Tendai
basketball
1983-86

Joe Whipple
football
1937-38
athletic letterman
alumni association
secretary-treasurer

1992-93 Induction

Debbie Allin
volleyball
1978-81

Mert Bancroft
basketball
1965-69

Cindy Bell Thompson
track
1973-77

Dick Bradley
basketball broadcaster
1952-80

Art Helms
basketball
1952-54

Natalie Hoberg Gresham
golf
1979-83

Terry Kasper
football
baseball
1974-77

Lisa Nicholson Reece
softball
basketball
1976-79

Ken Norton
cross country
track
1970-74

Pat Talburt
football
1964-67

1993-94 Induction

Tom Hamilton
football
1974-77

Dennis Heim
football
1974-77

Tammy Holloway
softball
1982-85

Chris Kage-Willis
track
cross country
1982-84

Larry Lewis
basketball
1976-80

Scott Lowery
wrestling
1976-81

Bill Rowe
baseball coach
1964-82
athletics director
1982-present

Dennis Strickland
baseball
1969-70

Lynn Strubberg Lottmann
basketball
1980-83

1994-95 Induction

Kenny Ault
cross country
track
1970-75

Mark Bailey
baseball
basketball
1979-82

Diane Barlow
cross country
track
1986-88

Bobby Biser
golf
1978-81

Kathy Crotty
volleyball
1983-86

Janie Gohn Richardson
volleyball
1969-72

Rick Iverson
swimming
1971-75

Dennis Scott
football
1963-66

Dave Sperry
tennis
1976-79

Sharon Thurman Partain
gymnastics
1970-73

1995-96 Induction

Bill Anderson
basketball
track
1955-58

Marcia Bisges
softball
basketball
1983-87

Dave Dickensheet
baseball
1979-82

Chuck Frederking
swimming
1973-77

Maureen Manda Campos
volleyball
1981-84

Mike Murphy
football
1975-78

Mike Robinson
basketball
1978-80

Linda Schachet Greve
field hockey
1980-83

Mitch Ware
football
1976-79
assistant football coach
1980-97

Terri Whitmarsh McClure
softball
1983-86

1996-97 Induction

Steve Anderson
baseball
1978-81

Mary Beck
volleyball
1981-84

Anthony Boggs
basketball
1980-84

Roger Buenemann
tennis
1975-79

Marjorie DeMarino
  Bankovich
field hockey
1986-87

John Gianini
football
track
1976-80

Chuck Hunsaker
track
cross country coach
1972-77

Kelly Mago Pesano
basketball
1994-00

Ardie McCoy
football
wrestling
1965-69

Joyce Swofford
track
cross country
1985-89

1997-98 Induction

Merry Crouch
gymnastics
1975-78

Lisa Einheuser Isaacs
track
cross country
1983-86

Mindy Struckhoff
  Gresham
volleyball
1985-88

1998-99 Induction

Mike Armentrout
football
1981-84

Sofie Bjorling
tennis
1982-85

Jesse Branch
football coach
1986-94

Jerry Kirksey
basketball
1958-61

Karen Rapier
basketball
1988-92
basketball assistant coach
1994-present

Dr. Mary Jo Wynn
coach
administration
1957-98

1999-2000 Induction

Erica Calhoun
track
1988-91

Barb Gaines
softball
1990-93

Steve Newbold
football
1977-80

Phil Schlegel
basketball
1983-86

Ron Snider
baseball
1976-79

Kelly Stuckel Yates
field hockey
1976-79

2000-01 Induction

Glenda Bond
basketball
softball
1973-76

Mark Garrett
baseball
1979-82

Melody Howard
basketball
1990-94

Susan Ruch
volleyball
1986-89

Randy Stange
basketball
1983-85
assistant basketball coach
1987-92

Rick Suchenski
football
1976-79

2001-02 Induction

Mike Ablard
swimming
1981-85

Kellie Becher Kessler
softball
1993-94

Winston Garland
basketball
1985-87

Janice Gibson Rudnick
volleyball
1974-77

Tina Robbins
basketball
1990-94

Jan Stahle
football
1976-78
soccer coach
1987-89

Christa Townsend
tennis
1971-74

2002-03 Induction

Cheryl Burnett
basketball coach
1984-02

Ron Golden
track
1962-65

Mark Mennemeier
baseball
1977-78

Darrin Newbold
football
1979-82

Melinda Sallins
track
1992-96

Sandy Seale Hamm
track
cross country
1981-85

Randy Towe
basketball
1974-79

Karen White Hardin
tennis
1971-73

❀ Contributors ❀

Albers, Lolita
Allee, Dale
Allen, Tom
Alter, William III
Amonker, Ravindra
Anderson, Jim
Aripoli, Don
Arvizu, Candida
Bagley, William C.
Baker, Anne
Baker, James P.
Banks, Larry
Bartee, Wayne
Bartley, Richard
Batchelder, Mike
Beckett, Robert
Belcher, David
Bell, Joe
Benton, Alan D.
Berriman, Howard
Bixler, Vencil
Black, John
Blackmon, W. D.
Blackwood, Byrne
Blackwood, Randy
Bosch, Allan W.
Botsford, Virginia
Bottin, Ron
Bowdidge, John
Bradley, Robert H.
Brandon, Wanda
Bridges, Wilbur
Brill, Colleen Marie
Briscoe, Beulah
Brown, Kenneth
Brown, Sam
Brown, Ted
Burilson, Miriam
Burton, David L.
Burris, Greg

Caldwell, Cheryl
Carroll, Dana
Carter, Lillian
Casady, Mona
Catau, John
Cavner, Howard
Chaney, Wilma Craig
Clark, Sara
Cochran, Richard M.
Cockrill, Belle
Coleman, Earlene
Collins, Colin C.
Combs, Billy C.
Conner, Kenneth R.
Cooper, Vernon
Copeland, Clint D.
Cox, Larry
Craig, Jim
Crow, Elizabeth Bryant
Crighton, William
Davidson, Carrick W.
Davis, Cliff
Deidiker, Floyd D.
Dennis, Marilyn
Diamond, Arlen
DiSarno, Neil
Dixon, David
Doman, Earle
Dudley, Paul
Dunn, Brent
Eagles, Karen
Ebersold, Julie
Einhellig, Frank
Ellis, Gene
Ellis, Judy
Ellis, Roy
Fairbairn, Ron
Falls, Harold
Fehler, Gretchen
Feraldi, Nancy

Ferguson, Carol Ann
Fisher, Bradley
Flanders, Robert
Freeman, Dale
Friedman, Gordon
Funderburk, Stacey
Galanes, Gloria
Gerwert, Hank
Gilbert, Peggy
Gleghorn, Allison
Gordon, Albert
Gordon, Marshall
Green, Marvin
Grindstaff, Wyman
Hinton, E. Jackie
Hoe, Ruan
Holm, Bill
Hope, Kathryn
Horacek, Mark
Horny, Karen
Howard, Mary
Hunter, Jack
Illum, Steve
Irwin, Lyndon
Jahnke, Tamara
Jensen, Nancy
Johnson, Julie
Johnson, Linda
Kaatz, Kris
Keck, Don
Keeling, Russell
Keiser, John H.
Kennon, Marvin
Kindhart, Richard
Kincaid, Paul
Kirker, Martha
Kovats, Julius A.
Krasner, Babs
Langston, Paul
Lawrence, Curtis

Learned, William S.
Leclaire, Marissa K.
Lederer, Katherine
Lin, Zhi
Loch, Teri
Long, Homer
Lopinot, Neal
Lysingring, Lyle
Mallory, Arthur
March, Julie
Marinec, Stephanie
Marty, Fred F.
Maxwell, Fred
May, Diane
McAlear, John
McDowell, Debra
McKinney, Wayne
Meyer, Duane
Moran, John
Morrow, Lynn
Mostyn, Andrea
Moore, Dale
Moore, Jim
Morris, Enoch
Morris, Todd
Morrissey, Jeff
Mortensen, Harley
Moyer, Jim
Muegge, Sarah
Murphy, Valerie
Napper, Lucille
Newman, Diane
Nowell, Anjanette
Nugent, Pauline
O'Dell, Kathleen
O'Neal, Camilla
Onstot, Greg
Pace, Julian
Pagnotta, Mary
Painter, Una

Pamperin, Neil
Pardeck, Terry
Patel, Kant
Parrott, Neva J.
Patton, John
Payton, Don
Pierce, Ed
Pierce, Patricia
Peterson, Jane
Pilant, Denny
Prescott, John
Presley, Janice
Pulley, Kathy
Purvis, Jennifer
Randall, Shirley
Redfearn, Paul
Reid, Helen
Rhodes, Russell
Richards, David
Rippee, Billy
Robinette, Steve
Robinson, Orin
Rowe, Bill
Sampson, Doug
Sandoval, Donna R.
Sanderson, Peter
Schilling, Mike
Schmidt, Bruno
Schmitt, Craig
Schmitt, Vicki
Scott, Bob
Shannahan, William J.
Shoptaugh, Carol
Silvey, Carol
Simpson, Don
Sims, Reba
Smith, Judi
Smith, Rathel
Snodgrass, Burnie
Snyder, Linda

Spicer, Holt
Spiva, Norman
Stanton, Donal
Stewart, Byron
Stillwell, Mark
Stillwell, Tina
Stone, Allan
Strong, Tom
Stroup, Kala M.
Sullivan, Betty Goza
Swann, Jan
Talbert, Dale
Taylor, Mary
Taylor, William J.
Thomas, Kent
Thompson, Wade
Tipling, Sheila
Tooley, Lois
Trewatha, Robert
Udell, Gerald
Van Cleave, William R.
Wall, John
Ward, Gary
Weaver, Margaret
Webb, Guy
Wedenoja, Bill
Whitaker, Robert
White, Kevin
Williams, Charles
Witt, Doris
Wolf, George
Woodward, Jim
Woolf, Beverly
Woolford, Jane
Wynn, Mary Jo

❦ Index ❦